UNCERTAINTY IN DATA ENVELOPMENT ANALYSIS

Uncertainty, Computational Techniques, and Decision Intelligence Book Series

Series Editors

Tofigh Allahviranloo, PhD
Faculty of Engineering and Natural Sciences, Istinye University, Istanbul, Turkey

Narsis A. Kiani, PhD
Algorithmic Dynamics Lab, Department of Oncology-Pathology & Center of Molecular Medicine, Karolinska Institute, Stockholm, Sweden

Witold Pedrycz, PhD
Department of Electrical and Computer Engineering, University of Alberta, Edmonton, AB, Canada

Volumes in Series

- Sahar Tahvili, Leo Hatvani, Artificial Intelligence Methods for Optimization of the Software Testing Process (2022)
- Farhad Lotfi, Masoud Sanei, Ali Hosseinzadeh, Sadegh Niroomand, Ali Mahmoodirad, Uncertainty in Data Envelopment Analysis (2023)
- Chun-Wei Tsai, Ming-Chao Chiang, Handbook of Metaheuristic Algorithms (2023)
- Stanislaw Raczynski, Reachable Sets of Dynamic Systems (2023)

For more information about the UCTDI series, please visit: https://www.elsevier.com/books-and-journals/book-series/uncertainty-computational-techniques-and-decision-intelligence

Uncertainty, Computational Techniques, and Decision Intelligence

UNCERTAINTY IN DATA ENVELOPMENT ANALYSIS

Fuzzy and Belief Degree-Based Uncertainties

FARHAD HOSSEINZADEH LOTFI

Department of Mathematics, Science and Research Branch, Islamic Azad University, Tehran, Iran

MASOUD SANEI

Department of Mathematics, Central Tehran Branch, Islamic Azad University, Tehran, Iran

ALI ASGHAR HOSSEINZADEH

Department of Mathematics, Lahijan Branch, Islamic Azad University, Lahijan, Iran

SADEGH NIROOMAND

Department of Industrial Engineering, Firouzabad Institute of Higher Education, Firouzabad, Fars, Iran

ALI MAHMOODIRAD

Department of Mathematics, Ayatollah Amoli Branch, Islamic Azad University, Amol, Iran

ELSEVIER

ACADEMIC PRESS

An imprint of Elsevier

Academic Press is an imprint of Elsevier
125 London Wall, London EC2Y 5AS, United Kingdom
525 B Street, Suite 1650, San Diego, CA 92101, United States
50 Hampshire Street, 5th Floor, Cambridge, MA 02139, United States
The Boulevard, Langford Lane, Kidlington, Oxford OX5 1GB, United Kingdom

ISBN 978-0-323-99444-6

For information on all Academic Press publications
visit our website at https://www.elsevier.com/books-and-journals

Publisher: Mara E. Conner
Editorial Project Manager: Howi M. De Ramos
Production Project Manager: Omer Mukthar
Cover Designer: Greg Harris

Typeset by STRAIVE, India

Contents

Preface

One of the appropriate and efficient tools in the field of productivity measurement and evaluation is data envelopment analysis (DEA), which is used as a nonparametric method to calculate the efficiency of decision-making units. Today, DEA is expanding rapidly and is used in the evaluation of various organizations and industries such as banking, post offices, hospitals, educational centers, power plants, refineries, etc. There have been many developments in theoretical and practical aspects in data coverage analysis models that make knowing DEA and its various aspects indispensable for more precise applications.

The classical DEA models use crisp data to measure the inputs and outputs of a given system. In many cases such as manufacturing systems, production processes, service systems, etc., the inputs and outputs may be volatile and complex, so that they are difficult to measure with classical DEA models.

The purpose of this book is to introduce some methods to deal with uncertain data in DEA models. The book presents two types of uncertain DEA methods: fuzzy DEA and belief degree-based uncertain DEA. Fuzzy DEA is a promising extension of classical DEA that is proposed for dealing with imprecise and ambiguous data in performance measurement problems. It is obvious that for obtaining the probability distribution of any uncertain data, a lot of samples or historical information are needed. In cases that due to economical or technological reasons no samples or historical information exist for an event, the domain experts are invited to evaluate the belief degree of the event occurring. These types of events are belief degree-based uncertainty. A DEA model containing belief degree-based uncertain inputs and outputs is called uncertain DEA and clearly is useful for cases where no historical information of an uncertain event is available.

In practice, some information and knowledge are usually represented by human language such as "about 100 km," "roughly 80 kg," "low speed," "middle age," and "big size." A lot of surveys showed that these imprecise quantities do not behave like randomness or fuzziness. Hence, in 2007, Prof. Baoding Liu introduced a typical uncertainty theory to model these imprecise quantities called belief degree-based uncertainty. This uncertainty theory is a branch of mathematics based on normality, monotonicity, self-duality, countable subadditive, and product measure axioms as other mathematical tools. Thus, belief degree-based uncertainty is neither random nor fuzzy. Up to now, this uncertainty theory has become a new tool to describe human uncertainty and has a wide application both in theory and engineering. Specifically, some applications such as performance assessment of service and manufacturing sectors, productivity analysis, alternative evaluation and ranking in multicriteria decision analysis problems, assessment of the banking sector, etc., can be mentioned.

The book is suitable for academicians, researchers, and engineers who perform optimization and evaluation duties in public and private businesses. Also, postgraduate students in all levels in applied mathematics, management science, economics, operations research, industrial engineering, computer science, information science, etc., may use this book for their optimization-based courses.

Credit authorship contribution statement is as follows:

Farhad Hosseinzadeh Lotfi devised the project and wrote Chapter 2. He also supervised the methodology, findings, and analysis. **Masoud Sanei** supervised the methodology, findings, and analysis. **Ali Asghar Hosseinzadeh** worked on Chapters 1, 3, and 4. **Sadegh Niroomand** worked on content preparation, writing, editing, and scientific reviewing of all chapters of the book. **Ali Mahmoodirad** devised the project, the main conceptual ideas, and the proof outline while also writing Chapters 1, 5, and 6. He also wrote an original draft of the book and helped in all stages. All authors discussed the results and contributed to the final book.

We gratefully acknowledge those who have contributed to the compilation of this book, and it is hoped that this book will be useful for readers, researchers, and managers.

Farhad Hosseinzadeh Lotfi
Department of Mathematics, Science and Research Branch, Islamic Azad University, Tehran, Iran

Masoud Sanei
Department of Mathematics, Central Tehran Branch, Islamic Azad University, Tehran, Iran

Ali Asghar Hosseinzadeh
Department of Mathematics, Lahijan Branch, Islamic Azad University, Lahijan, Iran

Sadegh Niroomand
Department of Industrial Engineering, Firouzabad Institute of Higher Education, Firouzabad, Fars, Iran

Ali Mahmoodirad
Department of Mathematics, Ayatollah Amoli Branch, Islamic Azad University, Amol, Iran

CHAPTER ONE

Uncertain theories

1.1 Introduction

In this section, some information about the book such as its importance, motivation, structure, etc., will be discussed.

1.1.1 Importance of the book

In today's organizations, performance assessment is important for top managers. This assessment could be used as a tool for recognizing the weaknesses and strengths of an organization. Any organization as a system uses some inputs to produce some outputs. A decision-making unit (DMU) is responsible for processing, employing, and combining the inputs to produce the outputs. In 1978, the first classical data envelopment analysis (DEA) model was introduced by Charnes et al. (1978) to evaluate educational units. Shortly after that, this technique was developed in such a way as to be used in many organizations. With such rapid development of this technique from theoretical and applied aspects, many scientific reports have been published in related conferences and journals of the field. Even some universities around the world started to introduce some courses on DEA and graduate experts in this field. In the rest of this subsection, some important concepts of DEA such as efficiency, benchmarking, ranking, returns to scale, congestion, progress/regress, input/output estimation, allocation, etc., are discussed.

1.1.1.1 Efficiency

DEA compares a DMU of a population with other DMUs of the population to measure its relative efficiency optimistically. For this aim, DEA estimates an upper bound for the production function of the population and calculates the relative efficiency of each DMU according to this upper bound.

Uncertainty in Data Envelopment Analysis
https://doi.org/10.1016/B978-0-323-99444-6.00004-9

1.1.1.2 Benchmarking

It is a very important goal in DEA to recognize the shortcomings of each criterion. In benchmarking, first a collection for production possibilities is constructed, then by use of a selected direction, one point of the efficiency boundary of DMU under evaluation is determined. This point is introduced as the benchmark coordinate of the DMU.

1.1.1.3 Ranking

As DEA measures the relative efficiency for DMUs and also because the estimated efficiency of each DMU may be high, in real cases with a high number of DMUs, there may be more than one efficient DMU. To overcome this issue, efficient DMUs will be ranked by DEA.

1.1.1.4 Returns to scale

In cases where returns to scale are considered to be fixed for population members without any variation, the type of return to scale for each DMU can be determined by DEA. The optimum measure of the highest productivity is one of the goals that can be achieved by this technique.

1.1.1.5 Congestion

In some DMUs, by overincreasing the value of the inputs, the value of some outputs may be decreased. This may happen when congestion occurs for those inputs. DEA can be applied to recognize such congestion and help managers increase the outputs by reducing costs.

1.1.1.6 Progress/regress

It is natural that all members of a population try to improve and upgrade their situation. In such a population, one important criterion for managers is the level of progress/regress of the DMUs. A comparison between the improvement of each DMU with the improvement of population can be a basis for the progress/regress of the DMU. It is notable to say that DEA can introduce a scale for measuring progress/regress.

1.1.1.7 Input/output estimation

Some managers claim that if they increase the value of their inputs, the performance will be improved. By use of DEA, we can estimate the amount of increase in the outputs to obtain better performance. In a similar way, DEA can be used to estimate the inputs. In some studies, this is known as reverse DEA.

1.1.1.8 Allocation

Allocation means assigning a part of the total cost to each DMU to produce outputs. The allocation is not under the control of the manager, so it is expected that this allocation does not affect the productivity of the DMUs.

In some organizations, because of unfair distribution of one or some inputs to the DMUs, the managers try to redistribute and allocate them to the DMUs in a fair way. This issue is known as reallocation or centralized allocation, and its purpose is to increase the outputs and improve the performance of the DMUs.

Except for the above-mentioned concepts that are important capabilities of DEA, the applications of DEA in complex structures such as supply chains and other structural networks are very important.

1.1.2 Motivation

Due to the recent progress of DEA and its applications in educational, healthcare, service-based, and production-based organizations, many new models of DEA with various goals have been developed and are available for scientists and researchers. Some good experiences on national projects and developing DEA models with real data are some reasons that the authors of book decided to write it.

As for collecting the required data and developing the DEA models for the collected data, some of the data have no exact and deterministic value. Therefore, researchers are motivated to develop inexact DEA models to overcome such a difficulty. This inexact situation may happen in different types of uncertainty.

In some real-world problems, the value of a parameter may be of the interval $[a, b]$ instead of an exact value. This means that these data are exact, but we are not aware of their exact value, and the only information is that the exact value is of interval $[a, b]$. The optimization problems with such data are called interval programming. DEA models with interval input, output, and DMUs are called interval DEA models. In an interval DEA model, the efficiency values of DMUs will be of the interval type. So, with the existence of interval-type data, all DEA models of ranking, return to scale, congestion, etc., should be developed in interval form. Another type of uncertainty that can be used to reflect the inexact nature of real-world data is fuzzy-type uncertainty. This type of uncertainty can happen when the DEA models deal with inputs and/or outputs measured with qualitative arguments. These qualitative arguments are converted to fuzzy values. For the problems with fuzzy-type values, the DEA models should be developed in fuzzy form as fuzzy DEA models. Other types of uncertainties that can be used to model inexact data are stochastic and belief degree-based uncertainties, where either can be used to develop uncertain DEA models to deal with the inexact data of real-world cases.

It is notable that DEA models are developed in two forms—an envelopment model and a multiplier model—where each is dual form of other one. Any of these forms represents good and useful information for researchers. It is very important that, with the existence of inexact data, these forms are not dual for each other and some primal-dual theorems of linear programming may not be correct for them in the case of inexact data. As in many cases, the data of DEA models are not exact. The main motivation of this book is to develop inexact models for DEA problems.

1.1.3 Structure of the book

The book is presented in six chapters. In this chapter, the basic concepts of fuzzy sets and numbers and belief degree-based uncertainty are reviewed. The presented concepts of this chapter later will be used to develop uncertain DEA models. In Chapter 2, some important and well-known DEA models are introduced and analyzed carefully. The required assumptions are presented and the application area of the proposed models is explained and discussed. In Chapter 3, the fuzzy form of the DEA models of Chapter 2 is presented and some approaches to the efficiency assessment are introduced based on different methods. Due to its wide practical use, DEA has been adapted to many fields to deal with problems that have occurred in practice. One adaptation has been in the field of ranking DMUs. Most methods of ranking DMUs assume that all input and output data are exactly known, but in real life, the data cannot be precisely measured. Thus, in Chapter 4 some methods for ranking DMUs under a fuzzy environment are developed. In Chapter 5, the belief degree-based uncertain form of the DEA models of Chapter 2 is presented and some solution approaches are introduced to obtain their equivalent crisp form. Finally, in Chapter 6 some methods for ranking DMUs under belief degree-based uncertainty are developed.

1.2 Fuzzy sets theory

Fuzzy sets theory was first introduced by Zadeh (1965). In that time, no one could imagine that that study would be the origin of a new perspective in mathematics and other sciences to merge theory and practice based on human nature. In the early years, there were many doubts and disagreements by scientists about the applicability of this theorem, but by realizing the real-life applications and applied logics of this theorem, many scientists were motivated to apply it. Today, although hundreds of books, papers, and studies have been published about fuzzy theory, there remain wide research areas available on this topic (Allahviranloo et al., 2009; Ezadi et al., 2018). In this section, some concepts, definitions, and theorems of fuzzy sets and systems are reviewed to be used in next chapters of the book. The contents of this section are taken from Lai and Hwang (1992), Dubois and Prade (1980), Zimmermann (1987), and Allahviranloo (2020).

1.2.1 Basic definitions of fuzzy sets theory

Definition 1.1 Suppose X is a nonempty set, then the set of ordered pairs $\tilde{A} = \{(x, \mu_{\tilde{A}}(x)) | x \in X\}$ where $\mu_{\tilde{A}} : X \to [0, 1]$ is called a fuzzy set on X. The membership function of fuzzy set $\tilde{A}$ is shown by $\mu_{\tilde{A}}(x)$ where it represents the degree of association of any $x \in X$ to the set $\tilde{A}$.

Definition 1.2 The fuzzy set $\tilde{A}$ is a subset of $\tilde{B}\left(\tilde{A} \subseteq \tilde{B}\right)$ if for any $x \in X$ the condition $\mu_{\tilde{A}}(x) \leq \mu_{\tilde{B}}(x)$ is true.

Definition 1.3 The fuzzy sets $\tilde{A}$ and $\tilde{B}$ are equal ($\tilde{A} = \tilde{B}$) if for any $x \in X$ the condition $\mu_{\tilde{A}}(x) = \mu_{\tilde{B}}(x)$ is true.

Definition 1.4 The support of a fuzzy set is shown by $\text{supp}\left(\tilde{A}\right)$ or $S\left(\tilde{A}\right)$ and is defined as $S\left(\tilde{A}\right) = \{x \in X | \mu_{\tilde{A}}(x) > 0\}$.

Definition 1.5 The height of a fuzzy set is shown by $hgt\left(\tilde{A}\right)$ and is defined as $hgt\left(\tilde{A}\right) = \sup \mu_{\tilde{A}}(x)$.

Definition 1.6 A fuzzy set is called normal if and only if $hgt\left(\tilde{A}\right) = 1$; otherwise, it is called subnormal.

Definition 1.7 The core of a fuzzy set is shown by $core\left(\tilde{A}\right)$ and is defined as $core\left(\tilde{A}\right) = \{x \in X | \mu_{\tilde{A}}(x) = 1\}$.

Definition 1.8 For two fuzzy sets $\tilde{A}$ and $\tilde{B}$, the following definitions are considered,

- $\tilde{A}^c = \left\{(x, \mu_{\tilde{A}^c}(x)) | x \in X, \mu_{\tilde{A}^c}(x) = 1 - \mu_{\tilde{A}}(x)\right\}$ where $\tilde{A}^c$ is the complement of fuzzy set $\tilde{A}$.
- $\tilde{A} \cup \tilde{B} = \left\{\left(x, \mu_{\tilde{A} \cup \tilde{B}}(x)\right) | x \in X, \mu_{\tilde{A} \cup \tilde{B}}(x) = \max\{\mu_{\tilde{A}}(x), \mu_{\tilde{B}}(x)\}\right\}$.
- $\tilde{A} \cap \tilde{B} = \left\{\left(x, \mu_{\tilde{A} \cap \tilde{B}}(x)\right) | x \in X, \mu_{\tilde{A} \cap \tilde{B}}(x) = \min\{\mu_{\tilde{A}}(x), \mu_{\tilde{B}}(x)\}\right\}$.

Definition 1.9 α-cut of a fuzzy set is shown by $\left[\tilde{A}\right]_\alpha$ and is obtained by the following relationship,

$$\left[\tilde{A}\right]_\alpha = \begin{cases} \{\, x\in X \mid \mu_{\tilde{A}}(x) \geq \alpha \} & \text{if } \alpha\in(0,1] \\ cl\left(S(\tilde{A})\right) & \text{if } \alpha = 0 \end{cases} \tag{1.1}$$

where $cl(U)$ is the closure of subset U where $U\subseteq X$.

It is notable to mention the following tips:

- if $0\leq\alpha\leq\beta\leq1$ then $\tilde{A}_\beta \subseteq \tilde{A}_\alpha$,
- $\tilde{A} = \underset{\alpha}{\cup}\tilde{A}_\alpha$.

Definition 1.10 A fuzzy set is convex if and only if for x_1, $x_2\in X$ and $\lambda\in[0,1]$ the following inequality is held (Fig. 1.1).

$$\mu_{\tilde{A}}(\lambda x_1 + (1-\lambda)x_2) \geq \min\,\{\mu_{\tilde{A}}(x_1), \mu_{\tilde{A}}(x_2)\} \tag{1.2}$$

Definition 1.11 Assume $\tilde{A}_1, \tilde{A}_2, \ldots, \tilde{A}_n$ are fuzzy subsets on X_1, X_2, …, X_n, respectively. Then the Cartesian product of the subsets on $X = X_1 \times X_2 \times \ldots \times X_n$ is defined as,

$$\tilde{A}_1 \times \tilde{A}_2 \times \cdots \times \tilde{A}_n = \Big\{\Big((x_1, x_2, \cdots, x_n), \mu_{\tilde{A}_1\times\tilde{A}_2\times\cdots\times\tilde{A}_n}(x_1, x_2, \cdots, x_n)\Big) \; | x_i\in X, i = 1, 2, \cdots, n\Big\} \tag{1.3}$$

where, $\mu_{\tilde{A}_1\times\tilde{A}_2\times\ldots\times\tilde{A}_n}(x_1, x_2, \ldots, x_n) = \min\{\mu_{\tilde{A}_i}(x_i), i = 1, 2, \ldots, n\}$.

Definition 1.12 (Extension principle). Assume $f: X\rightarrow Y$ is a mapping of $X = X_1 \times X_2 \times \ldots \times X_n$ to set Y, also $\tilde{A}_1, \tilde{A}_2, \ldots, \tilde{A}_n$ are fuzzy subsets of X_1, …, X_n, respectively. Fuzzy set $\tilde{B}$ from Y is defined as:

$$\tilde{B} = f\left(\tilde{A}_1, \ldots, \tilde{A}_n\right) = \{(y, \mu_{\tilde{B}}(y)) | y = f(x_1, \ldots, x_n), x_i\in X_i, i = 1, 2, \ldots, n\}$$

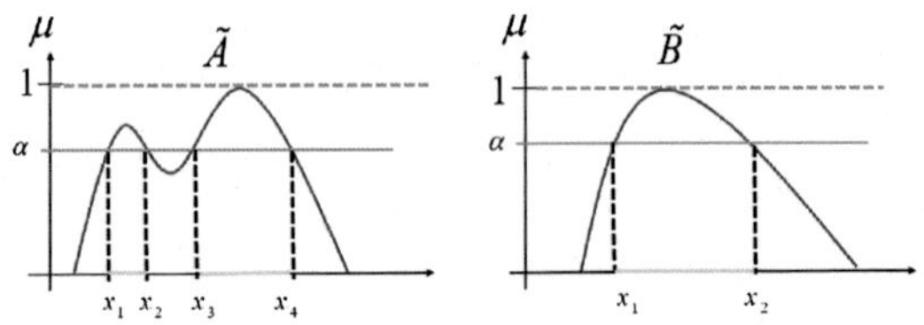

Fig. 1.1 A nonconvex fuzzy set ($\tilde{A}$) and a convex fuzzy set ($\tilde{B}$).

where,

$$\mu_{\tilde{B}}(y) = \begin{cases} \sup\limits_{(x_1, \ldots, x_n) \in f^{-1}(y)} \min\left\{\mu_{\tilde{A}_1}(x_1), \ldots, \mu_{\tilde{A}_n}(x_n)\right\}, & \text{if } y \in range(f) \\ 0, & \text{if } y \notin range(f) \end{cases} \tag{1.4}$$

Definition 1.13 The normal and convex fuzzy set $\tilde{A}$ is called a fuzzy number if its membership function is piecewise continuous on X.

Definition 1.14 The fuzzy number $\tilde{A}$ is nonnegative if for any $x < 0$ the equality $\mu_{\tilde{A}}(x) = 0$ is held.

Definition 1.15 Assume L and R are nonincreasing functions where L, R: $\mathbb{R}^+ \rightarrow [0, 1]$ and $L(0) = R(0) = 1$. Then the fuzzy number $\tilde{A}$ is called the $L\,R$ fuzzy number with the following membership function.

$$\mu_{\tilde{A}}(x) = \begin{cases} L\left(\dfrac{a_2 - x}{a_2 - a_1}\right), & a_1 \leq x \leq a_2 \\ 1, & a_2 \leq x \leq a_3 \\ R\left(\dfrac{x - a_3}{a_4 - a_3}\right), & a_3 \leq x \leq a_4 \end{cases} \tag{1.5}$$

This number is shown as $\tilde{A} = (a_1, a_2, a_3, a_4)_{LR}$ (see Fig. 1.2) where $a_1 \leq a_2 \leq a_3 \leq a_4$. Also L and R are reference functions.

Definition 1.16 The fuzzy number $\tilde{A} = (a_1, a_2, a_3, a_4)_{LR}$ is nonnegative if and only if $a_1 \geq 0$ and is negative if and only if $a_4 \leq 0$.

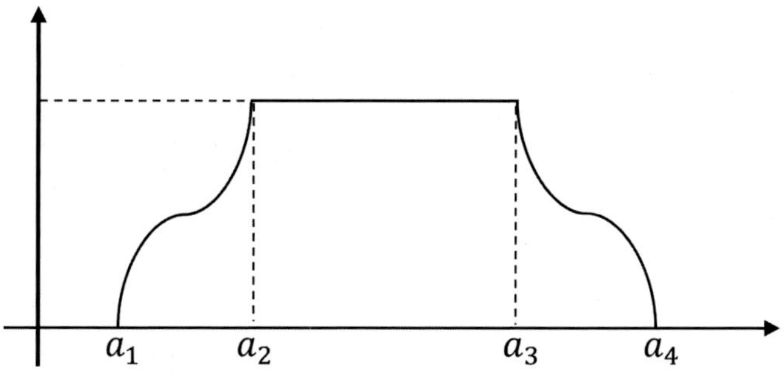

Fig. 1.2 Schematic representation of $\tilde{A} = (a_1, a_2, a_3, a_4)_{LR}$.

Definition 1.17 A *LR* fuzzy number with reference functions of $L(x) = R(x) = \max\{0, 1-x\}$ is called a trapezoidal fuzzy number and is shown by $\tilde{A} = (a_1, a_2, a_3, a_4)$. Its membership function is as below (see Fig. 1.3),

$$\mu_{\tilde{A}}(x) = \begin{cases} \dfrac{x-a_1}{a_2-a_1}, & a_1 \leq x \leq a_2 \\ 1, & a_2 \leq x \leq a_3 \\ \dfrac{a_4-x}{a_4-a_3}, & a_3 \leq x \leq a_4 \end{cases} \tag{1.6}$$

Definition 1.18 A *LR* fuzzy number with reference functions of $L(x) = R(x) = 1-x$ is called a triangular fuzzy number and is shown by $\tilde{A} = (a_1, a_2, a_3)$. Its membership function is as follows (see Fig. 1.4),

$$\mu_{\tilde{A}}(x) = \begin{cases} \dfrac{x-a_1}{a_2-a_1}, & a_1 \leq x \leq a_2 \\ 1, & x = a_2 \\ \dfrac{a_3-x}{a_3-a_2}, & a_2 \leq x \leq a_3 \end{cases} \tag{1.7}$$

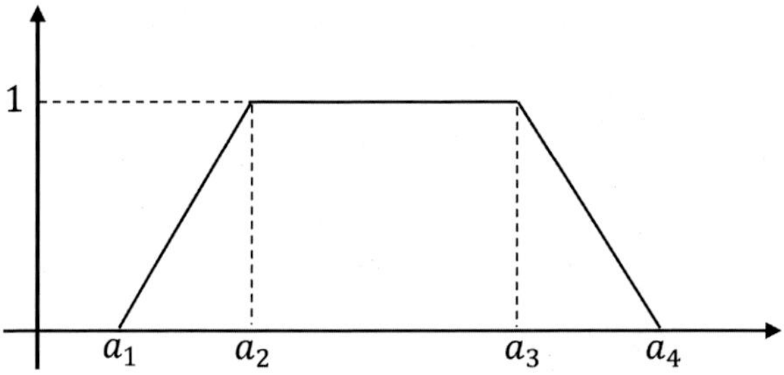

Fig. 1.3 Trapezoidal fuzzy number $\tilde{A} = (a_1, a_2, a_3, a_4)$.

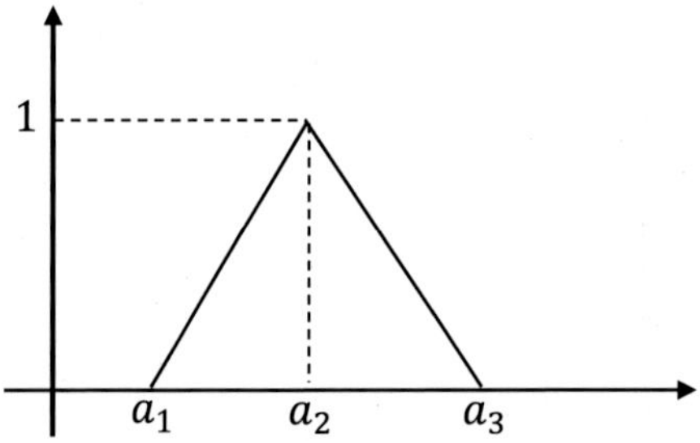

Fig. 1.4 Trapezoidal fuzzy number $\tilde{A} = (a_1, a_2, a_3)$.

It is notable that a triangular fuzzy number is a special form of trapezoidal number $\tilde{A} = (a_1, a_2, a_3, a_4)$ when $a_2 = a_3$.

Definition 1.19 Assume $\tilde{A} = (a_1, a_2, a_3)_{LR}$ and $\tilde{B} = (b_1, b_2, b_3)_{LR}$ as two fuzzy *LR* numbers and $\tilde{C} = (c_1, c_2, c_3)_{RL}$ as a fuzzy *RL* number. Then,

- $\tilde{A} + \tilde{B} = (a_1 + b_1, a_2 + b_2, a_3 + b_3)_{LR}$,
- $\tilde{A} - \tilde{C} = (a_1 - c_3, a_2 - c_2, a_3 - c_1)_{LR}$.
- $\tilde{A} \otimes \tilde{B} \approx (a_1 b_1, a_2 b_2, a_3 b_3)_{LR}$ if $a_1, b_1 > 0$.
- $\tilde{A} \odot \tilde{B} \approx \left(\frac{a_1}{b_3}, \frac{a_2}{b_2}, \frac{a_3}{b_1}\right)_{LR}$ if $a_1, b_1 > 0$.
- $t\tilde{A} = \begin{cases} (ta_1, ta_2, ta_3)_{LR}, & t \geq 0 \\ (ta_3, ta_2, ta_1)_{RL}, & t < 0 \end{cases}$.

Definition 1.20 Assume $\tilde{A} = (a_1, a_2, a_3, a_4)_{LR}$ and $\tilde{B} = (b_1, b_2, b_3, b_4)_{LR}$ as two fuzzy *LR* numbers and $\tilde{C} = (c_1, c_2, c_3, c_4)_{RL}$ as a fuzzy *RL* number. Then,

- $\tilde{A} + \tilde{B} = (a_1 + b_1, a_2 + b_2, a_3 + b_3, a_4 + b_4)_{LR}$.
- $\tilde{A} - \tilde{B} = (a_1 - b_4, a_2 - b_3, a_3 - b_2, a_4 - b_1)_{LR}$.
- $\tilde{A} \otimes \tilde{B} \approx (a_1 b_1, a_2 b_2, a_3 b_3, a_4 b_4)_{LR}$ if $a_1, b_1 > 0$.
- $\tilde{A} \odot \tilde{B} \approx \left(\frac{a_1}{b_4}, \frac{a_2}{b_3}, \frac{a_3}{b_2}, \frac{a_4}{b_1}\right)_{LR}$ if $a_1, b_1 > 0$.
- $t\tilde{A} = \begin{cases} (ta_1, ta_2, ta_3, ta_4)_{LR}, & t \geq 0 \\ (ta_4, ta_3, ta_2, ta_1)_{RL}, & t < 0 \end{cases}$.

Definition 1.21 α-cut of triangular fuzzy number $\tilde{A} = (a_1, a_2, a_3)$ and trapezoidal fuzzy number $\tilde{A} = (a_1, a_2, a_3, a_4)$ are obtained by the following relationships, respectively.

$$\begin{aligned} A_\alpha &= \{x | \mu_A(x) \geq \alpha\} = [A_1(\alpha), A_2(\alpha)] \\ &= [(a_2 - a_1\ )\alpha + a_1, a_3 - (a_3 - a_2)\alpha] \end{aligned} \tag{1.8}$$

$$\begin{aligned} A_\alpha &= \{x | \mu_A(x) \geq \alpha\} = [A_1(\alpha), A_2(\alpha)] \\ &= [(a_2 - a_1\ )\alpha + a_1, a_4 - (a_4 - a_3)\alpha] \end{aligned} \tag{1.9}$$

Definition 1.22 (Khezerloo et al., 2011). The parametric form of fuzzy number $\tilde{U}$ is the ordered pairs $(\underline{u}(r), \overline{u}(r)), 0 \leq r \leq 1$ where $\underline{u}(r) : [0, 1] \to \mathbb{R}$ and $\overline{u}(r) : [0, 1] \to \mathbb{R}$ are two functions with the following conditions:

- $\underline{u}(r)$ is a nondecreasing uniform function and left-continuous on $[0, 1]$,
- $\overline{u}(r)$ is a nonincreasing uniform function and left-continuous on,
- For any r where $0 \leq r \leq 1$ the condition $\underline{u}(r) \leq \overline{u}(r)$ should be held.

Definition 1.23 (Allahviranloo & Salahshour, 2011). For fuzzy numbers $\tilde{u} = (\underline{u}(r), \overline{u}(r))$ and $\tilde{v} = (\underline{v}(r), \overline{v}(r))$ where $0 \leq r \leq 1$ and $k \in \mathbb{R}$, the following mathematical operations are defined.

$$\tilde{u} + \tilde{v} = (\underline{u+v}(r), \overline{u+v}(r)), \quad 0 \leq r \leq 1 \tag{1.10}$$

$$\begin{cases} \underline{u+v}(r) = \underline{u}(r) + \underline{v}(r), \\ \overline{u+v}(r) = \overline{u}(r) + \overline{v}(r), \end{cases} \tag{1.11}$$

$$\tilde{u} - \tilde{v} = (\underline{u-v}(r), \overline{u-v}(r)) \qquad 0 \leq r \leq 1 \tag{1.12}$$

$$\begin{cases} \underline{u-v}(r) = \underline{u}(r) - \overline{v}(r), \\ \overline{u-v}(r) = \overline{u}(r) - \underline{v}(r), \end{cases} \tag{1.13}$$

$$k\tilde{u} = \begin{cases} (k\underline{u}(r), k\overline{u}(r)), & k \geq 0, \\ (k\overline{u}(r), k\underline{u}(r)), & k \leq 0, \end{cases} \quad 0 \leq r \leq 1 \tag{1.14}$$

$$\tilde{u} \otimes \tilde{v} = (\underline{uv}(r), \overline{uv}(r)), \quad 0 \leq r \leq 1 \tag{1.15}$$

$$\begin{cases} \underline{uv}(r) = \min\limits_{0 \leq r \leq 1} \{\underline{u}(r)\underline{v}(r), \underline{u}(r)\overline{v}(r), \overline{u}(r)\underline{v}(r), \overline{u}(r)\overline{v}(r)\} \\ \overline{uv}(r) = \max\limits_{0 \leq r \leq 1} \{\underline{u}(r)\underline{v}(r), \underline{u}(r)\overline{v}(r), \overline{u}(r)\underline{v}(r), \overline{u}(r)\overline{v}(r)\} \end{cases} \tag{1.16}$$

The following special cases are considered for the product of two fuzzy numbers:

- If $\tilde{u} \geq 0$ and $\tilde{v} \geq 0$, then,

$$\underline{uv}(r) = \underline{u}(r)\underline{v}(r), \quad 0 \leq r \leq 1 \tag{1.17}$$

$$\overline{uv}(r) = \overline{u}(r)\overline{v}(r) \quad 0 \leq r \leq 1 \tag{1.18}$$

- If $\tilde{u} \leq 0$ and $\tilde{v} \leq 0$, then,

$$\underline{uv}(r) = \overline{u}(r)\overline{v}(r) \quad 0 \leq r \leq 1 \tag{1.19}$$

$$\overline{uv}(r) = \underline{u}(r)\underline{v}(r) \quad 0 \leq r \leq 1 \tag{1.20}$$

- If $\tilde{u} \geq 0$ and $\tilde{v} \leq 0$, then,

$$\underline{uv}(r) = \overline{u}(r)\underline{v}(r) \quad 0 \leq r \leq 1 \tag{1.21}$$

$$\overline{uv}(r) = \underline{u}(r)\overline{v}(r) \quad 0 \leq r \leq 1 \tag{1.22}$$

- If $\tilde{u} \leq 0$ and $\tilde{v} \geq 0$, then,

$$\underline{uv}(r) = \underline{u}(r)\overline{v}(r) \quad 0 \leq r \leq 1 \tag{1.23}$$

$$\overline{uv}(r) = \overline{u}(r)\underline{v}(r) \quad 0 \leq r \leq 1 \tag{1.24}$$

1.2.2 Possibility measure

Possibility theory is a new method in mathematics that, like old methods of probability theory, tries to analyze uncertain events. This theory was first introduced by Zadeh (1978) to measure a fuzzy event. This theory later was extended by Dubois and Prade (1988). When analyzing the events and environmental conditions, we don't just seek certain events. According to this measure, in such conditions all possible events with their associated possibility degree are considered. Some concepts and definitions of the possibility measure are explained (Liu, 2002, 2004).

Definition 1.24 If X is a nonempty sample space with a power set of $\mathrm{P}(X)$, then the function $Pos: \mathrm{P}(X) \rightarrow [0,1]$ is a possibility measure of X, if it follows the conditions below,

- $Pos\{X\} = 1$,
- $Pos\{\varnothing\} = 0$,
- $Pos\left\{\bigcup_i A_i\right\} = \sup_i Pos\{A_i\}$, for any collection $\{A_i\}$ in $P(X)$.

Therefore, the triple $(X, \mathrm{P}(X), Pos)$ is called possibility space.

Theorem 1.1 According to the possibility space $(X, P(X), Pos)$,

- for any $A \in P(X)$, $0 \le Pos\{A\} \le 1$,
- if $A \subset B$, then $Pos\{A\} \le Pos\{B\}$,
- for any A, $B \in P(X)$, $Pos\{A \cup B\} \le Pos\{A\} + Pos\{B\}$.

Definition 1.25 The collection $X^+ = \{x \in X | \, Pos\{x\} > 0\}$ is called the kernel of the possibility space $(X, P(X), Pos)$.

Theorem 1.2 Suppose $(X_i, P(X_i), Pos_i)$ for $i = 1, 2, \ldots, n$ is some possibility space where $X = X_1 \times X_2 \times \ldots \times X_n$ and $Pos = Pos_1 \wedge Pos_2 \wedge \ldots \wedge Pos_n$. Then, the collective function Pos is a possibility measure on $P(X)$ and $(X, P(X), Pos)$.

Definition 1.26 Suppose $(X_i, P(X_i), Pos_i)$ for $i = 1, 2, \ldots, n$ is some possibility space where $X = X_1 \times X_2 \times \ldots d \times X_n$ and $Pos = Pos_1 \wedge Pos_2 \wedge \ldots \wedge Pos_n$. Then, $(X, P(X), Pos)$ is called the product possibility space of $(X_i, P(X_i), Pos_i)$.

Theorem 1.3 Suppose $(X_i, P(X_i), Pos_i)$ for $i = 1, 2, \ldots, n$ is some possibility space where $X = X_1 \times X_2 \times \ldots \times X_n$ and $Pos\{A\} = \sup_{(X_1, X_2, \ldots) \in X} Pos_1\{X_1\} \wedge Pos_2\{X_2\} \wedge \ldots$. Then, the collective function Pos is a possibility measure on $P(X)$ and $(X, P(X), Pos)$.

Definition 1.27 Suppose $(X_i, P(X_i), Pos_i)$ for $i = 1, 2, \ldots, n$ is some possibility space where $X = X_1 \times X_2 \times \ldots \times X_n$ and $Pos = Pos_1 \wedge Pos_2 \wedge \ldots \wedge Pos_n$. Then, $(X, P(X), Pos)$ is called the infinite product possibility space of $(X_i, P(X_i), Pos_i)$.

1.2.3 Necessity measure

The necessity measure of event A is equal to one minus the possibility of the supplement of A. It shows the amount of necessity of occurring the event.

Definition 1.28 Suppose $(X, P(X), Pos)$ as a possibility space and A as a collection of $P(X)$. Then, the necessity measure of A is defined as,

$$Nec\{A\} = 1 - Pos\{A^c\} \tag{1.25}$$

Therefore, an event happens necessarily when its supplement event has no possibility of occurring.

Theorem 1.4 According to the possibility space $(X, (X), Pos)$, the following is claimed,

- $Nec\{X\} = 1$,
- $Nec\{\varnothing\} = 1$,
- $Nec\{A\} = 0$ whenever $Pos\{A\} < 1$,
- $Nec\{A\} \leq Nec\{B\}$ whenever $A \subset B$,
- $Nec\{A\} + Pos\{A^c\} = 1$ for any $A \in P(X)$.

1.2.4 Credibility measure

The main disadvantage of the possibility theory is the lack of a self-duality property. Based on this disadvantage, Liu and Liu (2002a, 2002b) proposed the fuzzy credibility theory as an alternative to the possibility theory. As an example, the investors are aware of the possibility of a portfolio reaching its goal return (using possibility theory), but they cannot identify the possibility that the portfolio has not reached that goal. This issue can be a main concern for the investors. For this aim, Liu and Liu (2002a, 2002b) proposed the fuzzy credibility theory, which has a self-duality property as its main advantage. This theory was later extended to be applied in many optimization problems (Mahmoodirad et al., 2019; Mirzaei et al., 2019; Peykani et al., 2019, 2022; Pishvaee et al., 2012).

Definition 1.29 Suppose $(X, P(X), Pos)$ as a possibility space and A as a collection of $P(X)$. Then, the credibility measure of A is defined as,

$$Cr\{A\} = \frac{1}{2}(Pos\{A\} + Nec\{A\}) \tag{1.26}$$

Theorem 1.5 Suppose $(X, P(X), Pos)$ as a possibility space and A as a collection of P(X). Then,

$$Nec\{A\} \leq Cr\{A\} \leq Pos\{A\} \tag{1.27}$$

Theorem 1.6 Suppose $(X, P(X), Pos)$ as a possibility space, Then,

- $Cr\{X\} = 1$,
- $Cr\{\varnothing\} = 0$,
- $Cr\{A\} \leq Cr\{B\}$,if $A \subset B$,
- $Cr\{A\} + Cr\{A^c\} = 1$, for any $A \in P(X)$; (Cr is self-dual),
- $Cr\{A \cup B\} \leq Cr\{A\} + Cr\{B\}$, for any A, $B \in P(X)$.

Definition 1.30 A fuzzy variable is defined from possibility space $(X, P(X), Pos)$ to the set of real numbers.

Definition 1.31 Suppose ξ is a fuzzy variable of possibility space $(X, P(X), Pos)$. Then, the set $\xi_\beta = \{\xi(x) | x \in X, Pos\{x\} \geq \beta\}$ is the $\beta-$level set of ξ, and the set $\{\xi(x) | x \in X, Pos\{x\} > 0\} = \{\xi(x) | x \in X^+\}$ is its supports where X^+ is the core of $(X, P(X), Pos)$.

Definition 1.32 Consider fuzzy variable ξ. Then,

- It is a nonnegative fuzzy variable if and only if $Pos\{\xi < 0\} = 0$,
- It is a positive fuzzy variable if and only if $Pos\{\xi \leq 0\} = 0$,
- It is a continuous fuzzy variable if and only if $Pos\{\xi = x\}$ is a continuous function of x.

Theorem 1.7 If fuzzy variable ξ is continuous, then $Pos\{\xi \geq x\}$ and $Pos\{\xi \leq x\}$ are continuous functions of x. In addition, $Pos\{x \leq \xi \leq y\}$ is a continuous function on $\{(x, y) | x < y\}$.

Definition 1.33 The membership function of fuzzy variable ξ on possibility space $(X, P(X), Pos)$ is obtained by,

$$\mu(t) = Pos\{x \in X | \xi(x) = t\}, t \in \mathbb{R} \tag{1.28}$$

Theorem 1.8 Consider fuzzy variable ξ with a membership function of μ. Then,

- It is a nonnegative fuzzy variable if and only if $\mu(x) = 0$ for any $x < 0$,
- It is a positive fuzzy variable if and only if $\mu(x) = 0$ for any $x \leq 0$,
- It is a continuous fuzzy variable if and only if μ is a continuous function.

Definition 1.34 Suppose ξ_1 and ξ_2 as two fuzzy variables on possibility space $(X, P(X), Pos)$. Then, $\xi_1 = \xi_2$ if and only if $\xi_1(x) = \xi_2(x)$ for $x \in X$.

Definition 1.35 Suppose $f: \mathbb{R}^n \rightarrow \mathbb{R}$ is a function and for each $i = 1, 2, \ldots, n$, ξ_i is a fuzzy variable on possibility space $(X_i, P(X_i), Pos_i)$. Then, the fuzzy variable $\xi = f(\xi_1, \xi_2, \ldots, \xi_n)$ on the product possibility space $(X, P(X), Pos)$ is defined as below,

$$\xi(x_1, x_2, \ldots, x_n) = f(\xi_1(x_1), \xi_2(x_2), \ldots, \xi_n(x_n)), \text{for any } (x_1, x_2, \ldots, x_n) \in X \tag{1.29}$$

Definition 1.36 For fuzzy variable ξ with membership function μ and real number r,

$$Pos\{\xi \leq r\} = \sup_{x \leq r} \mu(x) \tag{1.30}$$

$$Nec\{\xi \leq r\} = 1 - \sup_{x > r} \mu(x) \tag{1.31}$$

Example 1.1 For triangular fuzzy variable $\xi = (a, b, c)$ and real number r, the above-mentioned measures are defined as below,

$$Pos\{\xi \leq r\} = \begin{cases} 0, & r \leq a \\ \dfrac{r-a}{b-a}, & a \leq r \leq b \\ 1, & b \leq r \end{cases} \tag{1.32}$$

$$Pos\{\xi \geq r\} = \begin{cases} 1, & r \leq b \\ \dfrac{c-r}{c-b}, & c \leq r \leq b \\ 0, & c \leq r \end{cases} \tag{1.33}$$

$$Nec\{\xi \leq r\} = \begin{cases} 0, & r \leq b \\ \dfrac{r-b}{c-b}, & b \leq r \leq c \\ 1, & c \leq r \end{cases} \tag{1.34}$$

$$Nec\{\xi \geq r\} = \begin{cases} 1, & r \leq a \\ \dfrac{b-r}{b-a}, & a \leq r \leq b \\ 0, & c \leq r \end{cases} \tag{1.35}$$

$$Cr\{\xi \leq r\} = \begin{cases} 0, & r \leq a \\ \dfrac{r-a}{2(b-a)}, & a \leq r \leq b \\ \dfrac{r+c-2b}{2(c-b)}, & b \leq r \leq c \\ 1, & c \leq r \end{cases} \tag{1.36}$$

$$Cr\{\xi \geq r\} = \begin{cases} 1, & r \leq a \\ \dfrac{2b-a-r}{2(b-a)}, & a \leq r \leq b \\ \dfrac{c-r}{2(c-b)}, & b \leq r \leq c \\ 0, & c \leq r \end{cases} \tag{1.37}$$

Example 1.2 For trapezoidal fuzzy variable $\zeta = (a, b, c, d)$ and real number α, the above-mentioned measures are defined as below,

$$Pos\{\zeta \geq \alpha\} = \begin{cases} 1, & \alpha \leq c \\ \dfrac{d-\alpha}{d-c}, & c \leq \alpha \leq d \\ 0, & d \leq \alpha \end{cases} \tag{1.38}$$

$$Pos\{\zeta \leq \alpha\} = \begin{cases} 0, & \alpha \leq a \\ \dfrac{\alpha-a}{b-a}, & a \leq \alpha \leq b \\ 1, & b \leq \alpha \end{cases} \tag{1.39}$$

$$Nec\{\zeta \geq \alpha\} = \begin{cases} 1, & \alpha \leq a \\ \dfrac{b-\alpha}{b-a}, & a \leq \alpha \leq b \\ 0, & b \leq \alpha \end{cases} \tag{1.40}$$

$$Nec\{\zeta \leq \alpha\} = \begin{cases} 0, & \alpha \leq c \\ \dfrac{\alpha-c}{d-c}, & c \leq \alpha \leq d \\ 1, & d \leq \alpha \end{cases} \tag{1.41}$$

$$Cr\{\zeta \leq \alpha\} = \begin{cases} 0, & \alpha \leq a \\ \dfrac{\alpha-a}{2(b-a)}, & a \leq \alpha \leq b \\ 0.5, & b \leq \alpha \leq c \\ \dfrac{\alpha-2c+d}{2(d-c)}, & c \leq \alpha \leq d \\ 1, & d \leq \alpha \end{cases} \tag{1.42}$$

$$Cr\{\zeta \geq \alpha\} = \begin{cases} 1, & \alpha \leq a \\ \dfrac{2b-a-\alpha}{2(b-a)}, & a \leq \alpha \leq b \\ 0.5, & b \leq \alpha \leq c \\ \dfrac{d-\alpha}{2(d-c)}, & c \leq \alpha \leq d \\ 0, & d \leq \alpha \end{cases} \tag{1.43}$$

Theorem 1.9 For triangular fuzzy variable $\xi=(a,b,c)$, trapezoidal fuzzy variable $\zeta=(a,b,c,d)$, and real number r, the following inequalities are defined for any confidence level β where $0<\beta\leq 1$.

$$\begin{aligned} Pos\{\xi \leq r\} \geq \beta &\Leftrightarrow (1-\beta)a+\beta b \leq r \\ Pos\{\xi \geq r\} \geq \beta &\Leftrightarrow \beta b+(1-\beta)c \geq r \\ Pos\{\zeta \leq r\} \geq \beta &\Leftrightarrow (1-\beta)a+\beta b \leq r \\ Pos\{\zeta \geq r\} \geq \beta &\Leftrightarrow \beta c+(1-\beta)d \geq r \end{aligned} \tag{1.44}$$

Corollary 1.1 The measure *Pos* is the most optimistic possibilistic confidence level for a fuzzy event. So, it is used by decision makers with optimistic opinions.

Theorem 1.10 For triangular fuzzy variable $\xi=(a,b,c)$, trapezoidal fuzzy variable $\zeta=(a,b,c,d)$, and real number r, the following inequalities are defined for any confidence level β where $0<\beta\leq 1$.

$$\begin{aligned} Nec\{\xi \leq r\} \geq \beta &\Leftrightarrow (1-\beta)b+\beta c \leq r \\ Nec\{\xi \geq r\} \geq \beta &\Leftrightarrow \beta a+(1-\beta)b \geq r \\ Nec\{\zeta \leq r\} \geq \beta &\Leftrightarrow (1-\beta)c+\beta d \leq r \\ Nec\{\zeta \geq r\} \geq \beta &\Leftrightarrow \beta a+(1-\beta)b \geq r \end{aligned} \tag{1.45}$$

Corollary 1.2 The measure *Nec* is the most pessimistic possibilistic confidence level for a fuzzy event. So, it is used by decision makers with high risk.

Theorem 1.11 For triangular fuzzy variable $\xi=(a,b,c)$, trapezoidal fuzzy variable $\zeta=(a,b,c,d)$, and real number r, the following inequalities are defined for any confidence level β where $0<\beta\leq 1$.

$$\begin{aligned} Cr\{\xi \leq r\} \geq \beta &\Leftrightarrow \begin{cases} (1-2\beta)a+2\beta b \leq r, & \beta \leq 0.5 \\ (2-2\beta)b+(2\beta-1)c \leq r, & \beta > 0.5 \end{cases} \\ Cr\{\xi \geq r\} \geq \beta &\Leftrightarrow \begin{cases} 2\beta b+(1-2\beta)c \geq r, & \beta \leq 0.5 \\ (2\beta-1)a+(2-2\beta)b \geq r, & \beta > 0.5 \end{cases} \\ Cr\{\zeta \leq r\} \geq \beta &\Leftrightarrow \begin{cases} (1-2\beta)a+2\beta b \leq r, & \beta \leq 0.5 \\ (2-2\beta)c+(2\beta-1)d \leq r, & \beta > 0.5 \end{cases} \\ Cr\{\zeta \geq r\} \geq \beta &\Leftrightarrow \begin{cases} 2\beta c+(1-2\beta)d \geq r, & \beta \leq 0.5 \\ (2\beta-1)a+(2-2\beta)b \geq r, & \beta > 0.5 \end{cases} \end{aligned} \tag{1.46}$$

1.2.5 General fuzzy measure

Suppose $(X, \mathrm{P}(X), Pos)$ as a possibility space and A the set of $(X, \mathrm{P}(X), Pos)$. Then, the general fuzzy measure of $A \in P(X)$ is defined as below (Xu & Zhou, 2013),

$$Me\{A\} = \gamma Pos\{A\} + (1-\gamma)Nec\{A\} \tag{1.47}$$

where γ $(0 \le \gamma \le 1)$ is an optimistic-pessimistic parameter for determining the combined attitude of the decision maker.

- If $\gamma = 0$, then $Me = Nec$, which shows the pessimistic attitude of the decision maker.
- If $\gamma = 0.5$, then $Me = Cr$, which shows the compromise attitude of the decision maker.
- If $\gamma = 1$, then $Me = Pos$, which shows the optimistic attitude of the decision maker.

Theorem 1.12 For possibility space $(X, (X), Pos)$ and set A from (X), there will be,

$$Me\{X\} = 1 \tag{1.48}$$

$$Me\{\varnothing\} = 0 \tag{1.49}$$

$$Nec\{A\} \le Me\{A\} \le Pos\{A\}, \text{for any } A \in P(X) \tag{1.50}$$

$$0 \le Me\{A\} \le 1, \text{ for any } A \in P(X) \tag{1.51}$$

$$Me\{A\} \le M\{B\}, \text{ if } A \subset B \tag{1.52}$$

$$0 \le Me\{A\} + Me\{A^c\} \le 1, \text{ for any } A \in P(X) \text{ and } \gamma \le 0.5 \tag{1.53}$$

$$1 \le Me\{A\} + Me\{A^c\} \le 2, \text{for any } A \in P(X) \text{ and } \gamma \ge 0.5 \tag{1.54}$$

$$Me\{A \cup B\} \le Me\{A\} + Me\{B\}, \text{for any } A, B \in P(X) \text{ and } \gamma \ge 0.5 \tag{1.55}$$

Example 1.3 For triangular fuzzy variable $\xi = (a, b, c)$ and real number α, the above-mentioned measures are defined as below,

$$Me\{\xi \le r\} = \begin{cases} 0, & r \le a \\ \gamma\left(\dfrac{r-a}{b-a}\right), & a \le r \le b \\ \gamma + (1-\gamma)\left(\dfrac{r-b}{c-b}\right), & b \le r \le c \\ 1, & c \le r \end{cases} \tag{1.56}$$

$$Me\{\xi \geq r\} = \begin{cases} 1, & r \leq a \\ \gamma + (1-\gamma)\left(\dfrac{b-r}{b-a}\right), & a \leq r \leq b \\ \gamma\left(\dfrac{c-r}{c-b}\right), & b \leq r \leq c \\ 1, & c \leq r \end{cases} \tag{1.57}$$

Example 1.4 For trapezoidal fuzzy variable $\zeta = (a, b, c, d)$ and real number α, the above-mentioned measures are defined as below,

$$Me\{\zeta \leq \alpha\} = \begin{cases} 0, & r \leq a \\ \gamma\left(\dfrac{\alpha - a}{b - a}\right), & a \leq r \leq b \\ \gamma, & b \leq r \leq c \\ \gamma + (1-\gamma)\left(\dfrac{\alpha - c}{d - c}\right), & c \leq r \leq d \\ 1, & d \leq r \end{cases} \tag{1.58}$$

$$Me\{\zeta \geq \alpha\} = \begin{cases} 1, & r \leq a \\ \gamma + (1-\gamma)\left(\dfrac{b - \alpha}{b - a}\right), & a \leq r \leq b \\ \gamma, & b \leq r \leq c \\ \gamma\left(\dfrac{d - \alpha}{d - c}\right), & c \leq r \leq d \\ 0, & d \leq r \end{cases} \tag{1.59}$$

Theorem 1.13 For triangular fuzzy variable $\xi = (a, b, c)$, trapezoidal fuzzy variable $\zeta = (a, b, c, d)$, and real number r, the following inequalities are defined for any confidence level β where $0 < \beta \leq 1$.

$$Me\{\xi \le r\} \ge \beta \Leftrightarrow \begin{cases} \left(\dfrac{\gamma-\beta}{\gamma}\right)a + \left(\dfrac{\beta}{\gamma}\right)b \le r, & \beta \le \gamma \\ \left(\dfrac{1-\beta}{1-\gamma}\right)b + \left(\dfrac{\beta-\gamma}{1-\gamma}\right)c \le r, & \beta > \gamma \end{cases}$$
$$Me\{\xi \ge r\} \ge \beta \Leftrightarrow \begin{cases} \left(\dfrac{\beta}{\gamma}\right)b + \left(\dfrac{\gamma-\beta}{\gamma}\right)c \ge r, & \beta \le \gamma \\ \left(\dfrac{\beta-\gamma}{1-\gamma}\right)a + \left(\dfrac{1-\beta}{1-\gamma}\right)b \ge r, & \beta > \gamma \end{cases}$$
$$Me\{\zeta \le r\} \ge \beta \Leftrightarrow \begin{cases} \left(\dfrac{\gamma-\beta}{\gamma}\right)a + \left(\dfrac{\beta}{\gamma}\right)b \le r, & \beta \le \gamma \\ \left(\dfrac{1-\beta}{1-\gamma}\right)c + \left(\dfrac{\beta-\gamma}{1-\gamma}\right)d \le r, & \beta > \gamma \end{cases} \quad (1.60)$$
$$Me\{\zeta \ge r\} \ge \beta \Leftrightarrow \begin{cases} \left(\dfrac{\beta}{\gamma}\right)c + \left(\dfrac{\gamma-\beta}{\gamma}\right)d \ge r, & \beta \le \gamma \\ \left(\dfrac{\beta-\gamma}{1-\gamma}\right)a + \left(\dfrac{1-\beta}{1-\gamma}\right)b \ge r, & \beta > \gamma \end{cases}$$

Definition 1.37 $\alpha-$optimistic value of fuzzy variable ξ ($\alpha \in [0,1]$) is calculated as,

$$\xi_{\sup}(\alpha) = \sup\{r | Cr\{\xi \ge r\} \ge \alpha\} \quad (1.61)$$

where this value is the supremum of the value obtained by ξ with credibility of α.

Definition 1.38 $\alpha-$ pessimistic value of fuzzy variable ξ ($\alpha \in [0,1]$) is calculated as,

$$\xi_{\inf}(\alpha) = \inf\{r | Cr\{\xi \le r\} \ge \alpha\} \quad (1.62)$$

where this value is the infimum of the value obtained by ξ with credibility of α. The optimistic and pessimistic values are used to rank fuzzy variables.

Example 1.5 For triangular fuzzy variable $\xi = (a, b, c)$, the $\alpha-$ optimistic and $\alpha-$ pessimistic values are obtained as below,

$$\xi_{\sup}(\alpha) = \begin{cases} 2\alpha b + (1-2\alpha)c & \alpha \le 0.5 \\ (2\alpha-1)a + (2-2\alpha)b & \alpha > 0.5 \end{cases} \quad (1.63)$$

$$\xi_{\inf}(\alpha) = \begin{cases} (1-2\alpha)a + 2\alpha b & \alpha \le 0.5 \\ (2-2\alpha)b + (2\alpha-1)c & \alpha > 0.5 \end{cases} \quad (1.64)$$

Example 1.6 For trapezoidal fuzzy variable $\zeta = (a, b, c, d)$, the $\alpha-$ optimistic and $\alpha-$ pessimistic values are obtained as below,

$$\zeta_{\sup}(\alpha) = \begin{cases} 2\alpha c + (1 - 2\alpha)d & \alpha \leq 0.5 \\ (2\alpha - 1)a + (2 - 2\alpha)b & \alpha > 0.5 \end{cases} \tag{1.65}$$

$$\zeta_{\inf}(\alpha) = \begin{cases} (1 - 2\alpha)a + 2\alpha b & \alpha \leq 0.5 \\ (2 - 2\alpha)c + (2\alpha - 1)d & \alpha > 0.5 \end{cases} \tag{1.66}$$

1.2.6 Expected value operator

In this section, the expected value of a fuzzy variable is explained by some definitions and theorems (Liu & Liu, 2002a, 2002b, 2003).

Definition 1.39 The expected value of fuzzy variable ξ is defined as below with the condition that at least one of the integrals be finite.

$$E[\xi] = \int_0^{\infty} Cr\{\xi \geq r\}dr - \int_{-\infty}^{0} Cr\{\xi \leq r\}dr \tag{1.67}$$

Example 1.7 The expected value of triangular fuzzy variable $\xi = (a, b, c)$ is defined as below,

$$E[\xi] = \frac{1}{4}(a + 2b + c) \tag{1.68}$$

Example 1.8 The expected value of trapezoidal fuzzy variable $\zeta = (a, b, c, d)$ is defined as below,

$$E[\zeta] = \frac{1}{4}(a + b + c + d) \tag{1.69}$$

Theorem 1.14 For fuzzy variable ξ and real numbers α and β,

$$E[a\xi + b] = aE[\xi] + b \tag{1.70}$$

Definition 1.40 The variance of fuzzy variable ξ is defined as below,

$$V[\xi] = E\left[(\xi - E)^2\right] \tag{1.71}$$

Theorem 1.15 For fuzzy variable ξ (where its variance exists) and real numbers α and β,

$$V[\alpha\xi + \beta] = \alpha^2 V[\xi] \tag{1.72}$$

1.3 Belief degree-based uncertainty theory

Usually, in real-world problems it is very difficult to know the value of the parameters exactly. To model such an inexact situation, there are two main methods of mathematics: probability theory and uncertainty theory. Probability theory is based on the abundance of uncertain events where uncertainty theory is based on the belief degree of people. If there are enough historical data about the inexact parameters, those can be modeled as stochastic variables with associated probability distributions. In cases where there are not enough historical data or there are invalid situations such as weather, accidents, etc., there is no probability distribution for the inexact parameters. In some cases, there is no possibility of collecting the required data by any experiment (e.g., evaluating the strength of a bridge against pressure or obtaining the number of volcanoes in a mountain). To model such uncertain cases, a solution is to use the ideas of field experts where they can express their opinion about the uncertain parameters based on their experience and existing evidence. To use the opinion of experts about uncertain events, several methods have been developed such as the Delphi method (Dalkey & Olaf, 1963), possibility theory (Sigarreta et al., 2007), the theory of Dempster-Shafer (Dempster, 1967; Shafer, 1967), etc. Therefore, the belief degree of experts can be used for evaluating any uncertain event and its inexact parameters.

Belief degree is a well-known concept and a belief-based concept is an event. For example, the claim that tomorrow will be sunny is an event that is believed and our belief degree about it shows how we believe this event will happen. It is questionable that why do we need to use belief degree for obtaining occurrence degree of an event instead of probability theory? To answer this question, assume a dark box with 100 balls in it where some of the balls are blue and others are red, and there is no information about the number of blue and red balls. If it is decided to take a ball from the box, the probability of selecting a blue or a red ball cannot be determined. As there is no information about the number of blue and red balls in the box, there is no priority for selecting a blue or red ball. Therefore, the belief degree of selecting a blue or red ball can be used and calculated to evaluate the event of selecting a ball.

The uncertainty theory was first introduced by Liu (2007) and later developed by Liu (2009). In recent years, this theory has been widely used in many studies, such as on the banking sector (Jamshidi et al., 2019, 2021, 2022), supply chain networks (Mahmoodirad & Niroomand, 2020a, 2020b), transportation problems (Sheng & Yao, 2012), network flows (Han et al., 2014), etc.

In the rest of this section, some basic concepts of belief degree-based uncertainty theory are explained; these are taken from the studies of Liu (2007, 2015), Liu and Ha (2010), Peng and Iwamura (2010), and Dai and Chen (2012).

1.3.1 Uncertainty measure

Definition 1.41 Suppose $\mathit{\Gamma}$ as a nonempty set (which later is called a reference set). The set L containing subsets of Γ is an algebra on Γ with the following conditions,

- $\Gamma \in L$,
- if $\mathit{\Lambda} \in L$ then $\mathit{\Lambda}^c \in L$, where Λ^c is the supplement of $\mathit{\Lambda}$,
- if $\Lambda_1, \Lambda_2, \ldots, \Lambda_n \in L$ then $\bigcup_{i=1}^{n} \Lambda_i \in L$.

Definition 1.42 Set L is called a σ-algebra on Γ, where for $\Lambda_1, \Lambda_2, \ldots, \Lambda_n \in L$ the condition $\bigcup_{i=1}^{\infty} \Lambda_i \in L$ is held.

Definition 1.43 Suppose Γ as a nonempty set and L as a σ-algebra on Γ, then (Γ, L) is a measurable space and each entity of Γ is also a measurable set or an event.

Definition 1.44 Suppose Δ is the smallest σ-algebra that contains all open intervals of $\mathbb{R}$. It is called a Borel algebra of the real numbers where each entity of Δ is called a Borel set.

Definition 1.45 Function f from measurable space (Γ, L) to the real numbers is a measurable function if and only if $f^{-1}(B) = \{\xi \in \Gamma | f(\xi) \in B\} \in L$ is true for any Borel set B of the real numbers.

Definition 1.46 Suppose L as a σ-algebra on nonempty set Γ. The collective function M is called an uncertain measure on L, where the following conditions are held,

- $M\{\Gamma\} = 1$,
- $M\{\Lambda\} + M\{\Lambda^c\} = 1$ for any $\Lambda \in L$,
- $M\left\{\bigcup_{i=1}^{\infty}\right\} \leq \sum_{i=1}^{\infty} M\{\Lambda_i\}$ for any countable sequence of $\{\mathit{\Lambda}_i\} \in L$.

The triple (Γ, L, M) is called uncertain space and each entity of Λ in L is called an event.

Remark 1.1 Uncertainty measure is the belief degree of people about an uncertain event that may happen. It is related to the personal knowledge of people about the event, so it is changed by variations in people's knowledge.

Definition 1.47 Suppose measurable space (Γ, L). Any entity Λ from L is called an event. The value $M\{\Lambda\}$ shows the belief degree of a person for occurring event Λ.

Reminder 1.1 As number 1 means full certainty, therefore, the belief degree of an event cannot be greater than 1. Also, the belief degree of the reference set is equal to 1 as its occurrence is fully believable.

Theorem 1.16 Assume M as an uncertain measure, then for any event Λ the condition $0 \leq M\{\Lambda\} \leq 1$ is held.

Theorem 1.17 Assume M as an uncertain measure, then the empty set ($\emptyset$) has the measure of $M\{\emptyset\}=0$.

Theorem 1.18 The uncertain measure M is increasingly uniform where for the events $\Lambda_1 \subset \Lambda_2$ the condition $M\{\Lambda_1\} \leq M\{\Lambda_2\}$ is held.

To obtain an uncertainty measure of events, the below uncertainty product measure has been defined by Liu (2009).

Definition 1.48 Assume (Γ_k, L_k, M_k) as uncertainty spaces for $k=1, 2, \ldots$. The product uncertain measure M is an uncertainty measure if it holds the condition $M\left\{\prod_{k=1}^{\infty} \Lambda_k\right\} = \min_{k=1}^{\infty} M_k\{\Lambda_k\}$ where Λ_k are arbitrary chosen events of L_k for $k=1, 2, \ldots$, respectively.

Definition 1.49 Assume (Γ_k, L_k, M_k) as uncertainty spaces for $k=1, 2, \ldots$, $\Gamma=\Gamma_1 \times \Gamma_2 \times \ldots$, $L=L_1 \times L_2 \times \ldots$, and $M=M_1 \times M_2 \times \ldots$. Then the triple (Γ, L, M) is called a product uncertainty space.

Definition 1.50 Assume Γ as a reference set. Then the events $\Lambda_1 \times \Lambda_2 \times \ldots \times \Lambda_n$ from Γ are independent if $M\left\{\bigcap_{i=1}^{n} \Lambda_i^*\right\} = \min_{i=1}^{n} M\{\Lambda_i^*\}$, where Λ_i^* are selected arbitrary chosen events from $\{\Lambda_i, \Lambda_i^c, \Gamma\}$ for $i=1, 2, \ldots, n$, respectively.

Theorem 1.19 Assume Γ as a reference set. Then the events $\Lambda_1 \times \Lambda_2 \times \ldots \times \Lambda_n$ from Γ are independent if and only if $M\left\{\bigcap_{i=1}^{n} \Lambda_i^*\right\} = \min_{i=1}^{n} M\{\Lambda_i^*\}$, where Λ_i^* are selected arbitrary chosen events from $\{\Lambda_i, \Lambda_i^c, \emptyset\}$ for $i=1, 2, \ldots, n$, respectively.

1.3.2 Uncertain variable

The uncertain variable is one of the basic concepts in uncertainty theory that is used to show the uncertain quantities.

Definition 1.51 The uncertain variable is a function, say ξ from uncertainty space (Γ, L, M) to real numbers, such that for any Borel set of real numbers the set $\{\xi \in B\} = \{\gamma \in \Gamma | \xi(\gamma) \in B\}$ is an event.

Definition 1.52 The uncertain variable ξ on uncertainty space (Γ, L, M) is,

- Nonnegative, if and only if $M\{\xi < 0\} = 0$,
- Positive, if and only if $M\{\xi \le 0\} = 0$.

Definition 1.53 Assume ξ and η as two uncertain variables of uncertainty space (Γ, L, M). For these variables $\xi = \eta$ if for approximately all $\gamma \in \Gamma$ the condition $\xi(\gamma) = \eta(\gamma)$ is met.

Definition 1.54 Suppose $\xi_1, \xi_2, \ldots, \xi_n$ as uncertain variables and f as a measurable function with real values. Then, $\xi = f(\xi_1, \xi_2, \ldots, \xi_n)$ is an uncertain variable defined as below,

$$\xi(\gamma) = f(\xi_1(\gamma), \xi_2(\gamma), \ldots, \xi_n(\gamma)), \quad \forall \gamma \in \Gamma \tag{1.73}$$

Theorem 1.20 Suppose $\xi_1, \xi_2, \ldots, \xi_n$ as uncertain variables and f as a measurable function with real values. Then, $f(\xi_1, \xi_2, \ldots, \xi_n)$ is an uncertain variable.

1.3.3 Uncertain distribution

To describe an uncertain variable, uncertain distribution has been introduced that contains incomplete information about the uncertain variable. In some situations, it is enough to know the uncertain distribution instead of the uncertain variable.

Definition 1.55 Uncertain distribution Φ is defined as below (where ξ is the uncertain variable),

$$\Phi(x) = M\{\xi \le x\}, \quad \forall x \in \mathbb{R} \tag{1.74}$$

Definition 1.56 Two uncertain variables are codistribution variables if their uncertain distributions are identical.

Theorem 1.21 The function $\Phi: \mathbb{R} \to [0, 1]$ is an uncertain distribution if and only if it is an increasingly uniform distribution, except in $\Phi(x) \equiv 0$ and $\Phi(x) \equiv 1$.

Definition 1.57 Uncertain distribution ξ is linear if and only if it follows the below uncertain distribution.

$$\Phi(x) = \begin{cases} 0, & x \le a \\ \dfrac{x-a}{b-a}, & a \le x \le b \\ 1, & b \le x \end{cases} \tag{1.75}$$

Linear uncertain distribution is shown by $l(a, b)$ where $a < b$ are real numbers. It is shown by Fig. 1.5.

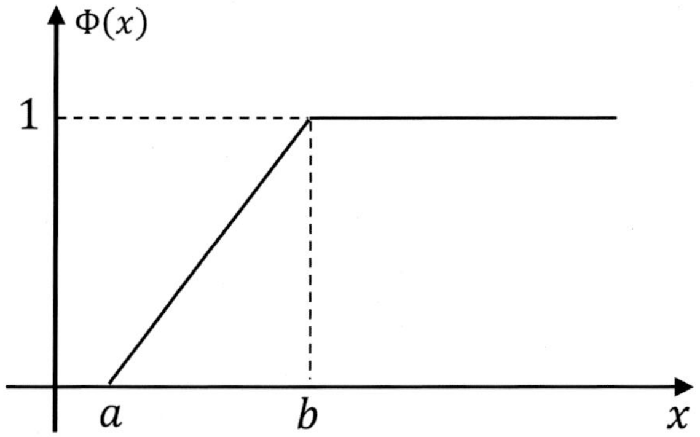

Fig. 1.5 A linear uncertain distribution (Liu, 2015).

Example 1.9 A student thinks that his/her final grade in a certain course will be between 14 and 17. So, the final grade is a linear uncertain variable $l(14, 17)$ with the following uncertain distribution,

$$\Phi(x) = \begin{cases} 0, & x \leq 14 \\ \dfrac{x-14}{3}, & 14 \leq x \leq 17 \\ 1, & 17 \leq x \end{cases} \tag{1.76}$$

Definition 1.58 The uncertain variable ξ is called zigzag if and only if it has the following uncertain distribution variable,

$$\Phi(x) = \begin{cases} 0, & x \leq a \\ \dfrac{x-a}{2(b-a)}, & a \leq x \leq b \\ \dfrac{x+c-2b}{2(c-b)}, & b \leq x \leq c \\ 1, & c \leq x \end{cases} \tag{1.77}$$

Zigzag uncertain distribution is shown by $Z(a, b, c)$ where $a < b < c$ are real numbers. It is shown by Fig. 1.6. The median of uncertain variable ξ with distribution Φ is the point with $\Phi(x) = 0.5$ (point b in Fig. 1.6).

Example 1.10 In the previous example, if the students think about the final grade by median and upper and lower bounds, it can be shown by zigzag uncertain variable $Z(14, 15, 17)$ with the following zigzag distribution,

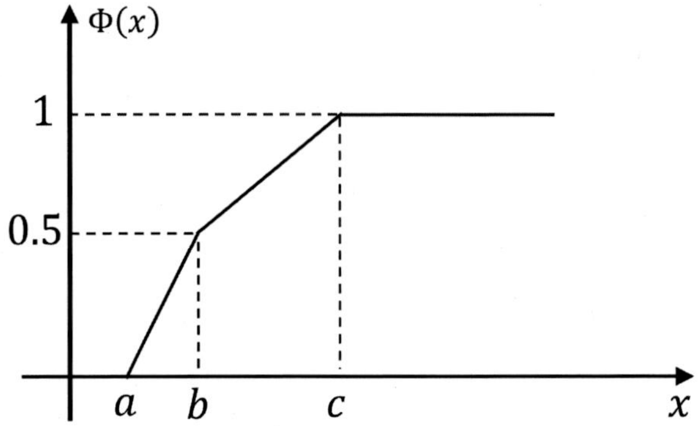

Fig. 1.6 A zigzag uncertain distribution (Liu, 2015).

$$\Phi(x) = \begin{cases} 0, & x \leq 14 \\ \dfrac{x-14}{2}, & 14 \leq x \leq 15 \\ \dfrac{x-13}{4}, & 15 \leq x \leq 17 \\ 1, & 17 \leq x \end{cases} \tag{1.78}$$

Definition 1.59 The uncertain variable ξ is normal if and only if it follows the below distribution.

$$\Phi(x) = \left(1 + \exp\left(\frac{\pi(\mu - x)}{\sqrt{3}\sigma}\right)\right)^{-1}, \quad x \in \mathbb{R} \tag{1.79}$$

Normal uncertain distribution is shown by $N(\mu, \sigma)$ where for the real numbers μ and σ, the condition $\sigma > 0$ is true. It is shown by Fig. 1.7.

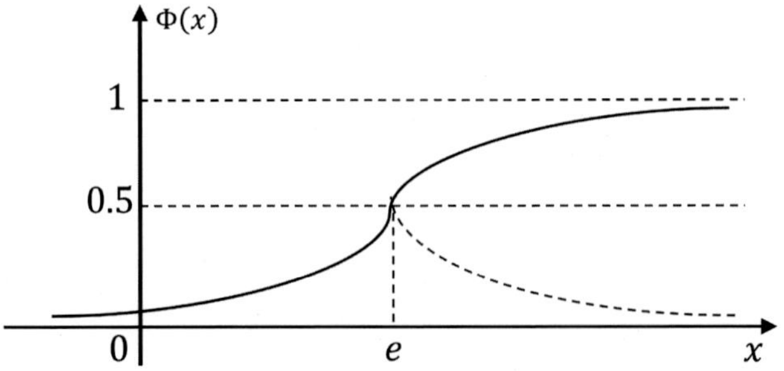

Fig. 1.7 A normal uncertain distribution (Liu, 2015).

Definition 1.60 The uncertain variable ξ is lognormal if and only if ξ is normal uncertain distribution $N(\mu, \sigma)$. Lognormal uncertain distribution is as follows,

$$\Phi(x) = \left(1 + \exp\left(\frac{\pi(t - \ln x)}{\sqrt{3}\sigma}\right)\right)^{-1}, \quad x \geq 0 \tag{1.80}$$

Lognormal uncertain distribution is shown by $LOGN(t, \sigma)$ where for the real numbers t and σ, the condition $\sigma > 0$ is true. It is shown by Fig. 1.8.
Definition 1.61 The uncertain variable ξ is called empirical if and only if it follows the below uncertain distribution where $x_1 < x_2 < \ldots < x_n$ and $0 \leq \beta_1 \leq \beta_2 \leq \ldots \leq \beta_n \leq 1$. It is shown by Fig. 1.9.

$$\Phi(x) = \begin{cases} 0, & x < x_1 \\ \beta_i + \dfrac{(\beta_{i+1} - \beta_i)(x - x_i)}{x_{i+1} - x_i}, & x_i \leq x \leq x_{i+1}, 1 \leq i \leq n \\ 1, & x > x_n \end{cases} \tag{1.81}$$

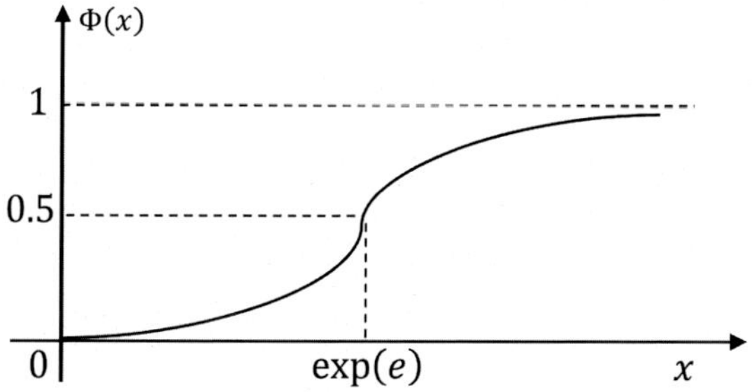

Fig. 1.8 A lognormal uncertain distribution (Liu, 2015).

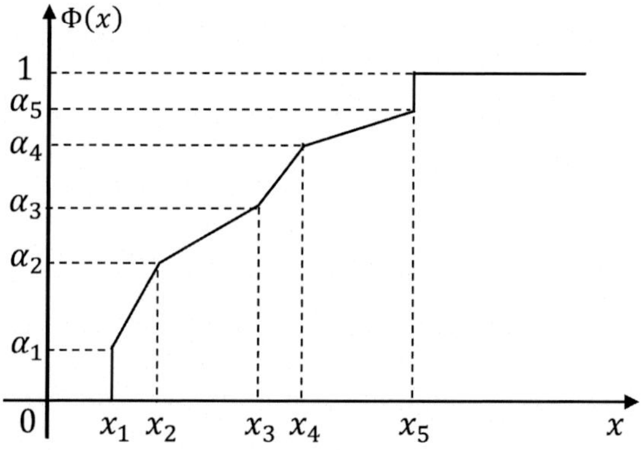

Fig. 1.9 An empirical uncertain distribution (Liu, 2015).

Theorem 1.22 Assume ξ as an uncertain variable with uncertain distribution Φ. Then, for any real number x, the equations $M\{\xi \leq x\} = \Phi(x)$ and $M\{\xi > x\} = 1 - \Phi(x)$ are held.

Reminder 1.2 If uncertain distribution Φ is a continuous function, then $M\{\xi < x\} = \Phi(x)$ and $M\{\xi \geq x\} = 1 - \Phi(x)$.

Theorem 1.23 Assume ξ as an uncertain variable with uncertain distribution Φ. Then, for any interval $[a, b]$ the following inequality is held.

$$\Phi(b) - \Phi(a) \leq M\{a \leq \xi \leq b\} \leq \min\{\Phi(b), 1 - \Phi(a)\} \tag{1.82}$$

Definition 1.62 Uncertain distribution $\Phi(x)$ is regular if it is a strictly ascending function of x where $0 < \Phi(x) < 1$, $\lim_{x \to -\infty} \Phi(x) = 0$, and $\lim_{x \to +\infty} \Phi(x) = 1$.

Example 1.11 The linear, zigzag, normal, and lognormal uncertain distributions are regular.

Definition 1.63 Suppose ξ as an uncertain variable with regular uncertain distribution of Φ. Then, inverse function Φ^{-1} is the inverse uncertain distribution of ξ. The inverse uncertain distribution $\Phi^{-1}(\alpha)$ is defined on interval $(0, 1)$, and it can be defined on interval $[0, 1]$ by considering $\Phi^{-1}(0) = \lim_{\alpha \downarrow 0} \Phi^{-1}(\alpha)$ and $\Phi^{-1}(1) = \lim_{\alpha \uparrow 1} \Phi^{-1}(\alpha)$.

Example 1.12 The inverse uncertain distribution of the linear uncertain variable $l(a, b)$ is $\Phi^{-1}(\alpha) = (1 - \alpha)a + \alpha b$.

Example 1.13 The inverse uncertain distribution of the zigzag uncertain variable $Z(a, b, c)$ is as follows,

$$\Phi^{-1}(\alpha) = \begin{cases} (1 - 2\alpha)a + 2\alpha b, & \alpha < 0.5 \\ (2 - 2\alpha)b + (2\alpha - 1)c, & \alpha \geq 0.5 \end{cases} \tag{1.83}$$

Example 1.14 The inverse uncertain distribution of the normal uncertain variable $N(\mu, \sigma)$ is $\Phi^{-1}(\alpha) = \mu + \frac{\sigma\sqrt{3}}{\pi} \ln\left(\frac{\alpha}{1-\alpha}\right)$.

Example 1.15 The inverse uncertain distribution of the normal uncertain variable $LOGN(t, \sigma)$ is $\Phi^{-1}(\alpha) = \exp\left(t + \frac{\sigma\sqrt{3}}{\pi} \ln\left(\frac{\alpha}{1-\alpha}\right)\right)$.

Theorem 1.24 The function Φ^{-1} is an inverse uncertain distribution of uncertain variable ξ if and only if $M\{\xi \leq \Phi^{-1}(\alpha)\} = \alpha$ for $\alpha \in [0, 1]$.

Theorem 1.25 The function $\Phi^{-1}: (0, 1) \to \mathbb{R}$ is an inverse uncertain distribution if and only if it is a continuous and strictly ascending function of α.

1.3.4 Independency of uncertain variables

Definition 1.64 Uncertain variables ξ_1, ξ_2, ..., ξ_n are independent if for Borel sets B_1, B_2, ..., B_n of the real numbers, the condition $M\left\{\bigcap_{i=1}^{n}(\xi_i \in B_i)\right\} = \min_{i=1}^{n}\{M\{\xi_i \in B_i\}\}$ is held.

Theorem 1.26 Uncertain variables $\xi_1, \xi_2, \ldots, \xi_n$ are independent if and only if for Borel sets B_1, B_2, ..., B_n of the real numbers, the condition $M\left\{\bigcup_{i=1}^{n}(\xi_i \in B_i)\right\} = \max_{i=1}^{n}\{M\{\xi_i \in B_i\}\}$ is held.

Theorem 1.27 Assume independent uncertain variables ξ_1, ξ_2, ..., ξ_n and measurable functions $f_1, f_2, \ldots, f_n$. Then, $f_1(\xi_1), f_2(\xi_2), \ldots, f_n(\xi_n)$ are independent uncertain variables.

1.3.5 Operational laws

Theorem 1.28 Assume independent uncertain variables ξ_1, ξ_2, ..., ξ_n and their regular uncertain distributions Φ_1, Φ_2, ..., Φ_n respectively. If f is a strictly ascending function, then $\xi = f(\xi_1, \xi_2, \ldots, \xi_n)$ has the inverse uncertain distribution $\Psi^{-1}(\alpha) = f(\Phi_1^{-1}(\alpha), \Phi_2^{-1}(\alpha), \ldots, \Phi_n^{-1}(\alpha))$.

Example 1.16 Assume independent uncertain variables ξ_1, ξ_2, ..., ξ_n and their regular uncertain distributions Φ_1, Φ_2, ..., Φ_n respectively. Then $\xi = \xi_1 + \xi_2 + \ldots + \xi_n$ has the inverse uncertain distribution $\Psi^{-1}(\alpha) = \Phi_1^{-1}(\alpha) + \Phi_2^{-1}(\alpha) + \ldots + \Phi_n^{-1}(\alpha)$.

Example 1.17 Assume independent uncertain variables ξ_1, ξ_2, ..., ξ_n and their regular uncertain distributions Φ_1, Φ_2, ..., Φ_n respectively. Then $\xi = \xi_1 \times \xi_2 \times \ldots \times \xi_n$ has the inverse uncertain distribution $\Psi^{-1}(\alpha) = \Phi_1^{-1}(\alpha) \times \Phi_2^{-1}(\alpha) \times \ldots \times \Phi_n^{-1}(\alpha)$.

Theorem 1.29 Assume ξ_1 and ξ_2 as independent linear uncertain variables shown by $l(a_1, b_1)$ and $l(a_2, b_2)$, respectively. Then, the summation $\xi_1 + \xi_2$ is a linear uncertain variable as $l(a_1, b_1) + l(a_2, b_2) = l(a_1 + a_2, b_1 + b_2)$. Also, the product of linear uncertain variable $l(a, b)$ and scaler $k > 0$ is a linear uncertain variable as $k.\ l(a, b) = l(ka, kb)$.

Theorem 1.30 Assume ξ_1 and ξ_2 as independent zigzag uncertain variables shown by $Z(a_1, b_1, c_1)$ and $Z(a_2, b_2, c_2)$, respectively. Then, the summation $\xi_1 + \xi_2$ is a zigzag uncertain variable as $Z(a_1, b_1, c_1) + Z(a_2, b_2, c_2) = Z(a_1 + a_2, b_1 + b_2, c_1 + c_2)$. Also, the product of zigzag uncertain variable $Z(a, b, c)$ and scaler $k > 0$ is a zigzag uncertain variable as $k.\ Z(a, b, c) = Z(ka, kb, kc)$.

Theorem 1.31 Assume ξ_1 and ξ_2 as independent normal uncertain variables shown by $N(\mu_1, \sigma_1)$ and $N(\mu_2, \sigma_2)$, respectively. Then, the summation

$\xi_1+\xi_2$ is a normal uncertain variable as $N(\mu_1,\sigma_1)+N(\mu_2,\sigma_2)=N(\mu_1+\mu_2,\sigma_1+\sigma_2)$. Also, the product of normal uncertain variable $N(\mu,\sigma)$ and scaler $k>0$ is a normal uncertain variable as $k.\ N(\mu,\sigma)=N(k\mu,k\sigma)$.

Theorem 1.32 Assume ξ_1 and ξ_2 as independent lognormal uncertain variables shown by $LOGN(t_1,\sigma_1)$ and $LOGN(t_2,\sigma_2)$, respectively. Then, the product $\xi_1\times\xi_2$ is a lognormal uncertain variable $LOGN(t_1+t_2,\sigma_1+\sigma_2)$, that is, $LOGN(t_1,\sigma_1)\times LOGN(t_2,\sigma_2)=LOGN(t_1+t_2,\sigma_1+\sigma_2)$. Also, the product of lognormal uncertain variable $LOGN(t,\sigma)$ and scaler $k>0$ is a lognormal uncertain variable as $k.\ LOGN(t,\sigma)=LOGN(t+\ln k,\sigma)$.

Reminder 1.3 The summation of two lognormal uncertain variables is not a lognormal uncertain variable.

Theorem 1.33 Assume independent uncertain variables ξ_1, ξ_2, ..., ξ_n and their regular uncertain distributions Φ_1, Φ_2, ..., Φ_n, respectively. If the function $f(x_1,x_2,\ldots,x_n)$ is strictly ascending for x_1, x_2, ..., x_m and strictly descending for x_{m+1}, x_{m+2}, ..., x_n, then $\xi=f(x_1,x_2,\ldots,x_n)$ has inverse uncertain distribution of $\Psi^{-1}(\alpha)=f(\Phi_1^{-1}(\alpha),\ldots,\Phi_m^{-1}(\alpha),\Phi_{m+1}^{-1}(1-\alpha),\ldots,\Phi_n^{-1}(1-\alpha))$.

Example 1.18 Assume ξ_1 and ξ_2 as positive and independent uncertain variables with regular uncertain distributions Φ_1 and Φ_2, respectively. Then, $\xi=\frac{\xi_1}{\xi_1+\xi_2}$ has inverse uncertain distribution of $\Psi^{-1}(\alpha)=\frac{\Phi_1^{-1}(\alpha)}{\Phi_1^{-1}(1-\alpha)+\Phi_2^{-1}(1-\alpha)}$.

Theorem 1.34 Assume independent uncertain variables ξ_1, ξ_2, ..., ξ_n and their regular uncertain distributions Φ_1, Φ_2, ..., Φ_n, respectively. If the function $f(\xi_1,\xi_2,\ldots,\xi_n)$ is strictly ascending for ξ_1, ξ_2, ..., ξ_m and strictly descending for ξ_{m+1}, ξ_{m+2}, ..., ξ_n, then $M\{f(\xi_1,\xi_2,\ldots,\xi_n)\le 0\}\ge\alpha$ if and only if $f(\Phi_1^{-1}(\alpha),\ldots,\Phi_m^{-1}(\alpha),\Phi_{m+1}^{-1}(1-\alpha),\ldots,\Phi_n^{-1}(1-\alpha))\le 0$.

1.3.6 Expected value

The expected value of an uncertain variable is the average value of the uncertain variable where it shows the magnitude of the uncertain variable.

Definition 1.65 Assume ξ as an uncertain variable. The expected value of this variable is defined as $E[\xi]=\int_0^{\infty}M\{\xi\ge r\}\,dr-\int_{-\infty}^{0}M\{\xi\le r\}\,dr$ where at least one of the integrals must be limited.

Theorem 1.35 Assume ξ as an uncertain variable with an uncertain distribution of Φ. Then, $E[\xi]=\int_0^{+\infty}(1-\Phi(x))\,dx-\int_{-\infty}^{0}\Phi(x)\,dx$.

Theorem 1.36 Assume ξ as an uncertain variable with an uncertain distribution of Φ. Then, $E[\xi]=\int_{-\infty}^{+\infty}x\,d\Phi(x)$.

Reminder 1.4 If $\varphi(x)$ is the derivative of uncertain variable $\Phi(x)$, then $E[\xi]=\int_{-\infty}^{+\infty}x\varphi(x)dx$.

Theorem 1.37 Assume ξ as an uncertain variable with a regular uncertain distribution of Φ. If its expected value exists, then $E[\xi]=\int_0^1\Phi^{-1}(\alpha)\,d\alpha$.

Example 1.19 The expected value of linear uncertain variable $\xi\sim l(a,b)$ is $E[\xi]=\frac{a+b}{2}$.

Example 1.20 The expected value of zigzag uncertain variable $\xi\sim Z(a,b,c)$ is $E[\xi]=\frac{a+2b+c}{4}$.

Example 1.21 The expected value of normal uncertain variable $\xi\sim N(\mu,\sigma)$ is $E[\xi]=\mu$.

Example 1.22 The expected value of lognormal uncertain variable $\xi\sim LOGN(t,\sigma)$ is

$$E[\xi]=\begin{cases}\sigma\sqrt{3}\exp(t)\csc\left(\sigma\sqrt{3}\right), & \sigma<\pi/\sqrt{3}\\ +\infty, & \sigma\geq\pi/\sqrt{3}\end{cases} \tag{1.84}$$

Example 1.23 The expected value of empirical uncertain variable ξ with the following uncertain distribution,

$$\Phi(x)=\begin{cases}0, & x<x_1\\ \beta_i+\dfrac{(\beta_{i+1}-\beta_i)(x-x_i)}{x_{i+1}-x_i}, & x_i\leq x\leq x_{i+1}, 1\leq i\leq n\\ 1, & x>x_n\end{cases} \tag{1.85}$$

where $x_1<x_2<\ldots<x_n$ and $0\leq\beta_1\leq\beta_2\leq\ldots\leq\beta_n\leq 1$, is

$$E[\xi]=\frac{\beta_1+\beta_2}{2}x_1+\sum_{i=2}^{n-1}\left(\frac{\beta_{i+1}-\beta_{i-1}}{2}\right)x_i+\left(1-\frac{\beta_{n-1}+\beta_n}{2}\right)x_n \tag{1.86}$$

Theorem 1.38 Assume independent uncertain variables ξ_1, ξ_2, …, ξ_n and their regular uncertain distributions Φ_1, Φ_2, …, Φ_n, respectively. If the function $f(x_1,x_2,\ldots,x_n)$ is strictly ascending for x_1, x_2, …, x_m and strictly descending for x_{m+1}, x_{m+2}, …, x_n, then the expected value of $\xi=f(x_1,x_2,\ldots,x_n)$ is $E[\xi]=\int_0^1 f(\Phi_1^{-1}(\alpha),\ldots,\Phi_m^{-1}(\alpha),\Phi_{m+1}^{-1}(1-\alpha),\ldots,\Phi_n^{-1}(1-\alpha))\,d\alpha$.

Example 1.24 Assume ξ and η as positive and independent uncertain variables with regular uncertain distributions Φ and Ψ, respectively. Then,

$$E\left[\frac{\xi}{\eta}\right]=\int_0^1\frac{\Phi^{-1}(\alpha)}{\Psi^{-1}(1-\alpha)}\,d\alpha \tag{1.87}$$

Theorem 1.39 Assume ξ and η as independent uncertain variables with limited expected values. Then,

$$E[a\xi + b\eta] = aE[\xi] + bE[\eta] \tag{1.88}$$

where a *and* b *are two real values.*

1.3.7 Variance

To determine the dispersion degree of distribution of an uncertain variable around its expected value, the variance of the uncertain variable is used. If the variance takes a small value, the uncertain variable is concentrated around its expected value. On the other hand, its large values show a high degree of dispersion around the expected value.

Definition 1.66 Assume ξ as an uncertain variable with a limited expected value of μ. Its variance is defined as

$$V[\xi] = E\left[(\xi - \mu)^2\right] = \int_0^{+\infty} M\left\{(\xi - \mu)^2 \geq x\right\} dx \tag{1.89}$$

Theorem 1.40 Assume ξ as an uncertain variable with a limited expected value of μ. Then, for any real numbers a and b, the equality $V[a\xi + b] = a^2 V[\xi]$ is correct.

Theorem 1.41 Assume ξ as an uncertain variable with a limited expected value of μ and a regular uncertain distribution Φ, then

$$V[\xi] = \int_0^1 \left(\Phi^{-1}(\alpha) - \mu\right)^2 d\alpha \tag{1.90}$$

Example 1.25 The variance of the linear uncertain variable $\xi \sim l(a, b)$ is $V[\xi] = \frac{(b-a)^2}{12}$, and the variance of the normal uncertain variable $\zeta \sim N(\mu, \sigma)$ is $V[\zeta] = \sigma^2$.

Definition 1.67 Assume ξ as an uncertain variable with an uncertain distribution Φ. Its entropy function is defined as $H[\xi] = \int_{-\infty}^{+\infty} S(\Phi(x))\, dx$ where $S(r) = -r \ln r - (1 - r) \ln(1 - r)$.

Example 1.26 The entropy function of the linear uncertain variable $\xi \sim l(a, b)$ is $H[\xi] = \frac{b-a}{2}$. The entropy function of the zigzag uncertain variable $\xi \sim Z(a, b, c)$ is $H[\xi] = \frac{c-a}{2}$. The entropy function of the normal uncertain variable $\xi \sim N(\mu, \sigma)$ is $H[\xi] = \frac{\pi\sigma}{\sqrt{3}}$.

Theorem 1.42 Assume ξ as an uncertain variable and c as an arbitrary real number. Then,

- $H[\xi] \geq 0$ (the equal form happens just when the uncertain variable is a constant),
- $H[\xi + c] = H[\xi]$.

Theorem 1.43 Assume ξ as an uncertain variable with uncertain distribution Φ. Then, $H[\xi] = \int_0^1 \Phi^{-1}(\alpha)\ln\left(\frac{\alpha}{1-\alpha}\right)d\alpha$.

Theorem 1.44 Assume independent uncertain variables $\xi_1, \xi_2, \ldots, \xi_n$ and their regular uncertain distributions $\Phi_1, \Phi_2, \ldots, \Phi_n$, respectively. If the function $f(x_1, x_2, \ldots, x_n)$ is strictly ascending for $x_1, x_2, \ldots, x_m$ and strictly descending for $x_{m+1}, x_{m+2}, \ldots, x_n$, then the entropy function of $\xi = f(x_1, x_2, \ldots, x_n)$ is $H[\xi] = \int_0^1 f\left(\Phi_1^{-1}(\alpha), \ldots, \Phi_m^{-1}(\alpha), \Phi_{m+1}^{-1}(1-\alpha), \ldots, \Phi_n^{-1}(1-\alpha)\right)\ln\left(\frac{\alpha}{1-\alpha}\right)d\alpha$.

Example 1.27 Assume ξ and η as positive and independent uncertain variables with regular uncertain distributions Φ and Ψ, respectively. Then, $H[\xi\eta] = \int_0^1 \Phi^{-1}(\alpha)\Psi^{-1}(\alpha)\ln\left(\frac{\alpha}{1-\alpha}\right)d\alpha$.

Example 1.28 Assume ξ and η as positive and independent uncertain variables with regular uncertain distributions Φ and Ψ, respectively. Then, $H\left[\frac{\xi}{\eta}\right] = \int_0^1 \frac{\Phi^{-1}(\alpha)}{\Psi^{-1}(1-\alpha)}\ln\left(\frac{\alpha}{1-\alpha}\right)d\alpha$.

Theorem 1.45 Assume ξ and η as independent uncertain variables. Then, $H[a\xi + b\eta] = |a|H[\xi] + |b|\,H[\eta]$ where a and b are real numbers.

Definition 1.68 Assume ξ_1 and ξ_2 as independent uncertain variables with regular uncertain distributions Φ and Ψ, respectively. The ranking of ξ_1 and ξ_2 is defined as follows:

- $\xi_1 \succ \xi_2$, if and only if $E[\xi_1] > E[\xi_2]$ or $E[\xi_1] = E[\xi_2]$, $V[\xi_1] < V[\xi_2]$,
- $\xi_1 \prec \xi_2$, if and only if $E[\xi_1] < E[\xi_2]$ or $E[\xi_1] = E[\xi_2]$, $V[\xi_1] > V[\xi_2]$,
- $\xi_1 \approx \xi_2$, if and only if $E[\xi_1] = E[\xi_2]$, $V[\xi_1] = V[\xi_2]$.

Then we formulate the order "$\succeq$"and "$\preceq$" as

$\xi_1 \succeq \xi_2$ if and only if $\xi_1 \succ \xi_2$ or $\xi_1 \approx \xi_2$,
$\xi_1 \preceq \xi_2$ if and only if $\xi_1 \prec \xi_2$ or $\xi_1 \approx \xi_2$.

1.3.8 Uncertain optimization

Uncertain optimization was introduced by Liu and Liu (2002a, 2002b) to deal with the problems with uncertain variables. Assume x as a crisp variable and ξ as an uncertain variable. The general form of the uncertain optimization problem is as follows (Liu & Liu, 2002a, 2002b),

$$\begin{aligned} &\min_x f(x, \xi) \\ &\text{subject to} \\ &g_i(x, \xi) \le 0 \quad i = 1, 2, \ldots, m \end{aligned} \tag{1.91}$$

It is notable that variations of the uncertain variable ξ are independent from x but the objective function $f(x, \xi)$ is varied based on both the variables. Because of the uncertain variable of the objective function, it is not possible to determine an exact value for x; therefore, traditional and popular optimization methods cannot be used for this aim. A method can use the expected value of the objective function as $\min_x E[f(x, \xi)]$. This expected value is independent from the uncertain variable and is dependent to x. On the other hand, the constraint $g_i(x, \xi) \leq 0$ does not determine any special feasible space. Therefore, it is reasonable that instead of each constraint use its belief degree value and its lower bound α_i , which is between 0 and 1. Thus, the above model is represented as below,

$$\begin{aligned} &\min_x E[f(x, \xi)] \\ &\text{subject to} \\ &M\{g_i(x, \xi) \leq 0\} \geq \alpha_i \quad i = 1, 2, \ldots, m \end{aligned} \tag{1.92}$$

If α_i is close to 1, it means that the belief of the satisfying constraint i is high. If $\alpha_i = 1$ then we believe that constraint i is satisfied in the obtained solution.

Definition 1.69 Vector x for model (1.92) is a feasible solution if and only if $M\{g_i(x, \xi) \leq 0\} \geq \alpha_i$ for $i = 1, 2, \ldots, m$.

Definition 1.70 Feasible solution x^* is the optimal solution of problem (1.92) if and only if $E[f(x^*, \xi)] \leq E[f(x, \xi)]$ for feasible solution x.

Theorem 1.46 Assume independent uncertain variables $\xi_1, \xi_2, \ldots, \xi_n$ and their regular uncertain distributions $\Phi_1, \Phi_2, \ldots, \Phi_n$, respectively. If the function $f(x_1, x_2, \ldots, x_n)$ is strictly ascending for $\xi_1, \xi_2, \ldots, \xi_m$ and strictly descending for $\xi_{m+1}, \xi_2, \ldots, \xi_n$, and the function $g_i(x, \xi_1, \xi_2, \ldots, \xi_n)$ for $i = 1, 2, \ldots, m$ is strictly ascending for $\xi_1, \xi_2, \ldots, \xi_k$ and strictly descending for $\xi_{m+1}, \xi_2, \ldots, \xi_n$, then the uncertain problem

$$\begin{aligned} &\min_x E[f(x, \xi_1, \xi_2, \ldots, \xi_n)] \\ &\text{subject to} \\ &M\{g_i(x, \xi_1, \xi_2, \ldots, \xi_n) \leq 0\} \geq \alpha_i \quad i = 1, 2, \ldots, m \end{aligned} \tag{1.93}$$

is equivalent to problem

$$\begin{aligned} &\min_x \int_0^1 f\left(x, \Phi_1^{-1}(\alpha), \ldots, \Phi_m^{-1}(\alpha), \Phi_{m+1}^{-1}(1-\alpha), \ldots, \Phi_n^{-1}(1-\alpha)\right) d\alpha \\ &\text{subject to} \\ &g_i\left(x, \Phi_1^{-1}(\alpha_i), \ldots, \Phi_k^{-1}(\alpha_i), \Phi_{k+1}^{-1}(1-\alpha_i), \ldots, \Phi_n^{-1}(1-\alpha_i)\right) \leq 0 \\ &i = 1, 2, \ldots, m \end{aligned} \tag{1.94}$$

Theorem 1.46 converts the uncertain objective function (1.93) to a crisp form and presents an equivalent constraint for uncertain constraint (1.93) that describes the feasible space based on α_i.

References

Allahviranloo, T. (2020). *Uncertain information and linear systems*. Berlin: Springer.

Allahviranloo, T., Mikaeilvand, N., & Barkhordary, M. (2009). Fuzzy linear matrix equation. *Fuzzy Optimization and Decision Making*, *8*(2), 165–177.

Allahviranloo, T., & Salahshour, S. (2011). Fuzzy symmetric solutions of fuzzy linear systems. *Journal of Computational and Applied Mathematics*, *235*(16), 4545–4553.

Charnes, A., Cooper, W. W., & Rhodes, E. L. (1978). Measuring the efficiency of decision making units. *European Journal of Operational Research*, *2*(6), 429–444.

Dai, W., & Chen, X. (2012). Entropy of function of uncertain variables. *Mathematical and Computer Modelling*, *55*(3), 754–760.

Dalkey, N., & Olaf, H. (1963). An experimental application of the Delphi method to the use of experts. *Management Science*, *9*(3), 458–467.

Dempster, A. P. (1967). Upper and lower probabilities induced by a multivalued mapping. *The Annals of Mathematical Statistics*, *38*(2), 325–339.

Dubois, D., & Prade, H. (1980). *Fuzzy sets and systems theory and applications*. New York: Academic Press.

Dubois, D., & Prade, H. (1988). Fuzzy numbers: An overview. In J. C. Bezdek (Ed.), *Vol. 2. Analysis of fuzzy information* (pp. 3–39). Boca Raton, FL: CRC Press.

Ezadi, S., Allahviranloo, T., & Mohammadi, S. (2018). Two new methods for ranking of Z-numbers based on sigmoid function and sign method. *International Journal of Intelligent Systems*, *33*(7), 1476–1487.

Han, S., Peng, Z., & Wang, S. (2014). The maximum flow problem of uncertain network. *Information Sciences*, *265*, 167–175.

Jamshidi, M., Sanei, M., & Mahmoodirad, A. (2022). An uncertain allocation models in data envelopment analysis: A case in the Iranian stock market. *Scintia Iranica*, 29(6), 3434–3454.

Jamshidi, M., Sanei, M., Mahmoodirad, A., Tohidi, G., & Hosseinzade Lotfi, F. (2021). Uncertain BCC data envelopment analysis model with belief degree: A case study in Iranian banks. *International Journal of Industrial Mathematics*, *13*(3), 239–249.

Jamshidi, M., Saneie, M., Mahmoodirad, A., Lotfi, F. H., & Tohidi, G. (2019). Uncertain RUSSEL data envelopment analysis model: A case study in Iranian banks. *Journal of Intelligent Fuzzy Systems*, *37*(2), 2937–2951.

Khezerloo, S., Allahviranloo, T., & Khezerloo, M. (2011). Ranking of fuzzy numbers based on alpha-distance. In *Proceedings of the 7th conference of the European Society for Fuzzy Logic and Technology (EUSFLAT-2011). Atlantis Press, Aix-les-Bains, France* (pp. 770–777).

Lai, Y. J., & Hwang, C. L. (1992). *Fuzzy mathematical programming*. Berlin: Springer.

Liu, B. (2002). Toward fuzzy optimization without mathematical ambiguity. *Fuzzy Optimization and Decision Making*, *1*(1), 43–63.

Liu, B. (2004). *Uncertainty theory*. Berlin: Springer.

Liu, B. (2007). *Uncertain theory* (2nd ed.). Berlin, Germany: Springer.

Liu, B. (2009). Some research problems in uncertainty theory. *Journal of Uncertain System*, *3* (1), 3–10.

Liu, B. (2015). *Uncertain theory* (4nd ed.). Berlin, Germany: Springer.

Liu, Y. H., & Ha, M. H. (2010). Expected value of function of uncertain variables. *Journal of Uncertain Systems*, *4*(3), 181–186.

Liu, B., & Liu, Y. K. (2002a). Expected value of fuzzy variable and fuzzy expected value models. *IEEE Transactions on Fuzzy Systems*, *10*(4), 445–450.

Liu, B., & Liu, B. (2002b). *Theory and practice of uncertain programming*. Heidelberg: Physica-Verlag.
Liu, Y. K., & Liu, B. (2003). Expected value operator of random fuzzy variable and random fuzzy expected value models. *International Journal of Uncertainty, Fuzziness and Knowledge-Based Systems, 11*(2), 195–215.
Mahmoodirad, A., Allahviranloo, T., & Niroomand, S. (2019). A new effective solution method for fully intuitionistic fuzzy transportation problem. *Soft Computing, 23*(12), 4521–4530.
Mahmoodirad, A., & Niroomand, S. (2020a). A belief degree-based uncertain scheme for a bi-objective two-stage green supply chain network design problem with direct shipment. *Soft Computing, 24*(24), 18499–18519.
Mahmoodirad, A., & Niroomand, S. (2020b). Uncertain location-allocation decisions for a bi-objective two-stage supply chain network design problem with environmental impacts. *Expert Systems, 37*, e12558.
Mirzaei, N., Mahmoodirad, A., & Niroomand, S. (2019). An uncertain multi-objective assembly line balancing problem: A credibility-based fuzzy modeling approach. *International Journal of Fuzzy Systems, 21*(8), 2392–2404.
Peng, Z. X., & Iwamura, K. (2010). A sufficient and necessary condition of uncertainty distribution. *Journal of Interdisciplinary Mathematics, 13*(3), 277–285.
Peykani, P., Hosseinzadeh Lotfi, F., Jafar Sadjadi, S. J., Ebrahimnejad, A., & Mohammadi, E. (2022). Fuzzy chance-constrained data envelopment analysis: A structured literature review, current trends, and future directions. *Fuzzy Optimization and Decision Making, 21*, 197–261.
Peykani, P., Mohammadi, E., Emrouznejad, A., Pishvaee, M. S., & Rostamy-Malkhalifeh, M. (2019). Fuzzy data envelopment analysis: An adjustable approach. *Expert Systems with Applications, 136*, 439–452.
Pishvaee, M. S., Torabi, S. A., & Razmi, J. (2012). Credibility-based fuzzy mathematical programming model for green logistics design under uncertainty. *Computers & Industrial Engineering, 62*, 624–632.
Shafer, G. (1967). *A mathematical theory of evidence*. Princeton: Princeton University Press.
Sheng, Y., & Yao, K. (2012). Fixed charge transportation problem in uncertain environment. *Industrial Engineering & Management Systems, 11*(2), 183–187.
Sigarreta, J. M., Ruesga, P., & Rodriguez, M. (2007). On mathematical foundations of the plausibility theory. *International Mathematical Forum, 2*(27).
Xu, J., & Zhou, X. (2013). Approximation based fuzzy multi-objective models with expected objectives and chance constraints: application to earth-rock work allocation. *Information Sciences, 238*, 75–95.
Zadeh, L. A. (1965). Fuzzy sets. *Information and Control, 8*(3), 338–353.
Zadeh, L. A. (1978). Fuzzy sets as a basis for a theory of possibility. *Fuzzy Sets and Systems, 1*, 3–28.
Zimmermann, H. J. (1987). *Fuzzy sets, decision making and expert systems*. Boston, MA: Kluwer Academic Publishers.

Further reading

Allahviranloo, T., & Saneifard, R. (2012). Defuzzification method for ranking fuzzy numbers based on center of gravity. *Iranian Journal of Fuzzy Systems, 9*(6), 57–67.
Dubois, D., & Prade, H. (1988). Possibility theory: An approach to computerized processing of uncertainty. New York: Plenum.
Lio, W., & Liu, B. (2017). Uncertain data envelopment analysis with imprecisely observed inputs and outputs. *Fuzzy Optimization and Decision Making, 17*(3), 357–373.

Lio, W., & Liu, B. (2018). Residual and confidence interval for uncertain regression model with imprecise observations. *Journal of Intelligent Fuzzy Systems*. https://doi.org/10.3233/JIFS-18353.
Liu, B. (2010a). *Uncertainty theory: A branch of mathematics for modeling human uncertainty*. Berlin: Springer Verlag.
Liu, B. (2010b). Uncertain risk analysis and uncertain reliability analysis. *Journal of Uncertain Systems, 4*(3), 163–170.
Liu, B. (2012). Why is there a need for uncertainty theory. *Journal of Uncertain Systems, 6*, 3–10.
Liu, B. (2013a). Toward uncertain finance theory. *Journal of Uncertainty Analysis and Applications, 1*, 1.
Liu, B. (2013b). Polyrectangular theorem and independence of uncertain vectors. *Journal of Uncertainty Analysis and Applications, 1*, 9.
Liu, B., & Chen, X. W. (2015). *Uncertain multi-objective programming and uncertain goal programming*. http://orsc.edu.cn/online/131020.pdf.
Wen, M. L. (2015). *Uncertain data envelopment analysis*. Berlin: Springer.
Wen, M. L., & Kang, R. (2014). Data envelopment analysis (DEA) with uncertain inputs and outputs. *Journal of Applied Mathematics, 2*, 1–7.

CHAPTER TWO

Introduction to data envelopment analysis

2.1 Introduction

Data envelopment analysis (DEA) (introduced by Charnes et al., 1978) is an approach for measuring and analyzing decision-making units (DMUs) as well as their comparison based on their efficient frontier. In this approach, a set of DMUs is measured and analyzed by a multiinput and multioutput linear mathematical programming model. In DEA, a production possibility set (PPS) for all DMUs is estimated and the efficiency of each DMU is evaluated based on this estimated set. The estimated production possibility set is an advantage of DEA as there is no assumption for the shape of this set (Allahviranloo et al., 2014; Saneifard et al., 2007).

Researchers in several fields have quickly recognized that DEA is an excellent methodology for modeling operational processes. Its empirical orientation and minimization of a priori assumptions have made possible its use in a number of studies involving efficient frontier estimation in the nonprofit sector, the regulated sector, and the private sector. At present, DEA encompasses a variety of alternate approaches to performance evaluation.

Many applications have been proposed for DEA in recent years. In these applications, the performance of DMUs is measured in operating firms (Farzipoor Sean et al., 2005; Nouri et al., 2013; Shirouyehzad et al., 2012), hospitals, the banking industry (Jamshidi et al., 2019, 2021, 2022; Roodposhti et al., 2010), cities (Pouriyeh et al., 2016; Tavana et al., 2018; Xue & Ye, 2021), universities (Hamdi et al., 2014), etc. Based on the original study of DEA made by Charnes et al. (1978), many studies in the literature have focused on improving and advancing this approach such as Seiford (1996), Gattoufi et al. (2004), Emrouznejad et al. (2008), Cook and Seiford (2009), Ebrahimnejad and Tavana (2014), etc.

Based on the importance and applicability of DEA, the literature on this topic contains many studies published in the form of books, journal papers,

Uncertainty in Data Envelopment Analysis
https://doi.org/10.1016/B978-0-323-99444-6.00002-5

conference papers, etc. Some important studies of the literature are reported here. The first book including a review and discussion of DEA models was written by Charnes et al. (1995). In this book, the theory, application, and methodology of DEA were discussed. A book describing static and dynamic network models of DEA was written by Färe and Grosskopf (1996). Cooper et al. (2005) introduced a systematic scheme of DEA models and their applications. A systematic presentation of the initial principles of DEA and also its developments was made by Cooper et al. (2006). Klemen (2009) deals with measuring and evaluating returns to scale by DEA models. Zhu and Cook (2013) described and represented mathematical models for the methodology of DEA.

The applications of DEA in healthcare systems are the focus of the book written by Ozcan and Tone (2014). The topic of nonparametric DEA is the focus of by the book by Blackburn et al. (2014). Hosseinzadeh Lotfi et al. (2016) wrote a book on the concepts, applications, and developments of the DEA approach.

For more information on the basic and advanced topics of DEA, the studies of Hosseinzadeh Lotfi et al. (2009), Ebrahimnejad and Hosseinzadeh Lotfi (2012), Molla-Alizadeh-Zavardehi et al. (2021), and Mahmoodirad et al. (2019) can be mentioned.

In the rest of this chapter, the basic definitions and concepts and basic models of DEA are presented and discussed.

2.2 Basic definitions

In many organizations, due to various factors with different behaviors, the assessment of organizational units may be difficult.

The efficiency of each unit is affected by the associated effective factors. If there are k effective factors, then the efficiency function of $E: \mathbb{R}^k \to \mathbb{R}$ can be defined. To recognize the relationship of function E, some assumptions should be considered in advance. Before explaining these assumptions, some definitions are given here.

Definition 2.1. (Maddahi et al., 2014) A DMU is a unit that decides on the production process and related facilities such as a factory, university, hospital, etc.

Definition 2.2. (Hosseinzadeh Lotfi, Jahanshahloo, et al., 2010) An input vector is a vector assigned to the DMU to complete its activities such as personnel, budget, equipment, etc.

Definition 2.3. An output vector is a vector obtained by the DMU using the input vector such as the selling amount, improvement, customer satisfaction, etc.

Therefore, each DMU uses the input vector to produce the output vector, according to Fig. 2.1.

In Fig. 2.1, $X_j^t = (x_{1j}, \ldots, x_{mj})$ and $Y_j^t = (y_{1j}, \ldots, y_{sj})$ are the input and output vectors of DMU_j respectively, where each DMU uses m inputs to produce s outputs. Therefore, the efficiency function is written as $E: \mathbb{R}^{m+s} \to \mathbb{R}$. So, a combination of input and output vectors of DMU_j is defined as the efficiency of that DMU as $E(X_j, Y_j)$.

Some assumptions for the estimation of the efficiency function are presented below.

- All inputs and outputs of each DMU are predetermined and nonnegative real values as $x_{ij}, y_{ij} \in \mathbb{R}_{\geq 0}$ $(\forall i, j, r)$.
- The input and output vectors of each DMU are nonzero vectors as $X_j \neq 0$, $Y_j \neq 0$ $(\forall j)$. It means that at least one value of each of these vectors must be positive.
- All inputs of vector X_j are used only for producing output values of vector Y_j and all values of output vector Y_j are produced only by input values of vector X_j.
- To compare the DMUs, all inputs and outputs of all DMUs should be time independent. Therefore, the required information of these vectors is gathered at the same time.
- There is no dependency among the values of the input vector and the values of the output vector of a DMU. This means that, for example, if an input value of the input vector of a DMU is changed, it will not affect the other values of that input vector.
- There is no dependency among the DMUs. This means that, for example, if the input vector of a DMU is changed, it will not affect the input vectors of other DMUs.
- Increasing each output will increase the efficiency and decreasing each input will increase the efficiency. Therefore,

$$\begin{cases} \dfrac{\partial E}{\partial x_i} < 0 \\ \dfrac{\partial E}{\partial y_r} > 0 \end{cases} \quad \forall i, r \tag{2.1}$$

Fig. 2.1 The schematic representation of input to output conversion by DMU *j*.

There are many efficiency functions that are suitable according to the above-mentioned assumptions. Among them, the following functions (here presented for the case of one input and one output) have been mainly used by researchers. These functions are either linear or can be linearized.

$$E(x, y) = \frac{y}{x} \tag{2.2}$$

$$E(x, y) = y - x \tag{2.3}$$

For the case of x as investment and y as income, the function (2.2) determines the percentage of the benefit and the function (2.3) determines the net benefit value.

For the case of n DMUs as $\left\{\begin{pmatrix} X_j \\ Y_j \end{pmatrix} | j = 1, \dots, n\right\}$ where $X_j \in \mathbb{R}^m_{\geq 0}$, $Y_j \in \mathbb{R}^s_{\geq 0}$, and $s = m = 1$, efficiency is defined by the following definition.

Definition 2.4. According to the function (2.2), the absolute efficiency of DMU_p is defined by the following equation as a positive value.

$$E_p = \frac{y_p}{x_p} \tag{2.4}$$

Definition 2.5. According to the function (2.2), the relative efficiency of DMU_p (shown by RE_p where $RE_p \in (0, 1]$) is defined by comparing its absolute efficiency value with the best absolute efficiency value of the population as the following formulation.

$$RE_p = \frac{E_p}{\max\{E_1, \dots, E_n\}} = \frac{\frac{y_p}{x_p}}{\max\left\{\frac{y_j}{x_j} : j = 1, \dots, n\right\}} \tag{2.5}$$

Note that for a general case of $m > 1$ or $s > 1$, this definition cannot be used.

Definition 2.6. DMU_p with coordinates $\begin{pmatrix} X_p \\ Y_p \end{pmatrix}$ is better than DMU_k with coordinates $\begin{pmatrix} X_k \\ Y_k \end{pmatrix}$ if and only if $\begin{pmatrix} -X_p \\ Y_p \end{pmatrix} \geq \begin{pmatrix} -X_k \\ Y_k \end{pmatrix}$. By this condition, DMU_p dominates DMU_k, or DMU_k is dominated by DMU_p. To interpret this situation, Fig. 2.2 is presented. In this figure, region (1) is the set of

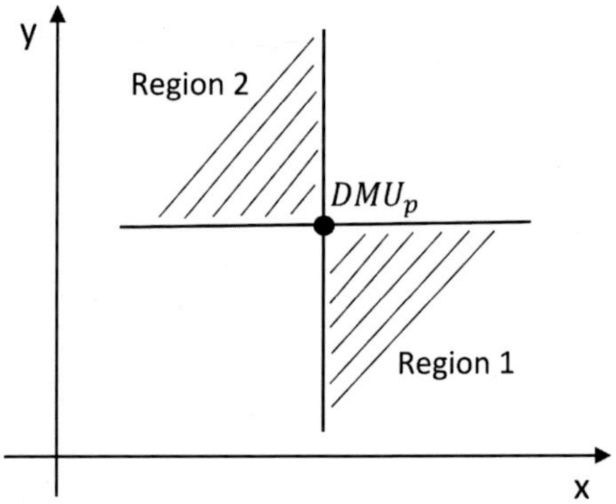

Fig. 2.2 The points dominated by DMU_p (region 1) and the points that dominate DMU_p (region 2).

points dominated by DMU_p and region (2) is the set of points that dominates DMU_p.

Definition 2.7. If all inputs and outputs can be presented by price values (assume u_r is the price of one unit of output r, and v_i is the price of one unit of input i), then the economic efficiency of DMU_p is defined by the below formulation.

$$EE_p = \frac{\sum_{r=1}^{s} u_r y_{rp}}{\sum_{i=1}^{m} v_i x_{ip}} \tag{2.6}$$

As in most real-world problems, the inputs and outputs are not of the economic type, so the economic efficiency cannot be used for such problems. Therefore, another method should be used to determine the weight (price) of the inputs and outputs of such problems.

If the weight vector of $U > 0$ for outputs (where $u_r > 0$ for any r) and the weight vector of $V > 0$ for inputs (where $v_i > 0$ for any i) can be considered, then the absolute efficiency of DMU_p can be calculated as,

$$EE_p = \frac{\sum_{r=1}^{s} u_r y_{rp}}{\sum_{i=1}^{m} v_i x_{ip}} = \frac{UY_p}{VX_p} \tag{2.7}$$

In DEA, the aim is to find the weight value where the absolute efficiency of a DMU is better than other DMUs. It means that the aim is to check the accuracy of the following statement.

$$\exists(U,V),\forall j\left[(U,V)>0\,\&\,j\in\{1,\ldots,n\}\Rightarrow\frac{UY_p}{VX_p}\geq\frac{UY_j}{VX_j}\right]\tag{2.8}$$

If statement (2.8) is not true, then there is no weight vector in which the absolute efficiency of DMU_p is greater than or equal to the absolute efficiency of other DMUs. It means that the statement $\exists(U,V)$, $\forall j\left[(U,V)>0\ \&\ j\in\{1,\ldots,n\}\Rightarrow\frac{UY_p}{VX_p}<\frac{UY_j}{VX_j}\right]$ is true.

The case of statement (2.8) means that for each positive weight vector of the inputs and outputs, there always exists a DMU in which its absolute efficiency is better than the absolute efficiency of the DMU under assessment (DMU_p). Therefore, DMU_p is inefficient. This is the advantage of DEA in that the inefficiency of a DMU is determined exactly.

If statement (2.8) is true, then positive weight vectors U and V are found where $\frac{UY_p}{VX_p}=\max\left\{\frac{UY_1}{VX_1},\ldots,\frac{UY_n}{VX_n}\right\}$. In this case, DMU_p is relatively efficient. This issue is the dis-advantage of DEA where for the mentioned positive weight vectors U and V, the absolute efficiency of DMU_p is greater than or equal to other DMUs. However, for other positive weight vectors U and V (if they exist), there is no information.

According to the above-mentioned discussions, to test the accuracy of statement (2.8) the following nonlinear model is written.

$$\begin{aligned}&\max\frac{\frac{UY_p}{VX_p}}{\max\left\{\frac{UY_j}{VX_j}:j=1,\ldots,n\right\}}\\&\text{subject to}\\&(U,V)>0\end{aligned}\tag{2.9}$$

Because the weight values of U and V are positive and the input and output values are nonnegative, the objective function value will be of the interval $(0,1]$.

To linearize the model (2.9), the Charnes-Cooper transformation (Charnes & Cooper, 1962) is used. For this aim, the conversion of $\frac{\frac{UY_p}{VX_p}}{\max\left\{\frac{UY_j}{VX_j}:j=1,\ldots,n\right\}}=q>0$ is considered and the model is converted to the below form.

$$\begin{aligned}&\max \frac{qUY_p}{VX_p}\\&\text{subject to}\\&q\left(\max\left\{\frac{UY_j}{VX_j}:j=1,\dots,n\right\}\right)=1\\&U\geq 1\varepsilon,\ V\geq 1\varepsilon,\ q\geq\varepsilon\end{aligned}\tag{2.10}$$

where $1=(1,1,\dots,1)$.

Considering $qU=U$, the model (2.10) is converted to the following model.

$$\begin{aligned}&\max \frac{UY_p}{VX_p}\\&\text{subject to}\\&\max\left\{\frac{UY_j}{VX_j}:j=1,\dots,n\right\}=1\\&U\geq 1\varepsilon,\ V\geq 1\varepsilon\end{aligned}\tag{2.11}$$

In the model (2.11), the first constraint is converted to two constraints and the model is written as the following.

$$\begin{aligned}&\max \frac{UY_p}{VX_p}\\&\text{subject to}\\&\frac{UY_j}{VX_j}\leq 1 \qquad j=1,\dots,n\\&\left(\frac{UY_1}{VX_1}=1\right)\vee\dots\vee\left(\frac{UY_n}{VX_n}=1\right)\\&U\geq 1\varepsilon,\ V\geq 1\varepsilon\end{aligned}\tag{2.12}$$

In this model, the second constraint means that at least one constraint of the first set of constraints should be satisfied in equal form. To cope with this issue, the following theorem is presented.

Theorem 2.1. Consider the problem $\max\left\{\frac{UY_p}{VX_p}\middle|\frac{UY_j}{VX_j}\leq 1, j=1,\dots, n\ \&\ U\geq q\varepsilon\ \&\ V\geq q\varepsilon\right\}$. If (U^*, V^*) is its optimal solution, then $\exists l;\ \frac{U^*Y_l}{V^*X_l}=1$.

According to Theorem 2.1, the model (2.12) is written as below.

$$\begin{aligned}
&\max \frac{UY_p}{VX_p} \\
&\text{subject to} \\
&\frac{UY_j}{VX_j} \leq 1 \qquad j = 1, \ldots, n \\
&(U, V) \geq 1\varepsilon
\end{aligned} \tag{2.13}$$

The model (2.13) is called a fractional-linear Charnes-Cooper-Rhodes (CCR) model (Charnes et al., 1978) where its objective function maximizes the absolute efficiency of DMU_p. As $\max\left\{\frac{UY_j}{VX_j} : j = 1, \ldots, n\right\} = 1$, then,

$$\frac{UY_p}{VX_p} = \frac{\frac{UY_p}{VX_p}}{\max\left\{\frac{UY_j}{VX_j} : j = 1, \ldots, n\right\} = 1}$$

which means that the model (2.13) maximizes the relative efficiency of DMU_p.

To linearize the model (2.13), the Charnes-Cooper transformation (Charnes & Cooper, 1962) is used once more. For this aim, consider $\frac{1}{VX_p} = q > 0$. Then the model (2.13) is written as

$$\begin{aligned}
&\max qUY_p \\
&\text{subject to} \\
&UY_j - VX_j \leq 0 \qquad j = 1, \ldots, n \\
&qVX_p = 1 \\
&U \geq 1\varepsilon, V \geq 1\varepsilon, q \geq \varepsilon
\end{aligned} \tag{2.14}$$

Both sides of the first and third constraints of model (2.14) are multiplied by q. Then, considering the conversions $qU \rightarrow U$, $qV \rightarrow V$, and $q\varepsilon \rightarrow \varepsilon$ (because both ε and $q\varepsilon$ have non-Archimedean properties), the model (2.14) is rewritten as follows,

$$\begin{aligned}
&\max UY_p \\
&\text{subject to} \\
&UY_j - VX_j \leq 0 \quad j = 1, \ldots, n \\
&VX_p = 1 \\
&U \geq 1\varepsilon, V \geq 1\varepsilon
\end{aligned} \tag{2.15}$$

The model (2.15) is known as an input-oriented CCR model (with envelopment form). In this model, the optimal value of the objective function is the relative efficiency of DMU_p. Therefore, if this optimal value for DMU_p is equal to 1, the DMU is relatively efficient, but for an optimal value less than 1, the DMU is relatively nonefficient.

According to the model (2.15), for the case of $j=p$ the first constraint is $UY_p - VX_p \leq 0$. As $Y_p \geq 0$, $Y_p \neq 0$, and $U > 0$, then by combining the first and second constraints the bounds of $0 < UY_p \leq 1$ can be obtained for the objective function. Because the model (2.15) always has a feasible solution, this model always has a bounded optimal solution.

Proposition 2.1. Assume (U^*, V^*) as the optimal solution of model (2.9). Then, for any scalar values $\alpha, \beta > 0$, the solution $(\alpha U^*, \beta V^*)$ also is optimal for the model (2.9).

Proposition 2.2. Assume (U^*, V^*) as the optimal solution of model (2.13). Then, for any scalar value $\alpha > 0$, the solution $(\alpha U^*, \alpha V^*)$ also is optimal for the model (2.13).

According to the above-mentioned theorems, it is obvious that the set of optimal solutions of model (2.13) is a subset of the set of optimal solutions of model (2.9). Similarly, the set of optimal solutions of model (2.15) is a subset of the set of optimal solutions of model (2.13).

According to the model (2.15), the constraint $VX_p = 1$ is a normalizer constraint and helps the model to select one of the feasible solutions with similar objective function values. The models (2.9), (2.13), and (2.15) will have similar optimal objective function values but their optimal solutions may not be similar. The model (2.13) consists of $n+1$ constraints and $m+s$ variables.

2.3 The DEA models based on production possibility set

In the previous subsection, the classical DEA models were developed based on the weights. In this section, these models will be developed based on the concept of the production possibility set. For this aim, some definitions are presented in advance.

Definition 2.8. The production possibility set (PPS) on the space $\mathbb{R}^{m+s}$ is defined as $PPS = \left\{ \begin{pmatrix} X \\ Y \end{pmatrix} \middle| \text{output vector } Y \text{ can be produced by input vector } X \right\}$.

In fact, the production possibility set is a collection of the points in which they can exist in the population under study. To find the production possibility set, first some principles should be considered. Some of these principles are explained below.

Principle 1: Inclusion of the observations (nonempty)

All the observations are elements of the production possibility set, meaning that $\begin{pmatrix} X_j \\ Y_j \end{pmatrix} \in PPS$ where $j=1, \ldots, n$. This principle is true for all populations and is necessary for constructing the PPS.

Principle 2: Convexity

The production possibility set is convex. It means that for any two points of this set, say $\begin{pmatrix} X' \\ Y' \end{pmatrix}$ and $\begin{pmatrix} X'' \\ Y'' \end{pmatrix}$, any point of their segment, say $\lambda \begin{pmatrix} X' \\ Y' \end{pmatrix} + (1-\lambda) \begin{pmatrix} X'' \\ Y'' \end{pmatrix}$ where $0 \leq \lambda \leq 1$, is an element of the PPS.

Principle 3: Returns to scale

This principle is divided into three principles, which are explained below.

Increasing returns to scale principle

Assume $\begin{pmatrix} X \\ Y \end{pmatrix}$ as an element of PPS. Then for any $k \geq 1$, the point $\begin{pmatrix} kX \\ kY \end{pmatrix}$ is an element of PPS. It means that if input X produces output Y, then the input kX (which is greater than X) should produce the output kY.

Decreasing returns to scale principle

Assume $\begin{pmatrix} X \\ Y \end{pmatrix}$ as an element of PPS. Then for any $0 \leq k \leq 1$, the point $\begin{pmatrix} kX \\ kY \end{pmatrix}$ is an element of PPS. It means that if input X produces output Y, then the input kX (which is less than X) should produce the output kY.

Constant returns to scale principle

Assume $\begin{pmatrix} X \\ Y \end{pmatrix}$ as an element of PPS. Then for any $k \geq 0$, the point $\begin{pmatrix} kX \\ kY \end{pmatrix}$ is an element of PPS. It means that if input X produces output Y, then the input kX should produce at least the output kY.

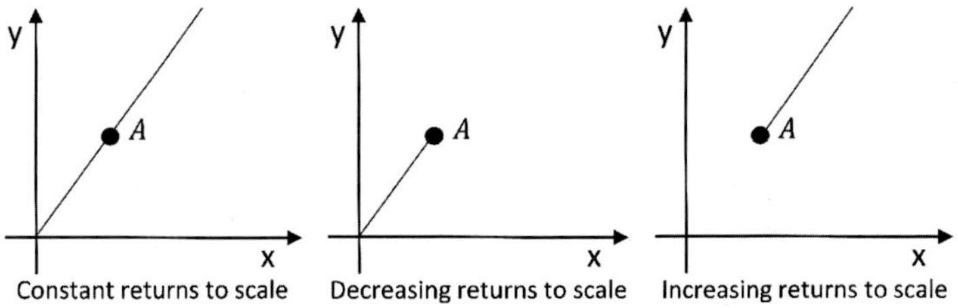

Fig. 2.3 Various returns to scale principles.

The returns to scale principle is shown in Fig. 2.3 schematically.

Principle 4: Possibility

This principle is divided into two principles, which are explained below.

Input possibility principle

If $\begin{pmatrix} X \\ Y \end{pmatrix} \in PPS$, then for any $\overline{X} \geq X$, the point $\begin{pmatrix} \overline{X} \\ Y \end{pmatrix}$ is an element of PPS too.

Output possibility principle

If $\begin{pmatrix} X \\ Y \end{pmatrix} \in PPS$, then for any $\overline{Y} \leq Y$, the point $\begin{pmatrix} X \\ \overline{Y} \end{pmatrix}$ is an element of PPS too.

Therefore, in the general form of the possibility principle, if $\begin{pmatrix} X \\ Y \end{pmatrix} \in PPS$, then for any $\overline{X} \geq X$ and $\overline{Y} \leq Y$, the point $\begin{pmatrix} \overline{X} \\ \overline{Y} \end{pmatrix}$ is an element of PPS too. It is easy to say that this principle may not be true for all populations. The possibility principle is shown in Fig. 2.4 schematically.

Principle 5: Minimum interpolation

PPS is the smallest set that is true for the above-mentioned principles 1–4. Theorem 2.2 is required for the relative comparison of DMUs and the calculation of relative efficiency.

It is notable that the existence of the above-mentioned principles in a population cannot be proved mathematically. The existence of any of these principles in a population depends on the situations of the population.

In the following, some PPSs developed by the above-mentioned principles are explained.

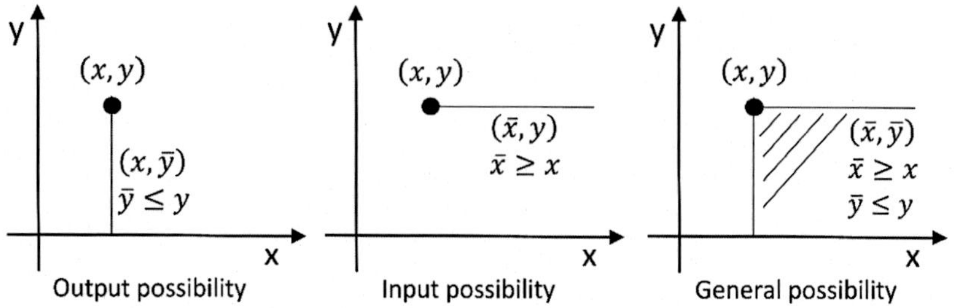

Fig. 2.4 Various possibility principles.

2.3.1 Production possibility set with variable and constant returns to scale

If we accept the principle of inclusion of the observations, convexity, possibility, and minimum interpolation, then we can construct a production possibility set (shown by T) with an observations set of $\left\{\begin{pmatrix} x_j \\ y_j \end{pmatrix} | j = 1, \ldots, n\right\}$ in the following four steps.

Step 1. By accepting the principle of inclusion of the observations, then $T = \left\{\begin{pmatrix} x_j \\ y_j \end{pmatrix} | j = 1, \ldots, n\right\}$.

Step 2. By accepting the principle of inclusion of the observations and convexity, then $T = \left\{\begin{pmatrix} X \\ Y \end{pmatrix} | \begin{pmatrix} X \\ Y \end{pmatrix} = \sum_{j=1}^{n} \lambda_j \begin{pmatrix} x_j \\ y_j \end{pmatrix} \& \sum_{j=1}^{n} \lambda_j = 1 \& \lambda_j \geq 0 \,\&\, j = 1, \ldots, n\right\}$.

Step 3. By accepting the principle of inclusion of the observations, convexity, possibility, and minimum interpolation, then,

$$T_v = \left\{\begin{pmatrix} X \\ Y \end{pmatrix} | X \geq \sum_{j=1}^{n} \lambda_j X_j \& Y \leq \sum_{j=1}^{n} \lambda_j Y_j \& \sum_{j=1}^{n} \lambda_j = 1 \& \lambda_j \geq 0 \& j = 1, \ldots, n\right\}.$$

If we accept none of the returns to scale principles, then instead of T, the notation T_v is used, which means variable returns to scale. A schematic representation of T_v is given in Fig. 2.5.

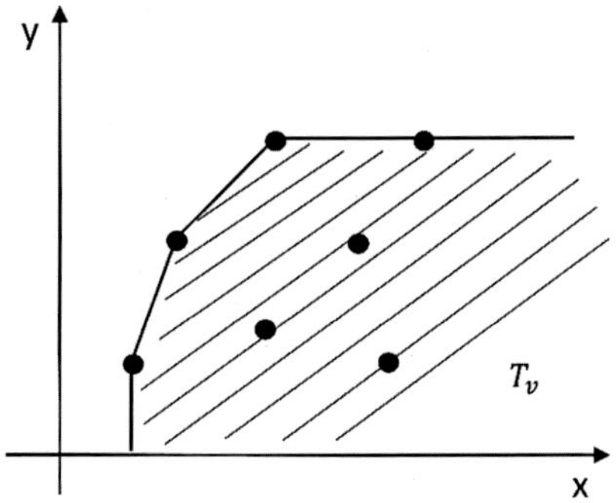

Fig. 2.5 Production possibility set of T_v.

Step 4. By accepting the principle of inclusion of the observations, convexity, constant returns to scale, possibility, and minimum interpolation, then a production possibility set of $T_C = \left\{ \begin{pmatrix} X \\ Y \end{pmatrix} | X \geq \sum_{j=1}^{n} \lambda_j X_j \& Y \leq \sum_{j=1}^{n} \lambda_j Y_j \& \lambda_j \geq 0 \& j = 1, \ldots, n \right\}$ is obtained. A schematic representation of T_C is given in Fig. 2.6.

2.3.2 CCR models

We assume that T is an arbitrary production possibility set and the aim is to investigate DMU_p with coordinates of $\begin{pmatrix} X_p \\ Y_p \end{pmatrix}$.

Definition 2.9. DMU_p is efficient if and only if there is no better point than $\begin{pmatrix} X_p \\ Y_p \end{pmatrix}$ in T.

To understand the above definition, we should check whether DMU_p has improving direction in T. As decreasing the input and increasing the output will improve the point p, therefore, an improving direction in any point of T should be like $\begin{pmatrix} -d^x \\ d^y \end{pmatrix} = d$ where d^x, $d^y \geq 0$ and $d \neq 0$. To prove that there is no point better than $\begin{pmatrix} X_p \\ Y_p \end{pmatrix}$ in direction d, the following problem is considered.

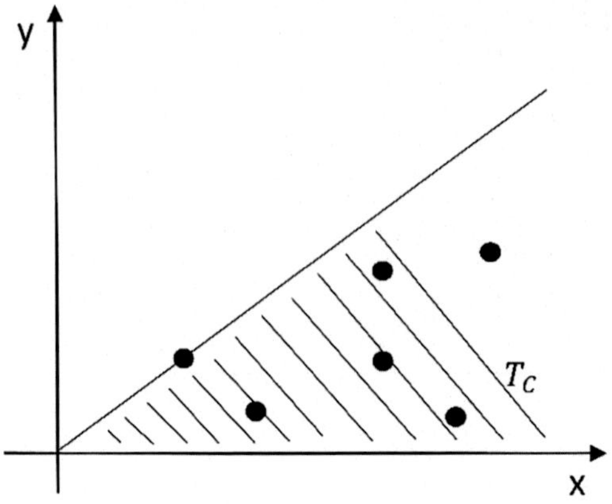

Fig. 2.6 Production possibility set of T_C.

$$\begin{aligned}&\max \alpha\\&\text{subject to}\\&\begin{pmatrix}X_p\\Y_p\end{pmatrix}+\alpha\begin{pmatrix}-d^x\\d^y\end{pmatrix}\in T\end{aligned} \tag{2.16}$$

This problem is simplified in the following.

$$\begin{aligned}&\max \alpha\\&\text{subject to}\\&\begin{pmatrix}X_p-\alpha d^x\\Y_p+\alpha d^y\end{pmatrix}\in T\end{aligned} \tag{2.17}$$

In the above problem for $\alpha^*>0$, the point $\begin{pmatrix}X_p-\alpha^* d^x\\Y_p+\alpha^* d^y\end{pmatrix}$ is better than $\begin{pmatrix}X_p\\Y_p\end{pmatrix}$ and DMU_p is inefficient where $\alpha^*=0$, which means that there is no better point than $\begin{pmatrix}X_p\\Y_p\end{pmatrix}$ in the direction d of T. As d is an arbitrary direction, this issue cannot be enough to say that DMU_p is efficient because there may be another direction that contains a point better than $\begin{pmatrix}X_p\\Y_p\end{pmatrix}$. Usually, two improving directions are considered by managers, the input-based improving direction $d = \begin{pmatrix} -X_p \\ 0 \end{pmatrix}$ and the output-based improving direction $\begin{pmatrix} 0 \\ Y_p \end{pmatrix}$. Applying $d = \begin{pmatrix} -X_p \\ 0 \end{pmatrix}$, the model (2.17) is written as,

$$\begin{aligned} &\max \alpha \\ &\text{subject to} \\ &\begin{pmatrix} (1-\alpha)X_p \\ Y_p \end{pmatrix} \in T \end{aligned} \tag{2.18}$$

Considering $1-\alpha=\theta$, the below model is obtained.

$$\begin{aligned} &\max\ (1-\theta) \\ &\text{subject to} \\ &\begin{pmatrix} \theta X_p \\ Y_p \end{pmatrix} \in T \end{aligned} \tag{2.19}$$

As $\max\ (1-\theta)$ and $1-\min\theta$ are identical, the following model is obtained instead of the model (2.19)

$$\begin{aligned} &\min \theta \\ &\text{subject to} \\ &\begin{pmatrix} \theta X_p \\ Y_p \end{pmatrix} \in T \end{aligned} \tag{2.20}$$

In the above problem for $\theta^* < 1$, there will be a point in T that is better than $\begin{pmatrix} X_p \\ Y_p \end{pmatrix}$ and DMU_p is inefficient where $\theta^* = 1$, which means that there is no better point than $\begin{pmatrix} X_p \\ Y_p \end{pmatrix}$ in the direction d of T. As d is an arbitrary direction, this issue cannot be enough to say that DMU_p is efficient because there may be another direction that contains a point better than $\begin{pmatrix} X_p \\ Y_p \end{pmatrix}$. Replacing T by T_c in (2.20), according to the definition of T_c the following model is obtained, which is called an input-oriented CCR model with envelopment form.

$$
\begin{aligned}
&\min \theta \\
&\text{subject to} \\
&\sum_{j=1}^{n} \lambda_j X_j \le \theta X_p \\
&\sum_{j=1}^{n} \lambda_j Y_j \ge \theta Y_p \\
&\lambda_j \ge 0 \qquad\qquad j = 1, \ldots, n
\end{aligned}
\tag{2.21}
$$

In the following, some properties of the model (2.21) are presented.

Lemma 2.1. For any feasible solution of the model (2.21), say (λ, θ), the condition $\lambda \neq 0$ is held.

Lemma 2.2. For any feasible solution of the model (2.21), say (λ, θ), the condition $\theta > 0$ is held.

Lemma 2.3. The model (2.21) has a bounded optimal solution where $0 < \theta^* \le 1$.

The dual form of the model (2.21) is given below, where V and U are vectors of dual variables associated with the first and second constraints of the model (2.21), respectively.

$$
\begin{aligned}
&\max UY_p \\
&\text{subject to} \\
&UY_j - VX_j \le 0 \quad j = 1, \ldots, n \\
&VX_p = 1 \\
&U \ge 0, V \ge 0
\end{aligned}
\tag{2.22}
$$

The model (2.22) is called an input-oriented CCR model with a multiplier form. This model is a typical version of the model (2.15) with $\varepsilon = 0$, which means that the efficiency obtained by the models (2.15) and (2.22) is the same. According to Lemma 2.3, the model (2.22) has a bounded optimal solution where $U^* Y_p = \theta^*$.

Lemma 2.4. If (V^*, U^*) is the optimal solution of the model (2.22), then $V^*, U^* \neq 0$.

Lemma 2.5. If (λ^*, θ^*) and (V^*, U^*) is the optimal solutions of the models (2.21) and (2.22), respectively, then,

- $\exists l;\ U^* Y_l - V^* X_l = 0$,
- $\exists i;\ \sum_{j=1}^{n} \lambda_j^* x_{ij} = \theta^* x_{ip}$,
- $\exists r;\ \sum_{j=1}^{n} \lambda_j^* y_{rj} = y_{rp}$.

Theorem 2.2. DMU_p is efficient in model (2.21) if and only if,

- $\theta^* = 1$,
- All slack variables of all constraints in any optimal solution are zero.

Definition 2.10. A hyperplane (H) in $\mathbb{R}^n$ is defined as follows,

$$H = \{X | p^t(X - \overline{X}) = 0\} = \{X | p^t X = \alpha\} \tag{2.23}$$

Where $p \neq 0$ is the normal vector.

Definition 2.11. The hyperplane H on the set S is called a supporting hyperplane if and only if,

- $S \subseteq H^+ \vee S \subseteq H^-$,
- $H \cap S \neq \varnothing$,

where $H^- = \{X | p^t X \leq \alpha\}$ and $H^+ = \{X | p^t X \geq \alpha\}$ are the half spaces of H.

To judge the efficiency of DMU_p in T_c according to Theorem 2.2, first the model (2.21) is solved. If $\theta^* < 1$, the DMU is inefficient. But if $\theta^* = 1$, to judge the efficiency, the second condition of Theorem 2.2 is required. So, the following model is solved.

$$\begin{aligned} & \max w = 1S^+ + 1S^- \\ & \text{subject to} \\ & \sum_{j=1}^{n} \lambda_j X_j + S^- = \theta^* X_p \\ & \sum_{j=1}^{n} \lambda_j Y_j - S^+ = Y_p \\ & \lambda \geq 0, \quad S^- \geq 0, \quad S^+ \geq 0 \end{aligned} \tag{2.24}$$

Now, by solving the model (2.24), if $w^* = 0$ both conditions of Theorem 2.2 are held (earlier $\theta^* = 1$) and DMU_p is efficient. For the case of $w^* > 0$, DMU_p is inefficient. In addition, the models (2.21) and (2.24) can be integrated as the following model, which is called an input-oriented CCR model with ε.

$$\begin{aligned} & \max z = \theta - \varepsilon(1S^+ + 1S^-) \\ & \text{subject to} \\ & \sum_{j=1}^{n} \lambda_j X_j + S^- = \theta X_p \\ & \sum_{j=1}^{n} \lambda_j Y_j - S^+ = Y_p \\ & \lambda \geq 0, \quad S^- \geq 0, \quad S^+ \geq 0 \end{aligned} \tag{2.25}$$

In this model, ε is a small positive non-Archimedean number that gives absolute priority to either θ or $1S^{+}+1S^{-}$. The objective function of the model (2.25) also can be written in the form of $M\theta-(1S^{+}+1S^{-})$, where M is a large positive number.

Definition 2.12. If the optimal solution of the model (2.25) is shown by $(\lambda^{*},S^{-*},S^{+*},\theta^{*})$, the vector $\begin{pmatrix}\sum_{j=1}^{n}\lambda_j^{*}X_j\\ \sum_{j=1}^{n}\lambda_j^{*}Y_j\end{pmatrix}$ is a projection of DMU_p on the frontier efficiency T_c. This vector is called the objective, benchmark, or projection coordinates of DMU_p.

Theorem 2.3. The benchmark coordinates $\begin{pmatrix}\sum_{j=1}^{n}\lambda_j^{*}X_j\\ \sum_{j=1}^{n}\lambda_j^{*}Y_j\end{pmatrix}$ are efficient.

Definition 2.13. The set of points of the production possibility set is divided into three types as follows,

- Inefficient points: The set of points that are inside of T (int T).
- Weak efficient points: The set of points that are on the frontier of T but there is a better point than them inside of T.
- Strong efficient points: The set of points of T where there is no point better than them in T.

It is obvious that there is a weak efficient point in T_c if and only if in the model (2.25), $\theta^{*}=1$ and $(S^{-*},S^{+*})\neq 0$.

Definition 2.14. An input-oriented reference set of DMU_p is defined as $RS_p=\{DMU_j\,|\,\lambda_j^{*}>0$ in an optimal solution of model (2.25)$\}$.

The coordinates of the pattern point and the reference set have many applications in management science. The coordinates of the pattern point for DMU_p are written as $\sum_{DMU_p\in RS_p}\lambda_j^{*}\begin{pmatrix}X_j\\ Y_j\end{pmatrix}$. By comparing the coordinates of the pattern point with DMU_p, the shortcomings of each input or output can be recognized. As $\sum_{DMU_p\in RS_p}\lambda_j^{*}X_j\leq X_p$ and $\sum_{DMU_p\in RS_p}\lambda_j^{*}Y_j\geq Y_p$, then the difference of DMU_p and the coordinates of the pattern point determine the amount of decrease in the inputs and the amount of increase in the outputs compared to society based on the existing historical data. If DMU_p has the coordinates of the pattern point, then it is a strong efficient point.

Otherwise, this DMU should define a strategy plan based on its strengths and weaknesses. To improve DMU_p to the coordinates of the pattern point, the members of RS_p can be used. This means that the policies and decisions made by the members of the reference set of DMU_p can be applied for DMU_p to improve it.

Theorem 2.4. All members of RS_p are strong efficient in T_c.

Definition 2.15. DMU_p is extremely efficient if and only if $RS_p = \{DMU_p\}$.

Definition 2.16. DMU_p is nonextremely efficient if and only if,

- DMU_p is strong efficient,
- $|RS_p| \geq 2$.

As T_c is a convex polyhedral cone, an extremely efficient DMU is always on the faces of T_c.

In the following, by applying $d = \begin{pmatrix} 0 \\ Y_p \end{pmatrix}$, the model (2.17) is written as,

$$\begin{aligned} &\max \alpha \\ &\text{subject to} \\ &\begin{pmatrix} X_p \\ (1-\alpha)Y_p \end{pmatrix} \in T_c \end{aligned} \tag{2.26}$$

According to the definition of T_c and the conversion $\varphi = 1 - \alpha$, this model is converted to the following model.

$$\begin{aligned} &\max \varphi \\ &\text{subject to} \\ &\sum_{j=1}^{n} \lambda_j X_j \leq X_p \\ &\sum_{j=1}^{n} \lambda_j Y_j \geq \varphi Y_p \\ &\lambda_j \geq 0 \qquad j = 1, \ldots, n \end{aligned} \tag{2.27}$$

This model is called an output-oriented CCR model with envelopment form and its dual problem is modeled as follows,

$$
\begin{aligned}
&\min VX_p \\
&\text{subject to} \\
&VX_j - UY_j \geq 0 \quad j = 1, \ldots, n \\
&UY_p = 1 \\
&U \geq 0, \quad V \geq 0
\end{aligned} \tag{2.28}
$$

The model (2.28) is called an output-oriented CCR model with multiplier form.

Obviously, $\lambda = e_p$ and $\varphi = 1$ are feasible solutions for the model (2.27), so its optimal objective function value is at least one that means $\varphi^* \geq 1$. Similar to the input-oriented model, to identify weak and strong efficiencies by the output-oriented CCR model, the following model is proposed,

$$
\begin{aligned}
&\max z = \varphi + \varepsilon(1S^+ + 1S^-) \\
&\text{subject to} \\
&\sum_{j=1}^{n} \lambda_j X_j + S^- = X_p \\
&\sum_{j=1}^{n} \lambda_j Y_j - S^+ = \varphi Y_p \\
&\lambda \geq 0, \quad S^- \geq 0, \quad S^+ \geq 0
\end{aligned} \tag{2.29}
$$

and its dual form is as follows,

$$
\begin{aligned}
&\min VX_p \\
&\text{subject to} \\
&VX_j - UY_j \geq 0 \quad j = 1, \ldots, n \\
&UY_p = 1 \\
&U \geq 1\varepsilon, \quad V \geq 1\varepsilon
\end{aligned} \tag{2.30}
$$

It is obvious that,

- For any feasible solution of the model (2.27) such as (λ, φ), the condition $\lambda \neq 0$ is held.
- If (U^*, V^*) is the optimal solution of the model (2.28), then $U^* \neq 0$ and $V^* \neq 0$.

Also, if (λ^*, φ^*) and (V^*, U^*) are the optimal solutions of the models (2.27) and (2.28), respectively, then,

- $\exists l;\ U^* Y_l - V^* X_l = 0$,
- $\exists i;\ \sum_{j=1}^{n} \lambda_j^* x_{ij} = x_{ip}$,

- $\exists r;\ \sum_{j=1}^{n} \lambda_j^* y_{rj} = \varphi^* y_{rp}$.

Theorem 2.5. DMU_p is efficient in the model (2.27), if and only if,

- $\varphi^* = 1$,
- All slack variables of all constraints in any optimal solution are zero.

Theorem 2.6. If (λ^*, θ^*) and $(\overline{\lambda}, \varphi^*)$ are optimal solutions of the models (2.20) and (2.27), respectively, then $\varphi^* = \frac{1}{\theta^*}$.

According to Theorem 2.6, the efficiency in both input-oriented and output-oriented CCR models is equal but the only difference is in the coordinates of pattern points. According to the decision maker, to improve the current situation of inefficient DMUs, either input-oriented or output-oriented models can be used. In the input-oriented model, improvement is done first by decreasing the inputs and then by increasing the outputs if necessary. But, in the output-oriented model, improvement is done first by increasing the outputs and then by decreasing the inputs if necessary. This is notable in that for most organizations, decreasing the inputs may be easier, less costly, and less time-consuming compared to increasing the outputs (e.g., increasing the production, the selling amount, the net benefit, etc.). Therefore, the managers according to the degree of urgency of their organizations can decide whether to use input-oriented or output-oriented models for improving the current situation.

2.3.3 BCC models

In this section, according to production possibility set T_v and some improving schemes, various models will be generated. As most of the generated models correspond to the models of T_c, the contents of this section are presented briefly.

According to the principles such as the inclusion of observations, convexity, possibility, and minimum interpolation, production possibility set T_v is defined as below.

$$T_v = \left\{ (X, Y) | X \geq \sum_{j=1}^{n} \lambda_j X_j \ \& \ Y \leq \sum_{j=1}^{n} \lambda_j Y_j \ \& \ \sum_{j=1}^{n} \lambda_j = 1 \ \& \ \lambda_j \geq 0, \quad j = 1, \ldots, n \right\} \tag{2.31}$$

2.3.3.1 Input-oriented models in T_v

Given $d = \begin{pmatrix} -X_p \\ 0 \end{pmatrix}$, $T = T_v$, and $\theta = 1 - \alpha$, the model (2.17) is reconstructed as follows,

$$
\begin{aligned}
&\min \theta \\
&\text{subject to} \\
&\sum_{j=1}^{n} \lambda_j X_j \leq \theta X_p \\
&\sum_{j=1}^{n} \lambda_j Y_j \geq Y_p \\
&\sum_{j=1}^{n} \lambda_j = 1 \\
&\lambda_j \geq 0 \qquad\qquad j = 1, \ldots, n
\end{aligned}
\tag{2.32}
$$

The above model is known as an input-oriented Banker-Charnes-Cooper (BCC) model (Banker et al., 1984) with envelopment form. All theorems presented for the input-oriented model with envelopment form are also true for the model (2.32), with the only difference that in the CCR model, if $\theta^* < 1$ then $\begin{pmatrix} X_p \\ Y_p \end{pmatrix} \in \text{int} T_c$ but this property may not be held by the BCC model.

The dual form of the model (2.32) is given below.

$$
\begin{aligned}
&\max UY_p + u_0 \\
&\text{subject to} \\
&UY_j - VX_j + u_0 \leq 0 \quad j = 1, \ldots, n \\
&VX_p = 1 \\
&U \geq 0, \quad V \geq 0
\end{aligned}
\tag{2.33}
$$

If $(V^*, U^*, u_0{}^*)$ is the optimal solution of the model (2.33), then, $H = \left\{ \begin{pmatrix} X \\ Y \end{pmatrix} | U^* Y - V^* X - u_0^* = 0 \right\}$ is a supporting hyperplane on the projection point in T_v.

Similar to the CCR model, strong efficiencies are recognized by the below two-phase model.

$$
\begin{aligned}
&\min z = \theta - \varepsilon(1S^+ + 1S^-) \\
&\text{subject to} \\
&\sum_{j=1}^{n} \lambda_j X_j + S^- = \theta X_p \\
&\sum_{j=1}^{n} \lambda_j Y_j - S^+ = Y_p \\
&\sum_{j=1}^{n} \lambda_j = 1 \\
&S^+ \geq 0, \quad S^- \geq 0, \quad \lambda_j \geq 0 \qquad j = 1, \ldots, n
\end{aligned} \tag{2.34}
$$

The dual form of the model (2.34) is written as follows,

$$
\begin{aligned}
&\max UY_p + u_0 \\
&\text{subject to} \\
&UY_j - VX_j + u_0 \leq 0 \quad j = 1, \ldots, n \\
&VX_p = 1 \\
&U \geq 1\varepsilon, \quad V \geq 1\varepsilon
\end{aligned} \tag{2.35}
$$

Obviously, in the model (2.34), if $z^* = 1$ then DMU_p is strongly efficient.

The models (2.34) and (2.35) are two-phase models. In the model (2.34), first $\min\theta$ respecting to all the constraints is solved and then in the second phase, $\max 1S^+ + 1S^-$ respecting to all the constraints is solved where $\theta = \theta^*$.

In the first phase of the model (2.35), the below problem is solved,

$$
\begin{aligned}
&\max z = UY_p + u_0 \\
&\text{subject to} \\
&UY_j - VX_j + u_0 \leq 0 \quad j = 1, \ldots, n \\
&VX_p = 1 \\
&U \geq 0, \quad V \geq 0
\end{aligned} \tag{2.36}
$$

where in the second phase, the problem to be solved is as follows,

$$
\begin{aligned}
&\max \gamma \\
&\text{subject to} \\
&UY_j - VX_j + u_0 \leq 0 \quad j = 1, \ldots, n \\
&VX_p = 1 \\
&UY_p + u_0 = z^* \\
&U \geq \gamma 1, \quad V \geq \gamma 1
\end{aligned} \tag{2.37}
$$

It is obvious that if $z^* = 1$ and $\gamma^* > 0$ then DMU_p is strongly efficient.

2.3.3.2 Output-oriented models in T_v

By considering $d = \begin{pmatrix} 0 \\ Y_p \end{pmatrix}$ and $T = T_v$ the model (2.17) is written as below

$$\begin{aligned} & \min \varphi \\ & \text{subject to} \\ & \sum_{j=1}^{n} \lambda_j X_j \le X_p \\ & \sum_{j=1}^{n} \lambda_j Y_j \ge \varphi Y_p \\ & \sum_{j=1}^{n} \lambda_j = 1 \\ & \lambda_j \ge 0 \qquad\qquad j = 1, \ldots, n \end{aligned} \tag{2.38}$$

The above model is known as an output-oriented BCC model with envelopment form and its optimal objective function value φ^* is at least 1.

The dual form of the model (2.32) is given below, and t is known as an output-oriented BCC model with multiplier form.

$$\begin{aligned} & \max VX_p + v_0 \\ & \text{subject to} \\ & VX_j - UY_j + v_0 \ge 0 \qquad j = 1, \ldots, n \\ & UY_p = 1 \\ & U \ge 0, \quad V \ge 0U, \quad V \ge 0 \end{aligned} \tag{2.39}$$

It is necessary to mention that in models (2.38) and (2.39), the relationship $\theta^* = \frac{1}{\varphi^*}$ may not always be true.

2.4 Nonincreasing and nondecreasing returns to scale models

According to principles such as the inclusion of observations, convexity, nondecreasing returns to scale, possibility, and minimum interpolation, production possibility set T_{ND} is defined as below.

$$T_{ND} = \left\{ (X, Y) | X \geq \sum_{j=1}^{n} \lambda_j X_j \ \& \ Y \leq \sum_{j=1}^{n} \lambda_j Y_j \& \ \sum_{j=1}^{n} \lambda_j \geq 1 \ \& \ \lambda_j \geq 0, j = 1, \ldots, n \right\} \tag{2.40}$$

According to the principles such as the inclusion of observations, convexity, nonincreasing returns to scale, possibility, and minimum interpolation, production possibility set T_{NI} is defined as below.

$$T_{NI} = \left\{ (X, Y) | X \geq \sum_{j=1}^{n} \lambda_j X_j \ \& \ Y \leq \sum_{j=1}^{n} \lambda_j Y_j \& \ \sum_{j=1}^{n} \lambda_j \leq 1 \ \& \ \lambda_j \geq 0, j = 1, \ldots, n \right\} \tag{2.41}$$

The models developed by T_{ND} are known as BCC-CCR models and the models developed by T_{ND} are known as CCR-BCC models. The input-oriented with envelopment form model and its variants are as follows,

$$\begin{aligned}
&\min z = \theta - \varepsilon(1S^+ + 1S^-) \\
&\text{subject to} \\
&\sum_{j=1}^{n} \lambda_j X_j + S^- = \theta X_p \\
&\sum_{j=1}^{n} \lambda_j Y_j - S^+ = Y_p \\
&S^+ \geq 0, \ \ S^- \geq 0, \ \ \lambda \in \Lambda
\end{aligned} \tag{2.42}$$

where, $\lambda_{CCR} = \{\lambda | \lambda \geq 0\}$, $\lambda_{BCC} = \left\{ \lambda | \lambda \geq 0, \ \sum_{j=1}^{n} \lambda_j = 1 \right\}$, $\lambda_{BCC-CCR} = \left\{ \lambda | \lambda \geq 0, \ \sum_{j=1}^{n} \lambda_j \geq 1 \right\}$, and $\lambda_{CCR-BCC} = \left\{ \lambda | \lambda \geq 0, \ \sum_{j=1}^{n} \lambda_j \leq 1 \right\}$.

The dual form of the model (2.42) is given below,

$$
\begin{aligned}
&\max UY_p + u_0 \\
&\text{subject to} \\
&UY_j - VX_j + u_0 \leq 0 \quad j = 1, \ldots, n \\
&VX_p = 1 \\
&U \geq 0, \quad V \geq 0
\end{aligned} \tag{2.43}
$$

where, $u_{0,CCR} = \{u_0 | \, u_0 = 0\}$, $u_{0,BCC} = \{u_0 | \, u_0 \in \mathbb{R}\}$, $u_{0,BCC-CCR} = \{u_0 | \, u_0 \geq 0\}$, and $u_{0,CCR-BCC} = \{u_0 | \, u_0 \leq 0\}$.

The output-oriented models also can be obtained by a similar way. The properties previously presented for CCR models are true for other models too.

2.5 Nonradial DEA models

In this section, the nonradial models of DEA are discussed. In the model (2.17), the behavior of a DMU is studied in an improving direction. Therefore, the route for finding a better point is like a radius. This means that all the previously presented models are called radial models. To construct nonradial models, it is necessary that improving direction be able to search in different routes. General form nonradial models are given below.

$$
\begin{aligned}
&\max\{\alpha_1, \ldots, \alpha_m, \beta_1, \ldots, \beta_s\} \\
&\text{subject to} \\
&\begin{pmatrix} x_{1p} - \alpha_1 d_1^x \\ \vdots \\ x_{mp} - \alpha_m d_m^x \\ y_{1p} + \beta_1 d_1^y \\ \vdots \\ y_{sp} + \beta_s d_s^y \end{pmatrix} \in T \\
&\alpha \geq 0, \quad \beta \geq 0
\end{aligned} \tag{2.44}
$$

In the above-mentioned model, in each of the input and output elements, the improving process happens independently where $d^x \geq 0$, $d^y \geq 0$, and $(d^x, d^y) \neq 0$. In the following, some nonradial models are presented.

2.5.1 Additive model

If in the model (2.44), $d_i^x = 1$ (for any i) and $d_r^y = 1$ (for any r), then the model is written as follows.

$$\begin{aligned} &\max\{\alpha_1, \ldots, \alpha_m, \beta_1, \ldots, \beta_s\} \\ &\text{subject to} \\ &\begin{pmatrix} X_p - \alpha \\ Y_p + \beta \end{pmatrix} \in T \\ &\alpha \geq 0, \quad \beta \geq 0 \end{aligned} \tag{2.45}$$

Assuming $T = T_c$ and using the weighted sum of the objective functions with weight values of 1, the following model is obtained.

$$\begin{aligned} &\max \sum_{i=1}^{m} \alpha_i + \sum_{r=1}^{s} \beta_r \\ &\text{subject to} \\ &\sum_{j=1}^{n} \lambda_j x_{ij} \leq x_{ip} - \alpha_i \qquad i = 1, \ldots, m \\ &\sum_{j=1}^{n} \lambda_j y_{rj} \geq y_{rp} + \beta_r \qquad r = 1, \ldots, s \\ &\lambda \geq 0, \quad \alpha \geq 0, \quad \beta \geq 0 \end{aligned} \tag{2.46}$$

Obviously, in any optimal solution, all the input and output constraints are effective; therefore, those can be considered in their equal form. In the case of equal form of the constraints of the model (2.46), the variables α_i and β_r play the role of slack variables and the model (2.46) is written as follows,

$$\begin{aligned} &\max \sum_{i=1}^{m} s_i^- + \sum_{r=1}^{s} s_r^+ \\ &\text{subject to} \\ &\sum_{j=1}^{n} \lambda_j x_{ij} + s_i^- = x_{ip} \qquad i = 1, \ldots, m \\ &\sum_{j=1}^{n} \lambda_j y_{rj} - s_r^+ = y_{rp} \qquad r = 1, \ldots, s \\ &\lambda \geq 0, \quad s^- \geq 0, \quad s^+ \geq 0 \end{aligned} \tag{2.47}$$

The model (2.47) is known as an additive model. In the optimal solution of this model, if $(s^{-*}, s^{+*}) \neq 0$, then DMU_p is not efficient and can be improved by the input(s)/output(s) associated with the positive variables. The optimal objective function value shows the highest distance of DMU_p from the efficiency frontier. This means that if the optimal objective function value of DMU_p is zero, then it is on the efficient frontier and it is efficient. So, if the optimal objective function value of DMU_p is positive, then it is inefficient. This model does not calculate the efficiency value, but it determines whether the DMU is strongly efficient. The dual form of the model (2.47) is presented below.

$$\begin{aligned}
&\max\ VX_p - UY_p \\
&\text{subject to} \\
&UY_j - VX_j \leq 0 \qquad j = 1, \dots, n \\
&U \geq 1_s, \quad V \geq 1_m
\end{aligned} \tag{2.48}$$

The most important advantage of models (2.47) and (2.48) is that just by solving one model, it is determined whether the DMU is strongly efficient. But as a shortage, these models cannot determine relative efficiency value. The models (2.47) and (2.48) can be written for T_v, T_{NI}, and T_{ND} easily in a similar way.

2.5.2 The Russell and SBM model

One of the nonradial models or determining the strong efficiency of a DMU is as follows,

$$\begin{aligned}
&\min\{\theta_1, \dots, \theta_m\} \\
&\max\{\varphi_1, \dots, \varphi_s\} \\
&\quad \text{subject to} \\
&\begin{pmatrix} \theta_1 x_{1p} \\ \vdots \\ \theta_m x_{mp} \\ \varphi_1 y_{1p} \\ \vdots \\ \varphi_s y_{sp} \end{pmatrix} \in T \\
&\quad \theta_i \leq 1 \qquad i = 1, \dots, m \\
&\quad \varphi_r \geq 1 \qquad r = 1, \dots, s \\
&\quad \lambda \geq 0
\end{aligned} \tag{2.49}$$

As the above model is in multiobjective form, the following single objective functions can be proposed instead of the multiobjective functions.

$$\min \frac{1}{m}\sum_{i=1}^{m}\theta_i + \frac{1}{\frac{1}{s}\sum_{r=1}^{s}\varphi_r} \tag{2.50}$$

$$\min \frac{1}{m}\sum_{i=1}^{m}\theta_i + \frac{1}{s}\sum_{r=1}^{s}\frac{1}{\varphi_r} \tag{2.51}$$

As both these single objective functions are nonlinear and so are difficult to solve, the following linear version for the objective function (2.51) is proposed.

$$\min \frac{1}{m}\sum_{i=1}^{m}\theta_i - \frac{1}{s}\sum_{r=1}^{s}\varphi_r \tag{2.52}$$

The objective function (2.52) is linear, but its value cannot be easily interpreted as a scale for measuring efficiency. Therefore, the following model was proposed by Pastor et al. (1999):

$$\begin{aligned}
&\min \rho = \frac{\frac{1}{m}\sum_{i=1}^{m}\theta_i}{\frac{1}{s}\sum_{r=1}^{s}\varphi_r} \\
&\text{subject to} \\
&\sum_{j=1}^{n}\lambda_j x_{ij} \le \theta_i x_{ip} \qquad i = 1, \ldots, m \\
&\sum_{j=1}^{n}\lambda_j y_{rj} \ge \varphi_r y_{rp} \qquad r = 1, \ldots, s \\
&\theta_i \le 1 \qquad i = 1, \ldots, m \\
&\varphi_r \ge 1 \qquad r = 1, \ldots, s \\
&\lambda \ge 0
\end{aligned} \tag{2.53}$$

The model (2.53) is called the enhanced Russell model (Pastor et al., 1999). In the model (2.53), the conditions $X_p > 0$ and $Y_p > 0$ should be held. If one of the elements of X_p such as x_{tp} is zero, then θ_t is removed from the model. This is because for this input, the value of zero is the best and there is no possibility of reducing it. If one of the elements of Y_p such as y_{lp} is zero, then φ_l is replaced by a small positive value (say ε) in the model because improvement cannot be done by a multiplier operation for zero value.

Lemma 2.6. The objective function value of the model (2.53) is in the interval $(0,1]$.

Lemma 2.7. According to the model (2.53), a DMU is efficient if and only if $\rho^*=1$.

Lemma 2.8. If $(\lambda^*,\ \theta^*,\ \varphi^*)$ is the optimal solution of the model (2.53), then $\sum_{j=1}^{n}\lambda_j^* x_{ij} = \theta_i^* x_{ip}$ and $\sum_{j=1}^{n}\lambda_j^* y_{rj} = \varphi_r^* y_{rp}$ for any i and r.

According to Lemma 2.8, the model (2.53) can be written as below,

$$
\begin{aligned}
&\min \rho = \frac{\frac{1}{m}\sum_{i=1}^{m}\theta_i}{\frac{1}{s}\sum_{r=1}^{s}\varphi_r}\\
&\text{subject to}\\
&\sum_{j=1}^{n}\lambda_j x_{ij} = \theta_i x_{ip} \qquad i=1,\ldots,m\\
&\sum_{j=1}^{n}\lambda_j y_{rj} = \varphi_r y_{rp} \qquad r=1,\ldots,s\\
&\theta_i \le 1 \qquad i=1,\ldots,m\\
&\varphi_r \ge 1 \qquad r=1,\ldots,s\\
&\lambda \ge 0
\end{aligned}
\tag{2.54}
$$

Assuming $\theta_i = \frac{x_{ip}-s_i^-}{x_{ip}}$ and $\varphi_r = \frac{y_{rp}+s_r^+}{y_{rp}}$ for any i and r, the following model is obtained.

$$
\begin{aligned}
&\min \rho = \frac{1-\frac{1}{m}\sum_{i=1}^{m}\frac{s_i^-}{x_{ip}}}{1+\frac{1}{s}\sum_{r=1}^{s}\frac{s_r^+}{y_{rp}}}\\
&\text{subject to}\\
&\sum_{j=1}^{n}\lambda_j x_{ij} = x_{ip} - s_i^- \qquad i=1,\ldots m\\
&\sum_{j=1}^{n}\lambda_j y_{rj} = y_{rp} + s_r^+ \qquad r=1,\ldots,s\\
&\lambda,\ s^-,\ s^+ \ge 0
\end{aligned}
\tag{2.55}
$$

The model (2.55) defines an efficiency measure according to the slack variables and is known as a slacks-based measure (SBM) model. According to the Charnes-Cooper transformation (Charnes & Cooper, 1962), it is linearized as follows,

$$
\begin{aligned}
&\min \rho = q - \frac{1}{m}\sum_{i=1}^{m}\frac{s_i^-}{x_{ip}} \\
&\text{subject to} \\
&\sum_{j=1}^{n}\lambda_j x_{ij} = q x_{ip} - s_i^- \qquad i = 1, \ldots, m \\
&\sum_{j=1}^{n}\lambda_j y_{rj} = q y_{rp} + s_r^+ \qquad r = 1, \ldots, s \\
&q + \frac{1}{s}\sum_{r=1}^{s}\frac{s_r^+}{y_{rp}} = 1 \\
&\lambda,\ s^-,\ s^+ \geq 0,\ \ q \geq \varepsilon
\end{aligned}
\tag{2.56}
$$

The models (2.54) and (2.56) can be written based on both inputs and outputs. For instance, the output-based SBM model can be written as follows,

$$
\begin{aligned}
&\max 1 + \frac{1}{s}\sum_{r=1}^{s}\frac{s_r^+}{y_{rp}} \\
&\text{subject to} \\
&\sum_{j=1}^{n}\lambda_j x_{ij} = x_{ip} - s_i^- \qquad i = 1, \ldots, m \\
&\sum_{j=1}^{n}\lambda_j y_{rj} = y_{rp} + s_r^+ \qquad r = 1, \ldots, s \\
&\lambda,\ s^-,\ s^+ \geq 0
\end{aligned}
\tag{2.57}
$$

It is notable that the objective function of the model (2.53) can be weighted as $\min \frac{\frac{\sum_{i=1}^{m}\alpha_i\theta_i}{\sum_{i=1}^{m}\alpha_i}}{\frac{\sum_{r=1}^{s}\beta_r\varphi_r}{\sum_{r=1}^{s}\beta_r}}$, where α_i and β_r are the weights of input i and output r, respectively.

2.6 Stability of DEA models for unit of scale change and transmission

In most DEA problems, an important question is how unit of scale changes in an input or output index are effective on the efficiency value of a DMU? Or how does the transmission of an input or output affect efficiency value? For example, if the costs of an organization are an input, how do different units of currency affect the efficiency values?

If a DEA model is stable for unit of scale changes, then all inputs and outputs can be normalized separately with infinity norm to be in the interval of [0, 1]. In this situation for problems with relatively large sizes, calculation errors are reduced significantly because of the similarity in the scales of the input and output parameters. Also, if a DEA model is stable for transmission, then if an index (e.g., net benefit) has negative value in some DMUs, these negative values can convert to positive values by transmission.

2.6.1 Stability of DEA models for unit of scale change

If input i of all DMUs is multiplied by $\alpha_i > 0$ ($x_{ij} \rightarrow \alpha_i x_{ij}$) and if output r of all DMUs is multiplied by $\beta_r > 0$ ($y_{rj} \rightarrow \beta_r y_{rj}$), the changes in the efficiency of each DMU are the focus here. For this aim, first the radial models are considered as follows,

$$
\begin{aligned}
& \min \theta \\
& \text{subject to} \\
& \sum_{j=1}^{n} \lambda_j \left(\alpha_i x_{ij}\right) \leq \theta\left(\alpha_i x_{ip}\right) \quad i = 1, \ldots, m \\
& \sum_{j=1}^{n} \lambda_j \left(\beta_r y_{rj}\right) \geq \beta_r y_{rp} \qquad r = 1, \ldots, s \\
& \lambda \in \Lambda
\end{aligned}
\tag{2.58}
$$

As the coefficients α_i and β_r are positive, the model (2.58) is written as follows,

$$
\begin{aligned}
&\min \theta \\
&\text{subject to} \\
&\sum_{j=1}^{n} \lambda_j x_{ij} \le \theta x_{ip} \quad i = 1, \dots, m \\
&\sum_{j=1}^{n} \lambda_j y_{rj} \ge y_{rp} \quad r = 1, \dots, s \\
&\lambda \in \Lambda
\end{aligned}
\tag{2.59}
$$

This means that unit scale changes in the input-based CCR, BCC, CCR-BCC, and BCC-CCR models have no impact on the value of efficiency and the values such as λ^* and θ^* are not changed. In fact, unit scale changes have no impact on the classification of the DMUs such as efficiency, nonefficiency, extreme efficiency, nonextreme efficiency, etc. Similarly, all output-based CCR, BCC, CCR-BCC, and BCC-CCR models have this property.

Now, unit scale changes in nonradial models are considered. For this aim, consider the below additive model where all of its inputs and outputs are multiplied by positive coefficients.

$$
\begin{aligned}
&\max \sum_{i=1}^{m} s_i^- + \sum_{r=1}^{s} s_r^+ \\
&\text{subject to} \\
&\sum_{j=1}^{n} \lambda_j (\alpha_i x_{ij}) + s_i^- = \alpha_i x_{ip} \quad i = 1, \dots, m \\
&\sum_{j=1}^{n} \lambda_j \left(\beta_r y_{rj}\right) - s_r^+ = \beta_r y_{rp} \quad r = 1, \dots, s \\
&s^-, \ s^+ \ge 0, \ \lambda \in \Lambda
\end{aligned}
\tag{2.60}
$$

In this model, as the coefficients α_i and β_r cannot be removed from all constraints, therefore the optimal solution of the model (2.60) is not equal to the optimal solution of the classical additive model. So, the additive model is not stable for unit scale changes. If the optimal solution of the classical additive model is shown by $(\lambda^*, \ s^{-*}, \ s^{+*})$ and the optimal solution of the model (2.60) is shown by $\left(\overline{\lambda}, \ \overline{s}^-, \ \overline{s}^+\right)$, then $\overline{\lambda} = \lambda^*$, $\overline{s}_i^- = \alpha_i s_i^{-*}$, and $\overline{s}_r^+ = \beta_r s_r^{-*}$ for any i and r. Therefore, $(\overline{s}^-, \ \overline{s}^+) = 0 \Leftrightarrow \left(s^{-*}, \ s^{+*}\right) = 0$, which means that if according to the additive model DMU_p is efficient, then according to the model (2.60) it is efficient too and vice versa. On the other hand, as $\bar{\lambda} = \lambda^*$, then the classification of DMUs to extremely efficient and nonextremely efficient in the additive model is stable for unit scale changes.

It is notable that unit scale changes in the enhanced Russell model are reflected as follows,

$$\begin{aligned}
&\min \rho = \frac{\frac{1}{m}\sum_{i=1}^{m}\theta_i}{\frac{1}{s}\sum_{r=1}^{s}\varphi_r} \\
&\text{subject to} \\
&\sum_{j=1}^{n}\lambda_j\alpha_i x_{ij} \le \theta_i\alpha_i x_{ip} \quad i = 1, \ldots, m \\
&\sum_{j=1}^{n}\lambda_j\beta_r y_{rj} \ge \varphi_r\beta_r y_{rp} \quad r = 1, \ldots, s \\
&\theta_i \le 1 \quad i = 1, \ldots, m \\
&\varphi_r \ge 1 \quad r = 1, \ldots, s \\
&\lambda \in \Lambda
\end{aligned} \tag{2.61}$$

It is obvious that for positive values of α_i and β_r, the optimal solution of the model (2.61) is equal to the optimal solution of the original enhanced Russell model (Hosseinzadeh Lotfi, Noora, et al., 2010). Therefore, the modified Russell model and the SBM model (as it is equivalent to the enhanced Russell model) are stable for unit scale changes.

In real-world applications of DEA models that are stable for unit scale changes, to avoid any error in solution algorithms, it is better to normalize all inputs and outputs with infinity norm such that $x_{ij} \to x_{ij}\frac{1}{\max_j\{x_{ij}\}}$ and $y_{rj} \to y_{rj}\frac{1}{\max_j\{y_{rj}\}}$ for all r, i, and j.

2.6.2 Stability of DEA models for transmission

Suppose the values of all inputs and outputs of all DMUs are transmitted by a constant value to obtain nonnegative new values as below,

$$x_{ij} \to x_{ij} + h_i \ge 0 \quad i = 1, \ldots m, \quad j = 1, \ldots, n \tag{2.62}$$

$$y_{rj} \to y_{rj} + f_r \ge 0 \quad r = 1, \ldots, s, \quad j = 1, \ldots, n \tag{2.63}$$

The impact of the above-mentioned transmissions first is studied on the radial models. So, the following model is considered.

$$
\begin{aligned}
&\min \theta \\
&\text{subject to} \\
&\sum_{j=1}^{n} \lambda_j \left(x_{ij} + h_i\right) \leq \theta\left(x_{ip} + h_i\right) \quad i = 1, \ldots m \\
&\sum_{j=1}^{n} \lambda_j \left(y_{rj} + f_r\right) \geq y_{rp} + f_r \qquad r = 1, \ldots, s \\
&\lambda \in \Lambda
\end{aligned}
\tag{2.64}
$$

For checking the equivalency of the model (2.64) and its original form, the first constraint is considered. The condition that makes this constraint equivalent to its classical form is $\sum_{j=1}^{n} \lambda_j = \theta$. As this condition is not true for all DMUs, therefore the classical input-based DEA models are not stable for transmission. Now, consider the second constraint of the model (2.64). The condition that makes this constraint equivalent to its classical form is $\sum_{j=1}^{n} \lambda_j = 1$. Therefore, the classical radial (BCC) DEA models are stable for transmission if the condition $\sum_{j=1}^{n} \lambda_j = 1$ is met. In summary,

- The input-oriented BCC models are not stable for input transmission and are stable for output transmission.
- The output-oriented radial BCC models are stable for input transmission and are not stable for output transmission.

Now, the following nonradial model is considered.

$$
\begin{aligned}
&\max \sum_{i=1}^{m} s_i^- + \sum_{r=1}^{s} s_r^+ \\
&\text{subject to} \\
&\sum_{j=1}^{n} \lambda_j x_{ij} + s_i^- = x_{ip} \qquad i = 1, \ldots m \\
&\sum_{j=1}^{n} \lambda_j y_{rj} - s_r^+ = y_{rp} \qquad r = 1, \ldots, s \\
&s^-, \ s^+ \geq 0, \lambda \in \Lambda
\end{aligned}
\tag{2.65}
$$

If transmissions (2.62) and (2.63) are done for the model (2.65), the obtained model will be equivalent to the model (2.65) if the condition $\sum_{j=1}^{n}\lambda_j = 1$ is met. Therefore, the additive model in T_v is stable for transmission of its inputs and outputs, and its optimal solution will not be changed. Therefore, the classification of DMUs to extremely efficient and nonextremely efficient will not be changed.

It is obvious that when data are transmitted, their relativity is changed but their distance (difference) is not changed. Therefore, the radial models where their efficiency values are obtained as a relative value are not stable for transmission in general. But the radial models with a distance-based efficiency measure with a convexity condition are stable for transmission. The enhanced Russell and SBM models are not stable for transmission as those apply a relativity-based efficiency measure.

2.7 Cost and revenue efficiencies

The classic DEA models assume that there is no price (cost) available for the inputs and outputs. In this section, a situation is considered in which the cost and income values of all inputs or all outputs are available.

2.7.1 Cost efficiency

Assume the cost value of $c_{ip} > 0$ for input i of DMU_p. It further can be assumed that the cost values of m inputs of the DMU are converted to a single cost-based input that can be used to assess the DMU. Therefore, any DMU_j can be considered with a single input of $\sum_{i=1}^{m} c_{ip}x_{ij}$ and outputs of $Y_j = (y_{1j}, \ldots, y_{sj})^T$. Then, the relative efficiency of DMU_p is obtained by solving the below model.

$$\begin{aligned} &\min \theta \\ &\text{subject to} \\ &\begin{pmatrix} \theta C_p X_p \\ Y_p \end{pmatrix} \in T_C^p \end{aligned} \tag{2.66}$$

The production possibility set in cost-based inputs is defined as follows,

$$T_C^p = \left\{ \begin{pmatrix} X \\ Y \end{pmatrix} \in \mathbb{R}_{\geq 0}^{1+s} | X \geq \sum_{j=1}^{n} \lambda_j C_p X_j \ \& \ Y \leq \sum_{j=1}^{n} \lambda_j Y_j \ \& \ \lambda_j \geq 0 \right\} \tag{2.67}$$

Note that this production possibility set is defined based on the input costs of DMU_p, so it depends on this DMU. If the costs of inputs are equal in all DMUs, then the production possibility set of all DMUs will be equivalent and there will be no index of p. According to T_C^p defined by Eq. (2.67), the model (2.66) is written as follows,

$$\begin{aligned} & \min \theta \\ & \text{subject to} \\ & \sum_{j=1}^{n} \lambda_j (C_p X_j) \leq \theta (C_p X_p) \\ & \sum_{j=1}^{n} \lambda_j Y_j \geq Y_p \\ & \lambda \geq 0 \end{aligned} \tag{2.68}$$

Note that in any optimal solution of the model (2.68), at least one of the input-based constraints is satisfied in equality form. In the optimal solution of the model (2.68) shown by $(\lambda^*, \ \theta^*)$, as this model has one input, the equation $\sum_{j=1}^{n} \lambda_j^* (C_p X_j) \leq \theta^* (C_p X_p)$ is held.

Further note that if some information of the optimal solution is available in advance, this information can be inserted into the model at the beginning and the optimal solution of this new model is not different than the initial model without the given information. Therefore, the model (2.68) is written as the following model.

$$\begin{aligned} & \min \theta \\ & \text{subject to} \\ & \sum_{j=1}^{n} \lambda_j (C_p X_j) = \theta (C_p X_p) \\ & \sum_{j=1}^{n} \lambda_j Y_j \geq Y_p \\ & \lambda \geq 0 \end{aligned} \tag{2.69}$$

In the above-mentioned model, as θ is free of sign, it can be obtained from the first constraint and we can remove this constraint. Therefore, the following model is obtained.

$$\begin{aligned} &\min \frac{\sum_{j=1}^{n} \lambda_j (C_p X_j)}{C_p X_p} \\ &\text{subject to} \\ &\sum_{j=1}^{n} \lambda_j Y_j \geq Y_p \\ &\lambda \geq 0 \end{aligned} \tag{2.70}$$

Assuming $\sum_{j=1}^{n} \lambda_j X_j = X$, the following model is obtained.

$$\begin{aligned} &\frac{1}{C_p X_p} \min C_p X \\ &\text{subject to} \\ &\sum_{j=1}^{n} \lambda_j X_j = X \\ &\sum_{j=1}^{n} \lambda_j Y_j \geq Y_p \\ &\lambda, \ X \geq 0 \end{aligned} \tag{2.71}$$

Note that in this model as $\lambda \geq 0$ and also $X_j \geq 0$ for any j, then $X \geq 0$.

Assuming $(\lambda^*, \ X^*)$ as the optimal solution of the model (2.71), the cost efficiency of DMU_p is obtained as $CE_p = \frac{C_p X^*}{C_p X_p}$. As $0 < CE_p \leq 1$, if $CE_p = 1$ then DMU_p is cost efficient and if $0 < CE_p < 1$ then it is not cost efficient. Note that as the vector X in the model (2.71) is variable, then if all constraints of the first constraints set of this model are written in $\leq$ form, these constraints in the optimal solution will be satisfied in equality form. Therefore, the model (2.71) is equivalent to the following model.

$$\begin{aligned} &\min C_p X \\ &\text{subject to} \\ &\begin{pmatrix} X \\ Y_p \end{pmatrix} \in T_C \end{aligned} \tag{2.72}$$

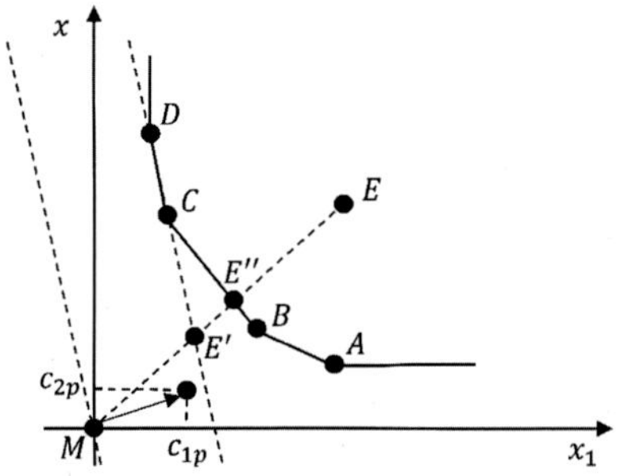

Fig. 2.7 A schematic example for cost-based efficiency.

For more explanation, an example with two inputs and one output is represented in Fig. 2.7. In this figure, if c_{1p} and c_{2p} are the costs of the first and second inputs of DMU_E, then only the points C and D are cost efficient and the cost efficiency of DMU_E is calculated as $CE_E = \frac{ME'}{ME}$, where the technical efficiency of this DMU is $\frac{ME''}{ME}$.

2.7.2 Revenue efficiency

Now, assume each output has a price such as R_{rp} is the price of output r of DMU_p. Similar to the cost efficiency concepts, when any of the inputs has a price value, each DMU produces only one output (called total **revenue**) from the given inputs. This single output for DMU_j is defined as $y_j = R_p Y_j = \sum_{r=1}^{s} R_{rp} y_{rj}$. The production possibility set in income-based inputs is defined as follows,

$$T_R^p = \left\{ \begin{pmatrix} X \\ Y \end{pmatrix} | X \geq \sum_{j=1}^{n} \lambda_j X_j \ \& \ y \leq \sum_{j=1}^{n} \lambda_j (R_p Y_j) \& \ \lambda_j \geq 0, \quad j = 1, \dots, n \right\} \tag{2.73}$$

The following output-oriented model is proposed for calculating the relative efficiency of DMU_p,

$$\begin{aligned} & \max \varphi \\ & \text{subject to} \\ & \begin{pmatrix} X_p \\ \varphi R_p Y_p \end{pmatrix} \in T_R^p \end{aligned} \tag{2.74}$$

where $T_R^p \in \mathbb{R}^{m+1}$. According to the production possibility set (2.73), this model is written as

$$\begin{aligned}&\max \varphi\\&\text{subject to}\\&\sum_{j=1}^{n}\lambda_j X_j \le X_p\\&\sum_{j=1}^{n}\lambda_j\left(R_p Y_j\right) \ge \varphi\left(R_p Y_p\right)\\&\lambda \ge 0\end{aligned} \tag{2.75}$$

Note that in any optimal solution of the model (2.75), at least one of the output-based constraints is satisfied in equality form. In the optimal solution of the model (2.75) shown by $(\lambda^*,\ \varphi^*)$, as this model has one output, the equation $\sum_{j=1}^{n}\lambda_j\left(R_p Y_j\right) \ge \varphi^*\left(R_p Y_p\right)$ is held. Therefore, the model (2.75) is written as the following model.

$$\begin{aligned}&\max \varphi\\&\text{subject to}\\&\sum_{j=1}^{n}\lambda_j X_j \le X_p\\&\sum_{j=1}^{n}\lambda_j\left(R_p Y_j\right) = \varphi\left(R_p Y_p\right)\\&\lambda \ge 0\end{aligned} \tag{2.76}$$

In the above-mentioned model, as φ is free of sign, it can be obtained from its related constraint and we can remove this constraint. Therefore, the following model is obtained.

$$\begin{aligned}&\max \frac{\sum_{j=1}^{n}\lambda_j\left(R_p Y_j\right)}{R_p Y_p}\\&\text{subject to}\\&\sum_{j=1}^{n}\lambda_j X_j \le X_p\\&\lambda \ge 0\end{aligned} \tag{2.77}$$

Assuming $\sum_{j=1}^{n}\lambda_j Y_j = Y$, the following model is obtained.

$$
\begin{aligned}
&\frac{1}{R_pY_p}\max R_pY\\
&\text{subject to}\\
&\sum_{j=1}^{n}\lambda_jX_j \leq X_p\\
&\sum_{j=1}^{n}\lambda_jY_j = Y\\
&\lambda,\quad Y \geq 0
\end{aligned}
\tag{2.78}
$$

Assuming $(\lambda^*,\quad Y^*)$ as the optimal solution of the model (2.78), the income efficiency of DMU_p is obtained as $RE_p = \frac{R_pY_p}{R_pY^*}$. Note that in output-oriented models, the efficiency is obtained as $\frac{1}{\varphi^*}$. If all constraints of the second constraints set of this model are written in $\geq$ form, these constraints in the optimal solution will be satisfied in equality form. Therefore, the model (2.78) is equivalent to the following model.

$$
\begin{aligned}
&\max R_pY\\
&\text{subject to}\\
&\begin{pmatrix} X_p\\ Y \end{pmatrix} \in T
\end{aligned}
\tag{2.79}
$$

In this model, T is the same as the production possibility set with a classical constant returns to scale assumption (T_C). In fact, the model (2.79) should find the vector Y such that this vector is the highest possible value that can be produced by X_p in the production possibility set based on the price R_p. For more explanation, an example with one input and two outputs is represented by Fig. 2.8. In this figure, R_{1p} and R_{2p} are the incomes of the first and second outputs and the aim is to calculate the income efficiency of DMU_p. Obviously, based on the vector $(R_{1p},\quad R_{2p})$, DMU_B has the highest income among other DMUs. This DMU is the only one that is income efficient based on the given prices vector. Note that the points A, B, and C are technically efficient. The income efficiency of DMU_p is calculated as $RE_p = \frac{MP}{MP''}$.

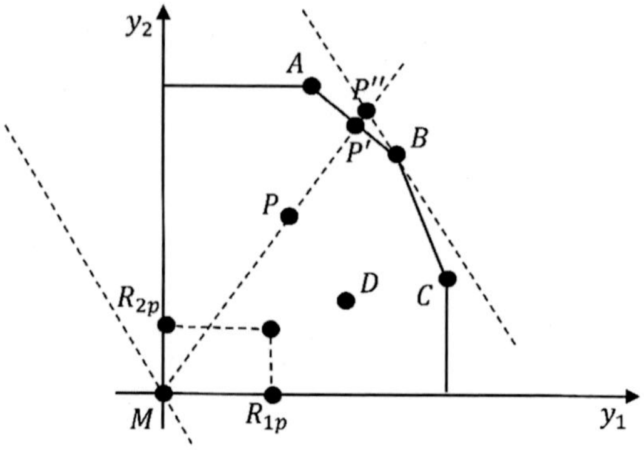

Fig. 2.8 A schematic example for income-based efficiency.

2.7.3 Profit efficiency

In this type of efficiency, the assumption is that all the inputs and outputs are priceable. The cost of input i is shown by c_{ip} and the income of output r is represented by R_{rp}. The aim is to assess the costs of inputs and the incomes of outputs for a DMU. The model for calculating the profit efficiency of DMU_p is given below.

$$
\begin{aligned}
&\max R_pY - C_pX \\
&\text{subject to} \\
&\begin{pmatrix} X \\ Y \end{pmatrix} \in T_C
\end{aligned}
\tag{2.80}
$$

In fact, based on the prices and costs determined by DMU_p, the model (2.80) will find such $\begin{pmatrix} X \\ Y \end{pmatrix}$ from the production possibility set to maximize the net profit. If $(X^*,\ Y^*)$ is the optimal solution of the model (2.80), the benefit efficiency of DMU_p is obtained as $PE_p = \frac{R_pY_p - C_pX_p}{R_pY^* - C_pX^*}$.

According to the definition of T_C, the model (2.80) is converted as follows,

$$
\begin{aligned}
&\max R_pY - C_pX \\
&\text{subject to} \\
&\sum_{j=1}^{n} \lambda_j X_j \le X \\
&\sum_{j=1}^{n} \lambda_j Y_j \ge Y \\
&\lambda,\ X,\ Y \ge 0
\end{aligned}
\tag{2.81}
$$

Note that in addition to the model presented for calculating profit efficiency, a model for economic efficiency also can be constructed easily. In the cases that the prices of only some inputs or outputs are available (not all of them), the efficiencies of cost, income, and profit cannot be calculated.

2.8 Weight restrictions

The classical DEA models calculate the optimistic efficiency for each DMU. This means that the DMU under assessment is compared to the others in its best conditions. For more clarification, refer to the following example.

Example 2.1. Two universities with the information in Table 2.1 are compared based on relative efficiencies.

Remember that DMU_p with a data vector of $(X_p, \ Y_p)$ is relatively efficient if and only if $\exists(V, \ U) > 0; \ \forall j: \ \frac{UY_p}{VX_p} \geq \frac{UY_j}{VX_j}$. To assess the efficiency of DMU_1, the condition $\frac{UY_1}{VX_1} = \frac{7u_1 + 100u_2}{100v} \geq \frac{100u_1 + 7u_2}{100v} = \frac{UY_2}{VX_2}$ is tested for u_1, u_2, $v > 0$. As this condition has the feasible solution of $u_1 = 1$, $u_2 = 150$, and $v = 1$, therefore DMU_1 is relatively efficient. If the above-mentioned condition is written to check the efficiency of DMU_2, the solution $(u_1, \ u_2, \ v) = (150, \ 1, \ 1)$ will exist that shows that DMU_2 is also relatively efficient. In this example, as the second output (Ph.D. graduates) is more important than the first one, the solution should be considered that $u_2 > u_1$ or $u_2 \geq \alpha u_1$ where $\alpha > 1$. Considering this condition, the solution $(u_1, \ u_2, \ v) = (150, \ 1, \ 1)$ is not acceptable. So, based on the obtained solutions, the reason for the efficiency of DMU_2 is that the weights are free in the interval $(0, \ +\infty)$. This issue reflects the concepts of optimistic efficiency that were explained earlier.

Table 2.1 Data of Example 2.1.

	Criteria		
University	**Input (Faculty members)**	**Output 1 (B.Sc. graduates)**	**Output 2 (Ph.D. graduates)**
1	100	7	100
2	100	100	7

References

Allahviranloo, T., Hosseinzadeh Lotfi, F., & Adabitabar Firozja, M. (2014). Efficiency in fuzzy production possibility set. *Iranian Journal of Fuzzy Systems*, *9*(4), 17–30.

Banker, R. D., Charnes, A., & Cooper, W. W. (1984). Some models for estimating technical and scale efficiencies in data envelopment analysis. *Management Science*, *30*, 1078–1092.

Blackburn, V., Brennan, S., & Ruggiero, J. (2014). Nonparametric estimation of educational production and costs using data envelopment analysis. In *International series in operations research & management science* Springer.

Charnes, A., & Cooper, W. W. (1962). Programming with linear fractional functionals. *Naval Research Logistics Quarterly*, *9*, 181–186.

Charnes, A., Cooper, W. W., Lewin, A. Y., & Seiford, L. M. (1995). *Data envelopment analysis: Theory, methodology, and applications*. Springer.

Charnes, A., Cooper, W. W., & Rhodes, E. L. (1978). Measuring the efficiency of decision making units. *European Journal of Operational Research*, *2*(6), 429–444.

Cook, W. D., & Seiford, L. M. (2009). Data envelopment analysis (DEA)—Thirty years on. *European Journal of Operational Research*, *192*(1), 1–17.

Cooper, W. W., Seiford, L. M., & Tone, K. (2005). *Introduction to data envelopment analysis and its uses: With DEA-solver software and references*. Springer.

Cooper, W. W., Seiford, L. M., & Tone, K. (2006). *Data envelopment analysis: A comprehensive text with models, applications, references and DEA-solver software*.

Ebrahimnejad, A., & Hosseinzadeh Lotfi, F. (2012). Equivalence relationship between the general combined-oriented CCR model and the weighted minimax MOLP formulation. *Journal of King Saud University-Science*, *24*(1), 47–54.

Ebrahimnejad, A., & Tavana, M. (2014). An interactive MOLP method for identifying target units in output-oriented DEA models: The NATO enlargement problem. *Measurement*, *52*, 124–134.

Emrouznejad, A., Parker, B. R., & Tavares, G. (2008). Evaluation of research in efficiency and productivity: A survey and analysis of the first 30 years of scholarly literature in DEA. *Socio-Economic Planning Sciences*, *42*(3), 151–157.

Färe, R., & Grosskopf, S. (1996). *Intertemporal production frontiers: With dynamic DEA*. Springer.

Farzipoor Sean, R., Memariani, A., & Hosseinzadeh Lotfi, F. (2005). Determining relative efficiency of slightly non-homogeneous decision making units by data envelopment analysis: A case study in IROST. *Applied Mathematics and Computation*, *165*(2), 313–328.

Gattoufi, S., Oral, M., & Reisman, A. (2004). A taxonomy for data envelopment analysis. *Economic Planning Sciences*, *38*(2–3), 141–158.

Hamdi, K., Hosseinzadeh Lotfi, F., & Moghaddas, Z. (2014). An application of DEA in efficiency evaluation of universities. *International Journal of Mathematics in Operational Research*, *6*(5), 550–566.

Hosseinzadeh Lotfi, F., Allahviranloo, T., Mozaffari, M. R., & Gerami, J. (2009). Basic DEA models in the full fuzzy position. *International Mathematical Forum*, *4*(20), 983–993.

Hosseinzadeh Lotfi, F., Jahanshahloo, G. R., Soltanifar, M., Ebrahimnejad, A., & Mansourzade, S. M. (2010). Relationship between MOLP and DEA based on output-orientated CCR dual model. *Expert Systems with Applications*, *37*(6), 4331–4336.

Hosseinzadeh Lotfi, F., Najafi, S. E., & Nozari, H. (2016). Data envelopment analysis and effective performance assessment. In *Advances in business information systems and analytics* IGI Global. ISBN-13: 978-1522505969.

Hosseinzadeh Lotfi, F., Noora, A. A., Jahanshahloo, G. R., Gerami, J., & Mozaffari, M. R. (2010). Centralized resource allocation for enhanced Russell models. *Journal of Computational and Applied Mathematics*, *235*(1), 1–10.

Jamshidi, M., Sanei, M., & Mahmoodirad, A. (2022). An uncertain allocation models in data envelopment analysis: A case in the Iranian stock market. Scintia Iranica, 29(6), 3434–3454.

Jamshidi, M., Sanei, M., Mahmoodirad, A., Tohidi, G., & Hosseinzade Lotfi, F. (2021). Uncertain BCC data envelopment analysis model with belief degree: A case study in Iranian banks. *International Journal of Industrial Mathematics*, *13*(3), 239–249.

Jamshidi, M., Saneie, M., Mahmoodirad, A., Hosseinzadeh Lotfi, F., & Tohidi, G. (2019). Uncertain RUSSEL data envelopment analysis model: A case study in Iranian banks. *Journal of Intelligent Fuzzy Systems*, *37*(2), 2937–2951.

Klemen, B. (2009). *Data envelopment analysis: Returns-to-scale measurement*. VDM Verlag.

Maddahi, R., Jahanshahloo, G. R., Hosseinzadeh Lotfi, F., & Ebrahimnejad, A. (2014). Optimizing proportional weights as a secondary goal in DEA cross-efficiency evaluation. *International Journal of Operational Research*, *19*(2), 234–245.

Mahmoodirad, A., Dehghan, R., & Niroomand, S. (2019). Modelling linear fractional transportation problem in belief degree-based uncertain environment. *Journal of Experimental & Theoretical Artificial Intelligence*, *31*(3), 393–408.

Molla-Alizadeh-Zavardehi, S., Mahmoodirad, A., Sanei, M., Niroomand, S., & Banihashemi, S. (2021). Metaheuristics for data envelopment analysis problems. *International Journal of Systems Science: Operations & Logistics*, *8*(4), 371–382.

Nouri, J., Hosseinzadeh Lotfi, F., Borgheipour, H., Atabi, F., Sadeghzadeh, S. M., & Moghaddas, Z. (2013). An analysis of the implementation of energy efficiency measures in the vegetable oil industry of Iran: A data envelopment analysis approach. *Journal of Cleaner Production*, *52*, 84–93.

Ozcan, Y. A., & Tone, K. (2014). Health care benchmarking and performance evaluation: An assessment using data envelopment analysis (DEA). In *International series in operations research & management science* Springer.

Pastor, J. T., Ruiz, J. L., & Sirvent, I. (1999). An enhanced DEA Russell graph efficiency measure. *European Journal of Operational Research*, *115*, 569–607.

Pouriyeh, A., Khorasani, N., Hosseinzadeh Lotfi, F., & Farshchi, P. (2016). Efficiency evaluation of urban development in Yazd City, Central Iran using data envelopment analysis. *Environmental Monitoring and Assessment*, *188*(11), 618.

Roodposhti, F. R., Hosseinzadeh Lotfi, F., & Ghasemi, M. V. (2010). Acquiring targets in balanced scorecard method by data envelopment analysis technique and its application in commercial banks. *Applied Mathematical Sciences*, *4*(69-72), 3549–3563.

Saneifard, R., Allahviranloo, T., Hosseinzadeh Lotfi, F., & Mikaeilvand, N. (2007). Euclidean ranking DMUs with fuzzy data in DEA. *Applied Mathematical Sciences*, *60*, 2989–2998.

Seiford, L. M. (1996). Data envelopment analysis: The evolution of the state of the art (1978–1995). *Journal of Productivity Analysis*, 7, 99–137.

Shirouyehzad, H., Hosseinzadeh Lotfi, F., Shahin, A., Aryanezhad, M. B., & Dabestani, R. (2012). Performance evaluation of hotels by data envelopment analysis based on customers' perception and gap analysis. *International Journal of Services and Operations Management*, *12*(4), 447–467.

Tavana, M., Ebrahimnejad, A., Santos-Arteaga, F. J., Mansourzadeh, S. M., & Kazemi Matin, R. (2018). A hybrid DEA-MOLP model for public school assessment and closure decision in the City of Philadelphia. *Socio-Economic Planning Sciences*, *61*, 70–89.

Xue, T., & Ye, C. (2021). The state of science on severe air pollution episodes: Quantitative and qualitative analysis. *Environment International*, *156*, 106732. https://doi.org/10.1016/j.envint.2021.106732.

Zhu, J., & Cook, W. D. (2013). *Data envelopment analysis: Balanced benchmarking*. Create Space Independent Publishing Platform.

CHAPTER THREE

Fuzzy data envelopment analysis

3.1 Introduction

In some operational systems, the decision-making units (DMUs) play a critical role in the overall performance of the system. According to limitations such as capital, time, energy, etc., in the DMU performance, managers always try to find the best strategy to use these factors for improving the overall performance of the system. The assessment of the DMUs is an important tool for reaching such an optimal strategy. In real-world situations, the parameters, indices, and types of decision making may be of a degree of uncertainty and in some cases may be of the fuzzy-type uncertainty. In such situations, to evaluate the DMUs, fuzzy data envelopment analysis (FDEA) can be applied. In such problems, the DMUs are fuzzy where their input and output values are represented by fuzzy numbers, and the aim is to assess these DMUs by introducing an assessment method and obtaining their performance. The α-cut based approach, the fuzzy ranking approach, the possibility approach, the fuzzy arithmetic approach, etc., are some of the most important approaches in the literature for evaluating fuzzy DMUs. The related references and features of these approaches are summarized in Table 3.1.

To define a fuzzy DEA model, we consider n fuzzy DMUs ($FDMU_j$, $j=1, \cdots, n$) with fuzzy input values of $\tilde{X}_j = \left(\tilde{x}_{1j}, \tilde{x}_{2j}, \cdots, \tilde{x}_{mj}\right)$ and fuzzy output values of $\tilde{Y}_j = \left(\tilde{y}_{1j}, \tilde{y}_{2j}, \cdots, \tilde{y}_{sj}\right)$.

Definition 3.1 Assume n fuzzy DMUs ($FDMU_j$, $j=1,\cdots,n$) with fuzzy input values of $\tilde{X}_j = \left(\tilde{x}_{1j}, \tilde{x}_{2j}, \cdots, \tilde{x}_{mj}\right)$ and fuzzy output values of $\tilde{Y}_j = \left(\tilde{y}_{1j}, \tilde{y}_{2j}, \cdots, \tilde{y}_{sj}\right)$, where $\tilde{x}_{ij}$ and $\tilde{y}_{ij}$ are fuzzy numbers with membership

https://doi.org/10.1016/B978-0-323-99444-6.00001-3

Table 3.1 Summary of the main studies of the literature on fuzzy DEA.

Approach	Reference	Features
α-cut based approach	Kao and Liu (2000)	Multiplier formulation; fractional parametric programming; fuzzy efficiency scores
	Saati et al. (2002)	Radial; input-oriented; multiplier formulation; interval linear programming; α-level efficiency scores
	Saati and Memariani (2009)	Nonoriented SBM; multiplier formulation; interval linear programming; α-level efficiency scores
	Hsiao et al. (2011)	Nonoriented SBM; envelopment formulation; fuzzy efficiency and superefficiency scores
	Hatami-Marbini et al. (2012)	Additive model; nonoriented; envelopment formulation; interval linear programming; α-level efficiency scores
	Puri and Yadav (2013)	Radial and nonradial models; input-oriented; envelopment formulations; fuzzy efficiency scores
	Wu et al. (2015)	Nonradial model; nonoriented ERGM envelopment formulation; undesirable outputs; fuzzy efficiency scores
Fuzzy ranking approach	Guo and Tanaka (2001)	Radial model; input-oriented; multiplier formulation; fuzzy linear programming; fuzzy efficiency scores
	León et al. (2003)	Radial model; input-oriented; envelopment formulation; fuzzy linear programming; possibility-level efficiency scores
	Soleimani-Damaneh et al. (2006)	Radial model; input-oriented; envelopment formulation; crisp efficiency scores; crisp targets
	Ghasemi et al. (2015)	Multiplier formulation; generalized DEA; fuzzy expected value; DMU ranking
	Khaleghi et al. (2015)	Radial model; input-oriented; multiplier formulation; fully fuzzy; level-sum method; fuzzy efficiency scores; DMU ranking
	Kordrostami et al. (2016)	Radial model; input-oriented; envelopment formulation; integer data; crisp efficiency scores; crisp targets
	Arana-Jimenez et al. (2020)	Radial model; input-oriented; envelopment formulation; fully fuzzy; fuzzy partial order; lexicographic weighted Tchebycheff method; fuzzy efficiency scores; fuzzy targets

Table 3.1 Summary of the main studies of the literature on fuzzy DEA—cont'd

Approach	Reference	Features
Possibility approach	Lertworasirikul, Fang, Nuttle, and Joines (2003)	Radial model; input-oriented; multiplier and envelopment formulations; possibility-level efficiency scores
	Wang and Chin (2011)	Radial model; input-oriented; multiplier formulation; fuzzy expected value; double frontier analysis; crisp efficiency scores; DMU ranking
	Ruiz and Sirvent (2017)	Radial model; input-oriented; multiplier formulation; benevolent and aggressive possibility-level cross-efficiency scores
	Izadikhah and Khoshroo (2018)	Nonradial model; nonoriented modified ERGM envelopment formulation; undesirable outputs; possibility-level superefficiency scores
	Peykani et al. (2019)	Radial model; input-oriented; multiplier formulation; adjustable pessimistic-optimistic parameter; possibility-level efficiency scores
Fuzzy arithmetic approach	Wang et al. (2009)	Radial model; input-oriented; multiplier formulation; fuzzy efficiency scores; DMU ranking
	Azar et al. (2016)	Additive model; nonoriented; multiplier formulation; common set of weights; fuzzy efficiency scores; DMU ranking

functions of $\mu_{\tilde{x}_{ij}}$ and $\mu_{\tilde{y}_{rj}}$, respectively. Then, the fuzzy relative efficiency (FRE) of DMU_p is defined as follows,

$$FRE_p = \frac{\tilde{y}_p/\tilde{x}_p{}^{O}}{Max\left\{\tilde{y}_j/\tilde{x}_j{}^{O} : j = 1, \cdots, n\right\}}$$

where $\tilde{y}_p/\tilde{x}_p{}^{O}$ is the fuzzy ratio of the fuzzy values $\tilde{x}_{ij}$ and $\tilde{y}_{ij}$, and can be interpreted mathematically and economically.

Definition 3.2 The vector $\tilde{X}_1$ is dominant to the vector $\tilde{X}_2$ (or $\tilde{X}_2$ is dominated by $\tilde{X}_1$) if and only if $\tilde{X}_1 \tilde{\geq} \tilde{X}_2$ and $\tilde{X}_1 \neq \tilde{X}_2$. The sign $\tilde{\geq}$ is used for the relationship of two fuzzy values and can be interpreted mathematically and economically.

There is a fuzzy relationship between the fuzzy performance of a DMU and its fuzzy input and output values. This relationship is called the fuzzy production function. Therefore, the fuzzy production function is such a function that produces the maximum fuzzy outputs from the available fuzzy inputs. This function is important for evaluating DMUs because it determines whether a DMU is efficient. In some cases because of the complexity of the production process, the variation of the production technology, the multivariability of the production function, etc., the fuzzy production function is not available and should be estimated.

3.2 Fuzzy production possibility set (FPPS)

As mentioned above, the fuzzy production function is not easily available. Therefore, the fuzzy production possibility set (FPPS) is constructed and its frontier is considered as an estimation of the fuzzy production function. The FPPS is denoted by $\tilde{T}$ and defined as,

$$\tilde{T} = \left\{ \left(\tilde{X}, \tilde{Y}\right) \mid \text{the output } \tilde{Y} \text{ be produced by the input } \tilde{X} \right\}$$

As the production function is not available exactly, therefore some general principles are considered to determine it. These principles are as follows,

- **Fuzzy envelopment**: All observations are the member of $\tilde{T}$ as $\left(\tilde{X}_j, \tilde{Y}_j\right) \tilde{\in} \tilde{T},\ j = 1, 2, \ldots, n$. The notation $\tilde{\in}$ shows the membership of a fuzzy element in a fuzzy set.
- **Fuzzy scalability**: If $\left(\tilde{X}_j, \tilde{Y}_j\right) \tilde{\in} T$ then $\left(\tilde{\lambda} \tilde{X}_j, \tilde{\lambda} \tilde{Y}_j\right) \tilde{\in} \tilde{T}$, for all $\tilde{\lambda} \geq 0$. Here, the value of $\tilde{\lambda}$ can even be of the deterministic type.
- **Fuzzy convexity**: If $\left(\tilde{X}_1, \tilde{Y}_1\right), \left(\tilde{X}_2, \tilde{Y}_2\right) \tilde{\in} \tilde{T}$ then $\lambda\left(\tilde{X}_1, \tilde{Y}\right) + (1 - \lambda)\left(\tilde{X}_2, \tilde{Y}_2\right) \tilde{\in} \tilde{T}$ for all $\lambda \in [0, 1]$.
- **Fuzzy free disposability**: If $\left(\tilde{X}, \tilde{Y}\right) \tilde{\in} \tilde{T}$ and $\tilde{Y} \tilde{\geq} \tilde{Y}', \tilde{X}' \tilde{\geq} \tilde{X}$ then $\left(\tilde{X}', \tilde{Y}'\right) \tilde{\in} \tilde{T}$.

According to these principles, the following FPPS is obtained,

$$\tilde{T}_c = \left\{ \left(\tilde{X}, \tilde{Y}\right) \middle| \tilde{X} \tilde{\geq} \sum_{j=1}^{n} \lambda_j \tilde{X}_j,\ \tilde{Y} \tilde{\leq} \sum_{j=1}^{n} \lambda_j \tilde{Y}_j,\ \lambda_j \geq 0, j = 1, \ldots, n \right\}$$

If we accept the fuzzy inclusion of observations, fuzzy convexity, and fuzzy possibility, the following FPPS is obtained.

$$\tilde{T}_v = \left\{ \left(\tilde{X}, \tilde{Y}\right) \middle| \tilde{X} \tilde{\geq} \sum_{j=1}^{n} \lambda_j \tilde{X}_j, \tilde{Y} \tilde{\leq} \sum_{j=1}^{n} \lambda_j \tilde{Y}_j, \sum_{j=1}^{n} \lambda_j = 1, \lambda_j \geq 0, j = 1, \dots, n \right\}$$

In the above $\tilde{T}_c$, the value of $\tilde{\lambda}$ can be either fuzzy (as $\left(\underline{\lambda}, \lambda, \overline{\lambda}\right)$) or deterministic (as $(\lambda, \lambda, \lambda)$). The set $\tilde{T}_c$ can be in different forms according to the type of $\tilde{\lambda}$ and the fuzzy sign $\tilde{\geq}$. Actually, 1-cut of the $\tilde{T}$ represents the deterministic production possibility set.

3.3 Fuzzy environment in DEA

Assume n fuzzy DMUs ($FDMU_j$, $j=1, \cdots, n$) with fuzzy input values of $\tilde{X}_j = \left(\tilde{x}_{1j}, \tilde{x}_{2j}, \cdots, \tilde{x}_{mj}\right)$ and fuzzy output values of $\tilde{Y}_j = \left(\tilde{y}_{1j}, \tilde{y}_{2j}, \cdots, \tilde{y}_{sj}\right)$, where $\tilde{x}_{ij}$ and $\tilde{y}_{ij}$ are fuzzy numbers with membership functions of $\mu_{\tilde{x}_{ij}}$ and $\mu_{\tilde{y}_{rj}}$, respectively. If there is no $\left(\tilde{X}, \tilde{Y}\right)$ in $\tilde{T}$ to dominate $\left(\tilde{X}_j, \tilde{Y}_j\right)$, then $FDMU_j$ is relatively efficient. To find a production possibility in $\tilde{T}$ to dominate $FDMU_j$, the following three cases are considered.

- **Case 1**. A production possibility (point) in $\tilde{T}$ that produces an output greater than or equal to $\tilde{Y}_O$ from an input less than $\tilde{X}_O$ (Fig. 3.1).

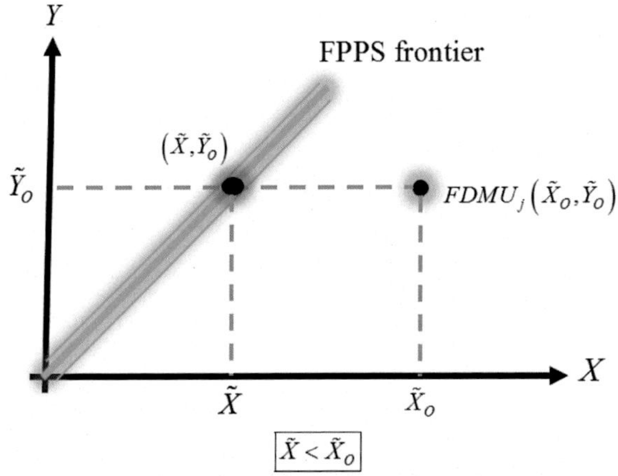

Fig. 3.1 The schematic representation of Case 1 (input oriented).

- **Case 2**. A production possibility (point) in $\tilde{T}$ that produces an output greater than $\tilde{Y}_O$ from an input less than or equal $\tilde{X}_O$ (Fig. 3.2).
- **Case 3**. A production possibility (point) in $\tilde{T}$ that produces an output greater than $\tilde{Y}_O$ from an input less than $\tilde{X}_O$ (Fig. 3.3).

In Fig. 3.1, the dummy DMU (projected on the frontier of $\tilde{T}$) with an input of $\tilde{X}$ that is less than $\tilde{X}_O$ produces an output greater than or equal to $\tilde{Y}_O$. If $\tilde{X} = \theta\tilde{X}_O$ where $0<\theta\leq 1$, then the value of $\tilde{\theta}$ should be minimized by the below model,

$$\begin{aligned}&\text{Min } \tilde{\theta}\\&\text{subject to}\\&(\tilde{\theta}\tilde{X}_O, \tilde{Y}_O)\in\tilde{T}\end{aligned} \tag{3.1}$$

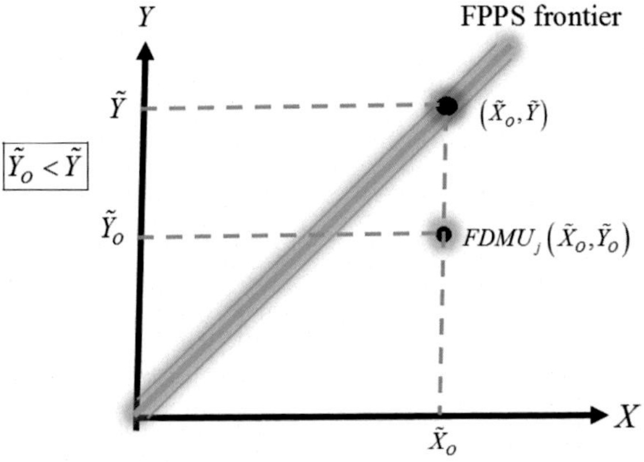

Fig. 3.2 The schematic representation of Case 2 (output oriented).

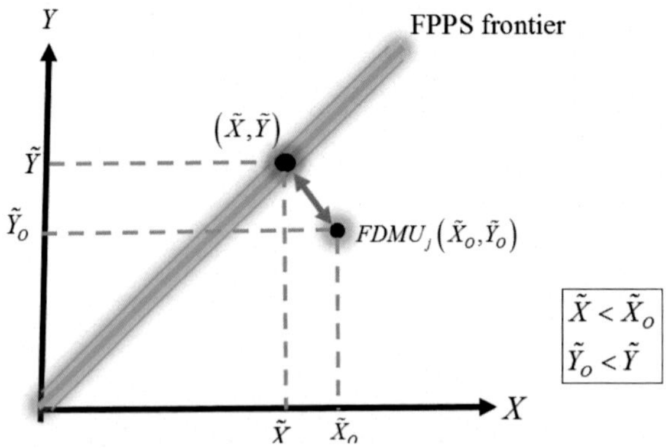

Fig. 3.3 The schematic representation of Case 3 (hybrid oriented).

where $\left(\tilde{X}_O, \tilde{Y}_O\right)$ is the vector of inputs and outputs of the DMU_o. If $\tilde{T} = \tilde{T}_c$, then model (3.1) is called an input-oriented Charnes-Cooper-Rhodes (CCR) envelopment model (Charnes et al., 1978). According to the definition of $\tilde{T}_c$ and considering the crisp form of $\tilde{\lambda}$, the model (3.1) is written as follows,

$$
\begin{aligned}
&\text{Min } \tilde{\theta} \\
&\text{subject to} \\
&\sum_{j=1}^{n} \lambda_j \tilde{x}_{ij} \tilde{\leq} \tilde{\theta} \tilde{x}_{io} \quad && i = 1, 2, \ldots, m \\
&\sum_{j=1}^{n} \lambda_j \tilde{y}_{rj} \tilde{\geq} \tilde{y}_{ro} \quad && r = 1, 2, \ldots, s \\
&\lambda_j \geq 0 \quad && j = 1, 2, \ldots, s
\end{aligned}
\tag{3.2}
$$

Considering $\tilde{T} = \tilde{T}_v$, the input-oriented Banker-Charnes-Cooper (BCC) envelopment model (Banker et al., 1984) for obtaining the value of $\tilde{\theta}$ is as follows,

$$
\begin{aligned}
&\text{Min } \tilde{\theta} \\
&\text{subject to} \\
&\sum_{j=1}^{n} \lambda_j \tilde{x}_{ij} \tilde{\leq} \tilde{\theta} \tilde{x}_{io} \quad && i = 1, 2, \ldots, m \\
&\sum_{j=1}^{n} \lambda_j \tilde{y}_{rj} \tilde{\geq} \tilde{y}_{ro} \quad && r = 1, 2, \ldots, s \\
&\sum_{j=1}^{n} \lambda_j = 1 \\
&\lambda_j \geq 0 \quad && j = 1, 2, \ldots, s
\end{aligned}
\tag{3.3}
$$

The fuzzy DEA (FDEA) models are of fuzzy linear programming models. In the literature, there are numerous studies on the solution approaches of fuzzy linear programming models (see Mahmoodirad, Allahviranloo, & Niroomand, 2019; Mahmoodirad, Dehghan, & Niroomand, 2019; Nasseri et al., 2019; Sigarpich et al., 2011).

As a fuzzy linear programming model consists of a fuzzy objective function and a set of fuzzy inequalities that determines the feasible region, the solution approaches of the fuzzy DEA models are related to the solution approaches of a system of fuzzy equations (see Allahviranloo, 2020; Allahviranloo et al., 2013; Allahviranloo & Salahshour, 2011;

Mahmoodirad, Allahviranloo, & Niroomand, 2019; Mahmoodirad, Dehghan, & Niroomand, 2019; Molla-Alizadeh-Zavardehi et al., 2014; Niroomand et al., 2020).

3.4 Solution approaches of the fuzzy DEA models

In general, the solution approaches of the FDEA models can be categorized into five types of approaches:

- α-cut-based solution approaches,
- Extension principle-based solution approaches,
- Fuzzy ranking-based solution approaches,
- Possibility-based solution approaches,
- Other solution approaches.

These approaches are explained briefly in the rest of this section.

3.4.1 α-cut-based solution approach

This approach is the most famous and popular approach for solving FDEA models. This approach works based on the α-cut values of the FPPS $\tilde{T}$.

Assume n fuzzy DMUs ($FDMU_j$, $j=1, \cdots, n$) with fuzzy input values of $\tilde{X}_j = (\tilde{x}_{1j}, \tilde{x}_{2j}, \cdots, \tilde{x}_{mj})$ and fuzzy output values of $\tilde{Y}_j = \left(\tilde{y}_{1j}, \tilde{y}_{2j}, \cdots, \tilde{y}_{sj}\right)$, where $\tilde{x}_{ij}$ and $\tilde{y}_{ij}$ are fuzzy numbers with membership functions of $\mu_{\tilde{x}_{ij}}$ and $\mu_{\tilde{y}_{rj}}$, respectively. Therefore, the FPPS is defined as follows and represented by Fig. 3.4.

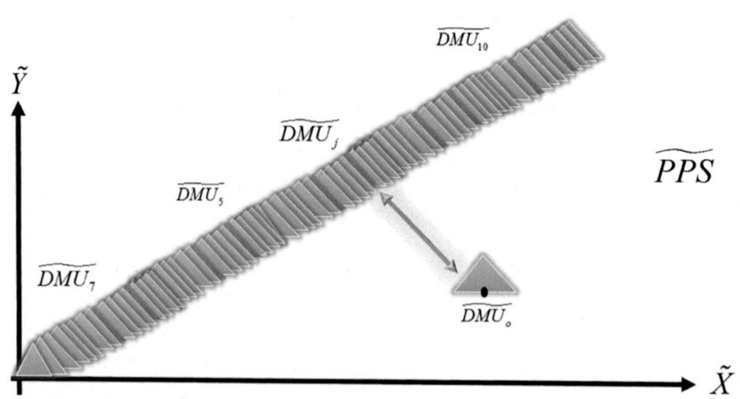

Fig. 3.4 The fuzzy production possibility set (FPPS).

$$\tilde{T} = \left\{ (\tilde{X}, \tilde{Y}) \middle| \tilde{X} \tilde{\geq} \sum_{j=1}^{n} \lambda_j \tilde{X}_j, \tilde{Y} \tilde{\leq} \sum_{j=1}^{n} \lambda_j \tilde{Y}_j, \lambda_j \geq 0, j = 1, \ldots, n \right\}$$

The input-oriented CCR with a multiplier form model for evaluating $FDMU_O$, $o \in \{1, \cdots, n\}$ is as follows,

$$\begin{aligned}
&\text{Max } \tilde{Z} = \sum_{r=1}^{s} u_r \tilde{y}_{ro} \\
&\text{subject to} \\
&\sum_{i=1}^{m} v_i \tilde{x}_{io} \cong 1 \\
&\sum_{r=1}^{s} u_r \tilde{y}_{rj} - \sum_{i=1}^{m} v_i \tilde{x}_{ij} \tilde{\leq} 0 \quad && r = 1, 2, \ldots, s \\
&u_r \geq 0 && r = 1, 2, \ldots, s \\
&v_i \geq 0 && i = 1, 2, \ldots, m
\end{aligned} \tag{3.4}$$

where the input-oriented CCR with an envelopment form model for evaluating the DMU is as follows,

$$\begin{aligned}
&\text{Min } \tilde{\theta} \\
&\text{subject to} \\
&\sum_{j=1}^{n} \lambda_j \tilde{x}_{ij} \tilde{\leq} \tilde{\theta} \tilde{x}_{io} \quad && i = 1, 2, \ldots, m \\
&\sum_{j=1}^{n} \lambda_j \tilde{y}_{rj} \tilde{\geq} \tilde{y}_{ro} && r = 1, 2, \ldots, s \\
&\lambda_j \geq 0 && j = 1, 2, \ldots, n
\end{aligned} \tag{3.5}$$

As the models (3.4), (3.5) are fuzzy linear programming models, first the following α-cuts of the parameters are defined.

$$\begin{aligned}
&[\tilde{x}_{ij}]_\alpha = \left\{ x_{ij} \in \mathbb{R} \middle| \mu_{\tilde{x}_{ij}}(x_{ij}) \geq \alpha \right\} = \left[x_{ij}^l, x_{ij}^u \right]_\alpha \\
&[\tilde{y}_{rj}]_\alpha = \left\{ y_{rj} \in \mathbb{R} \middle| \mu_{\tilde{y}_{rj}}(y_{rj}) \geq \alpha \right\} = \left[y_{rj}^l, y_{rj}^u \right]_\alpha \\
&[\tilde{z}]_\alpha = \left[z^l, z^u \right]_\alpha \\
&[\tilde{\theta}]_\alpha = \left[\theta^l, \theta^u \right]_\alpha \\
&\circ \leq \alpha \leq 1 \;\; r = 1, \ldots, s, \;\; i = 1, \ldots, m, \;\; j = 1, 2, \ldots, n
\end{aligned}$$

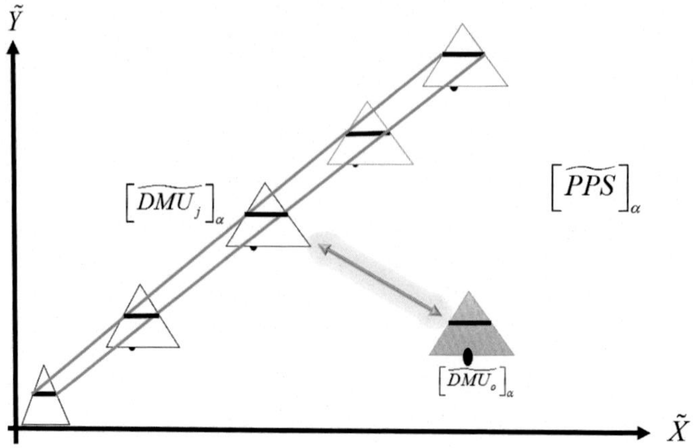

Fig. 3.5 The FPPS for the cut α_k ($[\tilde{T}]_{\alpha_k}$) for triangular fuzzy values.

Therefore, according to the above definitions, the FPPS for the cut α_k ($[\tilde{T}]_{\alpha_k}$) is defined as follows and represented by Fig. 3.5 for triangular fuzzy values.

$$[\tilde{T}]_{\alpha_k} = \left\{ \left([\underline{X}\overline{X}]_{\alpha_k}, [\underline{Y}\overline{Y}]_{\alpha_k} \right) \middle| [\underline{X}\overline{X}]_{\alpha_k} \tilde{\geq} \sum_{j=1}^{n} \lambda_j \left[\underline{X}_j \overline{X}_j \right]_{\alpha_k}, \left[\underline{Y}, \overline{Y} \right]_{\alpha_k} \tilde{\leq} \sum_{j=1}^{n} \lambda_j \left[\underline{Y}_j \overline{Y}_j \right]_{\alpha_k}, \lambda_j \geq 0, \forall j \right\}$$

Considering the α-cuts of the parameters and variables, the models (3.4), (3.5) are written as the below models, respectively.

$$\begin{aligned}
&\text{Max } \left[z^l, z^u\right]_\alpha = \sum_{r=1}^{s} u_r \left[y_{ro}^l, y_{ro}^u\right]_\alpha \\
&\text{subject to} \\
&\sum_{i=1}^{m} v_i \left[x_{io}^l, x_{io}^u\right]_\alpha = [1, 1] \\
&\sum_{r=1}^{s} u_r \left[y_{rj}^l, y_{rj}^u\right]_\alpha - \sum_{i=1}^{m} v_i \left[x_{ij}^l, x_{ij}^u\right]_\alpha \leq [0, 0] \quad r = 1, 2, \ldots, s \\
&u_r \geq 0 \quad r = 1, 2, \ldots, s \\
&v_i \geq 0 \quad i = 1, 2, \ldots, m
\end{aligned} \tag{3.6}$$

$$\begin{aligned}
&\text{Min } \left[\theta^l, \theta^u\right]_\alpha \\
&\text{subject to} \\
&\sum_{j=1}^{n} \lambda_j \left[x_{ij}^l, x_{ij}^u\right]_\alpha \tilde{\leq} \left[\theta^l, \theta^u\right]_\alpha \left[x_{io}^l, x_{io}^u\right]_\alpha \quad i = 1, 2, \ldots, m \\
&\sum_{j=1}^{n} \lambda_j \left[y_{rj}^l, y_{rj}^u\right]_\alpha \tilde{\geq} \left[y_{ro}^l, y_{ro}^u\right]_\alpha \quad r = 1, 2, \ldots, s \\
&\lambda_j \geq 0 \quad j = 1, 2, \ldots, n
\end{aligned} \tag{3.7}$$

Also, the α-cut of the input-oriented BCC with an envelopment model is written as follows,

$$\begin{aligned}
&\text{Min } \left[\theta^l, \theta^u\right]_\alpha \\
&\text{subject to} \\
&\sum_{j=1}^{n} \lambda_j \left[x_{ij}^l, x_{ij}^u\right]_\alpha \tilde{\leq} \left[\theta^l, \theta^u\right]_\alpha \left[x_{io}^l, x_{io}^u\right]_\alpha \quad i = 1, 2, \ldots, m \\
&\sum_{j=1}^{n} \lambda_j \left[y_{rj}^l, y_{rj}^u\right]_\alpha \tilde{\geq} \left[y_{ro}^l, y_{ro}^u\right]_\alpha \quad r = 1, 2, \ldots, s \\
&\sum_{j=1}^{n} \lambda_j = 1 \\
&\lambda_j \geq 0 \quad j = 1, 2, \ldots, n
\end{aligned} \tag{3.8}$$

The above-mentioned α-cut models are of the interval form where the approaches such as ranking method, algebraic method, and pointwise method can be used to solve them. These approaches are described in the following.

3.4.1.1 Ranking method

In this method, first a set of α values (better if uniformly generated) is considered as $\Delta = \{\alpha_1, \alpha_2, \ldots, \alpha_p\}$ where $1 = \alpha_1 > \alpha_2 > \ldots > \alpha_p = 0$. Then, for each α_j the models (3.6), (3.7) are written as follows, respectively, to evaluate $FDMU_O$ $(o \in \{1, \cdots, n\})$.

$$\begin{aligned}
&\text{Max } \left[z^l, z^u\right]_\alpha = \sum_{r=1}^{s} u_r \left[y_{ro}^l, y_{ro}^u\right]_\alpha \\
&\text{subject to} \\
&\sum_{i=1}^{m} v_i \left[x_{io}^l, x_{io}^u\right]_\alpha = [1, 1] \\
&\sum_{r=1}^{s} u_r \left[y_{rj}^l, y_{rj}^u\right]_\alpha - \sum_{i=1}^{m} v_i \left[x_{ij}^l, x_{ij}^u\right]_\alpha \leq [0, 0] \quad r = 1, 2, \ldots, s \\
&u_r \geq 0 \quad r = 1, 2, \ldots, s \\
&v_i \geq 0 \quad i = 1, 2, \ldots, m
\end{aligned} \tag{3.9}$$

$$\begin{aligned}
&\text{Min } \left[\theta^l, \theta^u\right]_\alpha \\
&\text{subject to} \\
&\sum_{j=1}^{n} \lambda_j \left[x_{ij}^l, x_{ij}^u\right]_\alpha \tilde{\leq} \left[\theta^l, \theta^u\right]_\alpha \left[x_{io}^l, x_{io}^u\right]_\alpha \quad i = 1, 2, \ldots, m \\
&\sum_{j=1}^{n} \lambda_j \left[y_{rj}^l, y_{rj}^u\right]_\alpha \tilde{\geq} \left[y_{ro}^l, y_{ro}^u\right]_\alpha \quad r = 1, 2, \ldots, s \\
&\sum_{j=1}^{n} \lambda_j = 1 \\
&\lambda_j \geq 0 \quad j = 1, 2, \ldots, n
\end{aligned} \tag{3.10}$$

Then, using the algebraic operations of interval numbers, the models (3.9), (3.10) are converted to the below models, respectively.

$$\begin{aligned}
&\text{Max } \left[z^{l\alpha_j}, z^{u\alpha_j}\right] = \sum_{r=1}^{s} \left[u_r y_{ro}^{l\alpha_j}, u_r y_{ro}^{u\alpha_j}\right] \\
&\text{subject to} \\
&\sum_{i=1}^{m} \left[v_i x_{io}^{l\alpha_j}, v_i x_{io}^{u\alpha_j}\right] = [1, 1] \\
&\sum_{r=1}^{s} \left[u_r y_{rj}^{l\alpha_j}, u_r y_{rj}^{u\alpha_j}\right] - \sum_{i=1}^{m} \left[v_i x_{ij}^{l\alpha_j}, v_i x_{ij}^{u\alpha_j}\right] \leq [0, 0] \quad j = 1, 2, \ldots, n \\
&u_r \geq 0 \quad r = 1, 2, \ldots, s \\
&v_i \geq 0 \quad i = 1, 2, \ldots, m
\end{aligned} \tag{3.11}$$

$$
\begin{aligned}
&\text{Min } \left[\theta^{l\alpha_j}, \theta^{u\alpha_j}\right]_{\alpha_j} \\
&\text{subject to} \\
&\sum_{j=1}^{n} \left[\lambda_j x_{ij}^{l\alpha_j}, \lambda_j x_{ij}^{u\alpha_j}\right] \tilde{\leq} \left[\theta^{l\alpha_j} x_{io}^{l\alpha_j}, \theta^{u\alpha_j} x_{io}^{u\alpha_j}\right], \quad i = 1, 2, \ldots, m \\
&\sum_{j=1}^{n} \left[\lambda_j y_{rj}^{l\alpha_j}, y_{rj}^{u\alpha_j}\right] \tilde{\geq} \left[y_{ro}^{l\alpha_j}, y_{ro}^{u\alpha_j}\right], \quad r = 1, 2, \ldots, s \\
&\lambda_j \geq 0 \quad j = 1, 2, \ldots, n
\end{aligned} \tag{3.12}
$$

The objective function and constraints of the models (3.11) and (3.12) should be linearized by a ranking function of interval numbers as R: $I \to \mathbb{R}$. Therefore, the following models are obtained instead of the models (3.11), (3.12), respectively.

$$
\begin{aligned}
&\text{Max } Z_R^{\alpha_j} = R\left(\left[z^l, z^u\right]_{\alpha_j}\right) = R\left(\sum_{r=1}^{s} u_r \left[y_{ro}^l, y_{ro}^u\right]_{\alpha_j}\right) \\
&\text{subject to} \\
&R\left(\sum_{i=1}^{m} v_i \left[x_{io}^l, x_{io}^u\right]_{\alpha_j}\right) = R([1, 1]) \\
&R\left(\sum_{r=1}^{s} u_r \left[y_{rj}^l, y_{rj}^u\right]_{\alpha_j} - \sum_{i=1}^{m} v_i \left[x_{ij}^l, x_{ij}^u\right]_{\alpha_j}\right) \leq R([0, 0]), \quad r = 1, 2, \ldots, s \\
&u_r \geq 0 \quad r = 1, 2, \ldots, s \\
&v_i \geq 0 \quad i = 1, 2, \ldots, m
\end{aligned} \tag{3.13}
$$

$$
\begin{aligned}
&\text{Min } R\left(\left[\theta^{l\alpha_j}, \theta^{u\alpha_j}\right]_{\alpha_j}\right) \\
&\text{subject to} \\
&R\left(\sum_{j=1}^{n} \left[\lambda_j x_{ij}^{l\alpha_j}, \lambda_j x_{ij}^{u\alpha_j}\right]\right) \tilde{\leq} R\left(\left[\theta^{l\alpha_j} x_{io}^{l\alpha_j}, \theta^{u\alpha_j} x_{io}^{u\alpha_j}\right]\right), \quad i = 1, 2, \ldots, m \\
&R\left(\sum_{j=1}^{n} \left[\lambda_j y_{rj}^{l\alpha_j}, \lambda_j y_{rj}^{u\alpha_j}\right]\right) \tilde{\geq} R\left(\left[y_{ro}^{l\alpha_j}, y_{ro}^{u\alpha_j}\right]\right), \quad r = 1, 2, \ldots, s \\
&\lambda_j \geq 0 \quad j = 1, 2, \ldots, n
\end{aligned} \tag{3.14}
$$

For example, consider the following ranking function of interval numbers.

$$\begin{aligned} &R : I \to \mathbb{R} \\ &R([a,b]) = w_1 a + w_2 b \qquad 0 < w_1 \le w_2 < 1, w_1 + w_2 = 1 \end{aligned} \tag{3.15}$$

If in the ranking function of (3.14) we consider $w_1 = w_2 = \frac{1}{2}$, then $R([a,b]) = \frac{a+b}{2}$. Therefore, the model (3.13) is converted to the below model.

$$\begin{aligned}
&\text{Max } Z^{\alpha_j} = z^{l\alpha_j} + z^{u\alpha_j} = \frac{1}{2}\sum_{r=1}^{s}\left(u_r^{l\alpha_j} y_{ro}^{l\alpha_j} + u_r^{u\alpha_j} y_{ro}^{u\alpha_j}\right) \\
&\text{subject to} \\
&\frac{1}{2}\sum_{i=1}^{m}\left(v_i x_{io}^{l\alpha_j} + v_i x_{io}^{u\alpha_j}\right) = 1 \\
&\frac{1}{2}\sum_{r=1}^{s}\left(u_r y_{rj}^{l\alpha_j} + u_r y_{rj}^{u\alpha_j}\right) - \frac{1}{2}\sum_{i=1}^{m}\left(v_i x_{ij}^{l\alpha_j} + v_i x_{ij}^{u\alpha_j}\right) \le 0 \quad j = 1, 2, \ldots, n \\
&u_r \ge 0 \qquad r = 1, 2, \ldots, s \\
&v_i \ge 0 \qquad i = 1, 2, \ldots, m
\end{aligned} \tag{3.16}$$

Finally, by solving the model (3.16) for different α-cut values, the set of objective function values of $\{Z^{\alpha_1}, Z^{\alpha_2}, \cdots, Z^{\alpha_p}\}$ is obtained. Using the obtained objective function values, the crisp value of $R(\tilde{Z})$ is calculated and is used for the efficiency of $FDMU_O$.

Similarly, using the ranking function of (3.15), the following models are obtained instead of the model (3.14) and the input-oriented BCC with the envelopment form model, respectively.

$$\begin{aligned}
&\text{Min } \theta^{\alpha_j} = \frac{1}{2}\left(\theta^{l\alpha_j} + \theta^{u\alpha_j}\right) \\
&\text{subject to} \\
&\sum_{j=1}^{n}\frac{\lambda_j}{2}\left(x_{ij}^{l\alpha_j} + x_{ij}^{u\alpha_j}\right) \tilde{\le} \frac{1}{2}\left(\theta^{l\alpha_j} x_{io}^{l\alpha_j} + \theta^{u\alpha_j} x_{io}^{u\alpha_j}\right), \quad i = 1, 2, \ldots, m \\
&\sum_{j=1}^{n}\frac{\lambda_j}{2}\left(y_{rj}^{l\alpha_j} + y_{rj}^{u\alpha_j}\right) \tilde{\ge} \frac{1}{2}\left(y_{ro}^{l\alpha_j} + y_{ro}^{u\alpha_j}\right), \quad r = 1, 2, \ldots, s \\
&\lambda_j \ge 0 \qquad j = 1, 2, \ldots, n
\end{aligned} \tag{3.17}$$

$$
\begin{aligned}
&\text{Min } \theta^{\alpha_j} = \frac{1}{2}\left(\theta^{l\alpha_j} + \theta^{u\alpha_j}\right) \\
&\text{subject to} \\
&\sum_{j=1}^{n} \frac{\lambda_j}{2}\left(x_{ij}^{l\alpha_j} + x_{ij}^{u\alpha_j}\right) \tilde{\leq} \frac{1}{2}\left(\theta^{l\alpha_j} x_{io}^{l\alpha_j} + \theta^{u\alpha_j} x_{io}^{u\alpha_j}\right), && i = 1, 2, \dots, m \\
&\sum_{j=1}^{n} \frac{\lambda_j}{2}\left(y_{rj}^{l\alpha_j} + y_{rj}^{u\alpha_j}\right) \tilde{\geq} \frac{1}{2}\left(y_{ro}^{l\alpha_j} + y_{ro}^{u\alpha_j}\right), && r = 1, 2, \dots, s \qquad (3.18) \\
&\sum_{j=1}^{n} \lambda_j = 1 \\
&\lambda_j \geq 0 && j = 1, 2, \dots, n
\end{aligned}
$$

Finally, by solving the model (3.18) for different α-cut values, the set of objective function values of $\{\theta^{\alpha_1}, \theta^{\alpha_2}, \dots, \theta^{\alpha_P}\}$ is obtained. Using the obtained objective function values, the crisp value of $R(\tilde{Z})$ is calculated and is used for the efficiency of $FDMU_O$.

To solve the model (3.17), two approaches can be considered:

- For each α_j-cut (where $j = 1, \dots, P$) assume that $\theta^{\alpha_j} = \theta^{l\alpha_j} = \theta^{u\alpha_j}$. Therefore, for each cut a different value of θ^{α_j} is obtained.
- For each α_j-cut (where $j = 1, \dots, P$) assume that $\theta^{l\alpha_j} \leq \theta^{u\alpha_j}$. Therefore, the obtained model is not an efficiency-related model, and its results do not have the concept of efficiency.

Some points can be highlighted about the ranking method:

- The results obtained by this method are related to the selected ranking function.
- The obtained crisp value $R(\tilde{Z})$ is not necessarily equal to the ranking function value of the exact solution of the model (3.1).
- A disadvantage of this method is that the feasibility of the model (3.11) for each α_j-cut should be proved, but this is not always possible.
- To consider the upper and lower bounds of the interval $[z^l, z^u]_{\alpha_j}$ as the upper and lower bounds of the fuzzy efficiency $\tilde{Z}$ in α_j-cut, by applying the model (3.16) for two consecutive cuts of α_j and α_{j+1}, the relation $[z^l, z^u]_{\alpha_j} \subseteq [z^l, z^u]_{\alpha_j+1}$ should be held. However, this is not always true.

Example 3.1 The triangular fuzzy data of 10 FDMUs including three inputs and two outputs are given in Table 3.2.

Table 3.2 The triangular fuzzy data of the inputs and outputs of Example 3.1.

DMU	x_1^L	x_1^C	x_1^U	x_2^L	x_2^C	x_2^U	x_3^L	x_3^C	x_3^U	y_1^L	y_1^C	y_1^U	y_2^L	y_2^C	y_2^U
1	1090	1350	1580	1870	2150	2380	1250	1600	1850	630	850	1040	650	870	1060
2	1570	1850	2080	2790	3050	3360	1600	1900	2350	1910	2150	2320	1940	2200	2400
3	2730	2950	3160	3550	3850	4040	2370	2850	3050	2390	2650	2900	2370	2630	2820
4	4630	4850	5700	5630	5850	6500	5050	5450	6300	1950	2750	2900	1650	2650	2820
5	2070	2350	2580	2600	2850	3100	2250	2700	3000	1300	1550	2100	1250	1600	2150
6	3650	4350	5100	3350	3850	4300	3450	4450	4900	1550	1850	2300	1560	1930	2350
7	5570	5850	6140	6570	6850	7140	5650	5900	6130	1150	1350	1500	1100	1450	1700
8	7450	7750	8020	7550	7850	8080	7600	8000	8400	1250	1550	1800	1200	1550	1750
9	5090	5350	5620	7430	7750	8000	5750	6250	6700	410	650	750	430	680	700
10	5950	6350	6660	8550	8850	9120	6650	7550	8600	470	750	810	450	790	800

To continue, the efficiency values of $\{Z^{\alpha_1}, Z^{\alpha_2}, \cdots, Z^{\alpha_P}\}$ are calculated for each FDMU. The set of $\Delta = \{\alpha_1 = 1, \alpha_2 = 0.8, \alpha_3 = 0.5, \alpha_4 = 0.3, \alpha_5 = 0\}$ is considered for α-cuts and the ranking function of $R([a, b]) = 0.3a + 0.7b$ is selected.

Considering different α_j values from the set Δ, and assuming $\theta^{\alpha_j} = \theta^{l\alpha_j} = \theta^{u\alpha_j}$, the results in Table 3.3 are obtained by the model (3.14).

The efficiencies of the FDMUs are also obtained by the input-oriented BCC with the envelopment form, as reported in Table 3.4.

Table 3.3 The efficiencies obtained for the FDMUs of Example 3.1 by the input-oriented CCR with the envelopment form model (3.14).

	$\tilde{\theta}$				
FDMU	**1**	**0.8**	**0.5**	**0.3**	**0**
1	0.5609937	0.5683047	0.5793885	0.5860730	0.5955785
2	1.000000	1.000000	1.000000	1.000000	1.000000
3	0.9764422	0.9860324	1.000000	1.000000	1.000000
4	0.6668654	0.6547287	0.6367020	0.6192145	0.5939945
5	0.9277140	0.8027035	0.8437771	0.8703703	0.9073799
6	0.6949823	0.7045720	0.7187708	0.7295047	0.7463293
7	0.2934638	0.2962927	0.3005144	0.3033144	0.3074929
8	0.2801067	0.2840022	0.2897391	0.2908639	0.2925253
9	0.1216422	0.1196291	0.1195559	0.1191793	0.1186037
10	0.1237545	0.1209253	0.1175588	0.1158927	0.1130125

Table 3.4 The efficiencies obtained for the FDMUs of Example 3.1 by the input-oriented BCC with the envelopment form model.

	$\tilde{\theta}$				
FDMU	**1**	**0.8**	**0.5**	**0.3**	**0**
1	1.000000	1.000000	1.000000	1.000000	1.000000
2	1.000000	1.000000	1.000000	1.000000	1.000000
3	1.000000	1.000000	1.000000	1.000000	1.000000
4	1.000000	1.000000	0.6367081	0.6198046	0.5968969
5	0.9277140	0.9393080	0.9590969	0.9733558	0.9951605
6	0.7447515	0.7491761	0.7558993	0.7612225	0.7714345
7	0.3711651	0.3730106	0.3757604	0.3775816	0.3802956
8	0.3356198	0.3383361	0.3424246	0.3451597	0.3492768
9	0.2774194	0.2788380	0.2809551	0.2823594	0.2844552
10	0.2429379	0.2441318	0.2459127	0.2470934	0.2488546

Finally, the fuzzy efficiencies of the FDMUs can be obtained, as the fuzzy efficiencies of $FDMU_5$ with the CCR and BCC models are obtained below, respectively.

$$\theta_5^{CCR} = \left\{ \begin{array}{lll} (0.9277140, 1), & (0.8027035, 0.8), & (0.8437771, 0.5), \\ (0.8703703, 0.3), & (0.9073799, 0) & \end{array} \right\}$$

$$\theta_5^{BCC} = \left\{ \begin{array}{lll} (0.9277140, 1), & (0.9393080, 0.8), & (0.9590969, 0.5), \\ (0.9733558, 0.3), & (0.9951605, 0) & \end{array} \right\}$$

3.4.1.2 Algebraic method

In this method, by applying the interval operators of the model (3.2), some α_j-cuts are constructed. The details of this method are described in this section.

Assume n fuzzy DMUs ($FDMU_j$, $j=1, \cdots, n$) with fuzzy input values of $\tilde{X}_j = \left(\tilde{x}_{1j}, \tilde{x}_{2j}, \cdots, \tilde{x}_{mj}\right)$ and fuzzy output values of $\tilde{Y}_j = \left(\tilde{y}_{1j}, \tilde{y}_{2j}, \cdots, \tilde{y}_{sj}\right)$, where $\tilde{x}_{ij}$ and $\tilde{y}_{ij}$ are fuzzy numbers with membership functions of $\mu_{\tilde{x}_{ij}}$ and $\mu_{\tilde{y}_{rj}}$, respectively. The fuzzy linear programming model for the input-oriented CCR with the multiplier form for $FDMU_O$ (where $o \in \{1, \cdots, n\}$) is as follows

$$\begin{aligned} & \text{Max } \tilde{Z} = \sum_{r=1}^{s} u_r \tilde{y}_{ro} \\ & \text{subject to} \\ & \sum_{i=1}^{m} v_i \tilde{x}_{io} \cong 1 \\ & \sum_{r=1}^{s} u_r \tilde{y}_{rj} - \sum_{i=1}^{m} v_i \tilde{x}_{ij} \lesssim 0 \quad r = 1, 2, \ldots, s \\ & u_r \geq 0 \qquad r = 1, 2, \ldots, s \\ & v_i \geq 0 \qquad i = 1, 2, \ldots, m \end{aligned} \tag{3.19}$$

Also, the fuzzy linear programming model for the input-oriented CCR with the envelopment form for $FDMU_O$ (where $o \in \{1, \cdots, n\}$) is as follows,

$$
\begin{aligned}
& \text{Min } \tilde{\theta} \\
& \text{subject to} \\
& \sum_{j=1}^{n} \lambda_j \tilde{x}_{ij} \tilde{\leq} \tilde{\theta} \tilde{x}_{io} \qquad i = 1, 2, \ldots, m \\
& \sum_{j=1}^{n} \lambda_j \tilde{y}_{rj} \tilde{\geq} \tilde{y}_{ro} \qquad r = 1, 2, \ldots, s \\
& \lambda_j \geq 0 \qquad j = 1, 2, \ldots, n
\end{aligned}
\tag{3.20}
$$

As the models (3.19), (3.20) are fuzzy models, the α-cuts of their fuzzy parameters and variables are defined as follows,

$$
\begin{aligned}
& [\tilde{x}_{ij}]_\alpha = \left\{ x_{ij} \in \mathbb{R} \middle| \mu_{\tilde{x}_{ij}}(x_{ij}) \geq \alpha \right\} = \left[x_{ij}^l, x_{ij}^u \right]_\alpha && \circ \leq \alpha \leq 1 \quad i = 1, \ldots, m, \; j = 1, \ldots, n \\
& [\tilde{u}_r]_\alpha = \left\{ u_r \in \mathbb{R} \middle| \mu_{\tilde{u}_r}(u_r) \geq \alpha \right\} = \left[u_r^l, u_r^u \right]_\alpha && \circ \leq \alpha \leq 1 \quad r = 1, \ldots, s \\
& [\tilde{v}_i]_\alpha = \left\{ v_i \in \mathbb{R} \middle| \mu_{\tilde{v}_i}(v_i) \geq \alpha \right\} = \left[v_i^l, v_i^u \right]_\alpha && \circ \leq \alpha \leq 1 \quad i = 1, \ldots, m, \\
& [\tilde{\lambda}_j]_\alpha = \left\{ \lambda_j \in \mathbb{R} \middle| \mu_{\tilde{\lambda}_j}(\lambda_j) \geq \alpha \right\} = \left[\lambda_j^l, \lambda_j^u \right]_\alpha && \circ \leq \alpha \leq 1 \quad j = 1, \ldots, n \\
& [\tilde{Z}]_\alpha = [z^l, z^u]_\alpha && \circ \leq \alpha \leq 1 \\
& [\tilde{\theta}]_\alpha = [\theta^l, \theta^u]_\alpha && \circ \leq \alpha \leq 1
\end{aligned}
$$

In the model (3.19), the values of $\tilde{0}$ and $\tilde{1}$ can be written in any of the forms $\tilde{0} = (0, 0, 0)$, $\tilde{0} = (-\varepsilon, 0, \varepsilon)$, $\tilde{0} = (-\varepsilon, -\delta, 0)$ and $\tilde{1} = (1, 1, 1)$, $\tilde{1} = (1 - \varepsilon, 1, 1 + \varepsilon)$, $\tilde{1} = (1 - \varepsilon, 1 - \delta, 1)$ where $\varepsilon \leq \delta$. Each of these forms has a different interpretation. In this chapter, we consider the values $\tilde{0} = (0, 0, 0)$, $\tilde{1} = (1, 1, 1)$. Now, the models (3.19), (3.20) can be written as follows, respectively.

$$
\begin{aligned}
&\text{Max } \left[z^l, z^u\right]_\alpha = \sum_{r=1}^{s} \left[u_r^l, u_r^u\right]_\alpha \left[y_{ro}^l, y_{ro}^u\right]_\alpha \\
&\text{subject to} \\
&\sum_{i=1}^{m} \left[v_i^l, v_i^u\right]_\alpha \left[x_{io}^l, x_{io}^u\right]_\alpha = [1, 1] \\
&\sum_{r=1}^{s} \left[u_r^l, u_r^u\right] \left[y_{rj}^l, y_{rj}^u\right]_\alpha - \sum_{i=1}^{m} \left[v_i^l, v_i^u\right]_\alpha \left[x_{ij}^l, x_{ij}^u\right]_\alpha \leq [0, 0], \quad j = 1, \ldots, n \\
&\left[u_r^l, u_r^u\right]_\alpha, \left[v_i^l, v_i^u\right]_\alpha \geq 0 \qquad r = 1, 2, \ldots, s \quad i = 1, 2, \ldots, m
\end{aligned}
\tag{3.21}
$$

$$
\begin{aligned}
&\text{Min } \left[\theta^l, \theta^u\right]_\alpha \\
&\text{subject to} \\
&\sum_{j=1}^{n} \left[\lambda_j^l, \lambda_j^u\right]_\alpha \left[x_{ij}^l, x_{ij}^u\right]_\alpha \tilde{\leq} \left[\theta^l, \theta^u\right]_\alpha \left[x_{io}^l, x_{io}^u\right]_\alpha, \quad i = 1, 2, \ldots, m \\
&\sum_{j=1}^{n} \left[\lambda_j^l, \lambda_j^u\right]_\alpha \left[y_{rj}^l, y_{rj}^u\right]_\alpha \tilde{\geq} \left[y_{ro}^l, y_{ro}^u\right]_\alpha, \quad r = 1, 2, \ldots, s \\
&\left[\lambda_j^l, \lambda_j^u\right]_\alpha \geq \circ, \quad j = 1, 2, \ldots, n
\end{aligned}
\tag{3.22}
$$

According to the operators of the interval numbers, the model (3.21) is converted to the below pair of models.

$$
\begin{aligned}
&\text{Max } z_\alpha^l = \sum_{r=1}^{s} u_r^{l\alpha} y_{ro}^{l\alpha} \\
&\text{subject to} \\
&\sum_{i=1}^{m} v_i^{l\alpha} x_{io}^{l\alpha} = 1 \\
&\sum_{r=1}^{s} u_r^{l\alpha} y_{rj}^{l\alpha} - \sum_{i=q}^{m} v_i^{u\alpha} x_{ij}^{u\alpha} \leq 0, \quad j = 1, 2, \ldots, n \\
&u_r^{u\alpha}, u_r^{l\alpha} \geq 0, \quad r = 1, 2, \ldots, s \\
&v_i^{u\alpha}, v_i^{l\alpha} \geq 0, \quad i = 1, 2, \ldots, m
\end{aligned}
\tag{3.23}
$$

$$\text{Max } z_\alpha^u = \sum_{r=1}^{s} u_r^{u\alpha} y_{ro}^{u\alpha}$$

subject to

$$\sum_{i=1}^{m} v_i^{u\alpha} x_{io}^{u\alpha} = 1$$

$$\sum_{r=1}^{s} u_r^{u\alpha} y_{rj}^{u\alpha} - \sum_{i=q}^{m} v_i^{l\alpha} x_{ij}^{l\alpha} \leq 0 \quad j = 1, 2, \ldots, n \tag{3.24}$$

$$u_r^{u\alpha}, u_r^{l\alpha} \geq 0 \quad r = 1, 2, \ldots, s$$

$$v_i^{u\alpha}, v_i^{l\alpha} \geq 0 \quad i = 1, 2, \ldots, m$$

Similarly, the model (3.22) can be written as the below pair of models.

$$\text{Min } z_\alpha^l = \theta^{l\alpha}$$

subject to

$$\sum_{j=1}^{n} \lambda_j^{l\alpha} x_{ij}^{l\alpha} \tilde{\leq} \theta^{l\alpha} x_{io}^{l\alpha} \quad i = 1, 2, \ldots, m \tag{3.25}$$

$$\sum_{j=1}^{n} \lambda_j^{l\alpha} y_{rj}^{l\alpha} \tilde{\geq} y_{ro}^{l\alpha} \quad r = 1, 2, \ldots, s$$

$$\lambda_j^{l\alpha} \geq \text{o} \quad j = 1, 2, \ldots, n$$

$$\text{Min } z_\alpha^u = \theta^{u\alpha}$$

subject to

$$\sum_{j=1}^{n} \lambda_j^{u\alpha} x_{ij}^{u\alpha} \tilde{\leq} \theta^{u\alpha} x_{io}^{u\alpha} \quad i = 1, 2, \ldots, m \tag{3.26}$$

$$\sum_{j=1}^{n} \lambda_j^{u\alpha} y_{rj}^{u\alpha} \tilde{\geq} y_{ro}^{u\alpha} \quad r = 1, 2, \ldots, s$$

$$\lambda_j^{u\alpha} \geq \text{o} \quad j = 1, 2, \ldots, n$$

In a similar way, the input-oriented BCC with the envelopment form model is written as the below pair of models.

$$
\begin{aligned}
&\text{Min } z_\alpha^l = \theta^{l\alpha} \\
&\text{subject to} \\
&\sum_{j=1}^{n} \lambda_j^{l\alpha} x_{ij}^{l\alpha} \tilde{\leq} \theta^{l\alpha} x_{io}^{l\alpha} \; i = 1, 2, \dots, m \\
&\sum_{j=1}^{n} \lambda_j^{l\alpha} y_{rj}^{l\alpha} \tilde{\geq} y_{ro}^{l\alpha} \; r = 1, 2, \dots, s \\
&\sum_{j=1}^{n} \lambda_j^{l\alpha} = 1 \\
&\lambda_j^{l\alpha} \geq \circ \; j = 1, 2, \dots, n
\end{aligned}
\tag{3.27}
$$

$$
\begin{aligned}
&\text{Min } z_\alpha^u = \theta^{u\alpha} \\
&\text{subject to} \\
&\sum_{j=1}^{n} \lambda_j^{u\alpha} x_{ij}^{u\alpha} \tilde{\leq} \theta^{u\alpha} x_{io}^{u\alpha} \; i = 1, 2, \dots, m \\
&\sum_{j=1}^{n} \lambda_j^{u\alpha} y_{rj}^{u\alpha} \tilde{\geq} y_{ro}^{u\alpha} \; r = 1, 2, \dots, s \\
&\sum_{j=1}^{n} \lambda_j^{u\alpha} = 1 \\
&\lambda_j^{u\alpha} \geq \circ \; j = 1, 2, \dots, n
\end{aligned}
\tag{3.28}
$$

Some important highlights for the algebraic method are given below,

- Referring to the fuzzy condition of the efficiency values, the values of z_α^l, z_α^u obtained by any pair of the models (3.23)–(3.24), (3.25)–(3.26), (3.27)–(3.28) must meet the condition $z_\alpha^l \leq z_\alpha^u$.
- To consider the bounds of the interval $[z_\alpha^l, z_\alpha^u]$ as the bounds of the α_j-cut of the fuzzy efficiency $\tilde{\theta}$, for two consecutive cuts of α_t, α_{t+1} the condition $[{z_{\alpha_t}}^l, {z_{\alpha_t}}^u] \subseteq [{z_{\alpha_{t+1}}}^l, {z_{\alpha_{t+1}}}^u]$ should be met where may not be held necessarily.

Example 3.2 The FDMUs of Example 3.1 are evaluated considering the α_j-cuts of $\Delta = \{\alpha_1 = 1, \alpha_2 = 0.8, \alpha_3 = 0.5, \alpha_4 = 0.3, \alpha_5 = 0\}$.

Using the models (3.25), (3.26), the efficiency value of each $FDMU_O$ for $o \in \{1, 2, 5, 7\}$ is obtained for the given α_j-cuts, as shown in Table 3.5.

Using the models (3.27), (3.28), the efficiency value of each $FDMU_O$ for $o \in \{1, 2, 5, 7\}$ is obtained for the given α_j-cuts, as is shown in Table 3.6.

Table 3.5 The efficiency values obtained for the FDMUs of Example 3.2 by the models (3.25), (3.26).

$\tilde{\theta}$		α-cut				
		1	**0.8**	**0.5**	**0.3**	**0**
$\tilde{\theta}_1$	θ_1^l	0.5609937	0.5505550	0.5333718	0.5207706	0.4998897
	θ_1^u	0.5609937	0.5761925	0.5974247	0.6098292	0.6269358
$\tilde{\theta}_2$	θ_2^l	1.000000	1.000000	1.000000	1.000000	1.000000
	θ_2^u	1.000000	1.000000	1.000000	1.000000	1.000000
$\tilde{\theta}_5$	θ_5^l	0.9277140	0.7640682	0.7522032	0.7437970	0.7303665
	θ_5^u	0.9277140	0.8191995	0.8794116	0.9190620	0.9746632
$\tilde{\theta}_7$	θ_7^l	0.2934638	0.2834986	0.2680403	0.2631347	0.2556839
	θ_7^u	0.2934638	0.3016689	0.3137567	0.3216716	0.3333333

Table 3.6 The efficiency values obtained for the FDMUs of Example 3.2 by the models (3.27), (3.28).

$\tilde{\theta}$		α-cut				
		1	**0.8**	**0.5**	**0.3**	**0**
$\tilde{\theta}_1$	θ_1^l	1.000000	1.000000	1.000000	1.000000	1.000000
	θ_1^u	1.000000	1.000000	1.000000	1.000000	1.000000
$\tilde{\theta}_2$	θ_2^l	1.000000	1.000000	1.000000	1.000000	1.000000
	θ_2^u	1.000000	1.000000	1.000000	1.000000	1.000000
$\tilde{\theta}_5$	θ_5^l	0.9277140	0.9207451	0.9149420	0.9108734	0.9044471
	θ_5^u	0.9277140	0.9474226	0.9768875	0.9979199	1.000000
$\tilde{\theta}_7$	θ_7^l	0.3711651	0.3639729	0.3531695	0.3485596	0.3415145
	θ_7^u	0.3711651	0.3768256	0.3852056	0.3907204	0.3941303

According to the results of Table 3.5, the fuzzy efficiency can be estimated by the linear weighted fitting and Gaussian models easily. If we consider a higher weight for 1-cut and 0-cut, the membership function for the efficiencies of the FDMUs are as follows, where for $FDMU_2$ this value is exactly 2 with no doubt (using the linear fitting model).

$$\tilde{\theta}_1 = \begin{cases} \mathbf{0.0609}x + \mathbf{0.5002} & \mathbf{0.4998897} \leq x \leq \mathbf{0.5609937} \\ 1 & x = \mathbf{0.5609937} \\ -\mathbf{0.0661}x + \mathbf{0.6273} & \mathbf{0.5609937} \leq x \leq \mathbf{0.6269358} \end{cases}$$

$$\tilde{\theta}_5 = \begin{cases} 0.1988x + 0.7219 & 0.7219 \le x \le 0.9211 \\ 1 & x = 0.9211 \\ -0.0457x + 0.9668 & 0.9211 \le x \le 0.9668 \end{cases}$$

$$\tilde{\theta}_7 = \begin{cases} 0.0381x + 0.2551 & 0.2551 \le x \le 0.2935 \\ 1 & x = 0.2935 \\ -0.0399x + 0.3334 & 0.2935 \le x \le 0.3334 \end{cases}$$

The fuzzy efficiency membership function obtained by fitting the linear function for the fuzzy DMUs is obtained as follows and the form of linear fitting of fuzzy efficiency of fuzzy DMUs are depicted by Figs. 3.6–3.8,

$$\tilde{\theta}_1 = \begin{cases} 0.0609x + 0.5002 & 0.4998897 \le x \le 0.5609937 \\ -0.0661x + 0.6273 & 0.5609937 \le x \le 0.6269358 \end{cases}$$

$$\tilde{\theta}_5 = \begin{cases} 0.1988x + 0.7219 & 0.7219 \le x \le 0.9211 \\ -0.0457x + 0.9668 & 0.9211 \le x \le 0.9668 \end{cases}$$

$$\tilde{\theta}_7 = \begin{cases} 0.0381x + 0.2551 & 0.2551 \le x \le 0.2935 \\ -0.0399x + 0.3334 & 0.2935 \le x \le 0.3334 \end{cases}$$

Applying the Gaussian model, the following membership functions for the fuzzy efficiencies of the DMUs are obtained.

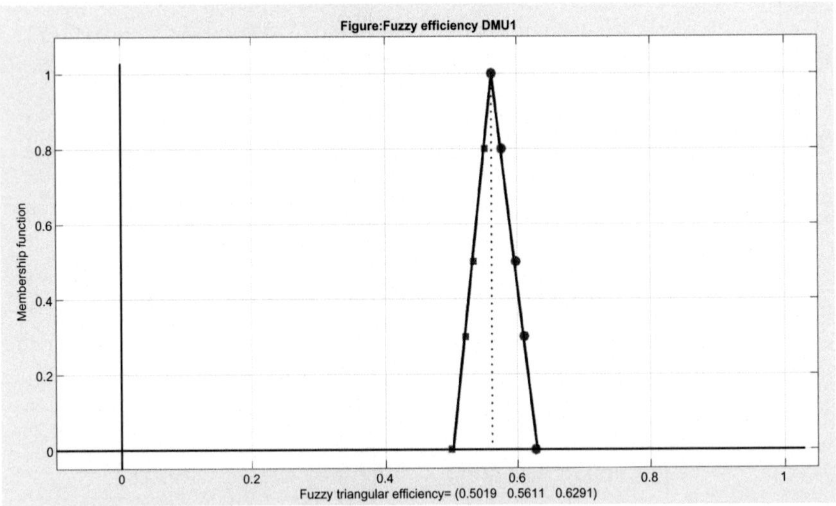

Fig. 3.6 The membership function of FDMU 1 of Example 3.2 by using the linear fitting model.

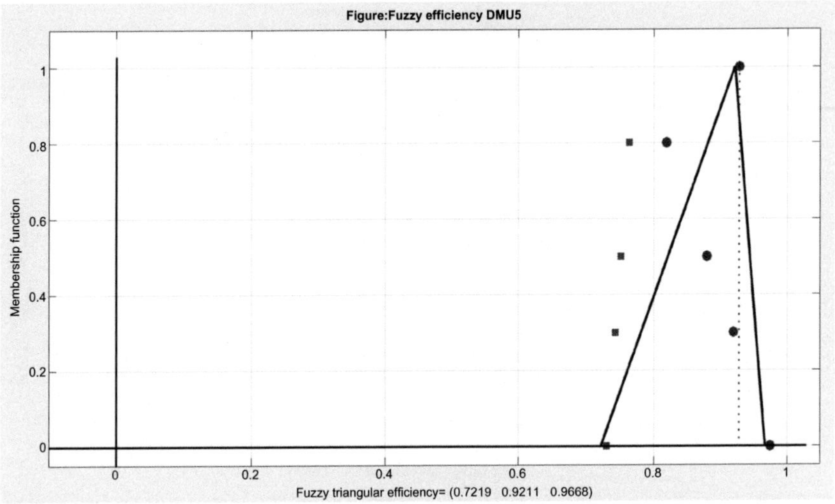

Fig. 3.7 The membership function of FDMU 5 of Example 3.2 by using the linear fitting model.

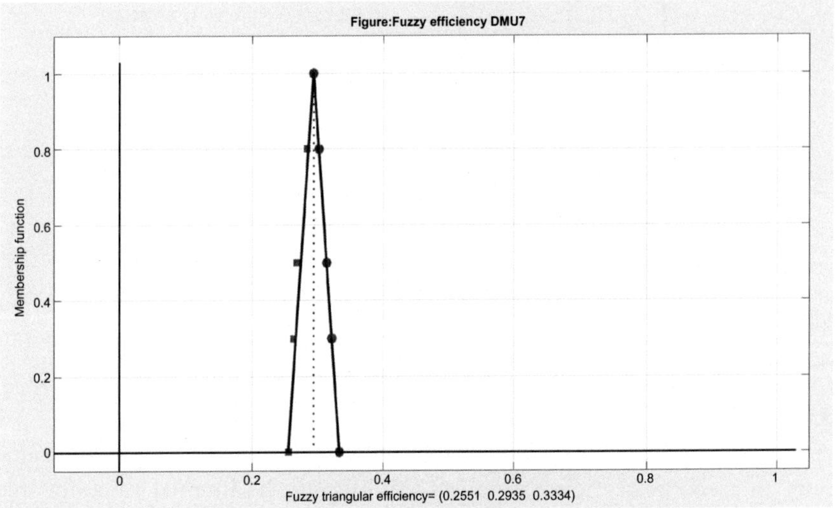

Fig. 3.8 The membership function of FDMU 7 of Example 3.2 by using the linear fitting model.

$$\tilde{\theta}_1 = \begin{cases} \dfrac{1}{1 + 3000(x - \mathbf{0.5609937})^2} & x \leq \mathbf{0.5609937} \\ \dfrac{1}{1 + 1000(x - \mathbf{0.5609937})^2} & x \geq \mathbf{0.5609937} \end{cases}$$

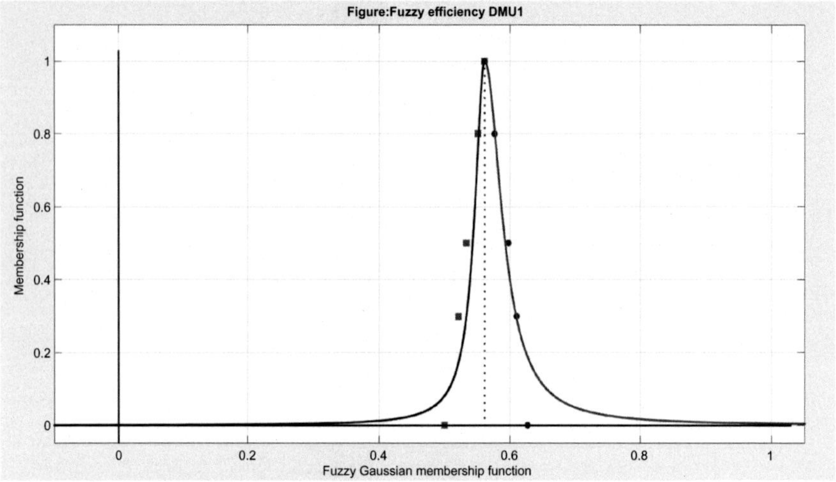

Fig. 3.9 The membership function of FDMU 1 of Example 3.2 by using the Gaussian model.

$$\tilde{\theta}_5 = \begin{cases} \dfrac{1}{1 + 1000000(x - 0.9277140)^2} & x \leq 0.9277140 \\ \dfrac{1}{1 + 100000(x - 0.9277140)^2} & x \geq 0.9277140 \end{cases}$$

$$\tilde{\theta}_7 = \begin{cases} \dfrac{1}{1 + 3000(x - \mathbf{0.2934638})^2} & x \leq \mathbf{0.2934638} \\ \dfrac{1}{1 + 5000(x - \mathbf{0.2934638})^2} & x \geq \mathbf{0.2934638} \end{cases}$$

The above-mentioned membership functions are shown in Figs. 3.9–3.11.

3.4.1.3 Pointwise method

According to the α-cut-based approaches, given the fuzzy inputs and outputs, in each cut of the fuzzy inputs and outputs the interval value for the efficiency of each FDMU is obtained. Actually, the FDMU under evaluation ($FDMU_o$) is compared to a dummy FDMU ($FDMU$) projected on the fuzzy production frontier and their maximum and minimum differences are considered as the interval efficiency value. Therefore, these DMUs are seen as $FDMU_o^\alpha = \left[FDMU_o^{L\alpha}, FDMU_o^{U\alpha}\right] = \begin{pmatrix} \left[x_{io}^l, x_{io}^u\right]_\alpha \\ \left[y_{ro}^l, y_{ro}^u\right]_\alpha \end{pmatrix}$, $FDMU^\alpha = \left[FDMU^{L\alpha}, FDMU^{U\alpha}\right] = \begin{pmatrix} \left[x_i^l, x_i^u\right]_\alpha \\ \left[y_r^l, y_r^u\right]_\alpha \end{pmatrix}$ according to the α-cut of their

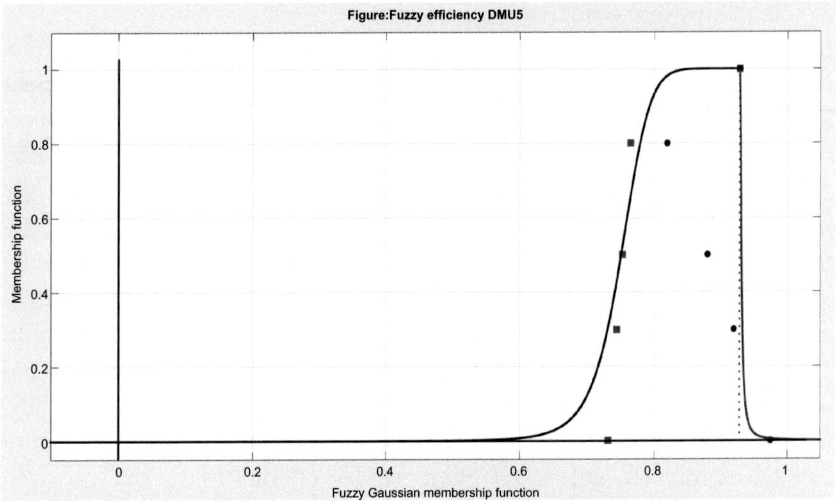

Fig. 3.10 The membership function of FDMU 5 of Example 3.2 by using the Gaussian model.

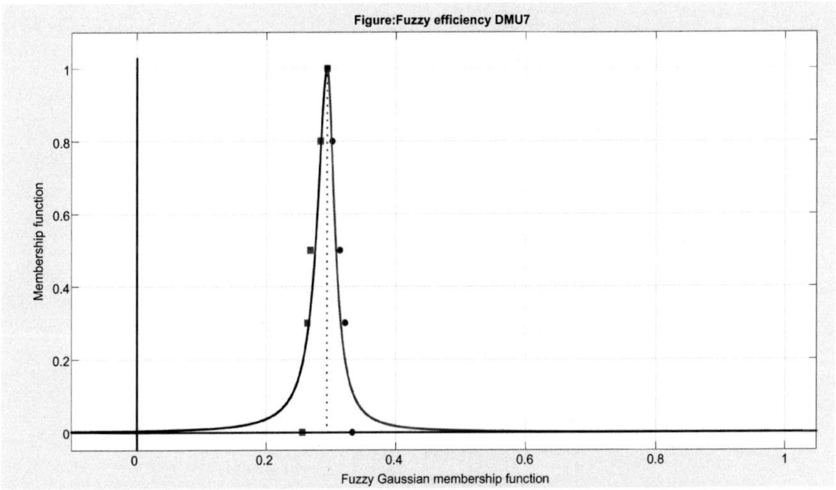

Fig. 3.11 The membership function of FDMU 7 of Example 3.2 by using the Gaussian model.

inputs and outputs. Therefore, for comparing the FDMUs, these intervals are compared. In this comparison, the lower bounds of the intervals are compared together and the upper bounds also are compared together. But in the pointwise method, the $FDMU_o$ and the projected dummy FDMU are considered according to different values of their intervals as $\begin{pmatrix} x_{io}^{l\alpha} \\ y_{ro}^{l\alpha} \end{pmatrix}, \begin{pmatrix} x_{io}^{u\alpha} \\ y_{ro}^{u\alpha} \end{pmatrix}, \begin{pmatrix} x_{io}^{l\alpha} \\ y_{ro}^{u\alpha} \end{pmatrix}, \begin{pmatrix} x_{io}^{u\alpha} \\ y_{ro}^{l\alpha} \end{pmatrix}, \begin{pmatrix} x_{i}^{l\alpha} \\ y_{r}^{l\alpha} \end{pmatrix}, \begin{pmatrix} x_{i}^{u\alpha} \\ y_{r}^{u\alpha} \end{pmatrix}, \begin{pmatrix} x_{i}^{l\alpha} \\ y_{r}^{u\alpha} \end{pmatrix}, \begin{pmatrix} x_{i}^{u\alpha} \\ y_{r}^{l\alpha} \end{pmatrix}.$

Simple pointwise method with domination

In this method for comparing the $FDMU_o$ and the projected dummy FDMU, two models are considered in each cut to calculate the upper and lower bounds of the interval efficiency value of the cut. To calculate the upper bound, the DMU under evaluation is fixed to its best possible efficiency, meaning the least input values and highest output values from the intervals of the cut of the inputs and outputs. However, other DMUs are fixed to their worst possible efficiency, meaning the highest input values and lowest output values. To calculate the lower bound, the DMU under evaluation is fixed to its worst possible efficiency, meaning the highest input values and least output values from the intervals of the cut of the inputs and outputs. However, other DMUs are fixed to their best possible efficiency, meaning the least input values and highest output values. Notably, the set of cut values $\Delta=\{\alpha_1,\alpha_2,\ldots,\alpha_p\}$ with similar conditions to the previous methods should be considered.

Using the simple pointwise method with domination, to evaluate $FDMU_O$ (where $o\in\{1,\cdots,n\}$) by the input-oriented CCR with multiplier form, the following models are obtained for the lower and upper bound calculations of the interval efficiency in cut α,

$$
\begin{aligned}
& z_\alpha^u = \text{Max} \sum_{r=1}^{s} u_r y_{ro}^{u\alpha} \\
& \text{subject to} \\
& \sum_{i=1}^{m} v_i x_{io}^{u\alpha} = 1 \\
& \sum_{r=1}^{s} u_r y_{rj}^{u\alpha} - \sum_{i=q}^{m} v_i x_{ij}^{l\alpha} \leq 0 \quad j = 1,2,\ldots,n \\
& u_r \geq 0 \qquad r = 1,2,\ldots,s \\
& v_i \geq 0 \qquad i = 1,2,\ldots,m
\end{aligned}
\tag{3.29}
$$

$$
\begin{aligned}
& z_\alpha^u = \text{Max} \sum_{r=1}^{s} u_r y_{ro}^{u\alpha} \\
& \text{subject to} \\
& \sum_{r=1}^{s} u_r y_{rj}^{l\alpha} - \sum_{i=q}^{m} v_i x_{ij}^{u\alpha} \leq 0 \quad j = 1,2,\ldots,n \\
& u_r \geq 0 \qquad r = 1,2,\ldots,s \\
& v_i \geq 0 \qquad i = 1,2,\ldots,m
\end{aligned}
\tag{3.30}
$$

Also, for the input-oriented CCR with envelopment form, the following models are obtained for lower and upper bound calculations of the interval efficiency in cut α,

$$
\begin{aligned}
&\text{Min } z_\alpha^l = \theta^\alpha \\
&\text{subject to} \\
&\sum_{\substack{j=1,\\ j\neq o}}^{n} \lambda_j x_{ij}^{l\alpha} + \lambda_j x_{io}^{u\alpha} \tilde{\leq} \theta^\alpha x_{io}^{u\alpha} \quad i = 1, 2, \ldots, m \\
&\sum_{\substack{j=1,\\ j\neq o}}^{n} \lambda_j y_{rj}^{u\alpha} + \lambda_j y_{ro}^{l\alpha} \tilde{\geq} y_{ro}^{l\alpha} \qquad r = 1, 2, \ldots, s \\
&\lambda_j \geq 0 \qquad\qquad j = 1, 2, \ldots, n
\end{aligned}
\tag{3.31}
$$

$$
\begin{aligned}
&\text{Min } z_\alpha^u = \theta^\alpha \\
&\text{subject to} \\
&\sum_{\substack{j=1,\\ j\neq o}}^{n} \lambda_j x_{ij}^{u\alpha} + \lambda_j x_{io}^{l\alpha} \tilde{\leq} \theta^\alpha x_{io}^{l\alpha} \quad i = 1, 2, \ldots, m \\
&\sum_{\substack{j=1,\\ j\neq o}}^{n} \lambda_j y_{rj}^{l\alpha} + \lambda_j y_{ro}^{u\alpha} \tilde{\geq} y_{ro}^{u\alpha} \qquad r = 1, 2, \ldots, s \\
&\lambda_j \geq 0 \qquad\qquad j = 1, 2, \ldots, n
\end{aligned}
\tag{3.32}
$$

Similarly, for the input-oriencodted BCC with envelopment form, the following models are obtained for lower and upper bound calculations of the interval efficiency in cut α,

$$\begin{aligned}
&\text{Min } z_\alpha^l = \theta^\alpha \\
&\text{subject to} \\
&\sum_{\substack{j=1,\\ j\neq o}}^{n} \lambda_j x_{ij}^{l\alpha} + \lambda_j x_{io}^{u\alpha} \tilde{\leq} \theta^\alpha x_{io}^{u\alpha} \quad i = 1, 2, \ldots, m \\
&\sum_{\substack{j=1,\\ j\neq o}}^{n} \lambda_j y_{rj}^{u\alpha} + \lambda_j y_{ro}^{l\alpha} \tilde{\geq} y_{ro}^{l\alpha} \quad r = 1, 2, \ldots, s \\
&\sum_{j=1}^{n} \lambda_j = 1 \\
&\lambda_j \geq 0 \quad j = 1, 2, \ldots, n
\end{aligned} \tag{3.33}$$

$$\begin{aligned}
&\text{Min } z_\alpha^u = \theta^\alpha \\
&\text{subject to} \\
&\sum_{\substack{j=1,\\ j\neq o}}^{n} \lambda_j x_{ij}^{u\alpha} + \lambda_j x_{io}^{l\alpha} \tilde{\leq} \theta^\alpha x_{io}^{l\alpha} \quad i = 1, 2, \ldots, m \\
&\sum_{\substack{j=1,\\ j\neq o}}^{n} \lambda_j y_{rj}^{l\alpha} + \lambda_j y_{ro}^{u\alpha} \tilde{\geq} y_{ro}^{u\alpha} \quad r = 1, 2, \ldots, s \\
&\sum_{j=1}^{n} \lambda_j = 1 \\
&\lambda_j \geq 0 \quad j = 1, 2, \ldots, n
\end{aligned} \tag{3.34}$$

By solving any pair of the models (3.29)–(3.34), in an α_j-cut, the interval of $[z_{\alpha_j}{}^L, z_{\alpha_j}{}^U]$ is obtained where $\theta_{\alpha_j}{}^L \leq \theta_{\alpha_j}{}^U$. Then, by considering all α_j-cuts for $FDMU_o$, its fuzzy relative efficiency can be estimated easily. Note that the condition $[z^l, z^u]_{\alpha_j} \subseteq [z^l, z^u]_{\alpha_j+1}$ should be met for any consecutive pairs of α-cuts.

Example 3.3 The data of Example 3.2 are solved by the models (3.31), (3.32) and the results of Table 3.7 are obtained.

Similar to Example 3.2, according to the results of Table 3.7 the fuzzy efficiency can be estimated by the linear weighted fitting and Gaussian models easily. If we consider a higher weight for 1-cut and 0-cut, the

Table 3.7 The results obtained for Example 3.3 by the CCR models (3.31), (3.32).

$\tilde{\theta}$		α-cut				
		1	**0.8**	**0.5**	**0.3**	**0**
$\tilde{\theta}_1$	θ_1^l	0.5609937	0.5038273	0.4268437	0.3806746	0.3183316
	θ_1^u	0.5609937	0.6282239	0.7508612	0.8557541	1
$\tilde{\theta}_2$	θ_2^l	1	1	1	1	0.8987328
	θ_2^u	1	1	1	1	1
$\tilde{\theta}_5$	θ_5^l	0.9277140	0.7100227	0.6257966	0.5745422	0.5043103
	θ_5^u	0.9277140	0.8847965	1	1	1
$\tilde{\theta}_7$	θ_7^l	0.2934638	0.2673686	0.2334681	0.2168484	0.1936939
	θ_7^u	0.2934638	0.3198682	0.3634258	0.3443404	0.4410792

membership functions for the efficiencies of the FDMUs are as follows where for $FDMU_2$ this value is exactly 2 with no doubt (using the linear fitting model). The membership functions are also shown in Figs. 3.12–3.15.

$$\tilde{\theta}_1 = \begin{cases} \mathbf{0.2506}x + \mathbf{0.3098} & \mathbf{0.3098} \leq x \leq \mathbf{0.5598} \\ 1 & x = \mathbf{0.5598} \\ -\mathbf{0.4251}x + \mathbf{0.9849} & \mathbf{0.5598} \leq x \leq \mathbf{0.9849} \end{cases}$$

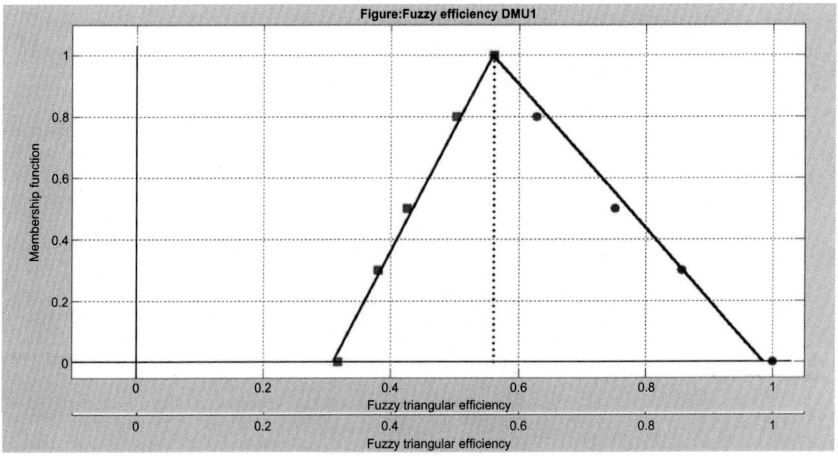

Fig. 3.12 The membership function of FDMU 1 of Example 3.3.

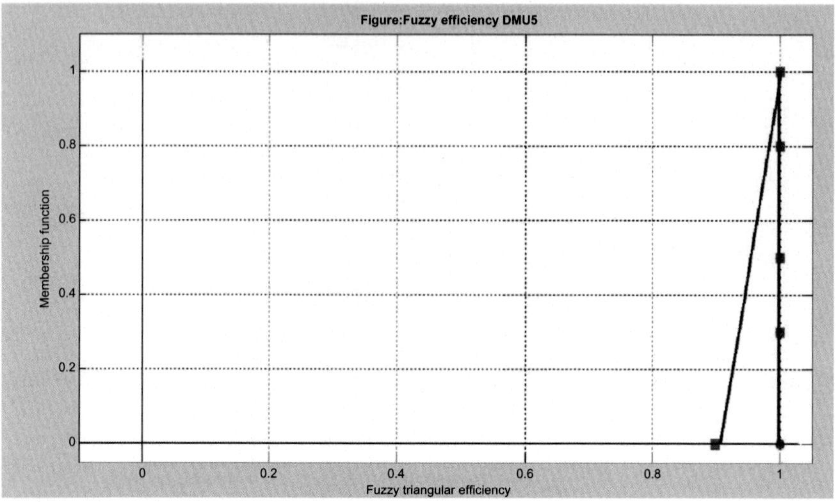

Fig. 3.13 The membership function of FDMU 2 of Example 3.3.

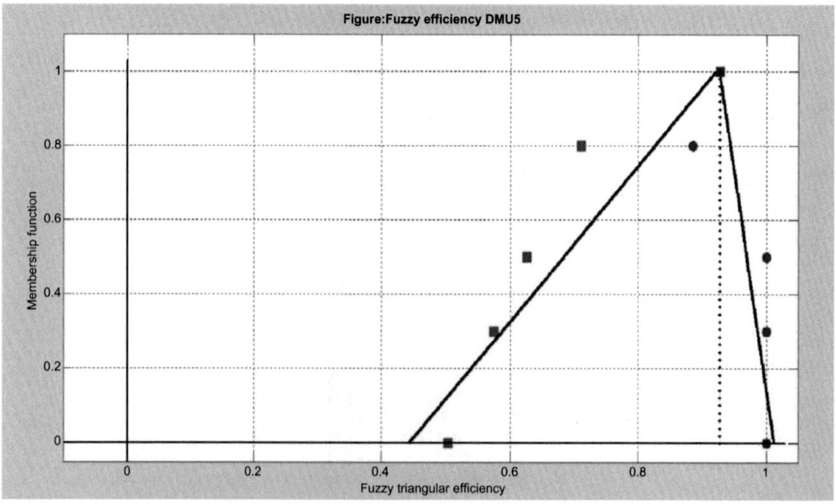

Fig. 3.14 The membership function of FDMU 5 of Example 3.3.

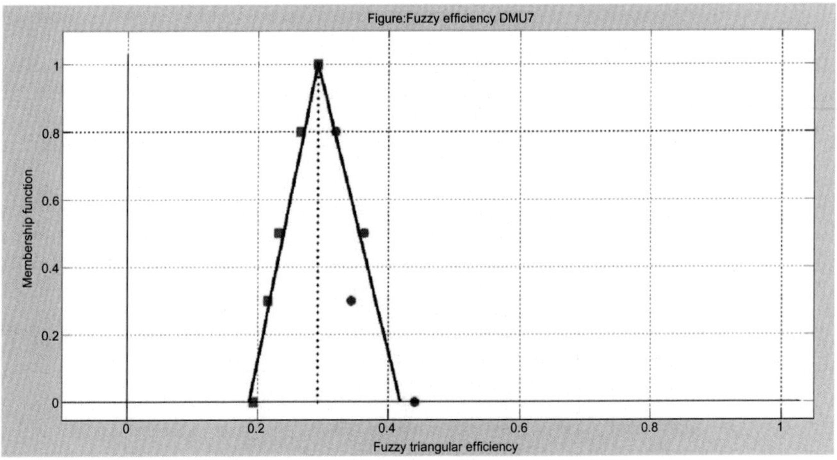

Fig. 3.15 The membership function of FDMU 7 of Example 3.3.

$$\tilde{\theta}_2 = \begin{cases} \mathbf{0.0969}x + \mathbf{0.9059} & \mathbf{0.9059} \leq x \leq 1 \\ 1 & x = 1 \\ 1 \quad 1 \leq x \leq 1 \end{cases}$$

$$\tilde{\theta}_5 = \begin{cases} \mathbf{0.4776}x + \mathbf{0.4439} & \mathbf{0.4439} \leq x \leq \mathbf{0.9263} \\ 1 & x = \mathbf{0.9263} \\ -\mathbf{0.0864}x + 1.0127 & \mathbf{0.9263} \leq x \leq 1.0127 \end{cases}$$

$$\tilde{\theta}_7 = \begin{cases} \mathbf{0.1054}x + \mathbf{0.1876} & \mathbf{0.1876} \leq x \leq \mathbf{0.2933} \\ 1 & x = \mathbf{0.2933} \\ -\mathbf{0.1260}x + \mathbf{0.4191} & \mathbf{0.2933} \leq x \leq \mathbf{0.4191} \end{cases}$$

Hybrid pointwise method

Assume n FDMUs with inputs of $\tilde{X}_j = \left(\left(x_{1j}^L, x_{1j}^C, x_{1j}^U\right), \left(x_{2j}^L, x_{2j}^C, x_{2j}^U\right), \ldots, \left(x_{mj}^L, x_{mj}^C, x_{mj}^U\right)\right)$ and outputs of $\tilde{Y}_j = \left(\left(y_{1j}^L, y_{1j}^C, y_{1j}^U\right), \left(y_{2j}^L, y_{2j}^C, y_{2j}^U\right), \ldots, \left(y_{mj}^L, y_{mj}^C, y_{mj}^U\right)\right)$, considering the constant returns to scale, the fuzzy production possibility set is $\tilde{T}_{CCR} = \left\{ \left(\tilde{X}, \tilde{Y}\right) \middle| \tilde{X} \gtrsim \sum_{j=1}^{n} \lambda_j \tilde{X}_j, \tilde{Y} \lesssim \sum_{j=1}^{n} \lambda_j \tilde{Y}_j, \lambda_j \geq 0, j = 1, \ldots n \right\}$

and assuming the variable returns to scale, the fuzzy production possibility set is as follows:

$$\tilde{T}_{BCC} = \left\{ (\tilde{X}, \tilde{Y}) | \tilde{X} \tilde{\geq} \sum_{j=1}^{n} \lambda_j \tilde{X}_j, \tilde{Y} \tilde{\leq} \sum_{j=1}^{n} \lambda_j \tilde{Y}_j, \sum_{j=1}^{n} \lambda_j = 1, \lambda_j \geq 0, \right.$$
$$\left. j = 1, \cdots, n \right\}$$

First, consider the uniform set of cuts $\Delta = \{\alpha_1, \alpha_2, \ldots, \alpha_P\}$ where $1 = \alpha_1 > \alpha_2 > \ldots > \alpha_P = 0$. Then the fuzzy efficiency of DMU_O is defined as $\tilde{\theta}_O = \{(\theta_{O1}^{\alpha_1}, \theta_{O2}^{\alpha_1}, \theta_{O3}^{\alpha_1}, \theta_{O4}^{\alpha_1}, \alpha_1), (\theta_{O1}^{\alpha_2}, \theta_{O2}^{\alpha_2}, \theta_{O3}^{\alpha_2}, \theta_{O4}^{\alpha_2}, \alpha_2), \ldots, (\theta_{O1}^{\alpha_P}, \theta_{O2}^{\alpha_P}, \theta_{O3}^{\alpha_P}, \theta_{O4}^{\alpha_P} \alpha_P)\}$ where $(\theta_{O1}^{\alpha_k}, \theta_{O2}^{\alpha_k}, \theta_{O3}^{\alpha_k}, \theta_{O4}^{\alpha_k})$ is the efficiency of DMU_O at α_k-cut, which is obtained by the CCR and BCC models in the following. For obtaining $(\theta_{O1}^{\alpha_k}, \theta_{O2}^{\alpha_k}, \theta_{O3}^{\alpha_k}, \theta_{O4}^{\alpha_k})$ by the CCR model, the α-cut of $\tilde{T}_{CCR}$ is obtained as $\left[\tilde{T}_{CCR}\right]_{\alpha_k} = \left\{ \left([\underline{X}, \overline{X}]_{\alpha_k}, [\underline{Y}, \overline{Y}]_{\alpha_k} \right) \middle| [\underline{X}, \overline{X}]_{\alpha_k} \tilde{\geq} \sum_{j=1}^{n} \lambda_j \left[\underline{X}_j, \overline{X}_j\right]_{\alpha_k}, \right.$ $[\underline{Y}, \overline{Y}]_{\alpha_k} \tilde{\leq} \sum_{j=1}^{n} \lambda_j \left[\underline{Y}_j, \overline{Y}_j\right]_{\alpha_k}, \lambda_j \geq 0, \left. j = 1, \ldots, n \right\}$ and then the following possibility sets are obtained.

$$T_{\alpha_k}^1 = \left\{ (X, Y) \middle| X \geq \sum_{j=1}^{n} \lambda_j \overline{X}_j, \ Y \leq \sum_{j=1}^{n} \lambda_j \underline{Y}_j, \ \lambda_j \geq 0, \ j = 1, \ldots, n \right\}$$

$$T_{\alpha_k}^2 = \left\{ (X, Y) \middle| X \geq \sum_{j=1}^{n} \lambda_j \underline{X}_j, \ Y \leq \sum_{j=1}^{n} \lambda_j \overline{Y}_j, \ \lambda_j \geq 0, \ j = 1, \ldots, n \right\}$$

$$T_{\alpha_k}^3 = \left\{ (X, Y) \middle| X \tilde{\geq} \sum_{j=1}^{n} \lambda_j \underline{X}_j, \ Y \tilde{\leq} \sum_{j=1}^{n} \lambda_j \underline{Y}_j, \ \lambda_j \geq 0, \ j = 1, \ldots, n \right\}$$

$$T_{\alpha_k}^4 = \left\{ (X, Y) \middle| X \tilde{\geq} \sum_{j=1}^{n} \lambda_j \overline{X}_j, \ Y \tilde{\leq} \sum_{j=1}^{n} \lambda_j \overline{Y}_j, \ \lambda_j \geq 0, \ j = 1, \ldots, n \right\}$$

Also for obtaining $(\theta_{O1}^{\alpha_k}, \theta_{O2}^{\alpha_k}, \theta_{O3}^{\alpha_k}, \theta_{O4}^{\alpha_k})$ by the BCC model, the α-cut of $\tilde{T}_{BCC}$ is obtained as $\left[\tilde{T}_{BCC}\right]_{\alpha_k} = \left\{ \left([\underline{X}, \overline{X}]_{\alpha_k}, [\underline{Y}, \overline{Y}]_{\alpha_k} \right) \middle| [\underline{X}, \overline{X}]_{\alpha_k} \tilde{\geq} \sum_{j=1}^{n} \lambda_j \right.$

$$\left[\underline{X}_j, \overline{X}_j\right]_{\alpha_k}, [\underline{Y}, \overline{Y}]_{\alpha_k} \tilde{\leq} \sum_{j=1}^{n} \lambda_j \left[\underline{Y}_j, \overline{Y}_j\right]_{\alpha_k}, \sum_{j=1}^{n} \lambda_j = 1, \lambda_j \geq 0, \ j = 1, \ldots, n.\}$$ and

then the following possibility sets are obtained.

$$T^1_{\alpha_k} = \left\{ (X, Y) \middle| X \geq \sum_{j=1}^{n} \lambda_j \overline{X}_j, Y \leq \sum_{j=1}^{n} \lambda_j \underline{Y}_j, \lambda_j \geq 0, \sum_{j=1}^{n} \lambda_j = 1, j = 1, \ldots, n \right\}$$

$$T^2_{\alpha_k} = \left\{ (X, Y) \middle| X \geq \sum_{j=1}^{n} \lambda_j \underline{X}_j, Y \leq \sum_{j=1}^{n} \lambda_j \overline{Y}_j, \lambda_j \geq 0, \sum_{j=1}^{n} \lambda_j = 1, j = 1, \ldots, n \right\}$$

$$T^3_{\alpha_k} = \left\{ (X, Y) \middle| X \tilde{\geq} \sum_{j=1}^{n} \lambda_j \underline{X}_j, Y \tilde{\leq} \sum_{j=1}^{n} \lambda_j \underline{Y}_j, \lambda_j \geq 0, \sum_{j=1}^{n} \lambda_j = 1, j = 1, \ldots, n \right\}$$

$$T^4_{\alpha_k} = \left\{ (X, Y) \middle| X \tilde{\geq} \sum_{j=1}^{n} \lambda_j \overline{X}_j, Y \tilde{\leq} \sum_{j=1}^{n} \lambda_j \overline{Y}_j, \lambda_j \geq 0, \sum_{j=1}^{n} \lambda_j = 1, \ j = 1, \ldots, n \right\}$$

Then, using the BCC and CCR models at α_k-cut,

- The optimistic value of the relative efficiency of $FDMU_o$ ($\theta^{\alpha_k}_{O1}$) is obtained by solving Min θ subject to $(\theta \underline{X}_o, \overline{Y}_o) \in T^1_{\alpha_k}$,
- The pessimistic value of the relative efficiency of $FDMU_o$ ($\theta^{\alpha_k}_{O2}$) is obtained by solving Min θ subject to $(\theta \overline{X}_o, \underline{Y}_o) \in T^2_{\alpha_k}$,
- The realistic values of the relative efficiency of $FDMU_o$ ($\theta^{\alpha_k}_{O3}$, $\theta^{\alpha_k}_{O4}$) are obtained by solving Min θ subject to $(\theta \underline{X}_o, \underline{Y}_o) \in T^3_{\alpha_k}$ and Min θ subject to $(\theta \overline{X}_o, \overline{Y}_o) \in T^4_{\alpha_k}$, respectively.

Here, the value $\begin{pmatrix} [\tilde{X}_O]_{\alpha_k} \\ [\tilde{Y}_O]_{\alpha_k} \end{pmatrix} = \begin{pmatrix} ([\underline{x}_{1O}, \overline{x}_{1O}], [\underline{x}_{2O}, \overline{x}_{2O}], \ldots, [\underline{x}_{mO}, \overline{x}_{mO}]) \\ ([\underline{y}_{1O}, \overline{y}_{1O}], [\underline{y}_{2O}, \overline{y}_{2O}], \ldots, [\underline{y}_{rO}, \overline{y}_{rO}]) \end{pmatrix}$ can be obtained easily. Finally, by calculating $\theta^{\alpha_k}_{O1}$, $\theta^{\alpha_k}_{O2}$, $\theta^{\alpha_k}_{O3}$, $\theta^{\alpha_k}_{O4}$ in the cut values α_1, α_2, …, α_P, the set of fuzzy efficiency of $\tilde{\theta}_O = \{(\theta^{\alpha_1}_{O1}, \theta^{\alpha_1}_{O2}, \theta^{\alpha_1}_{O3}, \theta^{\alpha_1}_{O4}, \alpha_1), (\theta^{\alpha_2}_{O1}, \theta^{\alpha_2}_{O2}, \theta^{\alpha_2}_{O3}, \theta^{\alpha_2}_{O4}, \alpha_2), \ldots, (\theta^{\alpha_P}_{O1}, \theta^{\alpha_P}_{O2}, \theta^{\alpha_P}_{O3}, \theta^{\alpha_P}_{O4}, \alpha_P)\}$ is obtained for $FDMU_o$.

Now, for calculating the triangular fuzzy efficiency of FDMUs, first by considering $(\theta^{\alpha_k}_{O1}, \theta^{\alpha_k}_{O2}, \theta^{\alpha_k}_{O3}, \theta^{\alpha_k}_{O4})$ for $FDMU_O$ in α_k-cut, the following arrangement is done.

$$\{\theta^{\alpha_k}_{O1}, \theta^{\alpha_k}_{O2}, \theta^{\alpha_k}_{O3}, \theta^{\alpha_k}_{O4}\} = \{\theta'^{\alpha_k}_{O1}, \theta'^{\alpha_k}_{O2}, \theta'^{\alpha_k}_{O3}, \theta'^{\alpha_k}_{O4}\}$$
$$\theta'^{\alpha_k}_{O1} \leq \theta'^{\alpha_k}_{O2} \leq \theta'^{\alpha_k}_{O3} \leq \theta'^{\alpha_k}_{O4}$$

Then, the lower and upper indices of $FDMU_O$ in α_k-cut are obtained as follows,

$$DMU_O \quad ---\rightarrow \quad \left[\underline{\theta}_{O1}^{\alpha_k}, \overline{\theta}_O^{\alpha_k}\right] \quad 1 < k < P$$

$$\underline{\theta}_O^{\alpha_k} = \delta_1 \theta_{O1}'^{\alpha_k} + \delta_2 \theta_{O2}'^{\alpha_k} + \delta_3 \theta_{O3}'^{\alpha_k} + \delta_4 \theta_{O4}'^{\alpha_k} \quad \delta_1 + \delta_2 + \delta_3 + \delta_4 = 1,$$
$$1 > \delta_1 > \delta_2 > \delta_3 > \delta_4 > 0$$

$$\overline{\theta}_O^{\alpha_k} = \gamma_1 \theta_{O1}'^{\alpha_k} + \gamma_2 \theta_{O2}'^{\alpha_k} + \gamma_3 \theta_{O3}'^{\alpha_k} + \gamma_4 \theta_{O4}'^{\alpha_k} \quad \gamma_1 + \gamma_2 + \gamma_3 + \gamma_4 = 1,$$
$$1 > \gamma_4 > \gamma_3 > \gamma_2 > \gamma_1 > 0$$

Finally, by solving the below model, an estimation of the triangular fuzzy efficiency $\tilde{\theta}_O = \left(\underline{\theta}_O, \theta_O, \overline{\theta}_O\right)$ from the data $\begin{pmatrix}\underline{\theta}_O^{\alpha_1} \\ \alpha_1\end{pmatrix}, \begin{pmatrix}\underline{\theta}_O^{\alpha_2} \\ \alpha_2\end{pmatrix}, \cdots, \begin{pmatrix}\underline{\theta}_O^{\alpha_P} \\ \alpha_P\end{pmatrix}, \begin{pmatrix}\overline{\theta}_O^{\alpha_1} \\ \alpha_1\end{pmatrix}, \begin{pmatrix}\overline{\theta}_O^{\alpha_2} \\ \alpha_2\end{pmatrix}, \cdots, \begin{pmatrix}\overline{\theta}_O^{\alpha_P} \\ \alpha_P\end{pmatrix}$ is obtained for $FDMU_O$.

$$\begin{aligned}
&\text{Min} \quad \text{Max}\left\{\left|\underline{\theta}_O^{\alpha_1} + b\alpha_1 + c\right|, \left|\underline{\theta}_O^{\alpha_2} + b\alpha_2 + c\right|, \cdots, \left|\underline{\theta}_O^{\alpha_P} + b\alpha_P + c\right|,\right. \\
&\left.\left|\overline{\theta}_O^{\alpha_1} + b'\alpha_1 + c'\right|, \left|\overline{\theta}_O^{\alpha_2} + b'\alpha_2 + c'\right|, \cdots, \left|\overline{\theta}_O^{\alpha_P} + b'\alpha_P + c'\right|\right\} \text{ subject to} \\
&b + c - b' - c' = 0 \\
&b < 0 \\
&b' > 0
\end{aligned} \tag{3.35}$$

As the optimal solution of the model (3.35), the values of b, c, b', c' are obtained and are used to calculate the triangular fuzzy efficiency $\tilde{\theta}_O = \left(\underline{\theta}_O = -c, \theta_O = -b - c, \overline{\theta}_O = -c'\right)$. As the model (3.35) is nonlinear, its linear form will be as follows,

$$\begin{aligned}
&\text{Min} \quad \Delta \\
&\text{subject to} \\
&-\Delta \le \underline{\theta}_O^{\alpha_t} + b\alpha_t + c \le \Delta \quad 1 \le t \le P \\
&-\Delta \le \overline{\theta}_O^{\alpha_t} + b'\alpha_t + c' \le \Delta \quad 1 \le t \le P \\
&b + c - b' - c' = 0 \\
&b < 0 \\
&b' > 0
\end{aligned}$$

$$
\begin{aligned}
&\text{Min } \Delta \\
&\text{subject to} \\
&-\Delta \leq \underline{\theta}_O^{\alpha_t} + b\alpha_t + c \leq \Delta \quad 1 \leq t \leq P \\
&-\Delta \leq \overline{\theta}_O^{\alpha_t} + b'\alpha_t + c' \leq \Delta \quad 1 \leq t \leq P \\
&b + c - b' - c' = 0 \\
&b < 0 \\
&b' > 0
\end{aligned}
$$

Example 3.4 Considering 10 *FDMU*, each with two inputs and one output, with the data of Table 3.8, the aim is to obtain the triangular fuzzy efficiency values of FDMUs 4, 5, and 6.

Based on the hybrid pointwise method, first the set of cut values $\Delta = \{1, 0.8, 0.5, 0.3, 0\}$ is determined. Then, in each cut of the fuzzy set $\tilde{T}_{BCC}$, the optimistic, pessimistic, and realistic values of the relative efficiency of the FDMUs are obtained and shown in Tables 3.9–3.11.

Table 3.8 Inputs and output of Example 3.4.

DMU	x_1^L	x_1^C	x_1^U	x_2^L	x_2^C	x_2^U	y_1^L	y_1^C	y_1^U
1	108	100	94	188	180	172	54	50	48
2	158	150	142	286	270	264	182	180	176
3	266	260	258	354	350	340	240	230	224
4	520	450	448	600	550	548	240	240	180
5	208	200	192	260	250	245	160	120	115
6	460	400	350	380	350	320	180	150	140
7	564	550	542	664	650	642	100	100	100
8	752	740	730	758	750	740	130	120	110
9	512	500	494	750	740	728	38	30	26
10	616	600	580	862	850	840	50	40	32

Table 3.9 The optimistic, pessimistic, and realistic values of the relative efficiency of $FDMU_4$.

α_k	$\theta_{41}^{\alpha_k}$	$\theta_{42}^{\alpha_k}$	$\theta_{43}^{\alpha_k}$	$\theta_{44}^{\alpha_k}$
$\alpha_1 = 1$	1	1	1	1
$\alpha_2 = 0.8$	1	0.6104651	0.6308635	1
$\alpha_3 = 0.5$	1	0.5371981	0.5791235	1
$\alpha_4 = 0.3$	1	0.4937588	0.5447326	1
$\alpha_5 = 0$	1	0.5699971	1	1

Table 3.10 The optimistic, pessimistic, and realistic values of the relative efficiency of $FDMU_5$.

α_k	$\theta_{51}^{\alpha_k}$	$\theta_{52}^{\alpha_k}$	$\theta_{53}^{\alpha_k}$	$\theta_{54}^{\alpha_k}$
$\alpha_1=1$	0.9138462	0.9138462	0.9138462	0.9138462
$\alpha_2=0.8$	0.9518568	0.8967127	0.9108781	0.9371595
$\alpha_3=0.5$	1	0.8713938	0.9063503	0.9730354
$\alpha_4=0.3$	1	0.8547609	0.9032805	0.9975516
$\alpha_5=0$	1	0.8301683	0.8985969	1

Table 3.11 The optimistic, pessimistic, and realistic values of the relative efficiency of $FDMU_6$.

α_k	$\theta_{61}^{\alpha_k}$	$\theta_{62}^{\alpha_k}$	$\theta_{63}^{\alpha_k}$	$\theta_{64}^{\alpha_k}$
$\alpha_1=1$	0.7120879	0.7120879	0.7120879	0.7120879
$\alpha_2=0.8$	0.7465188	0.6915730	0.7181309	0.7189728
$\alpha_3=0.5$	0.8015735	0.6619306	0.7275252	0.7297016
$\alpha_4=0.3$	0.8407021	0.6428785	0.7340213	0.7371125
$\alpha_5=0$	0.9114583	0.6084906	0.7441406	0.7460526

Then, by determining the weight values $\gamma_4=\delta_1=0.65 \quad \gamma_3=\delta_2=0.2 \quad \gamma_2=\delta_3=0.1 \quad \gamma_1=\delta_4=0.05$, the lower and upper indices of the relative efficiency of the FDMUs are calculated as follows,

$$\underline{\theta}_O^{\alpha_k} = 0.65\theta'^{\alpha_k}_{O1} + 0.2\theta'^{\alpha_k}_{O2} + 0.1\delta_3\theta'^{\alpha_k}_{O3} + 0.05\delta_4\theta'^{\alpha_k}_{O4}$$
$$\overline{\theta}_O^{\alpha_k} = 0.05\theta'^{\alpha_k}_{O1} + 0.1\theta'^{\alpha_k}_{O2} + 0.2\theta'^{\alpha_k}_{O3} + 0.65\theta'^{\alpha_k}_{O4}$$

The lower and upper indices of the relative efficiency of the FDMUs are obtained and shown in Table 3.12.

Finally, using the data of the example, the triangular fuzzy efficiency of the FDMUs are estimated by the model (3.35) and reported by Table 3.13.

The results obtained for Example 3.4 also are depicted by Figs. 3.16–3.24 schematically.

Table 3.12 The values of lower and upper indices for the FDMUs of Example 3.4.

	DMU₄		*DMU₅*		*DMU₆*	
α_k	$\underline{\theta}_4^{\alpha_k}$	$\overline{\theta}_4^{\alpha_k}$	$\underline{\theta}_5^{\alpha_k}$	$\overline{\theta}_5^{\alpha_k}$	$\underline{\theta}_6^{\alpha_k}$	$\overline{\theta}_6^{\alpha_k}$
$\alpha_1=1$	1	1	0.913846	0.913846	0.712088	0.712088
$\alpha_2=0.8$	0.672975	0.94361	0.906348	0.942062	0.702372	0.735424
$\alpha_3=0.5$	0.615003	0.934772	0.89498	0.978812	0.688809	0.772812
$\alpha_4=0.3$	0.57989	0.929161	0.886006	0.982576	0.680422	0.799425
$\alpha_5=0$	0.720498	0.9785	0.869329	0.981368	0.664525	0.846497

Table 3.13 The estimation of the triangular fuzzy efficiency of the FDMUs of Example 3.4.

	Triangular fuzzy efficiency
DMU_4	$\tilde{\theta}_4 = (0.5181739, 0.9645806, 0.9645806)$
DMU_5	$\tilde{\theta}_5 = (0.869329, 0.913846, 0.981368)$
DMU_6	$\tilde{\theta}_6 = (0.6645250, 0.712088, 0.8464970)$

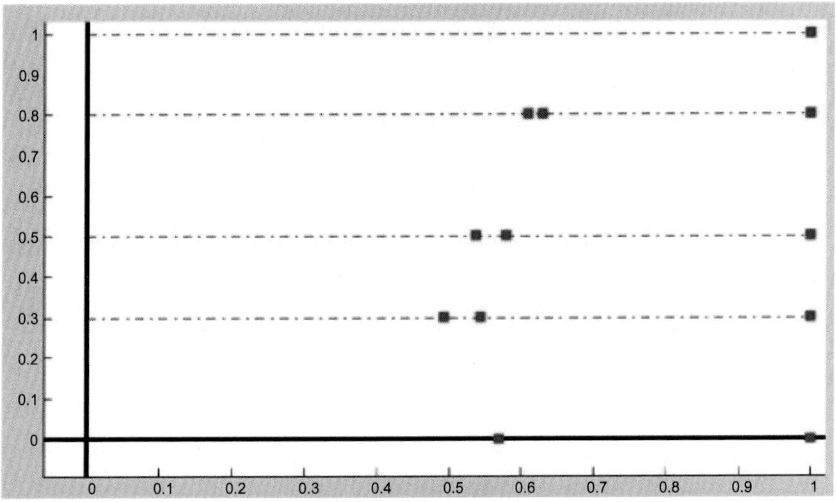

Fig. 3.16 The optimistic, pessimistic, and realistic values of the relative efficiency of $FDMU_4$.

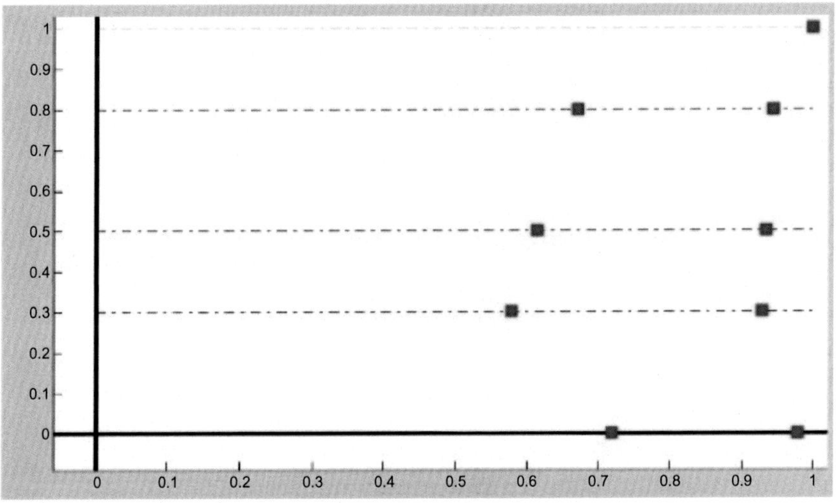

Fig. 3.17 The values of lower and upper indices for $FDMU_4$.

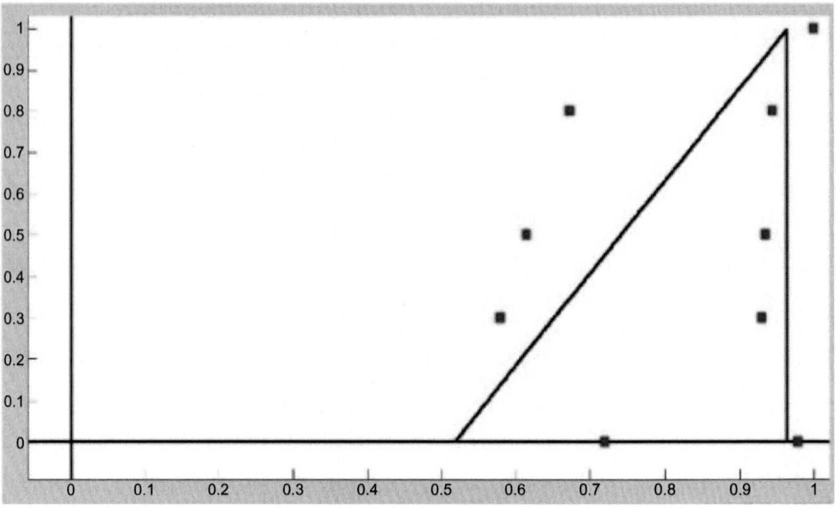

Fig. 3.18 The estimation of the triangular fuzzy efficiency of $FDMU_4$.

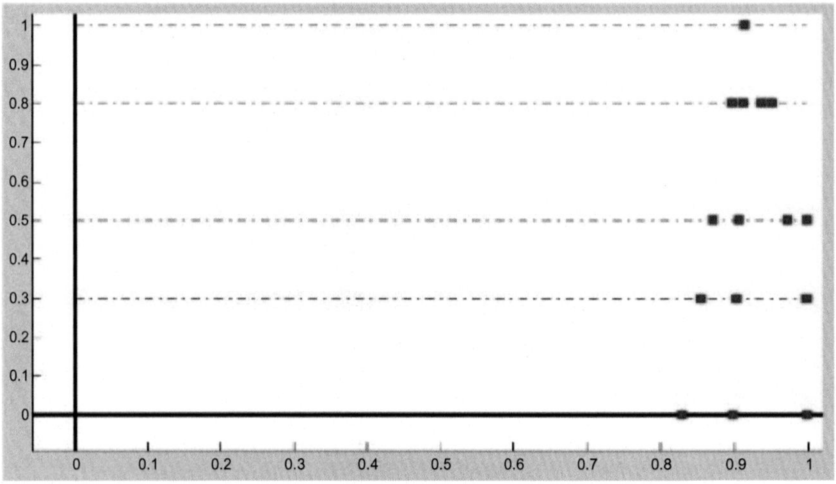

Fig. 3.19 The optimistic, pessimistic, and realistic values of the relative efficiency of $FDMU_5$.

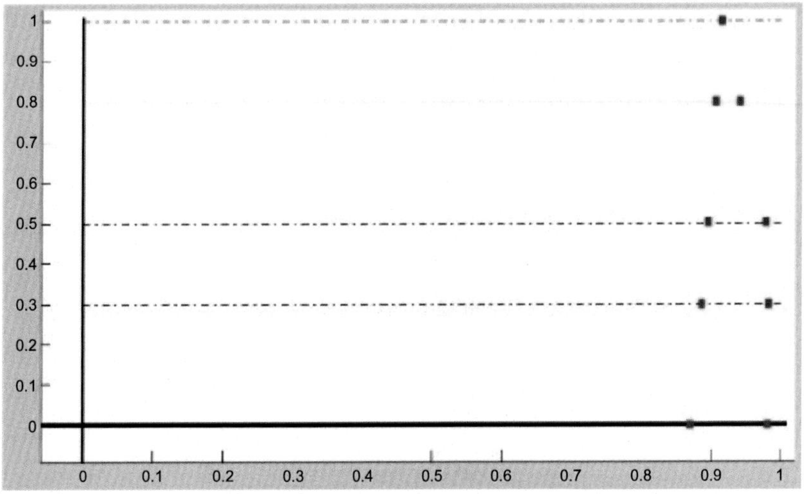

Fig. 3.20 The values of lower and upper indices for $FDMU_5$.

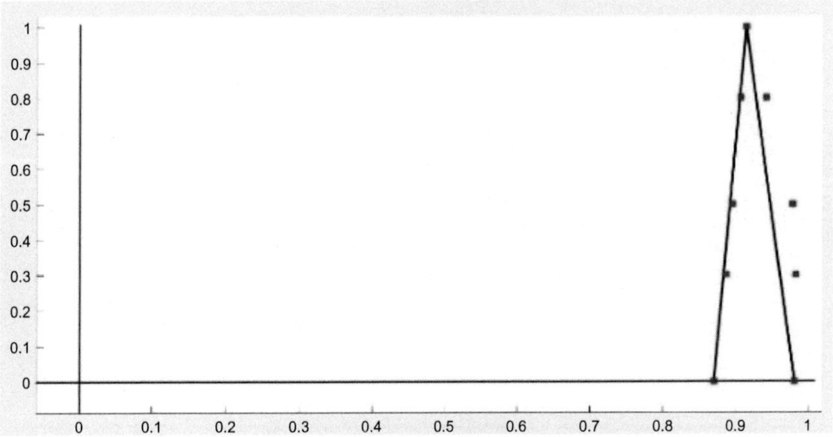

Fig. 3.21 The estimation of the triangular fuzzy efficiency of $FDMU_5$.

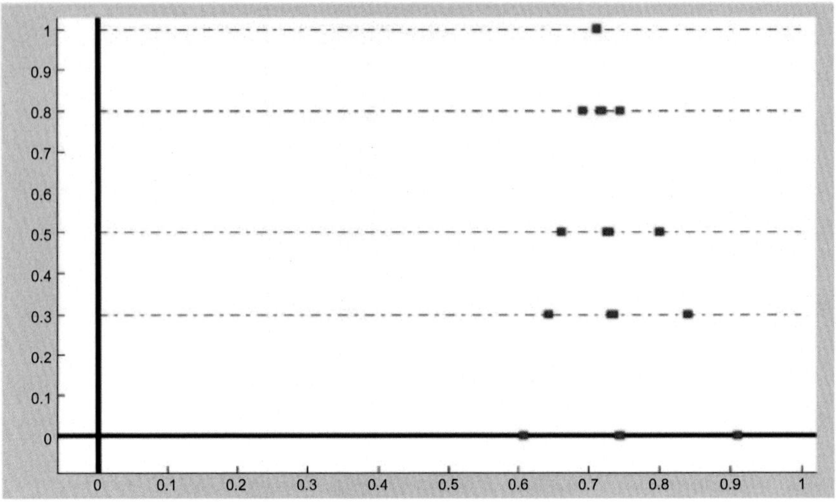

Fig. 3.22 The optimistic, pessimistic, and realistic values of the relative efficiency of $FDMU_6$.

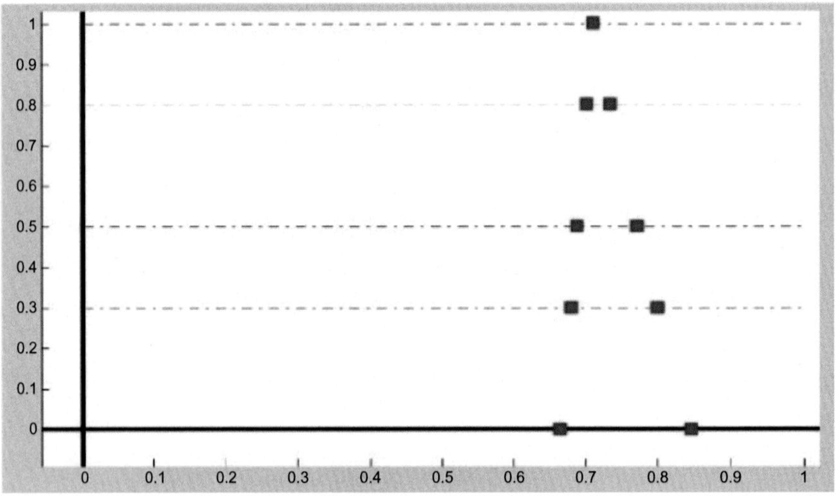

Fig. 3.23 The values of lower and upper indices for $FDMU_6$.

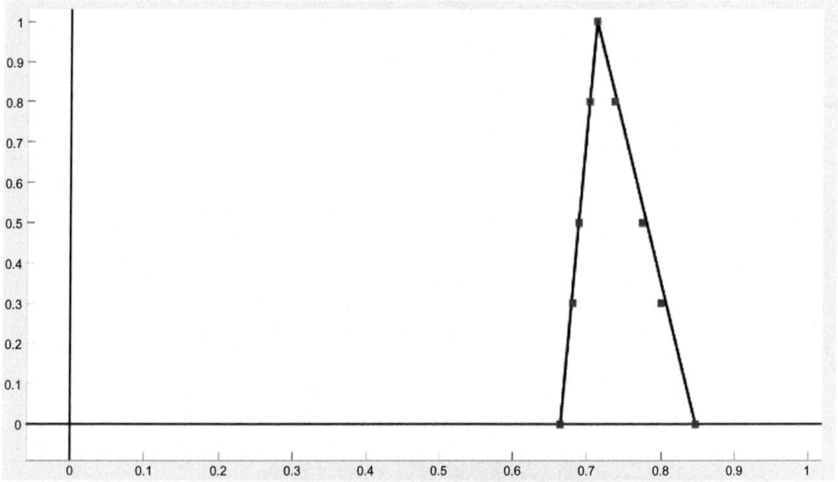

Fig. 3.24 The estimation of the triangular fuzzy efficiency of $FDMU_6$.

3.4.2 Extension principle based solution approach

This approach is based on Zadeh's extension principle. Considering the model (3.2) and assuming that the fuzzy efficiency ($\tilde{\theta}$) of $FDMU_o$ is obtained by the function f as follows where $\tilde{x}_j (j = 1, \ldots, n)$ are the input, $\tilde{y}_j (j = 1, \ldots, n)$ are the output, and $\tilde{u}_r, \tilde{v}_i (r = 1, 2, \ldots, s, \quad i = 1, 2, \ldots, m)$ are the coefficients.

$$\tilde{\theta} = f(\tilde{x}_{11}, \tilde{x}_{12}, \cdots, \tilde{x}_{mn}, \tilde{y}_{11}, \tilde{y}_{12}, \cdots, \tilde{y}_{sn}, \tilde{v}_1, \tilde{v}_2, \cdots, \tilde{v}_m, \tilde{u}_1, \tilde{u}_2, \cdots, \tilde{u}_s)$$

$$\begin{aligned}\tilde{\theta} = \Big\{ (t, \mu_{\tilde{\theta}}(t) | t = f(x_{11}, x_{12}, \cdots, x_{mn}, y_{11}, y_{12}, \cdots, y_{sn}, v_1, v_2, \cdots, v_m, u_1, u_2, \cdots, u_s) \\ \wp x_{11} \in S(\tilde{x}_{11}), x_{12} \in S(\tilde{x}_{12}), \cdots, x_{mn} \in S(\tilde{x}_{mn}), \\ y_{11} \in S(\tilde{y}_{11}), y_{12} \in S(\tilde{y}_{12}), \cdots, y_{sn} \in S(\tilde{y}_{sn}), \\ v_1 \in S(\tilde{v}_1), v_2 \in S(\tilde{v}_2), \cdots, v_1 \in S(\tilde{v}_m), u_1 \in S(\tilde{u}_1), u_2 \in S(\tilde{u}_2), \cdots u_s \in S(\tilde{u}_s) \}\end{aligned}$$

And the membership functions are defined as follows,

$$\mu_{\tilde{\theta}}(t) = \begin{cases} \sup\limits_{\substack{x_{11}, x_{12}, \cdots, x_{mn}, y_{11}, y_{12}, \cdots, \\ y_{sn}, v_1, v_2, \cdots, v_m, u_1, u_2, \cdots, u_s \\ t = f(x_{11}, x_{12}, \cdots, x_{mn}, y_{11}, y_{12}, \cdots,) \\ (y_{sn}, v_1, v_2, \cdots, v_m, u_1, u_2, \cdots, u_s)}} \left(\min\left\{ \mu_{\tilde{A}_1}(x_1), \ldots, \mu_{\tilde{A}_n}(x_n) \right\} \right) & f^{-1}(t) \neq \varnothing \\ 0 & f^{-1}(t) = \varnothing \end{cases}$$

This method is suitable to calculate and describe the fuzzy efficiency according to the fuzzy inputs and outputs, but it is notable that its application to a real case problem or a large DEA problem may be difficult and complex. This complexity is because that it is almost impossible to find all cases of the support of the fuzzy efficiency value.

Allahviranloo, Hosseinzadeh Lotfi, and AdabitabarFirozja (2012) introduced a new method based on the extension principle to evaluate FDMUs. This method is described by the rest of this subsection.

Definition 3.3 The α-cut of fuzzy number $\tilde{A}$ is defined as follows,

$$[\tilde{A}]^{\alpha} = [A^{l\alpha}, A^{u\alpha}]$$

where, $A^{l\alpha} = \min\{x \in X : \mu_{\tilde{A}}(x) \geq \alpha\}$ and $A^{u\alpha} = \max\{x \in X : \mu_{\tilde{A}}(x) \geq \alpha\}$.

Further, assume that S is a set of vectors in which,

$$\forall X \in S;\ \ X \geq \overline{X} \Leftrightarrow \overline{X} = \min S$$

$$FPPS^{\beta} = \left\{(X, Y) \middle| \left((X, Y), \mu_{\tilde{p}}(X, Y)\right) \in \tilde{P}, \mu_{\tilde{p}}(X, Y) \geq \beta\right\} = [\tilde{P}]^{\beta}$$

Definition 3.4 The FPPS for n FDMUs with fuzzy inputs of $\tilde{X}_j$ ($j=1, \ldots, n$), fuzzy outputs of $\tilde{Y}_j$ ($j=1, \ldots, n$), and membership functions of $\mu_{\tilde{x}_{ij}}$ and $\mu_{\tilde{y}_{rj}}$, respectively, is defined as follows,

$$\tilde{P} = \left\{(X, Y), \mu_{\tilde{p}}(X, Y) | X \in \Re^m, Y \in \Re^s\right\}$$

$$Y = (y_1, \ldots, y_r), \left(y_r, \mu_{\tilde{y}_r}(y_i)\right) \in \tilde{y}_r \qquad r = 1, \ldots, s$$

$$X = (x_1, \ldots, x_m), \left(x_1, \mu_{\tilde{x}_i}(x_i)\right) \in \tilde{x}_i \qquad i = 1, \ldots, m$$

The input-oriented CCR model for $FDMU_o$ is defined as follows,

$$\mu_{\tilde{p}}(X, Y) = \text{Max} \quad \min_{\lambda_j > \text{o}} \left\{\mu_{\tilde{x}_{lj}}(x_{lj}), \ldots, \mu_{\tilde{x}_{mj}}(x_{mj}), \mu_{\tilde{y}_{lj}}(x_{lj}), \ldots, \mu_{\tilde{y}_{sj}}(x_{sj})\right\}$$

subject to

$$X \geq \sum_{j=1}^{n} \lambda_j X_j$$

$$Y \geq \sum_{j=1}^{n} \lambda_j Y_j$$

$$\lambda_j \geq 0 \qquad j = 1, 2, \ldots n$$

$$(X_j, Y_j) \in \text{supp}(\tilde{X}_j, \tilde{Y}_j) \qquad j = 1, 2, \ldots, n$$

Accordingly, the following model for calculating the efficiency value is defined,

Max $\tilde{\theta}$

subject to

$(\tilde{\theta}\tilde{X}_\circ, \tilde{Y}_\circ) \in \tilde{P}$

where,

$$\left(\tilde{\theta}\tilde{X}_\circ, \tilde{Y}_\circ\right)\in\tilde{P} \Leftrightarrow \begin{cases} \left[\left(\tilde{\theta}\tilde{X}_\circ, \tilde{Y}_\circ\right)\right]^\alpha \subseteq \left[\tilde{P}\right]^\beta \\ \circ < \alpha \leq 1 \\ \circ < \beta \leq 1 \\ (X_\circ, Y_\circ)\in\left[\tilde{P}\right]^\beta \text{ for any } (X_\circ, Y_\circ)\in\left[\left(\tilde{X}_\circ, \tilde{Y}_\circ\right)\right]^\alpha \end{cases}$$

Assuming $\left[\tilde{\theta}\right]^\alpha = [E_1, E_2]$, the $\theta^{l.\alpha}$ is considered as the efficiency value with maximum input and minimum output, and, $\theta^{u\alpha}$ is considered as the efficiency value with minimum input and maximum output. Therefore,

$$E_1 = \min\left\{\theta\middle|(\theta X_\circ, Y_\circ)\in\left[\tilde{P}\right]^\beta, \theta\in\left[\tilde{\theta}\right]^\alpha, X_\circ\in\left[\tilde{X}_\circ\right]^\alpha, Y_\circ\in\left[\tilde{Y}_\circ\right]^\alpha\right\} = \theta^{l\alpha}$$

$$E_2 = \max\left\{\theta\middle|(\theta X_\circ, Y_\circ)\in\left[\tilde{P}\right]^\beta, \theta\in\left[\tilde{\theta}\right]^\alpha, X_\circ\in\left[\tilde{X}_\circ\right]^\alpha, Y_\circ\in\left[\tilde{Y}_\circ\right]^\alpha\right\} = \theta^{u\alpha}$$

where,

$$\left(\tilde{\theta}\tilde{X}_\circ, \tilde{Y}_\circ\right)\in\tilde{P} \Leftrightarrow \begin{cases} \left(\theta^{l\alpha}X_\circ^{u\alpha}, Y_\circ^{l\alpha}\right)\in\left[\tilde{P}\right]^\beta \\ \left(\theta^{u\alpha}X_\circ^{l\alpha}, Y_\circ^{u\alpha}\right)\in\left[\tilde{P}\right]^\beta \\ \left(X_\circ^{u\alpha}, Y_\circ^{l\alpha}\right)\in\left[\tilde{P}\right]^\beta \\ \left(X_\circ^{l\alpha}, Y_\circ^{u\alpha}\right)\in\left[\tilde{P}\right]^\beta \end{cases} \quad \circ < \alpha \leq 1, \ \circ < \beta \leq 1$$

If $(X_\circ, Y_\circ)\in\left[\left(\tilde{X}_\circ, \tilde{Y}_\circ\right)\right]^\alpha$ and $\mu_{\tilde{P}}(X_\circ, Y_\circ)\geq\beta$, then $\left[\tilde{\theta}\right]^{(\alpha,\beta)} = \left[\theta^{l(\alpha,\beta)}, \theta^{u(\alpha,\beta)}\right]$. Therefore, the following models are obtained.

$$\begin{aligned} &\theta^{l(\alpha,\beta)} = \text{Min } \theta \\ &\text{subject to} \\ &\theta X_\circ^{u\alpha} \geq \sum_{j=1}^{n} \lambda_j X_j \\ &Y_\circ^{l} \geq \sum_{j=1}^{n} \lambda_j Y_j \\ &X_\circ^{u\alpha} \geq \sum_{j=1}^{n} \lambda_j Y_j \\ &\lambda_j \geq \circ \qquad\qquad\qquad j = 1, \ldots, n \\ &\left(X_j, Y_j\right)\in\left[\left(\tilde{X}_j, \tilde{Y}_j\right)\right]^\beta \quad j = 1, \ldots, n \end{aligned}$$

$$
\begin{aligned}
&\theta^{u(\alpha,\beta)} = \text{Min } \theta \\
&\text{subject to} \\
&\theta X_{\circ}^{l\alpha} \geq \sum_{j=1}^{n} \lambda_j X_j \\
&Y_{\circ}^{u\alpha} \geq \sum_{j=1}^{n} \lambda_j Y_j \\
&X_{\circ}^{l\alpha} \geq \sum_{j=1}^{n} \lambda_j Y_j \\
&\lambda_j \geq \circ \qquad j = 1, \ldots, n \\
&(X_j, Y_j) \in \left[(\tilde{X}_j, \tilde{Y}_j) \right]^{\beta} \quad j = 1, \ldots, n
\end{aligned}
$$

Finally the α-cut values of the relative efficiency of $DMU_{\circ}$ are obtained by the below models.

$$
\begin{aligned}
&\theta'^{l(\alpha,\beta)} = \min \ \theta \\
&\text{subject to} \\
&\theta X_{\circ}^{l\alpha} \geq \sum_{j=1}^{n} \lambda_j X_{\circ}^{l\beta} + \sum_{j=1}^{n} \mu_j X_{\circ}^{u\beta} \\
&Y_{\circ}^{u\alpha} \geq \sum_{j=1}^{n} \lambda_j Y_{\circ}^{u\beta} + \sum_{j=1}^{n} \mu_j Y_{\circ}^{l\beta} \\
&X_{\circ}^{u\alpha} \geq \sum_{j=1}^{n} \lambda_j X_{\circ}^{l\beta} + \sum_{j=1}^{n} \mu_j X_{\circ}^{u\beta} \\
&\lambda_j \geq \circ \qquad j = 1, \ldots, n \\
&\mu_j \geq \circ \qquad j = 1, \ldots, n
\end{aligned}
\tag{3.36}
$$

$$
\begin{aligned}
&\theta'^{u(\alpha,\beta)} = \min \ \theta \\
&\text{subject to} \\
&\theta X_{\circ}^{l\alpha} \geq \sum_{j=1}^{n} \lambda_j X_{\circ}^{u\beta} + \sum_{j=1}^{n} \mu_j X_{\circ}^{l\beta} \\
&Y_{\circ}^{u\alpha} \geq \sum_{j=1}^{n} \lambda_j Y_{\circ}^{l\beta} + \sum_{j=1}^{n} \mu_j Y_{\circ}^{u\beta} \\
&X_{\circ}^{l\alpha} \geq \sum_{j=1}^{n} \lambda_j X_{\circ}^{u\beta} + \sum_{j=1}^{n} \mu_j X_{\circ}^{l\beta} \\
&\lambda_j \geq \circ \qquad j = 1, \ldots, n \\
&\mu_j \geq \circ \qquad j = 1, \ldots, n
\end{aligned}
\tag{3.37}
$$

3.4.3 Fuzzy ranking-based solution approach

A method for solving linear programming and DEA models with fuzzy-type data is to apply ranking functions of fuzzy numbers in the solution procedure. For this aim, three aspects can be considered.

- Using a comparison function as $F: F(R) \rightarrow R$ where $F(R)$ is the set of fuzzy numbers (see Allahviranloo, Abbasbandy, & Hajighasemi, 2012; Ezzati et al., 2012; Gu & Xuan, 2017).
- Determining a reference set used to compare the fuzzy values (see Kerre, 1982).
- Constructing a fuzzy relationship for comparing the fuzzy values (see Delgado et al., 1988; Koodziejczyk, 1986; Nakamura, 1986).

For solving the DEA models with fuzzy data, first by applying a suitable ranking function, the fuzzy model is converted to a crisp form. Then, the crisp form is solved by regular solution methods. Consider the following input-oriented CCR model with an envelopment form for calculating the relative efficiency of DMU_j.

$$
\begin{aligned}
&\text{Min } \tilde{\theta} \\
&\text{subject to} \\
&\sum_{j=1}^{n} \lambda_j \tilde{x}_{ij} \tilde{\leq} \tilde{\theta} \tilde{x}_{io} \qquad i = 1, 2, \ldots, m \\
&\sum_{j=1}^{n} \lambda_j \tilde{y}_{rj} \tilde{\geq} \tilde{y}_{ro} \qquad r = 1, 2, \ldots, s \\
&\lambda_j \geq 0 \qquad j = 1, 2, \ldots, n
\end{aligned}
\tag{3.38}
$$

Assuming $M: F(\mathbb{R}) \rightarrow \mathbb{R}$ as a fuzzy ranking function, the fuzzy vectors $\tilde{X}_j = \left(\tilde{x}_{1j}, \ldots, \tilde{x}_{mj}\right)$ and $\tilde{Y}_j = \left(\tilde{y}_{1j}, \ldots, \tilde{y}_{sj}\right)$ are converted to the real vectors $X_j = (x_{1j}, \ldots, x_{mj})$ and $Y_j = (y_{1j}, \ldots, y_{sj})$, respectively. Now, considering the crisp variables $\theta, \lambda_j \geq \circ, j = 1, 2, \ldots, n$ (obtained by the ranking function $M: F(\mathbb{R}) \rightarrow \mathbb{R}$), the following linear crisp model is obtained instead of the fuzzy model (3.38).

$$
\begin{aligned}
&\text{Min } Z = \theta \\
&\text{subject to} \\
&\sum_{j=1}^{n} \lambda_j x_{ij} \leq \theta x_{io} \qquad i = 1, 2, \ldots, m \\
&\sum_{j=1}^{n} \lambda_j y_{rj} \geq y_{ro} \qquad r = 1, 2, \ldots, s \\
&\lambda_j \geq 0 \qquad j = 1, 2, \ldots, n
\end{aligned}
\tag{3.39}
$$

There are some points to be highlighted in this approach:

- The results obtained by this approach highly depend on the selected ranking function.
- The optimal crisp value obtained by the model (3.39) is not necessarily equal to the value of the ranking function for the optimal solution of the model (3.38).
- The feasibility of the model (3.39) should be proved, which is not always easy.
- A shortcoming of the fuzzy ranking methods is that they assign small importance weight values to the lower and upper bounds of the support of a fuzzy number and higher weight values are assigned to the core of the support. Therefore, in the optimal solution, the values associated to the lower and upper bounds of the support become very small (almost zero). So, the models for efficiency evaluation after applying a ranking function will have crisp solutions.

A solution method using a ranking function of fuzzy numbers is presented in the rest of this section.

Allahviranloo and Adabitabar Firozja (2010) introduced a fuzzy norm of two fuzzy vectors as follows,

$$d_{TMI}^{(p)}([a,b],[c,d]) = \|(a-b-c-d)x+b-d\|_p$$

where $\|Y\|_p$ is the norm p of crisp values and the difference of $[a,b]$ and the origin $[0,0]$ is defined as $d_{TMI}^{(p)}([a,b]) = \|ax+b(1-x)\|_p$.

Definition 3.5 A meter between two fuzzy numbers is defined as follows,

$$d_{TMF}^{(p)}(\tilde{A},\tilde{B},s) = \frac{\int_0^1 s(\alpha)d_{TMI}^{(p)}([A]^\alpha,[B]^\alpha)d\alpha}{\int_0^1 s(\alpha)d\alpha}$$

where s is a continuous and positive weight function on $[0,1]$. Also, the absolute value of $\tilde{A}$, which means the meter between $\tilde{A}$ and the origin, is defined as follows.

$$d_{TMF}^{(p)}(\tilde{A},s) = \frac{\int_0^1 s(\alpha)d_{TMI}^{(p)}([A_l^\alpha,A_u^\alpha])d\alpha}{\int_0^1 s(\alpha)d\alpha}$$

Now, by considering the below statements,

$$\begin{aligned} d(\tilde{A}) &= d^{(1)}_{TMF}(\tilde{A}, 1) = \int_0^1 d^{(1)}_{TMI}([A^\alpha_l, A^\alpha_u])\,d\alpha \\ &= \int_0^1\int_0^1 \left|(1-x)A^\alpha_u + xA^\alpha_l\right| dx d\alpha \\ d(\tilde{A}, \tilde{B}) &= d^{(1)}_{TMF}(\tilde{A}, \tilde{B}, 1) = \int_0^1 d^{(1)}_{TMI}([A^\alpha_l, A^\alpha_u], [B^\alpha_l, B^\alpha_u])\,d\alpha \\ &= \int_0^1\int_0^1 \left|((1-x)A^\alpha_u + xA^\alpha_l) - ((1-x)B^\alpha_u + xB^\alpha_l)\right| dx d\alpha \end{aligned} \tag{3.40}$$

the ranking of two positive fuzzy values of $\tilde{A}, \tilde{B}$ is defined as follows,

$$\begin{cases} d(\tilde{A}) = d(\tilde{B}) \Leftrightarrow A \tilde{=} B \\ d(\tilde{A}) \geq d(\tilde{B}) \Leftrightarrow A \succsim B \\ d(\tilde{A}) \leq d(\tilde{B}) \Leftrightarrow A \precsim B \end{cases}$$

Definition 3.6 The norm of the fuzzy vector $\tilde{X} = (\tilde{x}_1, \cdots, \tilde{x}_n)$ is defined as follows,

$$\|\tilde{X}\|_p = \sum_{i=1}^{n} \left(d^{(p)}_{TMF}(\tilde{x}_i, s\ )^p\right)^{1/p}$$

Therefore, $\|\tilde{X}\|_1 = \sum_{i=1}^{n} d^{(1)}_{TMF}(\tilde{x}_i, s\ ) = \sum_{i=1}^{n} d(\tilde{x}_i)$.

Definition 3.7 The fuzzy PPS (FPPS) for n DMUs with fuzzy inputs and outputs using the meter of Definition 3.5 is defined as,

$$P\tilde{P}S = \left\{ (\tilde{X}, \tilde{Y}) \middle| d(\tilde{X}_j) \geq d\left(\sum_{j=1}^{n} \lambda_j \tilde{x}_{ij}\right) \wp d(\tilde{Y}_j) \leq d\left(\sum_{j=1}^{n} \lambda_j \tilde{y}_{rj}\right) \wp \lambda \geq 0 \right\}$$

The principles of the FPPS are discussed in the following.

Inclusion of the observations. For any $\alpha > 0$ for any $(\tilde{X}, \tilde{Y}) \in P\tilde{P}S$, there are $d(\tilde{x}_i) \geq d(\sum \lambda_j \tilde{x}_{ij})$ and $d(\tilde{y}_r) \leq d\left(\sum_{j=1}^{n} \lambda_j \tilde{y}_{rj}\right)$, therefore,

$$d(\alpha\tilde{x}_i) = \alpha d(\tilde{x}_i) \geq \alpha d\left(\sum_{j=1}^{n} \lambda_j \tilde{x}_{ij}\right) = d\left(\sum_{j=1}^{n} \alpha\lambda_j \tilde{x}_{ij}\right) = d\left(\sum_{j=1}^{n} \bar{\lambda}_j \tilde{x}_{ij}\right)$$

$$d(\alpha\tilde{y}_r) = \alpha d(\tilde{y}_r) \leq \alpha d\left(\sum_{j=1}^{n}\lambda_j\tilde{y}_{rj}\right) = d\left(\sum_{j=1}^{n}\alpha\lambda_j\tilde{y}_{rj}\right) = d\left(\sum_{j=1}^{n}\overline{\lambda}_j\tilde{y}_{rj}\right)$$

where, $\overline{\lambda}_j = \alpha\lambda_j$ $(j = 1, \cdots, n)$ and $(\alpha\tilde{X}, \alpha\tilde{Y}) \in P\tilde{P}S$.

Possibility. For any fuzzy vectors $(\tilde{X}, \tilde{Y}) \in P\tilde{P}S$ and $(\tilde{X}', \tilde{Y}') \in P\tilde{P}S$, if $d(\tilde{x}_i') \geq d(\tilde{x}_i)$ $i = 1, \cdots, m$ and $d(\tilde{y}_r') \leq d(\tilde{y}_r)$, then $d(\tilde{x}_i') \geq d\left(\sum_{j=1}^{n}\lambda_j\tilde{x}_{ij}\right)$ and $d(\tilde{y}_r') \leq d\left(\sum_{j=1}^{n}\lambda_j\tilde{y}_{rj}\right)$. Therefore, $(\tilde{X}', \tilde{Y}') \in P\tilde{P}S$.

Convexity. Assuming $(\overline{X}, \overline{Y}), (\tilde{X}, \tilde{Y}) \in P\tilde{P}S$, then it should be proved that

$$(\delta\tilde{X} + (1-\delta)\overline{X}, \delta\tilde{Y} + (1-\delta)\overline{Y}) \in P\tilde{P}S, \quad \forall\, \delta \in [0, 1]$$

It is obvious that,

$$\begin{aligned} d(\delta\tilde{x}_i + (1-\delta)\overline{x}_i) &= \delta d(\tilde{x}_i) + (1-\delta)d(\overline{x}_i) \qquad i = 1, \cdots, m \\ &\geq \delta d\left(\sum_{j=1}^{n}\lambda_j\tilde{x}_{ij}\right) + (1-\delta)d\left(\sum_{j=1}^{n}\overline{\lambda}_j\tilde{x}_{ij}\right) \geq d\left(\sum_{j=1}^{n}\lambda_j'\tilde{x}_{ij}\right) \end{aligned}$$

where, $\lambda_j' = \delta\lambda_j + (1-\delta)\overline{\lambda}_j$ $(j = 1, \cdots, n)$. Also, there is,

$$\begin{aligned} d(\delta\tilde{y}_r + (1-\delta)\overline{y}_r) &= \delta d(\tilde{y}_r) + (1-\delta)d(\overline{y}_r) \qquad r = 1, \cdots, s \\ &= \delta d\left(\sum_{j=1}^{n}\lambda_j\tilde{y}_{rj}\right) + (1-\delta)d\left(\sum_{j=1}^{n}\overline{\lambda}_j\tilde{y}_{rj}\right) \\ &= d\left(\sum_{j=1}^{n}\lambda_j'\tilde{y}_{rj}\right) \leq d\left(\sum_{j=1}^{n}\lambda_j'\tilde{y}_{rj}\right) \end{aligned}$$

where, $\lambda_j' = \delta\lambda_j + (1-\delta)\overline{\lambda}_j$ $(j = 1, \cdots, n)$, therefore,

$$(\delta\tilde{X} + (1-\delta)\overline{X}, \delta\tilde{Y} + (1-\delta)\overline{Y}) \in P\tilde{P}S.$$

Now, according to the $P\tilde{P}S$, the below CCR model is defined for the efficiency of DMU_O.

$$\begin{aligned} &\text{Min } \theta \\ &\text{subject to} \\ &(\theta\underline{X}_o, \overline{Y}_o) \in P\tilde{P}S \end{aligned}$$

Similarly, the below $\tilde{PPS}$ is defined for the BCC model.

$$P\tilde{P}S_{BCC} = \left\{ (\tilde{X}, \tilde{Y}) \middle| d\left(\tilde{X}_j\right) \geq d\left(\sum_{j=1}^{n} \lambda_j \tilde{x}_{ij}\right), d\left(\tilde{Y}_j\right) \leq d\left(\sum_{j=1}^{n} \lambda_j \tilde{y}_{rj}\right), \sum_{j=1}^{n} \lambda_j = 1, \lambda \geq 0 \right\}$$

and the below BCC model is defined for the efficiency of DMU_O,

$$\begin{aligned} &\text{Min } \theta \\ &\text{subject to} \\ &(\theta \underline{X}_o, \overline{Y}_o) \in P\tilde{P}S_{BCC} \end{aligned}$$

Example 3.5 The LR fuzzy data of two inputs and one output for 10 DMUs are given in Tables 3.14 and 3.15.

Table 3.14 The fuzzy inputs of the DMUs of Example 3.5.

DMU	x_1^L	x_1^C	x_1^U	x_2^L	x_2^C	x_2^U
1	108	100	94	188	180	172
2	158	150	142	286	270	264
3	266	260	258	354	350	340
4	454	450	442	558	550	542
5	208	200	192	260	250	242
6	412	400	390	366	350	340
7	564	550	542	664	650	642
8	752	740	730	758	750	740
9	512	500	494	750	740	728
10	616	600	580	862	850	840

Table 3.15 The fuzzy outputs of the DMUs of Example 3.5.

DMU	y_1^L	y_1^C	y_1^U
1	54	50	48
2	182	180	176
3	240	230	224
4	286	280	278
5	24	20	18
6	76	70	66
7	100	100	100
8	130	120	110
9	38	30	26
10	50	40	32

The following ranking function according to (3.40) is considered for this example as follows,

$$d : \mathbb{R} \rightarrow TF_{\mathbb{R}}$$
$$d(\tilde{A} = (a_1, a_2, a_3)) = 0.25a_1 + 0.5a_2 + 0.25a_3$$

where $TF_{\mathbb{R}}$ is the set of triangular fuzzy numbers. According to this ranking function, the crisp values of the inputs and outputs are obtained as reported by Table 3.16. Finally, using the crisp form of the CCR and BCC models, the efficiency values in Table 3.17 are obtained.

3.4.4 Probabilistic approach

The basic concepts of the probabilistic approach were proposed by Zadeh (1978). According to Zadeh (1978), the relationships of a fuzzy variable

Table 3.16 The crisp values of the inputs and outputs of the DMUs of Example 3.5.

DMU	$R(\tilde{X}_1)$	$R(\tilde{X}_2)$	$R(\tilde{Y})$
1	100.5	180	50.5
2	150	272.5	179.5
3	261	348.5	231
4	449	550	281
5	200	250.5	20.5
6	400.5	351.5	70.5
7	551.5	651.5	100
8	740.5	749.5	120
9	501.5	739.5	31
10	599	850.5	40.5

Table 3.17 The efficiency values obtained for the DMUs of Example 3.5 by the crisp CCR and BCC models.

DMU	Efficiency CCR	Efficiency BCC
1	0.4258072	1
2	1	1
3	1	1
4	0.7707871	1
5	0.1234630	0.7185629
6	0.3025900	0.5528907
7	0.2315668	0.3307662
8	0.2415463	0.3066515
9	0.6338392E-01	0.2434077
10	0.7194155E-01	0.2116402

and a stochastic variable with a probability distribution function are the same. As in the linear programming models, the coefficients and variables are fuzzy as well as the constraints. Therefore, the probabilities of the fuzzy constraints can be determined by probability theory.

First, Guo et al. (2000) constructed fuzzy DEA models based on the necessity measure. Then Lertworasirikul, Fang, Joines, and Nuttle (2002) and Lertworasirikul, Fang, Nuttle, and Joines (2002) proposed the credibility measure for solving fuzzy DEA models. They considered two aspects of optimistic and pessimistic for the probabilistic approach and replaced the fuzzy DEA model with a credibility-based fuzzy DEA model. Lertworasirikul, Fang, Joines, and Nuttle (2003a, 2003b) proposed a probabilistic approach for the fuzzy CCR model and considered the fuzzy constraints as fuzzy events. They converted the fuzzy DEA model to a probabilistic LP model; especially for the trapezoidal fuzzy-type data, an equivalent linear programming model is obtained instead of the fuzzy DEA model. To be more detailed, they considered the model of Lertworasirikul, Fang, Joines, and Nuttle (2003a) as follows,

$$
\begin{aligned}
&\text{Max } \theta_p = \bar{f} \\
&\text{subject to} \\
&\left(\sum_{r=1}^{s} u_r \tilde{y}_{rp}\right)_{\beta}^{U} \geq \bar{f} \\
&\left(\sum_{i=1}^{m} v_i \tilde{x}_{ip}\right)_{\alpha_0}^{L} \geq 1 \\
&\left(\sum_{i=1}^{m} v_i \tilde{x}_{ip}\right)_{\alpha_0}^{L} \leq 1 \\
&\left(\sum_{r=1}^{s} u_r \tilde{y}_{rj} - \sum_{i=1}^{m} v_i \tilde{x}_{ij}\right)_{\alpha}^{L} \leq 0, \quad j = 1, 2, \dots, n \\
&u_r \geq 0 \qquad r = 1, 2, \dots, s \\
&v_i \geq 0 \qquad i = 1, 2, \dots, m
\end{aligned}
\tag{3.41}
$$

In this model, $\beta \in [0, 1]$, $\alpha_0 \in [0, 1]$, and $\alpha \in [0, 1]$ are some predetermined confidence levels. $\bar{f}$ is maximized in a way that $\sum_{r=1}^{s} u_r \tilde{y}_{rp}$ is obtained at the β level or higher and the confidence level of other constraints is not less than

α_0 or α. In other words, in the optimal solution, the value of $\sum_{r=1}^{s} u_r \tilde{y}_{rp}$ is at least equal to $\overline{f}$ at the β level while other constraints are satisfied at their predetermined confidence levels.

3.4.5 Other approaches

Except for the previously mentioned solution approaches, there are some other approaches in the literature for tackling fuzzy DEA models. For example, Hougaard (1999) extended the technical efficiency of the DEA models to a fuzzy environment. Sheth and Triantis (2003) developed a DEA structure for evaluating the efficiency and effectiveness goals in fuzzy environment by assigning a membership function for each of the constraints related to the efficiency and effectiveness goals. Some approaches in the literature are discussed in the rest of this section.

3.4.5.1 Fuzzy efficiency approach for fuzzy DEA

Assume DMU_f, $1 \leq f \leq F$ with triangular fuzzy inputs of $\tilde{x}_{hf} = \left(x^o_{hf}, x^m_{hf}, x^p_{hf}\right) \in R^3$ and triangular fuzzy outputs of $\tilde{y}_{kf} = \left(y^p_{kf}, y^m_{kf}, y^o_{kf}\right) \in R^3$ where $h = 1, \ldots, H$ and $k = 1, \ldots, K$. Here, each triangular fuzzy value consists of a pessimistic, an average, and an optimistic value. According to this information, the Farrell efficiency frontier for one input and one output is represented by Fig. 3.25. The frontier is provided for two cases of producing the output y_o from the fuzzy input $\tilde{x} \equiv (x^o, x^m, x^p)$, and producing the fuzzy output $\tilde{y} \equiv (y^p, y^m, y^o)$ from the input x_o. As the inputs and outputs are fuzzy, the efficiency value cannot be crisp. Therefore, a fuzzy-based method is required to evaluate this system.

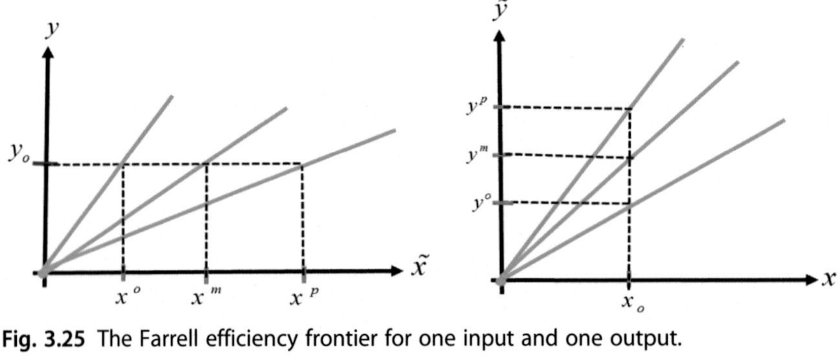

Fig. 3.25 The Farrell efficiency frontier for one input and one output.

Assume the below membership functions for the above-mentioned triangular inputs and outputs.

$$\mu_{x_{if}}(x) = \begin{cases} \dfrac{x_{hf} - x_{hf}^{o}}{x_{hf}^{m} - x_{hf}^{o}} & x_{hf}^{o} \leq x_{hf} \leq x_{hf}^{m} \\ \dfrac{x_{hf}^{p} - x_{hf}}{x_{hf}^{p} - x_{hf}^{m}} & x_{hf}^{m} \leq x_{hf} \leq x_{hf}^{p} \quad h = 1, \ldots, H \quad f = 1, \ldots, F \\ 0 & \text{otherwise} \end{cases}$$

$$\mu_{y_{kf}} = \begin{cases} \dfrac{y_{kf} - y_{kf}^{p}}{y_{kf}^{m} - y_{kf}^{p}} & y_{kf}^{p} \leq y_{kf} \leq y_{kf}^{m} \\ \dfrac{y_{kf}^{o} - y_{kf}}{y_{kf}^{o} - y_{kf}^{m}} & y_{kf}^{m} \leq y_{kf} \leq y_{kf}^{o} \quad k = 1, \ldots, K \quad f = 1, \ldots, F \\ 0 & \text{otherwise} \end{cases}$$

Now, similar to the classical DEA, in the fuzzy DEA the aim is to maximize the efficiency of DMUs where the model is to maximize the weighted ratio of the outputs and the inputs by determining the weight values. This model for DMU_{f_0} where $f_0 = 1, \ldots, F$ is represented as follows.

$$\begin{aligned} &\text{Max } \tilde{E}_{f_0} = \frac{\sum_{k=1}^{K} u_k . \tilde{y}_{kf_0}}{\sum_{h=1}^{H} v_h . \tilde{x}_{hf_0}} \\ &\text{subject to} \\ &\frac{\sum_{k=1}^{K} u_k . \tilde{y}_{kf}}{\sum_{h=1}^{H} v_h . \tilde{x}_{hf}} \leq 1 \qquad f = 1, \ldots, F \\ &u_k, v_h \geq 0 \qquad k = 1, \ldots, K, \quad h = 1, \ldots, H \end{aligned} \tag{3.42}$$

This model (3.42) has the general efficiency of DMU_{f_0} that is maximized where u_k and $v_h$are the weights of the k-th output and the h-th input, respectively. This model can be linearized as follows,

$$\begin{aligned} &\text{Max } \tilde{E}_{f_0} = \sum_{k=1}^{K} u_k \cdot \tilde{y}_{kf_0} \\ &\text{subject to} \\ &\sum_{k=1}^{K} u_k \cdot \tilde{y}_{kf} - \sum_{h=1}^{H} v_h \cdot \tilde{x}_{hf} \leq 0 \quad f = 1, \ldots, F \\ &\sum_{h=1}^{H} v_h \cdot \tilde{x}_{hf_0} = 1 \\ &u_k, v_h \geq 0 \qquad k = 1, \ldots, K, \quad h = 1, \ldots, H \end{aligned} \tag{3.43}$$

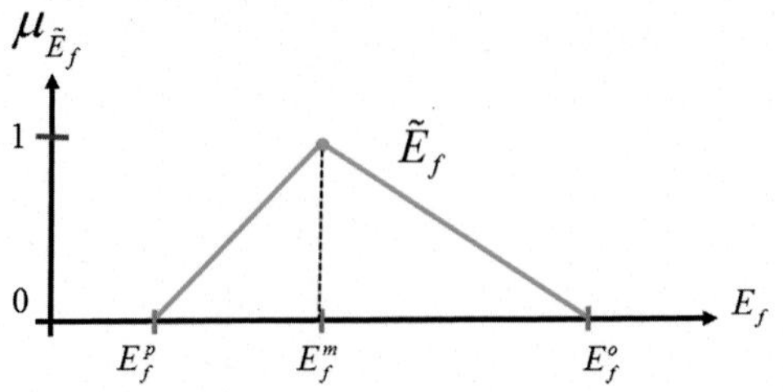

Fig. 3.26 The membership function of the fuzzy efficiency value $\tilde{E}_{f_0} = \left(E_{f_0}^p, E_{f_0}^m, E_{f_0}^o\right)$.

To solve the fuzzy model (3.43), Charnes-Cooper transformations (Charnes & Cooper, 1962) considered the fuzzy efficiency of the objective function as the fuzzy value of $\tilde{E}_{f_0} = \left(E_{f_0}^p, E_{f_0}^m, E_{f_0}^o\right)$ and then introduced the below models to obtain the fuzzy efficiency value. The schematic representation of the fuzzy efficiency value is given by Fig. 3.26.

$$\begin{aligned}
&\text{Max } E_{f_0}^p = \sum\nolimits_{k=1}^{K} \left(u_k \cdot y_{kf_0}\right)^P \\
&\text{subject to} \\
&\sum\nolimits_{k=1}^{K} \left(u_k \cdot y_{kf}\right)^P - \sum\nolimits_{h=1}^{H} \left(v_h \cdot x_{hf}\right)^P \leq 0 \quad f = 1, \ldots, F \\
&\sum\nolimits_{h=1}^{H} \left(v_h \cdot x_{hf_0}\right)^P = 1 \\
&u_k, v_h \geq 0 \qquad\qquad k = 1, \ldots, K, \;\; h = 1, \ldots, H
\end{aligned} \tag{3.44}$$

$$\begin{aligned}
&\text{Max } E_{f_0}^m = \sum\nolimits_{k=1}^{K} \left(u_k \cdot y_{kf_0}\right)^m \\
&\text{subject to} \\
&\sum\nolimits_{k=1}^{K} \left(u_k \cdot y_{kf}\right)^m - \sum\nolimits_{h=1}^{H} \left(v_h \cdot x_{hf}\right)^m \leq 0 \quad f = 1, \ldots, F \\
&\sum\nolimits_{h=1}^{H} \left(v_h \cdot x_{hf_0}\right)^m = 1 \\
&u_k, v_h \geq 0 \qquad\qquad k = 1, \ldots, K, \;\; h = 1, \ldots, H
\end{aligned} \tag{3.45}$$

$$\begin{aligned}
&\text{Max } E_{f_0}^o = \sum\nolimits_{k=1}^{K} \left(u_k \cdot y_{kf_0}\right)^o \\
&\text{subject to} \\
&\sum\nolimits_{k=1}^{K} \left(u_k \cdot y_{kf}\right)^o - \sum\nolimits_{h=1}^{H} \left(v_h \cdot x_{hf}\right)^o \leq 0 \quad f = 1, \ldots, F \\
&\sum\nolimits_{h=1}^{H} \left(v_h \cdot x_{hf_0}\right)^o = 1 \\
&u_k, v_h \geq 0 \qquad\qquad k = 1, \ldots, K, \;\; h = 1, \ldots, H
\end{aligned} \tag{3.46}$$

As in this method, different weight values are obtained by the models (3.44)–(3.46), and also three models have to be solved. Puri and Yadav (2013) introduced a new method to obtain the fuzzy efficiency value $\tilde{E}_{f_0} = \left(E^p_{f_0}, E^m_{f_0}, E^o_{f_0}\right)$ by considering the objectives; it is defined as follows:

- To maximize $E^m_{f_0}$,
- To minimize $E^m_{f_0} - E^p_{f_0}$,
- To maximize $E^o_{f_0} - E^m_{f_0}$.

According to this method, the positive ideal solution (PIS) and the negative ideal solution (NIS) for the fuzzy efficiency are introduced as follows,

$$\begin{aligned}
F^{PIS}_{1,f_0} &= \max\ E^m_{f_0} && f_0 = 1, \ldots, F \\
F^{PIS}_{2,f_0} &= \min\ \left[E^m_{f_0} - E^p_{f_0}\right] && f_0 = 1, \ldots, F \\
F^{PIS}_{3,f_0} &= \max\ \left[E^o_{f_0} - E^m_{f_0}\right] && f_0 = 1, \ldots, F \\
F^{NIS}_{1,f_0} &= \min\ E^m_{f_0} && f_0 = 1, \ldots, F \\
F^{NIS}_{2,f_0} &= \max\ \left[E^m_{f_0} - E^p_{f_0}\right] && f_0 = 1, \ldots, F \\
F^{NIS}_{3,f_0} &= \min\ \left[E^o_{f_0} - E^m_{f_0}\right] && f_0 = 1, \ldots, F
\end{aligned} \tag{3.47}$$

Then, the following membership functions are defined for $\tilde{E}_{f_0}$.

$$\begin{aligned}
\mu_{F_{1,f_0}} &= \begin{cases} 1 & \text{for } F_{1,f_0} > F^{PIS}_{1,f_0} \\ \dfrac{F_{1,f_0} - F^{NIS}_{1,f_0}}{F^{PIS}_{1,f_0} - F^{NIS}_{1,f_0}} & \text{for } F^{NIS}_{1,f_0} \le F_{1,f_0} \le F^{PIS}_{1,f_0} \\ 0 & \text{for } F_{1,f_0} < F^{NIS}_{1,f_0} \end{cases} \qquad f_0 = 1, \ldots, F \\
\mu_{F_{2,f_0}} &= \begin{cases} 1 & \text{for } F_{2,f_0} > F^{PIS}_{2,f_0} \\ \dfrac{F^{NIS}_{2,f_0} - F_{2,f_0}}{F^{NIS}_{2,f_0} - F^{PIS}_{2,f_0}} & \text{for } F^{PIS}_{2,f_0} \le F_{2,f_0} \le F^{NIS}_{2,f_0} \\ 0 & \text{for } F_{2,f_0} < F^{NIS}_{2,f_0} \end{cases} \qquad f_0 = 1, \ldots, F \\
\mu_{F_{3,f_0}} &= \begin{cases} 1 & \text{for } F_{3,f_0} > F^{PIS}_{3,f_0} \\ \dfrac{F_{3,f_0} - F^{NIS}_{3,f_0}}{F^{PIS}_{3,f_0} - F^{NIS}_{3,f_0}} & \text{for } F^{NIS}_{3,f_0} \le F_{3,f_0} \le F^{PIS}_{3,f_0} \\ 0 & \text{for } F_{3,f_0} < F^{NIS}_{3,f_0} \end{cases} \qquad f_0 = 1, \ldots, F
\end{aligned} \tag{3.48}$$

Finally, considering the slack variable λ_{f_0}, the below model is obtained for obtaining the fuzzy efficiency,

$$\begin{aligned}
&\text{Max } \lambda_{f_0} \\
&\text{subject to} \\
&1 \geq \mu_{F_{1,f_0}}(F_1(u_k, v_h)) \geq \lambda_{f_0} \geq 0 \\
&1 \geq \mu_{F_{2,f_0}}(F_2(u_k, v_h)) \geq \lambda_{f_0} \geq 0 \\
&1 \geq \mu_{F_{3,f_0}}(F_3(u_k, v_h)) \geq \lambda_{f_0} \geq 0 \\
&\sum_{k=1}^{K} u_k \cdot \left[w_1 \left(y_{kf}^o\right)_\alpha + w_2 \left(y_{kf}^m\right)_\alpha + w_3 \left(y_{kf}^p\right)_\alpha \right] \\
&\qquad - \sum_{h=1}^{H} v_h \cdot \left[w_1 \left(x_{hf}^o\right) + w_2 \left(x_{hf}^m\right) + w_3 \left(x_{hf}^p\right)_\alpha \right] \leq 0 \qquad f = 1, \ldots, F \\
&\sum_{h=1}^{H} v_h \left[w_1 \left(x_{hf_0}^o\right) + w_2 \left(x_{hf_0}^m\right) + w_3 \left(x_{hf_0}^p\right)_\alpha \right] = 1 \\
&u_k, v_h \geq 0 \qquad k = 1, \ldots, K, h = 1, \ldots, H
\end{aligned} \tag{3.49}$$

where,

$$\begin{aligned}
F_{f_0} &= E_{f_0}^m = \sum_{k=1}^{K} \left(u_k \cdot y_{kf_0}\right)^m \\
\mu_{F_{1,f_0}}(F_1(u_k, v_h)) &= \frac{F_{1,f_0} - F_{1,f_0}^{NIS}}{F_{1,f_0}^{PIS} - F_{1,f_0}^{NIS}} \\
\mu_{F_{2,f_0}}(F_2(u_k, v_h)) &= \frac{F_{2,f_0}^{NIS} - F_{2,f_0}}{F_{2,f_0}^{NIS} - F_{2,f_0}^{PIS}} \\
\mu_{F_{3,f_0}}(F_3(u_k, v_h)) &= \frac{F_{3,f_0} - F_{3,f_0}^{NIS}}{F_{3,f_0}^{PIS} - F_{3,f_0}^{NIS}}
\end{aligned} \tag{3.50}$$

In the model (3.49), by maximizing λ_{f_0} the membership functions $\mu_{F_{1,f0}}(F_1(u_k, v_h))$, $\mu_{F_{2,f0}}(F_2(u_k, v_h))$, and $\mu_{F_{3,f0}}(F_3(u_k, v_h))$ are maximized, which means that ${E_{f_0}}^p$, ${E_{f_0}}^m$, ${E_{f_0}}^o$ are maximized. The defuzzification of the constraints of the model (3.43) is done by considering the weight values of w_1, w_2, w_3 in an α-cut. Finally, as the obtained efficiency values are of the triangular fuzzy type ($\tilde{E}_{f_0} = \left(E_{f_0}^p, E_{f_0}^m, E_{f_0}^o\right)$), the simple formula $E_{f_0} = \frac{E_{f_0}^p + E_{f_0}^m + E_{f_0}^o}{3}$ is used to obtain their crisp values before comparing and ranking them.

3.5 The fuzzy additive DEA model

This model was introduced by Cooper et al. (1996) and is as follows,

$$
\begin{aligned}
&\text{Max } z=\sum_{i=1}^{m} s_i^- + \sum_{r=1}^{s} s_r^+\\
&\text{subject to}\\
&\sum_{j=1}^{n} \lambda_j x_{ij} + s_i^- = x_{io} \qquad i=1,2,\ldots,m\\
&\sum_{j=1}^{n} \lambda_j y_{rj} - s_r^+ = y_{ro} \qquad r=1,2,\ldots,s\\
&\sum_{j=1}^{n} \lambda_j = 1\\
&\lambda_j \geq 0, s_i^- \geq 0, s_r^+ \geq 0 \qquad j=1,2,\ldots,n, \quad i=1,2,\ldots,m, \quad r=1,2,\ldots,s
\end{aligned}
\tag{3.51}
$$

In this model, a DMU is efficient if and only if $z^* = 0$.

The fuzzy CCR additive model for $FDMU_O$ (where $o \in \{1, \cdots, n\}$) is written as follows,

$$
\begin{aligned}
&\text{Max } \tilde{z}=\sum_{i=1}^{m} \tilde{s}_i^- + \sum_{r=1}^{s} \tilde{s}_r^+\\
&\text{subject to}\\
&\sum_{j=1}^{n} \lambda_j \tilde{x}_{ij} + \tilde{s}_i^- \cong \tilde{x}_{io} \qquad i=1,2,\ldots,m\\
&\sum_{j=1}^{n} \lambda_j \tilde{y}_{rj} - \tilde{s}_r^+ \cong \tilde{y}_{ro} \qquad r=1,2,\ldots,s\\
&\lambda_j \geq 0, \ \tilde{s}_i^- \geq 0, \ \tilde{s}_r^+ \geq 0 \qquad j=1,2,\ldots,n, \quad i=1,2,\ldots,m, \quad r=1,2,\ldots,s
\end{aligned}
\tag{3.52}
$$

Also the fuzzy BCC additive model for $FDMU_O$ (where $o \in \{1, \cdots, n\}$) is written as follows,

$$
\begin{aligned}
&\text{Max } \tilde{z} = \sum_{i=1}^{m} \tilde{s}_i^- + \sum_{r=1}^{s} \tilde{s}_r^+ \\
&\text{subject to} \\
&\sum_{j=1}^{n} \lambda_j \tilde{x}_{ij} + \tilde{s}_i^- \cong \tilde{x}_{io} \qquad i = 1, 2, \ldots, m \\
&\sum_{j=1}^{n} \lambda_j \tilde{y}_{rj} - \tilde{s}_r^+ \cong \tilde{y}_{ro} \qquad r = 1, 2, \ldots, s \\
&\sum_{j=1}^{n} \lambda_j = 1 \\
&\lambda_j \geq 0,\ \tilde{s}_i^- \geq 0,\ \tilde{s}_r^+ \geq 0 \qquad j = 1, 2, \ldots, n,\ i = 1, 2, \ldots, m,\ r = 1, 2, \ldots, s
\end{aligned}
\tag{3.53}
$$

In the models (3.52), (3.53), the fuzzy equality constraints $\sum_{j=1}^{n} \lambda_j \tilde{x}_{ij} + \tilde{s}_i^- \cong \tilde{x}_{io} (i = 1, 2, \ldots, m)$ and $\sum_{j=1}^{n} \lambda_j \tilde{y}_{rj} - \tilde{s}_r^+ \cong \tilde{y}_{ro} (r = 1, 2, \ldots, s)$ are obtained from the constraints $\sum_{j=1}^{n} \lambda_j \tilde{x}_{ij} \leq \tilde{x}_{io} (i = 1, 2, \ldots, m)$ and $\sum_{j=1}^{n} \lambda_j \tilde{y}_{rj} \geq \tilde{y}_{ro}$ $(r = 1, 2, \ldots, s)$ by adding the slack variables $\tilde{s}_i^- (i = 1, 2, \ldots, m)$ and $\tilde{s}_r^+ (r = 1, 2, \ldots, s)$, respectively. The fuzzy equality constraints as the fuzzy equation of two values can be interpreted in two ways, as follows,

- The exact equality of two fuzzy values, which means the values must be exactly the same,
- The inexact equality of two fuzzy values, which means that the values are approximately equal.

In the solution of these models, the first concept is considered.

In general, solution approaches of fuzzy additive DEA models can be categorized as fuzzy ranking-based approaches and α-cut-based approaches. These methods are detailed in the rest of this section.

3.5.1 Fuzzy ranking-based approach for fuzzy additive DEA model

In this approach, by applying a suitable ranking function on the fuzzy parameters and variables of the models (3.52) and (3.53), the following crisp models are obtained. In these models, each notation is the crisp form of its related fuzzy form in the models (3.52), (3.53).

$$\text{Max } z = \sum_{i=1}^{m} s_i^- + \sum_{r=1}^{s} s_r^+$$

subject to

$$\sum_{j=1}^{n} \lambda_j x_{ij} + s_i^- = x_{io} \qquad i = 1, 2, \ldots, m$$

$$\sum_{j=1}^{n} \lambda_j y_{rj} - s_r^+ = y_{ro} \qquad r = 1, 2, \ldots, s$$

$$\lambda_j \geq 0, \ \ s_i^- \geq 0, \ \ s_r^+ \geq 0 \qquad j = 1, 2, \ldots, n, \ \ i = 1, 2, \ldots, m, \ \ r = 1, 2, \ldots, s \tag{3.54}$$

$$\text{Max } z = \sum_{i=1}^{m} s_i^- + \sum_{r=1}^{s} s_r^+$$

subject to

$$\sum_{j=1}^{n} \lambda_j x_{ij} + s_i^- = x_{io} \qquad i = 1, 2, \ldots, m$$

$$\sum_{j=1}^{n} \lambda_j y_{rj} - s_r^+ = y_{ro} \qquad r = 1, 2, \ldots, s$$

$$\sum_{j=1}^{n} \lambda_j = 1$$

$$\lambda_j \geq 0, \ \ s_i^- \geq 0, \ \ s_r^+ \geq 0 \qquad j = 1, 2, \ldots, n, \ \ i = 1, 2, \ldots, m, \ \ r = 1, 2, \ldots, s \tag{3.55}$$

Some points can be highlighted here.

- The solutions obtained by this approach highly depend on the ranking function applied.
- The crisp objective function value obtained by this approach is not necessarily equal to the ranking function value of the exact solution of the model (3.52).
- The feasibility of the models (3.54), (3.55) cannot always be proved easily.
- A shortcoming of the fuzzy ranking methods is that they assign small importance weight values to the lower and upper bounds of the support of a fuzzy number and higher weight values are assigned to the core of the support. Therefore, in the optimal solution, the values associated to the lower and upper bounds of the support become very small (almost zero).

So, the models for efficiency evaluation after applying the ranking function will have crisp solutions.

Example 3.6 The fuzzy data of 10 DMUs by two inputs and one output are given in Tables 3.18 and 3.19.

By applying the below ranking function

$$d : \mathbb{R} \to TF_{\mathbb{R}}$$
$$d\left(\tilde{A} = (a_1, a_2, a_3)\right) = 0.25a_1 + 0.5a_2 + 0.25a_3$$

where $TF_{\mathbb{R}}$ is the set of triangular fuzzy numbers, the crisp values of the fuzzy data of Tables 3.18 and 3.19 are calculated and reported in Table 3.20.

According to the models (3.54), (3.55), the DMUs are evaluated and the results of Table 3.21 are obtained.

Table 3.18 The fuzzy input values of the DMUs of Example 3.6.

DMU	x_1^L	x_1^C	x_1^U	x_2^L	x_2^C	x_2^U
1	108	100	94	188	180	172
2	158	150	142	286	270	264
3	266	260	258	354	350	340
4	454	450	442	558	550	542
5	208	200	192	260	250	242
6	412	400	390	366	350	340
7	564	550	542	664	650	642
8	752	740	730	758	750	740
9	512	500	494	750	740	728
10	616	600	580	862	850	840

Table 3.19 The fuzzy output values of the DMUs of Example 3.6.

DMU	y_1^L	y_1^C	y_1^U
1	54	50	48
2	182	180	176
3	240	230	224
4	286	280	278
5	24	20	18
6	76	70	66
7	100	100	100
8	130	120	110
9	38	30	26
10	50	40	32

Table 3.20 The crisp input and output values of the DMUs of Example 3.6.

DMU	$R(\tilde{X}_1)$	$R(\tilde{X}_2)$	$R(\tilde{Y})$
1	100.5	180	50.5
2	150	272.5	179.5
3	261	348.5	231
4	449	550	281
5	200	250.5	20.5
6	400.5	351.5	70.5
7	551.5	651.5	100
8	740.5	749.5	120
9	501.5	739.5	31
10	599	850.5	40.5

Table 3.21 The solutions obtained by the models (3.54), (3.55) for the DMUs of Example 3.6.

DMU	(s_1^*, s_2^*, s_3^*) model CCR	(s_1^*, s_2^*, s_3^*) model BCC
1	(0, 0, 0)	(58.29944, 103.3357, 0)
2	(0, 0, 0)	(0, 0, 0)
3	(0, 0, 0)	(0, 0, 0)
4	(0, 0, 0)	(214.1811, 123.4123, 0)
5	(99.5, 70.5, 30)	(182.8691, 219.3788, 0)
6	(292.3256, 157.1589, 0)	(341.5864, 244.4735, 0)
7	(432.0058, 436.0058, 0)	(467.9345, 499.6894, 0)
8	(613.3314, 519.6647, 0)	(640.2214, 567.3273, 0)
9	(0, 0, 0)	(0, 0, 0)
10	(498.5, 670.5, 10)	(565.156, 789.0167, 0)

According to the results of Table 3.21, the DMUs 1, 2, 3, 4, and 9 are efficient and the other DMUs are inefficient.

3.5.2 α-cut-based approach for fuzzy additive DEA model

In this approach, the α-cuts of the production possibility set ($\tilde{T}$) are obtained as crisp sets. Here, the aim is to obtain the fuzzy efficiency of a DMU by the α-cuts of its membership functions of the inputs and outputs. To solve the fuzzy linear models (3.52), (3.53), the following α-cuts are defined.

$$\left[\tilde{x}_{ij}\right]_\alpha = \left\{x_{ij} \in \mathbb{R} \middle| \mu_{\tilde{x}_{ij}}(x_{ij}) \geq \alpha\right\} = \left[x_{ij}^l, x_{ij}^u\right]_\alpha$$

$$\begin{aligned}
&\left[\tilde{y}_{rj}\right]_\alpha = \left\{y_{rj}\in\mathbb{R}\left|\mu_{\tilde{y}_{rj}}\left(y_{rj}\right)\geq\alpha\right.\right\} = \left[y^l_{rj}, y^u_{rj}\right]_\alpha \\
&[\tilde{z}]_\alpha = \left[z^l, z^u\right]_\alpha \\
&\left[\tilde{s}_i^-\right]_\alpha = \left[s_i^{-l}, s_i^{-u}\right]_\alpha \\
&\left[\tilde{s}_i^+\right]_\alpha = \left[s_i^{+l}, s_i^{+u}\right]_\alpha \\
&r = 1, \ldots, s \quad i = 1, \ldots, m, \quad \circ\leq\alpha\leq 1, \quad j = 1, \ldots, n
\end{aligned}$$

Then, the models (3.52), (3.53) are written as follows, respectively,

$$\begin{aligned}
&\text{Max } \left[z^l, z^u\right]_\alpha = \sum_{i=1}^{m}\left[s_i^{-l}, \tilde{s}_i^{-u}\right]_\alpha + \sum_{r=1}^{s}\left[s_i^{+l}, s_i^{+u}\right]_\alpha \\
&\text{subject to} \\
&\sum_{j=1}^{n}\lambda_j\left[x^l_{ij}, x^u_{ij}\right]_\alpha + \left[s_i^{-l}, s_i^{-u}\right]_\alpha = \left[x^l_{io}, x^u_{io}\right]_\alpha \qquad i = 1, 2, \ldots, m \\
&\sum_{j=1}^{n}\lambda_j\left[y^l_{rj}, y^u_{rj}\right]_\alpha - \left[s_i^{+l}, s_i^{+u}\right]_\alpha = \left[y^l_{ro}, y^u_{ro}\right]_\alpha \qquad r = 1, 2, \ldots, s \\
&\lambda_j\geq 0, \ \left[s_i^{-l}, s_i^{-u}\right]_\alpha\geq 0, \ \left[s_i^{+l}, s_i^{+u}\right]_\alpha\geq 0 \qquad j = 1, 2, \ldots, n, \ i = 1, 2, \ldots, m, \\
&\qquad r = 1, 2, \ldots, s
\end{aligned} \tag{3.56}$$

$$\begin{aligned}
&\text{Max } \left[z^l, z^u\right]_\alpha = \sum_{i=1}^{m}\left[s_i^{-l}, \tilde{s}_i^{-u}\right]_\alpha + \sum_{r=1}^{s}\left[s_i^{+l}, s_i^{+u}\right]_\alpha \\
&\text{subject to} \\
&\sum_{j=1}^{n}\lambda_j\left[x^l_{ij}, x^u_{ij}\right]_\alpha + \left[s_i^{-l}, s_i^{-u}\right]_\alpha = \left[x^l_{io}, x^u_{io}\right]_\alpha \qquad i = 1, 2, \ldots, m \\
&\sum_{j=1}^{n}\lambda_j\left[y^l_{rj}, y^u_{rj}\right]_\alpha - \left[s_i^{+l}, s_i^{+u}\right]_\alpha = \left[y^l_{ro}, y^u_{ro}\right]_\alpha \qquad r = 1, 2, \ldots, s \\
&\sum_{j=1}^{n}\lambda_j = 1 \\
&\lambda_j\geq 0, \ \left[s_i^{-l}, s_i^{-u}\right]_\alpha\geq 0, \ \left[s_i^{+l}, s_i^{+u}\right]_\alpha\geq 0 \qquad j = 1, 2, \ldots, n, \ i = 1, 2, \ldots, m, \\
&\qquad r = 1, 2, \ldots, s
\end{aligned} \tag{3.57}$$

For any α-cut where $(0 \leq \alpha \leq 1)$, each of the above models is an interval linear model. Therefore, the model (3.56) (the additive CCR model) by applying the operators and comparison logics of interval numbers is converted to the below models, respectively, (for α_j-cut).

$$\text{Max } z^l = \sum_{i=1}^{m} s_i^{-l} + \sum_{r=1}^{s} s_i^{+l}$$

subject to

$$\sum_{j=1}^{n} \lambda_j x_{ij}^l + s_i^{-l} = x_{io}^l \qquad i = 1, 2, \ldots, m$$

$$\sum_{j=1}^{n} \lambda_j y_{rj}^l - s_i^{+l} = y_{ro}^l \qquad r = 1, 2, \ldots, s$$

$$\lambda_j \geq 0, \quad s_i^{-l} \geq 0, \quad s_i^{+l} \geq 0 \qquad j = 1, 2, \ldots, n, \quad i = 1, 2, \ldots, m, \quad r = 1, 2, \ldots, s \tag{3.58}$$

$$\text{Max } z^l = \sum_{i=1}^{m} s_i^{-u} + \sum_{r=1}^{s} s_i^{+u}$$

subject to

$$\sum_{j=1}^{n} \lambda_j x_{ij}^u + s_i^{-u} = x_{io}^u \qquad i = 1, 2, \ldots, m$$

$$\sum_{j=1}^{n} \lambda_j y_{rj}^u - s_i^{+u} = y_{ro}^u \qquad r = 1, 2, \ldots, s$$

$$\lambda_j \geq 0, \quad s_i^{-u} \geq 0, \quad s_i^{+u} \geq 0 \qquad j = 1, 2, \ldots, n, \quad i = 1, 2, \ldots, m, \quad r = 1, 2, \ldots, s \tag{3.59}$$

Also, the model (3.57) (the additive BCC model) by applying the operators and comparison logics of interval numbers is converted to the below models, respectively, (for α_j-cut).

$$\text{Max } z^l = \sum_{i=1}^{m} s_i^{-l} + \sum_{r=1}^{s} s_i^{+l}$$

subject to

$$\sum_{j=1}^{n} \lambda_j x_{ij}^l + s_i^{-l} = x_{io}^l \qquad i = 1, 2, \ldots, m$$

$$\sum_{j=1}^{n} \lambda_j y_{rj}^l - s_i^{+l} = y_{ro}^l \qquad r = 1, 2, \ldots, s$$

$$\sum_{j=1}^{n} \lambda_j = 1$$

$$\lambda_j \geq 0, \ s_i^{-l} \geq 0, \ s_i^{+l} \geq 0 \qquad j = 1, 2, \ldots, n, \ i = 1, 2, \ldots, m, \ r = 1, 2, \ldots, s \tag{3.60}$$

$$\text{Max } z^l = \sum_{i=1}^{m} s_i^{-u} + \sum_{r=1}^{s} s_i^{+u}$$

subject to

$$\sum_{j=1}^{n} \lambda_j x_{ij}^u + s_i^{-u} = x_{io}^u \qquad i = 1, 2, \ldots, m$$

$$\sum_{j=1}^{n} \lambda_j y_{rj}^u - s_i^{+u} = y_{ro}^u \qquad r = 1, 2, \ldots, s$$

$$\sum_{j=1}^{n} \lambda_j = 1$$

$$\lambda_j \geq 0, \ s_i^{-u} \geq 0, \ s_i^{+u} \geq 0 \qquad j = 1, 2, \ldots, n, \ i = 1, 2, \ldots, m, \ r = 1, 2, \ldots, s \tag{3.61}$$

According to the models (3.58), (3.59), a DMU is efficient if for a partition of α values as $\Delta = \{\alpha_1, \alpha_2, \ldots, \alpha_p\}$ where $1 = \alpha_1 > \alpha_2 > \ldots > \alpha_p = 0$, $[z^l, z^u]_{\alpha_j} = [0, 0]$ for $j = 1, \cdots, p$.

Similarly, according to the models (3.60), (3.61), a DMU is efficient if for a partition of α values as $\Delta = \{\alpha_1, \alpha_2, \ldots, \alpha_p\}$ where $1 = \alpha_1 > \alpha_2 > \ldots > \alpha_p = 0$, $[z^l, z^u]_{\alpha_j} = [0, 0]$ for $j = 1, \cdots, p$.

Example 3.7 Consider the data of Example 3.6 and the set $\Delta = \{\alpha_1 = 1, \alpha_2 = 0.5, \alpha_3 = 0\}$. Using the additive CCR model (the model (3.58)) at $\alpha_1 = 1$, the results in Table 3.22 are obtained.

Table 3.22 The results obtained for Example 3.7 by the additive CCR model (3.58) at $\alpha_1 = 1$ cut.

DMU	(s_1^*, s_2^*, s_3^*) model (3.58)
1	(58.33, 104.44, 0)
2	(0, 0, 0)
3	(68.33, 2.44, 0)
4	(216.6667, 126.8889, 0)
5	(183.33, 219.7778, 0)
6	(341.6667, 244.2222, 0)
7	(466.6667, 498.8889, 0)
8	(640, 568.6667, 0)
9	(475, 694.6667, 0)
10	(566.6667, 789.5556, 0)

According to the results of Table 3.22, only DMU 2 can be efficient. Therefore, the additive CCR models (3.58), (3.59) at $\alpha_2 = 0.5$ and $\alpha_3 = 0$ are executed for this DMU and the results are shown by Tables 3.23 and 3.24, respectively.

According to the results of Tables 3.22–3.24, DMU 2 is efficient.

To continue, using the additive BCC model (the model (3.60)) at $\alpha_1 = 1$, the results in Table 3.25 are obtained.

According to the results of Table 3.25, the DMU_i, $i = 1, 2, 3, 4$ can be efficient. Therefore, the additive BCC models (3.60), (3.61) at $\alpha_2 = 0.5$ and $\alpha_3 = 0$ are executed for these DMUs and the results are shown in Tables 3.26 and 3.27, respectively.

According to the results of Tables 3.25–3.27, DMUs 1, 2, 3, and 4 are efficient.

Table 3.23 The results obtained for DMU 2 of Example 3.7 by the additive CCR models (3.58), (3.59) at $\alpha_2 = 0.5$ cut.

DMU	(s_1^*, s_2^*, s_3^*) model (3.58)	(s_1^*, s_2^*, s_3^*) model (3.59)
2	(0, 0, 0)	(0, 0, 0)

Table 3.24 The results obtained for DMU 2 of Example 3.7 by the additive CCR models (3.58), (3.59) at $\alpha_3 = 0$ cut.

DMU	(s_1^*, s_2^*, s_3^*)model (3.58)	(s_1^*, s_2^*, s_3^*) model (3.59)
2	(0, 0, 0)	(0, 0, 0)

Table 3.25 The results obtained for Example 3.7 by the additive BCC model (3.60) at $\alpha_1 = 1$ cut.

DMU	(s_1^*, s_2^*, s_3^*) model (3.60)
1	(0, 0, 0)
2	(0, 0, 0)
3	(0, 0, 0)
4	(0, 0, 0)
5	(100, 70, 30)
6	(292.3077, 155.8462, 0)
7	(430.7692, 434.6154, 0)
8	(613.0769, 520.4615, 0)
9	(400, 560, 20)
10	(500, 670, 10)

Table 3.26 The results obtained for DMU_i, $i = 1, 2, 3, 4$ of Example 3.7 by the additive BCC models (3.60), (3.61) at $\alpha_2 = 0.5$ cut.

DMU	(s_1^*, s_2^*, s_3^*) model (3.60)	(s_1^*, s_2^*, s_3^*) model (3.61)
1	(0, 0, 0)	(0, 0, 0)
2	(0, 0, 0)	(0, 0, 0)
3	(0, 0, 0)	(0, 0, 0)
4	(0, 0, 0)	(0, 0, 0)

Table 3.27 The results obtained for DMUs 1, 2, 3, and 4 of Example 3.7 by the additive BCC models (3.60), (3.61) at $\alpha_3 = 0$ cut.

DMU	(s_1^*, s_2^*, s_3^*) model (3.60)	(s_1^*, s_2^*, s_3^*) model (3.61)
1	(0, 0, 0)	(0, 0, 0)
2	(0, 0, 0)	(0, 0, 0)
3	(0, 0, 0)	(0, 0, 0)
4	(0, 0, 0)	(0, 0, 0)

3.6 The fuzzy SBM model

The slacks-based measure (SBM) model based on the slack variables was introduced by Tone (2001) as a nonlinear model as follows,

$$\text{Min } z_O = \frac{1 - \frac{1}{m}\sum_{i=1}^{m}\frac{s_i^-}{x_{io}}}{1 + \frac{1}{s}\sum_{r=1}^{s}\frac{s_r^+}{y_{ro}}}$$

subject to

$$\begin{aligned} &\sum_{j=1}^{n}\lambda_j\tilde{x}_{ij} + \tilde{s}_i^- \cong \tilde{x}_{io} && i = 1, 2, \dots, m \\ &\sum_{j=1}^{n}\lambda_j\tilde{y}_{rj} - \tilde{s}_r^+ \cong \tilde{y}_{ro} && r = 1, 2, \dots, s \\ &\lambda_j \geq 0, \ \tilde{s}_i^- \geq 0, \ \tilde{s}_r^+ \geq 0 && j = 1, 2, \dots, n, \ i = 1, 2, \dots, m, \ r = 1, 2, \dots, s \end{aligned} \tag{3.62}$$

In this model as $0 \leq z_O \leq 1$, DMU_o is efficient if and only if $z_{O^*} = 1$. The linearized forms of the model (3.62) as input-oriented CCR-SBM and output-oriented CCR-SBM models are, respectively, as follows,

$$\text{Min } z_O = 1 - \frac{1}{m}\sum_{i=1}^{m}\frac{s_i^-}{x_{io}}$$

subject to

$$\begin{aligned} &\sum_{j=1}^{n}\lambda_j x_{ij} + s_i^- = x_{io} && i = 1, 2, \dots, m \\ &\sum_{j=1}^{n}\lambda_j y_{rj} - s_r^+ = y_{ro} && r = 1, 2, \dots, s \\ &\lambda_j \geq 0, \ s_i^- \geq 0, \ s_r^+ \geq 0 && j = 1, 2, \dots, n, \ i = 1, 2, \dots, m, \ r = 1, 2, \dots, s \end{aligned} \tag{3.63}$$

$$
\begin{aligned}
&\text{Max } z_O = 1 + \frac{1}{s}\sum_{r=1}^{s}\frac{s_r^+}{y_{ro}} \\
&\text{subject to} \\
&\sum_{j=1}^{n}\lambda_j x_{ij} + s_i^- = x_{io} \qquad i = 1, 2, \ldots, m \\
&\sum_{j=1}^{n}\lambda_j y_{rj} - s_r^+ = y_{ro} \qquad r = 1, 2, \ldots, s \\
&\lambda_j \geq 0, \ s_i^- \geq 0, \ s_r^+ \geq 0 \qquad j = 1, 2, \ldots, n, \ i = 1, 2, \ldots, m, \ r = 1, 2, \ldots, s
\end{aligned} \tag{3.64}
$$

Also, the models (3.63), (3.64) by adding the constraint $\sum_{j=1}^{n}\lambda_j = 1$ are converted to the input-oriented BCC-SBM and output-oriented BCC-SBM model, respectively.

Considering fuzzy input and output values, the input-oriented CCR-SBM and output-oriented CCR-SBM models for $FDMU_O$ are, respectively, as follows,

$$
\begin{aligned}
&\text{Min } z_O = 1 - \frac{1}{m}\sum_{i=1}^{m}\frac{\tilde{s}_i^-}{x_{io}} \\
&\textit{subjectto} \\
&\sum_{j=1}^{n}\lambda_j \tilde{x}_{ij} + \tilde{s}_i^- \cong \tilde{x}_{io} \qquad i = 1, 2, \ldots, m \\
&\sum_{j=1}^{n}\lambda_j \tilde{y}_{rj} - \tilde{s}_r^+ \cong \tilde{y}_{ro} \qquad r = 1, 2, \ldots, s \\
&\sum_{j=1}^{n}\lambda_j = 1 \\
&\lambda_j \geq 0, \ \tilde{s}_i^- \geq 0, \ \tilde{s}_r^+ \geq 0 \qquad j = 1, 2, \ldots, n, \ i = 1, 2, \ldots, m, \ r = 1, 2, \ldots, s
\end{aligned} \tag{3.65}
$$

$$
\begin{aligned}
&\text{Max } z_O = 1 + \frac{1}{s}\sum_{r=1}^{s}\frac{\tilde{s}_r^+}{y_{ro}} \\
&\text{subject to} \\
&\sum_{j=1}^{n}\lambda_j\tilde{x}_{ij} + \tilde{s}_i^- \cong \tilde{x}_{io} && i = 1, 2, \ldots, m \\
&\sum_{j=1}^{n}\lambda_j\tilde{y}_{rj} - \tilde{s}_r^+ \cong \tilde{y}_{ro} && r = 1, 2, \ldots, s \\
&\sum_{j=1}^{n}\lambda_j = 1 \\
&\lambda_j \geq 0,\ \tilde{s}_i^- \geq 0,\ \tilde{s}_r^+ \geq 0 && j = 1, 2, \ldots, n,\ i = 1, 2, \ldots, m,\ r = 1, 2, \ldots, s
\end{aligned} \tag{3.66}
$$

Also, the models (3.65), (3.66) by adding the constraint $\sum_{j=1}^{n}\lambda_j = 1$ are converted to the input-oriented BCC-SBM and output-oriented BCC-SBM models, respectively.

In general, solution approaches of the fuzzy SBM models can be categorized as fuzzy ranking-based approaches and α-cut-based approaches. These methods are detailed in the rest of this section.

3.6.1 Fuzzy ranking-based approach

In this approach, by applying a suitable ranking function on the fuzzy parameters and variables of the model (3.65), the following crisp model is obtained. In this model, each notation is the crisp form of its related fuzzy form in the model (3.65)

$$
\begin{aligned}
&\text{Min } z_O = 1 - \frac{1}{m}\sum_{i=1}^{m}\frac{s_i^-}{x_{io}} \\
&\text{subject to} \\
&\sum_{j=1}^{n}\lambda_j x_{ij} + s_i^- = x_{io} && i = 1, 2, \ldots, m \\
&\sum_{j=1}^{n}\lambda_j y_{rj} - s_r^+ = y_{ro} && r = 1, 2, \ldots, s \\
&\lambda_j \geq 0,\ s_i^- \geq 0,\ s_r^+ \geq 0 && j = 1, 2, \ldots, n,\ i = 1, 2, \ldots, m,\ r = 1, 2, \ldots, s
\end{aligned} \tag{3.67}
$$

Similarly, the crisp form of the model (3.66) is as follows,

$$\text{Max } z_O = 1 + \frac{1}{s}\sum_{r=1}^{s}\frac{s_r^+}{y_{ro}}$$

subject to

$$\begin{aligned}
&\sum_{j=1}^{n}\lambda_j x_{ij} + s_i^- = x_{io} && i = 1,2,\dots,m\\
&\sum_{j=1}^{n}\lambda_j y_{rj} - s_r^+ = y_{ro} && r = 1,2,\dots,s\\
&\lambda_j \geq 0,\ s_i^- \geq 0,\ s_r^+ \geq 0 && j = 1,2,\dots,n,\ i = 1,2,\dots,m,\ r = 1,2,\dots,s
\end{aligned} \tag{3.68}$$

Also, the models (3.67), (3.68) by adding the constraint $\sum_{j=1}^{n}\lambda_j = 1$ are converted to the input-oriented BCC-SBM and output-oriented BCC-SBM models, respectively.

Some points can be highlighted here.

- The solutions obtained by this approach highly depend on the ranking function applied.
- The crisp objective function value obtained by this approach is not necessarily equal to the ranking function value of the exact solution of the model (3.52).
- Feasibility of the models (3.67), (3.68) cannot always be proved easily.
- A shortcoming of the fuzzy ranking methods is that they assign small importance weight values to the lower and upper bounds of the support of a fuzzy number and higher weight values are assigned to the core of the support. Therefore, in the optimal solution, the values associated to the lower and upper bounds of the support become very small (almost zero). So, the models for efficiency evaluation after applying the ranking function will have crisp solutions.

Example 3.8 Consider the data of Example 3.6. Using the below ranking function, the crisp data of the DMUs are obtained, as shown in Table 3.28.

$$d : \mathbb{R} \rightarrow TF_{\mathbb{R}}$$
$$d\big(\tilde{A} = (a_1, a_2, a_3)\big) = 0.3a_1 + 0.4a_2 + 0.3a_3$$

By assessing the DMUs using the CCR-SBM model (model (3.67)) and the BCC-SBM model, the results in Table 3.29 are obtained.

Table 3.28 The crisp data obtained for the fuzzy data of Example 3.6.

DMU	$R(\tilde{X}_1)$	$R(\tilde{X}_2)$	$R(\tilde{Y})$
1	100.6	180	50.6
2	150	273	179.4
3	261.2	348.2	231.2
4	448.8	550	281.2
5	200	250.6	20.6
6	400.6	351.8	70.6
7	551.8	651.8	100
8	740.6	749.4	120
9	501.8	739.4	31.2
10	598.8	850.6	40.6

Table 3.29 Results obtained for the DMUs of Example 3.8 using the CCR SBM model (the model (3.67)) and the BCC SBM model.

DMU	z_O model CCR	z_O model BCC
1	0.4241657	1.000000
2	1.000000	1.000000
3	1.000000	1.000000
4	0.6509515	1.000000
5	0.1056057	0.6106381
6	0.2263701	0.4114874
7	0.1924966	0.2737658
8	0.1895752	0.2394179
9	0.5809932E-01	0.2219595
10	0.6466251E-01	0.1898090

Based on the results of Table 3.29, according to the CCR-SBM model (model (3.67)) the DMUs 2 and 3 are efficient, and according to the BCC-SBM model the DMUs 1, 2, 3, and 4 are efficient.

3.6.2 α-cut-based approach

In this approach, the α-cuts of the production possibility set ($\tilde{T}$) are obtained as crisp sets. Here, the aim is to obtain the fuzzy efficiency of a DMU by the α-cuts of its membership functions of the inputs and the outputs. To solve the fuzzy models (3.65), (3.66), the following α-cut-based models are introduced, respectively.

$$\text{Min } \left[z_O^l, z_O^u\right]_\alpha = 1 - \frac{1}{m}\sum_{i=1}^{m}\frac{\left[s_i^{-l}, s_i^{-u}\right]_\alpha}{\left[x_{io}^l, x_{io}^u\right]_\alpha}$$

subject to

$$\sum_{j=1}^{n}\lambda_j\left[x_{ij}^l, x_{ij}^u\right]_\alpha + \left[s_i^{-l}, s_i^{-u}\right]_\alpha = \left[x_{io}^l, x_{io}^u\right]_\alpha \quad i = 1, 2, \ldots, m$$

$$\sum_{j=1}^{n}\lambda_j\left[y_{rj}^l, y_{rj}^u\right]_\alpha - \left[s_i^{+l}, s_i^{+u}\right]_\alpha = \left[y_{ro}^l, y_{ro}^u\right]_\alpha \quad r = 1, 2, \ldots, s$$

$$\lambda_j \geq 0, \ \left[s_i^{-l}, s_i^{-u}\right]_\alpha \geq 0, \ \left[s_i^{+l}, s_i^{+u}\right]_\alpha \geq 0 \quad j = 1, 2, \ldots, n, \ i = 1, 2, \ldots, m, \ r = 1, 2, \ldots, s \tag{3.69}$$

$$\text{Max } \left[z_O^l, z_O^u\right]_\alpha = 1 + \frac{1}{s}\sum_{r=1}^{s}\frac{\left[s_r^{+l}, s_r^{+u}\right]_\alpha}{\left[y_{ro}^l, y_{ro}^u\right]_\alpha}$$

subject to

$$\sum_{j=1}^{n}\lambda_j\left[x_{ij}^l, x_{ij}^u\right]_\alpha + \left[s_i^{-l}, s_i^{-u}\right]_\alpha = \left[x_{io}^l, x_{io}^u\right]_\alpha \quad i = 1, 2, \ldots, m$$

$$\sum_{j=1}^{n}\lambda_j\left[y_{rj}^l, y_{rj}^u\right]_\alpha - \left[s_i^{+l}, s_i^{+u}\right]_\alpha = \left[y_{ro}^l, y_{ro}^u\right]_\alpha \quad r = 1, 2, \ldots, s$$

$$\lambda_j \geq 0, \ \left[s_i^{-l}, s_i^{-u}\right]_\alpha \geq 0, \ \left[s_i^{+l}, s_i^{+u}\right]_\alpha \geq 0 \quad j = 1, 2, \ldots, n, \ i = 1, 2, \ldots, m, \ r = 1, 2, \ldots, s \tag{3.70}$$

For any α-cut where $(0 \leq \alpha \leq 1)$, each of the above models is an interval linear model. Therefore, applying the operators and comparison logics of the interval numbers, new models are obtained instead. So, the input-oriented CCR-SBM models are converted to the below models, respectively, (for α_j-cut).

$$\text{Min } z_O^1 = 1 - \frac{1}{m}\sum_{i=1}^{m}\frac{s_i^{-l}}{x_{io}^l}$$

subject to

$$\sum_{j=1}^{n}\lambda_j x_{ij}^l + s_i^{-l} = x_{io}^l \quad i = 1, 2, \ldots, m$$

$$\sum_{j=1}^{n}\lambda_j y_{rj}^l - s_i^{+l} = y_{ro}^l \quad r = 1, 2, \ldots, s$$

$$\lambda_j \geq 0, \ s_i^{-l} \geq 0, \ s_i^{+l} \geq 0 \quad j = 1, 2, \ldots, n, \ i = 1, 2, \ldots, m, \ r = 1, 2, \ldots, s \tag{3.71}$$

$$
\begin{aligned}
&\text{Min } z_O^2 = 1 - \frac{1}{m}\sum_{i=1}^{m}\frac{s_i^{-u}}{x_{io}^u}\\
&\text{subject to}\\
&\sum_{j=1}^{n}\lambda_j x_{ij}^u + s_i^{-u} = x_{io}^u \qquad i = 1,2,\ldots,m\\
&\sum_{j=1}^{n}\lambda_j y_{rj}^u - s_i^{+u} = y_{ro}^u \qquad r = 1,2,\ldots,s\\
&\lambda_j \geq 0,\ s_i^{-u} \geq 0,\ s_i^{+u} \geq 0 \qquad j = 1,2,\ldots,n,\ i = 1,2,\ldots,m,\ r = 1,2,\ldots,s
\end{aligned} \tag{3.72}
$$

The models (3.71) and (3.72) are converted to the input-oriented BCC-SBM models by adding the constraint $\sum_{j=1}^{n}\lambda_j = 1$. Also, similar to the models (3.71), (3.72), the output-oriented CCR-SBM models by applying the operators and comparison logics of interval numbers are converted to the below models, respectively, (for α_j-cut).

$$
\begin{aligned}
&\text{Max } z_O^3 = 1 + \frac{1}{s}\sum_{r=1}^{s}\frac{s_r^{+l}}{y_{ro}^l}\\
&\text{subject to}\\
&\sum_{j=1}^{n}\lambda_j x_{ij}^l + s_i^{-l} = x_{io}^l \qquad i = 1,2,\ldots,m\\
&\sum_{j=1}^{n}\lambda_j y_{rj}^l - s_i^{+l} = y_{ro}^l \qquad r = 1,2,\ldots,s\\
&\lambda_j \geq 0,\ s_i^{-l} \geq 0,\ s_i^{+l} \geq 0 \qquad j = 1,2,\ldots,n,\ i = 1,2,\ldots,m,\ r = 1,2,\ldots,s
\end{aligned} \tag{3.73}
$$

$$
\begin{aligned}
&\text{Max } z_O^4 = 1 + \frac{1}{s}\sum_{r=1}^{s}\frac{s_r^{+u}}{y_{ro}^u}\\
&\text{subject to}\\
&\sum_{j=1}^{n}\lambda_j x_{ij}^u + s_i^{-u} = x_{io}^u \qquad i = 1,2,\ldots,m\\
&\sum_{j=1}^{n}\lambda_j y_{rj}^u - s_i^{+u} = y_{ro}^u \qquad r = 1,2,\ldots,s\\
&\lambda_j \geq 0,\ s_i^{-u} \geq 0,\ s_i^{+u} \geq 0 \qquad j = 1,2,\ldots,n,\ i = 1,2,\ldots,m,\ r = 1,2,\ldots,s
\end{aligned} \tag{3.74}
$$

The models (3.73) and (3.74) are converted to the output-oriented BCC-SBM models by adding the constraint $\sum_{j=1}^{n} \lambda_j = 1$. The values of z_O^2, z_O^1 obtained from the models (3.71), (3.72) for each α_j-cut show the efficiency of $FDMU_O$ in that cut. Also, the values of z_O^4, z_O^3 obtained from the models (3.73), (3.74) for each α_j-cut show the efficiency of $FDMU_O$ in that cut that can be shown as $[\tilde{z}_O]_\alpha = [z_O^l, z_O^u]_\alpha$.

Example 3.9 Considering the data of Example 3.6 and the set $\Delta = \{\alpha_1 = 1, \alpha_2 = 0.5, \alpha_3 = 0\}$, the models (3.71), (3.72) (the CCR-BCC models) and also their related BCC-SBM models are used to evaluate the DMUs. The results in Tables 3.30–3.32 are obtained.

Table 3.30 The efficiency values z_O^1, z_O^2 obtained by the models (3.71), (3.72) (the CCR-BCC models) and also their related BCC-SBM models at $\alpha_1 = 1$ for Example 3.9.

DMU	$z_O^1 = z_O^2$ model CCR	$z_O^1 = z_O^2$ model BCC
1	0.4182099	1.000000
2	1.000000	1.000000
3	0.8650977	1.000000
4	0.6439057	1.000000
5	0.1021111	0.6100000
6	0.2240278	0.4119780
7	0.1919969	0.2740721
8	0.1884565	0.2387845
9	0.5563063E-01	0.2216216
10	0.6333333E-01	0.1892157

Table 3.31 The efficiency values z_O^1, z_O^2 obtained by the models (3.71), (3.72) (the CCR-BCC models) and also their related BCC-SBM models at $\alpha_2 = 0.5$ for Example 3.9.

DMU	z_O^1 model CCR	z_O^1 model BCC	z_O^2 model CCR	z_O^2 model BCC
1	0.4120667	1.000000	0.4297382	1.000000
2	1.000000	1.000000	1.000000	1.000000
3	0.8436792	1.000000	1.000000	1.000000
4	0.6326151	1.000000	0.6586497	1.000000
5	0.9659785E-01	0.6051726	0.1121330	0.6156863
6	0.2158386	0.4056851	0.2330851	0.4164581
7	0.1738981	0.2475074	0.1932643	0.2767070
8	0.1777710	0.2306917	0.1588770	0.2273847
9	0.5117950E-01	0.2174765	0.6363280E-01	0.2262567
10	0.5637810E-01	0.1863454	0.5429254E-01	0.1930030

Table 3.32 The efficiency values z_O^1, z_O^2 obtained by the models (3.71), (3.72) (the CCR-BCC models) and also their related BCC-SBM models at $\alpha_3=0$ for Example 3.9.

DMU	z_O^1 model CCR	z_O^1 model BCC	z_O^2 model CCR	z_O^2 model BCC
1	0.4152985	1.000000	0.4427169	1.000000
2	1.000000	1.000000	1.000000	1.000000
3	0.8443643	1.000000	1.000000	1.000000
4	0.6384142	1.000000	0.6761562	1.000000
5	0.9360473E-01	0.6001636	0.1226120	0.6211538
6	0.2138575	0.4011336	0.2432242	0.4213385
7	0.1912522	0.2677694	0.1952925	0.2797608
8	0.1722742	0.2266342	0.2097911	0.2539403
9	0.4801777E-01	0.2132736	0.7202535E-01	0.2308021
10	0.5082848E-01	0.1834154	0.8080770E-01	0.1967111

According to the results of the above tables, only DMU 2 is efficient. This is notable in that applying more cut values can better describe the efficiency of the DMUs.

References

Allahviranloo, T. (2020). *Uncertain information and linear systems*. Springer, International Publishing.

Allahviranloo, T., Abbasbandy, S., & Hajighasemi, S. (2012). A new similarity measure for generalized fuzzy numbers. *Neural Computing and Applications*, *21*(1), 289–294.

Allahviranloo, T., & Adabitabar Firozja, M. (2010). Ranking of fuzzy numbers by a new metric. *Soft Computing*, *14*(7), 773–782.

Allahviranloo, T., Hosseinzadeh Lotfi, F. H., & AdabitabarFirozja, M. (2012). Efficiency in fuzzy production possibility set. *Iranian Journal of Fuzzy Systems*, *9*(4), 17–30.

Allahviranloo, T., Lotfi, F. H., Kiasari, M. K., & Khezerloo, M. (2013). On the fuzzy solution of LR fuzzy linear systems. *Applied Mathematical Modelling*, *37*(3), 1170–1176.

Allahviranloo, T., & Salahshour, S. (2011). Fuzzy symmetric solutions of fuzzy linear systems. *Journal of Computational and Applied Mathematics*, *235*(16), 4545–4553.

Arana-Jimenez, M., Sánchez-Gil, M. C., & Lozano, S. (2020). Efficiency assessment and target setting using a fully fuzzy DEA approach. *International Journal of Fuzzy Systems*, *22*(4), 1056–1072.

Azar, A., Zarei Mahmoudabadi, M., & Emrouznejad, A. (2016). A new fuzzy additive model for determining the common set of weights in data envelopment analysis. *Journal of Intelligent Fuzzy Systems*, *30*(1), 61–69.

Banker, R. D., Charnes, A., & Cooper, W. W. (1984). Some models for estimating technical and scale efficiencies in data envelopment analysis. *Management Science*, 30, 1078–1092.

Charnes, A., & Cooper, W. W. (1962). Programming with linear fractional functionals. *Naval Research Logistics*, *9*, 181–186.

Charnes, A., Cooper, W. W., & Rhodes, E. L. (1978). Measuring the efficiency of decision making units. *European Journal of Operational Research*, 2(6), 429–444.

Cooper, W. W., Thompson, R. G., & Thrall, R. M. (1996). Exntensions and new developments in DEA. *Annals of Operations Research*, *66*, 3–45.

Delgado, M., Verdegay, J. L., & Vila, M. A. (1988). A procedure for ranking fuzzy numbers using fuzzy relations. *Fuzzy Sets and Systems*, *26*(1), 49–62.

Ezzati, R., Allahviranloo, T., Khezerloo, S., & Khezerloo, M. (2012). An approach for ranking of fuzzy numbers. *Expert Systems with Applications*, *39*(1), 690–695.

Ghasemi, M. R., Ignatius, J., Lozano, S., Emrouznejad, A., & Hatami-Marbini, A. (2015). A fuzzy expected value approach under generalized data envelopment analysis. *Knowledge-Based Systems*, *89*, 148–159.

Gu, Q., & Xuan, Z. (2017). A new approach for ranking fuzzy numbers based on possibility theory. *Journal of Computational and Applied Mathematics*, *309*, 674–682.

Guo, P., & Tanaka, H. (2001). Fuzzy DEA: A perceptual evaluation method. *Fuzzy Sets and Systems*, *119*(1), 149–160.

Guo, P., Tanaka, H., & Inuiguchi, M. (2000). Self-organizing fuzzy aggregation models to rank the objects with multiple attributes. *IEEE Transactions on Systems*, *30*(5), 573–580.

Hatami-Marbini, A., Tavana, M., Emrouznejad, A., & Saati, S. (2012). Efficiency measurement in fuzzy additive data envelopment analysis. *International Journal of Industrial and Systems Engineering*, *10*(1), 1–20.

Hougaard, J. L. (1999). Fuzzy scores of technical efficiency. *European Journal of Operational Research*, *115*(3), 529–541.

Hsiao, B., Chern, C. C., Chiu, Y. H., & Chiu, C. R. (2011). Using fuzzy super-efficiency slack-based measure data envelopment analysis to evaluate Taiwan's commercial bank efficiency. *Expert Systems with Applications*, *38*(8), 9147–9156.

Izadikhah, M., & Khoshroo, A. (2018). Energy management in crop production using a novel fuzzy data envelopment analysis model. *RAIRO-Operations Research*, *52*(2), 595–617.

Kao, C., & Liu, S. T. (2000). Fuzzy efficiency measures in data envelopment analysis. *Fuzzy Sets and Systems*, *113*(3), 427–437.

Kerre, E. E. (1982). The use of fuzzy set theory in electrocardiological diagnostics. In *Vol. 20. Approximate reasoning in decision analysis* (pp. 277–282).

Khaleghi, S., Noura, A., & Lotfi, F. H. (2015). Measuring efficiency and ranking fully fuzzy DEA. *Indian Journal of Science and Technology*, *8*(30), 84752.

Koodziejczyk, W. (1986). Orlovsky's concept of decision-making with fuzzy preference relation-further results. *Fuzzy Sets and Systems*, *19*(1), 11–20.

Kordrostami, S., Amirteimoori, A., & Jahani Sayyad Noveiri, M. (2016). Flexibility of variations in radial and non-radial data envelopment analysis models. *International Journal of Industrial Mathematics*, *8*(3), 269–278.

León, T., Liern, V., Ruiz, J. L., & Sirvent, I. (2003). A fuzzy mathematical programming approach to the assessment of efficiency with DEA models. *Fuzzy Sets and Systems*, *139*(2), 407–419.

Lertworasirikul, S., Fang, S. C., Joines, J. A., & Nuttle, H. L. W. (2002). A possibility approach to fuzzy data envelopment analysis. In *Vol. 6. Proceedings of the joint conference on information sciences* (pp. 176–179). Durham, NC: Duke University/Association for Intelligent Machinery.

Lertworasirikul, S., Fang, S. C., Joines, J. A., & Nuttle, H. L. W. (2003a). Fuzzy data envelopment analysis (DEA): A possibility approach. *Fuzzy Sets and Systems*, *139*(2), 379–394.

Lertworasirikul, S., Fang, S. C., Joines, J. A., & Nuttle, H. L. W. (2003b). Fuzzy data envelopment analysis (fuzzy DEA): A credibility approach. In J. L. Verdegay (Ed.), *Fuzzy sets based heuristics for optimization* (pp. 141–158). Physica Verlag.

Lertworasirikul, S., Fang, S. C., Nuttle, H. L. W., & Joines, J. A. (2002). Fuzzy data envelopment analysis. In *Proceedings of the 9th Bellman Continuum, Beijing* (p. 342).

Lertworasirikul, S., Fang, S. C., Nuttle, H. L., & Joines, J. A. (2003). Fuzzy BCC model for data envelopment analysis. *Fuzzy Optimization and Decision Making*, *2*(4), 337–358.

Mahmoodirad, A., Allahviranloo, T., & Niroomand, S. (2019). A new effective solution method for fully intuitionistic fuzzy transportation problem. *Soft Computing*, *23*(12), 4521–4530.

Mahmoodirad, A., Dehghan, R., & Niroomand, S. (2019). Modelling linear fractional transportation problem in belief degree-based uncertain environment. *Journal of Experimental & Theoretical Artificial Intelligence*, *31*(3), 393–408.

Molla-Alizadeh-Zavardehi, S., Mahmoodirad, A., & Rahimian, M. (2014). Step fixed charge transportation problems via genetic algorithm. *Indian Journal of Science and Technology*, 7 (7), 949–954.

Nakamura, K. (1986). Preference relations on a set of fuzzy utilities as a basis for decision making. *Fuzzy Sets and Systems*, *20*(2), 147–162.

Nasseri, S. H., Ebrahimnejad, A., & Cao, B. Y. (2019). *Fuzzy linear programming, fuzzy linear programming: Solution techniques and applications* (pp. 39–61). Berlin, Heidelberg: Springer.

Niroomand, S., Mosallaeipour, S., & Mahmoodirad, A. (2020). A hybrid simple additive weighting approach for constrained multi-criteria facilities location problem of glass production industries under uncertainty. *IEEE Transactions on Engineering Management*, *67* (3), 846–854.

Peykani, P., Mohammadi, E., Emrouznejad, A., Pishvaee, M. S., & Rostamy-Malkhalifeh, M. (2019). Fuzzy data envelopment analysis: An adjustable approach. *Expert Systems with Applications*, *136*, 439–452.

Puri, J., & Yadav, S. P. (2013). A concept of fuzzy input mix-efficiency in fuzzy DEA and its application in banking sector. *Expert Systems with Applications*, *40*(5), 1437–1450.

Ruiz, J. L., & Sirvent, I. (2017). Fuzzy cross-efficiency evaluation: A possibility approach. *Fuzzy Optimization and Decision Making*, *16*(1), 111–126.

Saati, S., & Memariani, A. (2009). SBM model with fuzzy input-output levels in DEA. *Australian Journal of Basic and Applied Sciences*, *3*(2), 352–357.

Saati, S. M., Memariani, A., & Jahanshahloo, G. R. (2002). Efficiency analysis and ranking of DMUs with fuzzy data. *Fuzzy Optimization and Decision Making*, *1*(3), 255–267.

Sheth, N., & Triantis, K. (2003). Measuring and evaluating efficiency and effectiveness using goal programming and data envelopment analysis in a fuzzy environment. *Yugoslav Journal of Operations Research*, *13*(1), 35–60.

Sigarpich, L. A., Allahviranloo, T., Lotfi, F. H., & Kiani, N. A. (2011). Degeneracy in fuzzy linear programming and its application. *International Journal of Uncertainty, Fuzziness and Knowledge-Based Systems*, *19*(06), 999–1012.

Soleimani-Damaneh, M., Jahanshahloo, G. R., & Abbasbandy, S. (2006). Computational and theoretical pitfalls in some current performance measurement techniques; and a new approach. *Applied Mathematics and Computation*, *181*(2), 1199–1207.

Tone, K. (2001). A slacks-based measure of efficiency in data envelopment analysis. *European Journal of Operational Research*, *130*, 498–509.

Wang, Y. M., & Chin, K. S. (2011). Fuzzy data envelopment analysis: A fuzzy expected value approach. *Expert Systems with Applications*, *38*(9), 11678–11685.

Wang, Y. M., Luo, Y., & Liang, L. (2009). Fuzzy data envelopment analysis based upon fuzzy arithmetic with an application to performance assessment of manufacturing enterprises. *Expert Systems with Applications*, *36*(3), 5205–5211.

Wu, J., Xiong, B., An, Q., Zhu, Q., & Liang, L. (2015). Measuring the performance of thermal power firms in China via fuzzy enhanced Russell measure model with undesirable outputs. *Journal of Cleaner Production*, *102*, 237–245.

Zadeh, L. A. (1978). Fuzzy sets as a basis for a theory of possibility. *Fuzzy Sets and Systems*, *1*, 3–28.

CHAPTER FOUR

Ranking, sensitivity and stability analysis in fuzzy DEA

4.1 Introduction

In data envelopment analysis (DEA), the value of the efficiency obtained for each decision-making unit (DMU) is between 0 and 1. Problems happen here when all or some of the DMUs are assessed as efficient DMUs and therefore theoretically cannot be differed. Considering this difficulty, in the literature some methods have been introduced to recognize efficient DMUs as well as compare and rank them. This procedure in DEA is known as ranking. There are numerous methods in the literature for this aim, and each considers typical criteria and characteristics.

The literature on this topic is briefly reviewed here. Saati et al. (2002) presented a linear programming model for ranking in fuzzy Charnes-Cooper-Rhodes (CCR) models (Charnes et al., 1978). Saneifard et al. (2007) presented a fuzzy L_2 norm for the ranking problem of DMUs. Jahanshahloo et al. (2009) applied a fuzzy L_1 norm for ranking DMUs. Wen et al. (2010) applied a credibility theory-based fuzzy Banker-Charnes-Cooper (BCC) model (Banker et al., 1984) to evaluate and rank DMUs. Alem et al. (2013) obtained triangular fuzzy efficiency values for DMUs by the fuzzy BCC model and then applied the fuzzy analytical hierarchy process (AHP) to rank them. Izadikhah et al. (2015) used a superefficiency model for evaluating and ranking DMUs. Also, the studies of Dotoli et al. (2015), Shahverdi (2016), Chen and Wang (2016), Mirzaei and Salehi (2019), etc., can be referenced for the ranking and stability analysis of DEA models.

In this chapter, methods such as fuzzy norm, fuzzy Chebyshev (infinite) norm, fuzzy cross-efficiency, etc., are presented for ranking models in fuzzy DEA.

Uncertainty in Data Envelopment Analysis
https://doi.org/10.1016/B978-0-323-99444-6.00003-7

4.2 Ranking models in fuzzy DEA

4.2.1 Ranking models based on fuzzy L_1 norm

Some ranking models based on the fuzzy L_1 norm are described in this section.

4.2.1.1 The ranking approach of efficient DMUs based on fuzzy L_1 norm

A ranking approach of efficient DMUs based on the fuzzy L_1 norm was proposed by Shahverdi (2016), and it is detailed here. Assume n DMUs where for DMU_j, the fuzzy input vector $\tilde{X}_j = \left(\left(x_{1j}^L, x_{1j}^C, x_{1j}^U\right), \left(x_{2j}^L, x_{2j}^C, x_{2j}^U\right), \ldots, \left(x_{mj}^L, x_{mj}^C, x_{mj}^U\right)\right)$ produces the fuzzy output vector $\tilde{Y}_j = \left(\left(y_{1j}^L, y_{1j}^C, y_{1j}^U\right), \left(y_{2j}^L, y_{2j}^C, y_{2j}^U\right) \ldots, \left(y_{mj}^L, y_{mj}^C, y_{mj}^U\right)\right)$. First by a DEA model, the DMUs are evaluated. Assume that DMU_o with input and output vectors of $\left(\tilde{X}_o, \tilde{Y}_o\right)$ is being evaluated. This DMU is removed from the fuzzy PPS $\tilde{T}_c$ and the new set is called $\tilde{T}_c'$; it is obtained as

$$\tilde{T}_c' = \left\{ (\tilde{X}, \tilde{Y}) | \tilde{X} \geq \sum_{\substack{j=1, \\ j \neq o}}^{n} \lambda_j \tilde{x}_{ij}, \tilde{Y} \leq \sum_{\substack{j=1, \\ j \neq o}}^{n} \lambda_j \tilde{y}_{rj}, \lambda \geq 0 \right\}.$$

The L_1 norm distance of DMU_o from $\tilde{T}_c'$ is considered as a criterion for ranking and is obtained by the below model,

$$\begin{aligned} &\text{Min} \;\; FNL_1\left(\left(\tilde{X}_o, \tilde{Y}_o\right), \left(\tilde{X}', \tilde{Y}'\right)\right) \\ &s.t. \;\; \left(\tilde{X}', \tilde{Y}'\right) \in \tilde{T}_c' \end{aligned}$$

where FNL_1 is the L_1 norm distance of fuzzy values, and the DMU with a higher L_1 norm distance from $\tilde{T}_c'$ obtains a better ranking. This model is rewritten as shown below,

$$
\begin{aligned}
&\text{Min } \widetilde{\Gamma}_c^o\left(\widetilde{X}, \widetilde{Y}\right) = FNL_1\left(\left(\widetilde{X}_o, \widetilde{Y}_o\right), \left(\widetilde{X}', \widetilde{Y}'\right)\right) \\
&\text{subject to} \\
&\qquad \widetilde{x}_i \geq \sum_{j=1, j\neq o}^{n} \lambda_j \widetilde{x}_{ij} \quad i=1,2,\ldots,m \\
&\qquad \widetilde{y}_r \leq \sum_{j=1, j\neq o}^{n} \lambda_j \widetilde{y}_{rj} \quad r=1,2,\ldots,s \\
&\qquad \widetilde{x}_i \geq 0 \qquad\quad i=1,2,\ldots,m \\
&\qquad \widetilde{y}_r \geq 0 \qquad\quad r=1,2,\ldots,s \\
&\qquad \lambda_j \geq 0 \qquad\quad j=1,2,\ldots,s
\end{aligned}
\tag{4.1}
$$

Based on the meter d defined in Chapter 3, the above model is written as shown below,

$$
\begin{aligned}
&\text{Min } \tilde{\Gamma}_c^o(X, Y) = \sum_{i=1}^{m} d(\tilde{x}_i, \tilde{x}_{io}) + \sum_{r=1}^{s} d(\tilde{y}_r, \tilde{y}_{ro}) \\
&\text{subject to} \\
&d(\tilde{x}_i) \geq \sum_{j=1}^{n} d\left(\lambda_j \tilde{x}_{ij}\right) \quad i = 1, 2, \ldots, m \\
&d(\tilde{y}_r) \leq \sum_{j=1}^{n} d\left(\lambda_j \tilde{y}_{rj}\right) \quad r = 1, 2, \ldots, s \\
&d(\tilde{x}_i) \geq 0 \qquad\qquad i = 1, 2, \ldots, m \\
&d(\tilde{y}_r) \geq 0 \qquad\qquad r = 1, 2, \ldots, s \\
&\lambda_j \geq 0 \qquad\qquad\quad j = 1, 2, \ldots, s
\end{aligned}
\tag{4.2}
$$

The model (4.2) is a nonlinear model. The below definition and theorem are used to linearize it.

Definition 4.1. The fuzzy sets $\tilde{T}, \tilde{P}''$ are defined as shown below,

$$
\begin{aligned}
&\tilde{T} = \left\{\left(\tilde{X}, \tilde{Y}\right) | d(\tilde{x}_i) \geq d(\tilde{x}_{io}) \wp \; d(\tilde{y}_r) \leq d(\tilde{y}_{ro})\right\} \\
&\tilde{P}'' = \tilde{T} \cap \tilde{P}'
\end{aligned}
$$

Theorem 4.1. Assume $(\tilde{X}_o, \tilde{Y}_o) \in \tilde{PPS}$ as an extreme efficient DMU. Then, for any $(\widehat{X}, \widehat{Y}) \in \tilde{P}' - \tilde{P}''$ there is at least a member of $\tilde{P}''$ like $(\tilde{X}, \tilde{Y})$ such that $\tilde{\Gamma}(\widehat{X}, \widehat{Y}) > \Gamma(\tilde{X}, \tilde{Y})$.

Proof. Assume $(\widehat{X}, \widehat{Y}) \in \tilde{P}' - \tilde{P}''$ where $1 \geq x \geq 0$. The sets M and N are defined as,

- if $\widehat{x}_u^l x + \widehat{x}_u^r(1-x) < \tilde{x}_{uo}^l x + \tilde{x}_{uo}^r(1-x)$ then $d(\widehat{x}_u) < d(\tilde{x}_{uo})$ and $u \in M$,
- if $\widehat{x}_i^l x + \widehat{x}_i^r(1-x) \geq \tilde{x}_{io}^l x + \tilde{x}_{io}^r(1-x)$ then $d(\hat{x}_i) \geq d(\tilde{x}_{io})$ and $i \in \{1, \cdots, n\} - M$,
- if $\widehat{y}_v^l x + \widehat{y}_v^r(1-x) > \tilde{y}_{vo}^l x + \tilde{y}_{vo}^r(1-x)$ then $d(\widehat{y}_v) > d(\tilde{y}_{vo})$ and $v \in N$,
- if $\widehat{y}_r^l x + \widehat{y}_r^r(1-x) \leq y_{ro}^l x + y_{ro}^r(1-x)$ then $d(\widehat{y}_r) \leq d(\tilde{y}_{ro})$ and $r \in \{1, \cdots, n\} - N$.

The vector $(\tilde{X}, \tilde{Y}) = ((\tilde{x}_1, \cdots, \tilde{x}_n), (\tilde{y}_1, \cdots, \tilde{y}_n))$ is defined such that,

- $d(\tilde{x}_u) = d(\tilde{x}_{uo})$ for $u \in M$,
- $d(\tilde{x}_i) = d(\tilde{x}_{io})$ for $i \in \{1, \cdots, n\} - M$,
- $d(\tilde{y}_v) = d(\tilde{y}_{vo})$ for $v \in N$,
- $d(\tilde{y}_r) = d(\tilde{y}_{ro})$ for $r \in \{1, \cdots, n\} - N$.

Therefore,

$$\forall i\, d(\tilde{x}_i) \geq d(\widehat{x}_i), \quad \forall i\, d(\tilde{y}_r) \geq d(\widehat{y}_r)$$
$$\forall i \;\; d(\tilde{x}_i) \geq d(\tilde{x}_{io}), \quad \forall i \;\; d(\tilde{y}_r) \geq d(\tilde{y}_{ro})$$

And,

$$\tilde{\Gamma}_c^o(\widehat{X}, \widehat{Y}) = \sum_{i=1}^{m} d(\widehat{x}_i, \tilde{x}_{io}) + \sum_{r=1}^{s} d(\widehat{y}_r, \tilde{y}_{ro})$$
$$= \sum_{pti08M} d(\widehat{x}_i, \tilde{x}_{io}) + \sum_{pti\notin M} d(\widehat{x}_i, \tilde{x}_{io}) + \sum_{ptr08N} d(\widehat{y}_r, \tilde{y}_{ro}) + \sum_{ptr\notin N} d(\widehat{y}_r, \tilde{y}_{ro})$$
$$> \sum_{pti\notin M} d(\widehat{x}_i, \tilde{x}_{io}) + \sum_{ptr\notin N} d(\widehat{y}_r, \tilde{y}_{ro}) = \sum_{pti\notin M} d(\tilde{x}_i, \tilde{x}_{io}) + \sum_{ptr\notin N} d(\tilde{y}_r, \tilde{y}_{ro}) = \tilde{\Gamma}_c^o(\tilde{X}, \tilde{Y})$$

According to Theorem 4.1, minimizing the function $\tilde{\Gamma}_c^o(X, Y)$ in the feasible region of the model (4.13) is equivalent to minimizing it in the feasible region $\tilde{P}''$.Therefore, the below model is proposed.

$$\text{Min } \tilde{\Gamma}_c^o(X,Y) = \sum_{i=1}^{m} d(\tilde{x}_i, \tilde{x}_{io}) + \sum_{r=1}^{s} d(\tilde{y}_r, \tilde{y}_{ro})$$

subject to

$$\begin{aligned}
&d(\tilde{x}_i) \geq \sum_{j=1}^{n} d(\lambda_j \tilde{x}_{ij}) && i = 1,2,\ldots,m\\
&d(\tilde{y}_r) \leq \sum_{j=1}^{n} d\left(\lambda_j \tilde{y}_{rj}\right) && r = 1,2,\ldots,s\\
&d(\tilde{x}_i) \geq d(\tilde{x}_{io}) && i = 1,2,\ldots,m\\
&d(\tilde{y}_r) \leq d(\tilde{y}_{ro}) && r = 1,2,\ldots,s\\
&d(\tilde{x}_i) \geq 0 && i = 1,2,\ldots,m\\
&d(\tilde{y}_r) \geq 0 && r = 1,2,\ldots,s\\
&\lambda_j \geq 0 && j = 1,2,\ldots,s
\end{aligned} \tag{4.3}$$

Further, if $(X, Y)\in\tilde{P}''$ then,

$$\begin{aligned}
\tilde{\Gamma}_c^o(X,Y) &= \sum_{i=1}^{m} d(\tilde{x}_i, \tilde{x}_{io}) + \sum_{r=1}^{s} d(\tilde{y}_r, \tilde{y}_{ro})\\
&= \sum_{i=1}^{m} \int_0^1\int_0^1 \left|\left((1-x)x_i^u + xx_i^l\right) - \left((1-x)x_{io}^u + xx_{io}^l\right)\right| dx d\alpha\\
&+ \sum_{r=1}^{s} \int_0^1\int_0^1 \left|\left((1-x)y_r^u + xy_r^l\right) - \left((1-x)y_{ro}^u + xy_{ro}^l\right)\right| dx d\alpha
\end{aligned}$$

and if,

$$\begin{aligned}
\tilde{\Gamma}_c^o(X,Y) &= \sum_{i=1}^{m} \int_0^1\int_0^1 \left(\left((1-x)x_i^u + xx_i^l\right) - \left((1-x)x_{io}^u + xx_{io}^l\right)\right) dx d\alpha\\
&+ \sum_{r=1}^{s} \int_0^1\int_0^1 \left(\left((1-x)y_{ro}^u + xy_{ro}^l\right) - \left((1-x)y_r^u + xy_r^l\right)\right) dx d\alpha\\
&= \sum_{i=1}^{m} \int_0^1 \frac{x_i^u + x_i^l}{2} d\alpha - \sum_{i=1}^{m} \int_0^1 \frac{x_{io}^u + x_{io}^l}{2} d\alpha + \sum_{i=1}^{m} \int_0^1 \frac{y_{ro}^u + y_{ro}^l}{2} d\alpha\\
&- \sum_{i=1}^{m} \int_0^1 \frac{y_r^u + y_r^l}{2} d\alpha
\end{aligned}$$

then the model (4.1) is converted to the below model.

$$\text{Min } \tilde{\Gamma}_c^o(X,Y) = \sum_{i=1}^{m}\int_0^1 \frac{x_i^u + x_i^l}{2}d\alpha - \sum_{i=1}^{m}\int_0^1 \frac{x_{io}^u + x_{io}^l}{2}d\alpha + \sum_{i=1}^{m}\int_0^1 \frac{y_{ro}^u + y_{ro}^l}{2}d\alpha - \sum_{i=1}^{m}\int_0^1 \frac{y_r^u + y_r^l}{2}d\alpha$$

subject to

$$\begin{aligned}
&\sum_{j=1}^{n}\lambda_j\left(\int_0^1 \frac{x_{ij}^l + x_{ij}^u}{2}d\alpha\right) \le \int_0^1 \frac{x_i^l + x_i^u}{2}d\alpha && i = 1,2,\ldots,m\\
&\sum_{j=1}^{n}\lambda_j\left(\int_0^1 \frac{y_{rj}^l + y_{rj}^u}{2}d\alpha\right) \ge \int_0^1 \frac{y_r^l + y_r^u}{2}d && r = 1,2,\ldots,s\\
&\int_0^1 \frac{x_i^l + x_i^u}{2}d\alpha \ge \int_0^1 \frac{x_{io}^l + x_{io}^u}{2}d\alpha && i = 1,2,\ldots,m\\
&\int_0^1 \frac{y_{ro}^l + y_{ro}^u}{2}d\alpha \le \int_0^1 \frac{y_r^l + y_r^u}{2}d\alpha && r = 1,2,\ldots,s\\
&d(\tilde{x}_i) \ge 0 && i = 1,2,\ldots,m\\
&d(\tilde{y}_r) \ge 0 && r = 1,2,\ldots,s\\
&\lambda_j \ge 0 && j = 1,2,\ldots,s
\end{aligned} \tag{4.4}$$

By considering the below terms,

$$\begin{aligned}
&\int_0^1 \frac{x_i^l + x_i^u}{2}d\alpha = x_i && i = 1,\cdots,m\\
&\int_0^1 \frac{x_{io}^l + x_{io}^u}{2}d\alpha = \overline{x}_{io} && i = 1,\cdots,m\\
&\int_0^1 \frac{y_r^l + y_r^u}{2}d\alpha = y_r && r = 1,\cdots,s\\
&\int_0^1 \frac{y_{ro}^l + y_{ro}^u}{2}d\alpha = \overline{y}_{ro} && r = 1,\cdots,s\\
&-\sum_{i=1}^{m}\overline{x}_{ij} + \sum_{i=1}^{m}y_{rj} = \gamma && j = 1,\cdots,n,\ \ i = 1,\cdots,m
\end{aligned}$$

the model (4.4) is converted to the below linear model.

$$\begin{aligned}
&\text{Min } \Gamma_c^o(X,Y) = \sum_{i=1}^{m} x_i - \sum_{r=1}^{s} y_r + \gamma \\
&\text{subject to} \\
&\sum_{j=1, j\neq o}^{n} \lambda_j \overline{x}_{ij} \leq x_{io} \quad i = 1,2,\ldots,m \\
&\sum_{j=1, j\neq o}^{n} \lambda_j \overline{y}_{rj} \geq y_{ro} \quad r = 1,2,\ldots,s \\
&x_i \geq \overline{x}_{io} \quad i = 1,2,\ldots,m \\
&y_r \geq \overline{y}_{ro} \quad r = 1,2,\ldots,s \\
&\lambda_j \geq 0 \quad j = 1,2,\ldots,s
\end{aligned} \tag{4.5}$$

Theorem 4.2. The model (4.5) is always feasible and bounded.
Proof. Assume $k \neq 0$, then,

$$\begin{aligned}
&\lambda_k = 1, \lambda_j = 0 \qquad j = 1, \cdots, n, \ j \neq o, k \\
&y_r = \text{Min}\{y_{rk}, y_{ro}\} \quad r = 1, \cdots, n \quad x_i = \text{Max}\{x_{ik}, x_{io}\} \quad i = 1, \cdots, n
\end{aligned}$$

It is obvious that (X, Y, λ) is a feasible solution of the model (4.5), so $\sum_{i=1}^{m} x_i - \sum_{r=1}^{s} y_r \geq \sum_{i=1}^{m} x_{io} - \sum_{r=1}^{s} y_{ro}$. Therefore, this model is always bounded.

Example 4.1. Consider 30 DMUs with four inputs and four outputs where the triangular fuzzy data of the DMUs are shown in Tables 4.1 and 4.2.

Using the meter *d* presented in Chapter 3, the fuzzy values of Tables 4.1 and 4.2 are converted to the crisp form and are shown in Tables 4.3 and 4.4.

The input-oriented BCC model is used for the crisp data of Tables 4.3 and 4.4 and the efficiency values are shown in Table 4.5.

Then, the model (4.5) is applied to the efficient DMUs and the results are shown in Table 4.6.

Finally, the ranking obtained for the efficient DMUs is shown in Table 4.7.

Table 4.1 The triangular fuzzy input values of Example 4.1.

DMU	*Ib*1	*Ic*1	*Ia*1	*Ib*2	*Ic*2	*Ia*2	*Ib*3	*Ic*3	*Ia*3	*Ib*4	*Ic*4	*Ia*4
1	73,504	86,523	59,153	86	87	84	4000	4000	4000	61,196,521	103,656,656	14,730,450
2	36,583	37,112	36,216	90	92	88	2565	2565	2565	66,287,095	95,701,909	41,144,517
3	25,002	25,369	24,566	87	89	85	1343	1343	1343	47,612,875	69,423,818	28,792,550
4	36,685	37,722	36,078	94	96	93	1500	1500	1500	349,278,139	2,592,824,900	24,277,018
5	36,835	39,445	34,734	83	87	83	1680	1680	1680	68,356,757	80,729,482	43,355,800
6	62,612	73,005	58,344	97	97	97	3750	3750	3750	75,508,661	139,483,237	8,425,500
7	41,573	42,573	38,849	91	92	90	3313	3313	3313	114,264,317	171,152,176	78,011,675
8	55,950	63,341	51,410	92	92	92	1500	1500	1500	74,950,922	135,858,469	14,969,393
9	95,523	100,220	91,930	90	92	84	1600	1600	1600	106,720,451	182,951,858	61,024,310
10	59,081	61,767	52,695	95	97	95	1725	1725	1725	66,010,355	94,511,449	21,625,962
11	40,736	54,521	33,285	78	79	78	1920	1920	1920	86,613,047	124,984,300	39,664,990
12	27,301	27,712	26,687	90	91	89	4433	4433	4433	69,942,333	139,888,000	23,106,000
13	63,295	65,026	61,716	106	111	103	2500	2500	2500	78,657,409	144,462,162	17,756,770
14	94,970	96,821	93,116	94	95	92	2800	2800	2800	78,951,534	168,961,589	30,082,208
15	50,062	52,856	44,305	93	95	92	1630	1630	1630	69,126,959	158,581,843	46,388,243
16	45,926	48,429	41,418	85	85	85	1127	1127	1127	146,206,909	827,138,457	35,631,132
17	82,203	82,923	81,588	104	104	104	3400	3400	3400	107,289,970	256,783,575	33,983,780
18	88,783	98,678	72,553	92	95	91	1304	1304	1304	165,532,950	389,185,592	37,568,447
19	87,247	89,844	84,905	96	98	95	4206	4206	4206	68,355,245	100,855,390	5,504,769
20	33,197	37,990	26,927	100	101	100	1340	1340	1340	92,342,642	136,748,402	52,060,934
21	28,403	29,058	27,744	89	90	88	1393	1393	1393	44,055,008	62,663,680	19,453,875
22	122,898	129,100	107,513	122	123	120	2191	2191	2191	94,312,914	190,535,604	45,229,750
23	32,588	35,194	27,704	100	100	100	2140	2140	2140	89,070,349	141,896,170	45,992,927
24	60,866	61,760	60,140	92	93	91	1231	1231	1231	69,549,539	113,530,688	5,099,980
25	86,430	88,038	83,940	90	90	90	1960	1960	1960	164,581,080	757,564,117	52,110,247
26	44,293	45,339	43,193	82	86	81	3375	3375	3375	63,963,409	109,022,822	33,088,649
27	81,566	83,148	80,107	101	103	101	2540	2540	2540	68,243,449	98,528,957	21,300,223
28	66,803	69,733	58,765	94	98	87	1603	1603	1603	143,921,178	537,844,764	45,363,108
29	40,156	40,860	39,142	82	86	81	2300	2300	2300	65,099,488	94,148,887	10,617,400
30	60,916	61,504	59,846	92	94	90	2930	2930	2930	82,182,154	113,930,230	57,568,217

Table 4.2 The triangular fuzzy output values of Example 4.2.

DMU	*Ob*1	*Oc*1	*Oa*1	*Ob*2	*Oc*2	*Oa*2	*Ob*3	*Oc*3	*Oa*3	*Ob*4	*Oc*4	*Oa*4
1	57,030	58,487	55,830	41	58	30	1269	1350	1117	175	219	145
2	36,872	37,110	36,740	19	35	0	8543	8776	8385	313	486	175
3	38,680	39,449	38,004	20	32	11	6595	6603	6588	275	585	113
4	35,933	36,651	35,469	32	59	10	10,517	10,821	8083	249	341	128
5	54,458	56,082	52,927	30	44	9	9685	9955	9493	222	299	101
6	72,277	78,574	70,254	12	19	0	8022	8752	7536	329	615	82
7	36,625	39,539	32,585	101	129	47	14,513	15,264	13,121	265	392	154
8	46,360	50,028	42,900	17	27	11	1623	1661	1563	226	634	54
9	86,063	87,858	84,531	71	111	43	10,645	11,080	10,206	298	616	179
10	47,242	47,800	46,924	26	36	9	6824	7472	6608	216	342	117
11	38,978	44,298	31,554	184	242	81	12,226	12,582	11,996	178	286	37
12	38,215	39,620	27,169	22	31	11	7562	7731	7422	157	184	124
13	58,340	60,545	56,144	45	77	30	7584	7936	7380	270	430	185
14	88,472	91,461	80,425	40	66	28	661	707	630	136	302	51
15	50,499	50,728	50,210	14	24	6	10,264	10,293	10,247	125	295	28
16	47,907	49,855	40,166	25	37	15	7492	7786	7302	189	286	85
17	59,580	82,222	52,923	20	29	14	4953	5205	4740	157	240	109
18	83,075	89,111	77,340	23	33	13	4917	5151	4745	142	247	72
19	51,027	86,330	46,154	18	25	13	1528	1636	825	218	477	129
20	29,658	33,038	27,978	77	325	23	14,766	15,125	14,473	306	411	190
21	27,735	28,297	27,128	19	36	0	941	973	921	165	275	55
22	102,855	103,641	102,175	48	77	31	2510	3577	252	238	414	120
23	34,064	36,205	31,819	23	32	12	2111	2257	1963	349	522	156
24	53,731	56,514	51,345	63	73	35	10,220	10,344	10,157	164	207	85
25	75,777	85,431	72,915	54	96	40	4480	4705	4193	253	427	112
26	43,845	45,396	42,887	26	36	11	611	658	560	283	390	218
27	79,968	82,314	78,068	43	60	26	9120	9338	8769	193	265	134
28	72,553	74,218	71,743	76	96	50	12,091	13,015	8762	185	240	102
29	38,631	39,065	38,054	25	39	13	1461	1516	1405	75	156	23
30	63,805	64,784	60,864	26	39	10	11,607	12,227	11,143	245	378	122

Table 4.3 The equivalent crisp values of the triangular fuzzy input values of Table 4.1.

DMU	I1	I2	I3	I4
1	73,171.13	132.25	4000	60,195,037
2	36,623.38	131.3889	2565	67,355,154
3	24,984.88	135.5	1343	48,360,529
4	36,792.38	139.25	1500	8.29E+08
5	36,962	130.2222	1680	65,199,699
6	64,143.06	139	3750	74,731,515
7	41,141.88	138.3333	3313	1.19E+08
8	56,662.56	131	1500	75,182,427
9	95,798.88	133.2778	1600	1.14E+08
10	58,155.81	147.1111	1725	62,039,530
11	42,319.56	124.4167	1920	84,468,846
12	27,250.06	135.8333	4433	75,719,667
13	63,333	149.1667	2500	79,883,437
14	94,969.19	145.6389	2800	89,236,716
15	49,321.25	138.9722	1630	85,806,001
16	45,424.88	132.5	1127	2.89E+08
17	82,229	154	3400	1.26E+08
18	87,199	136.6667	1304	1.89E+08
19	87,310.88	156.3056	4206	60,767,662
20	32,827.5	150.4722	1340	93,373,655
21	28,401.88	134.6667	1393	42,556,893
22	120,602.2	166.6944	2191	1.06E+08
23	32,018.38	140.5	2140	91,507,449
24	60,908.19	142.5	1231	64,432,436
25	86,209.44	133.5	1960	2.85E+08
26	44,279.44	123.25	3375	67,509,572
27	81,596.75	146.6667	2540	64,079,019
28	65,526.06	93.02778	1603	2.18E+08
29	40,078.56	82.91667	2300	58,741,316
30	60,795.5	92.05556	2930	83,965,689

Table 4.4 The equivalent crisp values of the triangular fuzzy output values of Table 4.2.

DMU	O1	O2	O3	O4
1	57,094.03	42.44444	1251.25	178.5
2	36,898.5	18.02778	8561.917	321.8056
3	38,703.25	20.86111	6595.139	311.9444
4	35,996.5	33.47222	9984.278	241.5278
5	54,481.14	28.30556	9704.333	210.8333
6	73,345.56	10.63889	8083	338.75
7	36,343.72	94.61111	14,352.92	268.8333
8	46,412.17	18.05556	1617.278	285.0556

Table 4.4 The equivalent crisp values of the triangular fuzzy output values of Table 4.2—cont'd

DMU	O1	O2	O3	O4
9	86,128.92	74.22222	10,644	347.6944
10	47,302.06	24.36111	6932.167	222.6389
11	38,451.89	172.8056	12,257.5	169.9167
12	35,804.69	21.38889	7569.139	155.7222
13	58,342.47	49.36111	7621	288.5278
14	87,207.67	43.5	664.8611	156.3611
15	50,484	14.66667	10,267.06	143.3056
16	46,458.86	25.5	7517.778	187.0278
17	63,576.14	20.69444	4962.639	165.9167
18	83,150.31	23.22222	4932.5	150.5278
19	58,634.28	18.27778	1379.417	260.3889
20	30,083.06	125.6667	14,782.67	303.3611
21	27,723.75	18.61111	943.8333	165.0556
22	102,881.6	50.77778	2212.472	252.5
23	34,037.83	22.55556	2110.444	344
24	53,830.42	58.66667	10,235.03	154.7778
25	77,474.78	60.94444	4464.667	261.4722
26	43,993.42	24.75	609.8333	293.5
27	80,079.72	42.77778	9086.861	196.3611
28	72,766.58	74.44444	11,489.86	177.8889
29	38,595.14	25.44444	1460.528	82.41667
30	63,314.39	25.30556	11,645.89	247.5

Table 4.5 The efficiency values of the DMUs of Example 4.1 obtained by the input-oriented BCC model.

DMU	Efficiency	DMU	Efficiency
1	0.882254	16	0.949552
2	1	17	0.699346
3	1	18	1
4	0.784789	19	0.925856
5	1	20	1
6	1	21	0.750145
7	1	22	1
8	0.892308	23	1
9	1	24	1
10	0.823018	25	0.862972
11	1	26	0.971798
12	0.925674	27	1
13	0.892031	28	1
14	0.992816	29	0.856841
15	0.894218	30	1

Table 4.6 The L_1 norm values obtained for the efficient DMUs.

DMU	Efficiency	Norm L_1
2	1	4.49076521
3	1	1.44E+03
5	1	1.38E+03
6	1	3.69E+01
7	1	0.73674693
9	1	4.44E+02
11	1	8.10E+01
18	1	3.27E+02
20	1	4.87E+03
22	1	4.89E+02
23	1	5.69963584
24	1	1.10E+03
27	1	2.01E+04
28	1	2.97E+02
30	1	5.54E+01

Table 4.7 The ranking obtained for the efficient DMUs of Example 4.1.

DMU	L_1	Rank
27	2.01E+04	1
20	4.87E+03	2
3	1.44E+03	3
5	1.38E+03	4
24	1.10E+03	5
22	4.89E+02	6
9	4.44E+02	7
18	3.27E+02	8
28	2.97E+02	9
11	8.10E+01	10
30	5.54E+01	11
6	3.69E+01	12
23	5.69963584	13
2	4.49076521	14
7	0.73674693	15

4.2.1.2 The hybrid ranking approach based on fuzzy L_1 norm

Assume n DMUs where for DMU_j, the fuzzy input vector $\tilde{X}_j = \left(\left(x_{1j}^L, x_{1j}^C, x_{1j}^U\right), \left(x_{2j}^L, x_{2j}^C, x_{2j}^U\right), \ldots, \left(x_{mj}^L, x_{mj}^C, x_{mj}^U\right)\right)$ produces the fuzzy output vector $\tilde{Y}_j = \left(\left(y_{1j}^L, y_{1j}^C, y_{1j}^U\right), \left(y_{2j}^L, y_{2j}^C, y_{2j}^U\right), \ldots, \left(y_{mj}^L, y_{mj}^C, y_{mj}^U\right)\right)$. First by a DEA model, the DMUs are evaluated. Then a fuzzy indicator is defined to rank the efficient DMUs.

To define a fuzzy indicator, an arbitrary set of fuzzy cuts such as $\Delta=\{\alpha_1,\alpha_2,\ldots,\alpha_p\}$ where $1=\alpha_1>\alpha_2>\ldots>\alpha_p=0$ is considered. Then the fuzzy indicator $IF_O=\{(if_1^L,if_1^U,\alpha_1),(if_2^L,if_2^U,\alpha_2),\ldots,(if_p^L,if_p^U,\alpha_p)\}$ for DMU_O is defined. In this indicator, to calculate if_v^L, if_v^U (where $1\leq v\leq p$) the following steps are done.

Step 1. The values $(LT')_V$, $(UT')_V$ are calculated. For this aim, first the new set $\tilde{T}'$ is constructed by removing DMU_O from the PPS. If the cut v for DMU_j is,

$$[DMU_O]_V=\begin{pmatrix}[\tilde{X}_O]_V\\ [\tilde{Y}_O]_V\end{pmatrix}=\begin{pmatrix}((\underline{x}_{1O},\overline{x}_{1O}),(\underline{x}_{2O},\overline{x}_{2O}),\ldots,(\underline{x}_{mO},\overline{x}_{mO}))\\ \left(\left(\underline{y}_{1O},\overline{y}_{1O}\right),\left(\underline{y}_{2O},\overline{y}_{2O}\right),\ldots,\left(\underline{y}_{rO},\overline{y}_{rO}\right)\right)\end{pmatrix}$$

then the fuzzy set $\tilde{T}'$ in the cut v is considered and the L_1 norm of $[DMU_j]_V$ is obtained from the v-cut of the fuzzy set $\tilde{T}'$ by the below two models.

$$\begin{aligned}
(LT')_V = \text{Min}\ z = &\sum_{i=1}^{m} x_i - \sum_{r=1}^{s} y_r + \Omega\\
\text{subject to}&\\
&\sum_{j=1,j\neq o}^{n} \lambda_j \underline{x}_{ij} \leq x_i \quad i=1,2,\ldots,m\\
&\sum_{j=1,j\neq o}^{n} \lambda_j \overline{y}_{rj} \geq y_r \quad r=1,2,\ldots,s\\
&x_i \geq \underline{x}_{io} \quad i=1,2,\ldots,m\\
&0 \leq y_r \leq \overline{y}_{ro} \quad r=1,2,\ldots,s\\
&\lambda_j \geq 0 \quad j=1,2,\ldots,s
\end{aligned} \tag{4.6}$$

where $\Omega=\sum_{r=1}^{s}\overline{y}_{ro}-\sum_{i=1}^{m}\underline{x}_{io}$ and

$$
\begin{aligned}
(UT')_V = \text{Min } z = \sum_{i=1}^{m} x_i - \sum_{r=1}^{s} y_r + \vartheta \\
\text{subject to} \\
\sum_{j=1, j\neq o}^{n} \lambda_j \overline{x}_{ij} \leq x_{io} \quad & i = 1, 2, \ldots, m \\
\sum_{j=1, j\neq o}^{n} \lambda_j \underline{y}_{rj} \geq y_{ro} \quad & r = 1, 2, \ldots, s \\
x_i \geq \overline{x}_{io} \quad & i = 1, 2, \ldots, m \\
0 \leq y_r \leq \underline{y}_{ro} \quad & r = 1, 2, \ldots, s \\
\lambda_j \geq 0 \quad & j = 1, 2, \ldots, s
\end{aligned}
\tag{4.7}
$$

where, $\vartheta = \sum_{r=1}^{s} \underline{y}_{ro} - \sum_{i=1}^{m} \overline{x}_{io}$.

Step 2. The values $(LT'')_V$, $(UT'')_V$ are calculated. The inefficient DMUs are removed from the *PPS* and a new *PPS* called T'' is constructed. The first step is repeated for T'' and DMU_O, and the values LT'', UT'' are obtained.

Step 3. Let,

$$
\begin{cases}
if_v^L = \delta_1 (LT')_V + \delta_2 (LT'')_V \\
if_v^U = \delta_1 (UT')_V + \delta_2 (UT'')_V
\end{cases}
\quad 1 \leq v \leq p, \ \ \delta_1 + \delta_2 = 1, \ \ 1 > \delta_1 > \delta_2 > 0
$$

Here, δ_1, δ_2 are the importance weights of the regions T', T'' in ranking the DMUs proposed by the decision maker (manager).

Finally, the fuzzy indicators IF_1, IF_2, …, IF_k for k number of efficient DMUs are obtained. By applying a suitable ranking method, these indicators can be ranked and accordingly, a ranking of the efficient DMUs is obtained.

The schematic representation of Step 1 and Step 2 is shown in Fig. 4.1.

Example 4.2. The triangular fuzzy data of 10 DMUs with two inputs and one output are given in Tables 4.8 and 4.9.

Using the below ranking function of triangular fuzzy numbers, the crisp values of Table 4.10 are obtained for the fuzzy data of Tables 4.8 and 4.9.

$$
d : \mathbb{R} \rightarrow TF_{\mathbb{R}}
$$

$$
d\big(\tilde{A} = (a_1, a_2, a_3)\big) = 0.25a_1 + 0.5a_2 + 0.25a_3
$$

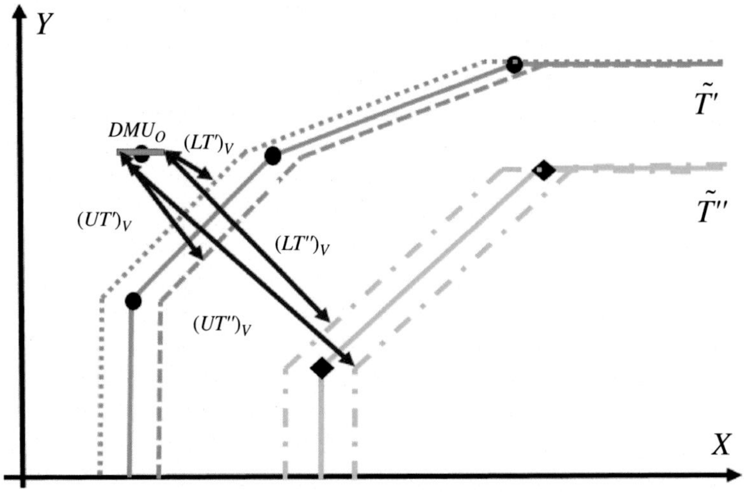

Fig. 4.1 The schematic representation of Step 1 and Step 2 for calculating a fuzzy indicator.

Table 4.8 The triangular fuzzy inputs of the DMUs of Example 4.2.

DMU	x_1^L	x_1^C	x_1^U	x_2^L	x_2^C	x_2^U
1	75.2	100	126.4	137.6	180	222.4
2	113.6	150	186.4	211.2	270	336.8
3	206.4	260	316.8	272	350	423.2
4	353.6	450	543.2	433.6	550	666.4
5	153.6	200	246.4	193.6	250	308
6	312	400	489.6	272	350	432.8
7	433.6	550	671.2	513.6	650	791.2
8	584	740	897.6	592	750	906.4
9	395.2	500	609.6	582.4	740	896
10	464	600	732.8	672	850	1029.6

Table 4.9 The triangular fuzzy output of the DMUs of Example 4.2.

DMU	y_1^L	y_1^C	y_1^U
1	38.4	50	63.2
2	140.8	180	217.6
3	179.2	230	284
4	222.4	280	340.8
5	14.4	20	27.2
6	52.8	70	88.8
7	80	100	120
8	88	120	152
9	20.8	30	42.4
10	25.6	40	56

Table 4.10 The equivalent crisp values of the fuzzy data of Example 4.2.

DMU	$R(\tilde{X}_1)$	$R(\tilde{X}_2)$	$R(\tilde{Y})$
1	100.4	180	50.4
2	150	272	179.6
3	260.8	348.8	230.8
4	449.2	550	280.8
5	200	250.4	20.4
6	400.4	351.2	70.4
7	551.2	651.2	100
8	740.4	749.6	120
9	501.2	739.6	30.8
10	599.2	850.4	40.4

Then, applying the input-oriented BCC model, the efficiency of the DMUs is obtained, as shown in Table 4.11.

The efficient DMUs of Table 4.11 are removed and the new efficiency values of the remaining DMUs are calculated, as shown in Table 4.12.

Table 4.11 The efficiency values obtained by the input-oriented BCC model for the DMUs of Example 4.2.

DMU	Efficiency
1	1
2	1
3	1
4	1
5	0.7188498
6	0.5530794
7	0.3306494
8	0.3062438
9	0.2433748
10	0.2116651

Table 4.12 The new efficiency values of the inefficient DMUs of Table 4.11.

DMU	Efficiency
5	1
6	1
7	1
8	1
9	0.4822091
10	0.4675567

Table 4.13 The rankings obtained for the efficient DMUs of Example 4.2.

DMU	$R(IF_j)$	Rank
1	350.68	1
2	240.80932	2
3	159.729239	4
4	198.067375	3

To rank the efficient DMUs of Table 4.11, the set of cuts $\Delta=\{\alpha_1=1,\alpha_2=0.5,\alpha_3=0\}$ is considered. Then, for each cut value, Steps 1–3 are done for each efficient DMU and the below fuzzy indicator values are obtained.

$$IF_1 = \{(159.12,1),(157.7,161.1,0.5),(157.4,164.2,0)\}$$
$$IF_2 = \{(113.2497,1),(110.7846,100.4292,0.5),(109.9667,109.5615,0)\}$$
$$IF_3 = \{(73.63891,1),(76.89502,64.53485,0.5),(80.29782,73.45587,0)\}$$
$$IF_4 = \{(93.64636,1),(93.86424,83.15696,0.5),(60.52236,98.58159,0)\}$$

Then, applying the ranking function $R\left(\tilde{A}=\{(a_1,1),(a_2,0.5),(a_3,0)\}\right)=a_1+0.5a_2+0.1a_3$ introduced by Yager (1979), the rankings of the efficient DMUs 1, 2, 3, and 4 are obtained and shown in Table 4.13.

4.2.2 The ranking models based on fuzzy L_∞ norm

Assume n DMUs where for DMU_j, the fuzzy input vector $\tilde{X}_j = \left(\left(x_{1j}^L,x_{1j}^C,x_{1j}^U\right),\left(x_{2j}^L,x_{2j}^C,x_{2j}^U\right),\ldots,\left(x_{mj}^L,x_{mj}^C,x_{mj}^U\right)\right)$ produces the fuzzy output vector $\tilde{Y}_j=\left(\left(y_{1j}^L,y_{1j}^C,y_{1j}^U\right),\left(y_{2j}^L,y_{2j}^C,y_{2j}^U\right),\ldots,\left(y_{mj}^L,y_{mj}^C,y_{mj}^U\right)\right)$. If d: $F\mathbb{R}\rightarrow\mathbb{R}$ is the ranking function, first by the ranking-based approaches the DMUs are evaluated and the efficient DMUs are determined. Suppose DMU_o is an efficient DMU. It is removed from the PPS $\tilde{T}$ and the new PPS $\tilde{T}^*$ is determined (for the CCR model $\tilde{T}^*=\left\{(\tilde{X},\tilde{Y})\middle|\tilde{X}\geq\sum_{j=1,j\neq o}^{n}\lambda_j\tilde{x}_{ij}\wp\tilde{Y}\leq\sum_{j=1,j\neq o}^{n}\lambda_j\tilde{y}_{rj}\wp\lambda\geq 0\right\}$). According to the ranking function d, the PPS $D\tilde{T}^*=$ $\left\{(\tilde{X},\tilde{Y})\middle|d(\tilde{x}_i)\geq d\left(\sum_{j=1}^{n}\lambda_j\tilde{x}_{ij}\right)\wp d(\tilde{y}_r)\leq d\left(\sum_{j=1}^{n}\lambda_j\tilde{y}_{rj}\right)\wp\,\lambda\geq 0\right\}$ is defined.

The L_1 norm distance of the vector $\left(d(\tilde{X}_o), d(\tilde{Y}_o)\right)$ from $D\tilde{T}_c'$ is considered as the ranking criterion of DMU_o where its higher value results in a better ranking.

The fuzzy L_∞ norm model for the efficient DMUs is as shown below,

$$\begin{aligned} &\text{Min } L_\infty\left(\left(d(\tilde{X}_o), d(\tilde{Y}_o)\right), \left(d(\tilde{X}), d(\tilde{Y})\right)\right) \\ &\text{subject to} \\ &(\tilde{X}, \tilde{Y}) \in D\tilde{T}^* \end{aligned} \tag{4.8}$$

As the model (4.8) is nonlinear, first we assume $x_{ij} = d(\tilde{x}_{ij}), y_{rj} = d\left(\tilde{y}_{rj}\right)$. Therefore,

$$\begin{aligned} &\text{Min } L_\infty\left(\left(d(\tilde{X}_o), d(\tilde{Y}_o)\right), \left(d(\tilde{X}), d(\tilde{Y})\right)\right) \\ &= \text{Min}\left\{ \underset{i=1,\cdots,m,\, r=1,\cdots,s}{\text{Max}} \left\{ \left| x_{iO} - \sum_{j=1, j\neq o}^{n} \lambda_j x_{ij} \right|, \left| y_{rO} - \sum_{j=1, j\neq o}^{n} \lambda_j y_{rj} \right| \right\} \right\} \end{aligned}$$

If we further consider $V_O = \underset{i=1,\cdots,m,\, r=1,\cdots,s}{\text{Max}} \left\{ \left(\sum_{j=1, j\neq o}^{n} \lambda_j x_{ij} - x_{iO} \right), \left(y_{rO} - \sum_{j=1, j\neq o}^{n} \lambda_j y_{rj} \right) \right\}$, the model (4.8) is linearized as shown below,

$$\begin{aligned} &\text{Min } V_O \\ &\text{subject to} \\ &\sum_{j=1, j\neq o}^{n} \lambda_j x_{ij} - x_{iO} \leq V_O \quad i = 1, 2, \ldots, m \\ &y_{rO} - \sum_{j=1, j\neq o}^{n} \lambda_j y_{rj} \leq V_O \quad r = 1, 2, \ldots, s \\ &\lambda_j \geq 0 \quad j = 1, 2, \ldots, s \end{aligned} \tag{4.9}$$

Similarly, the L_∞ norm BCC model is as shown below,

$$
\begin{aligned}
&\text{Min } V_O \\
&\text{subject to} \\
&\sum_{j=1, j\neq o}^{n} \lambda_j x_{ij} - x_{iO} \leq V_O \qquad i = 1, 2, \ldots, m \\
&y_{rO} - \sum_{j=1, j\neq o}^{n} \lambda_j y_{rj} \leq V_O \\
&\qquad\qquad\qquad\qquad\qquad\qquad r = 1, 2, \ldots, s \\
&\sum_{j=1}^{n} \lambda_j = 1 \\
&\lambda_j \geq 0 \qquad\qquad\qquad\qquad j = 1, 2, \ldots, s
\end{aligned}
\tag{4.10}
$$

In the models (4.9) and (4.10), the ranking criterion of DMU_o is V_O. Its higher value is favored.

Example 4.3. Consider the fuzzy data of Example 4.2. Applying the below ranking function, the crisp values for the fuzzy data of the example are obtained and shown in Table 4.14.

$$
\begin{aligned}
&d : \mathbb{R} \rightarrow TF_{\mathbb{R}} \\
&d\left(\tilde{A} = (a_1, a_2, a_3)\right) = 0.25a_1 + 0.5a_2 + 0.25a_3
\end{aligned}
$$

Then, applying the input-oriented BCC model on the crisp data of Table 4.14, the efficiency values of the DMUs are obtained and shown in Table 4.15.

Table 4.14 The equivalent crisp values of the fuzzy data of Example 4.3.

DMU	$R(\tilde{X}_1)$	$R(\tilde{X}_2)$	$R(\tilde{Y})$
1	100.4	180	50.4
2	150	272	179.6
3	260.8	348.8	230.8
4	449.2	550	280.8
5	200	250.4	20.4
6	400.4	351.2	70.4
7	551.2	651.2	100
8	740.4	749.6	120
9	501.2	739.6	30.8
10	599.2	850.4	40.4

Table 4.15 The efficiency values of the DMUs of Example 4.3 obtained by the input-oriented BCC model.

DMU	Efficiency
1	1
2	1
3	1
4	1
5	0.7188498
6	0.5530794
7	0.3306494
8	0.3062438
9	0.2433748
10	0.2116651

Table 4.16 The rankings of efficient DMUs of Example 4.3 obtained by the L_∞ norm ranking model.

DMU	V_j	Rank
1	79.20894	1
2	34.55352	3
3	17.03966	4
4	50.00000	2

The DMUs 1, 2, 3, and 4 are efficient. For these DMUs, the L_∞ norm ranking model is applied and the efficiency indicator and rankings in Table 4.16 are obtained.

4.2.3 The fuzzy cross-efficiency model

The fuzzy cross-efficiency model tries to improve the weakness of the classical DEA models by considering self-assessment and peer-assessment possibilities. Here, the cross-efficiency model proposed by Chen and Wang (2016) is the focus.

In the existence of n DMUs, m inputs, and s outputs, where x_{ij} is the value of input i for DMU_j and y_{rj} is the value of output r for DMU_j, the CCR efficiency of DMU_k is obtained by the below model.

$$
\begin{aligned}
&\text{Max } \theta_{kk} = \sum_{r=1}^{s} u_{rk} y_{rk} \\
&\text{subject to} \\
&\sum_{i=1}^{m} v_{ik} x_{ik} = 1 \\
&\sum_{r=1}^{s} u_{rk} y_{rj} - \sum_{i=1}^{m} v_{ik} x_{ij} \le 0 \quad j = 1, \ldots, n \\
&u_{rk}, v_{ik} \ge 0 \qquad r = 1, \ldots, s, \quad i = 1, \ldots, m
\end{aligned}
\tag{4.11}
$$

In this model, v_{ik} and u_{rk} are the coefficients of the i-th input and r-th output for DMU_k. If the optimal value θ^*_{kk} is equal to 1, then DMU_k is efficient. Otherwise, it is inefficient.

For the case of fuzzy input and output values, the model (4.11) is converted to the below fuzzy CCR model.

$$
\begin{aligned}
&\text{Max } \theta_{kk} = \sum_{r=1}^{s} u_{rk} \tilde{y}_{rk} \\
&\text{subject to} \\
&\sum_{i=1}^{m} v_{ik} \tilde{x}_{ik} = 1 \\
&\sum_{r=1}^{s} u_{rk} \tilde{y}_{rj} - \sum_{i=1}^{m} v_{ik} \tilde{x}_{ij} \le 0 \quad j = 1, \ldots, n \\
&u_{rk}, v_{ik} \ge 0 \qquad r = 1, \ldots, s, \quad i = 1, \ldots, m
\end{aligned}
\tag{4.12}
$$

The cross-efficiency model uses a secondary objective to optimize the coefficients of inputs and outputs based on the results of the CCR model. In this model, the results of the CCR model are represented as the results of self-assessment. But still, the efficiency should be evaluated according to the other DMUs, which means a peer assessment procedure also is required. So, the following model is used.

$$\begin{aligned}
&\min \quad \sum_{r=1}^{s} u_{rk}\left(\sum_{\substack{j=1\\ j\neq k}}^{n} y_{rj}\right) \\
&\text{subject to} \\
&\sum_{i=1}^{m} v_{ik}\sum_{\substack{j=1\\ j\neq k}}^{n} x_{ij} = 1 \\
&\sum_{r=1}^{s} u_{rk}y_{rk} - \theta_{kk}^{*}\sum_{i=1}^{m} v_{ik}x_{ik} = 0 \\
&\sum_{r=1}^{s} u_{rk}y_{rj} - \sum_{i=1}^{m} v_{ik}x_{ij} \leq 0 \qquad j = 1, \ldots, n \;\; j \neq k \\
&u_{rk}, v_{ik} \geq 0 \qquad r = 1, \ldots, s, \quad i = 1, \ldots, m
\end{aligned} \tag{4.13}$$

The model (4.13) is an offensive cross-efficiency model and its defensive form is obtained as shown below by considering its maximization form.

$$\begin{aligned}
&\max \quad \sum_{r=1}^{s} u_{rk}\left(\sum_{\substack{j=1\\ j\neq k}}^{n} y_{rj}\right) \\
&\text{subject to} \\
&\sum_{i=1}^{m} v_{ik}\sum_{\substack{j=1\\ j\neq k}}^{n} x_{ij} = 1 \\
&\sum_{r=1}^{s} u_{rk}y_{rk} - \theta_{kk}^{*}\sum_{i=1}^{m} v_{ik}x_{ik} = 0 \\
&\sum_{r=1}^{s} u_{rk}y_{rj} - \sum_{i=1}^{m} v_{ik}x_{ij} \leq 0 \qquad j = 1, \ldots, n \;\; j \neq k \\
&u_{rk}, v_{ik} \geq 0 \qquad r = 1, \ldots, s, \quad i = 1, \ldots, m
\end{aligned} \tag{4.14}$$

If the efficiency of DMU_k is θ_{kk}^{*}, the model (4.13) minimizes the cross-efficiency of other DMUs while the model (4.14) maximizes them. In this case, the optimal input and output weights obtained by the models (4.13) and (4.14) are used to calculate the offensive and defensive cross-efficiencies.

Considering fuzzy parameters such as $\tilde{x}_{ij}$, $\tilde{y}_{rj}$, and $\tilde{\theta}^*_{kk}$, the models (4.13) and (4.14) are converted to fuzzy cross-efficiency (FCE) models. However, the offensive and defensive models (4.13) and (4.14) cannot be the overall solution approaches of the cross-efficiency model. This is because of several reasons such as the unclear relationships of the DMUs, obtaining different results from different models, etc.

Among the methods for dealing with fuzzy numbers, the α-cut-based approach proposed by Hatami-Marbini et al. (2011) has been more attractive. Assume $\tilde{M}$ as a fuzzy number with a membership function of A and support of $S(\tilde{M})$. An α-cut of $\tilde{M}$ is shown by $[M^L, M^U]_\alpha$ where,

$$M^L = \min\{m \in S(\tilde{M}) | A(m) \geq \alpha\} \tag{4.15}$$

$$M^U = \max\{m \in S(\tilde{M}) | A(m) \geq \alpha\} \tag{4.16}$$

In this method, $\tilde{M}$ is converted to an interval number and a model with fuzzy data can be solved by interval methods.

4.2.3.1 A solution approach for the fuzzy CCR model

The α-cut of the inputs and outputs is shown by $[X^L, X^U]_\alpha$ and $[Y^L, Y^U]_\alpha$. The below models were introduced by Despotis and Smirlis (2002) for solving the fuzzy input-oriented CCR model with multiplier form using the upper and lower bounds of the efficiency values for DMU_k.

$$\begin{aligned}
&\max\ \theta^U_{kk} = \sum_{r=1}^{s} u_{rk} y^U_{rk} \\
&\text{subject to} \\
&\quad \sum_{i=1}^{m} v_{ik} x^L_{ik} = 1 \\
&\sum_{r=1}^{s} u_{rk} y^U_{rk} - \sum_{i=1}^{m} v_{ik} x^L_{ik} \leq 0 \\
&\sum_{r=1}^{s} u_{rk} y^L_{rj} - \sum_{i=1}^{m} v_{ik} x^U_{ij} \leq 0; \qquad j = 1, \ldots, n\ j \neq k \\
&\quad u_{rk}, v_{ik} \geq 0, \qquad r = 1, \ldots, s,\ \ i = 1, \ldots, m
\end{aligned} \tag{4.17}$$

$$
\begin{aligned}
&\max \ \theta_{kk}^{L} = \sum_{r=1}^{s} u_{rk} y_{rk}^{L} \\
&\text{subject to} \\
&\sum_{i=1}^{m} v_{ik} x_{ik}^{U} = 1 \\
&\sum_{r=1}^{s} u_{rk} y_{rk}^{L} - \sum_{i=1}^{m} v_{ik} x_{ik}^{U} \leq 0 \\
&\sum_{r=1}^{s} u_{rk} y_{rj}^{U} - \sum_{i=1}^{m} v_{ik} x_{ij}^{L} \leq 0 \qquad j = 1, \ldots, n \ j \neq k \\
&u_{rk}, v_{ik} \geq 0 \qquad r = 1, \ldots, s, \quad i = 1, \ldots, m
\end{aligned}
\tag{4.18}
$$

The objective functions of these models form the efficiency value of $[\theta_{kk}^{L*}, \theta_{kk}^{U*}]$, and if $\theta_{kk}^{L*} = \theta_{kk}^{U*} = 1$ then DMU_k is efficient. In the cases that there are more efficient DMUs among the given DMUs, these models are unable to identify them. Therefore, a secondary objective function may be required.

The inputs and outputs of DMU_k are considered as x_{ik}^{L} and y_{ik}^{U}, respectively. If other DMUs produce minimum output values from the maximum input values, then the optimal efficiency of θ_{kk}^{U*} is obtained for DMU_k. But if other DMUs produce maximum output values from the minimum input values, then the optimal efficiency of θ_{kk}^{L*} is obtained for DMU_k. Therefore, by combining the advantages of the offensive and defensive structures, the following cross-efficiency models are obtained.

$$
\begin{aligned}
&\max \ \sum_{r=1}^{s} u_{rk} \left(\sum_{\substack{j=1 \\ j \neq k}}^{n} y_{rj}^{U} \right) \\
&\text{subject to} \\
&\sum_{i=1}^{m} v_{ik} \sum_{\substack{j=1 \\ j \neq k}}^{n} x_{ij}^{L} = 1 \\
&\sum_{r=1}^{s} u_{rk} y_{rk}^{L} - \theta_{kk}^{L*} \sum_{i=1}^{m} v_{ik} x_{ik}^{U} = 0 \\
&\sum_{r=1}^{s} u_{rk} y_{rj}^{U} - \sum_{i=1}^{m} v_{ik} x_{ij}^{L} \leq 0 \qquad j = 1, \ldots, n \ j \neq k \\
&u_{rk}, v_{ik} \geq 0 \qquad r = 1, \ldots, s, \quad i = 1, \ldots, m
\end{aligned}
\tag{4.19}
$$

$$\min \quad \sum_{r=1}^{s} u_{rk}\left(\sum_{\substack{j=1\\ j\neq k}}^{n} y_{rj}^{L}\right)$$

subject to

$$\begin{aligned}
&\sum_{i=1}^{m} v_{ik}\sum_{\substack{j=1\\ j\neq k}}^{n} x_{ij}^{U} = 1\\
&\sum_{r=1}^{s} u_{rk}y_{rk}^{U} - \theta_{kk}^{U*}\sum_{i=1}^{m} v_{ik}x_{ik}^{L} = 0\\
&\sum_{r=1}^{s} u_{rk}y_{rj}^{L} - \sum_{i=1}^{m} v_{ik}x_{ij}^{U} \leq 0 \quad j = 1, \ldots, n \;\; j\neq k\\
&u_{rk}, v_{ik} \geq 0 \qquad\qquad r = 1, \ldots, s, \;\; i = 1, \ldots, m
\end{aligned} \tag{4.20}$$

The model (4.19) optimizes the weight values by considering the efficiency value of θ_{kk}^{L*} for DMU_k and the maximum cross-efficiency for other DMUs. Also, the model (4.20) optimizes the weight values by considering the efficiency value of θ_{kk}^{U*} for DMU_k and the minimum cross-efficiency for other DMUs. In both models, the second constraint guarantees that the efficiency of DMU_k is equal to the optimal CCR efficiency.

Considering DMU_k, the optimal efficiency value of θ_{kj}^{*} is calculated for DMU_j as shown below,

$$\theta_{kj}^{*} = \frac{\sum_{r=1}^{s} u_{rk}^{*} y_{rj}^{U}}{\sum_{i=1}^{m} v_{ik}^{*} x_{ij}^{L}} \qquad k, j = 1, \ldots, n; \;\; k\neq j \tag{4.21}$$

where v_{ik}^{*} and u_{rk}^{*} are the optimal weight values obtained by the model (4.19). Considering DMU_k, the worst efficiency value of θ_{kj}^{*} is calculated for DMU_j as shown below,

$$\theta_{kj}^{**} = \frac{\sum_{r=1}^{s} u_{rk}^{**} y_{rj}^{L}}{\sum_{i=1}^{m} v_{ik}^{**} x_{ij}^{U}} \qquad k, j = 1, \ldots, n; \;\; k\neq j \tag{4.22}$$

where v_{ik}^{**} and u_{rk}^{**} are the optimal weight values obtained by the model (4.20).

As the values θ_{kj}^{*} and θ_{kj}^{**} are not suitable to be the bounds of the efficiency of DMU_j, the upper bound of the efficiency of DMU_j is calculated by the below formula.

$$\overline{\theta}_{j}^{U} = \frac{1}{n}\left(\theta_{jj}^{U*} + \sum_{\substack{k=1\\ k\neq j}}^{n} \theta_{kj}^{*}\right) \qquad j = 1, \ldots, n \tag{4.23}$$

Actually, this upper bound is an average of the self-assessment and peer-assessment efficiencies. Similarly, the lower bound of the efficiency of DMU_j is calculated by the below formula with the same concept.

$$\overline{\theta}_j^L = \frac{1}{n}\left(\theta_{jj}^{L*} + \sum_{\substack{k=1\\k\neq j}}^{n}\theta_{kj}^{**}\right) \quad j = 1, \ldots, n \tag{4.24}$$

Finally, the cross-efficiency of DMU_j is represented as $\left[\overline{\theta}_j^L, \overline{\theta}_j^U\right]_\alpha$.

4.2.3.2 Ranking the DMUs according to the interval cross-efficiency values

As mentioned in the previous section, for a certain cut value the cross-efficiency of DMU_j is represented as $\left[\overline{\theta}_j^L, \overline{\theta}_j^U\right]_\alpha$. To rank the DMUs according to the obtained intervals of cross-efficiency values, the method proposed by Wang et al. (2005) is used. This method is based on minimizing the maximum loss and is suitable for comparing the interval values with a common center value.

For DMU_k assume $b = \max_{j\neq k}\left\{\overline{\theta}_j^U\right\}$. As $\overline{\theta}_k^L < b$, therefore the maximum loss of efficiency $r_k^U = \max_{j\neq k}\left\{\overline{\theta}_j^U\right\} - \overline{\theta}_k^L$ happens. This loss for DMU_k is calculated as shown below,

$$r_k^U = \max\left[\max_{j\neq k}\left\{\overline{\theta}_j^U\right\} - \overline{\theta}_k^L, 0\right] \tag{4.25}$$

Therefore, minimizing the maximum loss is a criterion to select the best interval as shown below,

$$\min_k\left\{r_k^U\right\} = \min_k\left\{\max\left[\max_{j\neq k}\left\{\overline{\theta}_j^U\right\} - \overline{\theta}_k^L, 0\right]\right\} \tag{4.26}$$

The decision should be made based on the minimum value obtained as $\min_k\left\{r_k^U\right\}$.

The procedure of this method is summarized in the following steps.

Step 1. The value of r_k^U for each DMU is calculated by formula (4.25) and the DMU with a minimum value is selected as the best one.

Step 2. The selected DMU of Step 1 is removed from the list of DMUs and Step 1 is repeated.

Step 3. Step 2 is repeated until the list of DMUs becomes empty. The ranking of DMUs is obtained by the order of the first selected DMU to the last selected DMU.

Example 4.4. A DEA problem with 10 DMUs, two inputs, and two outputs with triangular fuzzy data is considered to be evaluated by the above-mentioned FCE model. The data of this example are shown in Table 4.17.

The value of 0.75 is considered for α and the models (4.17) and (4.18) are solved to obtain the self-assessment efficiencies. Using the obtained efficiency values, the models (4.19) and (4.20) are solved to obtain the optimal weight values and also the cross-efficiency values. Then, using the obtained results and Eqs. (4.21) and (4.22), the estimated interval of the efficiency of DMU_j according to DMU_k is obtained (for all DMUs). The obtained results are shown in Tables 4.18–4.22.

In the following, the lower and upper bounds of the cross-efficiency of each DMU are obtained by formulas (4.23) and (4.24) as shown below. The complete results of this step are shown by Table 4.23.

$$\overline{\theta}_j^U = \frac{1}{n}\left(\theta_{jj}^{U*} + \sum_{\substack{k=1 \\ k\neq j}}^{n} \theta_{kj}^{*}\right) \quad j = 1, \ldots, n$$

$$\overline{\theta}_1^U = \frac{0.9092 + 7.4115}{10} = 0.8321, \quad \overline{\theta}_2^U = \frac{1 + 8.8004}{10} = 0.9800$$

Table 4.17 The data of Example 4.4.

	Inputs		Outputs	
DMU	***x*1**	***x*2**	***y*1**	***y*2**
1	[3.7, 4.0, 4.2]	[1.9, 2.1, 2.3]	[2.4, 2.6, 2.9]	[3.8, 4.1, 4.4]
2	[3.0, 3.0, 3.0]	[1.3, 1.5, 1.6]	[2.5, 2.5, 2.5]	[3.3, 3.5, 3.7]
3	[4.4, 4.9, 5.4]	[2.2, 2.6, 3.0]	[2.7, 3.2, 3.7]	[4.3, 5.1, 5.9]
4	[3.4, 4.2, 4.8]	[2.2, 2.3, 2.4]	[2.5, 2.9, 3.3]	[4.4, 5.1, 5.8]
5	[6.0, 6.5, 7.1]	[3.6, 4.1, 4.6]	[5.4, 6.1, 7.8]	[6.5, 7.4, 8.3]
6	[4.7, 4.7, 4.7]	[2.3, 2.8, 3.0]	[3.4, 3.9, 4.0]	[5.1, 5.4, 5.6]
7	[3.3, 3.9, 4.2]	[2.1, 2.1, 2.1]	[3.9, 4.0, 4.3]	[2.3, 2.7, 2.9]
8	[7.5, 7.8, 7.9]	[2.9, 3.3, 3.4]	[4.9, 5.2, 5.6]	[6.9, 6.9, 6.9]
9	[2.1, 2.3, 2.4]	[0.9, 1.3, 1.6]	[1.7, 1.7, 1.7]	[2.8, 3.0, 3.1]
10	[5.2, 5.6, 5.9]	[4.1, 4.1, 4.1]	[4.5, 4.5, 4.5]	[5.4, 5.7, 6.0]

Table 4.18 Interval form of the data of Example 4.4 by $\alpha = 0.75$.

$\alpha = 0.75$		$\alpha = 0.75$		$\alpha = 0.75$		$\alpha = 0.75$	
X11	[0.9375, 1]	X21	[0.6875, 0.8125]	Y11	[0.6875, 0.8125]	Y21	[0.9375, 1]
X12	[0.9375, 1]	X22	[0.4375, 0.5625]	Y12	[0.4375, 0.5625]	Y22	[0.9375, 1]
X13	[0.9375, 1]	X23	[0.9375, 1]	Y13	[0.6875, 0.8125]	Y23	[0.9375, 1]
X14	[0.9375, 1]	X24	[0.9375, 1]	Y14	[0.4375, 0.5625]	Y24	[0.9375, 1]
X15	[0.6875, 0.8125]	X25	[3.975, 1]	Y15	[0.4375, 0.5625]	Y25	[0.6875, 0.8125]
X16	[0.6875, 0.8125]	X26	[0.9375, 1]	Y16	[0.4375, 0.5625]	Y26	[0.6875, 0.8125]
X17	[0.9375, 1]	X27	[0.6875, 0.8125]	Y17	[0.6875, 0.8125]	Y27	[0.9375, 1]
X18	[0.4375, 0.5625]	X28	[0.6875, 0.8125]	Y18	[0.4375, 0.5625]	Y28	[0.4375, 0.5625]
X19	[0.4375, 0.5625]	X29	[0.4375, 0.5625]	Y19	[0.4375, 0.5625]	Y29	[0.4375, 0.5625]
X110	[0.6875, 0.8125]	X210	[0.9375, 1]	Y110	[0.6875, 0.8125]	Y210	[0.6875, 0.8125]

Table 4.19 The optimal weight values obtained by the model (4.19) for Example 4.4.

DMU	*OBJ*	*V1*	*V2*	*U1*	*U2*
1	0.9000454	0.014405347600293	0.016779339711083	0.011642689262978	0.010827989359015
2	0.9015077	0.008405901010408	0.026523208994910	0.013891922434096	0.008966895844412
3	0.8980738	0.014696264028874	0.017118198280551	0.011877813200864	0.011046661011622
4	0.8886659	0.014475637946865	0.016861213171255	0.011699498808567	0.010880824202112
5	0.9160121	0.025235679965870	0.000001678949068	0.017005844948597	0.009214002727099
6	0.8650574	0.024212444667754	0.000001139397014	0.007605259125594	0.013735678434827
7	0.8686779	0.008191063454651	0.027915798038037	0.020307513877264	0.004023186711534
8	0.8261916	0.000001490194514	0.044790278289136	0.020460113166779	0.003887349629815
9	0.8681940	0.022856844400060	0.000000536793315	0.006193580012060	0.013810020619687
10	0.8731349	0.024690617181619	0.000001400426810	0.007755556873565	0.014006982639919

Table 4.20 The optimal weight values obtained by the model (4.20) for Example 4.4.

DMU	*OBJ*	*V1*	*V2*	*U1*	*U2*
1	0.8198256	0.0079039489067090	0.0267474260483370	0.0000000000000000	0.0186961366503890
2	0.7214880	0.0000000000000000	0.0397614314115310	0.0000000000000000	0.0162405846610480
3	0.8218885	0.0080844574755680	0.0273620994542050	0.0000000000000000	0.0191248040853240
4	0.7534695	0.0231347599768650	0.0000000000000000	0.0000000000000000	0.0175429459540210
5	0.7161966	0.0244349419670130	0.0000000000000000	0.0238732191631730	0.0000000000000000
6	0.8739731	0.0233236151603500	0.0000000000000000	0.0120335237591220	0.0114475982567140
7	0.6699911	0.0000000000000000	0.0406917599186160	0.0209699867065260	0.0000000000000000
8	0.7972436	0.0000000000000000	0.0428265524625270	0.0194730639486960	0.0048193580674000
9	0.7044066	0.0000000000000000	0.0395256916996050	0.0000000000000000	0.0156796132362070
10	0.8877462	0.0238663484486870	0.0000000000000000	0.0135161812868340	0.0109585843985050

Table 4.21 The values of θ_{kj}^{*} for the DMUs of Example 4.4 when $\alpha = 0.75$.

DMU	$K=1$	$K=2$	$K=3$	$K=4$	$K=5$	$K=6$	$K=7$	$K=8$	$K=9$	$K=10$
1	**0.9092**	0.8539	0.8396	0.8396	0.8476	0.8175	0.7957	0.7728	0.8273	0.8175
2	1.0000	**1.0000**	1.0000	1.0000	0.9936	0.9330	1.0000	1.0000	0.9408	0.9330
3	0.8678	0.8804	**0.9472**	0.8678	0.8745	0.8484	0.8158	0.7915	0.8593	0.8484
4	0.9609	0.9469	0.9609	**1.0000**	0.9869	0.9837	0.8533	0.8036	1.0000	0.9837
5	1.0000	1.0000	1.0000	1.0000	**1.0000**	1.0000	1.0000	0.9163	1.0000	1.0000
6	0.9300	0.9361	0.9300	0.9300	0.9861	**1.0000**	0.8980	0.8470	0.9269	0.9201
7	0.8652	0.9318	0.8652	0.8652	1.0000	0.7573	**1.0000**	1.0000	0.7375	0.7573
8	0.8269	0.9045	0.8269	0.8269	0.7884	0.7222	0.8872	**0.9957**	0.7256	0.7222
9	1.0000	1.0000	1.0000	1.0000	1.0000	1.0000	0.8992	0.8659	**1.0000**	1.0000
10	0.7764	0.7375	0.7764	0.7764	0.9347	0.8526	0.7186	0.6236	0.8561	**0.9455**

Table 4.22 The values of θ_{kj}^{**} for the DMUs of Example 4.4 when $\alpha = 0.75$.

DMU	$K=1$	$K=2$	$K=3$	$K=4$	$K=5$	$K=6$	$K=7$	$K=8$	$K=9$	$K=10$
1	**0.7760**	0.7647	0.8406	0.7536	0.6152	0.8126	0.6112	0.7500	0.7426	0.8129
2	1.0000	**1.0000**	1.0000	0.8720	0.8142	0.9944	0.8448	1.0000	0.8974	1.0000
3	0.8184	0.7413	**0.7550**	0.7394	0.5979	0.7943	0.5869	0.7221	0.7199	0.7943
4	0.9535	0.8652	0.9535	**0.8451**	0.6289	0.8878	0.6206	0.7860	0.8403	0.8844
5	0.8102	0.6936	0.8102	0.8182	**0.9943**	0.9893	0.7227	0.8288	0.6737	1.0000
6	0.8781	0.7632	0.8781	0.8591	0.7847	**0.8950**	0.6826	0.8125	0.7412	0.9751
7	0.5550	0.5057	0.5550	0.4960	0.9770	0.8370	**1.0000**	1.0000	0.4911	0.8667
8	0.8556	0.8476	0.8556	0.6687	0.6399	0.7707	0.7943	**0.8841**	0.8232	0.7758
9	1.0000	0.8763	1.0000	0.9621	0.7144	1.0000	0.6371	0.8036	**0.9647**	0.9967
10	0.6806	0.5604	0.6806	0.7516	0.7747	0.8956	0.5656	0.6534	0.5442	**0.8113**

Table 4.23 The comparison of DMUs by the FCE model with $\alpha=0.75$ and the FDEA model.

DMU	FDEA	Rank	$FCE\alpha=0.75$	Rank
1	[0.7760, 0.9092]	10	[0.7479, 0.8321]	9
2	[1.0000, 1.0000]	1	[0.9423, 0.9800]	1
3	[0.7550, 0.9472]	9	[0.7270, 0.8601]	8
4	[0.8451, 1.0000]	6	[0.8265, 0.9480]	5
5	[0.9943, 1.0000]	3	[0.8341, 0.9916]	3
6	[0.8950, 1.0000]	5	[0.8270, 0.9304]	4
7	[1.0000, 1.0000]	1	[0.7283, 0.8779]	7
8	[0.8841, 0.9958]	7	[0.7915, 0.8227]	6
9	[0.9647, 1.0000]	4	[0.8955, 0.9765]	2
10	[0.8113, 0.9455]	8	[0.6918, 0.7998]	10

$$\overline{\theta}_j^L = \frac{1}{n}\left(\theta_{jj}^{L*} + \sum_{\substack{k=1 \\ k\neq j}}^{n} \theta_{kj}^{**}\right) \quad j = 1, \ldots, n$$

$$\overline{\theta}_1^L = \frac{0.7760 + 6.7034}{10} = 0.7479, \quad \overline{\theta}_2^L = \frac{1 + 8.4228}{10} = 0.9423$$

Considering the results of Table 4.23, for the FDEA model it is difficult to introduce an exact complete ranking. For example, between DMU_2 and DMU_7, introducing the better DMU is not possible as the same fuzzy CCR efficiency is obtained for both of them. This weakness is solved in the FCE model by considering the self-assessment and peer-assessment concepts. Also, the sensitivity of the fuzzy CCR and FCE models over different α values is shown in Table 4.24.

Now, the steps of the proposed algorithm for minimizing the maximum loss of efficiency are used to rank the DMUs. Therefore, applying Step 1, for all DMUs the maximum loss of efficiency values by Eq. (4.25) are calculated as shown below,

Table 4.24 The efficiency values obtained by the FCCR and FCE models at different α values for Example 4.4.

FCCR	$FCCR\alpha = 0$	$FCCR\alpha = 0.25$	$FCCR\alpha = 0.5$	$FCCR\alpha = 0.75$	$FCCR\alpha = 1$
DMU_1	[0.5863, 1.0000]	[0.6468, 1.0000]	[0.7091, 0.9716]	[0.7760, 0.9092]	0.8405
DMU_2	[0.7662, 1.0000]	[0.8470, 1.0000]	[0.9453, 1.0000]	[1.0000, 1.0000]	1
DMU_3	[0.5121, 1.0000]	[0.5868, 1.0000]	[0.6681, 1.0000]	[0.755, 0.9472]	0.8453
DMU_4	[0.6231, 1.0000]	[0.6904, 1.0000]	[0.7640, 1.0000]	[0.8451, 1.0000]	0.9582
DMU_5	[0.6814, 1.0000]	[0.7765, 1.0000]	[0.8829, 1.0000]	[0.9943, 1.0000]	1
DMU_6	[0.6752, 1.0000]	[0.7472, 1.0000]	[0.8230, 1.0000]	[0.8950, 1.0000]	0.9615
DMU_7	[0.8571, 1.0000]	[0.9440, 1.0000]	[1.0000, 1.0000]	[1.0000, 1.0000]	1
DMU_8	[0.7095, 1.0000]	[0.7857. 1.0000]	[0.8363, 1.0000]	[0.8841, 0.9958]	0.9335
DMU_9	[0.7003, 1.0000]	[0.7794, 1.0000]	[0.8671, 1.0000]	[0.9647, 1.0000]	1
DMU_{10}	[0.6257, 1.0000]	[0.6834, 1.0000]	[0.7460, 0.9880]	[0.8113, 0.9455]	0.8787
FCE	$FCE\alpha = 0$	$FCE\alpha = 0.25$	$FCE\alpha = 0.5$	$FCE\alpha = 0.75$	$FCE\alpha = 1$
DMU_1	[0.5565, 0.7865]	[0.6184, 0.8057]	[0.6856, 0.8231]	[0.7479, 0.8321]	[0.7938, 0.8225]
DMU_2	[0.7568, 0.8595]	[0.8226, 0.8998]	[0.8891, 0.9362]	[0.9423, 0.9800]	[0.9653, 0.9969]
DMU_3	[0.4932, 0.8624]	[0.5665, 0.8652]	[0.6486, 0.8684]	[0.7270, 0.8601]	[0.7985, 0.8282]
DMU_4	[0.5993, 0.9478]	[0.6747, 0.9381]	[0.7546, 0.9483]	[0.8265, 0.9480]	[0.8889, 0.9232]
DMU_5	[0.5902, 1.0000]	[0.6643, 1.0000]	[0.7555, 0.9972]	[0.8341, 0.9916]	[0.8659, 0.9231]
DMU_6	[0.6317, 0.8332]	[0.6965, 0.8675]	[0.7708, 0.8991]	[0.8270, 0.9304]	[0.8618, 0.9095]
DMU_7	[0.5888, 0.8302]	[0.6377, 0.8488]	[0.6806, 0.8557]	[0.7283, 0.8779]	[0.7406, 0.7887]
DMU_8	[0.6665, 0.7284]	[0.7200, 0.7741]	[0.7519, 0.7983]	[0.7915, 0.8227]	[0.8245, 0.8328]
DMU_9	[0.6607, 0.9427]	[0.7336, 0.9549]	[0.8257, 0.9673]	[0.8955, 0.9765]	[0.9366, 0.9761]
DMU_{10}	[0.5349, 0.7190]	[0.5808, 0.7398]	[0.6442, 0.7770]	[0.6918, 0.7998]	[0.7033, 0.7593]

$$r^u_{(DMU_1)} = \max[\max(0.98, 0.8601, 0.948, 0.9916, 0.9304, 0.8779, 0.8227, 0.9765, 0.7998) - 0.7479, 0] = 0.243681$$

$$\underline{r^u_{(DMU_2)}} = \max[\max(0.8321, 0.8601, 0.948, 0.9916, 0.9304, 0.8779, 0.8227, 0.9765, 0.7998) - 0.9423, 0] = 0.049346$$

$$r^u_{(DMU_3)} = \max[\max(0.8321, 0.98, 0.948, 0.9916, 0.9304, 0.8779, 0.8227, 0.9765, 0.7998) - 0.727, 0] = 0.264672$$

$$r^u_{(DMU_4)} = \max[\max(0.8321, 0.98, 0.8601, 0.9916, 0.9304, 0.8779, 0.8227, 0.9765, 0.7998) - 0.8265, 0] = 0.165101$$

$$r^u_{(DMU_5)} = \max[\max(0.8321, 0.98, 0.8601, 0.948, 0.9304, 0.8779, 0.8227, 0.9765, 0.7998) - 0.8341, 0] = 0.145954$$

$$r^u_{(DMU_6)} = \max[\max(0.8321, 0.98, 0.8601, 0.948, 0.9916, 0.8779, 0.8227, 0.9765, 0.7998) - 0.827, 0] = 0.164667$$

$$r^u_{(DMU_7)} = \max[\max(0.8321, 0.98, 0.8601, 0.948, 0.9916, 0.9304, 0.8227, 0.9765, 0.7998) - 0.7283, 0] = 0.263282$$

$$r^u_{(DMU_8)} = \max[\max(0.8321, 0.98, 0.8601, 0.948, 0.9916, 0.9304, 0.8779, 0.9765, 0.7998) - 0.7915, 0] = 0.200083$$

$$r^u_{(DMU_9)} = \max[\max(0.8321, 0.98, 0.8601, 0.948, 0.9916, 0.9304, 0.8779, 0.8227, 0.7998) - 0.8955, 0] = 0.096132$$

$$r^u_{(DMU_{10})} = \max[\max(0.8321, 0.98, 0.8601, 0.948, 0.9916, 0.9304, 0.8779, 0.8227, 0.9765) - 0.8918, 0] = 0.299812$$

Then, DMU_2 (with minimum loss of efficiency value) is removed and the calculations are done for the remaining DMUs as shown below,

$$
\begin{aligned}
r^{u}_{(DMU_1)} &= \max[\max(0.98, 0.8601, 0.948, 0.9916, 0.9304, 0.8779, 0.8227, 0.9765, 0.7998) - 0.7479, 0] = 0.243681\\
r^{u}_{(DMU_3)} &= \max[\max(0.8321, 0.98, 0.948, 0.9916, 0.9304, 0.8779, 0.8227, 0.9765, 0.7998) - 0.727, 0] = 0.264672\\
r^{u}_{(DMU_4)} &= \max[\max(0.8321, 0.98, 0.8601, 0.9916, 0.9304, 0.8779, 0.8227, 0.9765, 0.7998) - 0.8265, 0] = 0.165101\\
r^{u}_{(DMU_5)} &= \max[\max(0.8321, 0.98, 0.8601, 0.948, 0.9304, 0.8779, 0.8227, 0.9765, 0.7998) - 0.8341, 0] = 0.142414\\
r^{u}_{(DMU_6)} &= \max[\max(0.8321, 0.98, 0.8601, 0.948, 0.9916, 0.8779, 0.8227, 0.9765, 0.7998) - 0.827, 0] = 0.164667\\
r^{u}_{(DMU_7)} &= \max[\max(0.8321, 0.98, 0.8601, 0.948, 0.9916, 0.9304, 0.8227, 0.9765, 0.7998) - 0.7283, 0] = 0.263282\\
r^{u}_{(DMU_8)} &= \max[\max(0.8321, 0.98, 0.8601, 0.948, 0.9916, 0.9304, 0.8779, 0.9765, 0.7998) - 0.7915, 0] = 0.200083\\
\underline{r^{u}_{(DMU_9)}} &= \max[\max(0.8321, 0.98, 0.8601, 0.948, 0.9916, 0.9304, 0.8779, 0.8227, 0.7998) - 0.8955, 0] = 0.096132
\end{aligned}
$$

Then, DMU_9 (with a minimum loss of efficiency value) is removed and the calculations are done for the remaining DMUs as shown below,

$$
\begin{aligned}
r^{u}_{(DMU_1)} &= \max[\max(0.98, 0.8601, 0.948, 0.9916, 0.9304, 0.8779, 0.8227, 0.9765, 0.7998) - 0.7479, 0] = 0.243681\\
r^{u}_{(DMU_3)} &= \max[\max(0.8321, 0.98, 0.948, 0.9916, 0.9304, 0.8779, 0.8227, 0.9765, 0.7998) - 0.727, 0] = 0.264672\\
r^{u}_{(DMU_4)} &= \max[\max(0.8321, 0.98, 0.8601, 0.9916, 0.9304, 0.8779, 0.8227, 0.9765, 0.7998) - 0.8265, 0] = 0.165101\\
r^{u}_{(DMU_5)} &= \max[\max(0.8321, 0.98, 0.8601, 0.948, 0.9304, 0.8779, 0.8227, 0.9765, 0.7998) - 0.8341, 0] = 0.11388\\
r^{u}_{(DMU_6)} &= \max[\max(0.8321, 0.98, 0.8601, 0.948, 0.9916, 0.8779, 0.8227, 0.9765, 0.7998) - 0.827, 0] = 0.164667\\
r^{u}_{(DMU_7)} &= \max[\max(0.8321, 0.98, 0.8601, 0.948, 0.9916, 0.9304, 0.8227, 0.9765, 0.7998) - 0.7283, 0] = 0.263282\\
r^{u}_{(DMU_8)} &= \max[\max(0.8321, 0.98, 0.8601, 0.948, 0.9916, 0.9304, 0.8779, 0.9765, 0.7998) - 0.7915, 0] = 0.200083\\
r^{u}_{(DMU_{10})} &= \max[\max(0.8321, 0.98, 0.8601, 0.948, 0.9916, 0.9304, 0.8779, 0.8227, 0.9765) - 0.8918, 0] = 0.299812
\end{aligned}
$$

Then, DMU_5 (with minimum loss of efficiency value) is removed and the calculations are done for the remaining DMUs as shown below,

$$
\begin{aligned}
r^{u}_{(DMU_1)} &= \max[\max(0.98, 0.8601, 0.948, 0.9916, 0.9304, 0.8779, 0.8227, 0.9765, 0.7998) - 0.7479, 0] = 0.200023 \\
r^{u}_{(DMU_3)} &= \max[\max(0.8321, 0.98, 0.948, 0.9916, 0.9304, 0.8779, 0.8227, 0.9765, 0.7998) - 0.727, 0] = 0.221014 \\
\underline{r^{u}_{(DMU_4)}} &= \max[\max(0.8321, 0.98, 0.8601, 0.9916, 0.9304, 0.8779, 0.8227, 0.9765, 0.7998) - 0.8265, 0] = 0.103901 \\
r^{u}_{(DMU_6)} &= \max[\max(0.8321, 0.98, 0.8601, 0.948, 0.9916, 0.8779, 0.8227, 0.9765, 0.7998) - 0.827, 0] = 0.219624 \\
r^{u}_{(DMU_7)} &= \max[\max(0.8321, 0.98, 0.8601, 0.948, 0.9916, 0.9304, 0.8227, 0.9765, 0.7998) - 0.7283, 0] = 0.219624 \\
r^{u}_{(DMU_8)} &= \max[\max(0.8321, 0.98, 0.8601, 0.948, 0.9916, 0.9304, 0.8779, 0.9765, 0.7998) - 0.7915, 0] = 0.156425
\end{aligned}
$$

Then, DMU_4 (with a minimum loss of efficiency value) is removed and the calculations are done for the remaining DMUs as shown below,

$$
\begin{aligned}
r^{u}_{(DMU_1)} &= \max[\max(0.98, 0.8601, 0.948, 0.9916, 0.9304, 0.8779, 0.8227, 0.9765, 0.7998) - 0.7479, 0] = 0.182482 \\
r^{u}_{(DMU_3)} &= \max[\max(0.8321, 0.98, 0.948, 0.9916, 0.9304, 0.8779, 0.8227, 0.9765, 0.7998) - 0.727, 0] = 0.203473 \\
\underline{r^{u}_{(DMU_6)}} &= \max[\max(0.8321, 0.98, 0.8601, 0.948, 0.9916, 0.8779, 0.8227, 0.9765, 0.7998) - 0.827, 0] = 0.05098 \\
r^{u}_{(DMU_7)} &= \max[\max(0.8321, 0.98, 0.8601, 0.948, 0.9916, 0.9304, 0.8227, 0.9765, 0.7998) - 0.7283, 0] = 0.202083 \\
r^{u}_{(DMU_8)} &= \max[\max(0.8321, 0.98, 0.8601, 0.948, 0.9916, 0.9304, 0.8779, 0.9765, 0.7998) - 0.7915, 0] = 0.138884 \\
r^{u}_{(DMU_{10})} &= \max[\max(0.8321, 0.98, 0.8601, 0.948, 0.9916, 0.9304, 0.8779, 0.8227, 0.9765) - 0.8918, 0] = 0.238613
\end{aligned}
$$

Then, DMU_6 (with a minimum loss of efficiency value) is removed and the calculations are done for the remaining DMUs as shown below,

$$r^{u}_{(DMU_1)} = \max[\max(0.98, 0.8601, 0.948, 0.9916, 0.9304, 0.8779, 0.8227, 0.9765, 0.7998) - 0.7479, 0] = 0.129994$$
$$r^{u}_{(DMU_3)} = \max[\max(0.8321, 0.98, 0.948, 0.9916, 0.9304, 0.8779, 0.8227, 0.9765, 0.7998) - 0.727, 0] = 0.150985$$
$$r^{u}_{(DMU_7)} = \max[\max(0.8321, 0.98, 0.8601, 0.948, 0.9916, 0.9304, 0.8227, 0.9765, 0.7998) - 0.7283, 0] = 0.131771$$
$$\underline{r^{u}_{(DMU_8)}} = \max[\max(0.8321, 0.98, 0.8601, 0.948, 0.9916, 0.9304, 0.8779, 0.9765, 0.7998) - 0.7915, 0] = 0.086396$$
$$r^{u}_{(DMU_{10})} = \max[\max(0.8321, 0.98, 0.8601, 0.948, 0.9916, 0.9304, 0.8779, 0.8227, 0.9765) - 0.8918, 0] = 0.186125$$

Then, DMU_8 (with a minimum loss of efficiency value) is removed and the calculations are done for the remaining DMUs as shown below,

$$\underline{r^{u}_{(DMU_1)}} = \max[\max(0.98, 0.8601, 0.948, 0.9916, 0.9304, 0.8779, 0.8227, 0.9765, 0.7998) - 0.7479, 0] = 0.129994$$
$$r^{u}_{(DMU_3)} = \max[\max(0.8321, 0.98, 0.948, 0.9916, 0.9304, 0.8779, 0.8227, 0.9765, 0.7998) - 0.727, 0] = 0.150985$$
$$r^{u}_{(DMU_7)} = \max[\max(0.8321, 0.98, 0.8601, 0.948, 0.9916, 0.9304, 0.8227, 0.9765, 0.7998) - 0.7283, 0] = 0.131771$$
$$r^{u}_{(DMU_{10})} = \max[\max(0.8321, 0.98, 0.8601, 0.948, 0.9916, 0.9304, 0.8779, 0.8227, 0.9765) - 0.8918, 0] = 0.186125$$

Then, DMU_1 (with a minimum loss of efficiency value) is removed and the calculations are done for the remaining DMUs as shown below,

$$\begin{aligned} r^u_{(DMU_3)} &= \max[\max(0.8321, 0.98, 0.948, 0.9916, 0.9304, 0.8779, 0.8227, 0.9765, 0.7998) - 0.727, 0] = 0.150985 \\ \underline{r^u_{(DMU_7)}} &= \max[\max(0.8321, 0.98, 0.8601, 0.948, 0.9916, 0.9304, 0.8227, 0.9765, 0.7998) - 0.7283, 0] = 0.131771 \\ r^u_{(DMU_{10})} &= \max[\max(0.8321, 0.98, 0.8601, 0.948, 0.9916, 0.9304, 0.8779, 0.8227, 0.9765) - 0.8918, 0] = 0.186125 \end{aligned}$$

Then, DMU_7 (with a minimum loss of efficiency value) is removed and the calculations are done for the remaining DMUs as shown below,

$$\begin{aligned} \underline{r^u_{(DMU_3)}} &= \max[\max(0.8321, 0.98, 0.948, 0.9916, 0.9304, 0.8779, 0.8227, 0.9765, 0.7998) - 0.727, 0] = 0.072816 \\ r^u_{(DMU_{10})} &= \max[\max(0.8321, 0.98, 0.8601, 0.948, 0.9916, 0.9304, 0.8779, 0.8227, 0.9765) - 0.8918, 0] = 0.168302 \end{aligned}$$

Then, DMU_3 (with a minimum loss of efficiency value) is removed and DMU_{10} obtains the last ranking. The overall ranking is the order of DMUs 2, 9, 5, 4, 6, 8, 1, 7, 3, and 10.

The proposed algorithm for minimizing the maximum loss of efficiency is used for different α values and both of the FCE and FDEA models and the obtained rankings are reported by Tables 4.25 and 4.26.

The rankings of Tables 4.25 and 4.26 show that by changing the α value, the rankings. Obtained by the FCE model have more stability compared to the rankings obtained by the FDEA model. Also, the FCE model can easily introduce a unique rank for each DMU while in the FDEA model, a similar ranking may be obtained for more than one DMU. For example for $\alpha=1$, the DMUs 2, 5, and 7 have the rank of 1.

4.2.4 Other ranking models of fuzzy DEA

In this section, some other ranking models of fuzzy DEA are reviewed and discussed. These models are presented in the rest of this section.

4.2.4.1 The model of ranking the efficient DMUs by the inefficient DMUs

Assume DMU_j ($j=1, \cdots, n$) with fuzzy inputs $\tilde{X}_j = \left(\left(x_{1j}^L, x_{1j}^C, x_{1j}^U\right), \left(x_{2j}^L, x_{2j}^C, x_{2j}^U\right)\ldots, \left(x_{mj}^L, x_{mj}^C, x_{mj}^U\right)\right)$ produces fuzzy outputs $\tilde{Y}_j = \left(\left(y_{1j}^L, y_{1j}^C, y_{1j}^U\right), \left(y_{2j}^L, y_{2j}^C, y_{2j}^U\right), \ldots, \left(y_{mj}^L, y_{mj}^C, y_{mj}^U\right)\right)$. The following definition explains the efficiency concept of this DMU.

Definition 4.2. If the values $\theta_j^{l\alpha_c}$, $\theta_j^{u\alpha_c}$ are the efficiency of DMU_j obtained by the input-oriented BCC model in envelopment form, considering a set of cut values the following cases happen.

- If for all cut values $\theta_j^{u\alpha_c}=1$ then DMU_j is fuzzy efficient.
- If for one cut value $\theta_j^{u\alpha_c}=1$ and for one other cut value $\theta_j^{u\alpha_t}<1$ then DMU_j is fuzzy semiefficient.
- If for all cut values $\theta_j^{u\alpha_c}<1$ then DMU_j is fuzzy inefficient.

To rank the efficient DMUs according to the inefficient DMUs for any cut α_c from the set $\Delta=\{\alpha_1, \alpha_2, \ldots, \alpha_p\}$, the interval index of $\left[\underline{f}^c, \overline{f}^c\right]$ is calculated for the efficient DMU DMU_O. Then, the fuzzy index of $RF_O=\{(f_o^{\alpha_1}, \alpha_1), (f_o^{\alpha_2}, \alpha_2), \ldots, (f_o^{\alpha_p}, \alpha_p)\}$ is calculated for the efficient DMU DMU_O where $o=1, \cdots, k$. Then, applying a suitable ranking function, the fuzzy indexes $IF_1, IF_2, \cdots, IF_k$ are ranked and accordingly the ranking of DMUs is obtained.

For calculating if_v where $1\le v\le p$, first by removing DMU_O from the PPS, the set T'_O is constructed. Then, using the input-oriented BCC models with envelopment form, the inefficient DMUs are evaluated in any cut value of the set $\Delta=\{\alpha_1, \alpha_2, \ldots, \alpha_p\}$ in the set T'_O.

Table 4.25 The rankings obtained by the proposed algorithm for minimizing the maximum loss of efficiency at α values and the FCE model for Example 4.4.

Rank	1	2	3	4	5	6	7	8	9	10	
DMU	DMU_2	DMU_8	DMU_9	DMU_5	DMU_4	DMU_6	DMU_7	DMU_3	DMU_1	DMU_{10}	$\alpha=0$
Rank	1	2	3	4	5	6	7	8	9	10	$\alpha=0.25$
DMU	DMU_2	DMU_9	DMU_5	DMU_4	DMU_8	DMU_6	DMU_7	DMU_3	DMU_1	DMU_{10}	
Rank	1	2	3	4	5	6	7	8	9	10	$\alpha=0.5$
DMU	DMU_2	DMU_9	DMU_5	DMU_4	DMU_6	DMU_8	DMU_1	DMU_7	DMU_3	DMU_{10}	
Rank	1	2	3	4	5	6	7	8	9	10	$\alpha=0.75$
DMU	DMU_2	DMU_9	DMU_5	DMU_4	DMU_6	DMU_8	DMU_1	DMU_7	DMU_3	DMU_{10}	
Rank	1	2	3	4	5	6	7	8	9	10	$\alpha=1$
DMU	DMU_2	DMU_9	DMU_4	DMU_5	DMU_6	DMU_8	DMU_3	DMU_1	DMU_7	DMU_{10}	

Table 4.26 The rankings obtained by the proposed algorithm for minimizing the maximum loss of efficiency at α values and the FDEA model for Example 4.4.

Rank	1	2	3	4	5	6	7	8	9	10	
DMU	DMU_7	DMU_2	DMU_8	DMU_9	DMU_5	DMU_6	DMU_{10}	DMU_4	DMU_1	DMU_3	$\alpha=0$
Rank	1	2	3	4	5	6	7	8	9	10	$\alpha=0.25$
DMU	DMU_7	DMU_2	DMU_8	DMU_9	DMU_5	DMU_6	DMU_4	DMU_{10}	DMU_1	DMU_3	
Rank	1	2	3	4	5	6	7	8	9	10	$\alpha=0.5$
DMU	DMU_7	DMU_2	DMU_5	DMU_9	DMU_8	DMU_6	DMU_4	DMU_{10}	DMU_1	DMU_3	
Rank	1	3	4	5	6	7	8	9	10		$\alpha=0.75$
DMU	DMU_2 DMU_7	DMU_5	DMU_9	DMU_6	DMU_8	DMU_4	DMU_{10}	DMU_3	DMU_1		
Rank	1 DMU_2 DMU_7 DMU_5	4 DMU_9	5 DMU_6	6 DMU_4	7 DMU_8	8 DMU_{10}	9 DMU_3	10 DMU_1			$\alpha=1$

After removing DMU_O, the input-oriented BCC models with envelopment form for evaluating DMU_V (where $V\in\{k+1,\cdots,n\}$) are as follows,

$$
\begin{aligned}
&\min\ \widehat{\theta}_v^{l\alpha} \\
&\text{subject to} \\
&\sum_{j=1,j\neq o}^{n} \lambda_j^{l\alpha} x_{ij}^{l\alpha} \leq \widehat{\theta}_v^{l\alpha} x_{iv}^{l\alpha} \quad i=1,\ldots,m \\
&\sum_{j=1,j\neq o}^{n} \lambda_j^{l\alpha} y_{rj}^{l\alpha} \geq y_{rv}^{l\alpha} \\
&\qquad\qquad r=1,\ldots,s \\
&\sum_{j=1,j\neq o}^{n} \lambda_j = 1 \\
&\lambda_j^{l\alpha} \geq 0 \quad j=1,2,\ldots,n,\ j\neq o
\end{aligned}
\tag{4.27}
$$

$$
\begin{aligned}
&\min\ \widehat{\theta}_v^{u\alpha} \\
&\text{subject to} \\
&\sum_{j=1,j\neq o}^{n} \lambda_j^{u\alpha} x_{ij}^{u\alpha} \leq \widehat{\theta}_v^{u\alpha} x_{iv}^{u\alpha} \quad i=1,\ldots,m \\
&\sum_{j=1,j\neq o}^{n} \lambda_j^{u\alpha} y_{rj}^{u\alpha} \geq y_{rv}^{u\alpha} \quad r=1,\ldots,s \\
&\sum_{j=1,j\neq o}^{n} \lambda_j = 1 \\
&\lambda_j^{u\alpha} \geq 0 \quad j=1,2,\ldots,n,\ j\neq o
\end{aligned}
\tag{4.28}
$$

By the above-mentioned models, in each cut value of the set $\Delta=\{\alpha_1,\alpha_2,\ldots,\alpha_p\}$ the efficiency values $\widehat{\theta}_v^{l\alpha_c},\widehat{\theta}_v^{u\alpha_c}$ are obtained for DMU_V where $V\in\{k+1,\cdots,n\}$. Then, the following difference of efficiency values is calculated for each DMU.

$$
\mathrm{E}_v^{l\alpha_c}=\theta_v^{l\alpha_c}-\widehat{\theta}_v^{l\alpha_c},\quad \mathrm{E}_v^{u\alpha_c}=\theta_v^{u\alpha_c}-\widehat{\theta}_v^{u\alpha_c} \quad v=k+1,\cdots,n
$$

Then, the average of difference values is calculated as shown below.

$$
M\mathrm{E}_o^{l\alpha_c}=\frac{1}{v}\sum_{v=k+1}^{n}\mathrm{E}_v^{l\alpha_c},\qquad M\mathrm{E}_o^{u\alpha_c}=\frac{1}{v}\sum_{v=k+1}^{n}\mathrm{E}_v^{u\alpha_c}
$$

Considering the importance of values w_1, w_2 such that $w_1+w_2=1$, $0<w_1\le w_2<1$, the evaluation criterion of DMU_O (where $o=1, \cdots, k$) in cut value α_c (where $c=1, \cdots, p$) is obtained as,

$$f_o^{\alpha_c} = w_1 ME_o^{l\alpha_c} + w_2 ME_o^{u\alpha_c} \qquad c = 1, \cdots, p, \;\; v = k+1, \cdots, n$$

and finally the fuzzy evaluation index of $RF_O=\{(f_o^{\alpha_1},\alpha_1),(f_o^{\alpha_2},\alpha_2),\ldots,(f_o^{\alpha_p},\alpha_p)\}$ is obtained.

Example 4.5. Considering the data of Example 4.4 and the set of cut values $\Delta=\{\alpha_1=1,\alpha_2=0.5,\alpha_3=0.8,\alpha_4=0\}$, the DMUs are evaluated by the input-oriented BCC model with envelopment form in each cut value, and the results are shown in Table 4.27.

Table 4.27 The efficiency of the DMUs of Example 4.5 in the given cut values.

α_k-cut		$\alpha_1=1$	$\alpha_2=0.8$	$\alpha_3=0.5$	$\alpha_5=0$
DMU_1	$\theta_1^{l\alpha_c}$	1	1	1	1
	$\theta_1^{u\alpha_c}$		1	1	1
DMU_2	$\theta_2^{l\alpha_c}$	1	1	1	1
	$\theta_2^{u\alpha_c}$		1	1	1
DMU_3	$\theta_3^{l\alpha_c}$	1	1	1	1
	$\theta_3^{u\alpha_c}$		1	1	1
DMU_4	$\theta_4^{l\alpha_c}$	1	1	1	1
	$\theta_4^{u\alpha_c}$		1	1	1
DMU_5	$\theta_5^{l\alpha_c}$	0.7200000	0.7181965	0.7154472	0.7107438
	$\theta_5^{u\alpha_c}$		0.7936508	0.7215686	0.7230769
DMU_6	$\theta_6^{l\alpha_c}$	0.5547253	0.5519299	0.5468599	0.5439338
	$\theta_6^{u\alpha_c}$		0.5988738	0.5567104	0.5596824
DMU_7	$\theta_7^{l\alpha_c}$	0.3313609	0.3293577	0.2818792	0.3261293
	$\theta_7^{u\alpha_c}$		0.3489413	0.3332979	0.3361728
DMU_8	$\theta_8^{l\alpha_c}$	0.3060513	0.3022876	0.2953020	0.2926520
	$\theta_8^{u\alpha_c}$		0.3196046	0.2904201	0.3247856
DMU_9	$\theta_9^{l\alpha_c}$	0.2432432	0.2418655	0.2397820	0.2362637
	$\theta_9^{u\alpha_c}$		0.2695418	0.2469799	0.2506667
DMU_{10}	$\theta_{10}^{l\alpha_c}$	0.2117647	0.2103774	0.2082840	0.2047619
	$\theta_{10}^{u\alpha_c}$		0.2346316	0.2149533	0.2180974

In each cut value, the efficient DMUs of Table 4.27 (DMU_1, DMU_2, DMU_3, DMU_4) are removed from the *PPS* and the inefficient DMUs of Table 4.27 are evaluated again by the models (4.27) and (4.28).

By removing DMU_1, the efficiency values in Table 4.28 are obtained.

The average of the difference of the efficiency values is calculated as shown below,

$$\mathrm{E}^{l\alpha_1} = 0.15509656, \mathrm{E}^{l\alpha_2} = 0.15552592, \mathrm{E}^{l\alpha_3} = 0.1529058, \\ \mathrm{E}^{l\alpha_4} = 0.15989162$$

$$\mathrm{E}^{u\alpha_1} = 0.15509656, \mathrm{E}^{u\alpha_2} = 0.11608336, \mathrm{E}^{u\alpha_3} = 0.1582736, \\ \mathrm{E}^{u\alpha_4} = 0.15427314$$

Then, considering the weight values of $w_1 = 0.3$, $w_2 = 0.7$, the fuzzy index below is obtained for DMU_1.

$$RF_1 = \{(0.15509656, 1), (0.127916128, 0.8), (0.15666326, 0.5), (0.155958684, 0)\}$$

By removing DMU_2, the efficiency values in Table 4.29 are obtained.

The average of the difference of the efficiency values is calculated as shown below,

$$\mathrm{E}^{l\alpha_1} = 0.01076744, \mathrm{E}^{l\alpha_2} = 0.01122518, \mathrm{E}^{l\alpha_3} = 0.01258958, \\ \mathrm{E}^{l\alpha_4} = 0.01026758$$

Table 4.28 Efficiency of the inefficient DMUs of Table 4.27 in the given cut values by the models (4.27) and (4.28) when removing DMU_1.

		α-cut			
DMU		$\alpha_1 = 1$	$\alpha_2 = 0.8$	$\alpha_3 = 0.5$	$\alpha_5 = 0$
DMU_5	$\theta_5^{l\alpha_c}$	1	1	1	1
	$\theta_5^{u\alpha_c}$	1	**1**	**1**	**1**
DMU_6	$\theta_6^{l\alpha_c}$	0.7339286	0.7320111	0.7273357	0.7314222
	$\theta_6^{u\alpha_c}$	0.7339286	0.7324313	0.7328976	0.7337622
DMU_7	$\theta_7^{l\alpha_c}$	0.4015385	0.3989462	0.3934225	0.3947317
	$\theta_7^{u\alpha_c}$	0.4015385	0.4021451	0.4053014	0.4104011
DMU_8	$\theta_8^{l\alpha_c}$	0.3516667	0.3489003	0.3302013	0.3443380
	$\theta_8^{u\alpha_c}$	0.3516667	0.3531700	0.3531605	0.3660198
DMU_9	$\theta_9^{l\alpha_c}$	0.3520833	0.3499560	0.3456956	0.3453499
	$\theta_9^{u\alpha_c}$	0.3520833	0.3533740	0.3567747	0.3622766
DMU_{10}	$\theta_{10}^{l\alpha_c}$	0.3034111	0.3018300	0.2986264	0.2981008
	$\theta_{10}^{u\alpha_c}$	0.3034111	0.3045403	0.3071640	0.3113878

Table 4.29 Efficiency of the inefficient DMUs of Table 4.27 in the given cut values by the models (4.27) and (4.28) when removing DMU_2.

		α-cut			
DMU		$\alpha_1=1$	$\alpha_2=0.8$	$\alpha_3=0.5$	$\alpha_5=0$
DMU_5	$\theta_5^{l\alpha_c}$	0.7200000	0.7181965	0.7154472	0.7107438
	$\theta_5^{u\alpha_c}$	0.7200000	0.7936508	0.7215686	0.7230769
DMU_6	$\theta_6^{l\alpha_c}$	0.5682540	0.5659483	0.5624328	0.5564171
	$\theta_6^{u\alpha_c}$	0.5682540	0.6185265	0.5678176	0.5673071
DMU_7	$\theta_7^{l\alpha_c}$	0.3495726	0.3487045	0.3474015	0.3452280
	$\theta_7^{u\alpha_c}$	0.3495726	0.3745861	0.3471318	0.3449605
DMU_8	$\theta_8^{l\alpha_c}$	0.3281481	0.3250477	0.3203529	0.3124079
	$\theta_8^{u\alpha_c}$	0.3281481	0.3518381	0.3024742	0.3375039
DMU_9	$\theta_9^{l\alpha_c}$	0.2432432	0.2418655	0.2397820	0.2362637
	$\theta_9^{u\alpha_c}$	0.2432432	0.2695418	0.2469799	0.2506667
DMU_{10}	$\theta_{10}^{l\alpha_c}$	0.2117647	0.2103774	0.2082840	0.2047619
	$\theta_{10}^{u\alpha_c}$	0.2117647	0.2346316	0.2149533	0.2180974

$$\mathrm{E}^{u\alpha_1} = 0.01076744, \mathrm{E}^{u\alpha_2} = 0.0155062, \mathrm{E}^{u\alpha_3} = 0.00739904,$$
$$\mathrm{E}^{u\alpha_4} = 0.00582614$$

Then, considering the weight values of $w_1=0.3$, $w_2=0.7$, the fuzzy index below is obtained for DMU_2.

$$RF_2 = \{(0.01076744, 1), (0.014221894, 0.8), (0.008956202, 0.5), (0.007158572, 0)\}$$

By removing DMU_3, the efficiency values in Table 4.30 are obtained.

The average of the difference of the efficiency values is calculated as shown below,

$$\mathrm{E}^{l\alpha_1} = 0, \mathrm{E}^{l\alpha_2} = 0, \mathrm{E}^{l\alpha_3} = 0, \mathrm{E}^{l\alpha_4} = 0$$
$$\mathrm{E}^{u\alpha_1} = 0, \mathrm{E}^{u\alpha_2} = 0, \mathrm{E}^{u\alpha_3} = 0, \mathrm{E}^{u\alpha_4} = 0$$

Then, considering the weight values of $w_1=0.3$, $w_2=0.7$, the fuzzy index below is obtained for DMU_3.

$$RF_3 = \{(0, 1), (0, 0.8), (0, 0.5), (0, 0)\}$$

By removing DMU_4, the efficiency values in Table 4.31 are obtained.

The average of the difference of the efficiency values is calculated as shown below,

$$\mathrm{E}^{l\alpha_1} = 0, \mathrm{E}^{l\alpha_2} = 0, \mathrm{E}^{l\alpha_3} = 0, \mathrm{E}^{l\alpha_4} = 0$$
$$\mathrm{E}^{u\alpha_1} = 0, \mathrm{E}^{u\alpha_2} = 0, \mathrm{E}^{u\alpha_3} = 0, \mathrm{E}^{u\alpha_4} = 0$$

Table 4.30 Efficiency of the inefficient DMUs of Table 4.27 in the given cut values by the models (4.27) and (4.28) when removing DMU_3.

		α-cut			
DMU		$\alpha_1 = 1$	$\alpha_2 = 0.8$	$\alpha_3 = 0.5$	$\alpha_5 = 0$
DMU_5	$\theta_5^{l\alpha_c}$	0.7200000	0.7181965	0.7154472	0.7107438
	$\theta_5^{u\alpha_c}$	0.7200000	0.7936508	0.7215686	0.7230769
DMU_6	$\theta_6^{l\alpha_c}$	0.5547253	0.5519299	0.5468599	0.5439338
	$\theta_6^{u\alpha_c}$	0.5547253	0.5988738	0.5567104	0.5596824
DMU_7	$\theta_7^{l\alpha_c}$	0.3313609	0.3293577	0.3250774	0.3261293
	$\theta_7^{u\alpha_c}$	0.3313609	0.3489413	0.3332979	0.3361728
DMU_8	$\theta_8^{l\alpha_c}$	0.3060513	0.3022876	0.2953020	0.2926520
	$\theta_8^{u\alpha_c}$	0.3060513	0.3196046	0.2904201	0.3247856
DMU_9	$\theta_9^{l\alpha_c}$	0.2432432	0.2418655	0.2397820	0.2362637
	$\theta_9^{u\alpha_c}$	0.2432432	0.2695418	0.2469799	0.2506667
DMU_{10}	$\theta_{10}^{l\alpha_c}$	0.2117647	0.2103774	0.2082840	0.2047619
	$\theta_{10}^{u\alpha_c}$	0.2117647	0.2346316	0.2149533	0.2180974

Table 4.31 Efficiency of the inefficient DMUs of Table 4.27 in the given cut values by the models (4.27) and (4.28) when removing DMU_4.

		α-cut			
DMU		$\alpha_1 = 1$	$\alpha_2 = 0.8$	$\alpha_3 = 0.5$	$\alpha_5 = 0$
DMU_5	$\theta_5^{l\alpha_c}$	0.7200000	0.7181965	0.7154472	0.7107438
	$\theta_5^{u\alpha_c}$	0.7200000	0.7936508	0.7215686	0.7230769
DMU_6	$\theta_6^{l\alpha_c}$	0.5547253	0.5519299	0.5468599	0.5439338
	$\theta_6^{u\alpha_c}$	0.5547253	0.5988738	0.5567104	0.5596824
DMU_7	$\theta_7^{l\alpha_c}$	0.3313609	0.3293577	0.3250774	0.3261293
	$\theta_7^{u\alpha_c}$	0.3313609	0.3489413	0.3332979	0.3361728
DMU_8	$\theta_8^{l\alpha_c}$	0.3060513	0.3022876	0.2953020	0.2926520
	$\theta_8^{u\alpha_c}$	0.3060513	0.3196046	0.2904201	0.3247856
DMU_9	$\theta_9^{l\alpha_c}$	0.2432432	0.2418655	0.2397820	0.2362637
	$\theta_9^{u\alpha_c}$	0.2432432	0.2695418	0.2469799	0.2506667
DMU_{10}	$\theta_{10}^{l\alpha_c}$	0.2117647	0.2103774	0.2082840	0.2047619
	$\theta_{10}^{u\alpha_c}$	0.2117647	0.2346316	0.2149533	0.2180974

Then, considering the weight values of $w_1 = 0.3$, $w_2 = 0.7$, the fuzzy index below is obtained for DMU_4.

$$RF_4 = \{(0,1),(0,0.8),(0,0.5),(0,0)\}$$

Table 4.32 Ranking of the efficient DMUs of Example 4.5.

DMU	$R(RF_j)$	Rank
1	0.351356961	1
2	0.027338913	2
3	0	3
4	0	3

Now, the below ranking function introduced by Yager (1979) is used to rank the obtained fuzzy indexes as shown in Table 4.32.

$$R\big(\tilde{A} = \{(a_1, 1), (a_2, 0.8), (a_3, 0.5), (a_4, 0)\}\big) = a_1 + 0.8a_2 + 0.5a_3 + 0.1a_4$$

As can be seen from Table 4.32, a disadvantage of this method is that the same ranking can be obtained for more than one DMU. Also, in this method the selected ranking function can affect the obtained results, which may be a disadvantage.

4.3 Sensitivity analysis and stability of fuzzy DEA models

The sensitivity analysis of a DMU studies the effects of changes in its input and output values on its efficiency situation. Although this topic in regular DEA models has been a focus by researchers, the sensitivity analysis in fuzzy DEA models rarely has been considered in the literature. Some methods in the literature have studied the allowed changes of the inputs and outputs in fuzzy DEA models. Two of these methods are explained in this section.

4.3.1 Sensitivity analysis and stability of fuzzy DEA models by credibility theory

The sensitivity analysis and stability of fuzzy DEA models by credibility theory was first studied by Wen et al. (2011). This study focused on the sensitivity analysis of the changes in the inputs and outputs of the additive DEA model. As studying the behavior of the optimal solution in the case of changing the parameters and fixing the coefficients of the model is not easy, the credibility theory has been used for this aim.

The additive DEA model is as follows,

$$\begin{aligned}
&\text{Max } z = \sum_{i=1}^{p} s_i^- + \sum_{j=1}^{q} s_r^+ \\
&\text{subject to} \\
&\sum_{k=1}^{n} \lambda_k x_{ki} = x_{oi} - s_i^- \qquad i = 1, 2, \ldots, p \\
&\sum_{k=1}^{n} \lambda_k y_{kj} = y_{oj} + s_j^+ \qquad j = 1, 2, \ldots, q \\
&\sum_{k=1}^{n} \lambda_k = 1 \\
&\lambda_k \geq 0 \qquad k = 1, 2, \ldots, n \\
&s_i^- \geq 0 \qquad i = 1, 2, \ldots, p \\
&s_j^+ \geq 0 \qquad j = 1, 2, \ldots, q
\end{aligned} \tag{4.29}$$

Definition 4.3. In the model (4.29), a DMU is efficient if and only if $z^* = 0$ or $s_i^- = 0$, $s_j^+ = 0$ (for $j = 1, 2, \ldots, q$, $i = 1, 2, \ldots, p$).

Assume $FDMU_k$ ($k = 1, \cdots, n$) with fuzzy inputs $\tilde{X}_k = (\tilde{x}_{k1}, \tilde{x}_{k2}, \cdots, \tilde{x}_{kp})$ and fuzzy outputs $\tilde{Y}_k = (\tilde{y}_{k1}, \tilde{y}_{k2}, \cdots, \tilde{y}_{kp})$. The model (4.29), which is based on the approach of Wen and Li (2009) for evaluating $FDMU_O$, is shown below,

$$\begin{aligned}
&\text{Max } z = \sum_{i=1}^{p} s_i^- + \sum_{j=1}^{q} s_r^+ \\
&\text{subject to} \\
&Cr\left\{ \sum_{k=1}^{n} \lambda_k \tilde{x}_{ki} \leq \tilde{x}_{oi} - s_i^- \right\} \geq \alpha \quad i = 1, 2, \ldots, p \\
&Cr\left\{ \sum_{k=1}^{n} \lambda_k \tilde{y}_{kj} \geq \tilde{y}_{oj} + s_j^+ \right\} \geq \alpha \quad j = 1, 2, \ldots, q \\
&\sum_{k=1}^{n} \lambda_k = 1 \\
&\lambda_k \geq 0 \qquad k = 1, 2, \ldots, n \\
&s_i^- \geq 0 \qquad i = 1, 2, \ldots, p \\
&s_j^+ \geq 0 \qquad j = 1, 2, \ldots, q
\end{aligned} \tag{4.30}$$

Definition 4.4. DMU_O is α-efficient if $s_i^{-*}(\alpha)$ and $s_j^{+*}(\alpha)$ are zero for $j=1, 2, \ldots, q$, $i=1, 2, \ldots, p$ where $s_i^{-*}(\alpha)$ and $s_j^{+*}(\alpha)$ are optimal solutions of the model (4.30).

Theorem 4.3. If DMU_O is α-inefficient, then the optimal solution satisfying $\lambda_o^*(\alpha)=0$.

Proof. The proof is given by Wen et al. (2011).

Theorem 4.4. An α-inefficient DMU_O becomes α-efficient if $(\widehat{x}_O, \widehat{y}_O) = \left(\tilde{x}_O - s_i^{-*}(\alpha), \tilde{y}_O + s_r^{+}(\alpha)\right)$ in which $s_i^{-*}(\alpha)$ and $s_r^{+*}(\alpha)$ are optimal solutions of (4.30).

Proof. The proof is given by Wen et al. (2011).

By Theorem 4.4, the efficiency radius of an efficient DMU can be calculated. For this aim, the model of Wen et al. (2011) is shown below,

$$
\begin{aligned}
&\text{Max } z = \sum_{i=1}^{p} t_i^+ + \sum_{j=1}^{q} t_r^- \\
&\text{subject to} \\
&Cr\left\{ \sum_{k=1}^{n} \lambda_k \tilde{x}_{ki} \le \tilde{x}_{oi} + t_i^+ \right\} \ge \alpha \quad i = 1, 2, \ldots, p \\
&Cr\left\{ \sum_{k=1}^{n} \lambda_k \tilde{y}_{kj} \ge \tilde{y}_{oj} - t_j^- \right\} \ge \alpha \quad j = 1, 2, \ldots, q \\
&\sum_{k=1}^{n} \lambda_k = 1 \\
&\lambda_k \ge 0 \quad k = 1, 2, \ldots, n \\
&t_i^+ \ge 0 \quad i = 1, 2, \ldots, p \\
&t_j^- \ge 0 \quad j = 1, 2, \ldots, q
\end{aligned}
\tag{4.31}
$$

Theorem 4.5. The α-efficient DMU_O stays α-efficient if $(\widehat{x}_O, \widehat{y}_O) = \left(\tilde{x}_O - t^{-*}(\alpha), \tilde{y}_O + t^{+}(\alpha)\right)$, where $t^{+*}(\alpha)$ and $t^{-*}(\alpha)$ are optimal solutions of the model (4.31).

Proof. The proof is given by Wen et al. (2011).

According to Theorems 4.3, 4.4, and 4.5, the stability radius and regions of the inputs and outputs of DMU_o are obtained as shown below,

- If DMU_O is α-inefficient by solving model (4.30), then DMU_O stays α-inefficient if $(\widehat{x}_O, \widehat{y}_O) = (\tilde{x}_O - s_i^-, \tilde{y}_O + s_r^+)$ in which $s^- = \{(s_1^-, \dots, s_p^-) | 0 \le s_i^- \le s_i^{-*}(\alpha), i = 1, 2, \dots, p\}$, $s^+ = \{(s_1^+, \dots, s_q^+) | 0 \le s_j^+ \le s_j^{+*}(\alpha), j = 1, 2, \dots, q\}$, where $s_i^{-*}(\alpha)$ and $s_j^{+*}(\alpha)$ are optimal solutions of the model (4.30).
- If DMU_O is α-efficient by solving model (4.30), then we use model (4.31) to account for the efficient radius. DMU_O stays α-efficient if $(\widehat{x}_O, \widehat{y}_O) = (\tilde{x}_O - t^{-*}(\alpha), \tilde{y}_O + t^{+*}(\alpha))$ in which $t^+ = \{(t_1, \dots, t_p) | 0 \le t_i \le t_i^{+*}(\alpha), i = 1, 2, \dots, p\}$, and $t^- = \{(t_1, \dots, t_q) | 0 \le t_j \le t_j^{-*}(\alpha), j = 1, 2, \dots, q\}$, where $t_i^{+*}(\alpha)$ and $t_j^*(\alpha)$ are optimal solutions of the model (4.31).

Definition 4.5. For any $\alpha \in (0, 1]$, the α-optimistic and α-pessimistic values of a fuzzy variable such as ξ are defined as shown below,

$$\xi_{\sup}^{\alpha} = \sup\{Cr\{\xi \ge r\} \ge \alpha\}, \quad \xi_{\inf}^{\alpha} = \inf\{Cr\{\xi \le r\} \le a\}$$

According to the study of Wen et al. (2011), the following issues are considered.

- $\xi_{\inf}^{\alpha}$ is an increasing and left-continuous function of α.
- $\xi_{\sup}^{\alpha}$ is a decreasing and left-continuous function of α.
- If $c \ge 0$ then $c\xi_{\sup}^{\alpha} = c\xi_{\sup}^{\alpha}$ and $c\xi_{\inf}^{\alpha} = c\xi_{\inf}^{\alpha}$.
- If $c < 0$ then $c\xi_{\sup}^{\alpha} = c\xi_{\inf}^{\alpha}$ and $c\xi_{\inf}^{\alpha} = c\xi_{\sup}^{\alpha}$.
- If ξ and η are independent $(\xi + \eta)_{\sup}^{\alpha} = \xi_{\sup}^{\alpha} + \eta_{\sup}^{\alpha}$.

From the properties of the α-optimistic and α-pessimistic values, we can rewrite the fuzzy DEA models *(4.30) and (4.31) as follows,*

$$\text{Max } z = \sum_{i=1}^{p} s_i^- + \sum_{j=1}^{q} s_r^+$$

subject to

$$\sum_{k=1}^{n} \lambda_k (\tilde{x}_{ki})_{\inf}^{\alpha} + \lambda_O \left[(\tilde{x}_{Oi})_{\sup}^{\alpha} - (\tilde{x}_{Oi})_{\inf}^{\alpha} \right] \le (\tilde{x}_{Oi})_{\sup}^{\alpha} - s_i^- \qquad i = 1, 2, \dots, p$$

$$\sum_{k=1}^{n} \lambda_k \left(\tilde{y}_{kj}\right)_{\sup}^{\alpha} + \lambda_O \left[\left(\tilde{y}_{Oj}\right)_{\inf}^{\alpha} - \left(\tilde{y}_{Oj}\right)_{\sup}^{\alpha} \right] \ge \left(\tilde{y}_{Oj}\right)_{\inf}^{\alpha} + s_j^+ \quad j = 1, 2, \dots, q$$

$$\sum_{k=1}^{n} \lambda_k = 1$$

$$\lambda_k \ge 0 \qquad k = 1, 2, \dots, n$$

$$s_i^- \ge 0 \qquad i = 1, 2, \dots, p$$

$$s_j^+ \ge 0 \qquad j = 1, 2, \dots, q$$

(4.32)

$$
\begin{aligned}
&\text{Min } z = \sum_{i=1}^{p} t_i^+ + \sum_{j=1}^{q} t_r^- \\
&\text{subject to} \\
&\sum_{k=1,\,k\neq O}^{n} \lambda_k (\tilde{x}_{ki})_{\inf}^{\alpha} \le (\tilde{x}_{Oi})_{\sup}^{\alpha} - t_i^+ \qquad i = 1,2,\ldots,p \\
&\sum_{k=1,\,k\neq O}^{n} \lambda_k \left(\tilde{y}_{kj}\right)_{\sup}^{\alpha} \ge \left(\tilde{y}_{Oj}\right)_{\inf}^{\alpha} + t_j^- \qquad j = 1,2,\ldots,q \\
&\sum_{k=1}^{n} \lambda_k = 1 \\
&\lambda_k \ge 0 \qquad k = 1,2,\ldots,n \\
&t_i^+ \ge 0 \qquad i = 1,2,\ldots,p \\
&t_j^- \ge 0 \qquad j = 1,2,\ldots,q
\end{aligned}
\tag{4.33}
$$

The models (4.32) and (4.33) are linear and can be easily solved by the optimization software.

Example 4.6. Consider the DMUs of Table 4.33 with two fuzzy inputs and two fuzzy outputs of triangular type.

The DMUs are evaluated by the model (4.30) at the level of $\alpha = 0.6$. The obtained results are shown in Table 4.34.

Table 4.33 The data of Example 4.6.

DMU_i	1	2	3	4	5
Input 1	(3.5, 4.0, 4.5)	(2.9, 2.9, 2.9)	(4.4, 4.9, 5.4)	(3.4, 4.1, 4.8)	(5.9, 6.5, 7.1)
Input 2	(1.9, 2.1, 2.3)	(1.4, 1.5, 1.6)	(2.2, 2.6, 3.0)	(2.1, 2.3, 2.5)	(3.6, 4.1, 4.6)
Output 1	(2.4, 2.6, 2.8)	(2.2, 2.2, 2.2)	(2.7, 3.2, 3.7)	(2.5, 2.9, 3.3)	(4.4, 5.1, 5.8)
Output 2	(3.8, 4.1, 4.4)	(3.3, 3.5, 3.7)	(4.3, 5.1, 5.9)	(5.5, 5.7, 5.9)	(6.5, 7.4, 8.3)

Table 4.34 The results obtained for the DMUs of Example 4.6 by the model (4.30) at the level of $\alpha = 0.6$.

DMU_i	$(\lambda_1^*, \lambda_2^*, \lambda_3^*, \lambda_4^*, \lambda_5^*)$	$\sum_{i=1}^{p} s_i^{-*} + \sum_{j=1}^{q} s_r^{+*}$	The result of evaluating
DMU_1	(0, 0.74, 0, 0.09, 0.17)	0.75	Inefficiency
DMU_2	(0, 1, 0, 0, 0)	0	Efficiency
DMU_3	(0, 0, 1, 0, 0)	0.19	Inefficiency
DMU_4	(0, 0, 0, 1, 0)	0	Efficiency
DMU_5	(0, 0, 0, 0, 1)	0	Efficiency

Table 4.35 The results of a sensitivity analysis of the inefficient DMUs of Example 4.6.

DMUs	s_1^{-*}	s_2^{-*}	s_1^{+*}	s_2^{+*}
DMU_1	0.15	0.00	0.00	0.60
DMU_3	0.47	0.05	0.00	0.83

Table 4.36 The results for a sensitivity analysis of the inefficient DMUs of Example 4.6.

DMUs	s_1^{-*}	s_2^{-*}	s_1^{+*}	s_2^{+*}
DMU_1	0.15	0.00	0.00	0.60
DMU_3	0.47	0.05	0.00	0.83

According to the results of Table 4.34, DMUs 1 and 3 are inefficient and DMUs 2, 4, and 5 are efficient.

The results of a sensitivity analysis for the inefficient DMUs are given in Table 4.35. In this table, the lower bound values are shown by columns 2 and 3, and the upper bound values are shown by columns 4 and 5. For example, the first DMU remains inefficient when $(\widehat{x}_{11}, \widehat{x}_{12}, \widehat{y}_{11}, \widehat{y}_{12}) = (\tilde{x}_{11} - r_{x1}, \tilde{x}_{12}, \tilde{y}_{11}, \tilde{y}_{12} + r_{y1})$ where $0 \le r_{x1} \le 0.15$ and $0 \le r_{y1} \le 0.60$.

The results of a sensitivity analysis for the efficient DMUs are given in Table 4.36. In this table, the upper bound values are shown by columns 2 and 3, and the lower bound values are shown by columns 4 and 5. For example, DMU 4 remains efficient when $(\widehat{x}_{41}, \widehat{x}_{42}, \widehat{y}_{41}, \widehat{y}_{42}) = (\tilde{x}_{41}, \tilde{x}_{42} + r_{x2}, \tilde{y}_{41}, \tilde{y}_{42} - r_{y2})$ where $0 \le r_{x2} \le 0.17$ and $0 \le r_{y1} \le 1.01$.

4.3.2 Sensitivity analysis and stability of fuzzy DEA models by the concept of fuzzy efficiency

Assume n DMUs such as DMU_j (where $j=1, \cdots, n$) with fuzzy inputs $\tilde{X}_j = \left(\left(x_{1j}^L, x_{1j}^C, x_{1j}^U\right), \left(x_{2j}^L, x_{2j}^C, x_{2j}^U\right), \ldots, \left(x_{mj}^L, x_{mj}^C, x_{mj}^U\right)\right)^t$ and fuzzy outputs $\tilde{X}_j = \left(\left(x_{1j}^L, x_{1j}^C, x_{1j}^U\right), \left(x_{2j}^L, x_{2j}^C, x_{2j}^U\right), \ldots, \left(x_{mj}^L, x_{mj}^C, x_{mj}^U\right)\right)^t$. If DMU_j is efficient, the aim is to find the values δ^L, δ^C, δ^U such that if the vector $(\tilde{X}_j, \tilde{Y}_j)$ is changed to the vector $(((x_{1j}^L+\delta^L, x_{1j}^C+\delta^C, x_{1j}^U+\delta^U), \ldots, (x_{mj}^L+\delta^L, x_{mj}^C+\delta^C, x_{mj}^U+\delta^U)), ((y_{1j}^L-\delta^L, y_{1j}^C-\delta^C, y_{1j}^U-\delta^U), \ldots, (y_{sj}^L-\delta^L, y_{sj}^C-\delta^C, y_{sj}^U-\delta^U)))^t$, the DMU remains efficient. In this case, the values δ^L, δ^C, δ^U are called the stability radius of DMU_j.

Definition 4.6. For DMU_j as an efficient or semiefficient DMU, assume $\theta_j^{u\alpha_c}=1$. The values δ^1, δ^2 are the stability radius of DMU_j in the cut α, if by changing the vector $\begin{pmatrix} [\tilde{X}_j]_\alpha \\ [\tilde{Y}_j]_\alpha \end{pmatrix} = \begin{pmatrix} \left(\left[\underline{x}_{1j}, \overline{x}_{1j}\right], \left[\underline{x}_{2j}, \overline{x}_{2j}\right], \ldots, \left[\underline{x}_{mj}, \overline{x}_{mj}\right]\right)^t \\ \left(\left[\underline{y}_{1j}, \overline{y}_{1j}\right], \left[\underline{y}_{2j}, \overline{y}_{2j}\right], \ldots, \left[\underline{y}_{sj}, \overline{y}_{sj}\right]\right)^t \end{pmatrix}$ to the vector $\begin{pmatrix} \left(\left[\underline{x}_{1j} + \delta_1, \overline{x}_{1j} + \delta_2\right], \ldots, \left[\underline{x}_{mj} + \delta_1, \overline{x}_{mj} + \delta_2\right]\right)^t \\ \left(\left[\underline{y}_{1j} - \delta_1, \overline{y}_{1j} - \delta_2\right], \ldots, \left[\underline{y}_{sj} - \delta_1, \overline{y}_{sj} - \delta_2\right]\right)^t \end{pmatrix}$, still $\theta_j^{u\alpha_c}=1$.

For DMU_j as an efficient or semiefficient DMU, the stability radius values δ_1^α and δ_2^α in the cut α are obtained from the below input-oriented BCC models with envelopment form.

$$
\begin{aligned}
&\text{Min } \delta_1^\alpha \\
&\text{subject to} \\
&\sum_{j=1, j\neq o}^{n} \lambda_j^{l\alpha} x_{ij}^{l\alpha} \leq x_{io}^{l\alpha} + \delta_1^\alpha \qquad i = 1, 2, \ldots, m \\
&\sum_{j=1, j\neq o}^{n} \lambda_j^{l\alpha} y_{rj}^{l\alpha} \geq y_{ro}^{l\alpha} - \delta_1^\alpha \qquad r = 1, 2, \ldots, s \\
&\quad \sum_{j=1, j\neq o}^{n} \lambda_j^{l\alpha} = 1 \\
&\quad \delta_1^\alpha \geq 0 \\
&\quad \lambda_j^{l\alpha} \geq 0 \qquad j = 1, 2, \ldots, n,\ j \neq o
\end{aligned}
\tag{4.34}
$$

$$
\begin{aligned}
&\min \ \delta_2^{\alpha} \\
&\textit{subject to} \\
&\sum_{j=1, j \neq o}^{n} \lambda_j^{u\alpha} x_{ij}^{u\alpha} \leq x_{io}^{u\alpha} + \delta_2^{\alpha} \quad i = 1, 2, \dots, m \\
&\sum_{j=1, j \neq o}^{n} \lambda_j^{u\alpha} y_{rj}^{u\alpha} \geq y_{ro}^{u\alpha} - \delta_2^{\alpha} \quad r = 1, 2, \dots, s \\
&\sum_{j=1, j \neq o}^{n} \lambda_j^{u\alpha} = 1 \\
&\delta_2^{\alpha} \geq 0 \\
&\lambda_j^{u\alpha} \geq 0 \qquad j = 1, 2, \dots, n, \ j \neq o
\end{aligned}
\tag{4.35}
$$

Example 4.7. The data of Example 3.6 from Chapter 3 are considered. In that example, considering the set $\Delta = \{\alpha_1 = 1, \alpha_2 = 0.8, \alpha_3 = 0.5, \alpha_4 = 0\}$, DMU_1, DMU_2, DMU_3, DMU_4 were efficient in all cut values. Now, according to the models (4.34) and (4.35), the stability radius values of Table 4.37 are obtained.

Definition 4.7. According to the results of the models (4.34) and (4.35), the efficient DMUs are divided into the following groups.

- If $\delta_1^{\alpha} > 0$, $\delta_2^{\alpha} > 0$, then DMU_j is extreme efficient in the cut α.
- If $\delta_1^{\alpha} > 0$, $\delta_2^{\alpha} = 0$ or $\delta_1^{\alpha} = 0$, $\delta_2^{\alpha} > 0$, then DMU_j is semiextreme efficient in the cut α.
- If $\delta_1^{\alpha} = 0$, $\delta_2^{\alpha} = 0$, then DMU_j is nonextreme efficient in the cut α.

Table 4.37 The stability radius values obtained for the efficient DMUs of Example 4.7.

Cut $-\alpha_k$		$\alpha_1 = 1$	$\alpha_2 = 0.8$	$\alpha_3 = 0.5$	$\alpha_4 = 0$
DMU_1	δ_1^{α}	79.16667	78.57727	77.03030	78.55556
	δ_2^{α}	79.16667	63.19551	80.13699	81.57895
DMU_2	δ_1^{α}	34.70588	35.15106	35.81176	36.89412
	δ_2^{α}	34.70588	39.74349	33.21930	31.75581
DMU_3	δ_1^{α}	16.13757	9.279520	14.37143	14.71579
	δ_2^{α}	16.13757	13.74684	19.46032	23.14894
DMU_4	δ_1^{α}	50.00000	50.80000	52.00000	54.00000
	δ_2^{α}	50.00000	49.20000	48.00000	46.00000

In Example 4.7, DMU_1, DMU_2, DMU_3, DMU_4 are extreme efficient in each of the cut values.

In the following, the stability region of an efficient DMU is calculated. Assume DMU_o with fuzzy input vector $\tilde{X}_j$ and fuzzy output vector $\tilde{Y}_j$ is efficient or semiefficient in its fuzzy PPS. The aim is to calculate the vectors $\Delta X_i^{\alpha}=((\gamma_1^{1\alpha},\gamma_1^{2\alpha}),(\gamma_2^{1\alpha},\gamma_2^{2\alpha}),\cdots,(\gamma_m^{1\alpha},\gamma_m^{2\alpha}))^t$ and $\Delta Y_i^{\alpha}=((\sigma_1^{1\alpha},\sigma_1^{2\alpha}),(\sigma_2^{1\alpha},\sigma_2^{2\alpha}),\ \cdots,\ (\sigma_s^{1\alpha},\sigma_s^{2\alpha}))^t$ in each cut in a way that by changing vector $\begin{pmatrix}[\tilde{X}_O]_\alpha\\ [\tilde{Y}_O]_\alpha\end{pmatrix}=\begin{pmatrix}([\underline{x}_{1O},\overline{x}_{1O}],[\underline{x}_{2O},\overline{x}_{2O}],\ldots,[\underline{x}_{mO},\overline{x}_{mO}])^t\\ \left(\left[\underline{y}_{1O},\overline{y}_{1O}\right],\left[\underline{y}_{2O},\overline{y}_{2O}\right],\ldots,\left[\underline{y}_{sO},\overline{y}_{sO}\right]\right)^t\end{pmatrix}$ to $\begin{pmatrix}\left(\left[\underline{x}_{1O}+\gamma_1^{1\alpha},\overline{x}_{1O}+\gamma_1^{2}\right],\ldots,\left[\underline{x}_{mo}+\gamma_m^{1\alpha},\overline{x}_{mo}+\gamma_m^{2\alpha}\right]\right)^t\\ \left(\left[\underline{y}_{1O}-\sigma_1^{1\alpha},\overline{y}_{1O}-\sigma_1^{2}\right],\ldots,\left[\underline{y}_{so}-\sigma_s^{1\alpha},\overline{y}_{so}-\sigma_s^{2\alpha}\right]\right)^t\end{pmatrix}$, DMU_o remains efficient (or semiefficient). For this purpose, the following models are defined in each cut.

$$
\begin{aligned}
&\text{Min} \quad \sum_{i=1}^{m}\gamma_i^{1\alpha}+\sum_{r=1}^{s}\sigma_r^{1\alpha}\\
&\text{subject to}\\
&\sum_{j=1,j\neq o}^{n}\lambda_j^{l\alpha}x_{ij}^{l\alpha}\le x_{io}^{l\alpha}+\gamma_i^{1\alpha} \qquad i=1,2,\ldots,m\\
&\sum_{j=1,j\neq o}^{n}\lambda_j^{l\alpha}y_{rj}^{l\alpha}\ge y_{ro}^{l\alpha}-\sigma_r^{1\alpha} \qquad r=1,2,\ldots,s\\
&\sum_{j=1,j\neq o}^{n}\lambda_j^{l\alpha}=1\\
&\sigma_r^{1\alpha}\ge 0 \qquad r=1,2,\ldots,s\\
&\gamma_i^{1\alpha}\ge 0 \qquad i=1,2,\ldots,m\\
&\lambda_j^{l\alpha}\ge 0 \qquad j=1,2,\ldots,n,j\neq o
\end{aligned}
\tag{4.36}
$$

$$\begin{aligned}
&\text{Min} \quad \sum_{i=1}^{m} \gamma_i^{2\alpha} + \sum_{r=1}^{s} \sigma_r^{2\alpha} \\
&\text{subject to} \\
&\sum_{j=1, j\neq o}^{n} \lambda_j^{u\alpha} x_{ij}^{u\alpha} \le x_{io}^{u\alpha} + \gamma_i^{2\alpha} \quad i = 1, 2, \ldots, m \\
&\sum_{j=1, j\neq o}^{n} \lambda_j^{u\alpha} y_{rj}^{u\alpha} \ge y_{ro}^{u\alpha} - \sigma_r^{2\alpha} \quad r = 1, 2, \ldots, s \\
&\sum_{j=1, j\neq o}^{n} \lambda_j^{u\alpha} = 1 \\
&\sigma_r^{2\alpha} \ge 0 \quad r = 1, 2, \ldots, s \\
&\gamma_i^{2\alpha} \ge 0 \quad i = 1, 2, \ldots, m \\
&\lambda_j^{u\alpha} \ge 0 \quad j = 1, 2, \ldots, n, \; j \neq o
\end{aligned} \tag{4.37}$$

Assume $\{\gamma_1^{1\alpha}, \gamma_2^{1\alpha}, \cdots, \gamma_m^{1\alpha}, \sigma_1^{1\alpha}, \sigma_2^{1\alpha}, \cdots, \sigma_s^{1\alpha}\}$ as the optimal solution of the model (4.36) and $\{\gamma_1^{2\alpha}, \gamma_2^{2\alpha}, \cdots, \gamma_m^{2\alpha}, \sigma_1^{2\alpha}, \sigma_2^{2\alpha}, \cdots, \sigma_s^{2\alpha}\}$ as the optimal solution of the model (4.37). Then, the stability region of DMU_o in cut α is defined as Φ_O^α and calculated as shown below,

$$\Phi_O^\alpha = \left\{ \begin{pmatrix} \underline{X} \\ \overline{X} \\ \underline{Y} \\ \overline{Y} \end{pmatrix} \middle| \underline{X}_O^\alpha \le \underline{X} \le \underline{X}_O^\alpha + \underline{\gamma}^\alpha, \overline{X}_O^\alpha \le \overline{X} \le \overline{X}_O^\alpha + \overline{\gamma}^\alpha, \right.$$
$$\left. \underline{Y}_O^\alpha \le \underline{Y} \le \underline{Y}_O^\alpha + \underline{\sigma}^\alpha, \overline{Y}_O^\alpha \le \overline{Y} \le \overline{Y}_O^\alpha + \overline{\sigma}^\alpha \right\}$$

where,

$$\underline{\gamma}^\alpha = \left(\gamma_1^{1\alpha}, \gamma_2^{1\alpha}, \cdots, \gamma_m^{1\alpha}\right)', \underline{\sigma}^\alpha = \left(\sigma_1^{1\alpha}, \sigma_2^{1\alpha}, \cdots, \sigma_s^{1\alpha}\right)', \underline{Y}_O^\alpha = \left(\underline{y}_{1O}, \cdots, \underline{y}_{sO}\right)',$$
$$\overline{Y}_O^\alpha = (\overline{y}_{1O}, \cdots, \overline{y}_{sO})'$$
$$\overline{\gamma}^\alpha = \left(\gamma_1^{2\alpha}, \gamma_2^{2\alpha}, \cdots, \gamma_m^{2\alpha}\right)', \overline{\sigma}^\alpha = \left(\sigma_1^{2\alpha}, \sigma_2^{2\alpha}, \cdots, \sigma_s^{2\alpha}\right)', \underline{X}_O^\alpha = (\underline{x}_{1O}, \cdots, \underline{x}_{mO})',$$
$$\overline{X}_O^\alpha = (\overline{x}_{1O}, \cdots, \overline{x}_{mO})'$$
$$\underline{X} = (\underline{x}_1, \cdots, \underline{x}_m)', \overline{X} = (\overline{x}_1, \cdots, \overline{x}_m)', \underline{Y} = \left(\underline{y}_1, \cdots, \underline{y}_s\right)', \overline{Y} = (\overline{y}_1, \cdots, \overline{y}_s)'$$

Example 4.8. The data of Example 3.6 from Chapter 3 are considered where the DMUs 1, 2, 3, and 4 are efficient in each cut from the set $\Delta=\{\alpha_1=1,\alpha_2=0.8,\alpha_3=0.5,\alpha_4=0\}$. To calculate the stability region in each cut, the values $\{\gamma_1^{1\alpha},\gamma_2^{1\alpha},\cdots,\gamma_m^{1\alpha},\sigma_1^{1\alpha},\sigma_2^{1\alpha},\cdots,\sigma_s^{1\alpha}\}$ and $\{\gamma_1^{2\alpha},\gamma_2^{2\alpha},\cdots,\gamma_m^{2\alpha},\sigma_1^{2\alpha},\sigma_2^{2\alpha},\cdots,\sigma_s^{2\alpha}\}$ are obtained for the efficient DMUs from the models (4.36) and (4.37), respectively, and shown in Tables 4.38–4.41.

According to the results of Table 4.38, the stability region of DMU_1 in each cut is calculated in the following.

The stability region of DMU_1 in $\alpha=1$:

$$\Phi_1^1=\left\{\begin{pmatrix}\underline{x}_1\\ \underline{x}_2\\ \underline{y}_1\\ \overline{x}_1\\ \overline{x}_2\\ \overline{y}_1\end{pmatrix}\middle|\begin{array}{l}100\le\underline{x}_1\le150,180\le\underline{x}_2\le272,50\le\underline{y}_1\le50\\ 100\le\overline{x}_1\le150,180\le\overline{x}_2\le272,50\le\overline{y}_1\le50\end{array}\right\}$$

Table 4.38 The values of $\{\gamma_1^{1\alpha},\gamma_2^{1\alpha},\sigma_1^{1\alpha}\}$ and $\{\gamma_1^{2\alpha},\gamma_2^{2\alpha},\sigma_1^{2\alpha}\}$ obtained for DMU_1 by the models (4.36) and (4.37).

DMU_1	$\alpha_1=1$	$\alpha_2=0.8$	$\alpha_3=0.5$	$\alpha_4=0$
$\gamma_1^{1\alpha}$	50	49.6	49	48
$\gamma_2^{1\alpha}$	92	90.4	86	92
$\sigma_1^{1\alpha}$	0	0	0	0
$\gamma_1^{2\alpha}$	50	39.6	50	50
$\gamma_2^{2\alpha}$	92	73.2	94	98
$\sigma_1^{2\alpha}$	0	0	0	0

Table 4.39 The values of $\{\gamma_1^{1\alpha},\gamma_2^{1\alpha},\sigma_1^{1\alpha}\}$ and $\{\gamma_1^{2\alpha},\gamma_2^{2\alpha},\sigma_1^{2\alpha}\}$ obtained for DMU_2 by the models (4.36) and (4.37).

DMU_2	$\alpha_1=1$	$\alpha_2=0.8$	$\alpha_3=0.5$	$\alpha_4=0$
$\gamma_1^{1\alpha}$	36.58824	36.10943	33.43787	41.80952
$\gamma_2^{1\alpha}$	0	0	0	0
$\sigma_1^{1\alpha}$	32.58824	34.08302	38.42012	31.61905
$\gamma_1^{2\alpha}$	36.58824	31.81463	38.96429	43.27711
$\gamma_2^{2\alpha}$	0	0	0	0
$\sigma_1^{2\alpha}$	32.58824	48.72293	26.60714	18.19277

Table 4.40 The values of $\{\gamma_1^{1\alpha},\gamma_2^{1\alpha},\sigma_1^{1\alpha}\}$ and $\{\gamma_1^{2\alpha},\gamma_2^{2\alpha},\sigma_1^{2\alpha}\}$ obtained for DMU_3 by the models (4.36) and (4.37).

DMU_3	$\alpha_1=1$	$\alpha_2=0.8$	$\alpha_3=0.5$	$\alpha_4=0$
$\gamma_1^{1\alpha}$	0	0	0	0
$\gamma_2^{1\alpha}$	0	1.070225	0	0
$\sigma_1^{1\alpha}$	21.94245	12.38507	10.95667	20.11511
$\gamma_1^{2\alpha}$	0	0	0	0
$\gamma_2^{2\alpha}$	0	0	0	0
$\sigma_1^{2\alpha}$	21.94245	18.72414	26.65217	32

Table 4.41 The values of $\{\gamma_1^{1\alpha},\gamma_2^{1\alpha},\sigma_1^{1\alpha}\}$ and $\{\gamma_1^{2\alpha},\gamma_2^{2\alpha},\sigma_1^{2\alpha}\}$ obtained for DMU_4 by the models (4.36) and (4.37).

DMU_4	$\alpha_1=1$	$\alpha_2=0.8$	$\alpha_3=0.5$	$\alpha_4=0$
$\gamma_1^{1\alpha}$	0	0	0	0
$\gamma_2^{1\alpha}$	0	0	0	0
$\sigma_1^{1\alpha}$	50	50.8	52	54
$\gamma_1^{2\alpha}$	0	0	0	0
$\gamma_2^{2\alpha}$	0	0	0	0
$\sigma_1^{2\alpha}$	50	49.2	48	46

The stability region of DMU_1 in $\alpha=0.8$:

$$\Phi_1^1=\left\{\left(\begin{array}{c}\underline{x}_1\\ \underline{x}_2\\ \underline{y}_1\\ \overline{x}_1\\ \overline{x}_2\\ \overline{y}_1\end{array}\right)\left|\begin{array}{l}98.8\le\underline{x}_1\le148.4,178.4\le\underline{x}_2\le268.8,49.6\le\underline{y}_1\le49.6\\ 112\le\overline{x}_1\le151.6,200\le\overline{x}_2\le273.2,50.8\le\overline{y}_1\le50.8\end{array}\right.\right\}$$

The stability region of DMU_1 in $\alpha=0.5$:

$$\Phi_1^1=\left\{\left(\begin{array}{c}\underline{x}_1\\ \underline{x}_2\\ \underline{y}_1\\ \overline{x}_1\\ \overline{x}_2\\ \overline{y}_1\end{array}\right)\left|\begin{array}{l}97\le\underline{x}_1\le146,176\le\underline{x}_2\le262,49\le\underline{y}_1\le49\\ 130\le\overline{x}_1\le180,230\le\overline{x}_2\le324,52\le\overline{y}_1\le52\end{array}\right.\right\}$$

The stability region of DMU_1 in $\alpha = 0$:

$$\Phi_1^1 = \left\{ \begin{pmatrix} \underline{x}_1 \\ \underline{x}_2 \\ \underline{y}_1 \\ \overline{x}_1 \\ \overline{x}_2 \\ \overline{y}_1 \end{pmatrix} \middle| \begin{array}{l} 94 \le \underline{x}_1 \le 142, 172 \le \underline{x}_2 \le 264, 48 \le \underline{y}_1 \le 48 \\ 160 \le \overline{x}_1 \le 210, 280 \le \overline{x}_2 \le 378, 54 \le \overline{y}_1 \le 54 \end{array} \right\}$$

The stability regions of other efficient DMUs of this example are obtained in a similar way.

As mentioned earlier, the stability region directly depends on the definition of the fuzzy efficiency of the DMUs. As in this example, the efficiency is determined for different α-cuts, and the stability regions of the efficient DMUs also are calculated for different α-cuts. Based on different definitions of fuzzy efficiency (from Chapter 3), the stability region of each efficient DMU can be calculated.

References

Alem, S. M., Jolai, F., & Nazari-Shirkouhi, S. (2013). An integrated fuzzy DEA-fuzzy AHP approach: A new model for ranking decision-making units. *International Journal of Operational Research, 17*(1), 38–58.

Banker, R. D., Charnes, A., & Cooper, W. W. (1984). Some models for estimating technical and scale efficiencies in data envelopment analysis. *Management Science, 30*, 1078–1092.

Charnes, A., Cooper, W. W., & Rhodes, E. L. (1978). Measuring the efficiency of decision making units. *European Journal of Operational Research, 2*(6), 429–444.

Chen, L., & Wang, Y. M. (2016). Data envelopment analysis cross-efficiency model in fuzzy environments. *Journal of Intelligent Fuzzy Systems, 30*(5), 2601–2609.

Despotis, D. K., & Smirlis, Y. G. (2002). Data envelopment analysis with imprecise data. *European Journal of Operational Research, 140*(1), 24–36.

Dotoli, M., Epicoco, N., & Falagario, M. (2015). A technique for supply chain network design under uncertainty using cross-efficiency fuzzy data envelopment analysis. *IFAC-PapersOnLine, 48*(3), 634–639.

Hatami-Marbini, A., Emrouznejad, A., & Tavana, M. (2011). A taxonomy and review of the fuzzy data envelopment analysis literature: Two decades in the making. *European Journal of Operational Research, 214*(3), 457–472.

Izadikhah, M., Aliakbarpoor, Z., & Sharafi, H. (2015). Ranking DMUs by ideal points in the presence of fuzzy and ordinal data. *Theory of Approximation and Applications, 9*(2), 13–36.

Jahanshahloo, G. R., Lotfi, F. H., Shahverdi, R., Adabitabar, M., Rostamy-Malkhalifeh, M., & Sohraiee, S. (2009). Ranking DMUs by l1-norm with fuzzy data in DEA. *Chaos, Solitons & Fractals, 39*(5), 2294–2302.

Mirzaei, S. H., & Salehi, A. (2019). Ranking efficient DMUs using the Tchebycheff norm with fuzzy data in DEA. *International Journal of Research in Industrial Engineering, 8*(2), 158–175.

Saati, S. M., Memariani, A., & Jahanshahloo, G. R. (2002). Efficiency analysis and ranking of DMUs with fuzzy data. *Fuzzy Optimization and Decision Making*, *1*(3), 255–267.
Saneifard, R., Allahviranloo, T., Hosseinzadeh, F., & Mikaeilvand, N. (2007). Euclidean ranking DMUs with fuzzy data in DEA. *Applied Mathematical Sciences*, *60*, 2989–2998.
Shahverdi, R. (2016). Ranking DMUs by new metric DTM with fuzzy data in DEA. *International Journal of Data Envelopment Analysis*, *4*(3), 1039–1044.
Wang, Y. M., Greatbanks, R., & Yang, J. B. (2005). Interval efficiency assessment using data envelopment analysis. *Fuzzy Sets and Systems*, *153*(3), 347–370.
Wen, M., & Li, H. (2009). Fuzzy data envelopment analysis (DEA): Model and ranking method. *Journal of Computational and Applied Mathematics*, *223*(2), 872–878.
Wen, M., Qin, Z., & Kang, R. (2011). Sensitivity and stability analysis in fuzzy data envelopment analysis. *Fuzzy Optimization and Decision Making*, *10*(1), 1–10.
Wen, M., You, C., & Kang, R. (2010). A new ranking method to fuzzy data envelopment analysis. *Computers & Mathematics with Applications*, *59*(11), 3398–3404.
Yager, R. R. (1979). Ranking fuzzy subsets over the unit interval. In *1978 IEEE conference on decision and control including the 17th symposium on adaptive processes* (pp. 1435–1437). IEEE.

CHAPTER FIVE

Uncertain data envelopment analysis

5.1 Introduction

With the rapid development, increased complexity, and transferred information of industrial systems, the impact of environmental factors such as competition, economic fluctuations, politics, etc., has forced researchers to introduce exact scientific methods to evaluate the performance of such systems (Allahviranloo & Ezadi, 2019; Mahmoodirad & Sanei, 2016). In this context, data envelopment analysis (DEA) is a mathematical approach that assesses and evaluates the performance of real-life systems to analyze their productivity.

DEA is a nonparametric approach that measures the performance of decision-making units (DMUs) with multiple input and outputs with different technologies. In this approach, to measure performance the measure of "efficiency" is used. The efficiency of a DMU is based on various factors such as the number of DMUs, the input and output values, the number of inputs and outputs, etc. (Hosseinzadeh Lotfi, Jahanshahloo, et al., 2010; Jahanshahloo et al., 2007).

In classical and general models of DEA, the main assumption is that the input and output values are of the deterministic type, but in many cases the inputs and outputs are of the uncertain type because the experts should estimate them based on their experience. Examples include factors such as social advantages, air pollution, etc., in a production system (Allahviranloo, 2020; Broomandi et al., 2021; Hosseinzadeh Lotfi et al., 2013; Jahanshahloo et al., 2009; Molla-Alizadeh-Zavardehi et al., 2014; Niroomand et al., 2020).

As such uncertainty in DEA models is complex and cannot be handled by regular procedure and solution approaches (Allahviranloo et al., 2012), methods such as probability theory, belief degree-based uncertainty (Liu, 2007), etc., can be used to handle the uncertainty of such DEA models. In problems where there is a set of samples of the uncertain events,

https://doi.org/10.1016/B978-0-323-99444-6.00005-0

probability theory becomes useful. But for the case of uncertain problems where no sample of the uncertain events is available, calculating the belief degrees of the uncertain events by the experts in the field can be a useful method. As the experts usually estimate and weight the improbable events highly, the belief degree has higher variance than frequency; therefore, it cannot be considered as the probability function of a stochastic variable (Wen et al., 2020). In the case of using belief degree for uncertain events, the uncertain problem can be tackled and managed by uncertainty theory.

An event with an uncertain measure of 1 has no doubt and we believe that it will happen. On the other hand, an event with an uncertain measure of 0 again has no doubt as we believe that it will not happen. The highest uncertain measure for an event occurs at the value of 0.5, as the event and its complement event have the same possibility of happening. The belief degree-based uncertainty theory has been used in many studies to formulate uncertain problems (see Chen et al., 2017; Dalman, 2019; Ding, 2015; Mahmoodirad et al., 2019; Mahmoodirad & Niroomand, 2020a, 2020b).

Several models have been introduced in the literature for DEA with uncertainty theory. For the first time, Wen et al. (2014) applied uncertainty theory for DEA models. They considered uncertain variables for inputs and outputs of their models. Some other DEA models in uncertain environments were proposed by Wen et al. (2015) while in the study from Wen et al. (2015), the sensitivity analysis of the DEA models was the focus. Wen et al. (2017) introduced some DEA models with ranking index and uncertain inputs and outputs. Mohammad Nejad and Ghaffari-Hadigheh (2018) proposed a new model to calculate the maximum belief degree in which a DMU is efficient. However, the introduced model is infeasible for some especial cases.

Jiang et al. (2018) introduced an uncertain DEA model for scale efficiency with uncertain inputs and outputs. In addition, they presented a sensitivity and stability analysis for the uncertainty DEA model for scale efficiency. A new uncertain DEA model with uncertain inputs and outputs was proposed by Lio and Liu (2018). The proposed model is highly sensitive to the changes in data values and may not be useful for real problems. Wen et al. (2020) developed a new uncertain ranking method where DMUs are considered uncertain variables.

Jamshidi et al. (2019) developed Russel's DEA model using uncertainty theory and applied it for the banking sector. Jamshidi et al. (2022) focused on the allocation models in DEA where the costs of inputs and the prices of outputs are of uncertain variables. Jamshidi et al. (2021a) developed the slacks-based measure (SBM) model for linear uncertain inputs and outputs and applied it for banking sector problems. Jamshidi et al. (2021b) developed the Banker-Charnes-Cooper (BCC) model (Banker et al., 1984) for uncertain inputs and outputs and applied it for banking sector problems.

In the rest of this chapter, the concepts and DEA models presented in Chapter 2 are extended in uncertain environments. Some solution approaches are introduced to overcome the difficulty of the proposed uncertain form of the DEA models.

5.2 Deterministic PPS

Assume that n DMUs as DMU_j, $j=1, 2, \ldots, n$, apply the input vector $X_j=(x_{1j}, x_{2j}, \ldots, x_{mj})$ to produce the outputs $Y_j=(y_{1j}, y_{2j}, \ldots, y_{sj})$. In classical DEA models, the PPS (PPS) shown by T satisfies the following axioms (Arana-Jiménez et al., 2022):

- **Envelopment (A1)**: All observations as $(X_j, Y_j)\in T,\ j=1, 2, \ldots, n$.
- **Scalability (A2)**: If $(X_j, Y_j)\in T$ then $(tX_j, tY_j)\in T$, for all $t>0$.
- **Free disposability (A3)**: If $(X, Y)\in T$, then for all $\overline{X}, \overline{Y}$ where $\overline{X}\geq X$ and $\overline{Y}\leq Y$, then$(\overline{X}, \overline{Y})\in T$.
- **Convexity (A4)**: If (X', Y'), $(X, Y)\in T$ then $\delta(X, Y)+(1-\delta)(X', Y')$ $\in T$ for all $\delta\in[0, 1]$.

According to the minimum extrapolation principle (Banker et al., 1984), the PPS of DEA is the subscription of all sets that satisfies the axioms A1–A4, and is shown as $T_{PPS}=\left\{(X, Y)|X\geq\sum_{j=1}^{n}\lambda_j X_j,\ Y\leq\sum_{j=1}^{n}\lambda_j Y_j,\ \lambda_j\geq 0\right.$ $\left. j=1,2,\ldots n\right\}$.

5.3 Identification function

Like a stochastic variable shown by a probability density function and a fuzzy variable shown by a membership function, an uncertain variable is shown by an identification function (Liu, 2009a, 2009b).

Definition 5.1 Uncertain variable ξ has the identification function (λ, ρ) where,

- $\lambda(x)$ and $\rho(x)$ are nonnegative functions, $\rho(x)$ is an integrable function, and $\sup_{x\in\mathbb{R}}\lambda(x) + \int_{\mathbb{R}}\rho(x)\,dx = 1$.

- For any Borel set (B) of real numbers, we have:

$$\mathcal{M}\{\xi \in B\} = \frac{1}{2}\left(\sup_{x\in B}\lambda(x) + \sup_{x\in \mathbb{R}}\lambda(x) - \sup_{x\in B^c}\lambda(x)\right) + \int_B \rho(x)dx$$

It is notable that some uncertain variables have no identification function. So, it is not true to say that each uncertain variable is shown by an identification function.

Remark 5.1 An uncertain variable with identification function (λ, ρ) is a fuzzy variable if $\sup_{x\in\mathbb{R}}\lambda(x) = 1$. In this situation, λ is the membership function and $\rho = 0$.

Remark 5.2 Assume uncertain variable ξ with identification function (λ, ρ). If $\lambda(x)$ is a continuous function, then for all $x \in \mathbb{R}$, $\mathcal{M}\{\xi = x\} = \frac{\lambda(x)}{2}$.

5.4 Uncertain PPS (UPPS)

In this section, the deterministic PPS and its axioms are extended to an uncertain environment using the operator principles of Liu (2007).

Assume that n DMUs as DMU_j, $j = 1, 2, \ldots, n$, apply the uncertain input vector $\tilde{X}_j = (\tilde{x}_{1j}, \tilde{x}_{2j}, \ldots, \tilde{x}_{mj})$ to produce the uncertain outputs $\tilde{Y}_j = (\tilde{y}_{1j}, \tilde{y}_{2j}, \ldots, \tilde{y}_{sj})$ where $\tilde{x}_{ij}$ and $\tilde{y}_{rj}$ are uncertain variables with regular uncertain distributions $\phi_{ij}(x_{ij})$ and $\varphi_{rj}(y_{rj})$, respectively. Then, using the ranking of Definition 1.67, the below axioms are defined.

- **Envelopment (B1)**: All observations $(\tilde{X}_j, \tilde{Y}_j) \in T$, $j = 1, 2, \ldots, n$.
- **Scalability (B2)**: If $(\tilde{X}_j, \tilde{Y}_j) \in T$ then $(t\tilde{X}_j, t\tilde{Y}_j) \in T$, for all $t > 0$.
- **Free disposability (B3)**: If $(\tilde{X}, \tilde{Y}) \in T$ for all $\overline{\tilde{X}}, \overline{\tilde{Y}}$ where $\overline{\tilde{X}} \succeq \tilde{X}$ and $\overline{\tilde{Y}} \preceq \tilde{Y}$ then $\left(\overline{\tilde{X}}, \overline{\tilde{Y}}\right) \in T$.
- **Convexity (B4)**: If $\left(\tilde{X}', \tilde{Y}'\right), (\tilde{X}, \tilde{Y}) \in T$ then $\delta(\tilde{X}, \tilde{Y}) + (1-\delta)\left(\tilde{X}', \tilde{Y}'\right) \in T$ for all $\delta \in [0, 1]$.

According to the minimum extrapolation principle, the uncertain PPS (UPPS) of DEA is the subscription of all sets that satisfies the principles B1–B4, and is shown as $T_{UPPS} = \left\{ (\tilde{X}, \tilde{Y}) \middle| \tilde{X} \succeq \sum_{j=1}^{n} \lambda_j \tilde{X}_j, \tilde{Y} \preceq \sum_{j=1}^{n} \lambda_j \tilde{Y}_j, \lambda_j \geq 0, \ j = 1, 2, \ldots, n \right\}$.

Theorem 5.1 Based on the axioms B1–B4, T_{UPPS} is the PPS obtained by the minimum extrapolation principle.

Definition 5.2 $(\tilde{X}, \tilde{Y}) \in T_{UPPS}$ is efficient if for any $\left(\tilde{X}', \tilde{Y}'\right) \in T_{UPPS}$ the claim $\tilde{X}' \preceq \tilde{X}, \tilde{Y}' \succeq \tilde{Y} \Rightarrow \left(\tilde{X}', \tilde{Y}'\right) \approx (\tilde{X}, \tilde{Y})$ is true.

Proof. For this aim, it is enough to show that $T_1 = T_{UPPS}$ where T_1 is the results of the minimum extrapolation principle of the principles B1–B4. This means that the claims $T_1 \subseteq T_{UPPS}$ and $T_{UPPS} \subseteq T_1$ should be true.

To prove $T_1 \subseteq T_{UPPS}$, it is enough to show that T_{UPPS} is true for the axioms B1–B4. So, we check T_{UPPS} for these axioms.

Check B1. Given $j = 1, \ldots, n$, then $\left(\tilde{X}_j, \tilde{Y}_j\right)$, with $\lambda_j = 1$, $\lambda_k = 0$, for all $k \neq j$, satisfies the condition in T_{UPPS}.

Check B2. Assume $\left(\tilde{X}, \tilde{Y}\right) \in T_{UPPS}$, there is a $\lambda \geq 0$ where $\tilde{X} \succeq \sum_{j=1}^{n} \lambda_j \tilde{X}_j$, $\tilde{Y} \preceq \sum_{j=1}^{n} \lambda_j \tilde{Y}_j$, holds. If $t > 0$ is given and $\overline{\lambda} = t\lambda = (t\lambda_1, \ldots, t\lambda_n) \geq 0$, then $t\tilde{X} \succeq \sum_{j=1}^{n} t\lambda_j \tilde{X}_j = \sum_{j=1}^{n} \overline{\lambda}_j \tilde{X}_j$, $t\tilde{Y} \preceq \sum_{j=1}^{n} t\lambda_j \tilde{Y}_j = \sum_{j=1}^{n} \overline{\lambda}_j \tilde{Y}_j$. Therefore, $\left(t\tilde{X}, t\tilde{Y}\right) \in T_{UPPS}$.

Check B3. Assume $\left(\tilde{X}, \tilde{Y}\right) \in T_{UPPS}$, $\tilde{X}' \succeq \tilde{X}, \tilde{Y}' \preceq \tilde{Y}$, $\left(\tilde{X}', \tilde{Y}'\right)$ is the uncertain positive vector. It is enough to prove $\left(\tilde{X}', \tilde{Y}'\right) \in T_{UPPS}$. By hypothesis, there exists $\lambda \geq 0$, such that

$$\tilde{X} \succeq \sum_{j=1}^{n} \lambda_j \tilde{X}_j, \quad \tilde{Y} \preceq \sum_{j=1}^{n} \lambda_j \tilde{Y}_j \tag{5.1}$$

Combining (5.1) with $\tilde{X}' \succeq \tilde{X}, \tilde{Y}' \preceq \tilde{Y}$, it follows that:

$$\tilde{X}' \succeq \tilde{X} \succeq \sum_{j=1}^{n} \lambda_j \tilde{X}_j, \quad \tilde{Y}' \preceq \tilde{Y} \preceq \sum_{j=1}^{n} \lambda_j \tilde{Y}_j \tag{5.2}$$

Thus, $\left(\tilde{X}', \tilde{Y}'\right) \in T_{UPPS}$.

Check B4. Assume $\left(\tilde{X}, \tilde{Y}\right), \left(\tilde{X}', \tilde{Y}'\right) \in T_{UPPS}$, $\delta \in [0, 1]$. By hypothesis, there exists $\lambda, \lambda' \geq 0$, such that

$$\tilde{X} \succeq \sum_{j=1}^{n} \lambda_j \tilde{X}_j, \quad \tilde{X}' \succeq \sum_{j=1}^{n} \lambda'_j \tilde{X}_j \tag{5.3}$$

$$\tilde{Y} \preceq \sum_{j=1}^{n} \lambda_j \tilde{Y}_j, \quad \tilde{Y}' \preceq \sum_{j=1}^{n} \lambda'_j \tilde{Y}_j \tag{5.4}$$

If the first and second inequalities of (5.3) are multiplied by δ and $(1-\delta)$, respectively, then by combining them, the following inequality is obtained.

$$\delta\tilde{X} + (1-\delta)\tilde{X}' \succeq \sum_{j=1}^{n} \left(\delta\lambda_j + (1-\delta)\lambda'_j\right) \tilde{X}_j \tag{5.5}$$

Similarly, the following inequality is obtained from inequalities (5.4).

$$\delta\tilde{Y} + (1-\delta)\tilde{Y}' \preceq \sum_{j=1}^{n} \left(\delta\lambda_j + (1-\delta)\lambda'_j\right) \tilde{Y}_j \tag{5.6}$$

Define $\lambda'' = (\lambda''_1, \ldots, \lambda''_n)$, with $\lambda''_j = \delta\lambda_j + (1-\delta)\lambda'_j \geq 0$, $j=1, \ldots, n$ for all $j=1, \ldots, n$, and substitute them in inequalities (5.5) and (5.6). It follows that $\left(\delta\tilde{X} + (1-\delta)\tilde{X}', \delta\tilde{Y} + (1-\delta)\tilde{Y}'\right) = \delta(\tilde{X}, \tilde{Y}) + (1-\delta)\left(\tilde{X}', \tilde{Y}'\right) \in T_{UPPS}$.

To prove $T_{UPPS} \subseteq T_1$, assume $(\tilde{X}, \tilde{Y}) \in T_{UPPS}$, which means that there exists $\lambda \geq 0$, such that,

$$\tilde{X} \succeq \sum_{j=1}^{n} \lambda_j \tilde{X}_j, \quad \tilde{Y} \preceq \sum_{j=1}^{n} \lambda_j \tilde{Y}_j \tag{5.7}$$

Therefore, $(\tilde{X}_j, \tilde{Y}_j) \in T_1$ by (B1), for all $j=1, \ldots, n$. Then, by (B2), it follows that $(\lambda\tilde{X}_j, \lambda\tilde{Y}_j) \in T_1$, for all $j=1, \ldots, n$.

Now, by induction we prove that,

$$\left(\sum_{j=1}^{k} \lambda_j \tilde{X}_j, \sum_{j=1}^{k} \lambda_j \tilde{Y}_j\right) \in T_1 \quad k = 1, 2, \ldots, n \tag{5.8}$$

For $k=1$ as $(\tilde{X}_1, \tilde{Y}_1) \in T_1$, then according to (B4), it follows that $(\lambda_1\tilde{X}_1, \lambda_1\tilde{Y}_1) \in T_1$. If we assume that this claim is true for $k \leq q$, then we should prove that the claim is true for $k=q+1$ too. The point $\left(\sum_{j=1}^{q+1} \lambda_j \tilde{X}_j, \sum_{j=1}^{q+1} \lambda_j \tilde{Y}_j\right)$ can be written as the convex sum of two elements of T_1, multiplied by a scalar number. By defining $\gamma = 0.5$, $\gamma' = 2$, then

$\left(\sum_{j=1}^{q+1}\lambda_j\tilde{X}_j, \sum_{j=1}^{q+1}\lambda_j\tilde{Y}_j\right) = \left(\sum_{j=1}^{q}\lambda_j\tilde{X}_j, \sum_{j=1}^{q}\lambda_j\tilde{Y}_j\right) + \left(\lambda_{q+1}\tilde{X}_{q+1}, \lambda_{q+1}\tilde{Y}_{q+1}\right) =$ $\gamma'\left(\gamma\left(\sum_{j=1}^{q}\lambda_j\tilde{X}_j, \sum_{j=1}^{q}\lambda_j\tilde{Y}_j\right) + (1-\gamma)\left(\lambda_{q+1}\tilde{X}_{q+1}, \lambda_{q+1}\tilde{Y}_{q+1}\right)\right)$. Then, according to (B1) and (B4), the corollary of $\left(\sum_{j=1}^{q+1}\lambda_j\tilde{X}_j, \sum_{j=1}^{q+1}\lambda_j\tilde{Y}_j\right) \in T_1$ is obtained, which means the claim (5.8) is true. Because of (5.8), we have that $\left(\sum_{j=1}^{n}\lambda_j\tilde{X}_j, \sum_{j=1}^{n}\lambda_j\tilde{Y}_j\right) \in T_1$. Because $(\tilde{X}, \tilde{Y})$ verifies (5.7), then according to (B3), we conclude that $(\tilde{X}, \tilde{Y}) \in T_1$. Thus, $T_{UPPS} \subseteq T_1$, and the theorem is proved.

According to the uncertain PPS given in Theorem 5.1, and to provide a measure for the efficiency of each DMU, we can extend the classical DEA models to uncertain models in the rest of this section.

5.5 Belief degree-based uncertain DEA models

For evaluating DMUs by the classical DEA models, an important assumption is that the input and output data are of the exact and deterministic type. But in some real case problems, the data are not exact and cannot be measured as exact values. For such cases, the classical DEA models are not applicable. By considering such inexact data as uncertain variables, the classical DEA models also can be extended to uncertain DEA models to evaluate the DMUs with uncertain input and output data. The belief degree-based uncertain DEA models are developed for this aim in the rest of this chapter. The main notations for presenting uncertain DEA models are given below,

DMU_j	The jth DMU, $j=1, 2, \ldots, n$
DMU_o	The target DMU
$\tilde{X}_j = (\tilde{x}_{1j}, \ldots, \tilde{x}_{mj})$	The uncertain input vector of DMU_j, $j=1, 2, \ldots, n$,
$\tilde{X}_o = (\tilde{x}_{1o}, \ldots, \tilde{x}_{mo})$	The uncertain input vector of DMU_o
$\tilde{Y}_j = (\tilde{y}_{1j}, \ldots, \tilde{y}_{sj})$	The uncertain output vector of DMU_j, $j=1, 2, \ldots, n$
$\tilde{Y}_o = (\tilde{y}_{1o}, \ldots, \tilde{y}_{so})$	The uncertain output vector of DMU_o
ϕ_{ij}	The uncertainty distribution of $\tilde{x}_{ij}, j = 1, \ldots, n, \ i = 1, \ldots, m$
ϕ_{ij}^{-1}	The inverse uncertainty distribution of $\tilde{x}_{ij}, j = 1, \ldots, n,$ $i = 1, \ldots, m$

Continued

—cont'd

ϕ_{io}	The uncertainty distribution of $\tilde{x}_{io}$, $i = 1, \ldots, m$
ϕ_{io}^{-1}	The inverse uncertainty distribution of $\tilde{x}_{io}$, $i = 1, \ldots, m$
φ_{rj}	The uncertainty distribution of $\tilde{y}_{rj}$, $j = 1, \ldots, n$, $r = 1, \ldots, s$
φ_{rj}^{-1}	The inverse uncertainty distribution of $\tilde{y}_{rj}$, $j = 1, \ldots, n$, $r = 1, \ldots, s$
φ_{ro}	The uncertainty distribution of $\tilde{y}_{ro}$, $r = 1, \ldots, s$
φ_{ro}^{-1}	The inverse uncertainty distribution of $\tilde{y}_{ro}$, $r = 1, \ldots, s$
$v \in \mathbb{R}^m$	The vector of input weights
$u \in \mathbb{R}^s$	The vector of output weights
$\mathcal{M}$	The uncertain measure
E	The expected value operator
α	The predetermined confidence level

5.6 Uncertain input-oriented CCR envelopment model

In this section, an uncertain Charnes-Cooper-Rhodes (CCR) model (Charnes et al., 1978) with an envelopment form is presented to evaluate the DMUs with uncertain input and output values. Similar to the classic CCR model, the objective in the uncertain CCR model is to minimize θ. In the rest of this section, three procedures (expected value model, chance-constrained model, and mixed of expected value and chance-constrained models) are introduced to obtain the equivalent crisp form of the uncertain CCR model with an envelopment form.

5.6.1 Expected value input-oriented CCR envelopment model

The expected value criterion was first introduced by Liu (2007) for uncertain variables. According to this criterion, the uncertain objective function is optimized under the expected value of the uncertain objective function and constraints. Applying the expected value criterion, the uncertain CCR model for DMU_o is defined as below.

$$
\begin{aligned}
&\min\ \theta \\
&\text{subject to} \\
&E\left[\sum_{j=1}^{n} \lambda_j \tilde{x}_{ij} - \theta\,\tilde{x}_{io}\right] \le 0 \quad i = 1, 2, \ldots, m \\
&E\left[\sum_{j=1}^{n} \lambda_j \tilde{y}_{rj} - \tilde{y}_{ro}\right] \ge 0 \quad r = 1, 2, \ldots, s \\
&\lambda_j \ge 0,\ \ \theta \text{ is free of sign} \quad j = 1, 2, \ldots, s
\end{aligned}
\tag{5.9}
$$

Definition 5.3 DMU_o is efficient if and only if in model (5.9), the optimal value of the objective function is 1 ($\theta^* = 1$).

Theorem 5.2 Model (5.9) is always feasible and $0 < \theta^* \leq 1$.

Proof. By setting $\theta = 1$ and $\lambda_0 = 1$, $\lambda_j = 0$, $j \neq o$, a feasible solution is obtained for model (5.9). According to this solution, the optimal objective function value cannot be greater than 1.

According to Definition 5.3, model (5.9) can be used to measure the efficiency of DMU_o.

Theorem 5.3 Assume that the independent uncertain variables $\tilde{x}_{ij}$, $\tilde{x}_{io}$, $\tilde{y}_{rj}$, and $\tilde{y}_{ro}$ have regular uncertain distributions ϕ_{ij}, ϕ_{io}, φ_{rj}, and φ_{ro}, respectively. The uncertain formulation (5.9) is equivalent to the below model.

$$
\begin{aligned}
&\min \theta \\
&\text{subject to} \\
&\sum_{j=1}^{n} \lambda_j \int_0^1 \phi_{ij}^{-1}(\alpha)\, d\alpha - \theta \int_0^1 \phi_{io}^{-1}(1-\alpha)\, d\alpha \leq 0 \quad i = 1, 2, \ldots, m \\
&\sum_{j=1}^{n} \lambda_j \int_0^1 \varphi_{rj}^{-1}(\alpha)\, d\alpha - \int_0^1 \varphi_{ro}^{-1}(1-\alpha)\, d\alpha \geq 0 \quad r = 1, 2, \ldots, s \\
&\qquad \lambda_j \geq 0, \ \ \theta \ \text{is free of sign} \qquad j = 1, 2, \ldots, s
\end{aligned}
\tag{5.10}
$$

Proof. Based on the linearity property of the expected value criterion (Theorem 1.39), conversion $E\left[\sum_{j=1}^{n} \lambda_j \tilde{x}_{ij} - \theta \tilde{x}_{io}\right] = E\left[\sum_{j=1}^{n} \lambda_j \tilde{x}_{ij}\right] - E[\theta \tilde{x}_{io}] \leq 0 \Leftrightarrow \sum_{j=1}^{n} \lambda_j E\left[\tilde{x}_{ij}\right] - \theta E[\tilde{x}_{io}] \leq 0$ is considered. Then, according to Theorem 1.38, conversion $\sum_{j=1}^{n} \lambda_j E\left[\tilde{x}_{ij}\right] - \theta E[\tilde{x}_{io}] \leq 0 \Leftrightarrow \sum_{j=1}^{n} \lambda_j \int_0^1 \phi_{ij}^{-1}(\alpha)\, d\alpha - \theta \int_0^1 \phi_{io}^{-1}(1-\alpha)\, d\alpha \leq 0$ is concluded. The other constraint is converted similarly and this completes the proof.

Corollary 5.1 Considering linear regular uncertain distribution such as $\mathcal{L}(a, b)$ for the uncertain variables of Theorem 5.3, the following deterministic model is obtained instead of the model (5.10).

$$\begin{aligned}
&\min \ \theta \\
&\text{subject to} \\
&\sum_{j=1}^{n} \lambda_j \left(\frac{a_{\tilde{x}_{ij}} + b_{\tilde{x}_{ij}}}{2} \right) - \theta \left(\frac{a_{\tilde{x}_{io}} + b_{\tilde{x}_{io}}}{2} \right) \leq 0 \quad i = 1, 2, \ldots, m \\
&\sum_{j=1}^{n} \lambda_j \left(\frac{a_{\tilde{y}_{rj}} + b_{\tilde{y}_{rj}}}{2} \right) - \left(\frac{a_{\tilde{y}_{ro}} + b_{\tilde{y}_{ro}}}{2} \right) \geq 0 \quad r = 1, 2, \ldots, s \\
&\lambda_j \geq 0, \ \ \theta \text{ is free of sign} \quad j = 1, 2, \ldots, s
\end{aligned} \tag{5.11}$$

Corollary 5.2 Considering zigzag regular uncertain distribution such as $\mathcal{Z}(a, b, c)$ for the uncertain variables of Theorem 5.3, the following deterministic model is obtained instead of the model (5.10).

$$\begin{aligned}
&\min \ \theta \\
&\text{subject to} \\
&\sum_{j=1}^{n} \lambda_j \left(\frac{a_{\tilde{x}_{ij}} + 2b_{\tilde{x}_{ij}} + c_{\tilde{x}_{ij}}}{4} \right) - \theta \left(\frac{a_{\tilde{x}_{io}} + 2b_{\tilde{x}_{io}} + c_{\tilde{x}_{io}}}{4} \right) \leq 0 \quad i = 1, 2, \ldots, m \\
&\sum_{j=1}^{n} \lambda_j \left(\frac{a_{\tilde{y}_{rj}} + 2b_{\tilde{y}_{rj}} + c_{\tilde{y}_{rj}}}{4} \right) - \left(\frac{a_{\tilde{y}_{ro}} + b_{\tilde{y}_{ro}} + c_{\tilde{y}_{ro}}}{4} \right) \geq 0 \quad r = 1, 2, \ldots, s \\
&\lambda_j \geq 0, \theta \text{ is free of sign} \quad j = 1, 2, \ldots, s
\end{aligned} \tag{5.12}$$

Corollary 5.3 Considering normal regular uncertain distribution such as $\mathcal{N}(\mu, \sigma)$ for the uncertain variables of Theorem 5.3, the following deterministic model is obtained instead of the model (5.10).

$$\begin{aligned}
&\min \ \theta \\
&\text{subject to} \\
&\sum_{j=1}^{n} \lambda_j \mu_{\tilde{x}_{ij}} - \theta \mu_{\tilde{x}_{io}} \leq 0 \quad i = 1, 2, \ldots, m \\
&\sum_{j=1}^{n} \lambda_j \mu_{\tilde{y}_{rj}} - \mu_{\tilde{y}_{ro}} \geq 0 \quad r = 1, 2, \ldots, s \\
&\lambda_j \geq 0, \theta \text{ is free of sign} \quad j = 1, 2, \ldots, s
\end{aligned} \tag{5.13}$$

Example 5.1 There are five DMUs with zigzag uncertain data shown in Table 5.1.

Table 5.1 The input and output values of Example 5.1.

DMU_j	1	2	3	4	5
Input 1	$\mathcal{Z}(3.5, 4, 4.5)$	$\mathcal{Z}(2.9, 3.1, 3.5)$	$\mathcal{Z}(4.4, 4.9, 5.4)$	$\mathcal{Z}(3.4, 4.1, 4.8)$	$\mathcal{Z}(5.9, 6.5, 7.1)$
Input 2	$\mathcal{Z}(2.9, 3.1, 3.3)$	$\mathcal{Z}(1.4, 1.5, 1.6)$	$\mathcal{Z}(3.2, 3.6, 4)$	$\mathcal{Z}(2.1, 2.3, 2.5)$	$\mathcal{Z}(3.6, 4.1, 4.6)$
Output 1	$\mathcal{Z}(2.4, 2.6, 2.8)$	$\mathcal{Z}(2.2, 3, 3.5)$	$\mathcal{Z}(2.7, 3.2, 3.7)$	$\mathcal{Z}(2.5, 2.9, 3.3)$	$\mathcal{Z}(4.4, 5.1, 5.8)$
Output 2	$\mathcal{Z}(3.8, 4.1, 4.4)$	$\mathcal{Z}(3.3, 3.5, 3.7)$	$\mathcal{Z}(4.3, 5.1, 5.9)$	$\mathcal{Z}(5.5, 5.7, 5.9)$	$\mathcal{Z}(6.5, 7.4, 8.3)$

Table 5.2 The results obtained for Example 5.1.

DMUs	$(\lambda_1^*, \lambda_2^*, \lambda_3^*, \lambda_4^*, \lambda_5^*)$	θ^*	The result of evaluating
DMU_1	(0, 0.45, 0, 0.44, 0)	0.81	Inefficient
DMU_2	(0, 1, 0, 0, 0)	1	Efficient
DMU_3	(0, 0.53, 0, 0.57, 0)	0.82	Inefficient
DMU_4	(0, 0, 0, 1, 0)	1	Efficient
DMU_5	(0, 1.17, 0, 0.58, 0)	0.93	Inefficient

Applying model (5.13), the results of Table 5.2 are obtained, which means only DMUs 2 and 4 are efficient.

5.6.2 Chance-constrained input-oriented CCR envelopment model

Chance-constrained programming for uncertain models was introduced by Liu (2007). To apply this approach to the uncertain input-oriented CCR envelopment models, the following uncertain form is introduced.

$$
\begin{aligned}
& \min \ \theta \\
& \text{subject to} \\
& \mathcal{M}\left\{ \sum_{j=1}^{n} \lambda_j \tilde{x}_{ij} \preceq \theta \tilde{x}_{io} \right\} \geq \alpha \quad i = 1, 2, \ldots, m \\
& \mathcal{M}\left\{ \sum_{j=1}^{n} \lambda_j \tilde{y}_{rj} \succeq \tilde{y}_{ro} \right\} \geq \alpha \quad r = 1, 2, \ldots, s \\
& \lambda_j \geq 0, \theta \, \text{is free of sign} \qquad j = 1, 2, \ldots, s
\end{aligned}
\tag{5.14}
$$

In the above formulation, $\alpha \in (0, 1)$ is the predetermined confidence level for uncertain constraints.

Definition 5.4 The vector $(\lambda=(\lambda_1,\ldots,\lambda_n)\geq 0,\theta)$ is a feasible solution of model (5.14) in confidence level α if it satisfies the set of constraints $\mathcal{M}\left\{\sum_{j=1}^{n}\lambda_j\tilde{x}_{ij}\preceq\theta\tilde{x}_{io}\right\}\geq\alpha,\ i=1,\ 2,\ \ldots,\ m$, and $\mathcal{M}\left\{\sum_{j=1}^{n}\lambda_j\tilde{y}_{rj}\succeq\tilde{y}_{ro}\right\}\geq\alpha$, $r=1,2,\ldots,s$.

Definition 5.5 DMU_o is α-efficient if and only if in model (5.14), the optimal value of the objective function is 1 $(\theta^*=1)$.

By setting $\theta=1$ and $\lambda_0=1, \lambda_j=0, j\neq o$, a feasible solution is obtained for model (5.14). According to this solution, the optimal objective function value cannot be greater than 1. Therefore, $0<\theta^*\leq 1$.

The model (5.14) is a complex model and cannot be solved directly. So, in the next theorem its equivalent crisp form is obtained to be solvable directly.

Theorem 5.4 Assume that the independent uncertain variables $\tilde{x}_{ij}$, $\tilde{x}_{io}$, $\tilde{y}_{rj}$, and $\tilde{y}_{ro}$ have regular uncertain distributions ϕ_{ij}, ϕ_{io}, φ_{rj}, and φ_{ro}, respectively. The uncertain formulation (5.14) is equivalent to the below model.

$$
\begin{aligned}
&\min\ \theta\\
&\text{subject to}\\
&\sum_{j=1}^{n}\lambda_j\phi_{ij}^{-1}(\alpha)-\theta\phi_{io}^{-1}(1-\alpha)\leq 0 \quad i=1,2,\ldots,m\\
&\sum_{j=1}^{n}\lambda_j\varphi_{rj}^{-1}(1-\alpha)-\varphi_{ro}^{-1}(\alpha)\geq 0 \quad r=1,2,\ldots,s\\
&\lambda_j\geq 0, \theta \text{ is free of sign} \quad j=1,2,\ldots,s
\end{aligned}
\tag{5.15}
$$

Proof. Based on Theorem 1.46, conversion $\mathcal{M}\left\{\sum_{j=1}^{n}\lambda_j\tilde{x}_{ij}\preceq\theta\tilde{x}_{io}\right\}\geq\alpha\Leftrightarrow$ $\sum_{j=1}^{n}\lambda_j\phi_{ij}^{-1}(\alpha)-\theta\phi_{io}^{-1}(1-\alpha)\leq 0$, is performed easily. The other constraint is converted similarly.

Corollary 5.4 Considering linear regular uncertain distribution such as $\mathcal{L}(a, b)$ for the uncertain variables of Theorem 5.4, the following deterministic model is obtained instead of the model (5.15).

$$
\begin{aligned}
&\min \ \theta \\
&\text{subject to} \\
&\sum_{j=1}^{n} \lambda_j \left((1-\alpha_i)\, a_{\tilde{x}_{ij}} + \alpha_i\, b_{\tilde{x}_{ij}} \right) - \theta \left(\alpha_i\, a_{\tilde{x}_{io}} + (1-\alpha_i)\, b_{\tilde{x}_{io}} \right) \le 0 \quad i = 1, 2, \ldots, m \\
&\sum_{j=1}^{n} \lambda_j \left(\alpha\, a_{\tilde{y}_{ij}} + (1-\alpha) b_{\tilde{y}_{ij}} \right) - \left((1-\alpha)\, a_{\tilde{y}_{ro}} + \alpha\, b_{\tilde{y}_{ro}} \right) \ge 0 \quad r = 1, 2, \ldots, s \\
&\lambda_j \ge 0, \theta \text{ is free of sign} \quad j = 1, 2, \ldots, s
\end{aligned}
\tag{5.16}
$$

Corollary 5.5 Considering zigzag regular uncertain distribution such as $\mathcal{Z}(a, b, c)$ for the uncertain variables of Theorem 5.4, the following deterministic model is obtained instead of the model (5.15) for a confidence level of $0 < \alpha < 0.5$.

$$
\begin{aligned}
&\min \ \theta \\
&\text{subject to} \\
&\sum_{j=1}^{n} \lambda_j \left((1-2\alpha)\, a_{\tilde{x}_{ij}} + 2\alpha\, b_{\tilde{x}_{ij}} \right) - \theta \left(2\alpha\, b_{\tilde{x}_{io}} + (1-2\alpha) c_{\tilde{x}_{io}} \right) \le 0 \quad i = 1, 2, \ldots, m \\
&\sum_{j=1}^{n} \lambda_j \left(2\alpha\, b_{\tilde{y}_{rj}} + (1-2\alpha)\, c_{\tilde{y}_{rj}} \right) - \left((1-2\alpha)\, a_{\tilde{y}_{ro}} + 2\alpha\, b_{\tilde{y}_{ro}} \right) \ge 0 \quad r = 1, 2, \ldots, s \\
&\lambda_j \ge 0, \theta \text{ is free of sign} \quad j = 1, 2, \ldots, s
\end{aligned}
\tag{5.17}
$$

Corollary 5.6 Considering zigzag regular uncertain distribution such as $\mathcal{Z}(a, b, c)$ for the uncertain variables of Theorem 5.4, the following deterministic model is obtained instead of the model (5.15) for a confidence level of $0.5 \le \alpha < 1$.

$$
\begin{aligned}
&\min \ \theta \\
&\text{subject to} \\
&\sum_{j=1}^{n} \lambda_j \left((2-2\alpha)\, b_{\tilde{x}_{ij}} + (2\alpha-1) c_{\tilde{x}_{ij}} \right) - \theta \left((2\alpha-1)\, a_{\tilde{x}_{io}} + (2-2\alpha)\, b_{\tilde{x}_{io}} \right) \le 0 \quad i = 1, 2, \ldots, m \\
&\sum_{j=1}^{n} \lambda_j \left((2\alpha-1)\, a_{\tilde{y}_{rj}} + (2-2\alpha)\, b_{\tilde{y}_{rj}} \right) - \left((2-2\alpha)\, b_{\tilde{y}_{ro}} + (2\alpha-1)\, c_{\tilde{y}_{ro}} \right) \ge 0 \quad r = 1, 2, \ldots, s \\
&\lambda_j \ge 0, \theta \text{ is free of sign} \quad j = 1, 2, \ldots, s
\end{aligned}
\tag{5.18}
$$

Corollary 5.7 Considering normal regular uncertain distribution such as $\mathcal{N}(\mu, \sigma)$ for the uncertain variables of Theorem 5.4, the following deterministic model is obtained instead of the model (5.15).

$$\begin{aligned}
&\min \quad \theta \\
&\text{subject to} \\
&\sum_{j=1}^{n} \lambda_j \left(\mu_{\tilde{x}_{ij}} + \frac{\sigma_{\tilde{x}_{ij}}\sqrt{3}}{\pi} \ln\left(\frac{\alpha}{1-\alpha}\right) \right) - \theta_o \left(\mu_{\tilde{x}_{io}} + \frac{\sigma_{\tilde{x}_{io}}\sqrt{3}}{\pi} \ln\left(\frac{1-\alpha}{\alpha}\right) \right) \le 0 \qquad i = 1, 2, \ldots, m \\
&\sum_{j=1}^{n} \lambda_j \left(\mu_{\tilde{y}_{rj}} + \frac{\sigma_{\tilde{y}_{rj}}\sqrt{3}}{\pi} \ln\left(\frac{1-\alpha}{\alpha}\right) \right) - \left(\mu_{\tilde{y}_{ro}} + \frac{\sigma_{\tilde{y}_{ro}}\sqrt{3}}{\pi} \ln\left(\frac{\alpha}{1-\alpha}\right) \right) \ge 0 \qquad r = 1, 2, \ldots, s \\
&\lambda_j \ge 0, \theta \text{ is free of sign} \qquad j = 1, 2, \ldots, s
\end{aligned} \tag{5.19}$$

5.6.3 Expected value and chance-constrained input-oriented CCR envelopment model

By considering the expected value of the objective function and the chance-constrained form of the uncertain constraints, the expected value and chance-constrained input-oriented CCR envelopment model can be obtained easily.

Example 5.2 Consider the data of Example 5.1. Applying the models (5.17) and (5.18) with the confidence level values of 0.4 and 0.6, respectively, the results shown in Tables 5.3 and 5.4 are obtained.

Table 5.3 The results of Example 5.2 by model (5.17) and $\alpha = 0.4$.

DMUs	$(\lambda_1^*, \lambda_2^*, \lambda_3^*, \lambda_4^*, \lambda_5^*)$	θ^*	The result of evaluating
DMU_1	(0, 0.36, 0, 0.48, 0)	0.74	Inefficient
DMU_2	(0, 0.82, 0, 0.09, 0)	0.94	Inefficient
DMU_3	(0, 0.42, 0, 0.6, 0)	0.73	Inefficient
DMU_4	(0, 0, 0, 1, 0)	1	Efficient
DMU_5	(0, 0.96, 0, 0.67, 0)	0.84	Inefficient

Table 5.4 The results of Example 5.2 by model (5.17) and $\alpha = 0.6$.

DMUs	$(\lambda_1^*, \lambda_2^*, \lambda_3^*, \lambda_4^*, \lambda_5^*)$	θ^*	The result of evaluating
DMU_1	(0, 0.51, 0, 0.42, 0)	0.88	Inefficient
DMU_2	(0, 1, 0, 0, 0)	1	Efficient
DMU_3	(0, 0.61, 0, 0.56, 0)	0.9	Inefficient
DMU_4	(0, 1, 0, 0.95, 0)	1	Efficient
DMU_5	(0, 1.3, 0, 0.54, 0)	1	Efficient

5.7 Uncertain input-oriented CCR model with multiplier form

In this section, the uncertain CCR model with a multiplier form is presented to evaluate the DMUs with uncertain input and output values. Three procedures (expected value model, chance-constrained model, and mixed of expected value and chance-constrained models) are introduced to obtain the equivalent crisp form of the uncertain CCR model with multiplier form.

5.7.1 Expected value input-oriented CCR model with multiplier form

The expected value input-oriented CCR model with a multiplier form was introduced by Lio and Liu (2018) as below.

$$
\begin{aligned}
& \max \quad \theta = E\left[\frac{\sum_{r=1}^{s} u_r \tilde{y}_{ro}}{\sum_{i=1}^{m} v_i \tilde{x}_{io}}\right] \\
& \text{subject to} \\
& E\left[\frac{\sum_{r=1}^{s} u_r \tilde{y}_{rj}}{\sum_{i=1}^{m} v_i \tilde{x}_{ij}}\right] \le 1 \quad j = 1, 2, \ldots, n \\
& v_i \ge 0 \quad i = 1, 2, \ldots, m \\
& u_r \ge 0 \quad r = 1, 2, \ldots, s
\end{aligned}
\tag{5.20}
$$

Definition 5.6 DMU_o is efficient if and only if in model (5.20), the optimal value of the objective function is 1 ($\theta^* = 1$).

Theorem 5.5 Assume that the independent uncertain variables $\tilde{x}_{ij}$, $\tilde{x}_{io}$, $\tilde{y}_{rj}$, and $\tilde{y}_{ro}$ have regular uncertain distributions ϕ_{ij}, ϕ_{io}, φ_{rj}, and φ_{ro}, respectively. The uncertain formulation (5.20) is equivalent to the below model.

$$
\begin{aligned}
&\max_{u_r,\, v_i} \ \theta = \int_0^1 \frac{\sum_{r=1}^{s} u_r \varphi_{ro}^{-1}(\alpha)}{\sum_{i=1}^{m} v_i \phi_{io}^{-1}(1-\alpha)} d\alpha \\
&\text{subject to} \\
&\int_0^1 \frac{\sum_{r=1}^{s} u_r \varphi_{rj}^{-1}(\alpha)}{\sum_{i=1}^{m} v_i \phi_{ij}^{-1}(1-\alpha)} d\alpha \le 1 \quad j = 1, 2, \dots, n \\
&v_i \ge 0 \quad i = 1, 2, \dots, m \\
&u_r \ge 0 \quad r = 1, 2, \dots, s
\end{aligned}
\tag{5.21}
$$

Proof. As the function $\frac{\sum_{r=1}^{s} u_r \tilde{y}_{rj}}{\sum_{i=1}^{m} v_i \tilde{x}_{ij}}$ is absolutely increasing for $\tilde{y}_{rj}$ and absolutely decreasing for $\tilde{x}_{ij}$, according to Theorem 1.33 its uncertain distribution is $\Gamma_j^{-1}(\alpha) = \frac{\sum_{r=1}^{s} u_r \varphi_{rj}^{-1}(\alpha)}{\sum_{i=1}^{m} v_i \phi_{ij}^{-1}(1-\alpha)}$. Then, according to Theorem 1.38, the term $E\left[\frac{\sum_{r=1}^{s} u_r \tilde{y}_{rj}}{\sum_{i=1}^{m} v_i \tilde{x}_{ij}}\right] = \int_0^1 \frac{\sum_{r=1}^{s} u_r \varphi_{rj}^{-1}(\alpha)}{\sum_{i=1}^{m} v_i \phi_{ij}^{-1}(1-\alpha)} d\alpha$ is obtained and this completes the proof.

Example 5.3 (Lio & Liu, 2018). The data of five DMUs with three uncertain inputs and three uncertain outputs are given in Table 5.5.

By using the model (5.21), the results in Table 5.6 are obtained.

According to the results of this table, DMUs 2 and 5 are efficient and the other DMUs are inefficient.

Table 5.5 The dataset for Example 5.3.

DMU$_j$	**1**	**2**	**3**	**4**	**5**
Input 1	$\mathcal{L}(4,7)$	$\mathcal{L}(2,5)$	$\mathcal{L}(3,4)$	$\mathcal{L}(2,5)$	$\mathcal{L}(1,6)$
Input 2	$\mathcal{L}(5,8)$	$\mathcal{L}(3,6)$	$\mathcal{L}(4,6)$	$\mathcal{L}(1,6)$	$\mathcal{L}(1,3)$
Input 3	$\mathcal{L}(4,8)$	$\mathcal{L}(1,3)$	$\mathcal{L}(3,7)$	$\mathcal{L}(1,3)$	$\mathcal{L}(1,3)$
Output 1	$\mathcal{Z}(1,2,3)$	$\mathcal{Z}(4,7,10)$	$\mathcal{Z}(2,3,4)$	$\mathcal{Z}(4,6,8)$	$\mathcal{Z}(10,12,14)$
Output 2	$\mathcal{Z}(1,2,4)$	$\mathcal{Z}(8,10,12)$	$\mathcal{Z}(2,6,8)$	$\mathcal{Z}(5,7,8)$	$\mathcal{Z}(5,6,7)$
Output 3	$\mathcal{Z}(1,3,4)$	$\mathcal{Z}(9,11,13)$	$\mathcal{Z}(3,5,7)$	$\mathcal{Z}(5,7,9)$	$\mathcal{Z}(8,9,10)$

Table 5.6 The results of Example 5.3 by model (5.21).

DMU$_j$	1	2	3	4	5
θ^*	0.1465	1	0.5028	0.9407	1
Efficiency results	Inefficient	Efficient	Inefficient	Inefficient	Efficient

5.7.2 Chance-constrained input-oriented CCR model with multiplier form

To optimize the optimistic value of the objective function under a specified confidence level of chance constraints, Wen et al. (2017) proposed the following chance-constrained input-oriented CCR model with a multiplier form.

$$\begin{aligned}
&\max_{u_r,\, v_i} \ \overline{f} \\
&\text{subject to} \\
&\mathcal{M}\left\{ \frac{\sum_{r=1}^{s} u_r \tilde{y}_{ro}}{\sum_{i=1}^{m} v_i \tilde{x}_{io}} \succeq \overline{f} \right\} \geq 1-\alpha \\
&\mathcal{M}\left\{ \sum_{r=1}^{s} u_r \tilde{y}_{rj} \preceq \sum_{i=1}^{m} v_i \tilde{x}_{ij} \right\} \geq \alpha \quad j=1,2,\ldots,n \\
&v_i \geq 0 \quad i=1,2,\ldots,m \\
&u_r \geq 0 \quad r=1,2,\ldots,s
\end{aligned} \tag{5.22}$$

In this formulation, $\alpha \in (0,1)$ is a predetermined confidence level. In practical situations, the researchers usually do not select the DMUs with less than a 0.5 uncertainty measure. Therefore, $0.5 \leq \alpha < 1$.

Definition 5.7 The feasible solution (u_r^*, v_i^*) is an optimistic optimal solution for model (5.22) if for any feasible solution (u_r, v_i), the condition

$$\max\left\{ \overline{f} \,\middle|\, \mathcal{M}\left\{ \frac{\sum_{r=1}^{s} u_r^* \tilde{y}_{ro}}{\sum_{i=1}^{m} v_i^* \tilde{x}_{io}} \succeq \overline{f} \right\} \geq 1-\alpha \right\} \geq \max\left\{ \overline{f} \,\middle|\, \mathcal{M}\left\{ \frac{\sum_{r=1}^{s} u_r \tilde{y}_{ro}}{\sum_{i=1}^{m} v_i \tilde{x}_{io}} \succeq \overline{f} \right\} \geq 1-\alpha \right\}$$

is true.

It is notable that based on model (5.22), the DMUs with a greater objective function value are more efficient. Therefore, the DMUs can be ranked by decreasing order of their objective function values.

Theorem 5.6 Assume that the independent uncertain variables $\tilde{x}_{ij}$, $\tilde{x}_{io}$, $\tilde{y}_{rj}$, and $\tilde{y}_{ro}$ have regular uncertain distributions ϕ_{ij}, ϕ_{io}, φ_{rj}, and φ_{ro}, respectively. The optimistic uncertain formulation (5.22) is equivalent to the below model where $\alpha \in (0,1)$.

$$
\begin{aligned}
&\max \sum_{r=1}^{s} \overline{u}_r \varphi_{ro}^{-1}(\alpha) \\
&\text{subject to} \\
&\sum_{i=1}^{m} \overline{v}_i \phi_{io}^{-1}(1-\alpha) = 1 \\
&\sum_{r=1}^{s} \overline{u}_r \varphi_{rj}^{-1}(\alpha) \leq \sum_{i=1}^{m} \overline{v}_i \phi_{ij}^{-1}(1-\alpha) \quad j = 1,2,\ldots,n \\
&v_i \geq 0 \quad i = 1,2,\ldots,m \\
&u_r \geq 0 \quad r = 1,2,\ldots,s
\end{aligned}
\tag{5.23}
$$

Proof. The first constraint of model (5.22) is converted as follows,

$$
\mathcal{M}\left\{ \frac{\sum_{r=1}^{s} u_r \tilde{y}_{ro}}{\sum_{i=1}^{m} v_i \tilde{x}_{io}} \succeq \overline{f} \right\} \geq 1-\alpha \Leftrightarrow \mathcal{M}\left\{ \sum_{r=1}^{s} u_r \tilde{y}_{ro} \succeq \overline{f} \sum_{i=1}^{m} v_i \tilde{x}_{io} \right\} \geq 1-\alpha \Leftrightarrow
$$

$$
\mathcal{M}\left\{ -\sum_{r=1}^{s} u_r \tilde{y}_{ro} + \overline{f} \sum_{i=1}^{m} v_i \tilde{x}_{io} \preceq 0 \right\} \geq 1-\alpha
$$

$$
\Leftrightarrow -\sum_{r=1}^{s} u_r \phi_{ro}^{-1}(\alpha) + \overline{f} \sum_{i=1}^{m} v_i \phi_{io}^{-1}(1-\alpha) \leq 0
$$

$$
\Leftrightarrow \sum_{r=1}^{s} u_r \phi_{ro}^{-1}(\alpha) - \overline{f} \sum_{i=1}^{m} v_i \phi_{io}^{-1}(1-\alpha) \geq 0
$$

$$
\Leftrightarrow \frac{\sum_{r=1}^{s} u_r \phi_{ro}^{-1}(\alpha)}{\sum_{i=1}^{m} v_i \phi_{io}^{-1}(1-\alpha)} \geq \overline{f}
$$

Similarly, the second constraint of model (5.22) is converted as below,

$$\mathcal{M}\left\{\sum_{r=1}^{s}u_r\tilde{y}_{rj}\preceq\sum_{i=1}^{m}v_i\tilde{x}_{ij}\right\}\geq\alpha\Leftrightarrow\mathcal{M}\left\{\sum_{r=1}^{s}u_r\tilde{y}_{rj}-\sum_{i=1}^{m}v_i\tilde{x}_{ij}\preceq 0\right\}\geq\alpha$$
$$\Leftrightarrow\sum_{r=1}^{s}u_r\varphi_{rj}^{-1}(\alpha)-\sum_{i=1}^{m}v_i\phi_{ij}^{-1}(1-\alpha)\leq 0$$

Therefore, the following model is obtained.

$$\begin{aligned}
&\max \quad \frac{\sum_{r=1}^{s}u_r\varphi_{ro}^{-1}(\alpha)}{\sum_{i=1}^{m}v_i\phi_{io}^{-1}(1-\alpha)}\\
&\text{subject to}\\
&\sum_{r=1}^{s}u_r\varphi_{rj}^{-1}(\alpha)\leq\sum_{i=1}^{m}v_i\phi_{ij}^{-1}(1-\alpha)\quad j=1,2,\ldots,n\\
&v_i\geq 0\quad i=1,2,\ldots,m\\
&u_r\geq 0\quad r=1,2,\ldots,s
\end{aligned}\tag{5.24}$$

Applying the Charnes-Cooper transformation (Charnes & Cooper, 1962) and assuming $\sum_{i=1}^{m}v_i\phi_{io}^{-1}(\alpha)=\frac{1}{t}$, model (5.24) is rewritten as follows,

$$\begin{aligned}
&\max \quad \sum_{r=1}^{s}tu_r\varphi_{ro}^{-1}(\alpha)\\
&\text{subject to}\\
&\sum_{i=1}^{m}tv_i\phi_{io}^{-1}(1-\alpha)=1\\
&\sum_{r=1}^{s}tu_r\varphi_{rj}^{-1}(\alpha)\leq\sum_{i=1}^{m}tv_i\phi_{ij}^{-1}(1-\alpha)\quad j=1,2,\ldots,n\\
&v_i\geq 0\quad i=1,2,\ldots,m\\
&u_r\geq 0\quad r=1,2,\ldots,s
\end{aligned}\tag{5.25}$$

Finally, by applying the conversions $\overline{v}_i=tv_i,\overline{u}_i=tu_i$, model (5.25) is converted to model (5.23).

Corollary 5.8 Considering linear regular uncertain distribution such as $\mathcal{L}(a, b)$ for the uncertain variables of Theorem 5.6, the following deterministic model is obtained instead of the optimistic uncertain model (5.23).

$$\begin{aligned}
&\max \quad \sum_{r=1}^{s} \overline{u}_r\left((1-\alpha)\, a_{\tilde{y}_{ro}} + \alpha\, b_{\tilde{y}_{ro}}\right) \\
&\text{subject to} \\
&\sum_{i=1}^{m} \overline{v}_i\left(\alpha\, a_{\tilde{x}_{io}} + (1-\alpha)\, b_{\tilde{x}_{io}}\right) = 1 \\
&\sum_{r=1}^{s} \overline{u}_r\left((1-\alpha)\, a_{\tilde{y}_{rj}} + \alpha\, b_{\tilde{y}_{rj}}\right) \leq \sum_{i=1}^{m} \overline{v}_i\left(\alpha\, a_{\tilde{x}_{ij}} + (1-\alpha)\, b_{\tilde{x}_{ij}}\right) \quad j = 1, 2, \ldots, n \\
&\overline{v}_i \geq 0 \quad i = 1, 2, \ldots, m \\
&\overline{u}_r \geq 0 \quad r = 1, 2, \ldots, s
\end{aligned} \tag{5.26}$$

Corollary 5.9 Considering zigzag regular uncertain distribution such as $\mathcal{Z}(a, b, c)$ for the uncertain variables of Theorem 5.6, the following deterministic model is obtained instead of the optimistic uncertain model (5.23) where $0.5 \leq \alpha < 1$.

$$\begin{aligned}
&\max \quad \sum_{r=1}^{s} \overline{u}_r\left((2-2\alpha)\, b_{\tilde{y}_{ro}} + (2\alpha - 1)\, c_{\tilde{y}_{ro}}\right) \\
&\text{subject to} \\
&\sum_{i=1}^{m} \overline{v}_i\left((2\alpha-1)\, a_{\tilde{x}_{io}} + (2-2\alpha)\, b_{\tilde{x}_{io}}\right) = 1 \\
&\sum_{r=1}^{s} \overline{u}_r\left((2-2\alpha)\, b_{\tilde{y}_{rj}} + (2\alpha-1)\, c_{\tilde{y}_{rj}}\right) \\
&\quad \leq \sum_{i=1}^{m} \overline{v}_i\left((2\alpha-1)\, a_{\tilde{x}_{ij}} + (2-2\alpha)\, b_{\tilde{x}_{ij}}\right) \quad j = 1, 2, \ldots, n \\
&\overline{v}_i \geq 0 \quad i = 1, 2, \ldots, m \\
&\overline{u}_r \geq 0 \quad r = 1, 2, \ldots, s
\end{aligned} \tag{5.27}$$

Sometimes, the decision maker may decide to maximize the chance of the constraint $\frac{\sum_{r=1}^{s} u_r \tilde{y}_{ro}}{\sum_{i=1}^{m} v_i \tilde{x}_{io}} \succeq 1$. For such cases, the dependent chance programming approach (see Liu, 1997, 1999, 2002) can be applied. The dependent chance programming of a DEA model is represented below (Wen et al., 2017):

$$
\begin{aligned}
&\theta = \max_{u_r,\, v_i} \ \mathcal{M}\left\{ \frac{\sum_{r=1}^{s} u_r \tilde{y}_{ro}}{\sum_{i=1}^{m} v_i \tilde{x}_{io}} \succeq 1 \right\} \\
&\text{subject to} \\
&\mathcal{M}\left\{ \sum_{r=1}^{s} u_r \tilde{y}_{rj} \preceq \sum_{i=1}^{m} v_i \tilde{x}_{ij} \right\} \geq \alpha \quad j = 1, 2, \ldots, n \\
&v_i \geq 0 \quad i = 1, 2, \ldots, m \\
&u_r \geq 0 \quad r = 1, 2, \ldots, s
\end{aligned}
\tag{5.28}
$$

where $\alpha \in (0, 1)$.

Definition 5.8 (Wen et al., 2017). The feasible solution (u_r^*, v_i^*) is a maximum chance optimal solution for model (5.28) if for any feasible solution (u_r, v_i), the condition $\mathcal{M}\left\{ \frac{\sum_{r=1}^{s} u_r^* \tilde{y}_{ro}}{\sum_{i=1}^{m} v_i^* \tilde{x}_{io}} \succeq 1 \right\} \geq \mathcal{M}\left\{ \frac{\sum_{r=1}^{s} u_r \tilde{y}_{ro}}{\sum_{i=1}^{m} v_i \tilde{x}_{io}} \succeq 1 \right\}$ is true.

It is notable that based on model (5.28), the DMUs with a greater objective function value are more efficient. Therefore, the DMUs can be ranked by decreasing order of their objective function values.

Theorem 5.7 Assume that the independent uncertain variables $\tilde{x}_{ij}$, $\tilde{x}_{io}$, $\tilde{y}_{rj}$, and $\tilde{y}_{ro}$ have regular uncertain distributions ϕ_{ij}, ϕ_{io}, φ_{rj}, and φ_{ro}, respectively. The optimistic uncertain formulation (5.28) is equivalent to the below model where $\alpha \in (0, 1)$.

$$
\begin{aligned}
&\theta = \max_{\gamma,\, u_r,\, v_i} \ \gamma \\
&\text{subject to} \\
&\sum_{r=1}^{s} u_r \varphi_{ro}^{-1}(1-\gamma) - \sum_{i=1}^{m} v_i \phi_{io}^{-1}(\gamma) \geq 0 \\
&\sum_{r=1}^{s} u_r \varphi_{rj}^{-1}(\alpha) \leq \sum_{i=1}^{m} v_i \phi_{ij}^{-1}(1-\alpha) \quad j = 1, 2, \ldots, n \\
&v_i \geq 0 \quad i = 1, 2, \ldots, m \\
&u_r \geq 0 \quad r = 1, 2, \ldots, s
\end{aligned}
\tag{5.29}
$$

Proof. The model (5.28) is equivalent to the following model.

$$\theta = \max_{\gamma,\, u_r,\, v_i} \ \gamma$$

subject to

$$\begin{aligned}
&\mathcal{M}\left\{ \frac{\sum_{r=1}^{s} u_r \tilde{y}_{ro}}{\sum_{i=1}^{m} v_i \tilde{x}_{io}} \succeq 1 \right\} \geq \gamma \\
&\mathcal{M}\left\{ \sum_{r=1}^{s} u_r \tilde{y}_{rj} \preceq \sum_{i=1}^{m} v_i \tilde{x}_{ij} \right\} \geq \alpha \quad j = 1, 2, \ldots, n \\
&v_i \geq 0 \quad i = 1, 2, \ldots, m \\
&u_r \geq 0 \quad r = 1, 2, \ldots, s
\end{aligned} \tag{5.30}$$

The first constraint of model (5.30) is converted to a crisp form as follows,

$$\begin{aligned}
\mathcal{M}\left\{ \frac{\sum_{r=1}^{s} u_r \tilde{y}_{ro}}{\sum_{i=1}^{m} v_i \tilde{x}_{io}} \succeq 1 \right\} \geq \gamma &\Leftrightarrow \mathcal{M}\left\{ -\sum_{r=1}^{s} u_r \tilde{y}_{ro} + \sum_{i=1}^{m} v_i \tilde{x}_{io} \preceq 0 \right\} \geq \gamma \\
&\Leftrightarrow \ -\sum_{r=1}^{s} u_r \phi_{ro}^{-1}(1-\gamma) + \sum_{i=1}^{m} v_i \phi_{io}^{-1}(\gamma) \leq 0 \\
&\Leftrightarrow \ \sum_{r=1}^{s} u_r \phi_{ro}^{-1}(1-\gamma) - \sum_{i=1}^{m} v_i \phi_{io}^{-1}(\gamma) \geq 0
\end{aligned}$$

Similarly, the second constraint of model (5.30) is converted as below,

$$\begin{aligned}
\mathcal{M}\left\{ \sum_{r=1}^{s} u_r \tilde{y}_{rj} \preceq \sum_{i=1}^{m} v_i \tilde{x}_{ij} \right\} \geq \alpha &\Leftrightarrow \mathcal{M}\left\{ \sum_{r=1}^{s} u_r \tilde{y}_{rj} - \sum_{i=1}^{m} v_i \tilde{x}_{ij} \preceq 0 \right\} \geq \alpha \\
&\Leftrightarrow \sum_{r=1}^{s} u_r \varphi_{rj}^{-1}(\alpha) - \sum_{i=1}^{m} v_i \phi_{ij}^{-1}(1-\alpha) \leq 0
\end{aligned}$$

The theorem is proved.

Although Theorem 5.6 can be used for any type of uncertain distribution, its special cases for linear and zigzag type uncertain distributions are represented in the following.

Corollary 5.10 Considering linear regular uncertain distribution such as $4C(a, b)$ for the uncertain variables of Theorem 5.6, the following deterministic model is obtained instead of the model (5.29).

$$\begin{aligned}
&\max_{\gamma,\, u_r,\, v_i} \quad \sum_{i=1}^{m} \overline{p}_i + \sum_{r=1}^{s} \overline{w}_r \\
&\text{subject to} \\
&\sum_{i=1}^{m} p_i + \sum_{r=1}^{s} w_r = 1 \\
&\sum_{i=1}^{m} \overline{p}_i\left(b_{\tilde{x}_{io}} - a_{\tilde{x}_{io}}\right) - \sum_{r=1}^{s} \overline{w}_r\left(a_{\tilde{y}_{ro}} - b_{\tilde{y}_{ro}}\right) + \sum_{i=1}^{m} p_i\, a_{\tilde{x}_{io}} - \sum_{r=1}^{s} w_r\, b_{\tilde{y}_{ro}} \le 0 \\
&\sum_{r=1}^{s} w_r\left((1-\alpha)a_{\tilde{y}_{rj}} + \alpha\, b_{\tilde{y}_{rj}}\right) \le \sum_{i=1}^{m} p_i\left(\alpha\, a_{\tilde{x}_{ij}} + (1-\alpha)\, b_{\tilde{x}_{ij}}\right) \quad j = 1, 2, \ldots, n \\
&0 < \overline{p}_i \le p_i \quad i = 1, 2, \ldots, m \\
&0 < \overline{w}_r \le w_r \quad r = 1, 2, \ldots, s
\end{aligned} \tag{5.31}$$

Proof. According to the inverse of the linear uncertain distribution, the following form of model (5.29) is obtained.

$$\begin{aligned}
&\theta = \max_{\gamma,\, u_r,\, v_i} \quad \gamma \\
&\text{subject to} \\
&\sum_{i=1}^{m} v_i\left(\gamma\left(b_{\tilde{x}_{io}} - a_{\tilde{x}_{io}}\right) + a_{\tilde{x}_{io}}\right) - \sum_{r=1}^{s} u_r\left(\gamma\left(a_{\tilde{y}_{ro}} - b_{\tilde{y}_{ro}}\right) + b_{\tilde{y}_{ro}}\right) \le 0 \\
&\sum_{r=1}^{s} u_r\left((1-\alpha)a_{\tilde{y}_{rj}} + \alpha\, b_{\tilde{y}_{rj}}\right) \le \sum_{i=1}^{m} v_i\left(\alpha\, a_{\tilde{x}_{ij}} + (1-\alpha)\, b_{\tilde{x}_{ij}}\right) \quad j = 1, 2, \ldots, n \\
&v_i \ge 0 \quad i = 1, 2, \ldots, m \\
&u_r \ge 0 \quad r = 1, 2, \ldots, s
\end{aligned} \tag{5.32}$$

The above model is rewritten as,

$$\theta = \max_{\gamma,\, u_r,\, v_i} \ \gamma$$

subject to

$$\gamma \sum_{i=1}^{m} v_i\left(b_{\tilde{x}_{io}} - a_{\tilde{x}_{io}}\right) - \gamma \sum_{r=1}^{s} u_r\left(a_{\tilde{y}_{ro}} - b_{\tilde{y}_{ro}}\right) + \sum_{i=1}^{m} v_i a_{\tilde{x}_{io}} - \sum_{r=1}^{s} u_r b_{\tilde{y}_{ro}} \le 0$$

$$\sum_{r=1}^{s} u_r\left((1-\alpha)a_{\tilde{y}_{rj}} + \alpha\, b_{\tilde{y}_{rj}}\right) \le \sum_{i=1}^{m} v_i\left(\alpha\, a_{\tilde{x}_{ij}} + (1-\alpha)\, b_{\tilde{x}_{ij}}\right) j = 1, 2, \ldots, n$$

$$v_i \ge 0 \quad i = 1, 2, \ldots, m$$

$$u_r \ge 0 \quad r = 1, 2, \ldots, s \tag{5.33}$$

Assume $\overline{u}_r = \gamma u_r, \overline{v}_i = \gamma v_i$, then $\gamma = \left(\sum_{i=1}^{m} \overline{v}_i + \sum_{r=1}^{s} \overline{u}_r\right) \Big/ \left(\sum_{i=1}^{m} v_i + \sum_{r=1}^{s} u_r\right)$, $0 \le \overline{u}_r \le u_r, 0 \le \overline{v}_i \le v_i$. Then the model (5.33) can be written as,

$$\max_{\gamma,\, u_r,\, v_i} \frac{\sum_{i=1}^{m} \overline{v}_i + \sum_{r=1}^{s} \overline{u}_r}{\sum_{i=1}^{m} v_i + \sum_{r=1}^{s} u_r}$$

subject to

$$\sum_{i=1}^{m} \overline{v}_i\left(b_{\tilde{x}_{io}} - a_{\tilde{x}_{io}}\right) - \sum_{r=1}^{s} \overline{u}_r\left(a_{\tilde{y}_{ro}} - b_{\tilde{y}_{ro}}\right) + \sum_{i=1}^{m} v_i a_{\tilde{x}_{io}} - \sum_{r=1}^{s} u_r b_{\tilde{y}_{ro}} \le 0$$

$$\sum_{r=1}^{s} u_r\left((1-\alpha)a_{\tilde{y}_{rj}} + \alpha\, b_{\tilde{y}_{rj}}\right) \le \sum_{i=1}^{m} v_i\left(\alpha\, a_{\tilde{x}_{ij}} + (1-\alpha)\, b_{\tilde{x}_{ij}}\right) \quad j = 1, 2, \ldots, n$$

$$0 < \overline{v}_i \le v_i \quad i = 1, 2, \ldots, m$$

$$0 < \overline{u}_r \le u_r \quad r = 1, 2, \ldots, s \tag{5.34}$$

Assuming the conversions $\sum_{i=1}^{m} v_i + \sum_{r=1}^{s} u_r = \frac{1}{t}$, and $\overline{p}_i = t\overline{v}_i, \overline{w}_r = t\overline{u}_r, p_i = t v_i, w_r = t u_r$ the following model is obtained.

$$\max_{\gamma,\, u_r,\, v_i} \sum_{i=1}^{m} \overline{p}_i + \sum_{r=1}^{s} \overline{w}_r$$

subject to

$$\sum_{i=1}^{m} p_i + \sum_{r=1}^{s} w_r = 1$$

$$\sum_{i=1}^{m} \overline{p}_i (b_{\tilde{x}_{io}} - a_{\tilde{x}_{io}}) - \sum_{r=1}^{s} \overline{w}_r (a_{\tilde{y}_{ro}} - b_{\tilde{y}_{ro}}) + \sum_{i=1}^{m} p_i\, a_{\tilde{x}_{io}} - \sum_{r=1}^{s} w_r\, b_{\tilde{y}_{ro}} \le 0$$

$$\sum_{r=1}^{s} w_r \Big((1-\alpha) a_{\tilde{y}_{rj}} + \alpha\, b_{\tilde{y}_{rj}} \Big) \le \sum_{i=1}^{m} p_i \big(\alpha\, a_{\tilde{x}_{ij}} + (1-\alpha)\, b_{\tilde{x}_{ij}} \big) \quad j = 1, 2, \ldots, n$$

$$0 < \overline{p}_i \le p_i \quad i = 1, 2, \ldots, m$$

$$0 < \overline{w}_r \le w_r \quad r = 1, 2, \ldots, s$$

(5.35)

The proof is completed.

Corollary 5.11 Considering zigzag regular uncertain distribution such as $\mathcal{Z}(a, b, c)$ for the uncertain variables of Theorem 5.6, the following deterministic model is obtained instead of the model (5.29).

$$\max_{\gamma,\, u_r,\, v_i} \sum_{i=1}^{m} \overline{p}_i + \sum_{r=1}^{s} \overline{w}_r$$

subject to

$$\sum_{i=1}^{m} p_i + \sum_{r=1}^{s} w_r = 1$$

$$\sum_{i=1}^{m} 2\overline{p}_i \Big(c_{\tilde{x}_{io}} - b_{\tilde{x}_{io}} \Big) - \sum_{r=1}^{s} 2\overline{w}_r \Big(a_{\tilde{y}_{ro}} - b_{\tilde{y}_{ro}} \Big) + 2 \sum_{i=1}^{m} p_i\, b_{\tilde{x}_{io}} - 2 \sum_{r=1}^{s} w_r\, b_{\tilde{y}_{ro}} +$$

$$\sum_{r=1}^{s} w_r a_{\tilde{y}_{ro}} - \sum_{i=1}^{m} p_i c_{\tilde{x}_{io}} \le 0$$

$$\sum_{r=1}^{s} w_r \Big(2(1-\alpha) b_{\tilde{y}_{rj}} + (2\alpha - 1)\, c_{\tilde{y}_{rj}} \Big) \le \sum_{i=1}^{m} p_i \Big((2\alpha - 1)\, a_{\tilde{x}_{ij}} + 2(1-\alpha)\, b_{\tilde{x}_{ij}} \Big) \quad j = 1, 2, \ldots, n$$

$$\overline{p}_i \ge 0.5\, p_i, \quad i = 1, 2, \ldots, m$$

$$\overline{w}_r \le 0.5\, w_r \quad r = 1, 2, \ldots, s$$

(5.36)

Proof. According to the inverse of the zigzag uncertain distribution, the following form of model (5.29) is obtained.

$$\theta = \max_{\gamma,\, u_r,\, v_i} \gamma$$

subject to

$$\gamma \sum_{i=1}^{m} v_i\left(2\left(c_{\tilde{x}_{io}} - b_{\tilde{x}_{io}}\right)\right) - \gamma \sum_{r=1}^{s} u_r\left(2\left(a_{\tilde{y}_{ro}} - b_{\tilde{y}_{ro}}\right)\right) + 2\sum_{i=1}^{m} v_i\, b_{\tilde{x}_{io}} - 2\sum_{r=1}^{s} u_r\, b_{\tilde{y}_{ro}} +$$

$$\sum_{r=1}^{s} u_r\, a_{\tilde{y}_{ro}} - \sum_{i=1}^{m} v_i\, c_{\tilde{x}_{io}} \le 0$$

$$\sum_{r=1}^{s} u_r\left(2(1-\alpha)b_{\tilde{y}_{rj}} + (2\alpha-1)\,c_{\tilde{y}_{rj}}\right) \le \sum_{i=1}^{m} v_i\left((2\alpha-1)\,b_{\tilde{x}_{ij}} + (2\alpha-1)\,a_{\tilde{x}_{ij}}\right) \quad j = 1, 2, \ldots, n$$

$$\gamma \ge 0.5, v_i \ge 0 \quad i = 1, 2, \ldots, m$$

$$u_r \ge 0 \quad r = 1, 2, \ldots, s \qquad (5.37)$$

Assume $\overline{u}_r = \gamma u_r, \overline{v}_i = \gamma v_i$, then $\gamma = \left(\sum_{i=1}^{m} \overline{v}_i + \sum_{r=1}^{s} \overline{u}_r\right) / \left(\sum_{i=1}^{m} v_i + \sum_{r=1}^{s} u_r\right)$, $\overline{u}_r \ge 0.5u_r, \overline{v}_i \ge 0.5v_i$. Then the model (5.37) can be written as,

$$\max_{\gamma,\, u_r,\, v_i} \frac{\sum_{i=1}^{m} \overline{v}_i + \sum_{r=1}^{s} \overline{u}_r}{\sum_{i=1}^{m} v_i + \sum_{r=1}^{s} u_r}$$

subject to

$$\gamma \sum_{i=1}^{m} v_i\left(2\left(c_{\tilde{x}_{io}} - b_{\tilde{x}_{io}}\right)\right) - \gamma \sum_{r=1}^{s} u_r\left(2\left(a_{\tilde{y}_{ro}} - b_{\tilde{y}_{ro}}\right)\right) + 2\sum_{i=1}^{m} v_i\, b_{\tilde{x}_{io}} - 2\sum_{r=1}^{s} u_r\, b_{\tilde{y}_{ro}} +$$

$$\sum_{r=1}^{s} u_r\, a_{\tilde{y}_{ro}} - \sum_{i=1}^{m} v_i\, c_{\tilde{x}_{io}} \le 0$$

$$\sum_{r=1}^{s} u_r\left(2(1-\alpha)b_{\tilde{y}_{rj}} + (2\alpha-1)\,c_{\tilde{y}_{rj}}\right) \le \sum_{i=1}^{m} v_i\left((2\alpha-1)\,b_{\tilde{x}_{ij}} + (2\alpha-1)\,a_{\tilde{x}_{ij}}\right) \quad j = 1, 2, \ldots, n$$

$$\gamma \ge 0.5, v_i \ge 0 \quad i = 1, 2, \ldots, m$$

$$u_r \ge 0 \quad r = 1, 2, \ldots, s \qquad (5.38)$$

Assuming the conversions $\sum_{i=1}^{m} v_i + \sum_{r=1}^{s} u_r = \frac{1}{t}$, and $\overline{p}_i = t\overline{v}_i, \overline{w}_r = t\overline{u}_r, p_i = t v_i, w_r = t u_r$ the following model is obtained.

$$\max_{\gamma, u_r, v_i} \sum_{i=1}^{m} \overline{p}_i + \sum_{r=1}^{s} \overline{w}_r$$

subject to

$$\sum_{i=1}^{m} p_i + \sum_{r=1}^{s} w_r = 1$$

$$\sum_{i=1}^{m} 2\overline{p}_i\left(c_{\tilde{x}_{io}} - b_{\tilde{x}_{io}}\right) - \sum_{r=1}^{s} 2\overline{w}_r\left(a_{\tilde{y}_{ro}} - b_{\tilde{y}_{ro}}\right) + 2\sum_{i=1}^{m} p_i b_{\tilde{x}_{io}} - 2\sum_{r=1}^{s} w_r b_{\tilde{y}_{ro}} +$$

$$\sum_{r=1}^{s} w_r a_{\tilde{y}_{ro}} - \sum_{i=1}^{m} p_i c_{\tilde{x}_{io}} \leq 0$$

$$\sum_{r=1}^{s} w_r\left(2(1-\alpha)b_{\tilde{y}_{rj}} + (2\alpha-1)\,c_{\tilde{y}_{rj}}\right) \leq \sum_{i=1}^{m} p_i\left((2\alpha-1)\,a_{\tilde{x}_{ij}} + 2(1-\alpha)\,b_{\tilde{x}_{ij}}\right) \quad j = 1, 2, \ldots, n$$

$$\overline{p}_i \geq 0.5\,p_i \quad i = 1, 2, \ldots, m$$

$$\overline{w}_r \leq 0.5\,w_r \quad r = 1, 2, \ldots, s \tag{5.39}$$

The proof is completed.

Example 5.4 Considering the data of Table 5.1 from Example 5.1, the results of Tables 5.7 and 5.8 are obtained for the models (5.27) and (5.36), respectively.

Table 5.7 The results obtained for different confidence levels by model (5.27).

Confidence level α	DMU_1	DMU_2	DMU_3	DMU_4	DMU_5
0.5	0.82	1	0.89	1	1
0.6	0.85	1	0.91	1	1
0.7	0.89	1	0.94	1	1
0.8	0.9	1	0.98	1	1
0.9	0.91	0.99	1	1	1

Table 5.8 The results obtained for different confidence levels by model (5.36).

Confidence level α	DMU_1	DMU_2	DMU_3	DMU_4	DMU_5
0.5	0.1	0.5	0.31	0.5	0.5
0.6	0.06	0.4	0.26	0.4	0.4
0.7	0.03	0.3	0.22	0.3	0.3
0.8	0	0.2	0.19	0.2	0.2
0.9	0	0.08	0.1	0.1	0.1

5.7.3 Expected value and chance-constrained input-oriented CCR model with multiplier form

In this approach, the expected value of the objective function is optimized with respect to the chance constraint form of the constraints (see Liu, 2007, 2012). The value and chance-constrained input-oriented CCR model with multiplier form is given below,

$$\theta = \max_{u_r, v_i} E\left[\frac{\sum_{r=1}^{s} u_r \tilde{y}_{ro}}{\sum_{i=1}^{m} v_i \tilde{x}_{io}}\right]$$

subject to (5.40)

$$\mathcal{M}\left\{\sum_{r=1}^{s} u_r \tilde{y}_{rj} \preceq \sum_{i=1}^{m} v_i \tilde{x}_{ij}\right\} \geq \alpha \quad j = 1, 2, \ldots, n$$

$$v_i \geq 0 \quad i = 1, 2, \ldots, m$$

$$u_r \geq 0 \quad r = 1, 2, \ldots, s$$

where, $\alpha \in [0.5, 1]$.

Definition 5.9 (Wen et al., 2017). The vector $(u_r, v_i) \geq 0$ is a feasible solution for model (5.40) if $\mathcal{M}\left\{\sum_{r=1}^{s} u_r \tilde{y}_{rj} \preceq \sum_{i=1}^{m} v_i \tilde{x}_{ij}\right\} \geq \alpha, j = 1, 2, \ldots, n.$

Definition 5.10 (Wen et al., 2017). The solution (u_r^*, v_i^*) is an expected value optimal solution for model (5.40) if for any solution (u_r, v_i) the condition $E\left[\frac{\sum_{r=1}^{s} u_r^* \tilde{y}_{ro}}{\sum_{i=1}^{m} v_i^* \tilde{x}_{io}}\right] \geq E\left[\frac{\sum_{r=1}^{s} u_r \tilde{y}_{ro}}{\sum_{i=1}^{m} v_i \tilde{x}_{io}}\right]$ is met.

It is notable that based on model (5.40), the DMUs with a greater objective function value are more efficient. Therefore, the DMUs can be ranked by the decreasing order of their objective function values.

Theorem 5.8 Assume that the independent uncertain variables $\tilde{x}_{ij}$, $\tilde{x}_{io}$, $\tilde{y}_{rj}$, and $\tilde{y}_{ro}$ have regular uncertain distributions ϕ_{ij}, ϕ_{io}, φ_{rj}, and φ_{ro}, respectively. The uncertain formulation (5.40) is equivalent to the below model.

$$\theta = \max \int_0^1 \frac{\sum_{r=1}^{s} u_r \varphi_{ro}^{-1}(\alpha)}{\sum_{i=1}^{m} v_i \phi_{io}^{-1}(1-\alpha)} d\alpha$$

subject to (5.41)

$$\sum_{r=1}^{s} u_r \varphi_{rj}^{-1}(\alpha) \le \sum_{i=1}^{m} v_i \phi_{ij}^{-1}(1-\alpha) \quad j = 1, 2, \ldots, n$$
$$v_i \ge 0 \quad i = 1, 2, \ldots, m$$
$$u_r \ge 0 \quad r = 1, 2, \ldots, s$$

Proof. As for $j=1, 2, \ldots, n$ the function $\frac{\sum_{r=1}^{s} u_r \tilde{y}_{ro}}{\sum_{i=1}^{m} v_i \tilde{x}_{io}}$ is absolutely increasing for $\tilde{y}_{ro}$ and absolutely decreasing for $\tilde{x}_{io}$; according to Theorem 1.33, the uncertain distribution $\Gamma_o^{-1}(\alpha) = \frac{\sum_{r=1}^{s} u_r \varphi_{ro}^{-1}(\alpha)}{\sum_{i=1}^{m} v_i \phi_{io}^{-1}(1-\alpha)}$ is obtained. On the other hand, according to Theorem 1.38 the relation $E\left[\frac{\sum_{r=1}^{s} u_r \tilde{y}_{ro}}{\sum_{i=1}^{m} v_i \tilde{x}_{io}}\right] = \int_0^1 \frac{\sum_{r=1}^{s} u_r \varphi_{ro}^{-1}(\alpha)}{\sum_{i=1}^{m} v_i \phi_{io}^{-1}(1-\alpha)} d\alpha$ is obtained. Also, $\mathcal{M}\left\{\sum_{r=1}^{s} u_r \tilde{y}_{rj} \preceq \sum_{i=1}^{m} v_i \tilde{x}_{ij}\right\} \ge \alpha$, $j=1, 2, \ldots, n$ is claimed if and only if $\sum_{r=1}^{s} u_r \varphi_{rj}^{-1}(\alpha) \le \sum_{i=1}^{m} v_i \phi_{ij}^{-1}(1-\alpha)$. So, the theorem is proved.

Example 5.5 Considering the data of Table 5.1 from Example 5.1, the results of Table 5.9 are obtained for the model (5.40).

Table 5.9 The results obtained for different confidence levels by model (5.40).

Confidence level α	DMU_1	DMU_2	DMU_3	DMU_4	DMU_5
0.5	0.82	1	0.91	1	1
0.6	0.85	1	0.92	1	1
0.7	0.89	1	0.94	1	1
0.8	0.9	1	0.98	1	1
0.9	0.91	1	1	1	1

5.8 Uncertain DEA model for scale efficiency evaluation

An uncertain DEA model is able to measure the efficiency of an organization according to some inexact inputs and outputs. In many organizations, the inefficiency may happen because of using old technologies. Therefore, the measured efficiency is actually technical efficiency and the employed uncertain DEA model can be called an uncertain DEA model for technical efficiency (see Jiang et al., 2018).

Lio and Liu (2018) developed the uncertain DEA model, but the applications of their model are different than what happen in real case organizations and practical economics. In real competitive markets, organizations operate in a situation with incremental, decremental, or fixed returns to scale; therefore, just the recognition of the technical efficiency of such organizations cannot be enough. In such an environment, instead of pure technical efficiency, scale efficiency can be used. By applying a scale efficiency model, the performance of the DMUs can be measured and improved as well.

An uncertain DEA model for scale efficiency evaluation (proposed by Jiang et al., 2018) is given by the below formulation.

$$
\begin{aligned}
&\max \ \gamma = E\left[\frac{\sum_{r=1}^{s} u_r \tilde{y}_{ro} - w}{\sum_{i=1}^{m} v_i \tilde{x}_{io}}\right] \\
&\text{subject to} \\
&E\left[\frac{\sum_{r=1}^{s} u_r \tilde{y}_{rj} - w}{\sum_{i=1}^{m} v_i \tilde{x}_{ij}}\right] \leq 1 \quad j = 1, 2, \ldots, n \\
&v_i \geq 0 \quad i = 1, 2, \ldots, m \\
&u_r \geq 0 \quad r = 1, 2, \ldots, s
\end{aligned}
\tag{5.42}
$$

In this model, w is free of sign. If $w \leq 0$, the model works with an expansion assumption, but if $w \geq 0$, the model works with a contraction assumption. In fact, the value of w determines the behavior of the DMUs. A DMU is in an incremental returns to scale situation ($w \leq 0$) or in a decremental returns to scale situation ($w \geq 0$). It is notable that the model is not able to determine the type of returns to scale.

Definition 5.11 DMU_o is efficient if and only if the optimal value of the model (5.42) is 1 ($\gamma^* = 1$).

Theorem 5.9 Assume that the independent uncertain variables $\tilde{x}_{ij}$, $\tilde{x}_{io}$, $\tilde{y}_{rj}$, and $\tilde{y}_{ro}$ have regular uncertain distributions ϕ_{ij}, ϕ_{io}, φ_{rj}, and φ_{ro}, respectively. The uncertain formulation (5.42) is equivalent to the below model where $\alpha \in (0, 1)$.

$$\max \ \gamma = \int_0^1 \frac{\sum_{r=1}^{s} u_r \varphi_{ro}^{-1}(\alpha) - w}{\sum_{i=1}^{m} v_i \phi_{io}^{-1}(1-\alpha)} d\alpha$$

subject to

$$\int_0^1 \frac{\sum_{r=1}^{s} u_r \varphi_{rj}^{-1}(\alpha) - w}{\sum_{i=1}^{m} v_i \phi_{ij}^{-1}(1-\alpha)} d\alpha \leq 1 \quad j = 1, 2, \ldots, n \tag{5.43}$$

$$v_i \geq 0 \quad i = 1, 2, \ldots, m$$

$$u_r \geq 0 \quad r = 1, 2, \ldots, s$$

Proof. As the function $\frac{\sum_{r=1}^{s} u_r \tilde{y}_{rj} - w}{\sum_{i=1}^{m} v_i \tilde{x}_{ij}}$ is absolutely increasing for $\tilde{y}_{rj}$ and absolutely decreasing for $\tilde{x}_{ij}$, according to Theorem 1.33 its uncertain distribution is $\Gamma_j^{-1}(\alpha) = \frac{\sum_{r=1}^{s} u_r \varphi_{rj}^{-1}(\alpha) - w}{\sum_{i=1}^{m} v_i \phi_{ij}^{-1}(1-\alpha)}$. Then, according to Theorem 1.38 the term $E\left[\frac{\sum_{r=1}^{s} u_r \tilde{y}_{rj} - w}{\sum_{i=1}^{m} v_i \tilde{x}_{ij}}\right] = \int_0^1 \frac{\sum_{r=1}^{s} u_r \varphi_{rj}^{-1}(\alpha) - w}{\sum_{i=1}^{m} v_i \phi_{ij}^{-1}(1-\alpha)} d\alpha$ is obtained.

It can be claimed that if DMU_o is efficient by model (5.20), then it will be efficient by model (5.42) as well, but the inverse of this claim may not be true. To prove this claim, assume DMU_o is efficient by model (5.20), then there exists a $(u,v) \geq 0$ where $E\left[\frac{\sum_{r=1}^{s} u_r \tilde{y}_{ro}}{\sum_{i=1}^{m} v_i \tilde{x}_{io}}\right] = 1$ and $E\left[\frac{\sum_{r=1}^{s} u_r \tilde{y}_{rj}}{\sum_{i=1}^{m} v_i \tilde{x}_{ij}}\right] \leq 1$ (for $j=1$, 2, …, n). Now assume $w=0$, then $(u,v) \geq 0$ and (u,v,w) are true for the conditions $E\left[\frac{\sum_{r=1}^{s} u_r \tilde{y}_{ro} - w}{\sum_{i=1}^{m} v_i \tilde{x}_{io}}\right] = 1$ and $E\left[\frac{\sum_{r=1}^{s} u_r \tilde{y}_{rj} - w}{\sum_{i=1}^{m} v_i \tilde{x}_{ij}}\right] \leq 1$ (for $j=1$, 2, …, n). Therefore, the optimal value of model (5.42) will be 1, which means that DMU_o is efficient by this model too.

Example 5.6 This example is taken from Jiang et al. (2018). Consider a problem with five DMUs, three uncertain inputs, and three uncertain outputs with the uncertain data in Table 5.10.

Applying the models (5.20) and (5.43) for evaluating the DMUs, the results of Table 5.11 are obtained.

According to Table 5.11, considering the results of model 5.20, only the DMUs with an optimal value of 1 ($\theta^* = 1$) are technically efficient.

Table 5.10 The uncertain data of Example 5.6.

DMU_j	1	2	3	4	5
Input 1	$\mathcal{L}(13,15)$	$\mathcal{L}(20,21)$	$\mathcal{L}(30,33)$	$\mathcal{L}(20,23)$	$\mathcal{L}(10,12)$
Input 2	$\mathcal{L}(15,18)$	$\mathcal{L}(30,33)$	$\mathcal{L}(40,47)$	$\mathcal{L}(10,11)$	$\mathcal{L}(10,12)$
Input 3	$\mathcal{L}(25,28)$	$\mathcal{L}(10,11)$	$\mathcal{L}(30,36)$	$\mathcal{L}(10,12)$	$\mathcal{L}(10,11)$
Output 1	$\mathcal{Z}(25,26,27)$	$\mathcal{Z}(40,45,48)$	$\mathcal{Z}(20,22,24)$	$\mathcal{Z}(40,43,46)$	$\mathcal{Z}(100,110,120)$
Output 2	$\mathcal{Z}(26,27,28)$	$\mathcal{Z}(80,90,96)$	$\mathcal{Z}(20,21,22)$	$\mathcal{Z}(44,46,50)$	$\mathcal{Z}(50,51,56)$
Output 3	$\mathcal{Z}(27,28,30)$	$\mathcal{Z}(90,100,108)$	$\mathcal{Z}(30,31,34)$	$\mathcal{Z}(50,55,59)$	$\mathcal{Z}(80,90,96)$

Table 5.11 Results obtained by the models (5.20) and (5.43) for Example 5.6.

DMU_j		1	2	3	4	5
Model (5.20)	Optimal value θ^*	0.41	1	0.14	0.93	1
	Technical efficiency	Inefficient	Efficient	Inefficient	Inefficient	Efficient
Model (5.43)	Optimal value γ^*_{pure}	0.78	1	0.2	1	1
	Scale efficiency γ^*_{scale}	0.52	1	0.7	0.93	1
	Pure technical efficiency	Inefficient	Efficient	Inefficient	Efficient	Efficient

Therefore, DMU_2 and DMU_5 are technically efficient while DMU_1, DMU_3, and DMU_4 are technically inefficient. In addition to pure technical efficiency (γ^*_{pure}) and technical efficiency (θ^*), scale efficiency (γ^*_{scale}) can be obtained as a division of technical efficiency by pure technical efficiency. The results for scale efficiency are given in Table 5.11, where DMU_4 has an obtained value of 0.93 for this efficiency. It interprets the reason why DMU_4 is purely technically efficient rather than technically inefficient, and it occurs because of scale inefficiency. The scale efficiency shows the possibility that the average productivity at the most productive scale size may not be attainable for the other scale sizes at which a particular DMU may operate (Banker et al., 1984). Therefore, an uncertain DEA model for scale efficiency can estimate the most productive scale size for the given DMUs. According to Table 5.13, the scale efficiency values of DMU_2 and DMU_5 are 1, which means that they are performing in the most productive scale size. Furthermore, the technical efficiency and scale efficiency of DMU_4 are 1 and 0.93, respectively. This means that there is no excess in the inputs and no shortage in the outputs of this DMU; therefore, there is no way to improve its performance by assigning more resources. As the scale efficiency of DMU_4 is less than 1 (is not optimal), the decision maker should focus on improving the returns to scale.

5.9 Uncertain DEA model for special scale efficiency

The recognition of the special scale of a DMU by evaluating its scale efficiency is very crucial for decisions about improving the inefficiency of the DMU (Jiang et al., 2020). Although the classical DEA models can measure various scale efficiencies, these models cannot handle inexact data. To overcome this difficulty, Jiang et al. (2020) introduced two different uncertain DEA models with inexact input and output values for recognizing incremental and decremental returns to scales that can be used to improve inefficiency without needing exact data.

5.9.1 Uncertain DEA model for decreasing scale efficiency

In this section, an uncertain DEA model for decreasing scale efficiency is presented (Jiang et al., 2020) that is able to determine whether a DMU is in a decremental returns to scale situation. The model is given as below.

$$\max \ \gamma_1 = E\left[\frac{\sum_{r=1}^{s} u_r \tilde{y}_{ro} - w_1}{\sum_{i=1}^{m} v_i \tilde{x}_{io}}\right]$$

subject to

$$E\left[\frac{\sum_{r=1}^{s} u_r \tilde{y}_{rj} - w_1}{\sum_{i=1}^{m} v_i \tilde{x}_{ij}}\right] \leq 1 \quad j = 1, 2, \ldots, n \tag{5.44}$$

$$v_i \geq 0 \quad i = 1, 2, \ldots, m$$

$$u_r \geq 0 \quad r = 1, 2, \ldots, s$$

$$w_1 \geq 0$$

The only difference in models (5.44) and (5.42) is about the restriction of variable w_1 where in model (5.44) it is nonnegative and in model (5.42) it is free of sign. Therefore, model (5.44) is able to recognize whether a DMU is in a decremental returns to scale situation, where model (5.42) cannot recognize such a situation (Jiang et al., 2020).

Definition 5.12 *DMU_o* is efficient if and only if the optimal value of model (5.44) is 1 ($\gamma_1^* = 1$).

Theorem 5.10 Assume that the independent uncertain variables $\tilde{x}_{ij}$, $\tilde{x}_{io}$, $\tilde{y}_{rj}$, and $\tilde{y}_{ro}$ have regular uncertain distributions ϕ_{ij}, ϕ_{io}, φ_{rj}, and φ_{ro}, respectively. The uncertain formulation (5.44) is equivalent to the below model where $\alpha \in (0, 1)$.

$$\max \ \gamma_1 = \int_0^1 \frac{\sum_{r=1}^{s} u_r \varphi_{ro}^{-1}(\alpha) - w_1}{\sum_{i=1}^{m} v_i \phi_{io}^{-1}(1-\alpha)} d\alpha$$

subject to

$$\int_0^1 \frac{\sum_{r=1}^{s} u_r \varphi_{rj}^{-1}(\alpha) - w_1}{\sum_{i=1}^{m} v_i \phi_{ij}^{-1}(1-\alpha)} d\alpha \leq 1 \quad j = 1, 2, \ldots, n \tag{5.45}$$

$$v_i \geq 0 \quad i = 1, 2, \ldots, m$$

$$u_r \geq 0 \quad r = 1, 2, \ldots, s$$

$$w_1 \geq 0$$

Proof. The proof is similar to Theorem (5.11), and so the proof is omitted.

5.9.2 Uncertain DEA model for increasing scale efficiency

In this section, an uncertain DEA model for increasing scale efficiency is presented (Jiang et al., 2020) that is able to determine whether a DMU is in an incremental returns to scale situation. The model is given as below.

$$\max \ \gamma_2 = E\left[\frac{\sum_{r=1}^{s} u_r\tilde{y}_{ro} - w_2}{\sum_{i=1}^{m} v_i\tilde{x}_{io}}\right]$$

subject to

$$E\left[\frac{\sum_{r=1}^{s} u_r\tilde{y}_{rj} - w_2}{\sum_{i=1}^{m} v_i\tilde{x}_{ij}}\right] \leq 1 \quad j = 1, 2, \ldots, n \tag{5.46}$$

$$v_i \geq 0 \quad i = 1, 2, \ldots, m$$

$$u_r \geq 0 \quad r = 1, 2, \ldots, s$$

$$w_2 \leq 0$$

The only difference of models (5.46) and (5.42) is about the restriction of variable w_2 where in model (5.46) it is nonpositive and in model (5.42) it is free of sign. Therefore, model (5.46) is able to recognize whether a DMU is in an incremental returns to scale situation, where model (5.42) cannot recognize such a situation (Jiang et al., 2020).

Definition 5.13 DMU_o is efficient if and only if the optimal value of model (5.46) is 1 ($\gamma_2^* = 1$).

Theorem 5.11 Assume that the independent uncertain variables $\tilde{x}_{ij}$, $\tilde{x}_{io}$, $\tilde{y}_{rj}$, and $\tilde{y}_{ro}$ have regular uncertain distributions ϕ_{ij}, ϕ_{io}, φ_{rj}, and φ_{ro}, respectively. The uncertain formulation (5.46) is equivalent to the below model where $\alpha \in (0, 1)$.

$$\max \ \gamma_2 = \int_0^1 \frac{\sum_{r=1}^{s} u_r \varphi_{ro}^{-1}(\alpha) - w_2}{\sum_{i=1}^{m} v_i \phi_{io}^{-1}(1-\alpha)} d\alpha$$

subject to

$$\int_0^1 \frac{\sum_{r=1}^{s} u_r \varphi_{rj}^{-1}(\alpha) - w_2}{\sum_{i=1}^{m} v_i \phi_{ij}^{-1}(1-\alpha)} d\alpha \leq 1 \quad j = 1, 2, \ldots, n \tag{5.47}$$

$$v_i \geq 0 \quad i = 1, 2, \ldots, m$$

$$u_r \geq 0 \quad r = 1, 2, \ldots, s$$

$$w_2 \leq 0$$

Proof. The proof is similar to Theorem (5.11), and so the proof is omitted.

5.10 Uncertain BCC models

In this section, the classical BCC models in multiplier form are developed to an uncertain environment and some methods are presented to measure their efficiency.

5.10.1 Expected value and chance-constrained BCC models in multiplier form

The following expected value and chance-constrained BCC models in multiplier form were proposed by Jamshidi et al. (2021b) to measure the efficiency of DMUs in an uncertain environment.

$$\theta = \max \ E\left[\sum_{r=1}^{s} u_r \tilde{y}_{ro} + u_0\right]$$

subject to

$$\mathcal{M}\left\{\sum_{i=1}^{m} v_i \tilde{x}_{io} \preceq 1\right\} \geq \alpha \tag{5.48}$$

$$\mathcal{M}\left\{\sum_{r=1}^{s} u_r \tilde{y}_{rj} \preceq \sum_{i=1}^{m} v_i \tilde{x}_{ij} - u_0\right\} \geq \alpha \quad j = 1, 2, \ldots, n$$

$$v_i \geq 0 \quad i = 1, 2, \ldots, m$$

$$u_r \geq 0 \quad r = 1, 2, \ldots, s$$

Definition 5.14 (Jamshidi et al., 2021a, 2021b). The vector $(u_r, v_i, u_0) \geq 0$ is a feasible solution of model (5.48) if $\mathcal{M}\left\{\sum_{i=1}^{m} v_i\tilde{x}_{io} \preceq 1\right\} \geq \alpha$ and $\mathcal{M}\left\{\sum_{r=1}^{s} u_r\tilde{y}_{rj} \preceq \sum_{i=1}^{m} v_i\tilde{x}_{ij} - u_0\right\} \geq \alpha$ for $j=1, 2, \ldots, n$.

Definition 5.15 (Jamshidi et al., 2021a, 2021b). The feasible solution (u_r^*, v_i^*, u_0^*) is an optimal expected value solution of model (5.48), if for any feasible solution (u_r, v_i, u_0), there is $E\left[\sum_{r=1}^{s} u_r^*\tilde{y}_{ro} + u_0^*\right] \geq E\left[\sum_{r=1}^{s} u_r\tilde{y}_{ro} + u_0\right]$.

The DMUs are ranked according to the increasing order of the optimal objective function values, and the greater the optimal objective function value, the more efficient the DMU.

Theorem 5.12 Assume that the independent uncertain variables $\tilde{x}_{ij}$, $\tilde{x}_{io}$, $\tilde{y}_{rj}$, and $\tilde{y}_{ro}$ have regular uncertain distributions ϕ_{ij}, ϕ_{io}, φ_{rj}, and φ_{ro}, respectively. The uncertain formulation (5.48) is equivalent to the below model where $\alpha \in (0, 1)$.

$$
\begin{aligned}
&\theta = \max \quad \sum_{r=1}^{s} u_r \int_0^1 \varphi_{ro}^{-1}(\alpha)d\alpha + u_0 \\
&\text{subject to} \\
&\sum_{i=1}^{m} v_i\phi_{io}^{-1}(\alpha) \leq 1 \\
&\sum_{r=1}^{s} u_r\varphi_{rj}^{-1}(\alpha) - \sum_{i=1}^{m} v_i\phi_{ir}^{-1}(1-\alpha) + u_0 \leq 0 \quad j = 1, 2, \ldots, n \\
&v_i \geq 0 \quad i = 1, 2, \ldots, m \\
&u_r \geq 0 \quad r = 1, 2, \ldots, s
\end{aligned}
\tag{5.49}
$$

Proof. The proof is straightforward.

5.10.2 Expected value BCC models in multiplier form

The expected value BCC models in multiplier form are applied to evaluate DMUs under an uncertain environment. This model is presented below (Jamshidi et al., 2021a, 2021b).

$$\theta = \max \ E\left[\sum_{r=1}^{s} u_r \tilde{y}_{ro} + u_0\right]$$
subject to
$$E\left[\sum_{i=1}^{m} v_i \tilde{x}_{io}\right] \le 1$$
$$E\left[\sum_{r=1}^{s} u_r \tilde{y}_{rj} - \sum_{i=1}^{m} v_i \tilde{x}_{ij} + u_0\right] \le 0 \quad j = 1, 2, \ldots, n$$
$$v_i \ge 0 \quad i = 1, 2, \ldots, m$$
$$u_r \ge 0 \quad r = 1, 2, \ldots, s \tag{5.50}$$

Definition 5.16 (Jamshidi et al., 2021a, 2021b). The vector $(u_r, v_i, u_0) \ge 0$ is a feasible solution of model (5.50) if $E\left[\sum_{i=1}^{m} v_i \tilde{x}_{io}\right] \le 1$ and $E\left[\sum_{r=1}^{s} u_r \tilde{y}_{rj} - \sum_{i=1}^{m} v_i \tilde{x}_{ij} + u_0\right] \le 0$ for $j = 1, 2, \ldots, n$.

Definition 5.17 (Jamshidi et al., 2021a, 2021b). The feasible solution (u_r^*, v_i^*, u_0^*) is an optimal expected value solution of model (5.50), if for any feasible solution (u_r, v_i, u_0), there is $E\left[\sum_{r=1}^{s} u_r^* \tilde{y}_{ro} + u_0^*\right] \ge E\left[\sum_{r=1}^{s} u_r \tilde{y}_{ro} + u_0\right]$.

Definition 5.18 DMU_o is efficient for model (5.50) if its optimal objective function value is 1 ($\theta^* = 1$).

Theorem 5.13 Assume that the independent uncertain variables $\tilde{x}_{ij}$, $\tilde{x}_{io}$, $\tilde{y}_{rj}$, and $\tilde{y}_{ro}$ have regular uncertain distributions ϕ_{ij}, ϕ_{io}, φ_{rj}, and φ_{ro}, respectively. The uncertain formulation (5.50) is equivalent to the below model where $\alpha \in (0, 1)$.

$$\theta = \max \ \sum_{r=1}^{s} u_r \int_0^1 \varphi_{ro}^{-1}(\alpha) d\alpha + u_0$$
subject to
$$\sum_{i=1}^{m} v_i \int_0^1 \phi_{io}^{-1}(\alpha) d\alpha \le 1$$
$$\sum_{r=1}^{s} u_r \int_0^1 \varphi_{rj}^{-1}(\alpha)\, d\alpha - \sum_{i=1}^{m} v_i \int_0^1 \phi_{ir}^{-1}(1-\alpha)\, d\alpha + u_0 \le 0 \quad j = 1, 2, \ldots, n$$
$$v_i \ge 0 \quad i = 1, 2, \ldots, m$$
$$u_r \ge 0 \quad r = 1, 2, \ldots, s \tag{5.51}$$

Table 5.12 Data of Example 5.7.

	Inputs			Outputs		
DMU_i	1	2	3	1	2	3
1	$\mathcal{L}$ (60, 70)	$\mathcal{L}$ (10, 15)	$\mathcal{L}$ (5, 10)	$\mathcal{L}$ (50, 70)	$\mathcal{L}$ (70, 80)	$\mathcal{L}$ (40, 50)
2	$\mathcal{L}$ (70, 80)	$\mathcal{L}$ (6, 18)	$\mathcal{L}$ 40, 50)	$\mathcal{L}$ (20, 40)	$\mathcal{L}$ (50, 60)	$\mathcal{L}$ (40, 50)
3	$\mathcal{L}$ (80,90)	$\mathcal{L}$ (70, 80)	$\mathcal{L}$ (70, 80)	$\mathcal{L}$ (80, 90)	$\mathcal{L}$ (80, 90)	$\mathcal{L}$ (80, 90)
4	$\mathcal{L}$(70, 100)	$\mathcal{L}$ (50, 100)	$\mathcal{L}$ (40, 100)	$\mathcal{L}$ (50, 100)	$\mathcal{L}$ (70, 100)	$\mathcal{L}$ (80, 100)
5	$\mathcal{L}$ (10, 15)	$\mathcal{L}$ (10, 15)	$\mathcal{L}$ (5, 10)	$\mathcal{L}$ (10, 20)	$\mathcal{L}$ (10, 15)	$\mathcal{L}$ (5, 10)
6	$\mathcal{L}$ (30, 60)	$\mathcal{L}$ (30, 40)	$\mathcal{L}$ (30, 50)	$\mathcal{L}$ (30, 50)	$\mathcal{L}$ (30, 40)	$\mathcal{L}$ (30, 60)

Table 5.13 The results of Example 5.7 by model (5.48).

DMU_i	DMU_1	DMU_2	DMU_3	DMU_4	DMU_5	DMU_6
Optimal value θ^*	1	1	0.68	0.65	1	0.64
Efficiency	Efficient	Efficient	Inefficient	Inefficient	Efficient	Inefficient

Table 5.14 The results of Example 5.7 by model (5.50) for different confidence level.

Confidence level	DMU_i	DMU_1	DMU_2	DMU_3	DMU_4	DMU_5	DMU_6
$\alpha=0.2$	θ^*	4.95	13	3.68	1.9	2.71	1.22
	Efficiency	Inefficient	Inefficient	Inefficient	Inefficient	Inefficient	Inefficient
$\alpha=0.5$	θ^*	1	1	1	1	1	0.87
	Efficiency	Efficient	Efficient	Efficient	Efficient	Efficient	Inefficient
$\alpha=0.8$	θ^*	0.88	0.85	0.89	0.72	0.79	0.59
	Efficiency	Inefficient	Inefficient	Inefficient	Inefficient	Inefficient	Inefficient

Proof. The proof is straightforward.

Example 5.7 Consider the problem with the linear uncertain data in Table 5.12. The results of evaluating the DMUs by models (5.48) and (5.50) are given in Tables 5.13 and 5.14.

5.11 Uncertain additive model

Similar to the deterministic additive model, objective function of the uncertain additive model maximizes the sum of the slack variables of the inputs and outputs. The belief degree-based uncertain additive model is as follows (Wen et al., 2014):

$$
\begin{aligned}
&\max \sum_{i=1}^{m} s_i^- + \sum_{r=1}^{s} s_r^+ \\
&\text{subject to} \\
&\mathcal{M}\left\{ \sum_{j=1}^{n} \lambda_j \tilde{x}_{ij} \preceq \tilde{x}_{io} - s_i^- \right\} \geq \alpha \quad i = 1, 2, \ldots, m \\
&\mathcal{M}\left\{ \sum_{j=1}^{n} \lambda_j \tilde{y}_{rj} \succeq \tilde{y}_{ro} + s_r^+ \right\} \geq \alpha \quad r = 1, 2, \ldots, s \\
&\sum_{j=1}^{n} \lambda_j = 1 \\
&s_i^- \geq 0 \quad i = 1, 2, \ldots, m \\
&s_r^+ \geq 0 \quad r = 1, 2, \ldots, s \\
&\lambda_j \geq 0 \quad j = 1, 2, \ldots, n
\end{aligned}
\tag{5.52}
$$

Definition 5.19 (Wen et al., 2014). DMU_o is α-efficient if the optimal solutions of model (5.52) take the value of zero such as $s_i^{-*}=0$ and $s_r^{+*}=0$ for $i=1, 2, \ldots, m$ and $r=1, 2, \ldots, s$.

This definition is similar to that of the deterministic additive model. Because of the uncertain nature of model (5.52), there may be some differences between the definitions. For example, for a specific α value, DMU_o may satisfy Definition 5.19 but is not efficient.

In model (5.52), if $\lambda_0=1$ and $\lambda_j=0$ for $j\neq o$, a feasible solution is obtained. Therefore, we claim that this model is always feasible and its optimal objective function value is zero.

Theorem 5.14 Assume that the independent uncertain variables $\tilde{x}_{ij}$, $\tilde{x}_{io}$, $\tilde{y}_{rj}$, and $\tilde{y}_{ro}$ have regular uncertain distributions ϕ_{ij}, ϕ_{io}, φ_{rj}, and φ_{ro}, respectively. The uncertain formulation (5.52) is equivalent to the below model.

$$
\begin{aligned}
&\max \sum_{i=1}^{m} s_i^- + \sum_{r=1}^{s} s_r^+ \\
&\text{subject to} \\
&\sum_{\substack{j=1 \\ j\neq o}}^{n} \lambda_j \phi_{ij}^{-1}(\alpha) + \lambda_o \phi_{io}^{-1}(1-\alpha) \leq \phi_{io}^{-1}(1-\alpha) - s_i^- \quad i=1,2,\ldots,m
\end{aligned}
$$

$$\sum_{\substack{j=1 \\ j \neq o}}^{n} \lambda_j \varphi_{rj}^{-1}(1-\alpha) + \lambda_o \varphi_{ro}^{-1}(1-\alpha) \geq \varphi_{ro}^{-1}(\alpha) + s_r^+ \quad r=1,2,\ldots,s$$

$$\sum_{j=1}^{n} \lambda_j = 1$$

$$s_i^- \geq 0 \quad i=1,2,\ldots,m$$

$$s_r^+ \geq 0 \quad r=1,2,\ldots,s$$

$$\lambda_j \geq 0 \quad j=1,2,\ldots,n \tag{5.53}$$

Proof. Without a loss of generality, let $o=1$ and $x_o=x_1$. The constraint $\mathcal{M}\left\{\sum_{j=1}^{n} \lambda_j \tilde{x}_{1j} \leq \tilde{x}_{11} - s_i^-\right\} \geq \alpha$ can be rewritten as $\mathcal{M}\left\{\sum_{j=1}^{n} \lambda_j \tilde{x}_{1j} \preceq \tilde{x}_{11} - s_i^-\right\} = \mathcal{M}\left\{\sum_{j=2}^{n} \lambda_j \tilde{x}_{1j} + \lambda_1 \tilde{x}_{11} - \tilde{x}_{11} \preceq -s_i^-\right\} = \mathcal{M}\left\{\sum_{j=2}^{n} \lambda_j \tilde{x}_{1j} - (1-\lambda_1)\tilde{x}_{11} \preceq -s_i^-\right\} \geq \alpha$. As the term $-(1-\lambda_1)\tilde{x}_{11}$ is an uncertain variable that is decreasing for $\tilde{x}_{11}$, its inverse uncertain distribution is $\Omega_{11}^{-1}(\alpha) = -(1-\lambda_1)\phi_{11}^{-1}(1-\alpha)$ where $0<\alpha<1$. Also, $\lambda_j \tilde{x}_{1j}$ (for $2 \leq j \leq n$) is an uncertain variable with inverse uncertain distribution of $\Omega_{1j}^{-1}(\alpha) = \lambda_j \phi_{1j}^{-1}(\alpha)$ where $0<\alpha<1$. Therefore, for the uncertain variable $\sum_{j=2}^{n} \lambda_j \tilde{x}_{1j} - (1-\lambda_1)\tilde{x}_{11}$, the inverse uncertain distribution of $\Omega^{-1}(\alpha) = \sum_{j=2}^{n} \lambda_j \phi_{1j}^{-1}(\alpha) - (1-\lambda_1)\phi_{11}^{-1}(1-\alpha)$ is obtained where $0<\alpha<1$. A similar procedure is used for the constraint $\mathcal{M}\left\{\sum_{j=1}^{n} \lambda_j \tilde{y}_{rj} \succeq \tilde{y}_{ro} + s_r^+\right\} \geq \alpha$ and the proof is completed.

Corollary 5.12 Considering linear regular uncertain distribution such as $\mathcal{L}(a,b)$ for the uncertain variables of Theorem 5.16, the following deterministic model is obtained instead of the model (5.52) applying the chance-constrained criterion.

$$\max \sum_{i=1}^{m} s_i^- + \sum_{r=1}^{s} s_r^+$$

subject to

$$\sum_{\substack{j=1\\ j\neq o}}^{n} \lambda_j\left((1-\alpha_i)a_{\tilde{x}_{ij}} + \alpha_i b_{\tilde{x}_{ij}}\right) - (1-\lambda_o)\left(\alpha_i a_{\tilde{x}_{io}} + (1-\alpha_i)b_{\tilde{x}_{io}}\right) \leq -s_i^- \quad i=1,2,\ldots,m$$

$$\sum_{\substack{j=1\\ j\neq o}}^{n} \lambda_j\left(\alpha a_{\tilde{y}_{ij}} + (1-\alpha)b_{\tilde{y}_{ij}}\right) - (1-\lambda_o)\left((1-\alpha)a_{\tilde{y}_{ro}} + \alpha b_{\tilde{y}_{ro}}\right) \geq s_r^+ \quad r=1,2,\ldots,s$$

$$\sum_{j=1}^{n} \lambda_j = 1$$

$$s_i^- \geq 0 \quad i=1,2,\ldots,m$$

$$s_r^+ \geq 0 \quad r=1,2,\ldots,s$$

$$\lambda_j \geq 0 \quad j=1,2,\ldots,n \tag{5.54}$$

Corollary 5.13 Considering zigzag regular uncertain distribution such as $\mathcal{Z}(a, b, c)$ for the uncertain variables of Theorem 5.16, the following deterministic model is obtained instead of the model (5.52) applying the chance-constrained criterion where $0<\alpha<0.5$.

$$\max \sum_{i=1}^{m} s_i^- + \sum_{r=1}^{s} s_r^+$$

subject to

$$\sum_{\substack{j=1\\ j\neq o}}^{n} \lambda_j\left((1-2\alpha)a_{\tilde{x}_{ij}} + 2\alpha b_{\tilde{x}_{ij}}\right) - (1-\lambda_o)\left(2\alpha b_{\tilde{x}_{io}} + (1-2\alpha)c_{\tilde{x}_{io}}\right) \leq -s_i^- \quad i=1,2,\ldots,m$$

$$\sum_{\substack{j=1\\ j\neq o}}^{n} \lambda_j\left(2\alpha b_{\tilde{y}_{rj}} + (1-2\alpha)c_{\tilde{y}_{rj}}\right) - (1-\lambda_o)\left((1-2\alpha)a_{\tilde{y}_{ro}} + 2\alpha b_{\tilde{y}_{ro}}\right) \geq s_r^+ \quad r=1,2,\ldots,s$$

$$\sum_{j=1}^{n} \lambda_j = 1$$

$$s_i^- \geq 0 \quad i=1,2,\ldots,m$$

$$s_r^+ \geq 0 \quad r=1,2,\ldots,s$$

$$\lambda_j \geq 0 \quad j=1,2,\ldots,n \tag{5.55}$$

Corollary 5.14 Considering zigzag regular uncertain distribution such as $\mathcal{Z}(a, b, c)$ for the uncertain variables of Theorem 5.16, the following deterministic model is obtained instead of the model (5.52) applying the chance-constrained criterion where $0.5 \leq \alpha < 1$.

$$\max \sum_{i=1}^{m} s_i^- + \sum_{r=1}^{s} s_r^+$$

subject to

$$\sum_{\substack{j=1 \\ j \neq o}}^{n} \lambda_j \left((2-2\alpha)\, b_{\tilde{x}_{ij}} + (2\alpha-1) c_{\tilde{x}_{ij}} \right) - (1-\lambda_o)\left((2\alpha-1)\, a_{\tilde{x}_{io}} + (2-2\alpha)\, b_{\tilde{x}_{io}} \right) \leq -s_i^- \; i = 1, 2, \ldots, m$$

$$\sum_{\substack{j=1 \\ j \neq o}}^{n} \lambda_j \left((2\alpha-1)\, a_{\tilde{y}_{rj}} + (2-2\alpha)\, b_{\tilde{y}_{rj}} \right) - (1-\lambda_o)\left((2-2\alpha)\, b_{\tilde{y}_{ro}} + (2\alpha-1)\, c_{\tilde{y}_{ro}} \right) \geq s_r^+ \; r = 1, 2, \ldots, s$$

$$\sum_{j=1}^{n} \lambda_j = 1$$

$$s_i^- \geq 0 \; i = 1, 2, \ldots, m$$

$$s_r^+ \geq 0 \; r = 1, 2, \ldots, s$$

$$\lambda_j \geq 0 \; j = 1, 2, \ldots, n \tag{5.56}$$

Corollary 5.15 Considering normal regular uncertain distribution such as $\mathcal{N}(\mu, \sigma)$ for the uncertain variables of Theorem 5.16, the following deterministic model is obtained instead of the model (5.52).

$$\max \sum_{i=1}^{m} s_i^- + \sum_{r=1}^{s} s_r^+$$

subject to

$$\sum_{\substack{j=1 \\ j \neq o}}^{n} \lambda_j \left(\mu_{\tilde{x}_{ij}} + \frac{\sigma_{\tilde{x}_{ij}} \sqrt{3}}{\pi} \ln\left(\frac{\alpha}{1-\alpha}\right) \right) - (1-\lambda_o)\left(\mu_{\tilde{x}_{io}} + \frac{\sigma_{\tilde{x}_{io}} \sqrt{3}}{\pi} \ln\left(\frac{1-\alpha}{\alpha}\right) \right) \leq -s_i^- \quad i = 1, 2, \ldots, m$$

$$\sum_{\substack{j=1\\ j\neq o}}^{n} \lambda_j \left(\mu_{\widetilde{y}_{rj}} + \frac{\sigma_{\widetilde{y}_{rj}} \sqrt{3}}{\pi} \ln\left(\frac{1-\alpha}{\alpha}\right) \right) - (1-\lambda_o)\left(\mu_{\widetilde{y}_{ro}} + \frac{\sigma_{\widetilde{y}_{ro}} \sqrt{3}}{\pi} \ln\left(\frac{\alpha}{1-\alpha}\right) \right) \geq s_r^+ \quad r=1,2,\ldots,s$$

$$\sum_{j=1}^{n} \lambda_j = 1$$

$$s_i^- \geq 0 \quad i=1,2,\ldots,m$$

$$s_r^+ \geq 0 \quad r=1,2,\ldots,s$$

$$\lambda_j \geq 0 \quad j=1,2,\ldots,n \tag{5.57}$$

Example 5.8 According to the data of Example 5.1, the DMUs are evaluated using Theorem 5.14, Corollary 5.13 and 5.14. The detailed results for two confidence levels of 0.4 and 0.7 are reported in Tables 5.15 and 5.16 and a summary of the results for more confidence levels is reported in Table 5.17.

Table 5.15 Results obtained for a confidence level of 0.4.

DMUs	$(\lambda_1^*, \lambda_2^*, \lambda_3^*, \lambda_4^*, \lambda_5^*)$	$\sum_{i=1}^{m} s_i^- + \sum_{r=1}^{s} s_r^+$	The result of evaluating
DMU_1	(0, 0, 0, 1, 0)	3.14	Inefficiency
DMU_2	(0, 1, 0, 0, 0)	0	Efficiency
DMU_3	(0, 0, 0, 0.95, 0)	3.14	Inefficiency
DMU_4	(0, 0, 0, 1, 0)	0	Efficiency
DMU_5	(0, 0, 0, 0, 1)	0	Efficiency

Table 5.16 Results obtained for a confidence level of 0.7.

DMUs	$(\lambda_1^*, \lambda_2^*, \lambda_3^*, \lambda_4^*, \lambda_5^*)$	$\sum_{i=1}^{m} s_i^- + \sum_{r=1}^{s} s_r^+$	The result of evaluating
DMU_1	(0, 0.32, 0, 0.68, 0)	1.89	Inefficiency
DMU_2	(0, 1, 0, 0, 0)	0	Efficiency
DMU_3	(0, 0, 0, 0.78, 0.22)	1.54	Inefficiency
DMU_4	(0, 0, 0, 1, 0)	0	Efficiency
DMU_5	(0, 0, 0, 0, 1)	0	Efficiency

Table 5.17 Summary of the results obtained for all confidence levels.

α_i, β_r	DMU_1	DMU_2	DMU_3	DMU_4	DMU_5
0.1	Inefficiency	Efficiency	Inefficiency	Inefficiency	Efficiency
0.2	Inefficiency	Efficiency	Inefficiency	Efficiency	Efficiency
0.3	Inefficiency	Efficiency	Inefficiency	Efficiency	Efficiency
0.4	Inefficiency	Efficiency	Inefficiency	Efficiency	Efficiency
0.5	Inefficiency	Efficiency	Inefficiency	Efficiency	Efficiency
0.6	Inefficiency	Efficiency	Inefficiency	Efficiency	Efficiency
0.7	Inefficiency	Efficiency	Inefficiency	Efficiency	Efficiency
0.8	Efficiency	Efficiency	Efficiency	Efficiency	Efficiency
0.9	Efficiency	Efficiency	Efficiency	Efficiency	Efficiency

5.12 Uncertain SBM model

In this section, the uncertain form of the SBM model is considered. To evaluate DMUs by this uncertain model, two crisp versions are proposed in the rest of this section.

5.12.1 Expected value SBM model

The following expected value crisp form of the uncertain SBM model was proposed by Jamshidi et al. (2021a).

$$
\begin{aligned}
&\min \quad \rho = E\left[\frac{1-\dfrac{1}{m}\displaystyle\sum_{i=1}^{m}\frac{s_i^-}{\tilde{x}_{io}}}{1+\dfrac{1}{s}\displaystyle\sum_{r=1}^{s}\frac{s_r^+}{\tilde{y}_{ro}}}\right] \\
&\text{subject to} \\
&E\left[\sum_{j=1}^{n}\lambda_j\tilde{x}_{ij}-\tilde{x}_{io}+s_i^- \approx 0\right] i=1,2,\ldots,m \\
&E\left[\sum_{j=1}^{n}\lambda_j\tilde{y}_{rj}-\tilde{y}_{ro}-s_r^+ \approx 0\right] r=1,2,\ldots,s \\
&\sum_{j=1}^{n}\lambda_j=1 \\
&s_i^- \geq 0 \quad i=1,2,\ldots,m \\
&s_r^+ \geq 0 \quad r=1,2,\ldots,s \\
&\lambda_j \geq 0 \quad j=1,2,\ldots,n
\end{aligned}
\tag{5.58}
$$

Definition 5.20 The vector $(s_i^-, s_r^+, \lambda_j) \geq 0$ for $i=1, 2, \ldots, m$, $r=1, 2, \ldots, s$, and $j=1, 2, \ldots, n$ is a feasible solution of model (5.54), if and only if it satisfies the constraints $E\left[\sum_{j=1}^{n} \lambda_j \tilde{x}_{ij} - \tilde{x}_{io} + s_i^- \approx 0\right]$, for $i=1, 2, \ldots, m$, $E\left[\sum_{j=1}^{n} \lambda_j \tilde{y}_{rj} - \tilde{y}_{ro} - s_r^+ \approx 0\right]$, for $r=1, 2, \ldots, s$, and $\sum_{j=1}^{n} \lambda_j = 1$.

Definition 5.21 DMU_o is efficient for model (5.58) if its optimal objective function value is 1 ($\rho^* = 1$).

Theorem 5.15 Assume that the independent uncertain variables $\tilde{x}_{ij}$, $\tilde{x}_{io}$, $\tilde{y}_{rj}$, and $\tilde{y}_{ro}$ have regular uncertain distributions ϕ_{ij}, ϕ_{io}, φ_{rj}, and φ_{ro}, respectively. The uncertain formulation (5.58) is equivalent to the below model.

$$\min \ \rho = \int_0^1 \frac{1 - \dfrac{1}{m} \sum\limits_{i=1}^{m} \dfrac{s_i^-}{\phi_{io}^{-1}(1-\alpha)}}{1 + \dfrac{1}{s} \sum\limits_{r=1}^{s} \dfrac{s_r^+}{\varphi_{ro}^{-1}(\alpha)}} d\alpha$$

$$\begin{aligned}
&\text{subject to}\\
&\sum_{j=1}^{n} \lambda_j E[\tilde{x}_{ij}] - E[\tilde{x}_{io}] + s_i^- = 0 \quad i = 1, 2, \ldots, m\\
&\sum_{j=1}^{n} \lambda_j E[\tilde{y}_{rj}] - E[\tilde{y}_{ro}] - s_r^+ = 0 \quad r = 1, 2, \ldots, s\\
&\sum_{j=1}^{n} \lambda_j = 1\\
&s_i^- \geq 0 \quad i = 1, 2, \ldots, m\\
&s_r^+ \geq 0 \quad r = 1, 2, \ldots, s\\
&\lambda_j \geq 0 \quad j = 1, 2, \ldots, n
\end{aligned} \tag{5.59}$$

Proof. As the function $\frac{1 - \frac{1}{m}\sum_{i=1}^{m} \frac{s_i^-}{\tilde{x}_{io}}}{1 + \frac{1}{s}\sum_{r=1}^{s} \frac{s_r^+}{\tilde{y}_{ro}}}$ is absolutely increasing for $\tilde{y}_{ro}$ and absolutely decreasing for $\tilde{x}_{io}$, according to Theorem 1.33 its uncertain distribution is $\Gamma_o^{-1}(\alpha) = \frac{1 - \frac{1}{m}\sum_{i=1}^{m} \frac{s_i^-}{\phi_{io}^{-1}(1-\alpha)}}{1 + \frac{1}{s}\sum_{r=1}^{s} \frac{s_r^+}{\varphi_{ro}^{-1}(\alpha)}}$. Then, according to Theorem 1.38 the term

$E\left[\frac{1-\frac{1}{m}\sum_{i=1}^{m}\frac{s_i^-}{\tilde{x}_{io}}}{1+\frac{1}{s}\sum_{r=1}^{s}\frac{s_r^+}{\tilde{y}_{ro}}}\right]=\int_0^1\frac{1-\frac{1}{m}\sum_{i=1}^{m}\frac{s_i^-}{\phi_{io}^{-1}(1-\alpha)}}{1+\frac{1}{s}\sum_{r=1}^{s}\frac{s_r^+}{\varphi_{ro}^{-1}(\alpha)}}d\alpha$ is obtained. Conversion of the constraints is proved by the linearity of the expected value criterion (Theorem 1.39).

5.12.2 Expected value and chance-constrained SBM model

The expected value and chance-constrained SBM model is obtained by considering the expected value of the objective function and chance constraints as below (Jamshidi et al., 2021a).

$$
\begin{aligned}
&\min\ \rho=E\left[\frac{1-\dfrac{1}{m}\displaystyle\sum_{i=1}^{m}\frac{s_i^-}{\tilde{x}_{io}}}{1+\dfrac{1}{s}\displaystyle\sum_{r=1}^{s}\frac{s_r^+}{\tilde{y}_{ro}}}\right]\\
&\text{subject to}\\
&\mathcal{M}\left\{\sum_{j=1}^{n}\lambda_j\tilde{x}_{ij}\preceq\tilde{x}_{io}-s_i^-\right\}\geq\alpha\quad i=1,2,\dots,m\\
&\mathcal{M}\left\{\sum_{j=1}^{n}\lambda_j\tilde{y}_{rj}\succeq\tilde{y}_{ro}+s_r^+\right\}\geq\alpha\quad r=1,2,\dots,s\\
&\sum_{j=1}^{n}\lambda_j=1\\
&s_i^-\geq 0\quad i=1,2,\dots,m\\
&s_r^+\geq 0\quad r=1,2,\dots,s\\
&\lambda_j\geq 0\quad j=1,2,\dots,n
\end{aligned}
\tag{5.60}
$$

Definition 5.22 The vector $(s_i^-,s_r^+,\lambda_j)\geq 0$ for $i=1, 2, \dots, m$, $r=1, 2, \dots, s$, and $j=1, 2, \dots, n$ is a feasible solution of model (5.59), if and only if it satisfies the constraints $\mathcal{M}\left\{\sum_{j=1}^{n}\lambda_j\tilde{x}_{ij}\preceq\tilde{x}_{io}-s_i^-\right\}\geq\alpha$, for $i=1, 2, \dots, m$, $\mathcal{M}\left\{\sum_{j=1}^{n}\lambda_j\tilde{y}_{rj}\succeq\tilde{y}_{ro}+s_r^+\right\}\geq\alpha$, for $r=1, 2, \dots, s$, and $\sum_{j=1}^{n}\lambda_j=1$.

Definition 5.23 The feasible solution $(s_i^{-*}, s_r^{+*}, \lambda_j^*) \geq 0$ is an optimal expected value solution for model (5.60) if for any feasible solution $(s_i^-, s_r^+, \lambda_j) \geq 0$ the claim $E\left[\frac{1-\frac{1}{m}\sum_{i=1}^{m}\frac{s_i^{-*}}{\tilde{x}_{io}}}{1+\frac{1}{s}\sum_{r=1}^{s}\frac{s_r^{+*}}{\tilde{y}_{ro}}}\right] \leq E\left[\frac{1-\frac{1}{m}\sum_{i=1}^{m}\frac{s_i^{-}}{\tilde{x}_{io}}}{1+\frac{1}{s}\sum_{r=1}^{s}\frac{s_r^{+}}{\tilde{y}_{ro}}}\right]$ is true.

Definition 5.24 Applying model (5.60),$DMU_o$with the highest optimal objective function value is efficient.

Theorem 5.16 Assume that the independent uncertain variables $\tilde{x}_{ij}$, $\tilde{x}_{io}$, $\tilde{y}_{rj}$, and $\tilde{y}_{ro}$ have regular uncertain distributions ϕ_{ij}, ϕ_{io}, φ_{rj}, and φ_{ro}, respectively. The uncertain formulation (5.60) is equivalent to the below model.

$$\min \ \rho = \int_0^1 \frac{1 - \frac{1}{m}\sum_{i=1}^{m}\frac{s_i^-}{\phi_{io}^{-1}(1-\alpha)}}{1 + \frac{1}{s}\sum_{r=1}^{s}\frac{s_r^+}{\varphi_{ro}^{-1}(\alpha)}} d\alpha$$

subject to

$$\sum_{\substack{j=1 \\ j\neq o}}^{n} \lambda_j \phi_{ij}^{-1}(\alpha) + \lambda_o \phi_{io}^{-1}(1-\alpha) \leq \phi_{io}^{-1}(1-\alpha) - s_i^- \quad i = 1, 2, \ldots, m$$

$$\sum_{\substack{j=1 \\ j\neq o}}^{n} \lambda_j \varphi_{rj}^{-1}(1-\alpha) + \lambda_o \varphi_{ro}^{-1}(1-\alpha) \geq \varphi_{ro}^{-1}(\alpha) + s_r^+ \quad r = 1, 2, \ldots, s$$

$$\sum_{j=1}^{n} \lambda_j = 1$$

$$s_i^- \geq 0 \quad i = 1, 2, \ldots, m$$

$$s_r^+ \geq 0 \quad r = 1, 2, \ldots, s$$

$$\lambda_j \geq 0 \quad j = 1, 2, \ldots, n$$

(5.61)

Proof. The proof can be completed using Theorems 5.14 and 5.15.

5.13 Russel uncertainty model

The Russel model is nonradial and deals with inputs/outputs individually, unlike the radial DEA models where the variations of inputs/outputs are proportional (Hosseinzadeh Lotfi, Noora, et al., 2010). In this section, the uncertain form of the Russel model is used to evaluate DMUs with belief degree-based uncertain inputs and outputs. Two crisp forms for this uncertain model are proposed and presented in the rest of this section.

5.13.1 Expected value and chance-constrained uncertain Russel model

Jamshidi et al. (2019) proposed the following expected value and chance-constrained uncertain Russel model where $F(t_r) = (1 - \sqrt{t_r})^2$.

$$
\begin{aligned}
&\max\ E\left[-\eta + \sum_{r=1}^{s} u_r\tilde{y}_{ro} - \sum_{i=1}^{m} v_i\tilde{x}_{io} + 1 - \frac{1}{m+s}\sum_{r=1}^{s} F(t_r)\right] \\
&\text{subject to} \\
&\mathcal{M}\left\{\sum_{r=1}^{s} u_r\tilde{y}_{rj} - \sum_{i=1}^{m} v_i\tilde{x}_{ij} \preceq \eta\right\} \geq \alpha \quad j = 1, 2, \ldots, n \\
&\mathcal{M}\{(m+s)v_i\tilde{x}_{io} \succeq 1\} \geq \alpha \quad i = 1, 2, \ldots, m \\
&\mathcal{M}\{(m+s)u_r\tilde{y}_{ro} \succeq t_r\} \geq \alpha \quad r = 1, 2, \ldots, s
\end{aligned}
\tag{5.62}
$$

Definition 5.25 Vector (η, u_r, v_i, t_r) is a feasible solution of model (5.62) if and only if $\mathcal{M}\left\{\sum_{r=1}^{s} u_r\tilde{y}_{rj} - \sum_{i=1}^{m} v_i\tilde{x}_{ij} \preceq \eta\right\} \geq \alpha$, for j=1, 2, ..., n, $\mathcal{M}\{(m+s)v_i\tilde{x}_{io} \succeq 1\} \geq \alpha$, for i=1, 2, ..., m, and $\mathcal{M}\{(m+s)u_r \tilde{y}_{ro} \succeq t_r\} \geq \alpha$ for r=1, 2, ..., s.

Definition 5.26 Feasible solution $(\eta^*, u_r^*, v_i^*, t_r^*)$ is an expected optimal solution for model (5.62) if for the feasible solution (η, u_r, v_i, t_r), the condition $E\left[-\eta^* + \sum_{r=1}^{s} u_r^*\tilde{y}_{ro} - \sum_{i=1}^{m} v_i^*\tilde{x}_{io} + 1 - \frac{1}{m+s}\sum_{r=1}^{s} F\left(t_r^*\right)\right] \geq$ $E\left[-\eta + \sum_{r=1}^{s} u_r\tilde{y}_{ro} - \sum_{i=1}^{m} v_i\tilde{x}_{io} + 1 - \frac{1}{m+s}\sum_{r=1}^{s} F(t_r)\right]$ is true.

Theorem 5.17 Assume that the independent uncertain variables $\tilde{x}_{ij}$, $\tilde{x}_{io}$, $\tilde{y}_{rj}$, and $\tilde{y}_{ro}$ have regular uncertain distributions ϕ_{ij}, ϕ_{io}, φ_{rj}, and φ_{ro}, respectively. The uncertain formulation (5.62) is equivalent to the below model where $F(t_r) = (1 - \sqrt{t_r})^2$.

$$\max -\eta + \sum_{r=1}^{s} u_r \int_0^1 \varphi_{ro}^{-1}(\alpha)d\alpha - \sum_{i=1}^{m} v_i \int_0^1 \phi_{io}^{-1}(1-\alpha)d\alpha + 1 - \frac{1}{m+s}\sum_{r=1}^{s} F(t_r)$$

subject to

$$\sum_{r=1}^{s} u_r \varphi_{rj}^{-1}(\alpha) - \sum_{i=1}^{m} v_i \phi_{ij}^{-1}(1-\alpha) \le \eta \quad j = 1,2,\ldots,n$$

$$(m+s)v_i \phi_{io}^{-1}(1-\alpha) \ge 1 \quad i = 1,2,\ldots,m$$

$$(m+s)u_r \varphi_{ro}^{-1}(1-\alpha) \ge t_r \quad r = 1,2,\ldots,s$$

(5.63)

Proof. According to the linearity of the expected value criterion (Theorem 1.39), the objective function of model (5.62) is written as $E\left[-\eta + \sum_{r=1}^{s} u_r \tilde{y}_{ro} - \sum_{i=1}^{m} v_i \tilde{x}_{io} + 1 - \frac{1}{m+s}\sum_{r=1}^{s} F(t_r)\right] = -\eta + \sum_{r=1}^{s} u_r E[\tilde{y}_{ro}] - \sum_{i=1}^{m} v_i E[\tilde{x}_{io}] + 1 - \frac{1}{m+s}\sum_{r=1}^{s} F(t_r)$. Then according to Theorem 1.38 it is converted to $-\eta + \sum_{r=1}^{s} u_r \int_0^1 \varphi_{ro}^{-1}(\alpha)d\alpha - \sum_{i=1}^{m} v_i \int_0^1 \phi_{io}^{-1}(1-\alpha)d\alpha + 1 - \frac{1}{m+s}\sum_{r=1}^{s} F(t_r)$.

In the constraint $\mathcal{M}\left\{\sum_{r=1}^{s} u_r \tilde{y}_{rj} - \sum_{i=1}^{m} v_i \tilde{x}_{ij} \preceq \eta\right\} \ge \alpha$, the term $\sum_{r=1}^{s} u_r \tilde{y}_{rj}$ is increasing for $\tilde{y}_{rj}$ and the function $-\sum_{i=1}^{m} v_i \tilde{x}_{ij}$ is decreasing for $\tilde{x}_{ij}$. Therefore, according to Theorem 1.34 the conversion $\mathcal{M}\left\{\sum_{r=1}^{s} u_r \tilde{y}_{rj} - \sum_{i=1}^{m} v_i \tilde{x}_{ij} \preceq \eta\right\} \ge \alpha \Leftrightarrow \sum_{r=1}^{s} u_r \varphi_{rj}^{-1}(\alpha) - \sum_{i=1}^{m} v_i \phi_{ij}^{-1}(1-\alpha) \le \eta$ is done. Similarly, for other constraints the conversions $\mathcal{M}\{(m+s)v_i \tilde{x}_{io} \succeq 1\} \ge \alpha \Leftrightarrow (m+s)v_i \phi_{io}^{-1}(1-\alpha) \ge 1$ and $\mathcal{M}\{(m+s)u_r \tilde{y}_{ro} \succeq t_r\} \ge \alpha \Leftrightarrow (m+s)u_r \varphi_{ro}^{-1}(1-\alpha) \ge t_r$ are done.

5.13.2 Expected value uncertain Russel model

Jamshidi et al. (2019) proposed the following expected value uncertain Russel model where $F(t_r) = (1 - \sqrt{t_r})^2$.

$$\begin{aligned}
&\max \ E\left[-\eta + \sum_{r=1}^{s} u_r\tilde{y}_{ro} - \sum_{i=1}^{m} v_i\tilde{x}_{io} + 1 - \frac{1}{m+s}\sum_{r=1}^{s} F(t_r)\right] \\
&\text{subject to} \\
&E\left[\sum_{r=1}^{s} u_r\tilde{y}_{rj} - \sum_{i=1}^{m} v_i\tilde{x}_{ij} \preceq \eta\right] \quad j = 1, 2, \ldots, n \\
&E\left[(m+s)v_i\tilde{x}_{io} \succeq 1\right] \quad i = 1, 2, \ldots, m \\
&E\left[(m+s)u_r\tilde{y}_{ro} \succeq t_r\right] \quad r = 1, 2, \ldots, s
\end{aligned} \tag{5.64}$$

Definition 5.27 Vector (η, u_r, v_i, t_r) is a feasible solution of model (5.64) if and only if $E\left[\sum_{r=1}^{s} u_r\tilde{y}_{rj} - \sum_{i=1}^{m} v_i\tilde{x}_{ij} \preceq \eta\right]$, for $j = 1, 2, \ldots, n$, $E\left[(m+s)v_i\tilde{x}_{io} \succeq 1\right]$, for $i = 1, 2, \ldots, m$, and $E\left[(m+s)u_r\tilde{y}_{ro} \succeq t_r\right]$ for $r = 1, 2, \ldots, s$.

Definition 5.28 DMU_o is efficient if and only if it obtains the optimal objective function value of 1 by model (5.64).

Theorem 5.18 Assume that the independent uncertain variables $\tilde{x}_{ij}$, $\tilde{x}_{io}$, $\tilde{y}_{rj}$, and $\tilde{y}_{ro}$ have regular uncertain distributions ϕ_{ij}, ϕ_{io}, φ_{rj}, and φ_{ro}, respectively. The uncertain formulation (5.64) is equivalent to the below model where $F(t_r) = (1 - \sqrt{t_r})^2$.

$$\begin{aligned}
&\max \ -\eta + \sum_{r=1}^{s} u_r\int_0^1 \varphi_{ro}^{-1}(\alpha)d\alpha - \sum_{i=1}^{m} v_i\int_0^1 \phi_{io}^{-1}(1-\alpha)d\alpha + 1 - \frac{1}{m+s}\sum_{r=1}^{s} F(t_r) \\
&\text{subject to} \\
&\sum_{r=1}^{s} u_r\int_0^1 \varphi_{rj}^{-1}(\alpha)d\alpha - \sum_{i=1}^{m} v_i\int_0^1 \phi_{ij}^{-1}(1-\alpha)d\alpha \le \eta \quad j = 1, 2, \ldots, n \\
&(m+s)v_i\int_0^1 \phi_{io}^{-1}(1-\alpha)d\alpha \ge 1 \quad i = 1, 2, \ldots, m \\
&(m+s)u_r\int_0^1 \varphi_{ro}^{-1}(1-\alpha)\,d\alpha \ge t_r \quad r = 1, 2, \ldots, s
\end{aligned} \tag{5.65}$$

Proof. The proof for the objective function is similar to that of Theorem 5.19. According to the linearity of the expected value criterion

(Theorem 1.39), the first constraint of model (5.64) is written as $E\left[\sum_{r=1}^{s} u_r\tilde{y}_{rj} - \sum_{i=1}^{m} v_i\tilde{x}_{ij} \preceq \eta\right] = \sum_{r=1}^{s} u_r E\left[\tilde{y}_{rj}\right] - \sum_{i=1}^{m} v_i E\left[\tilde{x}_{ij}\right] \leq \eta$. Then, according to Theorem 1.38 it is converted to $\sum_{r=1}^{s} u_r \int_0^1 \varphi_{\tilde{y}_{rj}}^{-1}(\alpha)d\alpha - \sum_{i=1}^{m} v_i \int_0^1 \Phi_{\tilde{x}_{ij}}^{-1}(1-\alpha)d\alpha \leq \eta$. Other constraints are converted similarly.

Corollary 5.16 Considering linear regular uncertain distribution such as $\mathcal{L}(a, b)$ for the uncertain variables of Theorem 5.20, the following deterministic model is obtained instead of the model (5.64) applying the expected value criterion where $F(t_r) = (1-\sqrt{t_r})^2$.

$$\max \; -\eta + \sum_{r=1}^{s} u_r\left(\frac{a_{\tilde{y}_{ro}} + b_{\tilde{y}_{ro}}}{2}\right) - \sum_{i=1}^{m} v_i\left(\frac{a_{\tilde{x}_{io}} + b_{\tilde{x}_{io}}}{2}\right) + 1 - \frac{1}{m+s}\sum_{r=1}^{s} F(t_r)$$

subject to

$$\begin{aligned}
&\sum_{r=1}^{s} u_r\left(\frac{a_{\tilde{y}_{rj}} + b_{\tilde{y}_{rj}}}{2}\right) - \sum_{i=1}^{m} v_i\left(\frac{a_{\tilde{x}_{ij}} + b_{\tilde{x}_{ij}}}{2}\right) \leq \eta \quad j = 1, 2, \dots, n \\
&(m+s)v_i\left(\frac{a_{\tilde{x}_{io}} + b_{\tilde{x}_{io}}}{2}\right) \geq 1 \quad i = 1, 2, \dots, m \\
&(m+s)u_r\left(\frac{a_{\tilde{y}_{ro}} + b_{\tilde{y}_{ro}}}{2}\right) \geq t_r \quad r = 1, 2, \dots, s
\end{aligned} \tag{5.66}$$

Corollary 5.17 Considering zigzag regular uncertain distribution such as $\mathcal{Z}(a, b, c)$ for the uncertain variables of Theorem 5.20, the following deterministic model is obtained instead of the model (5.64) applying the expected value criterion where $F(t_r) = (1-\sqrt{t_r})^2$.

$$\max \; -\eta + \sum_{r=1}^{s} u_r\left(\frac{a_{\tilde{y}_{ro}} + 2b_{\tilde{y}_{ro}} + c_{\tilde{y}_{ro}}}{4}\right) - \sum_{i=1}^{m} v_i\left(\frac{a_{\tilde{x}_{io}} + 2b_{\tilde{x}_{io}} + c_{\tilde{x}_{io}}}{4}\right) + 1 - \frac{1}{m+s}\sum_{r=1}^{s} F(t_r)$$

subject to

$$\begin{aligned}
&\sum_{r=1}^{s} u_r\left(\frac{a_{\tilde{y}_{rj}} + 2b_{\tilde{y}_{rj}} + c_{\tilde{y}_{rj}}}{4}\right) - \sum_{i=1}^{m} v_i\left(\frac{a_{\tilde{x}_{ij}} + 2b_{\tilde{x}_{ij}} + c_{\tilde{x}_{ij}}}{4}\right) \leq \eta \quad j = 1, 2, \dots, n \\
&(m+s)v_i\left(\frac{a_{\tilde{x}_{io}} + 2b_{\tilde{x}_{io}} + c_{\tilde{x}_{io}}}{4}\right) \geq 1 \quad i = 1, 2, \dots, m \\
&(m+s)u_r\left(\frac{a_{\tilde{y}_{ro}} + 2b_{\tilde{y}_{ro}} + c_{\tilde{y}_{ro}}}{4}\right) \geq t_r \quad r = 1, 2, \dots, s
\end{aligned} \tag{5.67}$$

Corollary 5.18 Considering normal regular uncertain distribution such as $\mathcal{N}(\mu, \sigma)$ for the uncertain variables of Theorem 5.20, the following deterministic model is obtained instead of the model (5.64) applying the expected value criterion where $F(t_r) = (1 - \sqrt{t_r})^2$.

$$\begin{aligned}
&\max \; -\eta + \sum_{r=1}^{s} u_r \mu_{\tilde{y}_{ro}} - \sum_{i=1}^{m} v_i \mu_{\tilde{x}_{io}} + 1 - \frac{1}{m+s} \sum_{r=1}^{s} F(t_r) \\
&\text{subject to} \\
&\sum_{r=1}^{s} u_r \mu_{\tilde{y}_{rj}} - \sum_{i=1}^{m} v_i \mu_{\tilde{x}_{ij}} \le \eta \quad j = 1, 2, \ldots, n \\
&(m+s) v_i \mu_{\tilde{x}_{io}} \ge 1 \quad i = 1, 2, \ldots, m \\
&(m+s) u_r \mu_{\tilde{y}_{ro}} \ge t_r \quad r = 1, 2, \ldots, s
\end{aligned} \tag{5.68}$$

5.14 Uncertain cost and revenue DEA model

The economy plays a very important role in the world, and theoretical and practical science can be applied to improve the economy in today's world. DEA also as a mathematical approach can be used to evaluate organizations from the cost and revenue points of view. Farrell (1957) introduced cost efficiency, which played an important role in developing DEA concepts. Later, Färe et al. (1985) developed cost efficiency and obtained it using mathematical models. Their models in addition to the inputs and outputs values use the price of the inputs and outputs of DMUs. Tone (2002) explained the difficulties of cost efficiency evaluation rising from differences between the costs of the inputs and the assumed fixed values for the costs.

DEA models can be easily used to measure and analyze the concepts of cost and revenue (Charnes et al., 1985; Jahanshahloo et al., 2004; Sahoo & Tone, 2013). A cost efficiency model is used to identify the DMU that uses a minimum cost for the inputs not greater than the inputs of the evaluating DMU and for obtaining the outputs equal to the evaluating DMU. A revenue efficiency model applies a similar logic for maximizing the revenue of the outputs. For more details on the cost and revenue efficiency models, the study of Tone (2002) can be referenced.

5.14.1 Expected value uncertain cost efficiency model

Considering $\tilde{c}_i = (\tilde{c}_{i1}, \ldots, \tilde{c}_{im})$ as uncertain prices of the inputs of a DEA model, the expected value uncertain cost efficiency model for evaluating DMU_o is as follows (Jamshidi et al., 2022),

$$E\left[\tilde{c}x^*\right] = \min E[\tilde{c}_i x] = \min E\left[\sum_{i=1}^{m} \tilde{c}_{io} x_i\right]$$

subject to

$$E\left[x_i \succeq \sum_{j=1}^{n} \tilde{x}_{ij} \lambda_j\right] \quad i = 1, 2, \ldots, m \tag{5.69}$$

$$E\left[\tilde{y}_{ro} \preceq \sum_{j=1}^{n} \tilde{y}_{rj} \lambda_j\right] \quad r = 1, 2, \ldots, s$$

$$\lambda_j \geq 0, x_i \geq 0 \quad j = 1, \ldots, n, i = 1, 2, \ldots, m$$

Definition 5.29 DMU_o is efficient if and only if it obtains the optimal objective function value of 1 by model (5.69).

Theorem 5.19 Assume that the independent uncertain variables $\tilde{x}_{ij}$, $\tilde{c}_{ij}$, and $\tilde{y}_{rj}$ have regular uncertain distributions ϕ_{ij}, ψ_{ij}, and φ_{rj}, respectively. The uncertain formulation (5.69) is equivalent to the below model.

$$\min \sum_{i=1}^{m} x_i \int_0^1 \psi_{io}^{-1}(\alpha)\, d\alpha$$

subject to

$$\sum_{j=1}^{n} \lambda_j \int_0^1 \phi_{ij}^{-1}(\alpha)\, d\alpha - x_i \leq 0 \quad i = 1, 2, \ldots, m \tag{5.70}$$

$$\int_0^1 \varphi_{ro}^{-1}(\alpha) d\alpha - \sum_{j=1}^{n} \lambda_j \int_0^1 \varphi_{rj}^{-1}(1-\alpha) d\alpha \leq 0 \quad r = 1, 2, \ldots, s$$

$$\lambda_j \geq 0, x_i \geq 0 \quad j = 1, \ldots, n, i = 1, 2, \ldots, m$$

Proof. According to Theorems 1.38 and 1.39, this is proved easily.

5.14.2 Expected value uncertain revenue efficiency model

Considering $\tilde{p}_r = (\tilde{p}_{r1}, \ldots, \tilde{p}_{rs})$ as the uncertain prices of the outputs of a DEA model, the expected value and chance-constrained uncertain revenue efficiency model for evaluating DMU_o is as follows (Jamshidi et al., 2022),

$$E\left[\tilde{p}y^*\right] = \max E[\tilde{p}_r y] = \max E\left[\sum_{r=1}^{s} \tilde{p}_{ro} y_r\right]$$

subject to

$$E\left[\tilde{x}_{io} \succeq \sum_{j=1}^{n} \tilde{x}_{ij} \lambda_j\right] \quad i = 1, 2, \ldots, m \tag{5.71}$$

$$E\left[y_r \preceq \sum_{j=1}^{n} \tilde{y}_{rj} \lambda_j\right] \quad r = 1, 2, \ldots, s$$

$$\lambda_j \geq 0, x_i \geq 0 \quad j = 1, \ldots, n, i = 1, 2, \ldots, m$$

Definition 5.30 DMU_o is efficient if and only if it obtains the optimal objective function value of 1 by model (5.71).

Theorem 5.20 Assume that the independent uncertain variables $\tilde{x}_{ij}$, $\tilde{y}_{rj}$, and $\tilde{p}_{rj}$ have regular uncertain distributions ϕ_{ij}, φ_{rj}, and χ_{rj}, respectively. The uncertain formulation (5.71) is equivalent to the below model.

$$\max \sum_{r=1}^{s} y_r \int_0^1 \chi_{ro}^{-1}(\alpha)\, d\alpha$$

subject to

$$\sum_{j=1}^{n} \lambda_j \int_0^1 \phi_{ij}^{-1}(\alpha)\, d\alpha - \int_0^1 \phi_{io}^{-1}(1-\alpha)\, d\alpha \leq 0 \quad i = 1, 2, \ldots, m \tag{5.72}$$

$$y_r - \sum_{j=1}^{n} \lambda_j \int_0^1 \varphi_{rj}^{-1}(1-\alpha) d\alpha \leq 0 \quad r = 1, 2, \ldots, s$$

$$\lambda_j \geq 0, x_i \geq 0 \quad j = 1, \ldots, n, i = 1, 2, \ldots, m$$

Proof. According to Theorems 1.38 and 1.39, this is proved easily.

5.14.3 Expected value and chance-constrained uncertain cost efficiency model

Considering $\tilde{c}_i = (\tilde{c}_{i1}, \ldots, \tilde{c}_{im})$ as uncertain prices of the inputs of a DEA problem, the expected value and chance-constrained uncertain cost efficiency model for evaluating DMU_o is as follows (Jamshidi et al., 2022) where the expected value of the objective function and the chance-constrained form of the constraints are considered.

$$
\begin{aligned}
& E\left[\tilde{c}x^*\right] = \min E[\tilde{c}_i x] = \min E\left[\sum_{i=1}^{m} \tilde{c}_{io} x_i\right] \\
& \text{subject to} \\
& \mathcal{M}\left\{ x_i \succeq \sum_{j=1}^{n} \tilde{x}_{ij}\lambda_j \right\} \geq \alpha \quad i = 1, 2, \ldots, m \\
& \mathcal{M}\left\{ \tilde{y}_{ro} \preceq \sum_{j=1}^{n} \tilde{y}_{rj}\lambda_j \right\} \geq \alpha \quad r = 1, 2, \ldots, s \\
& \lambda_j \geq 0, x_i \geq 0 \quad j = 1, \ldots, n, i = 1, 2, \ldots, m
\end{aligned}
\tag{5.73}
$$

Definition 5.31 Vector (x_i, λ_j) is a feasible solution of model (5.73) if and only if $\mathcal{M}\left\{ x_i \succeq \sum_{j=1}^{n} \tilde{x}_{ij}\lambda_j \right\} \geq \alpha$, $\mathcal{M}\left\{ \tilde{y}_{ro} \preceq \sum_{j=1}^{n} \tilde{y}_{rj}\lambda_j \right\} \geq \alpha$, $\lambda_j \geq 0$, and $x_i \geq 0$ where $j=1, 2, \ldots, n$, $i=1, 2, \ldots, m$, and $r=1, 2, \ldots, s$.

Definition 5.32 Feasible solution (x_i^*, λ_j^*) is an expected optimal solution for model (5.73) if for any feasible solution (x_i, λ_j), the condition $E\left[\sum_{i=1}^{m} \tilde{c}_{io} x_i^*\right] \leq E\left[\sum_{i=1}^{m} \tilde{c}_{io} x_i\right]$ is true.

Definition 5.33 The DMU with the highest objective function value of model (5.73) is more efficient.

Theorem 5.21 Assume that the independent uncertain variables $\tilde{x}_{ij}$, $\tilde{c}_{ij}$, and $\tilde{y}_{rj}$ have regular uncertain distributions ϕ_{ij}, ψ_{ij}, and φ_{rj}, respectively. The uncertain formulation (5.73) is equivalent to the below model.

$$\min \sum_{i=1}^{m} x_i \int_0^1 \psi_{io}^{-1}(\alpha)\, d\alpha$$

subject to

$$\begin{aligned}
&\sum_{j=1}^{n} \lambda_j \phi_{ij}^{-1}(\alpha) - x_i \le 0 \quad i = 1, 2, \ldots, m \\
&\varphi_{ro}^{-1}(\alpha) - \sum_{j=1}^{n} \lambda_j \varphi_{rj}^{-1}(1-\alpha) \le 0 \quad r = 1, 2, \ldots, s \\
&\lambda_j \ge 0, x_i \ge 0 \quad j = 1, \ldots, n, i = 1, 2, \ldots, m
\end{aligned} \tag{5.74}$$

Proof. According to Theorems 1.34, 1.38, and 1.39, this is proved easily.

5.14.4 Expected value and chance-constrained uncertain revenue efficiency model

Considering $\tilde{p}_r = (\tilde{p}_{r1}, \ldots, \tilde{p}_{rs})$ as the uncertain prices of the outputs of a DEA problem, the expected value and chance-constrained uncertain revenue efficiency model for evaluating DMU_o is as follows (Jamshidi et al., 2022) where the expected value of the objective function and the chance-constrained form of the constraints are considered.

$$E\left[\tilde{p}y^*\right] = \max E[\tilde{p}_r y] = \max E\left[\sum_{r=1}^{s} \tilde{p}_{ro} y_r\right]$$

subject to

$$\begin{aligned}
&\mathcal{M}\left\{\tilde{x}_{io} \succeq \sum_{j=1}^{n} \tilde{x}_{ij}\lambda_j\right\} \ge \alpha \quad i = 1, 2, \ldots, m \\
&\mathcal{M}\left\{y_r \preceq \sum_{j=1}^{n} \tilde{y}_{rj}\lambda_j\right\} \ge \alpha \quad r = 1, 2, \ldots, s \\
&\lambda_j \ge 0, x_i \ge 0 \quad j = 1, \ldots, n, i = 1, 2, \ldots, m
\end{aligned} \tag{5.75}$$

Definition 5.34 Vector (y_r, λ_j) is a feasible solution of model (5.75) if and only if $\mathcal{M}\left\{\tilde{x}_{io} \succeq \sum_{j=1}^{n} \tilde{x}_{ij}\lambda_j\right\} \ge \alpha$, $\mathcal{M}\left\{\tilde{y}_r \preceq \sum_{j=1}^{n} \tilde{y}_{rj}\lambda_j\right\} \ge \alpha$, $\lambda_j \ge 0$, and $x_i \ge 0$ where $j = 1, 2, \ldots, n$, $i = 1, 2, \ldots, m$, and $r = 1, 2, \ldots, s$.

Definition 5.35 Feasible solution $(\gamma_r^*, \lambda_j^*)$ is an expected optimal solution for model (5.75) if for any feasible solution (γ_r, λ_j), the condition $E\left[\sum_{r=1}^{s} \tilde{p}_{ro}\gamma_r^*\right] \geq E\left[\sum_{r=1}^{s} \tilde{p}_{ro}\gamma_r\right]$ is true.

Theorem 5.22 Assume that the independent uncertain variables $\tilde{x}_{ij}$, $\tilde{p}_{rj}$, and $\tilde{\gamma}_{rj}$ have regular uncertain distributions ϕ_{ij}, φ_{rj}, and χ_{rj}, respectively. The uncertain formulation (5.75) is equivalent to the below model.

$$
\begin{aligned}
& \max \sum_{r=1}^{s} \gamma_r \int_0^1 \chi_{ro}^{-1}(\alpha)\, d\alpha \\
& \text{subject to} \\
& \sum_{j=1}^{n} \lambda_j \phi_{ij}^{-1}(\alpha) - \phi_{io}^{-1}(1-\alpha) \leq 0 \quad i = 1, 2, \ldots, m \\
& \gamma_r - \sum_{j=1}^{n} \lambda_j \varphi_{rj}^{-1}(1-\alpha) \leq 0 \quad r = 1, 2, \ldots, s \\
& \lambda_j \geq 0, x_i \geq 0 \quad j = 1, \ldots, n, i = 1, 2, \ldots, m
\end{aligned}
\tag{5.76}
$$

Proof. According to Theorems 1.34, 1.38, and 1.39, this is proved easily.

References

Allahviranloo, T. (2020). *Uncertain information and linear systems*. Berlin: Springer.

Allahviranloo, T., & Ezadi, S. (2019). Z-Advanced numbers processes. *Information Sciences, 480*, 130–143.

Allahviranloo, T., Hosseinzadeh Lotfi, F., & AdabitabarFirozja, M. (2012). Efficiency in fuzzy production possibility set. *Iranian Journal of Fuzzy Systems, 9*(4), 17–30.

Arana-Jiménez, M., Carmen Sánchez-Gil, M., Lozano, S., & Younesi, A. (2022). Efficiency assessment using fuzzy production possibility set and enhanced Russell Graph measure. *Computational and Applied Mathematics, 41*, 79. https://doi.org/10.1007/s40314-022-01780-y.

Banker, R. D., Charnes, A., & Cooper, W. W. (1984). Some models for estimating technical and scale efficiencies in data envelopment analysis. *Management Science, 30*, 1078–1092.

Broomandi, P., Geng, X., Guo, W., Pagani, A., Topping, D., & Kim, J. R. (2021). Dynamic complex network analysis of PM2.5 concentrations in the UK, using hierarchical directed graphs. *Sustainability, 2021*, 13.

Charnes, A., & Cooper, W. W. (1962). Programming with linear fractional functionals. *Naval Research Logistics Quarterly, 9*, 181–186.

Charnes, A., Cooper, W. W., Golany, B., Seiford, L., & Stutz, J. (1985). Foundations of data envelopment analysis for Pareto-Koopmans efficient empirical production functions. *Journal of Econometrics, 30*(1–2), 91–107.

Charnes, A., Cooper, W. W., & Rhodes, E. (1978). Measuring the efficiency of decision making units. *European Journal of Operational Research, 2*(6), 429–444.

Chen, L., Peng, J., & Zhang, B. (2017). Uncertain goal programming models for bicriteria solid transportation problem. *Applied Soft Computing, 51*, 49–59.

Dalman, H. (2019). Entropy-based multi-item solid transportation problems with uncertain variables. *Soft Computing*, *23*, 5931–5943.

Ding, S. (2015). The α-maximum flow model with uncertain capacities. *Applied Mathematical Modelling*, *39*(7), 2056–2063.

Färe, R., Grosskopf, S., & Lovell, C. A. K. (1985). *Measurment of efficient of production*. Boston: Kluwer-Nijhoff Publishing Co., Inc.

Farrell, M. J. (1957). The measurement of productive efficient. *Journal of the Royal Statistical Society A*, *120*, 253–281.

Hosseinzadeh Lotfi, F., Jahanshahloo, G. R., Ebrahimnejad, A., Soltanifar, M., & Mansourzadeh, S. M. (2010). Target setting in the general combined-oriented CCR model using an interactive MOLP method. *Journal of Computational and Applied Mathematics*, *234*(1), 1–9.

Hosseinzadeh Lotfi, F., Noora, A. A., Jahanshahloo, G. R., Gerami, J., & Mozaffari, M. R. (2010). Centralized resource allocation for enhanced Russell models. *Journal of Computational and Applied Mathematics*, *235*(1), 1–10.

Hosseinzadeh Lotfi, F., Rostamy-Malkhalifeh, M., Aghayi, N., Ghelej Beigi, Z., & Gholami, K. (2013). An improved method for ranking alternatives in multiple criteria decision analysis. *Applied Mathematical Modelling*, *37*(1–2), 25–33.

Jahanshahloo, G. R., Hosseinzadeh Lotfi, F., Adabitabar Firozja, M., & Allahviranloo, T. (2007). Ranking DMUs with fuzzy data in DEA. *International Journal Contemporary Mathematical Sciences*, *2*(5), 203–211.

Jahanshahloo, G. R., Hosseinzadeh Lotfi, F., Rostamy Malkhalifeh, M., & Ahadzadeh Namin, M. (2009). A generalized model for data envelopment analysis with interval data. *Applied Mathematical Modelling*, *33*(7), 3237–3244.

Jahanshahloo, G. R., Hosseinzadeh Lotfi, F., Shoja, N., & Sanei, M. (2004). An alternative approach for equitable allocation of shared costs by using DEA. *Applied Mathematics and Computation*, *153*(1), 267–274.

Jamshidi, M., Sanei, M., & Mahmoodirad, A. (2022). An uncertain allocation models in data envelopment analysis: A case in the Iranian stock market. *Scintia Iranica*, *29*(6), 3434–3454.

Jamshidi, M., Sanei, M., Mahmoodirad, A., Tohidi, G., & Hosseinzade Lotfi, F. (2021a). Uncertain SBM data envelopment analysis model: A case study in Iranian banks. *International Journal of Finance and Economics*, *26*(2), 2674–2689.

Jamshidi, M., Sanei, M., Mahmoodirad, A., Tohidi, G., & Hosseinzade Lotfi, F. (2021b). Uncertain BCC data envelopment analysis model with belief degree: A case study in Iranian banks. *International Journal of Industrial Mathematics*, *13*(3), 239–249.

Jamshidi, M., Saneie, M., Mahmoodirad, A., Hosseizadeh Lotfi, F., & Tohidi, G. (2019). Uncertain RUSSEL data envelopment analysis model: A case study in Iranian banks. *Journal of Intelligent Fuzzy Systems*, *37*(2), 2937–2951.

Jiang, B., Lio, W., & Li, X. (2018). An uncertain DEA model for scale efficiency evaluation. *IEEE Transactions on Fuzzy Systems*, *27*(8), 1616–1624.

Jiang, B., Zou, Z., Lio, W., & Li, J. (2020). The uncertain DEA models for specific scale efficiency identification. *Journal of Intelligent Fuzzy Systems*, *38*, 3403–3417.

Lio, W., & Liu, B. (2018). Uncertain data envelopment analysis with imprecisely observed inputs and outputs. *Fuzzy Optimization and Decision Making*, *17*, 357–373.

Liu, B. (1997). Dependent-chance programming: A class of stochastic programming. *Computers and Mathematics with Applications*, *34*(12), 89–104.

Liu, B. (1999). Dependent-chance programming with fuzzy decisions. *IEEE Transactions on Fuzzy Systems*, 7, 354–360.

Liu, B. (2002). Random fuzzy dependent-chance programming and its hybrid intelligent algorithm. *Information Sciences*, *141*(3–4), 259–271.

Liu, B. (2007). *Uncertain theory* (2nd ed.). Berlin, Germany: Springer-Verlag.

Liu, B. (2009a). Some research problems in uncertainty theory. *Journal of Uncertain System, 3*(1), 3–10.

Liu, B. (2009b). *Theory and practice of uncertain programming* (2nd ed.). Berlin, Germany: Springer.

Liu, B. (2012). Why is there a need for uncertainty theory? *Journal of Uncertain Systems, 6*(1), 3–10.

Mahmoodirad, A., Dehghan, R., & Niroomand, S. (2019). Modelling linear fractional transportation problem in belief degree-based uncertain environment. *Journal of Experimental & Theoretical Artificial Intelligence, 31*(3), 393–408.

Mahmoodirad, A., & Niroomand, S. (2020a). A belief degree-based uncertain scheme for a bi-objective two-stage green supply chain network design problem with direct shipment. *Soft Computing, 24*(24), 18499–18519.

Mahmoodirad, A., & Niroomand, S. (2020b). Uncertain location-allocation decisions for a bi-objective two-stage supply chain network design problem with environmental impacts. *Expert Systems, 37*, e12558.

Mahmoodirad, A., & Sanei, M. (2016). Solving a multi-stage multi-product solid supply chain network design problem by meta-heuristics. *Scientia Iranica, 23*(3), 1429–1440.

Mohammad Nejad, Z., & Ghaffari-Hadigheh, A. (2018). A novel DEA model based on uncertainty theory. *Annals of Operations Research, 264*, 367–389.

Molla-Alizadeh-Zavardehi, S., Mahmoodirad, A., & Rahimian, M. (2014). Step fixed charge transportation problems via genetic algorithm. *Indian Journal of Science and Technology*, 7(7), 949–954.

Niroomand, S., Garg, H., & Mahmoodirad, A. (2020). An intuitionistic fuzzy two stage supply chain network design problem with multi-mode demand and multi-mode transportation. *ISA Transactions, 107*, 117–133.

Sahoo, B. K., & Tone, K. (2013). Non-parametric measurement of economies of scale and scope in non-competitive environment with price uncertainty. *Omega, 41*, 97–111.

Tone, K. (2002). A strange case of the cost and allocative efficiencies in DEA. *Journal of Operation Research, 53*, 1225–1231.

Wen, M., Guo, L., Kang, R., & Yang, Y. (2014). Data envelopment analysis with uncertain inputs and outputs. *Journal of Applied Mathematics, 2014*, 307108.

Wen, M., Qin, Z., Kang, R., & Yang, Y. (2015). Sensitivity and stability analysis of the additive model in uncertain data envelopment analysis. *Soft Computing, 19*, 1987–1996.

Wen, M., Yu, X., & Wang, F. (2020). A new uncertain DEA model and application to scientific research personnel. *Soft Computing, 24*, 2841–2847.

Wen, M., Zhang, Q., Kang, R., & Yang, Y. (2017). Some new ranking criteria in data envelopment analysis under uncertain environment. *Computers and Industrial Engineering, 110*, 498–504.

Further reading

Färe, R., & Lovell, C. A. K. (1978). Measuring the technical efficient of production. *Journal of Economic Theory, 19*, 150–162.

Khanjani Shiraz, R., Fukuyama, H., & Vakili, J. (2019). A note on 'some new ranking criteria in data envelopment analysis under uncertain environment'. *Computers & Industrial Engineering, 131*, 259–262.

Liu, B. (2004). *Uncertainty theory*. Berlin: Springer.

Liu, B. (2010a). *Uncertainty theory: A branch of mathematics for modeling human uncertainty*. Berlin: Springer Verlag.

Liu, B. (2010b). Uncertain risk analysis and uncertain reliability analysis. *Journal of Uncertain Systems*, *4*(3), 163–170.
Liu, B. (2013). Poly rectangular theorem and independence of uncertain vectors. *Journal of Uncertainty Analysis and Applications*, *1*, 9.
Liu, B., & Chen, X. W. (2015). *Uncertain multi-objective programming and uncertain goal programming*. http://orsc.edu.cn/onLine/131020.pdf.
Wen, M. L. (2015). *Uncertain data envelopment analysis*. Berlin: Springer.

CHAPTER SIX

Ranking, sensitivity, and stability analysis in uncertain DEA

6.1 Introduction

The topic of sensitivity and stability in data envelopment analysis (DEA) has been introduced from different aspects in the literature. The sensitivity analysis of DEA was first focused on by Charnes et al. (1985) by changing the values of the inputs and outputs of a DEA problem and later was developed and improved upon by Charnes and Neralic (1992) and Neralic (1997). Another method was developed by Zhu (1996) and Seiford and Zhu (1998) that obtains the biggest stable region for changing the values of inputs and outputs. These two aspects are used to monitor the behavior of a decision-making unit (DMU) in a DEA problem. However, even if by changing all data the situation of at least one DMU is changed, the development of such methods for sensitivity analysis becomes important (see Seiford & Zhu, 1998, 1999; Thompson et al., 1994; Zhu, 1996).

Ranking of organizational units usually is done based on various criteria and models. The relative efficiency of each unit obtained by some inputs and outputs can be a good criterion for ranking the units. DEA is of linear programming methods that can be easily used to evaluate the relative efficiency and managerial outputs, and therefore determining the best performance. This method considers the most suitable weight values to rank the DMUs and compares the efficiency of a DMU to other DMUs considering a similar set of inputs and outputs. An important property of DEA is to use the weights obtained from the inputs and outputs of DMUs so that to rank DMUs, there is no need to determine the weight values of the inputs and outputs in advance.

Usually in a real case problem, the data cannot be determined as exact values. If the historical values of such data are available, the data can be considered as stochastic variables and their probability distribution can be estimated (Allahviranloo & Ghanbari, 2012; Broomandi et al., 2018;

Uncertainty in Data Envelopment Analysis
https://doi.org/10.1016/B978-0-323-99444-6.00006-2

Mahmoodirad & Sanei, 2016; Molla-Alizadeh-Zavardehi et al., 2021). But in the cases that historical data are not available, the experts in a field can be invited to determine the belief degree of the uncertain events. This type of uncertain value was introduced by Liu (2007) as belief degree-based uncertainty theory. Later, this type of uncertain number was applied in many optimization problems by Molla-Alizadeh-Zavardehi et al. (2014), Mahmoodirad et al. (2019), Allahviranloo (2020), Mahmoodirad and Niroomand (2020a, 2020b); Niroomand et al. (2020).

With the lack of exact information, DEA models also can be formulated and solved in a belief degree-based uncertain environment (Jamshidi et al., 2019, 2021a, 2021b, 2022). For the first time, Wen et al. (2014) developed DEA models in a belief degree-based uncertain environment. Later, the studies of Lio and Liu (2018) applied uncertain DEA models for efficiency evaluation purposes. In addition, Jiang et al. (2018) proposed an uncertain DEA model for evaluating scale efficiency where the proposed model is not able to distinguish between incremental and decremental returns to scale. This disadvantage was solved by the uncertain DEA model proposed by Jiang et al. (2020).

In the rest of this chapter, DMUs are ranked by some proposed models, and also the analysis and stability of inefficient and efficient DMUs are discussed in a belief degree-based uncertain environment.

The following notations are used to represent formulations in the rest of this chapter.

DMU_j	The jth DMU, $j=1, 2, \ldots, n$
DMU_o	The target DMU
$\tilde{X}_j = (\tilde{x}_{1j}, \ldots, \tilde{x}_{mj})$	The uncertain input vector of DMU_j, $j=1, 2, \ldots, n$
$\tilde{X}_o = (\tilde{x}_{1o}, \ldots, \tilde{x}_{mo})$	The uncertain input vector of DMU_o
$\tilde{Y}_j = \left(\tilde{y}_{1j}, \ldots, \tilde{y}_{sj}\right)$	The uncertain output vector of DMU_j, $j=1, 2, \ldots, n$
$\tilde{Y}_o = (\tilde{y}_{1o}, \ldots, \tilde{y}_{so})$	The uncertain output vector of DMU_o
ϕ_{ij}	The uncertainty distribution of $\tilde{x}_{ij}$, $j = 1, \ldots, n$, $i = 1, \ldots, m$
ϕ_{ij}^{-1}	The inverse uncertainty distribution of $\tilde{x}_{ij}$, $j = 1, \ldots, n$, $i = 1, \ldots, m$
ϕ_{io}	The uncertainty distribution of $\tilde{x}_{io}$, $i = 1, \ldots, m$
ϕ_{io}^{-1}	The inverse uncertainty distribution of $\tilde{x}_{io}$, $i = 1, \ldots, m$
φ_{rj}	The uncertainty distribution of $\tilde{y}_{rj}$, $j = 1, \ldots, n$, $r = 1, \ldots, s$
φ_{rj}^{-1}	The inverse uncertainty distribution of $\tilde{y}_{rj}$, $j = 1, \ldots, n$, $r = 1, \ldots, s$

φ_{ro}	The uncertainty distribution of $\tilde{y}_{ro}$, $r = 1, \ldots, s$
φ_{ro}^{-1}	The inverse uncertainty distribution of $\tilde{y}_{ro}$, $r = 1, \ldots, s$
$v \in \mathbb{R}^m$	The vector of input weights
$u \in \mathbb{R}^s$	The vector of output weights
$\mathcal{M}$	The uncertain measure
E	The expected value operator
α	The predetermined confidence level

6.2 Uncertain superefficiency model

The classical DEA models divide DMUs into two classes, efficient and inefficient. The inefficient DMUs can be ranked according to their efficiency points, but the problem is that all the efficient DMUs in a DEA problem gain an efficiency value of 1; therefore, they cannot be compared and ranked. To overcome this difficulty, Andersen and Petersen (1993) introduced the superefficiency model for the first time. The uncertain superefficiency model can be defined as below,

$$\begin{aligned} & \min \ \theta \\ & \text{subject to} \\ & \sum_{\substack{j=1, \\ j \neq o}}^{n} \lambda_j \tilde{x}_{ij} - \theta \tilde{x}_{io} \leq 0 \quad i = 1, 2, \ldots, m \\ & \sum_{\substack{j=1, \\ j \neq o}}^{n} \lambda_j \tilde{y}_{rj} - \tilde{y}_{ro} \geq 0 \quad r = 1, 2, \ldots, s \\ & \lambda_j \geq 0 \quad j = 1, \ldots, n, j \neq o \end{aligned} \tag{6.1}$$

6.2.1 Expected value uncertain superefficiency model

According to the expected value criterion introduced by Liu (2007), the following expected value uncertain superefficiency model is defined for DMU_o where the expected value of the objective function of model (6.1) is optimized under the expected value of its constraints.

$$
\begin{aligned}
&\min\ \theta \\
&\text{subject to} \\
&E\left[\sum_{\substack{j=1,\\ j\neq o}}^{n} \lambda_j \tilde{x}_{ij} - \theta \tilde{x}_{io}\right] \leq 0 \quad i = 1, 2, \ldots, m \\
&E\left[\sum_{\substack{j=1,\\ j\neq o}}^{n} \lambda_j \tilde{y}_{rj} - \tilde{y}_{ro}\right] \geq 0 \qquad r = 1, 2, \ldots, s \\
&\lambda_j \geq 0 \qquad\qquad\qquad\qquad j = 1, \ldots, n, j \neq o
\end{aligned}
\tag{6.2}
$$

Theorem 6.1. Assume that the independent uncertain variables $\tilde{x}_{ij}$, $\tilde{x}_{io}$, $\tilde{y}_{rj}$, and $\tilde{y}_{ro}$ have regular uncertain distributions ϕ_{ij}, ϕ_{io}, φ_{rj}, and φ_{ro}, respectively. The uncertain formulation (6.2) is equivalent to the below model.

$$
\begin{aligned}
&\min\ \theta \\
&\text{subject to} \\
&\sum_{\substack{j=1,\\ j\neq o}}^{n} \lambda_j \int_0^1 \phi_{ij}^{-1}(\alpha)\, d\alpha - \theta \int_0^1 \phi_{io}^{-1}(1-\alpha)\, d\alpha \leq 0 \quad i = 1, 2, \ldots, m \\
&\sum_{\substack{j=1,\\ j\neq o}}^{n} \lambda_j \int_0^1 \varphi_{rj}^{-1}(\alpha)\, d\alpha - \int_0^1 \varphi_{ro}^{-1}(1-\alpha)\, d\alpha \geq 0 \qquad r = 1, 2, \ldots, s \\
&\lambda_j \geq 0 \qquad\qquad\qquad\qquad j = 1, \ldots, n, j \neq o
\end{aligned}
\tag{6.3}
$$

Proof. According to the linearity property of the expected value criterion denoted by Theorem 1.39, the conversion $E\left[\sum_{\substack{j=1,\\ j\neq o}}^{n} \lambda_j \tilde{x}_{ij} - \theta \tilde{x}_{io}\right] = E\left[\sum_{\substack{j=1,\\ j\neq o}}^{n} \lambda_j \tilde{x}_{ij}\right] - E[\theta \tilde{x}_{io}] \leq 0 \Leftrightarrow \sum_{\substack{j=1,\\ j\neq o}}^{n} \lambda_j E\left[\tilde{x}_{ij}\right] - \theta E[\tilde{x}_{io}] \leq 0$ is done for the first constraint of model (6.2). Then, based on Theorem 1.37 the conversion $\sum_{j=1, j\neq o}^{n} \lambda_j E\left[\tilde{x}_{ij}\right] - \theta E[\tilde{x}_{io}] \leq 0 \Leftrightarrow \sum_{j=1, j\neq o}^{n} \lambda_j \int_0^1 \Phi_{ij}^{-1}(\alpha)\, d\alpha - \theta \int_0^1 \Phi_{io}^{-1}(1-\alpha)\, d\alpha \leq 0$ is done.

Similarly, the second constraint of model (6.2) is converted.

Corollary 6.1. Assume the independent uncertain variables $\tilde{x}_{ij}$, $\tilde{x}_{io}$, $\tilde{y}_{rj}$, and $\tilde{y}_{ro}$ are regular linear uncertain variables as $\mathcal{L}(a, b)$. Then, the crisp form of model (6.2) is represented as below.

$$\begin{aligned}
&\min\ \theta \\
&\text{subject to} \\
&\sum_{j=1, j\neq o}^{n} \lambda_j \left(\frac{a_{\tilde{x}_{ij}} + b_{\tilde{x}_{ij}}}{2}\right) - \theta\left(\frac{a_{\tilde{x}_{io}} + b_{\tilde{x}_{io}}}{2}\right) \leq 0 \quad i = 1, 2, \ldots, m \\
&\sum_{j=1, j\neq o}^{n} \lambda_j \left(\frac{a_{\tilde{y}_{rj}} + b_{\tilde{y}_{rj}}}{2}\right) - \left(\frac{a_{\tilde{y}_{ro}} + b_{\tilde{y}_{ro}}}{2}\right) \geq 0 \quad r = 1, 2, \ldots, s \\
&\lambda_j \geq 0 \quad j = 1, \ldots, n, j \neq o
\end{aligned} \tag{6.4}$$

Corollary 6.2. Assume the independent uncertain variables $\tilde{x}_{ij}$, $\tilde{x}_{io}$, $\tilde{y}_{rj}$, and $\tilde{y}_{ro}$ are regular zigzag uncertain variables as $\mathcal{Z}(a, b, c)$. Then, the crisp form of model (6.2) is represented as below.

$$\begin{aligned}
&\min\ \theta \\
&\text{subject to} \\
&\sum_{j=1, j\neq o}^{n} \lambda_j \left(\frac{a_{\tilde{x}_{ij}} + 2b_{\tilde{x}_{ij}} + c_{\tilde{x}_{ij}}}{4}\right) - \theta\left(\frac{a_{\tilde{x}_{io}} + 2b_{\tilde{x}_{io}} + c_{\tilde{x}_{io}}}{4}\right) \leq 0 \quad i = 1, 2, \ldots, m \\
&\sum_{j=1, j\neq o}^{n} \lambda_j \left(\frac{a_{\tilde{y}_{rj}} + 2b_{\tilde{y}_{rj}} + c_{\tilde{y}_{rj}}}{4}\right) - \left(\frac{a_{\tilde{y}_{ro}} + 2b_{\tilde{y}_{ro}} + c_{\tilde{y}_{ro}}}{4}\right) \geq 0 \quad r = 1, 2, \ldots, s \\
&\lambda_j \geq 0 \quad j = 1, \ldots, n, j \neq o
\end{aligned} \tag{6.5}$$

6.2.2 Chance-constrained uncertain superefficiency model

According to the chance-constrained programming approach introduced by Liu (2007), the following chance-constrained uncertain superefficiency model is defined for DMU_o where the objective function of model (6.1) is optimized under the chance-constrained form of its constraints.

$$
\begin{aligned}
&\min \ \theta \\
&\text{subject to} \\
&\mathcal{M}\left\{\sum_{\substack{j=1,\\ j\neq o}}^{n} \lambda_j \tilde{x}_{ij} - \theta \tilde{x}_{io} \preceq 0\right\} \geq \alpha \quad i = 1, 2, \ldots, m \\
&\mathcal{M}\left\{\sum_{\substack{j=1,\\ j\neq o}}^{n} \lambda_j \tilde{y}_{rj} - \tilde{y}_{ro} \succeq 0\right\} \geq \alpha \quad r = 1, 2, \ldots, s \\
&\lambda_j \geq 0 \quad j = 1, \ldots, n, j \neq o
\end{aligned}
\tag{6.6}
$$

In the above model, $\alpha \in (0,1)$ is a predetermined confidence level.

Theorem 6.2. Assume that the independent uncertain variables $\tilde{x}_{ij}$, $\tilde{x}_{io}$, $\tilde{y}_{rj}$, and $\tilde{y}_{ro}$ have regular uncertain distributions ϕ_{ij}, ϕ_{io}, φ_{rj}, and φ_{ro}, respectively. The uncertain formulation (6.6) is equivalent to the below model.

$$
\begin{aligned}
&\min \ \theta \\
&\text{subject to} \\
&\sum_{\substack{j=1,\\ j\neq o}}^{n} \lambda_j \phi_{ij}^{-1}(\alpha) - \theta \phi_{io}^{-1}(1-\alpha) \leq 0 \quad i = 1, 2, \ldots, m \\
&\sum_{\substack{j=1,\\ j\neq o}}^{n} \lambda_j \varphi_{rj}^{-1}(1-\alpha) - \varphi_{ro}^{-1}(\alpha) \geq 0 \quad r = 1, 2, \ldots, s \\
&\lambda_j \geq 0 \quad j = 1, \ldots, n, j \neq o
\end{aligned}
\tag{6.7}
$$

Proof. The first constraint of model (6.6) is converted to the first constraint of model (6.7) as $\mathcal{M}\left\{\sum_{\substack{j=1,\\ j\neq o}}^{n}\lambda_j\tilde{x}_{ij}-\theta\,\tilde{x}_{io}\preceq 0\right\}\geq\alpha\Leftrightarrow\sum_{\substack{j=1,\\ j\neq o}}^{n}\lambda_j\phi_{\tilde{ij}}^{-1}(\alpha)-\theta$ $\phi_{\tilde{io}}^{-1}(1-\alpha)\leq 0.$

Similarly, the second constraint of model (6.6) is converted to the second constraint of model (6.7).

Corollary 6.3. Assume the independent uncertain variables $\tilde{x}_{ij}$, $\tilde{x}_{io}$, $\tilde{y}_{rj}$, and $\tilde{y}_{ro}$ are regular linear uncertain variables as $\mathcal{L}(a,b)$. Then, the crisp form of model (6.6) is represented as below.

$$
\begin{aligned}
&\min\ \theta\\
&\text{subject to}\\
&\sum_{\substack{j=1,\\ j\neq o}}^{n}\lambda_j\Big((1-2\alpha)\,a_{\tilde{x}_{ij}}+\alpha\,b_{\tilde{x}_{ij}}\Big)-\theta\left(\alpha\,a_{\tilde{x}_{io}}+(1-\alpha)\,b_{\tilde{x}_{io}}\right)\leq 0 \quad i=1,2,\ldots,m\\
&\sum_{\substack{j=1,\\ j\neq o}}^{n}\lambda_j\Big(\alpha\,a_{\tilde{y}_{rj}}+(1-\alpha)\,b_{\tilde{y}_{rj}}\Big)-\left((1-\alpha)\,a_{\tilde{y}_{ro}}+\alpha\,b_{\tilde{y}_{ro}}\right)\geq 0 \quad r=1,2,\ldots,s\\
&\lambda_j\geq 0 \quad j=1,\ldots,n, j\neq o
\end{aligned}
\tag{6.8}
$$

Corollary 6.4. Assume the independent uncertain variables $\tilde{x}_{ij}$, $\tilde{x}_{io}$, $\tilde{y}_{rj}$, and $\tilde{y}_{ro}$ are regular zigzag uncertain variables as $\mathcal{Z}(a,b,c)$. Then, the crisp form of model (6.6) is represented as below where $0<\alpha<0.5$.

$$
\begin{aligned}
&\min\ \theta\\
&\text{subject to}\\
&\sum_{\substack{j=1,\\ j\neq o}}^{n}\lambda_j\Big((1-2\alpha)\,a_{\tilde{x}_{ij}}+2\alpha\,b_{\tilde{x}_{ij}}\Big)-\theta\left(2\alpha\,b_{\tilde{x}_{io}}+(1-2\alpha)c_{\tilde{x}_{io}}\right)\leq 0 \quad i=1,2,\ldots,m\\
&\sum_{\substack{j=1,\\ j\neq o}}^{n}\lambda_j\Big(2\alpha\,b_{\tilde{y}_{rj}}+(1-2\alpha)\,c_{\tilde{y}_{rj}}\Big)-\Big((1-2\alpha)\,a_{\tilde{y}_{ro}}+2\alpha\,b_{\tilde{y}_{ro}}\Big)\geq 0 \quad r=1,2,\ldots,s\\
&\lambda_j\geq 0 \quad j=1,\ldots,n, j\neq o
\end{aligned}
\tag{6.9}
$$

Corollary 6.5. Assume the independent uncertain variables $\tilde{x}_{ij}$, $\tilde{x}_{io}$, $\tilde{y}_{rj}$, and $\tilde{y}_{ro}$ are regular zigzag uncertain variables as $\mathcal{Z}(a, b, c)$. Then, the crisp form of model (6.6) is represented as below where $0.5 \le \alpha < 1$.

$$
\begin{aligned}
&\min \ \theta \\
&\text{subject to} \\
&\sum_{\substack{j=1,\\ j\neq o}}^{n} \lambda_j\left((2-2\alpha)\, b_{\tilde{x}_{ij}} + (2\alpha-1)c_{\tilde{x}_{ij}}\right) - \theta\left((2\alpha-1)\, a_{\tilde{x}_{io}} + (2-2\alpha)\, b_{\tilde{x}_{io}}\right) \le 0 \qquad i = 1,2,\ldots,m \\
&\sum_{\substack{j=1,\\ j\neq o}}^{n} \lambda_j\left((2\alpha-1)\, a_{\tilde{y}_{rj}} + (2-2\alpha)\, b_{\tilde{y}_{rj}}\right) - \left((2-2\alpha)\, b_{\tilde{y}_{ro}} + (2\alpha-1)\, c_{\tilde{y}_{ro}}\right) \ge 0 \qquad r = 1,2,\ldots,s \\
&\lambda_j \ge 0 \qquad j = 1,\ldots,n, j \neq o
\end{aligned}
\tag{6.10}
$$

Example 6.1. Consider five DMUs where each has two inputs and two outputs with zigzag-type uncertain data. The data of these DMUs are represented in Table 6.1.

The results for evaluating the DMUs with the expected value and chance-constrained uncertain superefficiency models are shown in Tables 6.2–6.5.

It is notable that (1) in all experiments, DMU_2 obtained the best ranking and DMU_1 obtained the worst ranking, and (2) by increasing the confidence level value, the efficiency values were increased.

Table 6.1 Data of the DMUs of Example 6.1.

DMU_j	1	2	3	4	5
Input 1	$\mathcal{Z}(3.5, 4, 4.5)$	$\mathcal{Z}(2.9, 3.1, 3.5)$	$\mathcal{Z}(4.4, 4.9, 5.4)$	$\mathcal{Z}(3.4, 4.1, 4.8)$	$\mathcal{Z}(5.9, 6.5, 7.1)$
Input 2	$\mathcal{Z}(2.9, 3.1, 3.3)$	$\mathcal{Z}(1.4, 1.5, 1.6)$	$\mathcal{Z}(3.2, 3.6, 4)$	$\mathcal{Z}(2.1, 2.3, 2.5)$	$\mathcal{Z}(3.6, 4.1, 4.6)$
Output 1	$\mathcal{Z}(2.4, 2.6, 2.8)$	$\mathcal{Z}(2.2, 3, 3.5)$	$\mathcal{Z}(2.7, 3.2, 3.7)$	$\mathcal{Z}(2.5, 2.9, 3.3)$	$\mathcal{Z}(4.4, 5.1, 5.8)$
Output 2	$\mathcal{Z}(3.8, 4.1, 4.4)$	$\mathcal{Z}(3.3, 3.5, 3.7)$	$\mathcal{Z}(4.3, 5.1, 5.9)$	$\mathcal{Z}(5.5, 5.7, 5.9)$	$\mathcal{Z}(6.5, 7.4, 8.3)$

Table 6.2 Efficiency values of the DMUs of Example 6.1 using the expected value uncertain superefficiency model.

DMU_1	DMU_2	DMU_3	DMU_4	DMU_5
0.81	1.55	0.82	1.23	0.93

Table 6.3 Ranking of the DMUs of Example 6.1 using the expected value uncertain superefficiency model.

DMU_1	DMU_2	DMU_3	DMU_4	DMU_5
5	1	4	2	3

Table 6.4 Efficiency values of the DMUs of Example 6.1 using the chance-constrained uncertain superefficiency model with different α values.

	Confidence level (α)					
DMUs	**0.5**	**0.6**	**0.7**	**0.8**	**0.9**	**1**
DMU_1	0.80	0.88	0.96	1.06	1.17	1.30
DMU_2	1.59	1.74	1.90	2.08	2.28	2.50
DMU_3	0.81	0.9	0.99	1.10	1.23	1.38
DMU_4	1.23	1.33	1.44	1.56	1.70	1.84
DMU_5	0.92	1.01	1.12	1.23	1.37	1.56

Table 6.5 Ranking of the DMUs of Example 6.1 using the chance-constrained uncertain superefficiency model with different α values.

	Confidence level (α)					
DMUs	**0.5**	**0.6**	**0.7**	**0.8**	**0.9**	**1**
DMU_1	5	5	5	5	5	5
DMU_2	1	1	1	1	1	1
DMU_3	4	4	4	4	4	4
DMU_4	2	2	2	2	2	2
DMU_5	3	3	3	3	3	3

6.3 Uncertain modified MAJ model

As classical uncertain DEA models do not clearly rank the DMUs after evaluating them, Mehrabian et al. (1999) introduced model for ranking the DMUs (it is known as MAJ model), which was later modified by Jahanshahloo et al. (2006). The uncertain modified MAJ model is as follows:

$$
\begin{aligned}
&\min \quad 1+\theta \\
&\text{subject to} \\
&\sum_{\substack{j=1,\\ j\neq o}}^{n} \lambda_j \tilde{x}_{ij} - \tilde{x}_{io} - \theta \leq 0 \quad i=1,2,\ldots,m \\
&\sum_{\substack{j=1,\\ j\neq o}}^{n} \lambda_j \tilde{y}_{rj} - \tilde{y}_{ro} + \theta \geq 0 \quad r=1,2,\ldots,s \\
&\lambda_j \geq 0 \qquad\qquad j=1,\ldots,n, j\neq o
\end{aligned}
\tag{6.11}
$$

6.3.1 Expected value uncertain modified MAJ model

The expected value uncertain modified MAJ model is defined by the following form.

$$
\begin{aligned}
&\min \quad 1+\theta \\
&\text{subject to} \\
&E\left[\sum_{\substack{j=1,\\ j\neq o}}^{n} \lambda_j \tilde{x}_{ij} - \tilde{x}_{io} - \theta\right] \leq 0 \quad i=1,2,\ldots,m \\
&E\left[\sum_{\substack{j=1,\\ j\neq o}}^{n} \lambda_j \tilde{y}_{rj} - \tilde{y}_{ro} + \theta\right] \geq 0 \quad r=1,2,\ldots,s \\
&\lambda_j \geq 0 \qquad\qquad j=1,\ldots,n, j\neq o
\end{aligned}
\tag{6.12}
$$

Theorem 6.3. Assume that the independent uncertain variables $\tilde{x}_{ij}$, $\tilde{x}_{io}$, $\tilde{y}_{rj}$, and $\tilde{y}_{ro}$ have regular uncertain distributions ϕ_{ij}, ϕ_{io}, φ_{rj}, and φ_{ro}, respectively. The uncertain formulation (6.12) is equivalent to the below model.

$$\min \quad 1+\theta$$

subject to

$$\sum_{\substack{j=1,\\ j\neq o}}^{n} \lambda_j \int_0^1 \phi_{ij}^{-1}(\alpha)\, d\alpha - \int_0^1 \phi_{io}^{-1}(1-\alpha)\, d\alpha - \theta \leq 0 \quad i=1,2,\ldots,m$$

$$\sum_{\substack{j=1,\\ j\neq o}}^{n} \lambda_j \int_0^1 \varphi_{rj}^{-1}(\alpha)\, d\alpha - \int_0^1 \varphi_{ro}^{-1}(1-\alpha)\, d\alpha + \theta \geq 0 \quad r=1,2,\ldots,s$$

$$\lambda_j \geq 0 \qquad j=1,\ldots,n, j\neq o \tag{6.13}$$

Proof. According to the linearity property of the expected value criterion denoted by Theorem 1.39, the conversion $E\left[\sum_{\substack{j=1,\\ j\neq o}}^{n} \lambda_j\tilde{x}_{ij} - \tilde{x}_{io} - \theta\right] = E\left[\sum_{\substack{j=1,\\ j\neq o}}^{n} \lambda_j\tilde{x}_{ij}\right] - E[\tilde{x}_{io}] - E[\theta] \leq 0 \Leftrightarrow \sum_{\substack{j=1,\\ j\neq o}}^{n} \lambda_j E[\tilde{x}_{ij}] - E[\tilde{x}_{io}] - \theta \leq 0$ is done for the first constraint of model (6.12). Then, based on Theorem 1.37, the conversion $\sum_{\substack{j=1,\\ j\neq o}}^{n} \lambda_j E[\tilde{x}_{ij}] - E[\tilde{x}_{io}] - \theta \leq 0 \Leftrightarrow \sum_{\substack{j=1,\\ j\neq o}}^{n} \lambda_j \int_0^1 \phi_{ij}^{-1}(\alpha)\, d\alpha - \int_0^1 \phi_{io}^{-1}(1-\alpha)\, d\alpha - \theta \leq 0$ is done.

Similarly, the second constraint of model (6.12) is converted.

Corollary 6.6. Assume the independent uncertain variables $\tilde{x}_{ij}$, $\tilde{x}_{io}$, $\tilde{y}_{rj}$, and $\tilde{y}_{ro}$ are regular linear uncertain variables as $\mathcal{L}(a,b)$. Then, the crisp form of model (6.12) is represented as below.

$$
\begin{aligned}
&\min \quad 1+\theta \\
&\text{subject to} \\
&\sum_{\substack{j=1,\\ j\neq o}}^{n} \lambda_j\left(\frac{a_{\tilde{x}_{ij}}+b_{\tilde{x}_{ij}}}{2}\right)-\theta\left(\frac{a_{\tilde{x}_{io}}+b_{\tilde{x}_{io}}}{2}\right)\leq 0 \quad i=1,2,\ldots,m \\
&\sum_{\substack{j=1,\\ j\neq o}}^{n} \lambda_j\left(\frac{a_{\tilde{y}_{rj}}+b_{\tilde{y}_{rj}}}{2}\right)-\left(\frac{a_{\tilde{y}_{ro}}+b_{\tilde{y}_{ro}}}{2}\right)\geq 0 \quad r=1,2,\ldots,s \\
&\lambda_j\geq 0 \quad j=1,\ldots,n, j\neq o
\end{aligned}
\tag{6.14}
$$

Corollary 6.7. Assume the independent uncertain variables $\tilde{x}_{ij}$, $\tilde{x}_{io}$, $\tilde{y}_{rj}$, and $\tilde{y}_{ro}$ are regular zigzag uncertain variables as $\mathcal{Z}(a, b, c)$. Then, the crisp form of model (6.12) is represented as below.

$$
\begin{aligned}
&\min \quad 1+\theta \\
&\text{subject to} \\
&\sum_{\substack{j=1,\\ j\neq o}}^{n} \lambda_j\left(\frac{a_{\tilde{x}_{ij}}+2b_{\tilde{x}_{ij}}+c_{\tilde{x}_{ij}}}{4}\right)-\theta\left(\frac{a_{\tilde{x}_{io}}+2b_{\tilde{x}_{io}}+c_{\tilde{x}_{io}}}{4}\right)\leq 0 \quad i=1,2,\ldots,m \\
&\sum_{\substack{j=1,\\ j\neq o}}^{n} \lambda_j\left(\frac{a_{\tilde{y}_{rj}}+2b_{\tilde{y}_{rj}}+c_{\tilde{y}_{rj}}}{4}\right)-\left(\frac{a_{\tilde{y}_{ro}}+2b_{\tilde{y}_{ro}}+c_{\tilde{y}_{ro}}}{4}\right)\geq 0 \quad r=1,2,\ldots,s \\
&\lambda_j\geq 0 \quad j=1,\ldots,n, j\neq o
\end{aligned}
\tag{6.15}
$$

6.3.2 Chance-constrained uncertain modified MAJ model

The chance-constrained uncertain modified MAJ model is presented by the following formulation.

$$\begin{aligned}
&\min \quad 1+\theta \\
&\text{subject to} \\
&\mathcal{M}\left\{\sum_{\substack{j=1,\\ j\neq o}}^{n} \lambda_j\tilde{x}_{ij} - \tilde{x}_{io} - \theta \preceq 0\right\} \geq \alpha \quad i=1,2,\ldots,m \\
&\mathcal{M}\left\{\sum_{\substack{j=1,\\ j\neq o}}^{n} \lambda_j\tilde{y}_{rj} - \tilde{y}_{ro} + \theta \succeq 0\right\} \geq \alpha \quad r=1,2,\ldots,s \\
&\lambda_j \geq 0 \qquad j=1,\ldots,n, j\neq o
\end{aligned} \tag{6.16}$$

In the above model, $\alpha \in (0,1)$ is a predetermined confidence level.

Theorem 6.4. Assume that the independent uncertain variables $\tilde{x}_{ij}$, $\tilde{x}_{io}$, $\tilde{y}_{rj}$, and $\tilde{y}_{ro}$ have regular uncertain distributions ϕ_{ij}, ϕ_{io}, φ_{rj}, and φ_{ro}, respectively. The uncertain formulation (6.16) is equivalent to the below model.

$$\begin{aligned}
&\min \quad 1+\theta \\
&\text{subject to} \\
&\sum_{\substack{j=1,\\ j\neq o}}^{n} \lambda_j\phi_{ij}^{-1}(\alpha) - \phi_{io}^{-1}(1-\alpha) - \theta \leq 0 \quad i=1,2,\ldots,m \\
&\sum_{\substack{j=1,\\ j\neq o}}^{n} \lambda_j\varphi_{rj}^{-1}(1-\alpha) - \varphi_{ro}^{-1}(\alpha) + \theta \geq 0 \quad r=1,2,\ldots,s \\
&\lambda_j \geq 0 \qquad j=1,\ldots,n, j\neq o
\end{aligned} \tag{6.17}$$

Proof. The first constraint of model (6.16) is converted to the first constraint of model (6.17) as $\mathcal{M}\left\{\sum_{\substack{j=1,\\ j\neq o}}^{n} \lambda_j\tilde{x}_{ij} - \tilde{x}_{io} - \theta \preceq 0\right\} \geq \alpha \Leftrightarrow \sum_{\substack{j=1,\\ j\neq o}}^{n} \lambda_j\phi_{ij}^{-1}(\alpha) - \phi_{io}^{-1}(1-\alpha) - \theta \leq 0$.

Similarly, the second constraint of model (6.16) is converted to the second constraint of model (6.17).

Corollary 6.8. Assume the independent uncertain variables $\tilde{x}_{ij}$, $\tilde{x}_{io}$, $\tilde{y}_{rj}$, and $\tilde{y}_{ro}$ are regular linear uncertain variables as $\mathcal{L}(a, b)$. Then, the crisp form of model (6.16) is represented as below.

$$
\begin{aligned}
&\min \ 1+\theta \\
&\text{subject to} \\
&\sum_{\substack{j=1,\\ j\neq o}}^{n} \lambda_j\left((1-\alpha)\,a_{\tilde{x}_{ij}} + \alpha\, b_{\tilde{x}_{ij}}\right) - \left(\alpha\, a_{\tilde{x}_{io}} + (1-\alpha)\, b_{\tilde{x}_{io}}\right) - \theta \le 0 \qquad i = 1, 2, \ldots, m \\
&\sum_{\substack{j=1,\\ j\neq o}}^{n} \lambda_j\left(\alpha\, a_{\tilde{y}_{rj}} + (1-\alpha)\, b_{\tilde{y}_{rj}}\right) - \left((1-\alpha)\, a_{\tilde{y}_{ro}} + \alpha\, b_{\tilde{y}_{ro}}\right) + \theta \ge 0 \qquad r = 1, 2, \ldots, s \\
&\lambda_j \ge 0 \qquad j = 1, \ldots, n, j \neq o
\end{aligned}
\tag{6.18}
$$

Corollary 6.9. Assume the independent uncertain variables $\tilde{x}_{ij}$, $\tilde{x}_{io}$, $\tilde{y}_{rj}$, and $\tilde{y}_{ro}$ are regular zigzag uncertain variables as $\mathcal{Z}(a, b, c)$. Then, the crisp form of model (6.16) is represented as below where $0<\alpha<0.5$.

$$
\begin{aligned}
&\min \ 1+\theta \\
&\text{subject to} \\
&\sum_{\substack{j=1,\\ j\neq o}}^{n} \lambda_j\left((1-2\alpha)\,a_{\tilde{x}_{ij}} + 2\alpha\, b_{\tilde{x}_{ij}}\right) - \left(2\alpha\, b_{\tilde{x}_{io}} + (1-2\alpha) c_{\tilde{x}_{io}}\right) - \theta \le 0 \qquad i = 1, 2, \ldots, m \\
&\sum_{\substack{j=1,\\ j\neq o}}^{n} \lambda_j\left(2\alpha\, b_{\tilde{y}_{rj}} + (1-2\alpha)\, c_{\tilde{y}_{rj}}\right) - \left((1-2\alpha)\, a_{\tilde{y}_{ro}} + 2\alpha\, b_{\tilde{y}_{ro}}\right) + \theta \ge 0 \qquad r = 1, 2, \ldots, s \\
&\lambda_j \ge 0 \qquad j = 1, \ldots, n, j \neq o
\end{aligned}
\tag{6.19}
$$

Corollary 6.10. Assume the independent uncertain variables $\tilde{x}_{ij}$, $\tilde{x}_{io}$, $\tilde{y}_{rj}$, and $\tilde{y}_{ro}$ are regular zigzag uncertain variables as $\mathcal{Z}(a, b, c)$. Then, the crisp form of model (6.6) is represented as below where $0.5\le\alpha<1$.

$$
\begin{aligned}
&\min\ \theta \\
&\text{subject to} \\
&\sum_{\substack{j=1,\\ j\neq o}}^{n} \lambda_j\left((2-2\alpha)\,b_{\tilde{x}_{ij}} + (2\alpha-1)c_{\tilde{x}_{ij}}\right) - \theta\left((2\alpha-1)\,a_{\tilde{x}_{io}} + (2-2\alpha)\,b_{\tilde{x}_{io}}\right) \le 0 \quad i = 1,2,\dots,m \\
&\sum_{\substack{j=1,\\ j\neq o}}^{n} \lambda_j\left((2\alpha-1)\,a_{\tilde{y}_{rj}} + (2-2\alpha)\,b_{\tilde{y}_{rj}}\right) - \left((2-2\alpha)\,b_{\tilde{y}_{ro}} + (2\alpha-1)\,c_{\tilde{y}_{ro}}\right) \ge 0 \quad r = 1,2,\dots,s \\
&\lambda_j \ge 0 \qquad\qquad j = 1,\dots,n, j\neq o
\end{aligned}
\tag{6.20}
$$

Example 6.2. Consider five DMUs where each has two inputs and two outputs with zigzag-type uncertain data. The data of these DMUs are represented in Table 6.6.

The results for evaluating the DMUs with the expected value and chance-constrained uncertain modified MAJ models are shown in Table 6.7–6.10.

It is notable that (1) in all experiments, DMU_4 obtained the best ranking, and (2) by increasing the confidence level value, the efficiency values were increased.

Table 6.6 Data of the DMUs of Example 6.6.

DMU_j	1	2	3	4	5
Input 1	$\mathcal{Z}(3.5, 4, 4.5)$	$\mathcal{Z}(2.9, 3.1, 3.5)$	$\mathcal{Z}(4.4, 4.9, 5.4)$	$\mathcal{Z}(3.4, 4.1, 4.8)$	$\mathcal{Z}(5.9, 6.5, 7.1)$
Input 2	$\mathcal{Z}(2.9, 3.1, 3.3)$	$\mathcal{Z}(1.4, 1.5, 1.6)$	$\mathcal{Z}(3.2, 3.6, 4)$	$\mathcal{Z}(2.1, 2.3, 2.5)$	$\mathcal{Z}(3.6, 4.1, 4.6)$
Output 1	$\mathcal{Z}(2.4, 2.6, 2.8)$	$\mathcal{Z}(2.2, 3, 3.5)$	$\mathcal{Z}(2.7, 3.2, 3.7)$	$\mathcal{Z}(2.5, 2.9, 3.3)$	$\mathcal{Z}(4.4, 5.1, 5.8)$
Output 2	$\mathcal{Z}(3.8, 4.1, 4.4)$	$\mathcal{Z}(3.3, 3.5, 3.7)$	$\mathcal{Z}(4.3, 5.1, 5.9)$	$\mathcal{Z}(5.5, 5.7, 5.9)$	$\mathcal{Z}(6.5, 7.4, 8.3)$

Table 6.7 Efficiency values of the DMUs of Example 6.2 using the expected value uncertain modified MAJ model.

DMU_1	DMU_2	DMU_3	DMU_4	DMU_5
0.61	1.46	0.55	1.49	0.78

Table 6.8 Ranking of the DMUs of Example 6.2 using the expected value uncertain modified MAJ model.

DMU_1	DMU_2	DMU_3	DMU_4	DMU_5
4	2	5	1	3

Table 6.9 Efficiency values of the DMUs of Example 6.2 using the chance-constrained uncertain modified MAJ model with different α values.

	Confidence level (α)					
DMUs	**0.5**	**0.6**	**0.7**	**0.8**	**0.9**	**1**
DMU_1	0.59	0.76	0.93	1.10	1.27	1.45
DMU_2	1.49	1.60	1.72	1.84	1.97	2.10
DMU_3	0.52	0.75	0.99	1.22	1.46	1.70
DMU_4	1.49	1.68	1.87	2.04	2.22	2.39
DMU_5	0.72	1.03	1.35	1.67	2.00	2.33

Table 6.10 Ranking of the DMUs of Example 6.2 using the chance-constrained uncertain modified MAJ model with different α values.

	Confidence level (α)					
DMUs	**0.5**	**0.6**	**0.7**	**0.8**	**0.9**	**1**
DMU_1	3	4	5	5	5	5
DMU_2	1	2	2	2	3	3
DMU_3	4	5	4	4	4	4
DMU_4	1	1	1	1	1	1
DMU_5	2	3	3	3	2	2

6.4 Sensitivity and stability analysis of the additive model

In this section, some theorems are introduced to recognize the stable region of the DMUs evaluated by an uncertain DEA model (5.52). For this aim, the stability of efficient and inefficient DMUs are focused on separately.

6.4.1 Stability region of inefficient DMUs

According to the literature, two theorems are used for the stability region of inefficient DMUs. These are presented in the rest of this section.

Theorem 6.5. (Wen et al., 2015) If DMU_o is α-inefficient, then in its optimal solution $\lambda_o^* = 0$.

Proof. Suppose DMU_1 is under evaluation. Now, we prove that $\lambda_1^* = 0$. For a fixed α, assume the optimal solution of $(s_i^{-*}, s_r^{+*}, \lambda_j^*) \geq 0$ and the optimal objective function value of $\sum_{i=1}^{m} s_i^- + \sum_{r=1}^{s} s_r^+$. If $\lambda_1^* = 0$ then the theorem is proved. But for the case of $\lambda_1^* > 0$ as the DMU is inefficient, there is at least one $s_i^{-*} > 0$ or $s_r^{+*} > 0$. Without a loss of generality, we assume $s_1^{-*} > 0$. If $\lambda_1^* = 1$ then $\mathcal{M}\{\tilde{x}_{11} \preceq \tilde{x}_{11} - s_1^{-*}\} = 0$ where this contradiction shows that $\lambda_1^* \neq 1$. Therefore, $0 < \lambda_1^* < 1$ and accordingly $\mathcal{M}\left\{\sum_{j=1}^{n} \lambda_j^* \tilde{x}_{ij} \preceq \tilde{x}_{i1} - s_i^{-*}\right\} =$

$$\mathcal{M}\left\{\sum_{j=2}^{n} \lambda_j^* \tilde{x}_{ij} \preceq (1 - \lambda_1^*)\tilde{x}_{i1} - s_i^{-*}\right\} = \mathcal{M}\left\{\frac{\sum_{j=2}^{n} \lambda_j^* \tilde{x}_{ij}}{1-\lambda_1^*} \preceq \tilde{x}_{i1} - \frac{s_i^{-*}}{1-\lambda_1^*}\right\} \geq \alpha.$$

Similarly, for assuming $s_r^{+*} > 0$, for $r = 1, 2, \ldots, s$ we obtain

$$\mathcal{M}\left\{\sum_{j=1}^{n} \lambda_j \tilde{y}_{rj} \succeq \tilde{y}_{r1} + s_r^+\right\} = \mathcal{M}\left\{\sum_{j=2}^{n} \lambda_j \tilde{y}_{rj} \succeq (1 - \lambda_1^*)\tilde{y}_{r1} + s_r^+\right\} =$$

$$\mathcal{M}\left\{\frac{\sum_{j=2}^{n} \lambda_j \tilde{y}_{rj}}{1-\lambda_1^*} \succeq \tilde{y}_{r1} + \frac{s_r^+}{1-\lambda_1^*}\right\} \geq \alpha.$$

As $\frac{\sum_{j=2}^{n} \lambda_j^*}{1-\lambda_1^*} = 1$ and $\left(0, \frac{\lambda_2^*}{\sum_{j=2}^{n} \lambda_j^*}, \frac{\lambda_3^*}{\sum_{j=2}^{n} \lambda_j^*}, \ldots, \frac{\lambda_n^*}{\sum_{j=2}^{n} \lambda_j^*}\right)$ form a feasible solution, by replacing this solution in the objective function, the inequality of $\frac{1}{1-\lambda_1^*}\left(\sum_{i=1}^{m} s_i^{-*} + \sum_{r=1}^{s} s_r^{+*}\right) > \sum_{i=1}^{m} s_i^{-*} + \sum_{r=1}^{s} s_r^{+*}$ is obtained.

As $0 < \lambda_1^* < 1$, the above-obtained inequality is in contradiction with the optimality of $(s_i^{-*}, s_r^{+*}, \lambda_j^*)$. Therefore, $\lambda_1^* = 0$ and the theorem is proved.

Theorem 6.6. (Wen et al., 2015) If DMU_o with an input and output of $(\tilde{x}_o, \tilde{y}_o)$ is inefficient by model (5.48), the modified DMU with data of $(\widehat{x}_o, \widehat{y}_o) = (\tilde{x}_o - s^{-*}, \tilde{y}_o + s^{+*})$ is α-inefficient where s^{-*} and s^{+*} are the optimal values of model (5.52).

Proof. The efficiency of $(\widehat{x}_o, \widehat{y}_o)$ is determined by solving the below model.

$$\max \sum_{i=1}^{m} s_i^- + \sum_{r=1}^{s} s_r^+$$

subject to

$$\mathcal{M}\left\{\sum_{\substack{j=1,\\ j\neq o}}^{n} \lambda_j \tilde{x}_{ij} + \lambda_o \widehat{x}_{io} \preceq \widehat{x}_{io} - s_i^- \right\} \geq \alpha \quad i = 1, 2, \ldots, m$$

$$\mathcal{M}\left\{\sum_{\substack{j=1,\\ j\neq o}}^{n} \lambda_j \tilde{y}_{rj} + \lambda_o \widehat{y}_{rj} \succeq \widehat{y}_{ro} + s_r^+ \right\} \geq \alpha \quad r = 1, 2, \ldots, s \tag{6.21}$$

$$\sum_{j=1}^{n} \lambda_j = 1$$

$$s_i^- \geq 0 \qquad i = 1, 2, \ldots, m$$

$$s_r^+ \geq 0 \qquad r = 1, 2, \ldots, s$$

$$\lambda_j \geq 0 \qquad j = 1, 2, \ldots, n$$

Assume the optimal solution of model (6.21) is $\left(\widehat{\lambda}, \widehat{s}^+, \widehat{s}^-\right)$ and the DMU with data of $(\widehat{x}_o, \widehat{y}_o)$ is inefficient. Then, according to Theorem 5.6 the value of $\lambda_o = 0$ is obtained. Replacing $(\widehat{x}_o, \widehat{y}_o) = \left(\tilde{x}_o - s^{-*}, \tilde{y}_o + s^{+*}\right)$ in the constraints of model (6.21), the constraints $\mathcal{M}\left\{\sum_{\substack{j=1\\ j\neq o}}^{n} \widehat{\lambda}_j \tilde{x}_{ij} \preceq \tilde{x}_{io} - \widehat{s}_i^- - s_i^{-*}\right\} \geq \alpha$ and $\mathcal{M}\left\{\sum_{\substack{j=1\\ j\neq o}}^{n} \widehat{\lambda}_j \tilde{y}_{rj} \succeq \tilde{y}_{ro} + \widehat{s}_r^+ + s_r^{+*}\right\} \geq \alpha$ are obtained. Then, considering $\overline{s}^+ = \widehat{s}^+ + s^{+*} \geq 0$ and $\overline{s}^- = \widehat{s}^- + s^{-*} \geq 0$, the constraints $\mathcal{M}\left\{\sum_{\substack{j=1\\ j\neq o}}^{n} \widehat{\lambda}_j \tilde{x}_{ij} \preceq \tilde{x}_{io} - \overline{s}_i^-\right\} \geq \alpha$ and $\mathcal{M}\left\{\sum_{\substack{j=1\\ j\neq o}}^{n} \widehat{\lambda}_j \tilde{y}_{rj} \succeq \tilde{y}_{ro} + \overline{s}_r^+\right\} \geq \alpha$ are obtained. Furthermore, the inequality $\sum_{i=1}^{m} \bar{s}_i^- + \sum_{r=1}^{s} \bar{s}_r^+ = \sum_{i=1}^{m} \left(\widehat{s}_i^- + s_i^{-*} \right) + \sum_{r=1}^{s} \left(\widehat{s}_r^+ + s_r^{+*} \right) \le \sum_{i=1}^{m} s_i^{-*} + \sum_{r=1}^{s} s_r^{+*}$ is obtained. As the obtained constraints form a feasible solution for model (5.52), by considering $\sum_{i=1}^{m} \bar{s}_i^- + \sum^{r=1} \bar{s}_r^+ \le \sum_{i=1}^{m} s_i^{-*} + \sum_{r=1}^{s} s_r^{+*}$, the equality $\sum_{i=1}^{m} \bar{s}_i^- + \sum_{r=1}^{s} \bar{s}_r^+ = 0$ is obtained, which means that all $\bar{s}_i^-$ and $\bar{s}_r^+$ values are zero and the theorem is proved.

6.4.2 Stability region of efficient DMUs

In this section, the stability analysis of efficient DMUs identified by model (5.25) is presented. To obtain the stability radius of efficient DMUs, the following model from Wen et al. (2015) is used.

$$
\begin{aligned}
& \max \quad \sum_{i=1}^{m} t_i^+ + \sum_{r=1}^{s} t_r^- \\
& \text{subject to} \\
& \mathcal{M}\left\{ \sum_{\substack{j=1,\\ j\neq o}}^{n} \lambda_j \tilde{x}_{ij} \preceq \tilde{x}_{io} + t_i^+ \right\} \ge \alpha \quad i = 1, 2, \ldots, m \\
& \mathcal{M}\left\{ \sum_{\substack{j=1,\\ j\neq o}}^{n} \lambda_j \tilde{y}_{rj} \succeq \tilde{y}_{ro} - t_r^- \right\} \ge \alpha \quad r = 1, 2, \ldots, s \\
& \sum_{j=1}^{n} \lambda_j = 1 \\
& s_i^- \ge 0 \qquad i = 1, 2, \ldots, m \\
& s_r^+ \ge 0 \qquad r = 1, 2, \ldots, s \\
& \lambda_j \ge 0 \qquad j = 1, 2, \ldots, n
\end{aligned}
\tag{6.22}
$$

Theorem 6.7. For a fixed value of α, the efficient DMU_o remains efficient if $(\widehat{x}_o, \widehat{y}_o) = \left(\tilde{x}_o + t^{+*}, \tilde{y}_o - t^{-*}\right)$ where t^{+*} and t^{-*} are the optimal solutions of model (6.22).

Proof. Consider the below model for measuring the relative efficiency of the adjusted DMU_o.

$$
\begin{aligned}
\max \quad & \sum_{i=1}^{m} s_i^- + \sum_{r=1}^{s} s_r^+ \\
\text{subject to} \quad & \\
& \mathcal{M}\left\{ \sum_{\substack{j=1,\\ j\neq o}}^{n} \lambda_j \tilde{x}_{ij} + \left(\tilde{x}_{io} + t_i^{+*}\right)\lambda_o \preceq \left(\tilde{x}_{io} + t_i^{+*}\right) - s_i^- \right\} \geq \alpha \quad i = 1, 2, \ldots, m \\
& \mathcal{M}\left\{ \sum_{\substack{j=1,\\ j\neq o}}^{n} \lambda_j \tilde{y}_{rj} + \left(\tilde{y}_{ro} - t_r^{-*}\right)\lambda_o \succeq \left(\tilde{y}_{ro} - t_r^{-*}\right) + s_r^+ \right\} \geq \alpha \quad r = 1, 2, \ldots, s \\
& \sum_{j=1}^{n} \lambda_j = 1 \\
& s_i^- \geq 0 \quad i = 1, 2, \ldots, m \\
& s_r^+ \geq 0 \quad r = 1, 2, \ldots, s \\
& \lambda_j \geq 0 \quad j = 1, 2, \ldots, n
\end{aligned}
\tag{6.23}
$$

Suppose that $(\lambda_j^*, \lambda_o^*, s^{-*}, s^{+*})$ is the optimal solution and DMU_o is inefficient. Applying Theorem 6.5 results in $\lambda_o^* = 0$ and therefore model (6.23) is converted to the below model.

$$
\begin{aligned}
&\max \quad \sum_{i=1}^{m} s_i^- + \sum_{r=1}^{s} s_r^+ \\
&\text{subject to} \\
&\mathcal{M}\left\{ \sum_{\substack{j=1,\\ j\neq o}}^{n} \lambda_j \tilde{x}_{ij} \preceq \tilde{x}_{io} + \left(t_i^{+*} - s_i^-\right) \right\} \geq \alpha \quad i = 1,2,\ldots,m \\
&\mathcal{M}\left\{ \sum_{\substack{j=1,\\ j\neq o}}^{n} \lambda_j \tilde{y}_{rj} \succeq \tilde{y}_{ro} - \left(t_r^{-*} - s_r^+\right) \right\} \geq \alpha \quad r = 1,2,\ldots,s \\
&\sum_{j=1}^{n} \lambda_j = 1 \\
&s_i^- \geq 0 \quad i = 1,2,\ldots,m \\
&s_r^+ \geq 0 \quad r = 1,2,\ldots,s \\
&\lambda_j \geq 0 \quad j = 1,2,\ldots,n
\end{aligned}
\tag{6.24}
$$

The optimal solution of model (6.24) is a feasible solution for model (6.22). Therefore $t_i^{+*} - s_i^{-*} \geq t_i^{+*}$ and $t_r^{-*} - s_r^{+*} \geq t_r^{-*}$, which means that $s_i^{-*} = 0$ and $s_r^{+*} = 0$. This result is in contradiction with the above-mentioned assumption and the theorem is proved.

6.4.3 Stability region calculations

In the latter two sections, some theoretical concepts of stability analysis were presented that may be difficult to use for calculating the stability region. In this section, some equivalent models are proposed to simplify the calculations. Theorem 5.16 has proved that the models (5.52) and (5.53) are equivalent. Similarly, it can be proved that model (6.22) is equivalent to the below model.

$$
\begin{aligned}
&\max \sum_{i=1}^{m} t_i^+ + \sum_{r=1}^{s} t_r^- \\
&\text{subject to} \\
&\sum_{\substack{j=1,\\ j\neq o}}^{n} \lambda_j \phi_{ij}^{-1}(\alpha) \le \phi_{io}^{-1}(1-\alpha) + t_i^+ \quad i=1,2,\ldots,m \\
&\sum_{\substack{j=1,\\ j\neq o}}^{n} \lambda_j \varphi_{rj}^{-1}(1-\alpha) \ge \varphi_{ro}^{-1}(\alpha) - t_r^- \quad r=1,2,\ldots,s \\
&\sum_{j=1}^{n} \lambda_j = 1 \\
&s_i^- \ge 0 \quad i=1,2,\ldots,m \\
&s_r^+ \ge 0 \quad r=1,2,\ldots,s \\
&\lambda_j \ge 0 \quad j=1,2,\ldots,n
\end{aligned}
\tag{6.25}
$$

Therefore, the input and output domains and the stability radius of DMU_o are calculated as below,

- If DMU_o is inefficient by model (5.53), then the inefficiency region is $\left(\tilde{x}_o - s^{-*}, \tilde{y}_o + s^{+*}\right)$ where s^{-*} and s^{+*} are the optimal solutions of model (5.49).
- If DMU_o is efficient by model (6.25), then the efficiency region is $\left(\widehat{x}_o + t^{+*}, \widehat{y}_o - t^{-*}\right)$ where t^{+*} and t^{-*} are the optimal solutions of model (6.25).

Example 6.3. Consider a problem with five DMUs, two inputs, and two outputs. The zigzag uncertain data of this example are given in Table 6.11.

For $\alpha=0.5$, the additive model (5.52) is used and the results in Table 6.12 are obtained.

Table 6.11 The data of Example 6.3.

DMU_j	1	2	3	4	5
Input 1	$\mathcal{Z}(3.5, 4, 4.5)$	$\mathcal{Z}(2.9, 3.1, 3.5)$	$\mathcal{Z}(4.4, 4.9, 5.4)$	$\mathcal{Z}(3.4, 4.1, 4.8)$	$\mathcal{Z}(5.9, 6.5, 7.1)$
Input 2	$\mathcal{Z}(2.9, 3.1, 3.3)$	$\mathcal{Z}(1.4, 1.5, 1.6)$	$\mathcal{Z}(3.2, 3.6, 4)$	$\mathcal{Z}(2.1, 2.3, 2.5)$	$\mathcal{Z}(3.6, 4.1, 4.6)$
Output 1	$\mathcal{Z}(2.4, 2.6, 2.8)$	$\mathcal{Z}(2.2, 3, 3.5)$	$\mathcal{Z}(2.7, 3.2, 3.7)$	$\mathcal{Z}(2.5, 2.9, 3.3)$	$\mathcal{Z}(4.4, 5.1, 5.8)$
Output 2	$\mathcal{Z}(3.8, 4.1, 4.4)$	$\mathcal{Z}(3.3, 3.5, 3.7)$	$\mathcal{Z}(4.3, 5.1, 5.9)$	$\mathcal{Z}(5.5, 5.7, 5.9)$	$\mathcal{Z}(6.5, 7.4, 8.3)$

Table 6.12 Results obtained for Example 6.3 using model (5.52) for $\alpha = 0.5$.

DMUs	$(\lambda_1^*, \lambda_2^*, \lambda_3^*, \lambda_4^*, \lambda_5^*)$	$(s_1^{-*}, s_2^{-*}, s_1^{+*}, s_2^{+*})$	Final decision
DMU_1	(0, 0.32, 0, 0.68, 0)	(0, 0.98, 0.19, 0.79)	Inefficiency
DMU_2	(0, 1, 0, 0, 0)	(0, 0, 0, 0, 0)	Efficiency
DMU_3	(0, 0, 0, 0.78, 0.22)	(0.03, 0.76, 0, 0.75)	Inefficiency
DMU_4	(0, 0, 0, 1, 0)	(0, 0, 0, 0, 0)	Efficiency
DMU_5	(0, 0, 0, 0, 1)	(0, 0, 0, 0, 0)	Efficiency

Based on the results in Table 6.12, the stability region of inefficient DMUs is determined and shown in Table 6.13, where s_1^{-*} and s_2^{-*} are the lower bounds for inputs and s_1^{+*} and s_2^{+*} are the upper bounds for outputs.

According to the results of Table 6.13, DMU_1 remains inefficient where $(\widehat{x}_{11}, \widehat{x}_{12}, \widehat{y}_{11}, \widehat{y}_{12}) = \left(\tilde{x}_{11}, \tilde{x}_{12} - \gamma_{x2}, \tilde{y}_{11} + \gamma_{y1}, \tilde{y}_{12} + \gamma_{y2}\right)$, $0 \le \gamma_{x2} < 0.98$, $0 \le \gamma_{y1} < 0.19$, and $0 \le \gamma_{y2} < 0.79$. A summary of the lower bounds for inputs and the upper bounds for outputs of the inefficient DMUs is shown in Tables 6.14 and 6.15 respectively.

Table 6.13 Results obtained for the stability region of the inefficient DMUs of Example 6.3.

DMUs	s_1^{-*}	s_2^{-*}	s_1^{+*}	s_2^{+*}
DMU_1	0	0.98	0.19	0.79
DMU_3	0.03	0.76	0	0.75

Table 6.14 Lower bounds for inputs of the inefficient DMUs of Example 6.3.

DMUs	Input 1	Input 2
DMU_1	$\mathcal{Z}(3.5, 4, 4.5)$	$\mathcal{Z}(1.92, 2.12, 2.32)$
DMU_3	$\mathcal{Z}(4.37, 4.87, 5.37)$	$\mathcal{Z}(2.44, 2.84, 3.24)$

Table 6.15 Upper bounds for outputs of the inefficient DMUs of Example 6.3.

DMUs	Output 1	Output 2
DMU_1	$\mathcal{Z}(2.59, 2.79, 2.99)$	$\mathcal{Z}(4.59, 4.89, 5.19)$
DMU_3	$\mathcal{Z}(2.7, 3.2, 3.7)$	$\mathcal{Z}(5.05, 5.85, 6.65)$

For example, if the input of DMU_1 is changed from $\mathcal{Z}(2.9, 3.1, 3.5)$ to $\mathcal{Z}(2.1, 2.3, 2.5)$, as its new value is not less than the lower bound $\mathcal{Z}(1.92, 2.12, 2.32)$, this DMU remains inefficient. If the output of DMU_3 is changed from $\mathcal{Z}(4.3, 5.1, 5.9)$ to $\mathcal{Z}(5.3, 6.1, 6.9)$, as its new value is not less than the upper bound $\mathcal{Z}(5.05, 5.85, 6.65)$, this DMU becomes efficient.

Based on the results in Table 6.12, the stability region of efficient DMUs is determined and shown in Table 6.13, where t_1^{+*} and t_2^{+*} are the upper bounds for inputs and t_1^{-*} and t_2^{-*} are the lower bounds for outputs.

According to the results in Table 6.16, DMU_4 remains efficient where $(\widehat{x}_{41}, \widehat{x}_{42}, \widehat{y}_{41}, \widehat{y}_{42}) = \left(\tilde{x}_{41}, \tilde{x}_{42} + \gamma_{x2}, \tilde{y}_{41}, \tilde{y}_{42} - \gamma_{y2}\right)$, $0 \leq \gamma_{x2} \leq 0.02$, and $0 \leq \gamma_{y2} < 1.21$. A summary of the upper bounds for inputs and the lower bounds for outputs of the efficient DMUs is reported in Tables 6.17 and 6.18, respectively.

For example, if the second input of DMU_2 is changed from $\mathcal{Z}(1.4, 1.5, 1.6)$ to $\mathcal{Z}(1.82, 1.92, 2.02)$, as its new value is not less than

Table 6.16 Results obtained for the stability region of the efficient DMUs of Example 6.3.

DMUs	t_1^{+*}	t_2^{+*}	t_1^{-*}	t_2^{-*}
DMU_2	0	0.23	0.16	0
DMU_4	0	0.02	0	1.21
DMU_5	0	0	3.11	2.06

Table 6.17 Upper bounds for inputs of the efficient DMUs of Example 6.3.

DMUs	Input 1	Input 2
DMU_2	$\mathcal{Z}(2.9, 3.1, 3.5)$	$\mathcal{Z}(1.63, 1.73, 1.83)$
DMU_4	$\mathcal{Z}(3.4, 4.1, 4.8)$	$\mathcal{Z}(2.12, 2.32, 2.52)$
DMU_5	$\mathcal{Z}(5.9, 6.5, 7.1)$	$\mathcal{Z}(3.6, 4.1, 4.6)$

Table 6.18 Lower bounds for outputs of the efficient DMUs of Example 6.3.

DMUs	Output 1	Output 2
DMU_2	$\mathcal{Z}(2.04, 2.44, 2.64)$	$\mathcal{Z}(3.3, 3.5, 3.7)$
DMU_4	$\mathcal{Z}(2.5, 2.9, 3.3)$	$\mathcal{Z}(4.29, 4.49, 4.69)$
DMU_5	$\mathcal{Z}(1.29, 1.99, 2.69)$	$\mathcal{Z}(4.44, 5.34, 6.24)$

the upper bound $\mathcal{Z}(1.63, 1.73, 1.83)$, this DMU becomes inefficient. If the second output of DMU_5 is changed from $\mathcal{Z}(6.5, 7.4, 8.3)$ to $\mathcal{Z}(4.76, 5.66, 6.56)$, as its new value is not less than the lower bound $\mathcal{Z}(4.44, 5.34, 6.24)$, this DMU remains efficient.

6.5 Analysis and stability of uncertain model (5.20)

To study the stability of uncertain model (5.20), this study is done in two directions of efficient and inefficient DMUs (Lio & Liu, 2018).

6.5.1 Analysis and stability of inefficient DMUs

Assume DMU_o as an inefficient DMU. Lio and Liu (2018) introduced the model for the obtain the maximum value for η such that the new form of this DMU with data of $(\tilde{x}_o + \eta e_m, \tilde{y}_o - \eta e_s)$ remains efficient, that $e_j = (1, 1, \ldots, 1)$ is a j-dimensional vector with values of 1.

$$
\begin{aligned}
& \min \ \eta \\
& \text{subject to} \\
& E\left[\frac{\sum_{r=1}^{s} u_r(\tilde{y}_{ro} + \eta)}{\sum_{i=1}^{m} v_i(\tilde{x}_{io} - \eta)}\right] = 1 \\
& E\left[\frac{\sum_{r=1}^{s} u_r\tilde{y}_{rj}}{\sum_{i=1}^{m} v_i\tilde{x}_{ij}}\right] \leq 1 \qquad j = 1, 2, \ldots, n \\
& v_i \geq 0 \qquad i = 1, 2, \ldots, m \\
& u_r \geq 0 \qquad r = 1, 2, \ldots, s
\end{aligned}
\tag{6.26}
$$

Theorem 6.8. (Lio & Liu, 2018) Assume that the independent uncertain variables $\tilde{x}_{ij}$, $\tilde{x}_{io}$, $\tilde{y}_{rj}$, and $\tilde{y}_{ro}$ have regular uncertain distributions ϕ_{ij}, ϕ_{io}, φ_{rj}, and φ_{ro}, respectively. The uncertain formulation (6.26) is equivalent to the below model.

$$\begin{aligned}
&\min \ \eta \\
&\text{subject to} \\
&\int_0^1 \frac{\sum_{r=1}^{s} u_r\left(\varphi_{ro}^{-1}(\alpha)+\eta\right)}{\sum_{i=1}^{m} v_i\left(\phi_{io}^{-1}(1-\alpha)-\eta\right)} d\alpha = 1 \\
&\int_0^1 \frac{\sum_{r=1}^{s} u_r\varphi_{rj}^{-1}(\alpha)}{\sum_{i=1}^{m} v_i\phi_{ij}^{-1}(1-\alpha)} d\alpha \le 1 \qquad j=1,2,\ldots,n \\
&v_i \ge 0 \qquad i=1,2,\ldots,m \\
&u_r \ge 0 \qquad r=1,2,\ldots,s
\end{aligned} \tag{6.27}$$

Proof. This is obvious that the inverse uncertain distributions of $\tilde{x}_{io}-\eta$ and $\tilde{y}_{ro}+\eta$ are $\phi_{io}^{-1}(\alpha)-\eta$ and $\varphi_{ro}^{-1}(\alpha)+\eta$, respectively. As the function $\frac{\sum_{r=1}^{s} u_r(\tilde{y}_{ro}+\eta)}{\sum_{i=1}^{m} v_i(\tilde{x}_{io}-\eta)}$ is absolutely increasing for $\tilde{y}_{ro}$ and absolutely decreasing for $\tilde{x}_{io}$, according to Theorem 1.33 its inverse uncertain distribution is obtained as $\psi_0^{-1}(\alpha)=\frac{\sum_{r=1}^{s} u_r\left(\varphi_{ro}^{-1}(\alpha)+\eta\right)}{\sum_{i=1}^{m} v_i\left(\phi_{io}^{-1}(1-\alpha)-\eta\right)}$. Therefore, according to Theorem 1.38 the conversion $E\left[\frac{\sum_{r=1}^{s} u_r(\tilde{y}_{ro}+\eta)}{\sum_{i=1}^{m} v_i(\tilde{x}_{io}-\eta)}\right]=\int_0^1 \frac{\sum_{r=1}^{s} u_r\left(\varphi_{ro}^{-1}(\alpha)+\eta\right)}{\sum_{i=1}^{m} v_i\left(\phi_{io}^{-1}(1-\alpha)-\eta\right)} d\alpha$is obtained and the theorem is proved.

Theorem 6.9. (Lio & Liu, 2018) Assume DMU_o is inefficient and η^* is the optimal solution value of model (6.27). Then,

- DMU_o remains inefficient for changing $\tilde{x}_o$ to $\tilde{x}_o-\eta e_m$, and $\tilde{y}_o$ to $\tilde{y}_o+\eta e_s$, if $\eta<\eta^*$.
- DMU_o becomes efficient for changing $\tilde{x}_o$ to $\tilde{x}_o-\eta e_m$, and $\tilde{y}_o$ to $\tilde{y}_o+\eta e_s$, if $\eta\ge\eta^*$.

Proof. Assume $(\tilde{x}_o - \eta e_m, \tilde{y}_o + \eta e_r)$ is efficient, then there exists a $(u,v) \geq 0$ where $\int_0^1 \frac{\sum_{r=1}^{s} u_r\left(\varphi_{ro}^{-1}(\alpha)+\eta\right)}{\sum_{i=1}^{m} v_i\left(\phi_{io}^{-1}(1-\alpha)-\eta\right)} d\alpha = 1$ and $\int_0^1 \frac{\sum_{r=1}^{s} u_r\varphi_{rj}^{-1}(\alpha)}{\sum_{i=1}^{m} v_i\phi_{ij}^{-1}(1-\alpha)} d\alpha \leq 1$. This means that (u,v,η) is a feasible solution of model (6.27), therefore, $\eta \geq \eta^*$. Thus, $(\tilde{x}_o - \eta e_m, \tilde{y}_o + \eta e_s)$ is inefficient for any $\eta < \eta^*$.

On the other hand, as η^* is the optimal solution value of model (6.27), then there exists $(u^*, v^*) \geq 0$ where (u^*, v^*, η^*) is a feasible solution, meaning that $\int_0^1 \frac{\sum_{r=1}^{s} u_r^*\left(\varphi_{ro}^{-1}(\alpha)+\eta^*\right)}{\sum_{i=1}^{m} v_i^*\left(\phi_{io}^{-1}(1-\alpha)-\eta^*\right)} d\alpha = 1$ and $\int_0^1 \frac{\sum_{r=1}^{s} u_r^*\varphi_{rj}^{-1}(\alpha)}{\sum_{i=1}^{m} v_i^*\phi_{ij}^{-1}(1-\alpha)} d\alpha \leq 1$. As $\int_0^1 \frac{\sum_{r=1}^{s} u_r^*\left(\varphi_{ro}^{-1}(\alpha)+\eta^*\right)}{\sum_{i=1}^{m} v_i^*\left(\phi_{io}^{-1}(1-\alpha)-\eta^*\right)} d\alpha$ is increasing for η^*, then the inequality $\int_0^1 \frac{\sum_{r=1}^{s} u_r^*\left(\varphi_{ro}^{-1}(\alpha)+\eta\right)}{\sum_{i=1}^{m} v_i^*\left(\phi_{io}^{-1}(1-\alpha)-\eta\right)} d\alpha \geq \int_0^1 \frac{\sum_{r=1}^{s} u_r^*\left(\varphi_{ro}^{-1}(\alpha)+\eta^*\right)}{\sum_{i=1}^{m} v_i^*\left(\phi_{io}^{-1}(1-\alpha)-\eta^*\right)} d\alpha = 1$ is held for $\eta \geq \eta^*$. The replacements $v_i = v_i^*$ and $u_r = \frac{u_r^*}{\int_0^1 \frac{\sum_{r=1}^{s} u_r^*\left(\varphi_{ro}^{-1}(\alpha)+\eta\right)}{\sum_{i=1}^{m} v_i^*\left(\phi_{io}^{-1}(1-\alpha)-\eta\right)} d\alpha} \leq u_r^*$ are considered. Now, as $(u,v) \geq 0$ and (u,v,η) are true for the conditions $\int_0^1 \frac{\sum_{r=1}^{s} u_r\left(\varphi_{ro}^{-1}(\alpha)+\eta\right)}{\sum_{i=1}^{m} v_i\left(\phi_{io}^{-1}(1-\alpha)-\eta\right)} d\alpha = 1$ and $\int_0^1 \frac{\sum_{r=1}^{s} u_r\varphi_{rj}^{-1}(\alpha)}{\sum_{i=1}^{m} v_i\phi_{ij}^{-1}(1-\alpha)} d\alpha \leq 1$, therefore $(\tilde{x}_o - \eta e_m, \tilde{y}_o + \eta e_s)$ is efficient for any $\eta \geq \eta^*$.

6.5.2 Analysis and stability of efficient DMUs

Assume DMU_o as an efficient DMU. In this section, the maximum value for η is obtained such that the new form of this DMU with data of $(\tilde{x}_o + \eta e_m, \tilde{y}_o - \eta e_s)$ remains efficient. Here, $e_j = (1,1,\ldots,1)$ is a j-dimensional vector with values of 1. For this aim, the below model has been introduced by Lio and Liu (2018).

$$\begin{aligned}
&\max\ \eta\\
&\text{subject to}\\
&E\left[\frac{\sum_{r=1}^{s} u_r(\tilde{y}_{ro}-\eta)}{\sum_{i=1}^{m} v_i(\tilde{x}_{io}+\eta)}\right]=1\\
&E\left[\frac{\sum_{r=1}^{s} u_r\tilde{y}_{rj}}{\sum_{i=1}^{m} v_i\tilde{x}_{ij}}\right]\le 1 \qquad j=1,2,\ldots,n,\ j\neq o\\
&v_i\ge 0 \qquad i=1,2,\ldots,m\\
&u_r\ge 0 \qquad r=1,2,\ldots,s
\end{aligned} \tag{6.28}$$

In this model, the exception $j \neq o$ means that when $(\tilde{x}_o + \eta e_m, \tilde{y}_o - \eta e_s)$ is evaluated, DMU_o should be excepted.

Theorem 6.10. (Lio & Liu, 2018) Assume that the independent uncertain variables $\tilde{x}_{ij}$, $\tilde{x}_{io}$, $\tilde{y}_{rj}$, and $\tilde{y}_{ro}$ have regular uncertain distributions ϕ_{ij}, ϕ_{io}, φ_{rj}, and φ_{ro}, respectively. The uncertain formulation (6.28) is equivalent to the below model.

$$\begin{aligned}
&\max\ \eta\\
&\text{subject to}\\
&\int_0^1 \frac{\sum_{r=1}^{s} u_r\left(\varphi_{ro}^{-1}(\alpha)-\eta\right)}{\sum_{i=1}^{m} v_i\left(\phi_{io}^{-1}(1-\alpha)+\eta\right)}\,d\alpha=1\\
&\int_0^1 \frac{\sum_{r=1}^{s} u_r\varphi_{rj}^{-1}(\alpha)}{\sum_{i=1}^{m} v_i\phi_{ij}^{-1}(1-\alpha)}\,d\alpha\le 1 \qquad j=1,2,\ldots,n,\ j\neq o\\
&v_i\ge 0 \qquad i=1,2,\ldots,m\\
&u_r\ge 0 \qquad r=1,2,\ldots,s
\end{aligned} \tag{6.29}$$

Proof. This is obvious that the inverse uncertain distributions of $\tilde{x}_{io} + \eta$ and $\tilde{y}_{ro} - \eta$ are $\phi_{io}^{-1}(\alpha) + \eta$ and $\varphi_{ro}^{-1}(\alpha) - \eta$, respectively. As the function $\frac{\sum_{r=1}^{s} u_r(\tilde{y}_{ro} - \eta)}{\sum_{i=1}^{m} v_i(\tilde{x}_{io} + \eta)}$ is absolutely increasing for $\tilde{y}_{ro}$ and absolutely decreasing for $\tilde{x}_{io}$, according to Theorem 1.33 its inverse uncertain distribution is obtained as $D_0^{-1}(\alpha) = \frac{\sum_{r=1}^{s} u_r\left(\varphi_{ro}^{-1}(\alpha) - \eta\right)}{\sum_{i=1}^{m} v_i\left(\phi_{io}^{-1}(1-\alpha) + \eta\right)}$. Therefore, according to Theorem 1.38 the conversion $E\left[\frac{\sum_{r=1}^{s} u_r(\tilde{y}_{ro} - \eta)}{\sum_{i=1}^{m} v_i(\tilde{x}_{io} + \eta)}\right] = \int_0^1 \frac{\sum_{r=1}^{s} u_r\left(\varphi_{ro}^{-1}(\alpha) - \eta\right)}{\sum_{i=1}^{m} v_i\left(\phi_{io}^{-1}(1-\alpha) + \eta\right)} d\alpha$ is obtained and the theorem is proved.

Theorem 6.11. (Lio & Liu, 2018) Assume DMU_o is efficient and η^* is the optimal solution value of model (6.27). Then,

- DMU_o remains efficient for changing $\tilde{x}_o$ to $\tilde{x}_o + \eta e_m$, and $\tilde{y}_o$ to $\tilde{y}_o - \eta e_s$, if $\eta \le \eta^*$.
- DMU_o becomes inefficient for changing $\tilde{x}_o$ to $\tilde{x}_o + \eta e_m$, and $\tilde{y}_o$ to $\tilde{y}_o - \eta e_s$, if $\eta > \eta^*$.

Proof. As η^* is the optimal solution value of model (6.28), then there exists $(u^*, v^*) \ge 0$ where (u^*, v^*, η^*) is a feasible solution, meaning that $\int_0^1 \frac{\sum_{r=1}^{s} u_r^*\left(\varphi_{ro}^{-1}(\alpha) - \eta^*\right)}{\sum_{i=1}^{m} v_i^*\left(\phi_{io}^{-1}(1-\alpha) + \eta^*\right)} d\alpha = 1$ and $\int_0^1 \frac{\sum_{r=1}^{s} u_r^* \varphi_{rj}^{-1}(\alpha)}{\sum_{i=1}^{m} v_i^* \phi_{ij}^{-1}(1-\alpha)} d\alpha \le 1$. As $\int_0^1 \frac{\sum_{r=1}^{s} u_r^*\left(\varphi_{ro}^{-1}(\alpha) - \eta^*\right)}{\sum_{i=1}^{m} v_i^*\left(\phi_{io}^{-1}(1-\alpha) + \eta^*\right)} d\alpha$ is decreasing for η^*, then the inequality $\int_0^1 \frac{\sum_{r=1}^{s} u_r^*\left(\varphi_{ro}^{-1}(\alpha) - \eta\right)}{\sum_{i=1}^{m} v_i^*\left(\phi_{io}^{-1}(1-\alpha) + \eta\right)} d\alpha \ge \int_0^1 \frac{\sum_{r=1}^{s} u_r^*\left(\varphi_{ro}^{-1}(\alpha) - \eta^*\right)}{\sum_{i=1}^{m} v_i^*\left(\phi_{io}^{-1}(1-\alpha) + \eta^*\right)} d\alpha = 1$ is held for $\eta \le \eta^*$.

The replacements $v_i = v_i^*$ and $u_r = \frac{u_r^*}{\int_0^1 \frac{\sum_{r=1}^{s} u_r^*\left(\varphi_{ro}^{-1}(\alpha) - \eta\right)}{\sum_{i=1}^{m} v_i^*\left(\phi_{io}^{-1}(1-\alpha) + \eta\right)} d\alpha} \le u_r^*$ are considered.

Now, as $(u, v) \ge 0$ and (u, v, η) are true for the conditions

$\int_0^1 \frac{\sum_{r=1}^{s} u_r\left(\varphi_{ro}^{-1}(\alpha)-\eta\right)}{\sum_{i=1}^{m} v_i\left(\phi_{io}^{-1}(1-\alpha)+\eta\right)} d\alpha = 1,$ and $\int_0^1 \frac{\sum_{r=1}^{s} u_r\, \varphi_{rj}^{-1}(\alpha)}{\sum_{i=1}^{m} v_i\, \phi_{ij}^{-1}(1-\alpha)} d\alpha \leq 1,$ therefore $(\tilde{x}_o + \eta e_m, \tilde{y}_o - \eta e_s)$ is efficient for any $\eta \leq \eta^*$.

On the other hand, assume $(\tilde{x}_o + \eta e_m, \tilde{y}_o - \eta e_s)$ is efficient, then there exists a $(u, v) \geq 0$ where $\int_0^1 \frac{\sum_{r=1}^{s} u_r\left(\varphi_{ro}^{-1}(\alpha)-\eta\right)}{\sum_{i=1}^{m} v_i\left(\phi_{io}^{-1}(1-\alpha)+\eta\right)} d\alpha = 1$ and $\int_0^1 \frac{\sum_{r=1}^{s} u_r \varphi_{rj}^{-1}(\alpha)}{\sum_{i=1}^{m} v_i \phi_{ij}^{-1}(1-\alpha)} d\alpha \leq 1.$

This means that (u, v, η) is a feasible solution of model (6.28), therefore, $\eta \leq \eta^*$. Thus, $(\tilde{x}_o + \eta e_m, \tilde{y}_o - \eta e_s)$ is inefficient for any $\eta > \eta^*$.

Example 6.4. (Lio & Liu, 2018) There are five DMUs to be evaluated according to three inputs and three outputs with uncertain values given in Table 6.19.

According to the results of Example 5.3, DMUs 2 and 5 are efficient and DMUs 1, 3, and 4 are inefficient. The results of the stability of the DMUs by models (6.27) and (6.29) are reported in Table 6.20.

Based on the results of Table 6.20, the stability radius η^* for DMU_1 (obtained by model (6.27)) is 3.58. This means that DMU_1, by at least a 3.58 decrease in all inputs and an increase in all outputs, can become efficient. For the changes of the inputs and outputs less than 3.58, the DMU cannot become efficient. A similar interpretation can be done for inefficient DMUs 3 and 4. On the other hand, the stability radius η^* for DMU_2 (obtained by model (6.29)) is 0.85. This means that DMU_2, by at most an 0.85 increase in all inputs and a decrease in all outputs, can remain

Table 6.19 Data of Example 6.4.

DMU_j	1	2	3	4	5
Input 1	$\mathcal{L}(4,7)$	$\mathcal{L}(2,5)$	$\mathcal{L}(3,4)$	$\mathcal{L}(2,5)$	$\mathcal{L}(1,6)$
Input 2	$\mathcal{L}(5,8)$	$\mathcal{L}(3,6)$	$\mathcal{L}(4,6)$	$\mathcal{L}(1,6)$	$\mathcal{L}(1,3)$
Input 3	$\mathcal{L}(4,8)$	$\mathcal{L}(1,3)$	$\mathcal{L}(3,7)$	$\mathcal{L}(1,3)$	$\mathcal{L}(1,3)$
Output 1	$\mathcal{Z}(1,2,3)$	$\mathcal{Z}(4,7,10)$	$\mathcal{Z}(2,3,4)$	$\mathcal{Z}(4,6,8)$	$\mathcal{Z}(10,12,14)$
Output 2	$\mathcal{Z}(1,2,4)$	$\mathcal{Z}(8,10,12)$	$\mathcal{Z}(2,6,8)$	$\mathcal{Z}(5,7,8)$	$\mathcal{Z}(5,6,7)$
Output 3	$\mathcal{Z}(1,3,4)$	$\mathcal{Z}(9,11,13)$	$\mathcal{Z}(3,5,7)$	$\mathcal{Z}(5,7,9)$	$\mathcal{Z}(8,9,10)$

Table 6.20 The results for the stability of the DMUs of Example 6.4.

DMU_j	1	2	3	4	5
Radius of stability η^*	3.58	0.85	1.44	0.09	2.67

efficient. For the changes of the inputs and outputs more than 0.85, the DMU cannot remain efficient. A similar interpretation can be done for DMU_5.

6.6 Analysis and stability of model (5.42)

To study the stability of uncertain model (5.42), this study is done in two directions of efficient and inefficient DMUs (Jiang et al., 2018).

6.6.1 Analysis and stability of inefficient DMUs

Assume DMU_o as an inefficient DMU. Jiang et al. (2018) introduced the model for the obtain the minimum value for η such that the new form of this DMU with data of $(\tilde{x}_o - \eta e_m, \tilde{y}_o + \eta e_s)$ becomes efficient, that $e_j = (1, 1, \dots, 1)$ is a j-dimensional vector with values of 1.

$$
\begin{aligned}
&\min \quad \eta \\
&\text{subject to} \\
&E\left[\frac{\sum_{r=1}^{s} u_r(\tilde{y}_{ro} - \eta) - w}{\sum_{i=1}^{m} v_i(\tilde{x}_{io} + \eta)}\right] = 1 \\
&E\left[\frac{\sum_{r=1}^{s} u_r\tilde{y}_{rj} - w}{\sum_{i=1}^{m} v_i\tilde{x}_{ij}}\right] \le 1 \qquad j = 1, 2, \dots, n \\
&v_i \ge 0 \qquad i = 1, 2, \dots, m \\
&u_r \ge 0 \qquad r = 1, 2, \dots, s
\end{aligned}
\tag{6.30}
$$

Theorem 6.12. (Jiang et al., 2018) Assume that the independent uncertain variables $\tilde{x}_{ij}$, $\tilde{x}_{io}$, $\tilde{y}_{rj}$, and $\tilde{y}_{ro}$ have regular uncertain distributions ϕ_{ij}, ϕ_{io}, φ_{rj}, and φ_{ro}, respectively. The uncertain formulation (6.30) is equivalent to the below model.

$$
\begin{aligned}
&\min \ \eta \\
&\text{subject to} \\
&\int_0^1 \frac{\sum_{r=1}^{s} u_r\left(\varphi_{ro}^{-1}(\alpha) + \eta\right) - w}{\sum_{i=1}^{m} v_i\left(\phi_{io}^{-1}(1-\alpha) - \eta\right)} d\alpha = 1 \\
&\int_0^1 \frac{\sum_{r=1}^{s} u_r\varphi_{rj}^{-1}(\alpha) - w}{\sum_{i=1}^{m} v_i\phi_{ij}^{-1}(1-\alpha)} d\alpha \leq 1 \qquad j = 1, 2, \ldots, n, \ j \neq o \\
&v_i \geq 0 \qquad i = 1, 2, \ldots, m \\
&u_r \geq 0 \qquad r = 1, 2, \ldots, s
\end{aligned}
\tag{6.31}
$$

Proof. This is obvious that the inverse uncertain distributions of $\tilde{x}_{io} - \eta$ and $\tilde{y}_{ro} + \eta$ are $\phi_{io}^{-1}(\alpha) - \eta$ and $\varphi_{ro}^{-1}(\alpha) + \eta$, respectively. As the function $\frac{\sum_{r=1}^{s} u_r(\tilde{y}_{ro} + \eta) - w}{\sum_{i=1}^{m} v_i(\tilde{x}_{io} - \eta)}$ is absolutely increasing for $\tilde{y}_{ro}$ and absolutely decreasing for $\tilde{x}_{io}$, according to Theorem 1.33 its inverse uncertain distribution is obtained as $H_0^{-1}(\alpha) = \frac{\sum_{r=1}^{s} u_r\left(\varphi_{ro}^{-1}(\alpha) + \eta\right) - w}{\sum_{i=1}^{m} v_i\left(\phi_{io}^{-1}(1-\alpha) - \eta\right)}$. Therefore, according to Theorem 1.38, the conversion $E\left[\frac{\sum_{r=1}^{s} u_r(\tilde{y}_{ro} + \eta) - w}{\sum_{i=1}^{m} v_i(\tilde{x}_{io} - \eta)}\right] = \int_0^1 \frac{\sum_{r=1}^{s} u_r\left(\varphi_{ro}^{-1}(\alpha) + \eta\right) - w}{\sum_{i=1}^{m} v_i\left(\phi_{io}^{-1}(1-\alpha) - \eta\right)} d\alpha$ is obtained and the theorem is proved.

Theorem 6.13. (Jiang et al., 2018) Assume DMU_o is inefficient and η^* is the optimal solution value of model (6.31). Then,

- DMU_o remains inefficient for changing $\tilde{x}_o$ to $\tilde{x}_o - \eta e_m$, and $\tilde{y}_o$ to $\tilde{y}_o + \eta e_s$, if $\eta < \eta^*$.
- DMU_o becomes efficient for changing $\tilde{x}_o$ to $\tilde{x}_o - \eta e_m$, and $\tilde{y}_o$ to $\tilde{y}_o + \eta e_s$, if $\eta \geq \eta^*$.

Proof. Assume $(\tilde{x}_o - \eta e_m, \tilde{y}_o + \eta e_r)$ is efficient, then there exists a $(u, v) \geq 0$ where $\int_0^1 \frac{\sum_{r=1}^{s} u_r\left(\varphi_{ro}^{-1}(\alpha) + \eta\right) - w}{\sum_{i=1}^{m} v_i\left(\phi_{io}^{-1}(1-\alpha) - \eta\right)} d\alpha = 1$ and $\int_0^1 \frac{\sum_{r=1}^{s} u_r \varphi_{rj}^{-1}(\alpha) - w}{\sum_{i=1}^{m} v_i \phi_{ij}^{-1}(1-\alpha)} d\alpha \leq 1$. This means that (u, v, η) is a feasible solution of model (6.31), therefore $\eta \geq \eta^*$. Thus, $(\tilde{x}_o - \eta e_m, \tilde{y}_o + \eta e_s)$ is inefficient for any $\eta < \eta^*$.

On the other hand, as η^* is the optimal solution value of model (6.31), then there exists $(u^*, v^*) \geq 0$ and w^* where (u^*, v^*, w^*, η^*) is a feasible solution, meaning that $\int_0^1 \frac{\sum_{r=1}^{s} u_r^*\left(\varphi_{ro}^{-1}(\alpha) + \eta^*\right) - w^*}{\sum_{i=1}^{m} v_i^*\left(\phi_{io}^{-1}(1-\alpha) - \eta^*\right)} d\alpha = 1$ and $\int_0^1 \frac{\sum_{r=1}^{s} u_r^* \varphi_{rj}^{-1}(\alpha) - w^*}{\sum_{i=1}^{m} v_i^* \phi_{ij}^{-1}(1-\alpha)} d\alpha \leq 1$. As $\int_0^1 \frac{\sum_{r=1}^{s} u_r^*\left(\varphi_{ro}^{-1}(\alpha) + \eta^*\right) - w^*}{\sum_{i=1}^{m} v_i^*\left(\phi_{io}^{-1}(1-\alpha) - \eta^*\right)} d\alpha$ is increasing for η^*, then the inequality $\int_0^1 \frac{\sum_{r=1}^{s} u_r^*\left(\varphi_{ro}^{-1}(\alpha) + \eta\right) - w^*}{\sum_{i=1}^{m} v_i^*\left(\phi_{io}^{-1}(1-\alpha) - \eta\right)} d\alpha \geq \int_0^1 \frac{\sum_{r=1}^{s} u_r^*\left(\varphi_{ro}^{-1}(\alpha) + \eta^*\right) - w^*}{\sum_{i=1}^{m} v_i^*\left(\phi_{io}^{-1}(1-\alpha) - \eta^*\right)} d\alpha = 1$ is held for $\eta \geq \eta^*$.

The replacements $v_i = v_i^*$, $w = w^*$, and $u_r = \frac{u_r^*}{\int_0^1 \frac{\sum_{r=1}^{s} u_r^*\left(\varphi_{ro}^{-1}(\alpha) + \eta\right) - w^*}{\sum_{i=1}^{m} v_i^*\left(\phi_{io}^{-1}(1-\alpha) - \eta\right)} d\alpha} \leq u_r^*$ are considered. Now, as $(u, v) \geq 0$, and (u, v, w, η) is true for the conditions $\int_0^1 \frac{\sum_{r=1}^{s} u_r\left(\varphi_{ro}^{-1}(\alpha) + \eta\right) - w}{\sum_{i=1}^{m} v_i\left(\phi_{io}^{-1}(1-\alpha) - \eta\right)} d\alpha = 1$ and $\int_0^1 \frac{\sum_{r=1}^{s} u_r \varphi_{rj}^{-1}(\alpha) - w}{\sum_{i=1}^{m} v_i \phi_{ij}^{-1}(1-\alpha)} d\alpha \leq 1$, therefore $(\tilde{x}_o - \eta e_m, \tilde{y}_o + \eta e_s)$ is efficient for any $\eta \geq \eta^*$.

6.6.2 Analysis and stability of efficient DMUs

Assume DMU_o as an efficient DMU. In this section, the maximum value for η is obtained such that the new form of this DMU with data of $(\tilde{x}_o + \eta e_m, \tilde{y}_o - \eta e_s)$ remains efficient. Here, $e_j = (1, 1, \ldots, 1)$ is a j-dimensional vector with values of 1. For this aim, the below model has been introduced by Jiang et al. (2018).

$$\begin{aligned}
&\max\ \eta \\
&\text{subject to} \\
&E\left[\frac{\sum_{r=1}^{s} u_r(\tilde{y}_{ro}-\eta)-w}{\sum_{i=1}^{m} v_i(\tilde{x}_{io}+\eta)}\right]=1 \\
&E\left[\frac{\sum_{r=1}^{s} u_r\tilde{y}_{rj}-w}{\sum_{i=1}^{m} v_i\tilde{x}_{ij}}\right]\le 1 \qquad j=1,2,\ldots,n,\ j\neq o \\
&v_i\ge 0 \qquad i=1,2,\ldots,m \\
&u_r\ge 0 \qquad r=1,2,\ldots,s
\end{aligned} \tag{6.32}$$

In this model, the exception $j \neq o$ means that when $(\tilde{x}_o + \eta e_m, \tilde{y}_o - \eta e_s)$ is evaluated, DMU_o should be excepted.

Theorem 6.14. (Jiang et al., 2018) Assume that the independent uncertain variables $\tilde{x}_{ij}$, $\tilde{x}_{io}$, $\tilde{y}_{rj}$, and $\tilde{y}_{ro}$ have regular uncertain distributions ϕ_{ij}, ϕ_{io}, φ_{rj}, and φ_{ro}, respectively. The uncertain formulation (6.32) is equivalent to the below model.

$$\begin{aligned}
&\max\ \eta \\
&\text{subject to} \\
&\int_0^1 \frac{\sum_{r=1}^{s} u_r\left(\varphi_{ro}^{-1}(\alpha)-\eta\right)-w}{\sum_{i=1}^{m} v_i\left(\phi_{io}^{-1}(1-\alpha)+\eta\right)}\,d\alpha=1 \\
&\int_0^1 \frac{\sum_{r=1}^{s} u_r\varphi_{rj}^{-1}(\alpha)-w}{\sum_{i=1}^{m} v_i\phi_{ij}^{-1}(1-\alpha)}\,d\alpha\le 1 \qquad j=1,2,\ldots,n,\ j\neq o \\
&v_i\ge 0 \qquad i=1,2,\ldots,m \\
&u_r\ge 0 \qquad r=1,2,\ldots,s
\end{aligned} \tag{6.33}$$

Proof. This is obvious that the inverse uncertain distributions of $\tilde{x}_{io}+\eta$ and $\tilde{y}_{ro}-\eta$ are $\phi_{io}^{-1}(\alpha)+\eta$ and $\varphi_{ro}^{-1}(\alpha)-\eta$, respectively. As the function $\frac{\sum_{r=1}^{s} u_r(\tilde{y}_{ro}-\eta)-w}{\sum_{i=1}^{m} v_i(\tilde{x}_{io}+\eta)}$ is absolutely increasing for $\tilde{y}_{ro}$ and absolutely decreasing for $\tilde{x}_{io}$, according to Theorem 1.33 its inverse uncertain distribution is obtained as $M_0^{-1}(\alpha)=\frac{\sum_{r=1}^{s} u_r\left(\varphi_{ro}^{-1}(\alpha)-\eta\right)-w}{\sum_{i=1}^{m} v_i\left(\phi_{io}^{-1}(1-\alpha)+\eta\right)}$. Therefore, according to Theorem 1.38, the conversion $E\left[\frac{\sum_{r=1}^{s} u_r(\tilde{y}_{ro}-\eta)-w}{\sum_{i=1}^{m} v_i(\tilde{x}_{io}+\eta)}\right]=\int_0^1 \frac{\sum_{r=1}^{s} u_r\left(\varphi_{ro}^{-1}(\alpha)-\eta\right)-w}{\sum_{i=1}^{m} v_i\left(\phi_{io}^{-1}(1-\alpha)+\eta\right)}d\alpha$ is obtained and the theorem is proved.

Theorem 6.15. (Jiang et al., 2018) Assume DMU_o is efficient and η^* is the optimal solution value of model (6.33). Then,

- DMU_o remains efficient for changing $\tilde{x}_o$ to $\tilde{x}_o+\eta e_m$, and $\tilde{y}_o$ to $\tilde{y}_o-\eta e_s$, if $\eta\leq\eta^*$.
- DMU_o becomes inefficient for changing $\tilde{x}_o$ to $\tilde{x}_o+\eta e_m$, and $\tilde{y}_o$ to $\tilde{y}_o-\eta e_s$, if $\eta>\eta^*$.

Proof. As η^* is the optimal solution value of model (6.33), then there exists $(u^*,v^*)\geq 0$ and w^* where (u^*,v^*,w^*,η^*) is a feasible solution, meaning that $\int_0^1 \frac{\sum_{r=1}^{s} u_r^*\left(\varphi_{ro}^{-1}(\alpha)-\eta^*\right)-w^*}{\sum_{i=1}^{m} v_i^*\left(\phi_{io}^{-1}(1-\alpha)+\eta^*\right)}d\alpha=1$ and $\int_0^1 \frac{\sum_{r=1}^{s} u_r^*\varphi_{rj}^{-1}(\alpha)-w^*}{\sum_{i=1}^{m} v_i^*\phi_{ij}^{-1}(1-\alpha)}d\alpha\leq 1.$ As $\int_0^1 \frac{\sum_{r=1}^{s} u_r^*\left(\varphi_{ro}^{-1}(\alpha)-\eta^*\right)-w^*}{\sum_{i=1}^{m} v_i^*\left(\phi_{io}^{-1}(1-\alpha)+\eta^*\right)}d\alpha$ is decreasing for η^*, then the inequality $\int_0^1 \frac{\sum_{r=1}^{s} u_r^*\left(\varphi_{ro}^{-1}(\alpha)-\eta\right)-w^*}{\sum_{i=1}^{m} v_i^*\left(\phi_{io}^{-1}(1-\alpha)+\eta\right)}d\alpha\geq\int_0^1 \frac{\sum_{r=1}^{s} u_r^*\left(\varphi_{ro}^{-1}(\alpha)-\eta^*\right)-w^*}{\sum_{i=1}^{m} v_i^*\left(\phi_{io}^{-1}(1-\alpha)+\eta^*\right)}d\alpha=1$ is held for $\eta\leq\eta^*$.

The replacements $v_i=v_i^*$, $w=w^*$, and $u_r=\frac{u_r^*}{\int_0^1 \frac{\sum_{r=1}^{s} u_r^*\left(\varphi_{ro}^{-1}(\alpha)-\eta\right)}{\sum_{i=1}^{m} v_i^*\left(\phi_{io}^{-1}(1-\alpha)+\eta\right)}d\alpha}\leq u_r^*$ are considered. Now, as $(u,v)\geq 0$, and (u,v,w,η) is true for the conditions

$\int_0^1 \frac{\sum_{r=1}^{s} u_r\left(\varphi_{ro}^{-1}(\alpha)-\eta\right)-w}{\sum_{i=1}^{m} v_i\left(\phi_{io}^{-1}(1-\alpha)+\eta\right)} d\alpha = 1$, and $\int_0^1 \frac{\sum_{r=1}^{s} u_r\,\varphi_{rj}^{-1}(\alpha)-w}{\sum_{i=1}^{m} v_i\,\phi_{ij}^{-1}(1-\alpha)} d\alpha \le 1$, therefore $(\tilde{x}_o + \eta e_m, \tilde{y}_o - \eta e_s)$ is efficient for any $\eta \le \eta^*$.

On the other hand, assume $(\tilde{x}_o + \eta e_m, \tilde{y}_o - \eta e_s)$ is efficient, then there exists a $(u, v) \ge 0$ where $\int_0^1 \frac{\sum_{r=1}^{s} u_r\left(\varphi_{ro}^{-1}(\alpha)-\eta\right)-w}{\sum_{i=1}^{m} v_i\left(\phi_{io}^{-1}(1-\alpha)+\eta\right)} d\alpha = 1$ and $\int_0^1 \frac{\sum_{r=1}^{s} u_r\varphi_{rj}^{-1}(\alpha)-w}{\sum_{i=1}^{m} v_i\phi_{ij}^{-1}(1-\alpha)} d\alpha \le 1$. This means that (u, v, w, η) is a feasible solution of model (6.33), therefore $\eta \le \eta^*$. Thus, $(\tilde{x}_o + \eta e_m, \tilde{y}_o - \eta e_s)$ is inefficient for any $\eta > \eta^*$.

Example 6.5. (Jiang et al., 2018) There are five DMUs to be evaluated according to three inputs and three outputs with uncertain values given in Table 6.21.

The results of the stability analysis of the DMUs by the models from Lio and Liu (2018) and Jiang et al. (2018) are reported in Tables 6.22 and 6.23, respectively.

Table 6.21 Data of Example 6.5.

DMU_j	1	2	3	4	5
Input 1	$\mathcal{L}(13,15)$	$\mathcal{L}(20,21)$	$\mathcal{L}(30,33)$	$\mathcal{L}(20,23)$	$\mathcal{L}(10,12)$
Input 2	$\mathcal{L}(15,18)$	$\mathcal{L}(30,33)$	$\mathcal{L}(40,47)$	$\mathcal{L}(10,11)$	$\mathcal{L}(10,12)$
Input 3	$\mathcal{L}(25,28)$	$\mathcal{L}(10,11)$	$\mathcal{L}(30,36)$	$\mathcal{L}(10,12)$	$\mathcal{L}(10,11)$
Output 1	$\mathcal{Z}(25,26,27)$	$\mathcal{Z}(40,45,48)$	$\mathcal{Z}(20,22,24)$	$\mathcal{Z}(40,43,46)$	$\mathcal{Z}(100,110,120)$
Output 2	$\mathcal{Z}(26,27,28)$	$\mathcal{Z}(80,90,96)$	$\mathcal{Z}(20,21,22)$	$\mathcal{Z}(44,46,50)$	$\mathcal{Z}(50,51,56)$
Output 3	$\mathcal{Z}(27,28,30)$	$\mathcal{Z}(90,100,108)$	$\mathcal{Z}(30,31,34)$	$\mathcal{Z}(50,55,59)$	$\mathcal{Z}(80,90,96)$

Table 6.22 The results for the stability of the DMUs of Example 6.5 by the model from Lio and Liu (2018).

DMU_j	1	2	3	4	5
Radius of stability η^*	6.82	22.3	0.57	6.21	28.3

Table 6.23 The results for the stability of the DMUs of Example 6.5 by the model from Jiang et al. (2018).

DMU_j	1	2	3	4	5
Radius of stability η^*	3	30.8	20.46	0.48	65.51

According to Table 6.23, the stability radius of DMU_1 is 3. It means that this DMU can be only technologically efficient by at least a 3 unit increase in all inputs and a decrease in all outputs. On the other hand, based on the results of Table 6.22, these changes should be at least 6.82 for DMU_1 to achieve technological and scale efficiencies. A similar interpretation can be done for inefficient DMUs 3 and 4.

The stability radius of the efficient DMUs shows that a new efficiency frontier is created when the inefficient DMUs are efficient by decreasing the inputs and increasing the outputs. Consider DMU_2. If all inputs are increased by not more than 30.8 and all outputs are decreased by not more than 30.8 (see Table 6.23), the DMU remains technologically efficient. But if these changes are not more than 22.3 (see Table 6.22), the DMU achieves technological and scale efficiencies. A similar interpretation can be considered for DMU_5.

6.7 A model for obtaining maximum possible belief degree for an efficient DMU

Mohammad Nejad and Ghaffari-Hadigheh (2018) proposed a model to find the maximum possible belief degree for an efficient DMU. They first assumed a DMU with uncertain inputs and outputs was efficient, then introduced a model to maximize the belief degree of such an uncertain environment considering the DMU in an efficient situation. The presented model was not optimistic, unlike the model from Wen et al. (2014).

Consider uncertain model (5.52) and its equivalent crisp form presented by model (5.53). In an uncertain environment, constraint satisfaction with higher rate of confidence is practically desirable. Therefore, the higher values of α are selected in practice. In model (5.53), as φ_{rj} and ϕ_{ij} are regular, their inverse functions φ_{rj}^{-1} and ϕ_{ij}^{-1} are strictly increasing for α. Therefore, by increasing α, the value of $\varphi_{ro}^{-1}(\alpha)$ is increased and $\phi_{io}^{-1}(1-\alpha)$ is decreased. This means that an input of the evaluated DMU is decreased to its minimum possible value and an output of this DMU is increased to its maximum possible value. So, DMU_o comes close to its favorable situation. On the other hand, $\varphi_{rj}^{-1}(1-\alpha)$ is decreasing and $\phi_{ij}^{-1}(\alpha)$ is increasing for values of α. This means that other DMUs come close to their most unfavorable situation. Therefore, the model from Wen et al. (2014) is optimistic and more DMUs may be evaluated as efficient (see Example 5.8 where all DMUs for $\alpha=0.8$ and $\alpha=0.9$ are efficient).

Mohammad Nejad and Ghaffari-Hadigheh (2018) presented the following uncertain model to obtain the maximum belief degree value that evaluates DMU_o as efficient,

$$\begin{aligned}
&\max\ \mathcal{M}\left\{\frac{\sum_{r=1}^{s} u_r\tilde{y}_{ro}}{\sum_{i=1}^{m} v_i\tilde{x}_{io}} \geq \theta_0\right\}\\
&\text{subject to}\\
&\mathcal{M}\left\{\frac{\sum_{r=1}^{s} u_r\tilde{y}_{rj}}{\sum_{i=1}^{m} v_i\tilde{x}_{ij}} \preceq 1\right\} \geq \alpha_j \quad j = 1, 2, \ldots, n\\
&v_i \geq \varepsilon \quad i = 1, 2, \ldots, m\\
&u_r \geq \varepsilon \quad r = 1, 2, \ldots, s
\end{aligned} \tag{6.34}$$

where $\theta_0 \in [0, 1]$ is a predetermined lower bound for the efficiency of DMU_o, α_j is the minimum confidence level of constraint j, and ε is a small positive value determined by a decision maker. This small value avoids obtaining zero value for the variables.

Model (6.34) is written as below.

$$\begin{aligned}
&\max\ \beta\\
&\text{subject to}\\
&\mathcal{M}\left\{-\sum_{r=1}^{s} u_r\tilde{y}_{ro} + \theta_0 \sum_{i=1}^{m} v_i\tilde{x}_{io} \preceq 0\right\} \geq \beta\\
&\mathcal{M}\left\{\sum_{r=1}^{s} u_r\tilde{y}_{rj} - \sum_{i=1}^{m} v_i\tilde{x}_{ij} \preceq 0\right\} \geq \alpha_j \quad j = 1, 2, \ldots, n\\
&v_i \geq \varepsilon \quad i = 1, 2, \ldots, m\\
&u_r \geq \varepsilon \quad r = 1, 2, \ldots, s
\end{aligned} \tag{6.35}$$

Theorem 6.16. (Mohammad Nejad & Ghaffari-Hadigheh, 2018) Models (6.34) and (6.35) are equivalent.

Proof. Assume (u, v) as a feasible solution of model (6.34) with an objective function value of $f(u, v)$. So, (μ, v, β) is a feasible solution of model (6.35) with the same objective function value where $\mu_r = \frac{u_r}{\sum_{i=1}^{m} v_i \tilde{x}_{io}}$, $v_i = \frac{v_i}{\sum_{i=1}^{m} v_i \tilde{x}_{io}}$, and $\beta = f(u, v)$. Furthermore, assume (μ, v, β) as a feasible solution of model (6.35). Then, (u, v) is a feasible solution of model (6.34) where $u_r = \frac{\mu_r}{\sum_{i=1}^{m} v_i \tilde{x}_{io}}$, and $v_i = \frac{v_i}{\sum_{i=1}^{m} v_i \tilde{x}_{io}}$.

Theorem 6.17. (Mohammad Nejad & Ghaffari-Hadigheh, 2018) Assume (β^*, u^*, v^*) as the optimal solution of model (6.35). The optimal solution satisfies the condition $\mathcal{M}\left\{-\sum_{r=1}^{s} u_r^* \tilde{y}_{ro} + \theta_o \sum_{i=1}^{m} v_i^* \tilde{x}_{io} \preceq 0\right\} = \beta^*$.

Proof. If $\mathcal{M}\left\{-\sum_{r=1}^{s} u_r^* \tilde{y}_{ro} + \theta_o \sum_{i=1}^{m} v_i^* \tilde{x}_{io} \preceq 0\right\} > \beta^*$ then $\mathcal{M}\left\{-\sum_{r=1}^{s} u_r^* \tilde{y}_{ro} + \theta_0 \sum_{i=1}^{m} v_i^* \tilde{x}_{io} \preceq 0\right\} = \beta^* + s$ and $s > 0$. This a contradiction and the theorem is proved.

For an optimal solution of model (6.35) such as (u^*, v^*), based on Definition 1.46 the equation $\mathcal{M}\left\{\sum_{r=1}^{s} u_r^* \tilde{y}_{ro} - \sum_{i=1}^{m} v_i^* \tilde{x}_{ij} \preceq 0\right\} + \mathcal{M}\left\{-\sum_{r=1}^{s} u_r^* \tilde{y}_{ro} + \sum_{i=1}^{m} v_i^* \tilde{x}_{ij} \preceq 0\right\} = 1$ is held, and according to Theorem 6.17 the inequality $\beta^* = 1 - \left\{\sum_{r=1}^{s} u_r^* \tilde{y}_{ro} - \sum_{i=1}^{m} v_i^* \tilde{x}_{ij} \preceq 0\right\} \leq 1 - \alpha_o$ is true, where α_0 is the minimum possible belief degree for satisfying the constraints of DMU_o in model (6.35).

Definition 6.1. (Mohammad Nejad & Ghaffari-Hadigheh, 2018) DMU_o is uncertainly efficient for $\theta_o = 1$ if $\beta = 1 - \alpha_o$, and it is uncertainly inefficient if $\beta < 1 - \alpha_0$.

Suppose $g_o(u, v, \tilde{x}_o, \tilde{y}_o) = -\sum_{r=1}^{n} u_r \tilde{y}_{ro} + \theta_o \sum_{i=1}^{m} v_i \tilde{x}_{io}$ and $g_j\left(u, v, \tilde{x}_j, \tilde{y}_j\right) = \sum_{r=1}^{n} u_r \tilde{y}_{rj} - \sum_{i=1}^{m} v_i \tilde{x}_{ij}$. As $g_o(u, v, \tilde{x}_o, \tilde{y}_o)$ is strictly increasing for $\tilde{x}_{io}$ and strictly decreasing for $\tilde{y}_{ro}$, according to Theorem 1.34 $\mathcal{M}\{g_o(u, v, \tilde{x}_o, \tilde{y}_o) \leq 0\} \geq \beta$ if and only if,

$$g_o\left(u, v, \phi_{1o}^{-1}(\beta), \ldots, \phi_{mo}^{-1}(\beta), \varphi_{1o}^{-1}(1-\beta), \ldots, \varphi_{no}^{-1}(1-\beta)\right) \leq 0 \quad (6.36)$$

Similarly, as $g_j\left(u, v, \tilde{x}_j, \tilde{y}_j\right)$ is strictly decreasing for $\tilde{x}_{io}$ and strictly increasing for $\tilde{y}_{ro}$, according to Theorem 1.34 $\mathcal{M}\left\{g_j\left(u, v, \tilde{x}_j, \tilde{y}_j\right) \leq 0\right\} \geq \alpha_j$ if and only if,

$$g_j\left(u, v, \phi_{1j}^{-1}(1-\alpha_j), \ldots, \phi_{mj}^{-1}(1-\alpha_j), \varphi_{1j}^{-1}(\alpha_j), \ldots, \varphi_{nj}^{-1}(\alpha_j)\right) \leq 0 \quad (6.37)$$

Considering inequalities (6.36) and (6.37), uncertain formulation (6.35) is rewritten as below

$$\begin{aligned}
&\max \ \beta \\
&\text{subject to} \\
&-\sum_{r=1}^{s} u_r \varphi_{ro}^{-1}(1-\beta) + \theta_0 \sum_{i=1}^{m} v_i \phi_{io}^{-1}(\beta) \leq 0 \\
&\sum_{r=1}^{s} u_r \varphi_{rj}^{-1}(\alpha_j) - \sum_{i=1}^{m} v_i \phi_{ij}^{-1}(1-\alpha_j) \leq 0 \qquad j = 1, 2, \ldots, n \\
&v_i \geq \varepsilon \qquad i = 1, 2, \ldots, m \\
&u_r \geq \varepsilon \qquad r = 1, 2, \ldots, s \\
&0 \leq \beta \leq 1
\end{aligned} \quad (6.38)$$

In the above model, as $\varphi_{ro}^{-1}(1-\beta)$ and $\phi_{io}^{-1}(\beta)$ are the functions of β, therefore $u_r\varphi_{ro}^{-1}(1-\beta)$ and $v_i\phi_{io}^{-1}(\beta)$ are nonlinear terms. So model (6.38) is nonlinear.

In the following, we show that considering linear and zigzag uncertain variables, model (6.38) can be written in linear form.

Assume uncertain variables $\tilde{x}_{ij}$ and $\tilde{y}_{rj}$ have zigzag uncertain distributions of $\mathcal{Z}\left(a'_{ij}, b'_{ij}, c'_{ij}\right)$ and $\mathcal{Z}\left(a_{rj}, b_{rj}, c_{rj}\right)$, respectively. According to the value of β, two cases happen (Mohammad Nejad & Ghaffari-Hadigheh, 2018).

Case 1. For $\beta \geq 0.5$ and considering zigzag-type uncertain variables, model (6.38) is written as follows,

$$
\begin{aligned}
&\max \ \beta \\
&\text{subject to} \\
&-\sum_{r=1}^{s} u_r\left((2\beta-1)a_{ro}+2(1-\beta)b_{ro}\right)+\theta_0\sum_{i=1}^{m} v_i\left((2-2\beta)b'_{io}+(2\beta-1)c'_{io}\right)\leq 0 \\
&\sum_{r=1}^{s} u_r\varphi_{rj}^{-1}(\alpha_j)-\sum_{i=1}^{m} v_i\phi_{ij}^{-1}(1-\alpha_j)\leq 0 \qquad j=1,2,\dots,n \\
&v_i\geq\varepsilon \qquad i=1,2,\dots,m \\
&u_r\geq\varepsilon \qquad r=1,2,\dots,s \\
&0.5\leq\beta\leq 1
\end{aligned}
\tag{6.39}
$$

Lemma 6.1. (Mohammad Nejad & Ghaffari-Hadigheh, 2018) Model (6.39) is feasible for $\alpha_o \leq 0.5$.

Proof. The constraint $\mathcal{M}\left\{-\sum_{r=1}^{s} u_r\tilde{y}_{ro}+\theta_0\sum_{i=1}^{m} v_i\tilde{x}_{io}\preceq 0\right\}\geq\beta$ from model (6.35) can be written as $\beta\leq\mathcal{M}\left\{-\sum_{r=1}^{s} u_r\tilde{y}_{ro}+\theta_0\sum_{i=1}^{m} v_i\tilde{x}_{io}\preceq 0\right\}\leq 1-\alpha_o$, which means $\beta\leq 1-\alpha_o$. As $\beta\geq 0.5$, we conclude that $\alpha_o\leq 0.5$. Therefore, the lemma is proved.

If β_1^* is the optimal objective function value of model (6.39), the first constraint of this model creates the upper bound of $k(u,v)$ for β as below.

$$
k(u,v)=\frac{1}{2}+\frac{\sum_{r=1}^{s} u_r b_{ro}-\theta_o\sum_{i=1}^{m} v_i b'_{io}}{2\left(\sum_{r=1}^{s} u_r(b_{ro}-a_{ro})-\theta_o\sum_{i=1}^{m} v_i\left(c'_{io}-b'_{io}\right)\right)}
\tag{6.40}
$$

Theorem 6.18. (Mohammad Nejad & Ghaffari-Hadigheh, 2018) Model (6.39) is equivalent to the below linear fractional model.

$$
\begin{aligned}
&\max \quad k(u, v) \\
&\text{subject to} \\
&\sum_{r=1}^{s} u_r \varphi_{rj}^{-1}(\alpha_j) - \sum_{i=1}^{m} v_i \phi_{ij}^{-1}(1-\alpha_j) \le 0 \quad j = 1, 2, \ldots, n \\
&\sum_{r=1}^{s} u_r b_{ro} + \theta_0 \sum_{i=1}^{m} v_i b'_{io} \ge 0 \\
&v_i \ge \varepsilon \qquad i = 1, 2, \ldots, m \\
&u_r \ge \varepsilon \qquad r = 1, 2, \ldots, s
\end{aligned}
\tag{6.41}
$$

Proof. Assume (β^*, u^*, v^*) as the optimal solution of model (6.39). It is obvious that $0.5 \le \beta^* = \min\{1, k(u^*, v^*)\}$ and therefore $k(u^*, v^*) \ge 0.5$. According to equality (6.40), the following equality is obtained.

$$
\frac{\sum_{r=1}^{s} u_r b_{ro} - \theta_o \sum_{i=1}^{m} v_i b'_{io}}{2\left(\sum_{r=1}^{s} u_r (b_{ro} - a_{ro}) - \theta_o \sum_{i=1}^{m} v_i (c'_{io} - b'_{io})\right)} \ge 0 \tag{6.42}
$$

As the denominator of fraction (6.42) is positive, we need to prove that its numerator is positive. As this condition should be held for the optimal solution of model (6.39), therefore, the below bi-level model is considered.

$$
\begin{aligned}
&\max \quad \min \{1, k(u, v)\} \\
&\text{subject to} \\
&\sum_{r=1}^{s} u_r \varphi_{rj}^{-1}(\alpha_j) - \sum_{i=1}^{m} v_i \phi_{ij}^{-1}(1-\alpha_j) \le 0 \quad j = 1, 2, \ldots, n \\
&\sum_{r=1}^{s} u_r b_{ro} + \theta_0 \sum_{i=1}^{m} v_i b'_{io} \ge 0 \\
&v_i \ge \varepsilon \qquad i = 1, 2, \ldots, m \\
&u_r \ge \varepsilon \qquad r = 1, 2, \ldots, s
\end{aligned}
\tag{6.43}
$$

If $k(u, v) \le 1$, the minimum lower bound of this problem will be $k(u, v)$. Therefore, bi-level model (6.43) is converted to a model with a single objective function of $\max \ k(u, v)$. If $k(u, v) > 1$, the minimum lower bound of this problem will be equal to 1 and the bi-level model (6.43) is converted to a model with a constant single objective function. In fact, model (6.43) is reduced to a one-level model. Therefore, the optimal solution of the model is the feasible solution that maximizes $k(u, v)$. So, for solving model (6.41), it is enough to solve bi-level model (6.43), and the theorem is proved.

Model (6.41) can be converted to the below linear form using the Charnes and Cooper (1962) transformation.

$$
\begin{aligned}
p^* = \max \quad & \sum_{r=1}^{s} u_r b_{ro} - \theta_0 \sum_{i=1}^{m} v_i b'_{io} \\
\text{subject to} \quad & \\
& \sum_{r=1}^{s} u_r \left(b_{ro} - a_{ro}\right) + \theta_o \sum_{i=1}^{m} v_i \left(c'_{io} - b'_{io}\right) = 1 \\
& \sum_{r=1}^{s} u_r \varphi_{rj}^{-1}(\alpha_j) - \sum_{i=1}^{m} v_i \phi_{ij}^{-1}(1-\alpha_j) \leq 0 \qquad j = 1, 2, \ldots, n \\
& \sum_{r=1}^{s} u_r b_{ro} - \theta_0 \sum_{i=1}^{m} v_i b'_{io} \geq 0 \\
& v_i \geq \varepsilon \qquad i = 1, 2, \ldots, m \\
& u_r \geq \varepsilon \qquad r = 1, 2, \ldots, s
\end{aligned}
\tag{6.44}
$$

Therefore, in Case 1 it is enough to consider $\beta_1^* = \min\left\{1, \frac{1}{2} + \frac{p^*}{2}\right\}$.

Case 2. For $\beta \leq 0.5$, considering zigzag-type uncertain variables, model (6.38) is written as follows,

$$
\begin{aligned}
\max \quad & \beta \\
\text{subject to} \quad & \\
& -\sum_{r=1}^{s} u_r \left(2\beta b_{ro} + (1-2\beta) c_{ro}\right) + \theta_0 \sum_{i=1}^{m} v_i \left((1-2\beta) d'_{io} + 2\beta b'_{io}\right) \leq 0 \\
& \sum_{r=1}^{s} u_r \varphi_{rj}^{-1}(\alpha_j) - \sum_{i=1}^{m} v_i \phi_{ij}^{-1}(1-\alpha_j) \leq 0 \quad j = 1, 2, \ldots, n \\
& v_i \geq \varepsilon \qquad i = 1, 2, \ldots, m \\
& u_r \geq \varepsilon \qquad r = 1, 2, \ldots, s \\
& 0 \leq \beta \leq 0.5
\end{aligned}
\tag{6.45}
$$

From the first constraint of the above model, we conclude that $\beta \leq h(u, v)$. Therefore,

$$h(u,v)=\frac{1}{2}\frac{\sum_{r=1}^{s}u_r c_{ro}-\theta_o\sum_{i=1}^{m}v_i d'_{io}}{\left(\sum_{r=1}^{s}u_r(c_{ro}-b_{ro})+\theta_o\sum_{i=1}^{m}v_i(b'_{io}-d'_{io})\right)} \tag{6.46}$$

Theorem 6.19. (Mohammad Nejad & Ghaffari-Hadigheh, 2018) The nonlinear model (6.45) is linearized as the below model.

$$\begin{aligned}
q^* = \max\ & \sum_{r=1}^{s}u_r c_{ro}-\theta_0\sum_{i=1}^{m}v_i d'_{io}\\
\text{subject to}\ & \\
& \sum_{r=1}^{s}u_r(c_{ro}-b_{ro})+\theta_o\sum_{i=1}^{m}v_i(b'_{io}-d'_{io})\le 1\\
& \sum_{r=1}^{s}u_r\varphi_{rj}^{-1}(\alpha_j)-\sum_{i=1}^{m}v_i\phi_{ij}^{-1}(1-\alpha_j)\le 0 \qquad j=1,2,\ldots,n\\
& \sum_{r=1}^{s}u_r c_{ro}-\theta_0\sum_{i=1}^{m}v_i d'_{io}\ge 0\\
& v_i\ge\varepsilon \qquad i=1,2,\ldots,m\\
& u_r\ge\varepsilon \qquad r=1,2,\ldots,s
\end{aligned} \tag{6.47}$$

Proof. Assume (β^*,u^*,v^*) as the optimal solution of model (6.45). It is obvious that $\beta^*=\min\{\frac{1}{2},h(u^*,v^*)\}$. Similar to Case 1, the below bi-level model is defined.

$$\begin{aligned}
\max\ \min\ & \left\{\frac{1}{2},h(u,v)\right\}\\
\text{subject to}\ & \\
& \sum_{r=1}^{s}u_r\varphi_{rj}^{-1}(\alpha_j)-\sum_{i=1}^{m}v_i\phi_{ij}^{-1}(1-\alpha_j)\le 0 \quad j=1,2,\ldots,n\\
& \sum_{r=1}^{s}u_r c_{ro}-\theta_0\sum_{i=1}^{m}v_i d'_{io}\ge 0\\
& v_i\ge\varepsilon \qquad i=1,2,\ldots,m\\
& u_r\ge\varepsilon \qquad r=1,2,\ldots,s
\end{aligned} \tag{6.48}$$

The above bi-level model is reduced to the below one-level model.

$$
\begin{aligned}
&\max \ h(u, v) \\
&\text{subject to} \\
&\sum_{r=1}^{s} u_r \varphi_{rj}^{-1}(\alpha_j) - \sum_{i=1}^{m} v_i \phi_{ij}^{-1}(1-\alpha_j) \le 0 \quad j = 1, 2, \ldots, n \\
&\sum_{r=1}^{s} u_r c_{ro} - \theta_0 \sum_{i=1}^{m} v_i d'_{io} \ge 0 \\
&v_i \ge \varepsilon \quad\quad i = 1, 2, \ldots, m \\
&u_r \ge \varepsilon \quad\quad r = 1, 2, \ldots, s
\end{aligned}
\tag{6.49}
$$

Finally, it is easy to linearize model (6.49) and obtain the linear model (6.47).

Similar to Case 1, in Case 2 it is enough to consider $\beta_2^* = \min\left\{\frac{1}{2}, \frac{q^*}{2}\right\}$.

In models (6.44) and (6.47), the continuous and linear functions $\varphi_{rj}^{-1}(\alpha_j)$ and $\phi_{ij}^{-1}(1-\alpha_j)$ are respectively increasing and decreasing for α_j. So, $\varphi_{rj}^{-1}(\alpha_j)$ and $\phi_{ij}^{-1}(1-\alpha_j)$ move respectively to c_{rj} and a_{ij}', as α_j moves to 1. As the outputs of DMUs determine the range of $\varphi_{rj}^{-1}(\alpha_j)$, and the inputs of DMUs determine the range of $\phi_{ij}^{-1}(1-\alpha_j)$, the outputs of each DMU move to the best possible value and the inputs move to the worst possible value when α_j moves to 1. It means that each DMU is driven to the most favorable situation by moving α_j to 1.

Comparing models (6.44) and (6.47) to DEA models shows that the efficiency frontiers of models (6.44) and (6.47) are on $\varphi_{rj}^{-1}(\alpha_j)$ and $\phi_{ij}^{-1}(1-\alpha_j)$, respectively In other words, $\varphi_{rj}^{-1}(\alpha_j)$ and $\phi_{ij}^{-1}(1-\alpha_j)$ are respectively the output and input of DMU_j in the uncertain DEA model.

Assume uncertain variables $\tilde{x}_{ij}$ and $\tilde{y}_{rj}$ are of linear uncertain distributions $\mathcal{L}(a_{ij}', b_{ij}')$ and $\mathcal{L}(a_{rj}, b_{rj})$, respectively. Model (6.38) is converted to the below model.

$$
\begin{aligned}
&\max \ \beta \\
&\text{subject to} \\
&-\sum_{r=1}^{s} u_r(\beta a_{ro} + (1-\beta) b_{ro}) + \theta_0 \sum_{i=1}^{m} v_i((1-\beta) d'_{ro} + \beta b'_{ro}) \le 0 \\
&\sum_{r=1}^{s} u_r \varphi_{rj}^{-1}(\alpha_j) - \sum_{i=1}^{m} v_i \phi_{ij}^{-1}(1-\alpha_j) \le 0 \quad j = 1, 2, \ldots, n \\
&v_i \ge \varepsilon \quad\quad i = 1, 2, \ldots, m \\
&u_r \ge \varepsilon \quad\quad r = 1, 2, \ldots, s \\
&0 \le \beta \le 1
\end{aligned}
\tag{6.50}
$$

The first constraint of the above model is nonlinear and can be written as below.

$$\beta\left(\sum_{r=1}^{n} u_r(b_{ro} - a_{ro}) + \sum_{i=1}^{m} v_i(b'_{ro} - a'_{ro})\right) \leq \sum_{r=1}^{n} u_r b_{ro} - \sum_{i=1}^{m} v_i a'_{ro} \quad (6.51)$$

As β is positive, the following inequality is obtained.

$$\beta \leq \frac{\sum_{r=1}^{n} u_r b_{ro} - \sum_{i=1}^{m} v_i a'_{ro}}{\sum_{r=1}^{n} u_r(b_{ro} - a_{ro}) + \sum_{i=1}^{m} v_i(b'_{ro} - a'_{ro})} \quad (6.52)$$

Therefore, model (6.50) is converted to the below model.

$$\begin{aligned} & \max \ \beta \\ & \text{subject to} \\ & \beta \leq \frac{\sum_{r=1}^{n} u_r b_{ro} - \sum_{i=1}^{m} v_i a'_{ro}}{\sum_{r=1}^{n} u_r(b_{ro} - a_{ro}) + \sum_{i=1}^{m} v_i(b'_{ro} - a'_{ro})} \\ & \sum_{r=1}^{s} u_r \varphi_{rj}^{-1}(\alpha_j) - \sum_{i=1}^{m} v_i \phi_{ij}^{-1}(1-\alpha_j) \leq 0 \quad j = 1, 2, \ldots, n \\ & v_i \geq \varepsilon \quad i = 1, 2, \ldots, m \\ & u_r \geq \varepsilon \quad r = 1, 2, \ldots, s \\ & 0 \leq \beta \leq 1 - \alpha_o \end{aligned} \quad (6.53)$$

Applying the Charnes & Cooper, 1962) transformation, the following linear model is obtained instead of nonlinear model (6.51).

$$
\begin{aligned}
\max \quad & \sum_{r=1}^{n} u_r b_{ro} - \sum_{i=1}^{m} v_i d'_{ro} \\
\text{subject to} \quad & \\
& \sum_{r=1}^{n} u_r (b_{ro} - a_{ro}) + \sum_{i=1}^{m} v_i (b'_{ro} - d'_{ro}) = 1 \\
& \sum_{r=1}^{s} u_r \varphi_{rj}^{-1}(\alpha_j) - \sum_{i=1}^{m} v_i \phi_{ij}^{-1}(1-\alpha_j) \le 0 \quad j = 1, 2, \ldots, n \\
& v_i \ge \varepsilon \quad i = 1, 2, \ldots, m \\
& u_r \ge \varepsilon \quad r = 1, 2, \ldots, s \\
& 0 \le \sum_{r=1}^{n} u_r b_{ro} - \sum_{i=1}^{m} v_i d'_{ro} \le 1 - \alpha_o
\end{aligned}
\tag{6.54}
$$

Example 6.6. (Mohammad Nejad & Ghaffari-Hadigheh, 2018) Consider 10 DMUs, each with two inputs and two outputs with zigzag-type uncertain values shown in Table 6.24.

Considering $\varepsilon = 0.001$, the results of evaluating the DMUs are represented in Tables 6.25 and 6.26 for different values of α. For each value of α, three columns are represented for each DMU. The first column shows the optimal objective function value of model (5.52), the second column shows the optimal value of model (6.47), and the last column shows the rankings of the DMUs by β^* values.

Table 6.24 Data of Example 6.6.

DMUs	Input 1	Input 2	Output 1	Output 2
1	$\mathcal{Z}(58.5, 95, 97)$	$\mathcal{Z}(85.8, 135, 137)$	$\mathcal{Z}(62, 67, 126)$	$\mathcal{Z}(153, 159, 289.8)$
2	$\mathcal{Z}(52, 83, 90)$	$\mathcal{Z}(97.5, 154, 157)$	$\mathcal{Z}(71, 75, 142.5)$	$\mathcal{Z}(189, 191, 351)$
3	$\mathcal{Z}(39, 69, 70)$	$\mathcal{Z}(91, 145, 150)$	$\mathcal{Z}(58, 59, 108)$	$\mathcal{Z}(200, 204, 374.4)$
4	$\mathcal{Z}(45.5, 78, 90)$	$\mathcal{Z}(58.5, 99, 107)$	$\mathcal{Z}(91, 93, 171)$	$\mathcal{Z}(175, 178, 324)$
5	$\mathcal{Z}(52.65, 85, 86)$	$\mathcal{Z}(78, 121, 122)$	$\mathcal{Z}(80, 84, 153)$	$\mathcal{Z}(180, 183, 333)$
6	$\mathcal{Z}(37.05, 59, 64)$	$\mathcal{Z}(71.5, 112, 114)$	$\mathcal{Z}(61, 65, 126)$	$\mathcal{Z}(141, 149, 273.6)$
7	$\mathcal{Z}(57.85, 90, 92)$	$\mathcal{Z}(130, 201, 205)$	$\mathcal{Z}(51, 58, 120.6)$	$\mathcal{Z}(190, 200, 369)$
8	$\mathcal{Z}(39, 67, 70)$	$\mathcal{Z}(65, 109, 110)$	$\mathcal{Z}(72.7, 74, 140.4)$	$\mathcal{Z}(188, 189, 343.8)$
9	$\mathcal{Z}(58.5, 96, 100)$	$\mathcal{Z}(74, 119, 122)$	$\mathcal{Z}(48, 49, 95.4)$	$\mathcal{Z}(170, 174, 315)$
10	$\mathcal{Z}(65, 101, 110)$	$\mathcal{Z}(64.5, 131, 132)$	$\mathcal{Z}(86, 91, 171)$	$\mathcal{Z}(150, 151, 279)$

Table 6.25 Results obtained for Example 6.6 for $\alpha=0.6$ and $\alpha=0.7$.

	$\alpha=0.6$			$\alpha=0.7$		
DMUs	w^*	β^*	**Rank**	w^*	β^*	**Rank**
1	35.6	0.2007	9	0	0.0902	9
2	0	0.2976	5	0	0.1893	5
3	0	0.3941	2	0	0.2961	2
4	0	0.4	1	0	0.3	1
5	0	0.3229	4	0	0.2134	4
6	0	0.374	3	0	0.2717	3
7	0	0.2499	8	0	0.14	7
8	0	0.4	1	0	0.3	1
9	0	0.2728	6	0	0.1618	6
10	0	0.2502	7	0	0.1369	8

Table 6.26 Results obtained for Example 6.6 for $\alpha=0.8$ and $\alpha=0.9$.

	$\alpha=0.8$			$\alpha=0.9$		
DMUs	w^*	β^*	**Rank**	w^*	β^*	**Rank**
1	0	0.0855	5	0	Infeasible	
2	0	0.0819	6	0	Infeasible	
3	0	0.1978	2	0	0.0992	2
4	0	0.2	1	0	0.1	1
5	0	0.1049	4	0	Infeasible	
6	0	0.1680	3	0	0.061	3
7	0	0.0308	8	0	Infeasible	
8	0	0.2	1	0	0.1	1
9	0	0.0525	7	0	Infeasible	
10	0	0.0242	9	0	Infeasible	

According to the obtained results, w^* for all cases takes a value of zero, except DMU_1 for $\alpha=0.6$. This means that based on the model from Wen et al. (2014), for $\alpha=0.6$ all DMUs are uncertainly efficient except DMU_1. For other α values, all DMUs are evaluated as uncertainly efficient. But applying model (6.47) for all α values, only DMUs 4 and 8 are uncertainly efficient. For the case of inefficient DMUs determined by model (6.47), by changing α values, the ranking of some DMUs is changed in the obtained order while it is fixed for some other DMUs. Therefore, it can be concluded that the ranking of DMUs over changes of α can be not exactly but approximately stable.

References

Allahviranloo, T. (2020). *Uncertain information and linear systems*. Berlin: Springer.

Allahviranloo, T., & Ghanbari, M. (2012). A new approach to obtain algebraic solution of interval linear systems. *Soft Computing*, *16*(1), 121–133.

Andersen, P., & Petersen, N. C. (1993). A procedure for ranking efficient units in data envelopment analysis. *Management Science*, *39*(10), 1261–1264.

Broomandi, P., Dabir, B., Bonakdarpour, B., Rashidi, Y., & Akherati, A. (2018). Simulation of mineral dust aerosols in southwestern Iran through numerical prediction models. *Environmental Progress & Sustainable Energy*, *37*, 1380–1393. https://doi.org/10.1002/ep.12805.

Charnes, A., & Cooper, W. W. (1962). Programming with linear fractional functionals. *Naval Research Logistics Quarterly*, *9*, 181–186.

Charnes, A., Cooper, W. W., Lewin, A. Y., Morey, R. C., & Rousseau, J. (1985). Sensitivity and stability analysis in DEA. *Annals of Operations Research*, *2*, 139–150.

Charnes, A., & Neralic, L. (1992). Sensitivity analysis of the proportionate change of inputs (or outputs) in data envelopment analysis. *Glasnik Matematički*, *1*(27), 393–405.

Jahanshahloo, G. R., Pourkarimi, L., & Zarepisheh, M. (2006). Modified MAJ model for ranking decision making units in data envelopment analysis. *Applied Mathematics and Computation*, *174*(2), 1054–1059.

Jamshidi, M., Sanei, M., & Mahmoodirad, A. (2022). An uncertain allocation models in data envelopment analysis: A case in the Iranian stock market. *Scintia Iranica*, 29(6), 3434–3454.

Jamshidi, M., Sanei, M., Mahmoodirad, A., Tohidi, G., & Hosseinzade Lotfi, F. (2021a). Uncertain SBM data envelopment analysis model: A case study in Iranian banks. *International Journal of Finance and Economics*, *26*(2), 2674–2689.

Jamshidi, M., Sanei, M., Mahmoodirad, A., Tohidi, G., & Hosseinzade Lotfi, F. (2021b). Uncertain BCC data envelopment analysis model with belief degree: A case study in Iranian banks. *International Journal of Industrial Mathematics*, *13*(3), 239–249.

Jamshidi, M., Saneie, M., Mahmoodirad, A., Hosseizadeh Lotfi, F., & Tohidi, G. (2019). Uncertain RUSSEL data envelopment analysis model: A case study in Iranian banks. *Journal of Intelligent Fuzzy Systems*, *37*(2), 2937–2951.

Jiang, B., Lio, W., & Li, X. (2018). An uncertain DEA model for scale efficiency evaluation. *IEEE Transactions on Fuzzy Systems*, *27*(8), 1616–1624.

Jiang, B., Zou, Z., Lio, W., & Li, J. (2020). The uncertain DEA models for specific scale efficiency identification. *Journal of Intelligent Fuzzy Systems*, *38*, 3403–3417.

Lio, W., & Liu, B. (2018). Uncertain data envelopment analysis with imprecisely observed inputs and outputs. *Fuzzy Optimization and Decision Making*, *17*, 357–373.

Liu, B. (2007). *Uncertain theory* (2nd ed.). Berlin, Germany: Springer.

Mahmoodirad, A., Dehghan, R., & Niroomand, S. (2019). Modelling linear fractional transportation problem in belief degree-based uncertain environment. *Journal of Experimental & Theoretical Artificial Intelligence*, *31*(3), 393–408.

Mahmoodirad, A., & Niroomand, S. (2020a). A belief degree-based uncertain scheme for a bi-objective two-stage green supply chain network design problem with direct shipment. *Soft Computing*, *24*(24), 18499–18519.

Mahmoodirad, A., & Niroomand, S. (2020b). Uncertain location-allocation decisions for a bi-objective two-stage supply chain network design problem with environmental impacts. *Expert Systems*, *37*, e12558.

Mahmoodirad, A., & Sanei, M. (2016). Solving a multi-stage multi-product solid supply chain network design problem by meta-heuristics. *Scientia Iranica*, *23*(3), 1429–1440.

Mehrabian, S., Alirezaee, M. R., & Jahanshahloo, G. R. (1999). A complete efficiency ranking of decision making units in data envelopment analysis. *Commutational Optimization and Applications*, *14*, 261–266.

Mohammad Nejad, Z., & Ghaffari-Hadigheh, A. (2018). A novel DEA model based on uncertainty theory. *Annals of Operations Research, 264*, 367–389.
Molla-Alizadeh-Zavardehi, S., Mahmoodirad, A., & Rahimian, M. (2014). Step fixed charge transportation problems via genetic algorithm. *Indian Journal of Science and Technology, 7*(7), 949–954.
Molla-Alizadeh-Zavardehi, S., Mahmoodirad, A., Sanei, M., Niroomand, S., & Banihashemi, S. (2021). Metaheuristics for data envelopment analysis problems. *International Journal of Systems Science: Operations & Logistics, 8*(4), 371–382.
Neralic, L. (1997). Sensitivity in data envelopment analysis for arbitrary perturbations of data. *Glasnik Matematički, 32*, 315–335.
Niroomand, S., Garg, H., & Mahmoodirad, A. (2020). An intuitionistic fuzzy two stage supply chain network design problem with multi-mode demand and multi-mode transportation. *ISA Transactions, 107*, 117–133.
Seiford, L. M., & Zhu, J. (1998). Stability regions for maintaining efficiency in data envelopment analysis. *European Journal of Operational Research, 108*(1), 127–139.
Seiford, L. M., & Zhu, J. (1999). Infeasibility of super efficiency data envelopment analysis models. *Infor, 37*(2), 174–187.
Thompson, R. G., Dharmapala, P. S., & Thrall, R. M. (1994). Sensitivity analysis of efficiency measures with applications to Kansas farming and Illinois coalmining. In A. Charnes, W. W. Cooper, A. Y. Lewin, & L. M. Seiford (Eds.), *Data envelopment analysis: Theory, methodology and applications* (pp. 393–422). Massachusetts: Norwell Kluwer Academic Publishers.
Wen, M., Guo, L., Kang, R., & Yang, Y. (2014). Data envelopment analysis with uncertain inputs and outputs. *Journal of Applied Mathematics, 2014*, 307108.
Wen, M., Qin, Z., Kang, R., & Yang, Y. (2015). Sensitivity and stability analysis of the additive model in uncertain data envelopment analysis. *Soft Computing, 19*, 1987–1996.
Zhu, J. (1996). Robustness of the efficient DMUs in data envelopment analysis. *European Journal of Operational Research, 90*, 451–460.

Index

Note: Page numbers followed by *f* indicate figures and *t* indicate tables.

Printed in the United States
by Baker & Taylor Publisher Services